PENGUIN BOOKS

MILLIONS LIKE US

'A triumph of research and organization – but also of sympathy' *Observer*

'Wide-ranging. Covers all aspects of their war in detail, from death and destruction to stockings and lipstick' *Sunday Times*

'Ambitious, humane and absorbing. A revelation. Nicholson's research has been phenomenally thorough and her narrative control is equally impressive. As a way of rescuing human feeling and individual experience from the fossilization of time and received opinion this book could not be better. I shall try to ensure my granddaughters read it' *Spectator*

D0510015

ABOUT THE AUTHOR

Virginia Nicholson was born in Newcastle-upon-Tyne and grew up in Yorkshire and Sussex. She studied at Cambridge University and lived abroad in France and Italy, then worked as a documentary researcher for BBC Television. Her books include the acclaimed social history *Among the Bohemians: Experiments in Living 1900–1939*, and *Singled Out: How Two Million Women Survived Without Men after the First World War*, published by Penguin in 2002 and 2007. She is married to a writer, has three children and lives in Sussex.

Millions Like Us

Women's Lives in the Second World War

VIRGINIA NICHOLSON

PENGUIN BOOKS

PENGUIN BOOKS

Published by the Penguin Group
Penguin Books Ltd, 80 Strand, London WC2R 0RL, England
Penguin Group (USA), Inc., 375 Hudson Street, New York, New York 10014, USA
Penguin Group (Canada), 90 Eglinton Avenue East, Suite 700, Toronto, Ontario, Canada M4P 2Y3
(a division of Pearson Penguin Canada Inc.)
Penguin Ireland, 25 St Stephen's Green, Dublin 2, Ireland (a division of Penguin Books Ltd)
Penguin Group (Australia), 250 Camberwell Road, Camberwell, Victoria 3124, Australia
(a division of Pearson Australia Group Pty Ltd)
Penguin Books India Pvt Ltd, 11 Community Centre, Panchsheel Park, New Delhi – 110 017, India
Penguin Group (NZ), 67 Apollo Drive, Rosedale, Auckland 0632, New Zealand
(a division of Pearson New Zealand Ltd)
Penguin Books (South Africa) (Pty) Ltd, 24 Sturdee Avenue, Rosebank, Johannesburg 2196, South Africa

Penguin Books Ltd, Registered Offices: 80 Strand, London WC2R 0RL, England

www.penguin.com

First published by Viking 2011
Published in Penguin Books 2012

002

Copyright © Virginia Nicholson, 2011

The moral right of the author has been asserted

The Acknowledgements on pp. 489–93 constitute an extension of this copyright page

Typeset by Palimpsest Book Production Limited, Falkirk, Stirlingshire
Printed in Great Britain by Clays Ltd, St Ives plc

A CIP catalogue record for this book is available from the British Library

ISBN: 978–0–141–03789–9

www.greenpenguin.co.uk

ALWAYS LEARNING   PEARSON

For my mother, Anne Olivier Bell

Contents

List of Illustrations

Inset Illustrations

1. Two young women from the Worthing 'Blackout Corps' paint their local hospital windows. (Fox Photos)
2. Spirit of the Blitz: a West End hairdressing salon picks up where it left off – in an air-raid shelter. (Popperfoto)
3. Cross-section of a life: the bombs exposed and revealed women's interior-based existence as never before. (Getty Images)
4. A cosy, if cramped, scene at Holborn station, September 1940. (London Transport Executive)
5. As the threat to Britain intensified, every mother had to choose between her children's safety and her maternal instincts. (Getty Images)
6. Volunteers like Joan Wyndham helped trained nurses to staff the first aid posts established across the city. (From *Love in Blue*)
7. Teenager Phyllis Noble, photographed at the time of Dunkirk, 1940. (From *Coming of Age in Wartime*)
8. First aid post, Notting Hill Gate, London. (Imperial War Museum)
9. For women, joining up often meant carrying out domestic tasks in a military context. (Imperial War Museum A23966)
10. A London Labour Exchange, 1941. (Imperial War Museum HU90889)
11. The Navy, Army and Air Force Institutes, or NAAFI, which ran canteens and shops for the forces, was 'a forgotten army'. (Getty Images)
12. Dorothy ('Doffy') Brewer went for training with the ATS in autumn 1941. (From *The Girls behind the Guns*)
13. Barbara Cartland with her ATS hat on, plus lipstick. (From *The Years of Opportunity*)
14. Unsuspecting ATS recruits arriving at Aldershot in 1941. (Fox Photos)
15. Wartime diarist Nella Last and her son Cliff. (From *Nella Last's War*)

Illustrations in the Text

Author's Note

In July 2005 the Queen unveiled a memorial in Whitehall dedicated to 'The Women of World War Two'. This massive bronze structure, twenty-two feet high, is studded with a row of oddly spooky disembodied uniforms. Hanging from the monument are the clothes and belongings of the servicewomen, factory workers, farm-workers and women who worked in hospitals, emergency services and volunteer bodies across the nation between 1939 and 1945. They are suspended in a featureless void, with no faces, no personalities. In its way the monument is a perfect metaphor for our state of national amnesia. Six million-odd women threw their energies into the home front. 640,000 British servicewomen played their part in helping to win the war. Of these, 624 died for their country.* But many of them are still alive.

Surely their endurance, their adventures, their sacrifices, their personalities are worthy of a deeper appreciation. This book asks, who were they? And what did it feel like to be them? I wanted to find out not only what they did in the war, but what the war did to them and how it changed their subsequent lives and relationships.

The chapters that follow are arranged chronologically, with the personal stories of a fifty-strong cast of characters in the spotlight against a backdrop of important social, political and international events: a momentous decade, seemingly familiar to many of us, but seen entirely through the eyes of the women who lived it. My approach to historical research is, as far as possible, to merge it with biography, and the telling of stories. I believe that the personal and idiosyncratic reveal more about the past than the generic and comprehensive. (A small note here: my intermittent – but, I think, authentic – use of the word 'girl' to describe the young women of the 1940s may sound a little patronising today, but back then it was

---

* See Appendix, p. 449, for a breakdown of women's military and civilian casualties.

their own preferred term, and was also universally used in the press and literature.)

Among the many elderly women whom I interviewed and whose stories appear in these pages is my mother, Anne Popham, as she then was. Not because her experiences were unusual or heroic, but precisely because they weren't. There have been numerous books celebrating the courage of women agents parachuted behind enemy lines in France, women in Japanese prisoner-of-war camps, women pilots from the Air Transport Auxiliary who delivered Spitfires to their airfields. Odette Hallowes and Dame Margot Turner have earned their place in history alongside Douglas Bader and Stanley Hollis. My mother is now ninety-four years old. Like most of our mothers and grandmothers, and like the majority of women in this narrative, she grew up in a world that seemed small and sedate and did nothing starry or distinguished in the war. When it was declared in 1939 she was ordinary, frightened and unsuspecting. But six years of conflict reordered that world; along with an entire generation, she awoke to her own post-war potential. In all these respects she was entirely typical of the many millions for whose sake I have borrowed my title. (*Millions Like Us* was a propaganda movie made by Frank Launder and Sidney Gilliat in 1943, to persuade women to join the war effort.)

If I could have chosen another title, it might have been 'We Just Got on with It' – the mantra of every woman I spoke to who lived through the war. So this book is not only an attempt to characterise that faceless war memorial, it is also my tribute to a generation of brave, stoical, unselfish, practical and uncomplaining women, whose values, along with their deeds, seem to be passing into history.

Prelude

A little over eighty years ago a very ordinary girl named Phyllis Noble was growing up in a terraced house with an outside toilet in Lewisham, south London. She was born in 1922. Her dad was a jobbing builder, and like many in the 1930s his trade was falling off; the Nobles' financial situation was not improved by his fondness for the pub. Phyllis's mum looked after the extended family of grandparents, in-laws and her own three children, who all lived under the same roof. As a role model Mum never overstepped the limits; she was first, foremost and exclusively a housewife, whose life revolved around the daily routine of shopping, cooking and washing. Despite the family's straitened circumstances Phyllis had a happy, rumbustious childhood. The kitchen in their cramped terrace house was a haven, and even when Dad had had a drop too much the family was united, roaring and joking when he let out one of his spectacularly loud farts. Phyllis was clever; but when she succeeded in winning a scholarship to a grammar school in Greenwich, Mum, disgusted at the expense of the uniform, launched a family battle to stop her daughter going. In any case getting educated would, in her view, be a pointless waste of time, since there was no alternative to the trap that she had herself been forced to enter twenty years earlier: that of marriage and motherhood.

To Phyllis's relief Mum was overruled by Dad, and in 1933 she took her first apprehensive steps away from the crowded, working-class, patriarchal world of her childhood. A better accent and a better life beckoned, alongside dreams of romance and escape from her proletarian background. But by the time she was sixteen it was 1938. Dad sat gloomily at home reading the newspaper reports about mass unemployment and the threat of war.

In June 1939, aged seventeen, Phyllis Noble joined the ranks of the so-called 'business girls'. She was to be a ledger clerk at the National Provincial Bank in Bishopsgate. Her workplace was a gloomy, noisy Victorian hall. Seated on a backless stool before her cumbersome ledger machine (a kind of monstrous typewriter), Phyllis was one of hundreds like her who spent their days sorting through piles of cheques, orders and statements to reconcile the bank's accounts. Prospects for women in this world were 'virtually nil'. Like their working-class counterparts, the maidservants in their basements and pantries, the business girls tended to be time-servers, dreaming of ensnaring their boss or male colleague into marriage. Then they could leave:

For women the main road was to matrimony. Judging by the total absence of married women and the scarcity of older, unmarried ones, this was a destination which most women who strayed into the banking world reached soon enough. And indeed with so many young men around, head office at least served well as a marriage market.

Years later, Phyllis told the story of her teenage years and early adult-hood in two short memoirs entitled *A Green Girl* (1983) and *Coming of Age in Wartime* (1988). She had grown up, married a man named Peter Willmott and become, not a film star or a literary virtuoso, but a respected social scientist. There is little to set her early life apart from the great mass of the working class to which she belonged – so what made her think her unexceptional adolescence was interesting enough to be the material for a book? And yet it is, for the reason that she lived through extraordinary times. Phyllis's life, like that of millions of her contemporaries in mid-twentieth century Britain, was about to be shaken to its foundations by uncontrollable international events. It would never recover its stability.

For skinny Jean McFadyen – like Phyllis, born in 1922 – a life of obscurity and narrow horizons was also about to be changed for ever. Jean had been brought up in a remote country area of Argyllshire. With an ailing mother and little twin sisters who needed looking after, she left school at thirteen-and-a-half to help. But when her mother regained her health the family couldn't afford to keep Jean in education. There was no local work for girls, so at the earliest oppor-tunity her parents sent her off to be housemaid to a landowner in Inveraray. 'I was the junior of the housemaids, so I got all the dirty work to do . . .' From morning till night there were beds to make, commodes to empty, grates to black-lead. Eighty years ago there was nothing unusual in such a life for a country-born Scottish teenager, but even then Jean could sense that there was no future in it. 'It was a dead-end job,' she recalls. 'I was seventeen – very quiet and shy, and I hadna mixed very much with people my own age. But I knew there was other things in the world. I knew there was something that I was not having, and I wanted a share of it.' The disaster that befell Europe a few years later brought untold evil and tribulation, but for Jean the Second World War was to offer an education, a chance of liberty and a source of self-confidence.

Five hundred miles away in Somerset, Patience Chadwyck-Healey, the daughter of a city businessman, was growing up to be waited on by young women like Jean. The Chadwyck-Healey family divided its time between London and a country residence near to Exmoor. 'We rode and hunted all day - I lived in the saddle. There was a large staff who looked after us, and we were brought up not to go into the kitchen or do anything for ourselves. In fact my aunt was proud of the fact that she didn't know how to make a cup of tea.' Patience was born in 1917; in her nineties she is still poised and sprightly, a product of her class. Her education consisted of day school in London, followed by six months being 'finished' in Paris ('as so many of us did'). In 1935 she donned her ostrich feathers and was presented at Court, before 'doing' two glitzy seasons as a debutante. 'We were very ignorant and romantic . . . attracted in a starry-eyed way to the young chaps we were dancing with. I had no ambitions. I lived very much in the present and enjoyed what there was. I don't ever remember thinking ahead as to what my eventual life might be. I think I hoped that it would be rather nice if I met a young man . . .' For a brief moment Patience considered doing an outside course at university, '. . . but I had no idea how it worked. Then they wrote back and told me I had to sit some exams, so I thought better of it.' Nothing had prepared this young lady for the approaching derailment of her privileged life at the age of just twenty-two.

*

As 'children of the Armistice', growing up in the 1930s, these women were just three of millions swept into the conflict that descended on our nation in 1939. The men who embarked on that war certainly did so in part to secure and perpetuate a way of life in which young women like Phyllis, Jean and Patience continued to take after their maternal role models, flush away the contents of commodes for their betters and look decorative in the saddle and at dances. Those men dared all, flew Spitfires, fought Fascism, suffered in prison camps and died in their thousands to preserve an ideal – an ideal of womanhood.

The story told in this book is the story of that ideal: of what it was, what became of it and the reality that lay beneath it. It's the story of a generation of young women caught up by the whirlwind of war and dropped down again in a different world not of their own making. And it sets out to tell how and why their stable position in that pre-war world, along with so much that they had taken for granted, was dislodged and blown apart by the Second World War, only to be reconstituted after 1945.

They were schoolgirls and business girls, brides, mothers and daughters, poor and privileged; some settled in the marital groove, others looking for love; reaching out to adulthood, or in their prime. These women were preoccupied by concerns that have always filled the minds of their sex: home and husband, boyfriends, family, work, exams, money, social life. If contemporary newspapers and magazines are anything to go on, shopping, childcare, the talkies, wireless programmes, Agatha Christie, knitting patterns, beauty and recipes preoccupied the waking hours of many of them. They revered the royal family. Despite the rise of socialism and industrial unrest, their media were as obsessed with the ruling classes as ours are with celebrities, and any class mobility there might have been in the 1930s was still only superficial. At the opposite end of the social scale from Patience Chadwyck-Healey and her kind was the 'socially lower' girl: meek and passive, she knew that the world of the posh girl who 'talked lovely' was beyond her reach. And yet the poor girl and the deb shared something. Neither looked for any other escape route than marriage.

But happiness was within easy grasp. Kay Mellis, now in her late eighties, was brought up in Edinburgh in the late 1930s. She speaks with the light, tripping accents of a town-bred Scot – in what she calls her 'how d'ye do' way of talking. Kay left school at fourteen and was bound apprentice to an Edinburgh dressmaker for five shillings a week. But she felt young for her age:

I was still going out to play on my bike when I was fifteen. In those days people were more satisfied with their way of life. Our expectations were to be able to live comfortably from Friday to Friday. We were far, far more

content than they are nowadays – we didn't expect the man in the moon to
come down and say hello to us! At that age we had no idea what a war was
going to *be* . . .

Kay's community was tightly knit. On Sunday nights teenagers
would meet at Bible class; Kay had known Alastair Wight, whom she
would eventually marry, since their schooldays together. His brother
had married her sister – why look further?

Privileged and unprivileged, most of them were innocent about
sex. Margaret Herbertson, a diplomat's daughter born in 1922, was
entirely unacquainted with the most basic facts of life: 'My mother
said nothing at all about it to me. Zero. I had an idea that if you were
married you had a baby, but how you had the baby I had *no* idea
whatever. We were all very, very naive.' For the vast majority in the
years leading up to the Second World War the walls of home were
their fortress. Life for them rolled securely on, seemingly untouched
by military build-up and a botched European peace.

*

The main purpose of this book is to see the world of war – and of the
ensuing peace - through their eyes. These women were entering
maturity in a world overshadowed by unemployment and Fascism.
In order to follow their stories over the ensuing chapters, we need to
start to get to know some of them in the last months before the Nazi
crisis erupted in late summer 1939.

Phyllis ('Pip') Beck, impressionable, naive, poetry-loving and dazzlingly pretty, is growing up in the little market town of Buckingham.
Pip is sixteen years old. Here in Middle England she has started her first
job working in a small bakery shop. The income will help her parents,
who have fallen on hard times during the Depression. So now she is
learning to count out change and display iced fancies on their silver
platters in the shop window, while flirting nervously with the boys
who bring in the bread deliveries. Soon after, she moves on to train as
a hairdresser and beautician – 'I was fascinated by cosmetics, though I
wasn't allowed to use them yet.' That year Pip also has her first kiss in
a summer meadow with Ron Race, a dashing telegraph boy from the
local post office. The occasion, for all its glamorous echoes of movie
romance, leaves her with mixed feelings. 'Supposing I had a baby? Had

I done anything that could result in having one? I simply didn't know.'
Scared, Pip ends the friendship. For such an attractive girl there will be
other boyfriends, and better ones.

Twenty-five-year-old Margery Berney is working for her father as
a clerk in his Portsmouth building business. Margery is alight with
unconfined ambitions. 'From my earliest memory I was rehearsing
for success in my daydreams.' But in 1939 she is still unsure what form
her future will take – tennis champion, pantomime fairy or movie
star? Two years at the Royal Academy of Dramatic Art have convinced her that the stage is not for her, but her true talents have yet
to surface. So, like many other middle-class young women, Margery
has learned to type. It seems improbable that days spent tapping on a
keyboard in an office will lead to the fulfilment of her vague but
over-arching ambitions to become something or somebody. 'But my
own sense of purpose was just beginning to develop.'

Mary Cornish shares a flat in Baker Street, London, with a female
friend. She is thirty-nine. Both are musicians. Miss Cornish is the
elder of two sisters, and Eileen, the younger, has always looked up to
her for guidance and leadership. She has also had the fortune, unlike
Eileen, to escape the parental home; in the 1920s she studied the piano
in Vienna and has since travelled alone. A forthright and fearless person, she has turned her back on marriage and made her own life
among like-minded musical friends. Like so many educated spinsters
in the 1930s,* she has chosen to teach and since 1928 has been employed
as a music teacher at a private girls' school in Wokingham, returning
to London at weekends. There is something in Miss Cornish of the
'universal aunt'. She combines patriotism and religion and is always
willing to be of service to friends, family and pupils.

Thelma Ryder, at seventeen, is a home-loving teenager who lacks
confidence. She lives with her mum and stepfather, who run a pub
just outside the Marine barracks in Plymouth. The family don't have
much money, but Thelma's mother takes good care of them; as a
tailoress, she makes all her daughter's clothes. Unusually for a girl of
her class, Thelma stays on at school until the age of fifteen. 'I didn't
want to go to work. I was a proper mummy's girl really. I wanted to

---

* See Virginia Nicholson *Singled Out – How Two Million Women Survived without
Men after the First World War* (2007)

stay at home. I said, "I'll do the cooking and the housework, and you can do the sewing and bring in the money."' Her mother's attempts to send her for jobs fail, until finally Thelma finds herself marched to the door of the Initial Towel Company; a job in laundry may not have a future, but it will do till she finds a husband. There, Thelma spends the next three years packing towels for the company's clients.

Clara Milburn is fifty-five years old. Her home is at Balsall Common, near Coventry, in the heart of the Midlands. Mrs Milburn is a woman of such unimpeachable middle-aged, middle-class respectability that she might be held up as a model for English womanhood. Happily married to a skilled machine tool engineer, she and her husband Jack have one boy, Alan, now twenty-four years old, and a faithful live-in servant named Kate. Mrs Milburn has never been employed, but willingly gives her energies to the Women's Institute and the church. She is a friend of Coventry Cathedral. She loves her husband, her house, her dog Twink and her garden. But most of all she loves her son.

Helen Vlasto is spending her summer holidays with her family at a capacious house rented by her wealthy grandparents at Frinton-on-Sea in East Anglia. The drawing room is scented with great bowls of roses and cut lavender. It's a break from nineteen-year-old Helen's busy life in London, where she has combined training to be a nurse by day with debutante dances by night. That summer, when not playing tennis or golf, the stunningly pretty girl (who has inherited her Greek grandparents' Mediterranean features) attends to the manicuring of her nails and the applying of face cream.

Monica Littleboy, daughter of a manager with the Colman's Mustard company, is wondering what to do with her life. There are so few possibilities for girls, especially in Norwich. Discouraged from aiming high by her teachers, she leaves school at sixteen and does a domestic science course – it's not a success. Early in 1939 she sets out for London to train as a beautician. She lodges in Earl's Court; London seems 'exciting but sordid', but is soon transformed when she meets George Symington, a young man who travels the same journey each day by Underground. George, handsome and educated, is from a different world; though not wealthy he is well-connected. Soon seventeen-year-old Monica is 'swimming in an endless round of happiness with the one I loved. Our young lives were as yet untouched by the bad news of the war clouds gathering over Europe.'

Anne Popham, aged twenty-two, daughter of a dignified museum official, has also had her world turned upside down. A shy, serious, unconfident student, she is studying Art History in London and has fallen deeply and passionately in love with a married artist. Graham's good looks and bohemianism, his left-wing politics, his subversive intelligence, his pleas, promises and seductive skill have all thrown her off her preordained course. He has separated from his wife, but will they ever be able to marry? The ups and downs of their illicit affair dominate her waking hours.

Nella Last has lived for the best part of her forty-nine years in Barrow-in-Furness, Cumbria, twenty-seven of these under the same roof as her somewhat gloomy and angry husband, William Last, who runs a joinery business. The Lasts have two sons, but since the boys have grown up Nella feels redundant. Life seems to her a treadmill, her husband is uncommunicative, and, bogged down with housewifely chores, she has no outlet for her feelings or latent creativity. She suffers a nervous breakdown, which coincides with the founding of the Mass Observation project, an anthropological initiative by three young men who are calling on ordinary members of the public to submit diaries recording their everyday lives. The following year, Nella Last decides to join them. It is the first step on the road to her recovery.

Mavis Lever, a well-read sixth-former, has persuaded her parents (who have never before travelled further than Bournemouth) to take up one of the cheap holidays offered by the German government in an effort to propagandise to other Europeans about the virtues of Aryan culture. They are travelling in the Rhineland – now occupied by Hitler. Already a talented German linguist, Mavis now steeps herself in Wagnerian legends, travelling past fairy-tale castles and listening to lieder sung in view of the Lorelei rock. Swept up in a fever of romanticism, she makes up her mind to study German literature at university.

Helen Forrester's family is painfully poor. In the Depression Helen's public-school-educated father has gone bankrupt; with seven children the family live on the brink of absolute penury. Their tiny terrace house in a run-down area of Liverpool stinks of 'neglect and malnutrition'. Helen, who is nineteen, earns a scanty living as a social worker for a charity in Bootle, supplementing her income by teaching shorthand in the evenings. She describes herself as 'struggling to stay alive'. After she has contributed to her keep there is nothing to spare for clothes, a perm, or beauty aids. Painfully thin, Helen suffers from spots and, unable to afford the hairdresser, scrapes her long hair into an unfashionable bun. She has never been kissed by a man.

Madeleine Henrey, the chic French wife of Robert Henrey, an upper-class English gossip columnist, is out with her husband in the West End looking for copy. London's aristocratic night life is their raw material. They dine together at Quaglino's, a famous restaurant patronised by the younger generation of royals. Madeleine has diamonds in her hair. Later she swathes her gleaming shoulders in an ermine cape and they go on to the Embassy Club in Old Bond Street. Princes, courtiers and leaders of fashion dance here; it is Madeleine's job to note every nuance of dress and coiffure, from lipstick to handbag. In those days, she wrote, 'every woman's dress was a masterpiece. My husband and I went out every evening during this fabulous period. For me this life was a continual joy, the sort that every girl dreams of. I would never be so young, so full of laughter again.'

*

Pip Beck, Margery Berney, Mary Cornish, Thelma Ryder, Clara Milburn, Helen Vlasto, Monica Littleboy, Anne Popham, Nella Last, Mavis Lever, Helen Forrester and Madeleine Henrey ... twelve glimpses of twelve lives. Few of the many names which will appear over the course of this book are any more conspicuous or celebrated than these, but every one of them was to have their lives changed by the war.

Twelve women ... but there were 'millions like us'.

1 We're at War

Ready for the Fray

In August 1939 sixteen-year-old Joan Wyndham started to keep a diary. Spending that summer at her grandmother's palatial house in Wiltshire, she recorded her teenage crush on the butler, point-to-points, charades in the drawing room and cream teas with Daddy in Marlborough. And also the weather:

22nd August

It's the hottest summer I can remember for years. There's thunder in the air which gives me a headache. I wish the rain would come to cool everything down.

August slid into September. Flies buzzed, fruit ripened; the still heat of late summer held fears in suspension. 'Nobody talks about Hitler,' wrote Joan.

Denial gripped the nation. Few of Britain's teenagers were readers of newspapers. Many of them barely knew where Germany, Poland or Czechoslovakia were. Margaret Perry from Nottingham was surely a typical seventeen-year-old. She had been taught in the schoolroom that the British Empire was coloured a lovely red across the globe. She also knew that Europe was 'full of foreigners who couldn't speak English', while 'tea came from India, and Africa was full of little black pygmies':

War didn't happen in England; any fighting that might occur would take place over the channel – in France. I had no idea what had been happening in Europe during the last six years . . . Why my mother was getting so upset I couldn't imagine. I did recall she'd mentioned something about Zepperlins [sic] whatever they were, flying over England, and Uncle Harry loosing [sic] a leg in the trenches. Yes I'd heard a lot about trenches but they were in France weren't they?

Another bewildered young working-class woman was Mary Hewins from Stratford-upon-Avon:

I couldn't understand the war, really. You know, what it was really *for*.

Debutante Susan Meyrick was also oblivious, preoccupied by her coming-out commitments: 'I had no idea of the world situation. None. I had no idea the war was so close.' Sixteen at the time, Mary Angove down in the West Country recalls, 'Nobody knew what was coming. We were living in a Fools' Paradise. We all thought Germans were 6 foot tall and blond. People saw Hitler as some kind of comedian – he looked so like Charlie Chaplin, jumping up and down and screaming.'

A sex divide that allocated home-making to women and world affairs to men left Margaret, Mary, Susan and many like them across Britain clueless about the reality. With international tension mounting, and reduced to guessing about their future, such young women looked to the comfortingly familiar. They turned to their mothers. And their mothers, who remembered how the First World War had affected them, had words of reassuring wisdom: 'I can remember my mum saying we must stock up on sugar and tea,' remembers Flo Mahony, now in her late eighties. Other prescient advice included: 'get a little extra soap darling, because soap rationing may well come in' and 'buy up hairpins, Kirby grips and elastic for knickers'.

Minds conditioned by decades of domesticity reached out for domestic solutions to the enemy's menace, and women prepared themselves in the way they knew best: by shopping. Dolly Scannell's baby was born in July 1939; the way things were going, little Susan was off to a rocky start in life, but her provident mother had seen things coming and purchased enough baby food to last a year. Kathleen Hale's husband had been prophesying war for years, telling her that England would be blockaded and that they would probably be reduced to eating rats. Kathleen bought a large supply of curry powder and tomato sauce, 'to make the rats more palatable'. Virginia Graham ordered two entire cases of Bronco lavatory paper (it turned out to be far more than needed and she gave it away as Christmas presents for years afterwards), and her best friend, Joyce Grenfell, cautiously purchased six pairs of silk stockings: not enough, it turned out. Young Edna Hughes from Liverpool filled up a tea-chest with necessities for her family. It was

early 1939, and soon they were ready to withstand a siege, stocked with
tins of corned beef, tea, cocoa and sugar. Months passed. Every so often
Edna's mother would find there was nothing for tea and suggest raiding
the chest – 'Come on, Ed, let's open another tin of salmon.' And, alas,
when war finally came the tea-chest was empty.

Before the Munich agreement trenches had been dug in the parks,
gas-masks had been fitted and issued, sandbags filled. Then Chamberlain returned and delivered his 'Peace for our Time' speech. There
would be no war. The gas-masks had been dumped on rubbish heaps
and the sandbags left leaking out their contents where they were
abandoned. But by summer 1939 even the most resolutely withdrawn
and unobservant members of the population could hardly fail to
notice the build-up.

*

In 1939 the women's auxiliary services started to muster, though as
yet there was no formal recruiting drive. Any woman with an urge to
serve her country could choose from the ATS (Auxiliary Territorial
Service), the WRNS (Women's Royal Naval Service, commonly
known as the Wrens), the WAAF (Women's Auxiliary Air Force), the
Women's Land Army, the FANY (First Aid Nursing Yeomanry) or
various other nursing services. With the exception of the ATS, all of
these services had played their part in the First World War, so it was
simply a question of reviving their numbers and bringing them up to
speed. Publicity made the services sound benign and appealing, like a
glorified Girl Guide camp:

Some are learning to be cooks, others are doing orderly and clerical work
. . . The Woman's Army is a very human institution – the use of powder is
allowed, and even a touch of natural lipstick . . . Not an easy life, perhaps,
but a healthy, friendly one. And a grand Army . . .

though, reading between the lines, there is little to distinguish these
female soldiers from militarised maidservants or secretaries. Not
surprisingly, a popular perception of the ATS was that its members
did nothing but peel potatoes.

Recruits were volunteers. At this stage a girl joining up was likely to
be met with mixed reactions; the public was by no means ready for
female soldiers. Parents were reluctant to let their daughters join the

ATS. Its existence upset many preconceived ideas. It was barely ten years since women under thirty had had the vote, and now here they were, belted and booted, square-bashing like the men. At this stage only a minority were working-class. The underprivileged had more pressing concerns, like having enough to eat, while better-off girls responded to the hint of glamour and adventure in the promotional material.

Some of these, with time on their hands – like Patience Chadwyck-Healey – enrolled in the FANYs. Patience admits that the fact that no qualifications were required helped: 'You just had to be able to drive.' Twenty-four-year-old Verily Bruce, the daughter of a Sussex rector, had been a debutante in 1934. She too joined the FANYs 'in a burst of mixed patriotism and fear soon after Munich'. Verily went off once a week to train, 'learning to change wheels of army vehicles, [and] do a bit of "left-right, left-right"'. Others joined, perhaps, with a wary eye on the probable alternative (work in munitions factories or making aircraft). By the time Hitler invaded Poland, there were 20,000 female auxiliaries in this country ready to play their part.

From the Women's Institute to the Townswomen's Guild, the Council of Voluntary Welfare Workers to the Blue Cross, women across the land were putting their organisations on to a wartime footing. The Citizens' Advice Bureaux set up in 1938 to coordinate information and inquiries were largely staffed by women. You could take your pick, and certainly the more prescient and experienced took what training was on offer.

*

Frances Faviell,* thirty-seven, educated, independent and artistically talented, had been living in a spacious studio flat at 33 Cheyne Place, Chelsea, through most of the 1930s. She loved the borough, with all its bohemianism and raffish social life, and, after many travels and upheavals – to Europe, India and the Far East – had become engaged to a strong, intelligent man named Richard Parker.

In 1939 Frances was one of those who decided that learning to

---

*Frances Faviell is the *nom de plume* of Olivia Parker (born Olive Frances Lucas in 1902). Confusingly, she also painted under the name Olivia Fabri – this being the surname of her first husband, a Hungarian painter named Karoy Fabri. Having largely drawn my account of her life in the 1940s from her published (but now, sadly, out of print) books, I have presented her under the name she chose as a writer.

administer first aid was a good idea and early that year she attended a
course. The trainees were told how to care for air-raid casualties.
'You must be prepared for anything,' they were told by the lecturer.
There would be no sterile bandages or boiled water at hand. 'Anything' included filth, blood, torn tissue – and spilled guts.

They *smell*, ladies and gentlemen. You'll have to get used to that. If you
come across a casualty with half his stomach laid open and his guts hanging
out, thrust your hands unhesitatingly into the wound and pack them back,
hold your fists there to keep them in position if you have nothing else. The
mess and smell may revolt you, *but that man needs his guts* – keep them in for
him till medical help arrives.

The lecturer's words, emphatic as they were, seemed detached from
any reality Frances had ever known.

   Later, there were trial runs for the blackout and rehearsals for air
raids. On a lovely June morning in 1939 Frances and her upstairs
neighbour Kathleen Marshman joined other members of their borough in a grand-scale Civil Defence exercise. At 12 noon the traffic
was stopped for the duration of fifteen minutes. Air-raid wardens
told everyone what to do, but – perhaps because of their ridiculous
appearance, dressed in regulation brown overalls so ill-fitting that the
pants seats were between their knees – nobody took them seriously.
Everybody was joking at the absurdity of the role-playing expected
of them. Frances and Kathleen were told to be casualties. Mrs Freeth,
her housekeeper, cradling Frances's dachshund in her arms, was told
to 'take shelter' in an area of pavement marked out with white paint.
There was some disagreement as to whether dogs were allowed in
this 'shelter', but, as Mrs Freeth pointed out, the shelter was entirely
imaginary so the dog was coming 'inside' whether she was permitted
or not.

   At midday the siren wailed. Mrs Freeth and the dog took up their
places; the 'casualties' were given their instructions. Frances lay flat
on the pavement in her allotted spot and awaited the arrival of the
giggling first aid party who enthusiastically and with much chaffing
bandaged up her imaginary wounds, then loaded her on to a stretcher
to be taken to an imaginary ambulance. Seeing her mistress being
assaulted, the dachshund went frantic; it was all Mrs Freeth could do
to hold her still. The exercise proceeded: 'a flurry of violent activity

in the deathless silence of the trafficless streets'. Many of the participants were contemptuous:

'Lot of tommy-rot, won't be no air raids here. All this silly play-acting!' I heard fellow casualties grumbling. Those in the imaginary shelters echoed their comments . . . There would be no air raids on England! It was unthinkable . . . At last the continuous flute-like voice of the All-Clear sirens sounded. The exercise was over! With relief and more grumbling we could all go home.

Frances tried to imagine what it would be like if the exercise had been real. Vivid pictures came to her mind: guns, crashing buildings, droning bombers above. 'It was horrible.' She shook herself back to reality. It was a beautiful June day; down by the Embankment the river glittered in the sunshine; in the nearby Physic Garden the trees were full of chirping birds. Crowds thronged Royal Hospital Road. Kathleen invited Frances upstairs for a restorative drink, and they had a good laugh at the absurdity of the proceedings. From below, Mrs Freeth called, 'Come and have your lunch.'

★

In Liverpool that summer twenty-year-old Helen Forrester was also aware of the preparations for war. The city would be hit, there was no doubt about that: it was the most important western port in the country.

Now the family's gas-masks had arrived and been tried on. Innumerable leaflets had landed on the doormat – what to do in the event of an air raid or a gas attack, how to handle food shortages and petrol rationing. The air-raid warden came round and told Helen's mother to arrange for the house to be blacked out.

Young Helen's life was already so wretched that death held few terrors. But the thought of dying did frighten her. The prospect of lying trapped, suffering, beneath the rubble of their home was a dreadful prospect, and the atmosphere of tension that August only added to her woes. 'To say that in the summer of 1939 we were scared would have been an understatement. Almost everybody in Liverpool was obsessed by a dread of the unknown.' Mother was drained and exhausted. 'There she sat, drinking tea and popping aspirins into her mouth, while Poland was decimated and we waited for our turn.'

Heaven Help Us

Back in London at the end of August Joan Wyndham was busy with
her drama school colleagues rehearsing *Hedda Gabler*. At sixteen she
was stage-struck, artistic and living in Chelsea. Dick Wyndham, her
father, was a wealthy *demi-mondain* and aspiring artist, now separated
from her devoutly religious mother. Joan lived in Redcliffe Gardens
with 'Mummy' and her eccentric female companion Sidonie – 'Sid'.
Despite (or because of) her unconventional upbringing, Joan's appetite for life and eager embrace of what Chelsea's bohemia had to offer
make her published diaries delectably entertaining – even with doom
impending. By this time parents were being advised to have their
children evacuated from the cities:

Friday 1st September
The posters say HITLER INVADES POLAND. Everywhere children
are waiting in expectant noisy herds, but the mothers are quiet, grey, and
some of them are crying . . . Mummy and Sid went to church so I sat in my
room and got completely drunk for the first time in my life – on rum. It
was a very nice experience indeed. I no longer cared a damn what happened
to anybody.
    I rang up Dorothea: 'I'm completely drunk.'
    'That's right, so are we.'
    'Goodbye and good luck.'
    'Goodbye, darling.' Everything now is goodbye and good luck.

The world seemed to be shutting down. On Saturday 2 September
Joan was panic-stricken to hear that 'they are planning to close the
theatres!' It was her last chance to see Edith Evans in *The Importance of
Being Earnest*. Mummy and Sid disapproved, but Joan's desire to seize
at pleasures was not so much frivolous as a fear that everything she
enjoyed was coming to an end.
    Another woman recollected the final days before the declaration
of war as being a time of heightened impressions, when to 'look your
last on all things lovely' was an imperative of the greatest urgency.
With the awful conviction that everything beloved and ordinary was
under threat, the familiar became beautiful. Images were indelibly
printed on people's minds with the clarity of a photograph: the sun

shining on a pane of glass, swans on the Thames, barrage balloons glittering in the evening sunlight. 'We believed that everything we had known was going to be wiped out.'

All that Saturday the BBC Home Service interrupted its schedule of gramophone records with gloomy announcements. Helen Vlasto, on holiday with her family on the Essex coast, recalled that the bulletins served only to undermine morale, already low. It was a day 'full of fore-boding'. That evening a terrific storm hit areas of northern England. Rain came down in sheets, and continuous thunder crashed overhead; in Derby lightning struck five barrage balloons, which burst dramatically into flame and came down over the town. 'Nature is providing the finishing touches to these poignant, horrible days,' wrote another young woman, unable to sleep as the elements raged above her. 'This storm makes one feel that perhaps God is wishful of reminding us that our little wars are as nothing compared with His awful power.'

Sunday morning dawned crystal clear. Shortly before 11 o'clock Helen Vlasto dropped by the kitchen to check that her grandmother's servants were going to be listening in at 11.15 to the expected broadcast from Number 10 Downing Street. The staff looked grim and white-faced, though Ella, the family cook, continued to prepare vegetables for dinner. 'Oh, Miss Helen dear, what is to become of us?' As the maids awaited the news below stairs, she made her way to the drawing room. There, the family were gathered in front of the wireless to listen to the Prime Minister:

This morning the British Ambassador in Berlin handed the German Government a final note stating that, unless we heard from them by 11 o'clock that they were prepared at once to withdraw their troops from Poland, a state of war would exist between us. I have to tell you now that no such undertaking has been received, and that consequently this country is at war with Germany.

As she listened to Chamberlain's announcement, Helen Vlasto told herself: 'This is the most poignant moment of your life to date, and you will never forget it.' The time and place remained engraved on her memory – the sun streaming through the latticed panes, dappling the swathes of lavender left out to dry on the broad window-seats, the scent of Turkish tobacco and rose petals in great bowls. There was silence.

But out in the garden nothing had changed. The September sun still shone thoughtlessly down, unmindful of the new and monstrous turn of events. The bees continued to bumble amongst the roses, and the butterflies to weave their erratic and inconsequential course towards the early Michaelmas daisies and the Buddleias.

My tiny erect grandmother watched grimly as her family made its urgent plans to scatter, and prayed that we might all be spared to meet again. How were we to find our way, and how should we come to know how best to use this emergency constructively and fruitfully?

★

Eighty years ago Sunday was a day when all the bustle of the week came to a stop. Shops closed, workers and traders downed tools for a lie-in. There was church, roast lunch, a day's dozing in the parlour over cups of tea. The country was suspended, hushed and stilled. The impact of Chamberlain's declaration would penetrate every home in the land.

Sixteen-year-old Pip Beck was exhilarated: '"Well, at least we know where we stand now!" I said.' But her parents were silent. Phyllis Noble was 'very scared . . . I'm afraid I'm not of the stuff that heroes are made of.' Some wept. 'I get emotional remembering it. Old age I suppose,' says Mary Davis (née Angove). Mary was a trainee nursing assistant. 'It was a beautiful sunny day, not a cloud in the sky. I went out on the verandah of our lodging, and I just stood there, trying to make my mind think: "War – we're at War." It was unreal.'

Deeply stirred, feminine hearts beat faster at the thought of our brave soldiers setting off to fight for king and country; one sixteen-year-old promptly got dressed in her Sunday navy-blue and white best and set off down Hereford High Street to wave goodbye to all the gallant lads. 'Nothing happened.' Where were the brass bands, the stirring processions she had seen in the movies? She cried all the way home. 'The glamour of war wasn't true and someone had lied.' Another – in the middle of cutting her toenails – stopped to listen to the broadcast with terror and bated breath, before reapplying herself to her task.

That same weekend Marguerite Eave had just moved into a small flat in Bradford. Aged twenty-two that summer, Marguerite was due to start on Monday with a brand-new job as a senior home economist, demonstrating appliances for the Lincolnshire and York-shire Electric Power Company. For Marguerite, that Sunday remains unforgettable:

It was an extraordinary day – one of those September days when you really feel, God's in His Heaven and all's well with the world. Well, I bumped into the girl who lived across the landing, and she introduced herself. She was the manageress of a Jaeger shop. 'Would you like to come and listen to the broadcast and share a cup of coffee?' she said.

Well, listening, it was the most terrifying thing one could possibly imag-ine. I felt, 'We are alone. Heaven help us' – a terrible fear and loneliness. And indeed we had everything to fear. And yet in a very short time – I was still with my neighbour listening to the radio – came the messages from Canada, Australia, South Africa: and they all said: 'We are with you. You are not alone.' And the feeling that they were with us was simply amazing . . . we knew that the whole Empire was behind us.

Within minutes of the announcement the Sabbath hush was bro-ken by the eerie wailing of sirens, unmistakably sounding the alert. Frances Faviell, who, together with a group of friends in her studio and in common with the entire nation, had just finished listening to Chamberlain's broadcast, suddenly woke up to the fact that this time it wasn't play-acting. The party scattered, Frances to her landlord's reinforced shelter in the rear courtyard of her building at 33 Cheyne Place. As a trained first-aider, should she go to her post? By the time she'd made up her mind to set out, the all-clear was sounding its war-bling note. The Cheyne Place community gathered in the street to compare notes – 'I saw neighbours who never spoke to one another chatting excitedly' – and it was soon revealed that the alarm had been false, triggered by the sighting of a lone plane, 'one of ours'. Later, Frances walked in Battersea Park with a friend. They gazed in bemused wonder at the massive silver barrage balloons bobbing above them, iridescent in the sky 'like drunken fish'. She counted eighty of them from her vantage point on Battersea Bridge. 'The scene was so peaceful . . . It was impossible to realise that these silver roach in the sky were there because we were at war. War seemed too remote and archaic a word to contemplate.'

In Streatham, Pat Bawland, the fifteen-year-old daughter of an itinerant confectionery salesman, and her young brother were at

Sunday church. Pat's feckless mother had insisted that her children attend regularly – it was one way of ensuring they got enough to eat, as the deaconess could be relied upon to give food handouts to the poorer families. 'My brother was in the choir. Mum and Dad had told us that if the warning went we were to come home immediately – and while we were there on that Sunday morning the siren went; it sounded in the middle of the service. So I got up and grabbed my brother out of the choir stalls and took him out of the church and ran all the way home.'

Meanwhile, in Barrow-in-Furness, the forty-nine-year-old housewife Nella Last reacted to the declaration of war with the realisation that she could not share her feelings with Will, her husband. 'Sunday, 3 September, 1939. Bedtime . . . Today I've longed for a close woman friend – for the first time in my life.' An image came vividly to Nella's mind. It was 'July, before the last crisis' – 1938. The Lasts had been visiting Portsmouth, and hundreds of young sailors, ratings, had arrived with the fleet from Weymouth in response to the military build-up. Nella saw the look on their faces – 'a slightly brooding, faraway look. They all had it . . . and I felt I wanted to rush up and ask them what they could see that I could not. And now I know . . . All I can see are those boys with their look of "beyond".'

Nella's moment of intuition serves to locate a point of no return. The onward march of history was carrying the men beyond our shores, beyond family, home and all its comforts, to an uncertain destiny – to a place where the nation's women could not follow them.

The next day Nella Last had a bad headache: 'Monday, 4 September, 1939 . . . a cap of pain has settled down firmly and defies aspirin.' Nella had two sons. Cliff, the younger, was twenty-one. He would be joining the Army as a PT instructor. Her diary shows a woman trying to keep a domestic lid on the mounting fear of losing all she held dear. There was the cleaning to do; the tidying and the washing. More urgently, Nella felt the need to contribute, so she sat down to sew cot blankets for the evacuees out of remnants. A plan now took shape in her aching head. The garden would have to go. She would keep hens on half the lawn and grow vegetables on the other half.

Domesticity seemed to Nella Last and thousands more like her to be under fundamental threat. Her life up to now had consisted of creating a home for her family and preparing their meals, of knitting, needlework and cosy evenings around the hearth. War struck fiercely at all these things. More than any ideology or notion of sovereignty, the preservation of her own world in Barrow-in-Furness was of paramount importance to Nella. Only when she felt sure that the semi in Ilkley Road and all it represented was safe could she contribute to the greater work of winning the war for Britain, and this she would do in the way she knew best: using her skills as a mother and housewife.

Patience Chadwyck-Healey was short on such skills. Nobody had ever taught her to boil an egg or sweep a hearth. She could dance, and she could ride a horse to hounds. Best of all she could drive a car, and in 1938 this had qualified her to join the FANYs. The approaching conflict filled her with mounting excitement. The FANY authorities had promised to keep Patience informed about her mobilisation, and the thought of it set her pulse racing: 'Hurrah, I'm already organised to be in the FANYs, and I can drive, and I'm going to be called up!' Now, at last, Patience had something real to do, but *when* would it start? For the first time in what had been a mainly ornamental life, she could envisage serving a greater purpose. 'The first two weeks after Chamberlain's declaration were the longest I've ever spent. The days passed so slowly. I kept thinking, "Hurry up, for goodness' sake, the war'll be *over* before I get called up!" Anyway, finally, on my birthday which is in mid-September, I got a telegram to say "Please report to Bovington Camp by noon tomorrow." And I said to my parents, "I have no idea what to expect, but this is something I've *got* to do . . ." And by the 20th September there I was, in khaki, and for me that was the beginning of the war.'

The Children

The evacuation of Britain's children was an undertaking that had been long anticipated. Arrangements had been made, surplus accommodation identified, camps built. Many city families didn't wait for the declaration of war to start sending their children to safety. The exodus had started in June. By September a figure approaching 3.75 million people (children, their mothers and their teachers, and expectant mums) had moved from areas of the country regarded as unsafe to areas regarded as safe. At the end of August Frances Faviell watched carloads of children jamming the Chelsea arteries – 'toys, perambulators, dogs, cats, and birds all piled in with them or balanced on top of them'. But some of the pugs and canaries had to be left behind. There were queues at vets' surgeries for pets that couldn't accompany their owners to be put down.

Goodmayes, near Ilford, the home of fourteen-year-old Nina Mabey, was uncomfortably close to the docks. For Nina, the evacuation of her school to Suffolk couldn't come too soon, but not because she feared for her own safety. From an early age Nina had been a storyteller, a creator of invented lives; her appetite for books served only to increase her discontent with suburbia, and her vivid imagination conjured up a 'dazzling future' in some aristocratic country mansion where people fell in love over candlelit dinners. The reality of her arrival in Ipswich a few days before war was declared was, inevitably, a disappointment. 'I was billeted on a family who lived in a council house and were definitely "common".' Nina's experience was standard; the reluctance of the well-to-do to house evacuees is well documented. A fellow pupil was billeted with her in this inferior house; they shared a bed, and the last night of peace was made extra memorable by the unfortunate girl having her first period. There was blood all over the sheet, and Nina, who knew about these things, had difficulty persuading the totally uninformed teenager that she was not dying. The girls did their best, creeping secretly to the bathroom, to wash the sheet out, but it remained stained. Next day they sat in the garden drinking fizzy lemonade, listening to the Prime Minister's announcement and worrying about the sheet. Not long after this the school relocated to Wales and new billets, which years later were to provide a setting for the wartime story *Carrie's War* (1973), which would bring Nina fame under her married name of Bawden.

In Liverpool, as the Germans rolled into Poland, the Forrester family were visited by the local schoolmistress, a tweedy spinster with false teeth, who explained that the younger children of the family would be safer away from the city. Little Brian, Tony, Avril and Edward stared as she explained that they could choose between being sent off with their class or staying with relatives in the country. The government would provide an allowance for the evacuees' board. Two maiden aunts in nearby Hoylake agreed to take Tony and Edward, while Avril would be accommodated by a nearby friend of the aunts. Small suitcases were packed, goodbyes said. 'I will never forget their tight, white little faces,' recalled Helen. Poor Brian was packed off with the school to Wales, where he was billeted with a postman.

If any picture encapsulates those early days of the war it is the heart-wrenching images of small children clutching teddy bears, labels round their neck and gas-mask boxes strapped to them, gallantly grinning at the camera as they wait to board special trains. Behind each picture lay a tale of soul-searching, uncertainty and loss. Few mothers wanted their little ones' safety on their conscience, and yet sending them away felt like a violation of their deepest instincts. In a sense, sending their children away denatured them as women. Mrs Lilian Roberts obediently tied her children's gas-mask boxes on strings and pinned their names to their lapels before delivering all five, aged between five and thirteen, to catch the bus to the railway station. 'The police on duty told us to turn our backs, so as not to upset the children if we could not hold back the tears. We had no idea where they were to be taken, and it was a most dreadful feeling, losing my five children in one day.' Mrs Roberts had to wait several days before she heard where her children had been taken. They had been dispersed around Sussex between Brighton and Hailsham. 'With the children gone, I felt completely at a loss.'

All over the country little flocks of desolate six-year-olds arrived, not knowing where they would be sleeping that night. The evacuee hosts were equally unprepared for what to expect. Though superficially the entire undertaking was a model of calm organisation, in the circumstances many of the best-laid plans collapsed. In the cities, the children had been loaded unceremoniously on to whatever trains happened to be waiting. Friends were separated, schools scattered. Dirty, hungry, tired and bewildered families arrived at unknown destinations after hours spent in crowded trains with no food or toilet facilities. Dismal scenes ensued as the evacuees were taken first to 'dispersal centres', then paraded before the householders commandeered to take them in. The diarist Frances Partridge recalled one scene at Hungerford in Berkshire:

The bus came lumbering in . . .

[They] stood like sheep beside the bus looking infinitely pathetic. 'Who'll take these?' 'How many are you?' 'Oh well, I can have these two but no more,' and the piteous cry, 'But we're *together*.' It was terrible. I felt we were like sharp-nosed housewives haggling over fillets of fish.

Nothing except the widespread certainty of serious and imminent danger could have persuaded Britain's housewives that such an upheaval to their lives was a necessity. But if there were any sector deserving of praise throughout the evacuation proceedings, it was surely the WVS.

The Women's Voluntary Service had been set up initially in 1938, under the chairmanship of the formidable Stella, Marchioness of Reading. Stella Reading was more than a chairman – she was the founder and inspiration of one of the largest voluntary bodies this country has ever seen. Already in the 1930s such organisations were on the increase. This was the era of the 'do-gooder', the 'Lady Bountiful', the charity ball and the charity pageant. With vigour and single-mindedness Lady Reading now marshalled the energies of legions of Christian, patriotic and unselfish women. In September 1939 there were 165,000 members of the WVS, by which time the organisation was already making far-reaching plans for the feeding and care of thousands of evacuees. By 1942 that number would grow to more than 1 million – all dressed in green tweed uniform suits with red piping. From the outset these ladies (and 'ladies' they mostly were: at least 60 per cent of them came from income groups A and B) dealt with the domestic nuts and bolts of the war. They played to their perceived strengths as women, making innumerable cups of tea. With zeal and a vengeance they cooked, clothed, knitted and sewed, washed, mothered, nursed and organised as the circumstances demanded. They set up an official sock-mending scheme for soldiers. At Lady Reading's behest they neglected their own housework in favour of 'the national job'.

A total of 30,000 children were looked after by them. Evacuees were sent to the WVS to be deloused, anointed for scabies and given clean clothes if required. One WVS member claimed to have escorted a total of 2,526 under-fives and travelled 126,490 miles in three years. A typical WVS lady was Mrs Warren of Cambridge: 'When I saw all those hundreds of little children taken away from their mothers . . . a lump came into my throat,' she said, whereupon she promptly accepted nine into her capacious home. She then took on the task of disinfecting their heads, laundering their socks and feeding them. She collected clothes for them, and at night she patched their knickers. Her two maids helped out and reprimanded the children when they walked on Mrs Warren's flower-beds.

Helen Forrester's little sister Avril was lucky. Removed from her impoverished family, the child was put into the care of a benevolent lady, and for the first time 'knew what it was to have good, new clothes bought for her, sleep in a properly equipped bed and be decently fed.' But evacuation was an imperfect solution. The uprooting of children from deprived, but familiar, backgrounds required huge adjustments. Rene Smith, a respectable newlywed living in Wolverhampton, got her choice of two little girls 'with fair hair and blue eyes, please'. The children arrived in rags: hand-me-down dresses beyond any repair, underclothes in shreds, crawling with lice. They smelled foul, wet the beds, didn't know how to eat with cutlery and had never seen domesticated animals. Rene launched herself into caring for her ready-made family. She bought them brand-new clothes and fed them up, and soon saw the rewards. 'It was most heartening and gratifying to see them develop into two plump, healthy, well-behaved, really very nice little girls.' History does not relate how the nice little girls' parents reacted to this transformation.

Class collisions of this kind weren't always so happily handled. The Tyson family took in a couple of little boys aged six and nine. They had come from a poor area of Manchester, and Joan, the daughter of the house, was dismayed at their savage state. At mealtimes they preferred to sit under the table than at it. Evenings were spent delousing the boys with a fine-tooth comb with newspaper spread out below to catch the nits. From time to time their parents would come to visit, always arriving drunk. These were common themes: the evacuees ate fried eggs with their fingers, never washed, slept under the beds, urinated against the walls and used incomprehensible language. House-proud women experienced a culture clash as feral children who had never seen toothbrushes or hand-towels were thrust into their nice middle-class accommodation. Rural communities felt invaded by loud-mouthed city evacuees who drank and swore. Soon village shops were selling out of Keating's insect powder, soap and disinfectant.

For their part, the city women couldn't get used to country ways. Who were these uncivilised bumpkins? Where were all the cinemas? Where on earth could you get your hair permed? Was it really three miles from the nearest bus stop? And how disgusting it was to have to use an earth closet. But in the various billets she stayed in over three years, Nina Mabey was primarily dismayed by the lack of books – 'What did these people do for pleasure? Did they read only in bed? But there were no books in the bedrooms either.'

Worse, there were horror stories - accounts of hostility, neglect, abuse, starvation. These were a minority, but even where 'foster' parents were kind and loving the separation and dispersal of families wrought damage. 'Despite much kindness,' wrote Helen Forrester about her little brothers and sister, '. . . none of the children came through that traumatic time without scars.'

The Darkness

The radio reported alarming news. The first ship to be sunk in the war was the SS *Athenia*, a passenger liner torpedoed off Rockall on 3 September, followed less than a fortnight later by the sinking of HMS *Courageous* in the Atlantic, with the loss of 519 lives.

'Our familiar world seemed to be disintegrating round us,' recalled Phyllis Noble. Phyllis was still travelling from Lewisham to her 'business girl' job at the National Provincial Bank in Bishopsgate, but her days were haunted by the fear of air raids. She envisaged skies blackened with bombers, the city toppling in ruins around her. 'I was terrified . . . more afraid during that first week of the war than I ever was later.' Stress made her family quarrelsome, and rows broke out with unnerving frequency.

In the early days of the Second World War the unchanging world of the pre-war woman was being slowly eroded. Community, family, routine, order, stability and plenty were still evident, but no longer carried any certainty. Nella Last recorded in her diary that her younger son, Cliff, would leave for the Army on 15 September: 'I have a cold feeling inside.' After his departure she noticed a crop of white hairs springing from her dark temples, and inexplicable lumpy ridges appeared on her fingernails – from shock, the doctor said. By the 25th she was writing:

I miss my Cliff more every day . . . I miss his cheeky ways . . .

It's no use making ginger-bread or new rolls or pies now, for my husband does not care for them . . . I smelled ginger-bread baking in a confectioner's, and it brought back memories of two hungry schoolboys who would insist on a piece of ginger-bread before tea if it was hot out of the oven. I've always had rather a narrow life and my joys have been so simple. I seem to have built a house like a jackdaw – straw by straw – and now my straws are all blowing away!

The known landscape of life, with all its comforts, its knitting needles and gingerbread, was taking on a new face: a face of necessity. Early in 1939 the newly formed Ministry of Information had devised a 'Careless Talk' campaign, specifically targeting housewives who were seen as the purveyors of harmful tittle-tattle. In late August the government took on powers to issue hundreds of new regulations to ensure public safety, order, supplies and services, and now instructions flooded in: *Make Your Room Gas-proof, Always Carry Your Gas-mask, Protect Your Home against Air-Raids, Mask Your Windows, First Aid Advice, Safety in the Blackout, What You Must KNOW, What You Must DO . . .*

How to look stylish in a gas-mask. The advertisers of this necessity promoted it alarmingly: 'The ravages of gas can be frightful, especially to women.'

Abiding by the new rules meant never going anywhere without a gas-mask. The masks came in compact cardboard containers, but a brisk business was done in cases and straps to render them more portable – and stylish. A woman spotted carrying hers in a satchel of violet velvet decked out with artificial roses caused a stir, as reported by the *Daily Telegraph*. Nella Last was very struck by the sight of a string of courting couples smooching in her local lovers' lane, all of them virtuously kitted out with the mandatory gear – 'a sign of the times'.

The blackout rules favoured such intimate activities. In this time before the bombs, many people rejoiced in the romance of moonlit nights, visible for the first time without garish sodium lighting. In cities lovers took advantage of the sandbagged doorways and the enveloping darkness for their pleasures. One young woman literally bumped into a soldier who had lost his way in the pitch darkness; two years later they were married. Other accidents were less happy, as one stumbled over fire hydrants, parked bicycles, letter boxes and cats; blood and bruises were often the result. The blackout was initially imposed strictly from sunset to sunrise; the nightly task of covering windows with heavy black curtains or, in many cases, thick black paper attached with drawing pins being a tedious but compulsory chore. In Balsall Common near Coventry, the housewife Clara Milburn spent the first week of the war alternately helping to billet several hundred Coventry children with their teachers in the locality, and making up blackout curtains for her windows. With heavy demand the price of blackout fabric had rocketed by over a shilling a yard, and it was, as Mrs Milburn noted with a housewifely eye, 'of decidedly inferior quality'. In the hot September weather the new curtains made the house stifling, 'but it is wonderful how one can conform to an order when it is absolutely necessary to do so'. Doing one's duty brought satisfaction.

There was a sense of the world shutting down. By common consent the social season was suspended entirely. Though they were to reopen within weeks, orders were issued for all theatres, cinemas and dance-halls to close. Three weeks after the declaration of war petrol rationing came in. Throughout the war the writer and journalist Mollie Panter-Downes indefatigably reported on Londoners' doings to the American press. On 17 September her weekly bulletin informed the readers of the *New Yorker* that nearly everything the British enjoyed was now banned:

Happy accidents in the blackout.

With, on the whole, astounding good humor and an obedience remarkable in an effete democracy, they have accepted a new troglodyte existence in which there are few places of entertainment, no good radio programs, little war news, and nothing to do after dark except stay in the cave . . . 'So we'll go no more a-roving so late into the night' has taken on a significance that Byron never intended.

The characteristics of good humour and stoicism were to be tested to the full, but at this time cheerfulness still came easily to teenagers like Joan Wyndham. 'This war really isn't at all bad,' she wrote in her diary during the second week of September. 'We make the best of things.' However, she noticed her own tendency to say 'bugger' when beaten at ping-pong and to crave French books 'of an immoral nature'. A fortnight in, very little had happened, but stresses were starting to show.

By October Clara Milburn noted: 'The paralysing effect of the first few weeks of war [have begun] to wear off . . .' But a shocking reminder of war's reality came on 14 October with the loss of another British ship. The *Royal Oak* was sunk, lying at anchor in Scapa Flow, with the loss of 800 lives. But the promised enemy air raids had failed to materialise. During this so-called 'phoney war' fears of disaster were allayed, but were replaced by endless inconveniences and intrusions. You couldn't get a seat on the train, or a cup of tea; you might twist your ankle falling off a pavement in the blackout; and with petrol rationing came the imposition of a 20 mph speed limit. Housewives oiled their old bicycles and pedalled out to do the shopping; in the country pensioned-off ponies were rehabilitated and ancient carts and traps refurbished. Income tax went up, and so did the price of many basic groceries. War and its fearsome realities loured in the background like an incipient headache. The majority of wives and mothers continued their primary activities. In the circumstances of the blackout people stayed in. Everything associated with home assumed increased importance: its safety, its cosiness and its guiding deity – 'Mum' – all took on the roseate glow of something loved, and something under threat.

Though two months into the war not a bomb had been dropped, women listening to a speech broadcast on the wireless by the Queen on 11 November, Armistice Day, would have felt boosted by Her Majesty's acknowledgement of the part they would play in the imminent conflict:

War has at all times called for the fortitude of women . . . we, no less than men, have real and vital work to do. To us also is given the proud privilege of serving our country in her hour of need. The call has come, and from my heart I thank you, the women of our great Empire, for the way in which you have answered it . . .

Women of all lands yearn for the day when it will be possible to set about building a new and better world, where peace and goodwill shall abide. That day must come. We all have a part to play. I know you will not fail in yours.

But while playing that part would surely involve unimagined adventures and hazards, right now the requirement appeared for the most part to be more prosaic.

Mum kept house, looked after her children, got her hair done and occasionally (when it reopened) braved the blackout to go to the cinema. She also went shopping – with a cautious eye on cost and durability. Fish was dear, bacon scarce. West End stores reported buoyant sales in indestructible tweed suits and tough but colourful housecoats. The factories that made them would soon switch to making uniforms, and those who had bought their tweeds early felt smug as woollen goods began to disappear from the shops. Trivial annoyances loomed large. There was a run on number 8 torch batteries, and queues formed wherever they appeared. Orders were issued regarding paper salvage, and a packet of paper handkerchiefs which had once contained fifty now only contained forty. In a St Albans store the shop assistants – once prohibited from being rude to their customers – were told by their managers that the rule had been relaxed; from now on it was all right to answer back to selfish shoppers who grumbled when they couldn't get swansdown powder puffs.

For downtrodden women in underpaid jobs like this, the scenery was beginning to change. Some found themselves redundant when firms producing unnecessary goods were forced to scale down. In 1939 the government took a laissez-faire attitude to women's employment. The frenzy to get women into war work was still to come, but in that first autumn of the war there were already openings for women in engineering, in the vehicle industries, in metals and chemicals, utilities and even ship-building.

Those openings were to siphon off almost half of all those working in domestic service over the course of the Second World War. Now, in 1939, the servants were already starting to leave, causing upheavals for their mistresses, and for many middle- and upper-class women it was a question of starve or learn to cook. How did one set about it? One approach was to ignore economy altogether, still possible in the early days before rationing turned cheese and chocolate into scarce luxuries. In September *Woman's Own* was still publishing recipes that needed three eggs, six ounces of margarine and twelve ounces of icing sugar. If making breakfast proved too challenging, there were still croissants to be bought from the Chelsea patisseries, as Joan Wyndham's mother found out after their cook deserted them. She also discovered how to make hot chocolate by melting down a bar of Cadbury's and adding cream. For dinner they had baked oysters in cheese sauce. 'Everybody was sick,' recorded Joan in her diary. 'Maybe somebody should give Mummy a pep talk about wartime austerity.'

'Women are busier than ever before,' claimed *Woman's Own* that autumn. 'And if there are any who aren't busy, I'm sorry for them! There is nothing like a definite job, and now there is no excuse for moping at home.' Skilled and non-skilled found niches, some obvious, others obscure. Young and old took on fire-watching duties – one of these was music teacher Mary Cornish, who sternly applied herself to her nightly vigil in the vicinity of her Baker Street flat. Telephonists and drivers adapted to work in exchanges and ambulance units; for others the outbreak of war shifted their career on to unexpected paths. The daughter of a plumber, Vera Welch's career as a popular vocalist was just getting off the ground when war was declared. She had chosen the stage surname Lynn, her grandmother's maiden name.

Vera remembers how she and her parents had been sitting in the garden when the announcement came over the air, dashing her hopes of a successful singing future. 'I thought, that's the end of my career . . . There won't be any call for frivolities and entertainment with a war going on.' Happily for everyone, radio broadcasts remained an outlet for the singer's silvery, heart-stopping vocals, and before long parted families were sending in requests for Vera to sing what was to become the Second World War's best-loved refrain, 'We'll Meet Again'. At the same time up in the north of England Marguerite Eave found herself promoted to a job as senior home economist demonstrating kitchen appliances in the Lincoln area. Marguerite, then as now, had confidence, charisma and aplomb. With food shortages already starting to have an impact, the Council hired her to go out to remote villages and educate the local housewives about how to cope with limited ingredients. Setting herself up in disused schoolrooms with archaic equipment, Marguerite now started out on a career that – after her marriage to RAF officer Bob Patten – was to bring her nationwide acclaim on the radio show *The Kitchen Front*.

Meanwhile, many women who had got left behind in the pre-war rush to join training schemes joined the war effort in droves. If they weren't in the WVS washing nits out of evacuees' hair, learning to cook, knitting cot blankets or obeying orders with the FANY or ATS, they were doing jobs with new status. Office workers had to adapt to new surroundings as their firms evacuated to country locations away from the bomb threat. Schoolteachers, workers in food production and supply, nurses and certain clerical jobs – all of which employed large numbers of women - were on the schedule of reserved occupations.

Uncharted Territory

Helen Forrester was one of these; she did not volunteer. Her existence was so hand-to-mouth that she could not afford to give up her job as a social worker in Bootle; even then she walked daily to work to save the twopenny bus fare. When her shorthand pupil was evacuated to Southport money became even tighter. In the long, dull autumn evenings Helen sat in silence with her bullying, unresponsive

mother over cups of tea. An envious, unfeeling woman, Mrs Forrester kept her daughter on a tight rein. What money Helen earned,
she pilfered. What clothes she owned, she pawned. And any independence that she had, she resented. At twenty, she was drained,
physically and mentally.

The nights drew in, blackout came earlier, but as the fear of being
bombed receded that autumn, Helen Forrester's depression deepened.
Finally there was a crisis. It came after she had to spend twopence on
a phone call for work and as a result found herself without the tram
fare to get home. At intervals on the long trudge down Stanley Road
she sat down on a wall or on the steps of a church. She was completely
exhausted. The future seemed an abyss. Finally at home her last
reserves gave out; leaning over the kitchen sink she gasped out her
misery in shuddering sobs. The suppressed anguish from years of
neglect broke out of her in uncontrollable howls of unhappiness –
'the revolt of a human creature nearly pressed out of existence'.

They put her to bed. As Helen lay weeping in the dark, her parents
quarrelled downstairs. She confided in her sister Fiona: how penuri-
ous she was, how she could never make any headway in her job
without a proper education, and how frightened and crushed she felt.
How their mother pocketed everything she earned. How she had no
clothes and never went out – 'I want to have fun, and go dancing.'
Fiona had seen her sister as 'the clever one', with no desires in that
direction. 'I didn't think you were interested in clothes and things like
that.' But Helen's collapse had frightened the family, and soon it was
established that a financial compromise would have to be agreed. Her
mother couldn't provide love, which was all Helen really wanted, but
now she was offering a modest gift of second-hand clothes from the
pawn shop, weekly pocket money and a three-and-sixpenny hairdo.

A week later, still sodden with weeping, Helen was sitting with
her head studded with metal curlers and her hair doused in chemicals
as Betty at 'Lady Fayre' plugged her into an electrical contraption
hanging from the ceiling. There was a strong smell of burning, and
smoke rose up as the perm took effect. Betty took pride in giving
Helen her first make-over: 'Yer know, yer could do quite well for
yourself – if yer wanted. If you like, luv, I'll make your face up too.
Just so you can see what a difference it can make.'

The result was striking; as Betty said, tweezering a few stray hairs from between her brows, 'proper pretty'. The salon girls gathered round to admire Helen's new halo of soft curls, her lightly pinked-up cheeks and touch of lipstick. 'You've missed your vocation – you could do real well for yourself. Why, Nick was only saying the other day, you got style – only needs bringing out.' Nick? It dawned on Helen, as the girls grinned admiringly, who he was. She passed his beat most evenings on her walk home past the Rialto cinema – he was a well-known pimp.

'Sure. He's set up a lot of girls in his time. Buys 'em clothes. Finds them flats. He's fair . . . Yer should get to know him better – you'd do fine with him. He moves his girls into real good districts.'

I was shocked. 'Oh, Betty. I'm not that kind.'

Betty's face lost its smile, and hardened. 'We're all that kind, luv, when times are like they are. Better'n slaving in service or standing on your feet in a factory all day – or being so clemmed in like you are.'

Betty meant well. From her perspective there weren't that many options for girls without an education. There was a sadness in her voice as she took Helen's three-and-sixpence: 'Don't be offended. Some nice lad'll know a good thing when he sees it – and take proper care of you.'

Poor as she was, Helen's background was profoundly middle-class, her values fundamentally respectable. Prostitution could not be, for her, an escape route; she knew too, from her work with the unemployed, that the reality of that profession was often far from pretty clothes and nice flats, and that there was a price to pay. But what else did life have to offer in wartime Liverpool? If poverty didn't get you first, the bombs surely would. Ultimately Betty and Helen were in the same boat, with a three-and-sixpenny permanent wave and a splash of lipstick spelling the difference between hope and a dead end. The future was bleak unless you were pretty enough to make a man want to care for you, one way or another.

*

The future in any case had little meaning in those early days of the war. Over by Christmas? Over in three months? Three years was being predicted by some as the worst possible scenario. Each day was measured out with BBC bulletins, beyond which lay uncharted territory. But the nation stepped up its readiness, and partings and upheavals started to become the norm. Male conscription proceeded slowly; by the end of 1939 the army numbered 1,128,000 men. Smaller numbers joined the navy and the RAF. The streets were full of young people in uniforms, and the trains were clogged up with troops. By December five regular divisions had been sent out to France to help man the allegedly impregnable Maginot line. For Frances Faviell in Chelsea 'life resembled a transit camp', with friends using the camp-bed in her studio for a couple of nights before leaving en route to unknown destinations.

For Helen Forrester the family scare and the perm were liberating; lipstick and new underwear released a new confidence. A Liverpool Cinderella, she decided to go to ballroom-dancing classes. Rigged up in sparkly taffeta redeemed from the pawn shop, she managed each week to extract the necessary shilling from her mother and braved the blackout to learn waltzing and fox-trotting to the music of a wind-up gramophone. Norm and Doris, the instructors, recognised her aptitude and encouraged her to try for her silver medal. Dancing now became her lifeline – 'I always put on my little satin slippers with a feeling of pure joy' – and wounds inflicted by years of poverty and unhappiness started to heal. Though still crippled by shyness, Helen's undeniable talent on the dance floor meant she was rarely without a partner.

Harry O'Dwyer wasn't a regular at Norm and Doris's dancing class, and Helen nearly tripped over him one blacked-out Saturday evening as she made her way up the steps to the makeshift ballroom in a working-class area of the city. Harry was ten years older than her, strong and lively, his face ruddy and battered, but etched with laughter lines. From the outset he made a beeline for her. They waltzed, sat one out and talked. He put his arm round her – 'It was exceedingly comforting, quite the snuggest feeling I had ever experienced.' Harry was a sailor – an engineer. On Thursday he would sail . . . but the next dancing night was Tuesday.

On Tuesday evening Helen worked late, but her mind was not on her job. 'I ached with impatience . . . Would he be there?'

He was. They danced, and Harry was quiet. 'Couldn't we go somewhere and get a cup of tea – and talk a while?' Over buns in a steamy café they shared confidences. Harry's Catholic family had destined him for the priesthood; he had lacked the vocation and pulled out. Then he joined the Merchant Navy. Unusually for a sailor, he didn't go in for dissipations – the seminary years had damp-ened the desire to drink or womanise. Reading, dancing, a game of billiards or a show were more in his line. As they walked home Harry placed his arm round Helen's waist; in the dark it was easier to talk, and she told him shyly about the distress her family had fallen into, and its dire consequences for her. At the top of the road he carefully kissed her on the cheek. 'You poor kid,' he said. 'I was trembling in his confining arms, with a scarifying, overwhelmingly strange feel-ing within me.' It was eleven o'clock; she had to be home. Harry told her that his ship would be at sea for at least five weeks; he couldn't tell exactly when he would be back. Then he took her office phone number, and they parted.

For her many loyal Liverpudlian readers, Helen Forrester's war memories hold a special place in their hearts. *Twopence to Cross the Mersey*, *By the Waters of Liverpool* and *Lime Street at Two* still carry a powerful hit of youthful anguish. It's not hard to identify with Helen's painful insecurities, her brittle family relationships and her young love. Helen was the heroine of her own story, which is not one of martial valour or courage in the face of the enemy, but tells of a primary battle to transcend her circumstances. Downtrodden and poverty-stricken as she was, the war and its consequences should surely have pulverised her. Instead, she lived to tell a tale of struggle and loneliness, of love and partings, of loss and self-reliance, which has echoes among multitudes of her contemporaries.

It has echoes in the life of the young trainee beautician Monica Littleboy, who had met her boyfriend, George Symington, in Lon-don in the spring of 1939. Their blissful summer together ended on 3 September – a day of 'dark, dead shock'. George was patriotic. He promptly left for Scotland to join the Black Watch and was soon after commissioned into his grandfather's regiment, the Gordon High-landers. 'It was as if one more light had gone out of my life. London now seemed empty.' In the face of the reality of war, a career doing manicures and facial treatments for rich ladies seemed meaningless. Monica packed it in and returned to her family in Norwich. 'I offered my services to the Land Army.'

It has echoes too in the story of Anne Popham, whose married lover, Graham, decided early in the war to train to be a pilot. 'I didn't like it at all; I tried to dissuade him. He thought it was important the war should be won as soon as possible.' After he left Anne decided to stay in London. And at least the vexed question of where their relationship was going could be temporarily shelved. From the beginning of the war Anne did air-raid warden duties three nights a week.

Young Pip Beck was not even eighteen when she waved goodbye to her boyfriend, Norman, a Territorial. He was sent off for training in Aylesbury – less than 20 miles away, but almost beyond her reach. Pip cajoled her mother into letting her spend an hour and a half with him, before he was posted abroad with the British Expeditionary Force. Mrs Beck didn't like the thought of her pretty daughter spending time on an army camp, which she feared was full of 'licentious soldiery'. 'I said it wouldn't be like that at all, and Norman would be with me, and I might never see him again.' They walked around together, but there was no privacy. He kissed her in the bus shelter before she left. 'Where would we meet again . . . would we ever? Tears flowed down my cheeks.'

Countless young women were confronting the removal of all they held dear – like Frances Campbell-Preston (née Grenfell), who had married her sweetheart, a young officer in the Black Watch, after a whirlwind romance at the end of 1938. A year later she was pregnant while Patrick, her husband, prepared for the inevitable. Patrick left for France with the British Expeditionary Force late in 1939:

It was the end of our idyllic time . . .

At the end of the week the Battalion marched through Aldershot and I found myself lining the street to wave goodbye, just like the women pictured in all wars . . .

I was homeless . . .

Awaiting her baby, Frances went to stay first with her mother-in-law in Argyllshire, then to her married sister in Somerset – 'the nearest thing to a maternity home'. At this point in the war changes of address were bewilderingly frequent as a frightened population packed and unpacked, scattered and relocated.

★

For fifteen-year-old Pat Bawland, travelling daily from Streatham to her job as invoice typist for a firm in Tower Bridge that made brassières and sanitary products, life as yet held no prospect of any more ambitious journeys. Pat had loved school. She wanted to learn, and her ability with figures had always earned her top marks in class. But the Bawlands, like the Forresters, lived hand to mouth. Their horizons were narrow, and there was never any question of Pat being able to pursue her education. 'We were very poor. I grew up in an extended family with my Irish granny and granddad – he used to get drunk and knock her about at weekends. There was fourteen of us in the house. My mother loved us, but she didn't know how to make a penny stretch. I knew more about pawn tickets and bailiffs and moon-light flits than most fifteen-year-olds.' The family needed every shilling Pat could earn. 'My dad took me to work the first day. I cried all the way on the bus.' But within a few months of working at the Tower Bridge firm her ability showed itself, and Pat graduated from sorting the piles of orders – brassières for Birmingham, bias bindings for Liverpool – to invoice clerk. And because the company produced such essentials as sanitary towels and baby clothes, Pat soon found that she was regarded as being in a reserved occupation. In 1939 it was looking as if, whatever the war held in store for others, for her it would be spent nine to five in front of a typewriter.

Pat was unquestioning. There was nothing new about money worries. In 1938 there were 2 million families in Britain living, as Kay Mellis in Edinburgh remembered, 'from Friday to Friday', crushed and undernourished, with no margin and no savings; but until the Second World War even the Mellises, the Bawlands and the Forresters had certain fundamental securities. They could turn on the tap, fill the kettle, boil it on the gas, buy a packet of cigarettes or an ounce of Murray Mints. To the best of their ability the men of such families would provide, the mums would keep house, and the daughters would bring home whatever earnings they could until they married. As with many women of similar background in this country, the outbreak of war was seen as adding worrying burdens to an already hard life. The British have always grumbled, but now they grumbled more.

In his Christmas broadcast, the King spoke to the nation, quoting a favourite poem: 'Give me a light that I may tread safely into the unknown . . .' Though many children were restored to their parents for the festivities, celebrations were muted. As 1939 drew to a close the Second World War was, for people on these shores, still more menacing than life-threatening. But with the Nazis now in occupation in Poland, the Russians attacking Finland, and battles in the Atlantic threatening to increase in ferocity, the future seemed full of fear.

2 All Our Prayers

Behind the Maginot

Madeleine Henrey felt that her life was full of promise. Madeleine was French; as a child she had emigrated with her mother to London and in the 1920s had found work as a manicurist at the Savoy Hotel. It was there that she met the handsome Robert Henrey, a gossip columnist, whom she married in 1928. They were madly in love, and Madeleine was entranced by his world of smoky night clubs, fashion and expensive jewellery.

But there was another side to Madeleine, and she yearned to revisit her French roots. In 1937, together with Madame Gal, her adored mother, the Henreys had set out from London and travelled to Normandy, where they bought a picturesque farm just outside Villers-sur-Mer on the coast near Le Havre. 'It was the house of a fairy-tale.' Here Madeleine kept chickens and cultivated cider-apple trees, transforming the farmhouse with her own dainty taste, relishing the skills of the local craftsmen, from joiners to mattress-makers. 'It was a little jewel, sparkling in new paint.' To cap her joy, she became pregnant and, in the summer of 1939, with her mother at her side, Madeleine gave birth to a son, Bobby.

The baby's eyes opened to a world at war. The Henreys spent the early months of his life hunkering down in Villers; they stocked the house with coffee and sugar, and watched with dismay as peasants and tenant farmers alike were called up and sent off to man the Maginot line, leaving the village populated largely by women, small children and dogs. They spent Christmas 1939 in their Normandy farm, doing their best to keep warm. Outside the fields were wintry, the orchard branches laden with snow.

★

The early months of 1940 were bitterly cold. Two hundred miles away near the Belgian border, Lorna Bradey, aged twenty-four, found herself with the British Expeditionary Force, in the process of converting a small school into a hospital. Lorna, the intelligent, intrepid daughter of a colonial official, had been looking for a challenge. In 1936 she had trained as a nurse; now, with her colleagues from Queen Alexandra's Imperial Military Nursing Service, she was billeted with the army in France. Her accommodation was in an unheated house. That January her face flannel froze to the basin every night. After work the weary, chilled British nurses stoked up with hot food at the local bistro, where Madame would regale them with omelettes and shots of Pernod.

At this stage in the phoney war, Lorna didn't have serious casualties to deal with; she was kept as busy as in a normal hospital. But in France that winter Lorna finally felt, having got through four gruelling years of training, that she was fulfilling her ambition. 'The world was at my feet, or so I thought. I would travel, see everything and have plenty of fun . . . I felt that no one could possibly win the war without me!'

Lorna was as innocent as any other well brought-up middle-class girl; and yet there was a spirited sexiness about her, a broad-mindedness and vitality that got her noticed by men. Her pre-war posting with the QAs at the Millbank military hospital had given her her first contacts with the British Tommy, and even though she didn't always understand their language, it was hard to ignore how attractive some of them found her. She was busy sterilising instruments when one young soldier commented to his pal, 'She's a good bit of cunt that one – I wouldn't mind having a go at her.' Lorna had no idea what the word meant, but was deeply embarrassed. The incident – a one-off – didn't change her deep-seated understanding of her role as a nurse:

In the main they never swore or were familiar with us, and it was born then, my admiration of the British Soldier. I was to spend many years trying to save his life, comfort him and make his dying more bearable. There were to be some terrible years ahead.

But in France, in early 1940, the champagne was flowing. 'We girls were in great demand . . .'

The nurse in wartime carried an unusual load of projected urges – from lust to homesickness, physical and emotional dependence, to what Lorna called 'unhappy married man syndrome'. Visually, the

QAs were already elevated above the common herd of womankind by their angelic, but subtly thrilling, appearance. It was an elegant look, full of suggestiveness. The sober grey dresses were immaculate, the white collar, cuffs and aprons spotlessly starched. Floating white veils gave a hint of the convent, while racy red capes imparted, perhaps, less virginal messages. 'We were generally a very attractive bunch of women,' recalled Lorna. Detached from any kind of normality, the nurses were to find themselves on the receiving end of every male nineteen-year-old's fantasy life for the next five years. Soldiers and male medics alike hugely outnumbered them. At this point, before danger added its own special charge of eroticism, many of these young men behaved as if they were on paid holiday – away from home for the first time. They appeared brave and glamorous; their wives, if they had them, were far away, 'and we were ready victims'

At twenty-four one is very vulnerable, when the tall handsome surgeon you assist is the man you fall in love with . . . We spent every moment of our spare time together. I got the whole story – unhappy marriage, unwanted son. Would I wait and on return live with him until he got his divorce? I agreed to everything . . .

Suddenly he was recalled . . . to Scotland. I thought my heart would break, but promises, promises, never to be fulfilled . . .

By early April, much to Lorna's relief, she was moved to Casualty Clearing Station No. 5 just outside Arras. Here her unit was outside the supposedly inviolable safety zone created by the Maginot line, but Lorna was pleased to be 'going into action'; it would distract her from her broken-up love affair. So far the German army had not penetrated the Netherlands, but as the threat intensified more British troops were arriving in France by the day. Lorna's field hospital was the nearest to the front line in her area, and it promised to be busy. Five sisters, five medical officers, fourteen orderlies and a surgeon now readied themselves for a bloody defence.

It Couldn't Happen to Us

On 8 January 1940 the government introduced food rationing. The lack of shipping space for food cargo made restrictions inevitable,

and everybody knew it was coming. The ration books were ready.
Towards the end of 1939 people had been told they must register
with their chosen suppliers. Now every person was allowed four
ounces of bacon, four ounces of butter and twelve ounces of sugar
per week. In a matter of weeks butchers' meat was also put on the
ration: no more than 1s 10d-worth a week for each adult, 11d-worth
for each child under six, not including offal. Fish was unrationed,
but scarce.

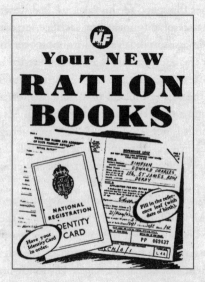

From the start food rationing was seen as tough but fair.

The effects were felt straight away. In her Midlands village Clara
Milburn was exasperated when her usual meat delivery failed and she
and her husband Jack had to survive on larder remains. Mrs Milburn
was a stern patriot, however, so when, eventually, a small boy
appeared on a bicycle, bearing with him an even smaller joint, she
reminded herself that restraint was a duty:

Such little joints, too, these days . . . It is a good thing to get down to hard
facts, though, and make everyone come under the same rule and help to
win the war . . .

We have a wicked enemy to encounter and there is only one way of dealing with so ruthless a foe, and that is to fight him until he is beaten.

Clara's fierce patriotism was driven by a personal motive. As a Territorial, the Milburns' only son, Alan, aged twenty-five, had been called up early in September 1939. He was now in France with the British Expeditionary Force, from where his intermittent letters were impatiently awaited by his anxious mother back in Balsall Common. Every week she mailed him biscuits, cakes and other small comforts. For her, as for so many, the fate of the army was her son's fate; defeating the Nazis meant defeating those who wished him harm. Alan was never out of her thoughts; for his sake, we had to win the war. No wonder that her resolve to make any sacrifice, or comply with any order that might assist in the eventual triumph over his enemies, was unwavering. It was a resolve due to be severely tested.

This focus on Alan didn't prevent Clara from intently following the course of the war in Finland that arctic winter, as the Russians advanced against a fiercely resisting nation until March 1940. 'The news of the Finns is not good . . . We have sent aeroplanes, medical supplies, ambulances, clothes and money, and still they cry in their agony,' she wrote. Finland capitulated to the Soviet aggressors on 12 March.

The freezing winter was followed by a ravishing and balmy spring. In early April Mrs Milburn walked Twink down to the corner baker's and was pleased to notice that they were still selling biscuits, though 'fewer cakes than in pre-war days'. On Monday the 8th she went to see Deanna Durbin in *First Love* at the Regal. The following day she heard on the radio that the Nazis had invaded neutral Norway: the next phase of the war had begun, Norway's fate precipitating Winston Churchill into the premiership on 10 May. 'The most eventful day of the war!' wrote Clara. She and Jack had been up early. At 8 o'clock they switched on the radio, continuing to listen at intervals all day. The political convulsions were matched by those abroad, as the war now escalated into the Low Countries. Another diarist, later the novelist Barbara Pym, tried to analyse her feelings about the events of that day:

Friday 10th May

Today Germany invaded Holland and Belgium. It may be a good thing to put down how one felt before one forgets it. Of course the first feeling was the usual horror and disgust, and the impossibility of finding words to describe this latest *Schweinerei* by the Germans. Then came the realisation that war was coming a lot nearer to us – airbases in Holland and Belgium would make raids on England a certainty . . . I think I was rather frightened, but hope I didn't show it, and anyway one still has the 'it couldn't happen to us' feeling . . . Winston Churchill will be better for this war – as Hilary [her sister] said, he is such an old beast! The Germans loathe and fear him and I believe he can do it.

On 14 May Rotterdam was obliterated by bombs. The Belgian border with France was the next obstacle ahead of the Nazi advance, which for Clara Milburn meant only one thing: would Alan's regiment, stationed in France, cross the border into Belgium? If so he would find himself in dreadful peril. The new Prime Minister's unambiguous message resonated with Mrs Milburn: 'You ask what is our aim? I can answer it in one word, VICTORY.'

Warm spring day followed warm spring day. The Milburns worked in their garden. The war news grew ever more grave, as Allied troops pulled back. Alan's twenty-sixth birthday fell on 18 May. The night before, just as she was dropping off, Clara had the sense of a visual image pressing against her closing lids. She saw a face, which at first she couldn't identify; fighting sleep, she attempted to focus on the features before it faded from her vision. For a moment it cleared, before being lost to the shadows: it was Alan.

On the morning of his birthday she pedalled into Balsall for their rations, pinned a poster discouraging waste on to the WI noticeboard and returned to her gardening. 'All day long we were thinking and talking of Alan, recalling other birthdays when he was a little boy and invited the three dogs to tea in the nursery!'

*

Refugees from the Low Countries were starting to arrive in London. Frances Faviell went to Chelsea Town Hall and offered her services as an interpreter. Among Frances's many talents was an impressive linguistic ability. She spoke Dutch, having lived in that 'kindly, tolerant' country for more than two years; its language was closely similar to the Flemish tongue, and she was confident that she could help. The people's plight tore at her heart; here, for the first time, was the desperate human face of war: terrified, frozen, sick and shocked. Inevitably, the majority were women with children. They had fled to the ports and begged for a place in any boat which would have them. Now it was Frances's task to explain as far as she could what would happen to these unhappy refugees. At Dover the stalwart women of the WVS had seen to their immediate needs: hot drinks, blankets, first aid. In London an appeal had been answered with donations of clothes and other domestic essentials. Frances helped with their distribution, before taking on the next job of cleaning the disused houses allocated to them. She and a group of volunteers got pails, soap and brushes, and spent several days on hands and knees scrubbing them out. Soon the Flemish women under Frances's care were clothed and housed; from now on she would share her time between refugee duties and the first aid post for which she had trained.

At the FAP there were quiet times when she could draw or read. But helping the displaced women fleeing from their ruined lives left Frances Faviell with very little time to herself, and from now on she laid all thought of her work as an artist to one side.

Joan Wyndham, aged seventeen, was of another type, breathlessly and insatiably interested in her own love life and the artistic milieu which furnished it. So on 1 April 1940, eager for new experiences, she signed up at Chelsea Polytechnic to study Art. From the outset everything looked extremely promising:

the students began to arrive: young men slouched in with hair flopping over their foreheads, lots of well-developed healthy girls with flat feet, in dirndls and brightly checked blouses. They fell on each other's necks with cries of 'Nuschka darling!' or 'Bobo!' and so on . . .

– kindred spirits, clearly.

That spring, as the home front accustomed itself to the new rations and feverishly listened to the bulletins, Joan was modelling clay under the tuition of Henry Moore, attending life-drawing classes and adoringly pursuing Gerhardt, the moody German sculptor she had met at a party the previous autumn. 'I would die for him tomorrow.' Gerhardt was non-committal, but there were distractions: Jo, proprietor of the Artists' Café, for whom she felt 'a certain tenderness', and Rupert – 'devastatingly attractive'. Anyway, there were serious worries about Gerhardt, who was fearful of being interned. 'If I'm not . . . and the Germans come, will I be able to shoot myself before they can get me? You know of course that I am Jewish?'

Gerhardt also took time to advise Joan: 'You know it's time you went to bed with someone.' Since this well-intentioned recommendation appeared not to include him, it spelt the blighting of all her hopes. On 14 April she wrote: 'I wish I was dead.' But flirting with Jo, art school and drunken studio parties made life bearable. As Churchill's leadership hung in the balance at the beginning of May, Joan found a new interest: Leonard, a painter who wore green trousers and sandals and explained to her about masturbation. But he wasn't moody and handsome enough to be Joan's type, so when he started groping inside her blouse she made her excuses and left. Instead she drifted back to Gerhardt's studio – if he couldn't love her, perhaps he could be her friend? That bright May afternoon everything was bursting into bud. As the sun dropped they stood on the balcony overlooking the Chelsea treetops. The vast blimps bobbed in the night sky, while across the Channel the German juggernaut was crushing everything in its path. 'I don't think they'll ever raid London,' said Gerhardt.

With Gerhardt off limits, Joan got her sex education where she could. She had her breasts caressed by Jo from the café; then there was an energetic kissing session with Leonard, who was amazing when it came to sheer technique. Though she turned down an offer to touch his penis, Leonard was a fund of information, demystifying orgasms, fellatio and unusual sex positions 'with scholarly enthusiasm'.

Monday 27th May

The Germans are in Calais. I don't seem to be able to react or to feel anything. I don't know what's real any more . . .

The bombs, which I know must come, hardly enter my fringe of consciousness. Bombs and death are real, and I and all the other artists around here are only concerned with unreality. We live in a dream.

Joan Wyndham's frank introduction to the facts of life place her in a minority, but the dreamlike, dizzying quality of those days was shared by many. During the Phoney War bombs and death had seemed remote; but in spring 1940 they were remote no longer, and everyone was talking about invasion.

In the Face of Danger

Urgent times demanded urgent responses. 'Everyone is getting married and engaged,' wrote one young diarist in April that year, while also recording the reaction of a columnist in the *Daily Express*, that 'any girl [who] ends up in this war not married . . . is simply not trying.'

In 1940 there were 534,000 weddings: nearly 40,000 more than in the previous year, and 125,000 more than in 1938. The brides were younger too – three in every ten were under twenty-one. At this time, before men's long absences abroad made nuptials impossible, there was a peak in the phenomenon of the hasty war marriage. The world seemed so full of danger that prudent delay simply looked pointless – you could be dead if you waited till tomorrow, so better to seize the day. Randolph Churchill, son of the Prime Minister, set the tone. As he hurtled round the revolving doors of the Ritz he managed to get the friend galloping through in the opposite direction to give him a phone number for a blind date. He rushed to the phone, called the number and promptly inquired of the young lady who picked it up what her name was and what she looked like. 'I'm Pamela Digby . . . Red-headed and rather fat, but Mummy says that puppy fat disappears.' Churchill was charmed. Three days later they were engaged, and within a month they were married. No wedding bells, however, as that would have signified a German invasion.

Margery Berney was another young woman who launched hastily into marriage at this time. Ignoring the promptings of ambition – for since childhood Margery had known she would *be* somebody – she took the conjugal plunge with an army officer named Major William Baines after an exceptionally brief courtship. Their wedding was followed by an equally brief few months together before her major was posted abroad. 'People become reckless in the face of danger,' was Margery's only comment on their impromptu commitment.

Seizing the day might turn out all well and fine, but war weddings were often beset by worries as to whether both parties would actually make it to the ceremony. In the emergency climate of spring 1940 the forces refused to release their men for leave under any circumstances. On 10 May, the eve of her planned wedding to Victor, her RAF sweetheart, young Eileen Hunt made her way to King's Cross to meet him, only to find the station closed and swarming with police and soldiers. All leave had been cancelled; there would be no wedding. Heartbroken, clasping her bouquet of lilies-of-the-valley, Eileen went home and cancelled church, car and flowers. But her brother and Victor's brother were not so easily deterred. They rushed up to Victor's base near Cambridge, kidnapped him and hid him on the floor of a borrowed van, which they then drove at breakneck speed back to London. Eileen's plans went into reverse; she put on her bridal gown and hastened to the church, where Victor appeared, and they were married without more ado. There was just time for the family to toast the couple, before Victor was bundled back to Cambridge and sneaked into his camp. A month later Victor and Eileen finally managed to get some time alone together – at the start of what was to be forty-nine years of marriage.

Afterwards, the newlywed Eileen returned to her job with Grubert's furriers. The company had contracted with the Red Cross to make musquash coats to be shipped out by the Merchant Navy to aid Russian children. As the war news worsened, so women sought to contribute to the best of their ability. The qualifications of trained women were at a premium, and nobody now doubted that nurses, first-aiders, volunteers and forces auxiliaries of every kind were going to prove indispensable; but with the fear of invasion growing daily, ordinary females from all backgrounds now added their voices to the patriotic clamour. 'Women want to be partners in the nation's war effort,' claimed an article in *Woman's Magazine*. Mrs 'NOT TOO OLD AT 46' pleaded to be allowed to join the anti-parachute corps – 'I, for one, would gladly offer my services.' Miss E. de Langlois of Ewell wrote with a suggestion for wires to be suspended between pylons 'to prevent parachute troops reaching the ground', while Mrs Gilroy of Rudwick wrote to the paper calling for a ban on iced cakes – 'a luxury we could dispense with'. Mrs Hope of Torquay added her voice to the numbers calling for 'aliens and Pacifists' to be rounded up and interned. The propagandising tone of the press aimed at women was relentlessly upbeat, stressing the gay willingness of countless women to give of their best. Typically, such journalism was aimed at cheering on factory workers, who, already at this stage in the war, were regarded as key to the anti-German effort:

WAR WORKERS' SUNDAY DASH

Hundreds of thousands of women rose early from their beds and rushed to work . . . with a smile.

There was no grousing at the loss of leisure. Everybody wanted to get on with the job . . .

'My boy friend is in France with the B.E.F.' said one girl working in a fuse factory, 'so I'll work 15 hours a day if necessary.'

Probably the morale-boosting, chin-up message helped. Despite the general willingness, there is evidence that at this stage the speed of events left many women bewildered, shocked and subject to mood swings. Mass Observation took daily soundings in late May 1940. On the 18th women were much more worried than men, with reactions ranging from terror to incomprehension. On the 21st morale had improved slightly. On the 22nd anxiety and depression among women hit a new low; some had weeping fits. This survey also showed that working-class women were on the whole more bewildered by events and unable to give a name to their emotions, whereas middle- and upper-class women were coherent in expressing their anxiety. A response from a Birmingham housewife must have echoed the reactions of many after Belgium surrendered:

A BLACK DAY. We need all our prayers now . . . the 1 o'c news has made me feel sick . . . I don't think France will give in, but neither did I think Belgium would. We *must* win – we *must* win, I could not live beneath a brutal power. I said to my husband Sunday, I would die fighting rather than live the life of a slave.

At this time the news on the radio was so dreadful that many just stopped listening to it. The distress in Europe was dreadful to witness, but worse still was the prospect of a German invasion. Fear of the unknown dominated. The average housewife, accustomed to leaving difficult decisions about politics and world affairs to her husband, was simply out of her depth:

So cruel. I don't know what's going to happen now, I really don't. It seems all up. You don't know what to do for the best. I don't know whether to send my children away, or not . . . I don't know whether to apply for a shelter or not. I think perhaps I ought to join the ARP; then I think I've got my duty to the home first. Oh dear . . .

4. *My nerves went to pieces. So did my work. One morning, I took a long memorandum in shorthand and* couldn't *read it back. I'll never forget it. I actually cried in the office!*

A shattered secretary, used by the advertiser to show that only Horlicks can help with war stress.

The writer Naomi Mitchison was not one to duck problems, intellectually at least. The Mitchisons were well-off and middle-aged, and from 1939 Naomi, who was expecting her seventh child, had been safely ensconced in Kintyre, a fishing village in rural Scotland. As Socialists, she and her husband Dick both hated the war while knowing it had to be fought. Day by day Naomi's wartime diary grapples with the issues of work, war, love, motherhood and the future. In May 1940 she was sick and experiencing nightmares – 'almost inevitable'. In the light northerly summer evenings she had leisure to read, and a book about the history of the Scottish kirk set her thinking about ideology and hate. 'Must there be hate in order to be life?' As France retreated before the invasion, what did it tell its young men as they prepared to die for their country? The early Scottish martyrs had been certain of heaven. Was courage dependent on superstition? Was the cowardice that she felt a luxury, to be shed if her own family were threatened? Dick and her oldest son were in London at this time, potentially in danger. She had her unborn child to protect. 'Would I hate if my immediate family were killed? . . . I don't know. But I rather doubt it.' She and Dick agreed that, as committed left-wing activists, they might have to flee the country if the Germans came. Naomi found herself imagining an Atlantic crossing in a herring boat, wondering how much luggage she could fit in alongside the diesel oil. 'It seems fantastic . . .' Everyone was talking about German agents landing – would they come disguised as clergymen or nuns, as many people thought? Naomi tried to look coolly at the likely outcome of an invasion, and concluded that she would almost certainly be sent to a concentration camp. On 30 May she noticed that she had bitten her nails very badly, 'a thing I have not done for months'.

Naomi Mitchison's contemporary, Frances Partridge, also took a committed and rational stance to the war at this time. She and her husband, Ralph, were pacifists. They lived in Wiltshire with their small son, Burgo, and for much of the war their home was a refuge for their many London friends who came to Ham Spray House for the intelligent conversation and plentiful food it offered. Throughout, Frances was writing a searchingly honest diary:

May 15th

In no time – days even – we may all be enduring the same horrors as Holland and Belgium. We talked about suicide . . . R. said we could easily gas ourselves in the car, all three of us. We were still talking of this as we went along to the bath, and of how happy our lives have been, and so has Burgo's, though there has been so little of it . . .

My greatest preoccupation is with the question of how to get a supply of lethal pills . . .

May 19th

The perfection of the weather is getting on all our nerves. It is too phenomenal and everything super-normal is unnerving; also it's impossible not to remember that it is ideal weather for air-raids. The German advance into France goes on . . .

We all sank into our private worlds of despair . . .

These two examples of the reflections of women intellectuals on the 1940 crisis raise fascinating questions about women's attitudes to war. Frances Partridge and Naomi Mitchison were both deeply thoughtful, educated individuals, and they were products of their time. Both had benefited from the advanced, emancipated atmosphere of the 1920s, which had brought women the franchise and opened up the world of active politics and other hitherto 'masculine' concerns. They saw no reason for 'womanish' submission. They rejected war and all it stood for. In Frances's case, she refused absolutely to play any part in it. Both women could see that the Nazi threat had provoked a military response which was bound to cause terrible loss of life and huge unhappiness. Against this, all their instincts as thinking people, but also as women and mothers, recoiled. They would save themselves and their families, or they would turn on the car and gas themselves. Was this a kind of intellectual paralysis, reserved for the over-educated minority – thinkers not doers – or was it the involuntary reflex of every woman who has ever lived and loved to save, to hide and to protect? Organised violence revolted such women; the expression of hate through force offended against the deep-seated need of their sex to build nests and to nurture. 'Can we also not love?' cried Naomi Mitchison. But if the wartime leadership had been female, how would it have responded to Hitler? The despairing reality that now had to be faced as the Nazi armies rolled inexorably across northern France was, simply, how to stop them. Intellectual toughness was no longer enough, and nor was loving. History was now on the side of the doers.

Beached

The British Expeditionary Force was now cornered by advancing German forces. Casualty Clearing Station No. 5 was in their path; the medical staff there were ordered to pack up and move towards the port of Dunkirk. On 20 May QA Lorna Bradey and her fellow nurses found themselves in a Red Cross ambulance as part of a troop convoy en route to the coast. That first day they travelled twenty miles to a small town named Frévent, where they spent the night in the château, converted into a hospital. They woke next morning to find their accompanying troops had departed, leaving a note from the Commanding Officer: 'We have moved forward – you are to turn back.' Unknown to the nurses, orders had been received that no women were to proceed to Dunkirk from that point. The CO's command saved the nurses' lives.

By the time they could organise their departure going south the countryside was a battle zone. Eventually the ambulance convoy set off, heading for Dieppe, designated a hospital port. A terrifying journey now began, in a vehicle which moved painfully slowly along a road crammed with refugees who clung to its sides; they had been forbidden to open the doors in case the panicked crowds attempted to get in. Every half-hour Stukas sprayed the fleeing civilians with fire. 'They were remorseless, the Red Cross meant nothing to them.' Peering out through the small slit windows of the ambulance, Lorna could see carnage. It went against all her instincts and training to abandon wounded civilians, but they had no medical equipment.

Stopping was out of the question. Lorna became desperate to find a toilet. 'You can't just do it here,' they all said. Relief came in the form of a large tin containing peaches, the last one they had left:

Solemnly we opened it and shared the contents; most delicious under the circumstances. One empty tin was now to be used for other purposes! Me first, nothing daunted and with an audience I balanced in that jolting ambulance.

By the time another eight hours had passed all the nurses were glad of that large tin.

The convoy passed through Abbeville; as they left the town was bombarded behind them. The next day they reached Arques-la-Bataille, just outside Dieppe, where they joined a hospital train for Dieppe Harbour, only to find the harbour in flames. As they stood at a loss, the hospital ship the *Maid of Kent* was blown up and sunk in front of their eyes; twenty-eight crew and medical personnel were drowned that day. Fear set in. Nobody knew where to go. Their train crawled through France, loaded with hospital staff and wounded; at night they shunted into a siding near Rouen, where, as darkness fell, the bombing started up again.

The nurses were coping, but near to hysterical. Lorna asked a friend sitting on the top bunk to pass something down to her; as the girl leaned over a bullet struck the panel where seconds before she had been resting her head. 'We were still laughing, too frightened, too terrified to cry.' Another girl lay chalk-faced and wide-eyed on the floor – 'she couldn't take any more.' At dawn they started up again. Orderlies brought the nurses buckets of hot sweet tea – 'we could have kissed them all'. Slowly the train zig-zagged across France to the southern Brittany coast, making for St Nazaire:

Miraculously no one on that journey south was hit. Midday – hot meat and veg on a tin plate – this was luxury indeed and we had a loo! [The journey] took us all of that day, but the sun was shining, the bombers were behind us and we were alive!

In those grim days, Dunkirk engrossed the nation. Like thousands upon thousands of mothers across the country, Clara Milburn was consumed by anxiety as news of the catastrophe became public. Her son Alan, unlike Lorna Bradey, was in the thick of it.

On Wednesday 29 May Mrs Milburn heard on the radio of the Belgian surrender and the withdrawal. On Friday the 31st her hopes for Alan were raised after a neighbour telephoned to say she had heard that the Royal Warwickshire Regiment was safely evacuated, only to be dashed on discovering that the news appeared ill founded. 'Our spirits went down and down and the day wore slowly on. We worked in the garden.' Saturday came, and 'still no news'. Tales came through of the evacuation: the horrors as the men on the beach were bombarded; the nightmare of their escape on the armada of small ships. A local boy, Philip Winser, had been killed. By the following Wednesday Clara broke down on discovering a box of Alan's sports trophies put away at the beginning of the war. 'To cry a bit relieved the tension.' On Friday Mrs Winser called by. They talked about the boys. Philip was dead. And Alan? Nobody knew. 'I felt how splendidly brave and calm she is.' Impossible for Clara not to imagine herself in Mrs Winser's shoes; would she, too, be splendidly brave and calm? A fortnight after the withdrawal of the BEF Mrs Milburn wrote:

One's mind seems numbed, and the last day or two I go on, keeping on the surface of things as it were, lest I go down and be drowned. Every moment Alan is in my thoughts, every hour I send out my love to him – and wonder and wonder.

For the 224,585 British troops who escaped from Dunkirk alive the reception was unstinting. The British woman lived up to her image during this most mortifying episode of the war. Tirelessly angelic, patient, nurturing and endlessly kind, she was the apotheosis of the perfect housewife. She cut sandwiches, washed up for hours on end, bandaged, healed and produced inexhaustible supplies of clean clothes. As the trains bearing the exhausted evacuees rolled slowly into London the WVS parked their mobile canteen beside the railway line and handed buttered buns and sandwiches to them through the train windows.

At Joyce Green Hospital in Dartford the message arrived over-night that the hospital must start preparing to receive wounded soldiers arriving from Dunkirk. At 2 a.m. the nurses were woken; Peggy Priestman, a twenty-year-old nurse, worked fifteen-hour shifts from then on, dealing with injuries ranging from broken arms to shrapnel wounds. Peggy had not been trained to extract shrapnel, but the doctors were too busy to do everything. She had to dig frag-ments out of the patients' heads, and then stitch them back up. 'You just got on with it and did the best you could.' Worse than shrapnel was gangrene. In many cases there was nothing for it but amputation. Another nurse, VAD Lucilla Andrews, received wounded evacuees arriving at a military hospital on Salisbury Plain and took notes on her experiences, which later ended up in a war memoir:

Men too tired to remember to swallow a mouthful of soup or keep their eyes open, but not to mumble, 'Thanks, nurse . . . ta, duck . . . that's great, hen . . . grand, luv . . . I say thanks awfully.'

Day after day of washing from the bodies of exhausted men the sand of Dunkirk, the grime of St Malo, of Brest, of Cherbourg, the oil of wrecked ships, the salt from the Channel.

The ATS came into its own. Kathy Kay's platoon was based at a militia camp in Cambridgeshire. Here, hundreds of straggling evacuees arrived, many in tatters, all needing food and beds. The platoon was immediately detailed to undertake the 'hard and tedious' jobs required to care for them: food preparation and washing up, re-equipping them with clothes and other necessities. Like all the others, Kathy was un-grudging. She knew how grateful the troops were, how glad they were to be back on home soil. Mary Angove was another, a seventeen-year-old based at Penhill camp near Newquay: 'We got thrown in the deep end. There was no bread-cutting machine – I was cutting hundreds of slices of bread and laying on liver sausage sandwiches. No dishwasher either – I was sleeves rolled up with my hands in a deep sink full of greasy washing-up water. The men were coming back all over the country . . . and they were just so tired. They didn't seem to want to talk about it. Not that we asked, we didn't have time, we just had to look after them, and then they got sorted and sent on leave.'

WAAF Joan Davis, based at Calshot near Southampton, witnessed the Dunkirk evacuation, both before and after. As the rescue vessels slipped into Southampton Water there was an atmosphere of anticipation and dread. Within a short time many of the small ships returned, bearing exhausted soldiers. Many of them were half-naked. Joan and a companion were ordered to collect as much clothing as possible from the stores. The spring weather was unnaturally hot, and the pair worked for hours on the dock, distributing garments to tattered, filthy men. 'The stench was terrible.' Inevitably the soldiers were in great distress; most of them had lost their belongings, all they had were a few wet remnants and some mementoes and photographs. The young WAAFs were harrowed with pity for these abject survivors. 'On our return to Calshot my companion, Air Craft Woman Foote, said to me, "I think the real war now begins."'

⋆

The German army proceeded remorselessly across France. In Villers-sur-Mer the Henreys believed that Normandy was still protected by the French lines of defence behind Amiens. Their smallholding was Madeleine's pride. Feminine to the core, she had poured into it all her love for home, for the *finesses* of everyday life. Her identity as a Frenchwoman – her 'chic', her *savoir faire*, her domestic artistry – were all bound up in the Normandy farm. That June the garden was a mass of roses, the grass a perfect green, grazed down by her cows. The air was scented with new-mown hay.

At midday on 9 June, without any warning, the sky darkened, the breeze stilled, and the day turned deathly cold. Madeleine and Robert walked out to the Point beyond the village, from where there was a panoramic view across the Seine estuary. They looked out and saw a vast plume of smoke billowing up like a volcano – it was the oil refinery at Port Jérôme, upriver from Le Havre. This refinery held the biggest petrol storage tanks in France. The allies had fired the tanks at dawn to prevent them from falling into enemy hands, and by lunchtime the cloud of smog had completely blotted out the sun. That evening while eating dinner with Mme Gal they heard planes overhead; bombs were being dropped on Le Havre. Bobby slept in his cot. As the sun set they walked up to the Point again, and watched as the coastline burned. With horror they now learned that German tanks were in Rouen. 'We both knew only too well what would happen if we left things to the last moment. The baby might get crushed or machine-gunned.' If they were not to be caught up in the advance they must flee.

As early as possible the next morning Madeleine rose. She made the bed, tidied her room, dusted and put away her treasures. 'I was determined that our house should be trim when we left it.' As a final touch she went out to the garden and cut roses to adorn the sitting room. But there was no more time to lose. A neighbour had agreed to drive the four of them ninety miles across country to St Malo, from where they hoped to escape to England. They packed what they could.

We took a last look round the house. The bedroom was bathed in sunshine, and I opened my wardrobes, filled with my dresses, my furs and hats, and looked at them with tears in my eyes. My linen cupboard, scented with lavender from my garden, was my pride . . . my baby's cot was all ready for him to sleep in.

I kissed the pillow in the cot when nobody was looking, and I steeled my nerves, driving my nails into the flesh of my hands. I knew there must be no choosing of this or that to take away. The sacrifice must be complete or it might cost us our lives.

Thus the family took to the road. They were refugees. 'The bottom had fallen out of my dream farm . . . Would I ever see it again? . . . It hurts to love.' Madeleine had stamped this little corner of Normandy so indelibly with her own personality that leaving it was a kind of annihilation.

Two days later, after getting transport and lodging through a combination of persuasion and bribery, they arrived at St Malo, the last of the major Channel ports still not bombed. Here, despite an abundance of luxuries in the shops, the signs of suffering were everywhere. St Malo was overrun with flotsam from all over northern France; they had arrived, like the Henreys, weighed down with prams and suitcases, and now haunted the picturesque streets, helplessly trying to find some means of getting away.

Transports arrived from England and tied up at the quay. The Henreys went to the British Consulate. Madeleine had a British passport, her son had a British father; there would be no problem for the three of them. Madeleine's mother was a different matter, however, and the Consular bureaucrat who guarded the gate was deaf to all entreaties. Nothing would persuade him that Madame Gal had a case for returning to London, where she had lived for years, and which she had left in order to help look after the grandchild she had loved, nursed and cherished since the day he was born. 'My pleading was in vain.'

Afterwards Madeleine saw that she had no real choice in doing what she did; as British citizens she and Robert would have been interned by the Nazis, and their baby might have died. They had to leave France. But on that June day she felt like a criminal. Robert thrust a bundle of banknotes into his mother-in-law's hand. Madeleine climbed the companion-way carrying the struggling Bobby in her arms, her eyes filled with tears. The danger was still terrible; their little steamer might be strafed or torpedoed. The Henreys stood on the boat deck as Madame Gal's figure on the shore became smaller and smaller, until she was out of sight. 'We were free. We were to be given a second chance ... The next morning we sailed into Southampton Water.'

Five years would pass before she saw her mother, or her farm, again.

★

The news worsened. Italy joined the conflict. Paris fell. But the ordeal of the French invasion wasn't over for Lorna Bradey. At St Nazaire in Brittany her nursing unit was assimilated into the Base Hospital, awaiting casualties from the fighting. Everyone there was still in total ignorance of the Dunkirk tragedy. But before long wounded men began to arrive, and the QAs were working flat out, knowing that the Germans were gaining ground by the day, and that they would be forced to flee yet again. Rescue arrived in the form of nineteen troop ships which arrived in St Nazaire harbour, and on 16 and 17 June a mass exodus took place, with thousands of troops inching their way on to the vessels waiting to carry them to safety.

With difficulty, Lorna helped to get her patients on board. As the stretchers were carried up the gangplank, the sky was black with Messerschmitts. The killing was indiscriminate, and chaos reigned. As soon as the patients were loaded the nurses headed below decks to settle them, from where they could hear the ceaseless crump of bombs above them, climaxing with a number of terrifyingly huge explosions, which, they were later to learn, had sunk the nearby *Lancastria*, killing at least 3,000 of the troops who were on board.

'Our turn next we thought. We never thought we'd get away alive.' Panic started to erupt among the passengers, with a civilian woman screaming uncontrollably; Lorna slapped her face and shook her until she stopped. With great courage the ship's captain held out till night fell and took the ship out into the Atlantic under cover of darkness. Two days later they docked in Southampton.

Lorna was in rags. Issued with a travel warrant she made her way back to her parents' home in Bedford, where she rang the doorbell. Her mother answered it and promptly fainted. Lorna was ignorant – till that moment – of what had been unfolding in Dunkirk.

When she recovered I learned that I had been reported missing, presumed killed, for the past ten days. News that No 5 C.C.S. had been wiped out had got to the War Office from Dunkirk, and the War Office presumed we were with them. All those men, all our comrades had been killed. I felt very humble. We had been pointed in the opposite direction by the foresight of our Commanding Officer.

Nobody knows exactly how many men were killed at Dunkirk, but at least 5,000 soldiers from the BEF lost their lives. People all over Britain quaked to think of what the future might bring, but for women whose waking thoughts were with the soldiers in France whom they loved, the lack of concrete news was a daily, hourly ordeal. It was not until Tuesday 16 July, after weeks of rumour and uncertainty – and nearly seven weeks after the army's withdrawal – that Clara Milburn heard the fate of her son.

That afternoon she had dropped in at the Women's Institute to see how the local produce exhibition was progressing. The judges were busy testing the range of jams, jellies, chutneys and bottled fruit. At 5.30 it was time to take Twink for a walk and, feeling rather heavy-hearted, she made her way out of the village. Two fields away, she caught sight of Jack waving wildly to her from beyond the hedge. Struggling to dampen the hopes and fears that now surged up, she strode to meet him – the telegram had come:

'Alan is a prisoner of war,' he said. There and then, saying 'Thank God', we embraced each other for sheer joy at the good news. Oh, how delighted we were to hear at last that he is still alive – and apparently unwounded . . .

My darling dear, you are alive!

Frances Campbell-Preston, recently married and with a baby daughter, had to wait even longer to hear that her husband, Patrick, a young officer in the Black Watch, was missing in action. Frances had friends in high places, and the officer network did their best to reassure her that he was a captive, but nothing concrete came through until late August, when one of Patrick's fellow officers arrived in Britain, having daringly escaped from German clutches. He was finally able to tell Frances that her husband too was a prisoner, and alive – 'Oh the excitement, joy and God knows what, I can hardly bear it, it is so marvellous.' Finally, in late autumn, she heard from Patrick himself. A letter arrived addressed Lager Bezefchung Oflag VIIC, Deutschland. He had been wounded in the head, he was safe and he was settling in for a long captivity.

News was even slower for Barbara Cartland, who heard early in June 1940 that both her brothers, Ronald and Tony, had gone missing at Dunkirk. But she and her mother had to wait until January 1941 for confirmation that Ronald was dead. Tony's death was not confirmed until the end of 1942.

So Naked, So Alone

As prisoners-of-war, Alan Milburn and Patrick Campbell-Preston were to endure much through the next five years. The women who loved them, and countless others, had to display endurance of a different kind. Mrs Milburn used her diaries to rally her spirits: 'Today I have just heard of someone who has been waiting longer than we have and had news of her prisoner son yesterday. Hope is a great thing and patience a real virtue in these times, but difficult for me,' she wrote sorrowfully.

The nation now entered the most dangerous phase of the war. The raids began to be stepped up, and some military targets were bombed, though these were pinpricks, compared with what was to come. Seventy years on, we know that the German leadership made mistakes which would eventually cost them victory. But in summer 1940 nobody in Britain could ignore the extreme threat of invasion, which, after France's surrender, now moved up several notches.

The 'it couldn't happen to us' feeling had evaporated. The reality of fear is very evident in contemporary accounts, many of which suggest women reacting to events with a sense of utter impotence. 'Is it any good fighting? Is it any good living at all?' reflected one young diarist. On the day that France surrendered an office worker recounted hearing the news, and how one of the typists became hysterical, uncontrollably shrieking, 'Whatever will we do now?' On that day Nella Last was listening to the radio too, in Barrow-in-Furness; the announcement left her close to breakdown as she felt all her courage and faith in the future ebb away. 'I felt if I could only cry – or better still scream and scream – it would have taken the sharp pain away . . . Never have I felt so naked, never so alone.' The racking anguish left Nella hardly able to stand. She dragged herself to the medicine cupboard, got out some smelling salts, doused her neck and shoulders with cold water and howled like a child. In Essex, a woman with a four-year-old daughter was gripped with the need to save her child from the German soldiers. Her home was by the coast, within easy reach of the occupied Channel ports – 'I used to get up on those lovely summer mornings and . . . wonder whether hordes of Germans would come in. It seemed so very, very possible.' After much thought she decided to put aside a bottle containing a hundred aspirins. 'If the Germans came, we'd have dissolved them in some milk and given them to her to drink . . . That's how real it was.' Up in Kintyre and away from the proximity of danger, Naomi Mitchison had given birth to a girl; the baby, so wanted and loved, who among so much death and destruction had come to symbolise life and creativity, lived for one day and then died. In the following days the horrible irrelevance of her 'little' distress taunted Naomi. 'I realise perfectly that much worse things are happening at this moment to thousands of people . . . but one cannot generalise as simply as that . . . All the little things hurt, hurt, hurt, and there is nothing to be done.'

Personal hopes and plans were shelved in the knowledge that the future was entirely without certainty. Shirley Hook, a diarist for Mass Observation, had been happily engaged to marry her boyfriend Jack Goodhart, a doctor. That June, with 'our world toppling round our shoulders', she began to think that it might have been better if the two of them had met their end the previous year, when they had both had a narrow escape in a climbing accident. Where did her hopes stand in relation to the awful prospect of a German invasion? Shirley felt demoralised, and utterly insignificant. 'We're so scared that something may happen to prevent [our marriage] . . . The war has succeeded in shattering our real hopes for the future very successfully.' In summer 1940 it seemed that the war had, with biblical impartiality, robbed many women even of the little self-worth that they already had, leaving them destitute of hope, of ambition, even of the will to live.

Adding insult to injury, the Ministry of Information now issued advice aimed at householders telling them what to do if Germans arrived by parachute. Since thousands of women were now *the* sole householders, it was readily understood that the advice was aimed at them. 'Do not believe rumours,' it said. 'Be calm, quick, exact . . . Do not give any German anything . . . Hide your food, your bicycles, your maps. See that the enemy get no petrol.' The recommendations, and the publicity picture showing a smiling mum in a housecoat secreting a biscuit tin at the back of her coal cellar, were met with ridicule. Did the Ministry really believe that a sweetly smiling lady politely protesting that she was not allowed to give him any biscuits would deter a tough Nazi paratrooper with a rifle? Frances Faviell tacked the pamphlet to the wall of her FAP. 'It never failed to amuse me when I was depressed.'

But on the whole Britain was still a nation which held authority in respect. 'The old beast', as Barbara Pym's sister had called Churchill, broadcast to the nation on 18 June:

What General Weygand called the Battle of France is over. I expect that the Battle of Britain is about to begin . . .

The whole fury and might of the enemy must very soon be turned on us. Hitler knows that he will have to break us in this island or lose the war. If we can stand up to him, all Europe may be free and the life of the world may move forward into broad, sunlit uplands . . .

Let us therefore brace ourselves to our duties, and so bear ourselves that if the British Empire and its Commonwealth last for a thousand years, men will still say, 'This was their finest hour.'

Few were impervious to his words. One London woman would never cease being grateful to Churchill: 'When people have decried [him], I've always said, "Yes, but he stopped me being afraid."' Another woman remembered: 'We would really have all gone down on to the beaches with broken bottles. We would have done anything – *anything* – to stop them.' The Trades Union Congress called on all British workers: 'Every man and woman in our movement is now a soldier in this war for the liberation of humanity.'

Such stirring sentiments might have echoed with a certain hollowness for the many women who would have liked to get down on to the beaches and hurl broken bottles at the Germans. For them, the chance of real combat was never on offer. Soldiering, for women, took other forms. In the case of twenty-two-year-old WAAF Aileen Morris, an educated, spirited and trenchant young woman, fluent in German, the first nine months of the war had been spent tied to a typewriter in the RAF Casualties Office at Ruislip. But that was about to change.

To her family, Aileen was always known as 'Mike'. Before the war Mike, the daughter of a civil servant, had studied in Germany for two years, finishing up at Halle-an-der-Saale near Leipzig. There she enjoyed the attentions of the smart German Luftwaffe officers who were in training at the Air Wireless School. But although she enjoyed their flattering company, she remained deeply disgusted by the political regime they espoused. Back in England in September 1939, Mike joined the WAAFs. 'I had seen the evils of Hitler's regime and, if there was to be a war against the Nazis, I wanted to have a hand in it.' At Ruislip her main function was sending letters of condolence to the families of killed or missing airmen. Though disciplined and courageous, Mike was also young, and highly strung; streaming with tears, she often worked late into the night typing out the fateful messages destined to break the hearts of the mothers and wives who read them: 'It is my painful duty to inform you that your son (or husband), Sergeant X, has been reported Missing (or Missing, believed killed) as the result of operations.' The girls were told that no typing errors were admissible. These were letters that the families would keep for ever.

Mike's distressing but menial employment in the Casualties Section might have continued like this throughout the war – there would be many more such letters to write – had it not been for her ability to speak German.

By the time of the Second World War the governments of most European countries were pouring resources into intelligence; it was clear that electronic eavesdropping on the enemy was going to play a vital part in complementing military might. Key to these operations in Britain was the section known as the 'Y' Service, responsible for the interception of communications. In spring 1940, as the German army across the Channel moved nearer, an important breakthrough was made: it was found that voice transmissions (as opposed to Morse) from the Luftwaffe could be picked up on VHF. The 'Y' Service officers celebrated – until they realised with dismay that there had been an oversight: nobody in the unit could understand German. Action was prompt, however; a message duly arrived at Ruislip asking them to locate German-speaking WAAFs. Mike, luckily, was there 'on the doorstep'.

After undergoing an interview to test her linguistic ability, followed by security clearance, Mike was told only that her new employment was 'hush-hush', before being presented with a sealed envelope containing a railway warrant for her new destination, Hastings, and sent on her way:

Under normal peacetime circumstances, as a happy young daughter of middle-class parents, I would most probably have been thinking about the next tennis party or perhaps planning a weekend picnic by the sea. Now it was June 1940, and although on that fine summer's day I did indeed find myself going to the seaside, I was very apprehensive.

But Mike Morris's arrival at Fairlight station above Hastings was a case of perfect timing. There was a pressing need for her linguistic talents, and it only remained to train her to operate radio receivers before she could be put to work. Soon she was on terms of easy familiarity with the knobs and dials and could twiddle them with the best. Installed in a humble caravan close to the towering Fairlight cliff-edge (so placed as to get the best cross-Channel reception), Mike and her fellow WAAF operators did six-hour shifts listening in to the messages transmitted between Luftwaffe pilots and control stations, earphones clamped to their heads, ears straining to catch coherent words. Everything she heard had to be logged, then translated into English. She had to become familiar with a range of German regional accents and found after a while that she could even distinguish the voices of individuals, any of whom, she reflected, could have been one of her dancing partners from the Air Wireless School at Halle-an-der-Saale. Cracking the simpler aspects of the pilots' code was a matter of time. For example, *Indianer* meant Indians – or enemy aircraft; *Kirchturm* meant church tower – or height. The girls' logged interceptions were all sent via the Air Ministry to 'Station X', the code-breaking headquarters at Bletchley in Buckinghamshire, where their 'raw material' was meticulously analysed and compared with other intelligence material.

Hitler planned to annihilate the RAF and mount attacks on Allied shipping. The WAAF operators could overhear German pilots communicating with their bases about shipping movements in the Channel. From Fairlight, the overheard message would go through warning the Navy and No. 11 Fighter Command at Uxbridge, who would immediately despatch air cover to protect the convoy. Mike and her colleagues knew that these convoys, containing fuel and food for the nation, had to get through, and that every message they intercepted could be vital. The operators were also gradually building up a fuller picture of the workings of the Luftwaffe. As German attacks increased in intensity, Mike's 'Y' Service unit moved to Hawkinge near Folkestone – a corner of Kent which was to become known as 'Hellfire Corner'. In their quarters, the WAAFs had no peace, with ceaseless fighter planes landing and taking off, and the nearby harbours constantly under attack.

Aircraft zoomed and twirled overhead like some ghastly aerial ballet dancing to the fiendish rhythm of machine-gun and anti-aircraft fire . . . I shall never forget the screaming whine of an aircraft crashing to earth out of control, followed by the dull crump as it hit the ground . . . each time I heard it I felt physically sick.

As the Battle of Britain reached fever pitch Folkestone and Hawkinge were repeatedly shelled from across the Channel. If they weren't at their posts, tracking the choreography of that *danse macabre*, the girls were dashing in and out of air-raid shelters. But despite the ceaseless bombing and shelling – under which some nearly cracked – they never left their sets while they were on watch.

Mike was one of those who, on the whole, managed to keep control under the severe strain of these conditions – more so than the men in the unit. On one occasion a man broke down completely. Mike, by now promoted to Corporal Morris, was the senior WAAF on duty, and she sensed that his hysteria, alongside exhaustion, was beginning to infect her unit. 'I had to act quickly, and so for the first time in my life I slapped a man across the face hard, and several times. It had the desired effect.' The man was senior to her, and she feared she might be court-martialled. But no more was heard about the affair.

She was not always so composed. Reconnaissance flights operated under an internationally agreed immunity. By now the German reconnaissance pilots' voices had become so familiar that the girls looked forward to hearing them come on air. One in particular, known to them as 'Amsel Eins' (from his callsign), was quite a character. He knew perfectly well that the WAAFs were listening in to him and would banter away to them flirtatiously in English:

'I know, you English listening station, can you hear me?' he would cheerfully declare. 'Would you like me to drop a bomb on you? Listen – whee! – boomp!' and he would chuckle into his microphone.

Anselm's witticisms ended in grief. His operations were suspected of breaching the immunity agreements, and the WAAFs were under orders to inform Fighter Group 11 when they heard him operating. His plane was shot down in flames by a flight of Spitfires.

He was unable to get out and we listened to him as he screamed and screamed for his mother and cursed the Fuehrer. I found myself praying: 'Get out, bale out – oh, please dear God, get him out.' But it was no use, he could not make it. We heard him the whole way down until he fell below reception range. I went outside and was sick.

Only then did I realise that I was in part his executioner; only then did I realise what I had done to that young pilot. I thought of the sad letters I had written when I was in the Casualties Section . . . and I knew that tomorrow a German mother's heart would break. It was then I made a vow to end the carnage as soon as possible. 'Amsel Eins' was just as brave as our pilots, for the demands of duty spell the same meaning in any language. We missed him sadly, for we had known him as such a happy young man.

On this occasion, and others, Mike Morris could not stifle her almost debilitating feelings of empathy; nevertheless during her time in the 'Y' Service she acted with consummate professionalism. This was no tennis party or seaside picnic. In 1940 many women like Mike Morris were being thrown into situations of the greatest urgency, demanding the coolest of heads. The rigours of the 'Y' Service required them to deny everything that, as women, they had hitherto been expected to embrace. They must not give life, they must kill. They must hate, not love; spurn, not pity. Their atavistic nature was being challenged by the circumstances of war; sex differences that had once seemed immutable now seemed precarious. Not surprisingly, Mike's bred-in sensitivity could not be extinguished so easily; her vow to 'end the carnage as soon as possible' was not the choice a soldier would have made.

She herself observed that men and women responded differently to battle conditions. Her cool view was that, at the outset, women tended to be braver than men under bombardment, but that demoralisation set in over time. Men, however, tended to panic at the beginning. Their morale emerged more slowly.

In the end, there is little to choose between men and women.

Would war prove a catalyst for some new kind of androgynous being? As Britain braced itself for the Blitz, Mike's assertion was very soon to be put to the most extreme of tests.

3   Wreckage

The Love of Her Life

Britain now stood isolated. Surviving on this island depended on importing foodstuffs – the role of the Merchant Navy. But from summer 1940 the U-boat threat to naval vessels in the Atlantic began to grow.

From the moment she first met the merchant seaman Harry O'Dwyer, Helen Forrester was under no illusions regarding the danger of his occupation. She knew that the submarines were out in the bay, 'like cats waiting at a mousehole'. Merchant shipping had to be protected by convoys of freighters. But sinkings were frequent, and there was huge loss of life. 'Allow five weeks, OK?' Harry had said to her when they parted. During his absence she was consumed with anxiety. Through her job, Helen knew at first hand what it was like for the women mourning their lost menfolk. She also had access to more information than most girls had about their sailor boyfriends. At that time there was a news embargo on British losses at sea, but next of kin were informed. If Harry's ship had gone to the bottom, Helen would have heard about it when the relatives came to her Bootle office to claim a pension. So when six weeks passed without a word from Harry, Helen became increasingly moody and despondent. Whatever had possessed her to trust a sailor?

And then, at last, he called. 'We've just berthed . . . wait for me if I'm late.' Helen took the call in her office, rapidly agreed to meet in Ma Ambleton's café at 7.30, then rushed downstairs to the cobwebby basement and burst into huge sobs of relief.

At 8 he finally appeared. 'I was all curled up inside with pure joy. I wanted to hug him.' Harry was exhausted and hungry. Over ravenous mouthfuls of steak and kidney pie, Harry let her know that his ship had got separated from the escorting convoy – 'Been chasing all over the bloody Atlantic, if you'll pardon the language.' Listening to him, Helen had a horrible premonition:

Suddenly I felt the icy Atlantic waters with its surface mist drifting over struggling men.

'Do you have to do another voyage? Can't you stay ashore – do something else?' . . .

I was in love.

After Harry had eaten, they walked down to the Mersey and boarded the ferry. Helen tucked herself under the curve of his arm, and they talked, crossing and recrossing the stretch of dark water in the blackout. Harry told her about his family. His mother had never forgiven him for quitting the seminary, and now he never went home. But he had been saving money and had put enough by for a house – would she come and help him look at some small properties in Allerton? 'My mind leaped ahead with all kinds of wild hopes.'

In her hungry, sad life, Helen had never known such happiness. She met Harry the next day at Norm and Doris's, and there they waltzed to the old wind-up gramophone. Her steps were as light as her heart, and when the music stopped it seemed far too soon. Harry took her back in his arms, and they swayed in gentle rhythm down the pavement; halfway along the avenue he stopped and kissed her, passionately.

Love, I know this is too quick. But I want to marry you, if you'll have me – soon as I can get a house ready to put you in safe and sound. Be my girl – I'll never let you down, I promise.

The Liverpool mist was swirling about them. Helen barely knew him, they were from different classes, different religions too; but even with the short time they had had together, she knew that Harry's offer meant the chance of something she had never dared hope for: a future. And she loved him. There and then, afloat in gratitude, Helen agreed. 'I'll try to be a good wife – I know how to keep house – and, oh, Harry, I want to make you happy.'

★

Love was in the air in 1940, and war often favoured romance in the most unexpected quarters.

Perhaps it was something in the water in Liverpool that year. Sonia Wilcox, the twenty-four-year-old daughter of an amiable Merseyside shipping pilot, might have been doomed to remain at home for all her adult life had it not been for the outbreak of war. Sonia was squashed by her recalcitrant and unloving mother, who stamped on all her ambitions. But in 1939 Mrs Wilcox ran out of excuses. Sonia went to work for an all-female team of censors who examined the documents and papers of travellers who might be suspected of passing information to the enemy – everything from personal correspondence to bibles, maps and recipe books. One morning a set of marine engravings came under Sonia's scrutiny, the property of a man claiming to be a Jewish refugee travelling to New York. Something about these engravings made Sonia linger over them – surely, between the cross-hatchings, she could detect minute lines of text? She took them up to the intelligence officers and asked for a second opinion. Lieutenant Keates, a handsome, educated-sounding young man, was dismissive. 'Nothing there. Waste of my time,' he said. Sonia, however, believed in her hunch and told the lieutenant that she would not go away until he had examined the engravings under an ultra-violet lamp. This time he was away for a considerable time, returning eventually to inform her that the cross-hatchings had, indeed, concealed information, in German, regarding shipping movements in and out of British ports, and that the so-called 'refugee' had been detained for questioning. 'You're rather a clever girl, aren't you?' he said. 'Patronising so-and-so' was Sonia's private reaction, before returning to her office. An hour later she found Lieutenant Keates waiting for her outside, with tickets for a performance at the Liverpool Playhouse.

After that Sonia met Basil Keates every night for a week, saying nothing to her parents, who were accustomed to her working long hours and catching the late ferry home across the Mersey. Love blossomed. Basil Keates turned out not only to have a captivating sense of humour, but also beautiful ankles. On the sixth day Basil appeared long-faced and told her that he was about to be posted to Iceland. They passed the evening together and he saw her to the quay. As the ferry gates clanked back and Sonia turned to depart he stopped her: 'Will you marry me, darling?' 'Yes,' she answered, and stepped aboard. The ferry pulled out into the great river, and suddenly Sonia realised that another vessel was churning up the water beside them, with none other than her father, its pilot, up on the top deck. Perhaps it was the radiance of her expression, or perhaps it was simply extraordinary fatherly intuition, but William Wilcox immediately guessed that his daughter had met the love of her life.

In February 1940 Basil managed to get leave, and the pair were married.*

Shirley Hook's wedding plans dominate her Mass Observation diary towards the end of the year. At that time she was working in the office of an engineering works. There was the excitement of showing off her engagement ring to her colleagues, followed by the announcement that she was leaving to get married. It was, however, a low-key wedding, in keeping with the times. On the day, she and Jack Goodhart were married in Leicester, 'most informally by an agreeable registrar', then went for a 'very good' two-and-sixpenny lunch at the Empire Café. It poured with rain, so they decided not to go away for the weekend. Shirley proudly headed her next diary entry 'Mrs Goodhart, Housewife, age 25'.

Marriage gave a sense of direction to Verily Bruce's otherwise meandering existence. The Sussex rector's daughter had always wanted to be a writer, but it would take another twenty years for her name to appear on a published book. Insouciant, funny and loveable, she found herself adrift in her early twenties.

Joining the FANYs in 1938 had helped. 'Somebody else does your thinking for you in the army, and even your feeling.' But despite being under orders she didn't find enough to keep her occupied. A dance band tune popular in spring 1940 seemed to reflect her sense of futility: 'I'm nothing but a nothing. I'm not a thing at all'. And work in the Corps held few attractions by comparison with the charming and debonair love of her life, writer Donald Anderson, whom she had met playing ping-pong with friends in 1936. More than seventy years later, Verily sighs romantically as she recalls their momentous first encounter:

Ah, God sent him I think.

On that occasion the sight of a large hole in his otherwise smart socks stirred something deep inside her:

*I am indebted to the author and teacher Jonathan Keates for telling me this endearing story about how his parents met; it was sad to hear that the charming Lieutenant Keates died of tuberculosis in 1949, when his younger son was only three years old. Sonia never remarried.

I just yearned to mend it. And I knew that we'd fallen in love.

By 1940 Donald was working in London in the Ministry of Information. Verily, now aged twenty-five, was based at a FANY depot in the Midlands. One afternoon that July her sergeant called her to the telephone, telling her to keep it quick. It was Donald, calling to ask her size in wedding rings.

'I don't know, darling. Why? Are we going to be married?'
   'That's what I should like. Can you get leave?'
   'Of course, darling.'
   'What about tomorrow?'

It was time to hang up.

'All right, darling. Of course.'

Duty called. So much for leave and browsing round ring shops. Verily was promptly detailed to pick up a captain at the depot and drive him to Birmingham. She drove the 30 miles in dreamy silence; once there, she took the first opportunity to park the vehicle outside a jeweller's. Courteously and quickly the assistant measured her wedding finger. It was P. Verily hastened to the nearest post office and drafted a telegram: 'P DARLING STOP YOUR ADORING V'.
   Back at the depot she requested forty-eight hours' leave. It was refused, but, noting that Verily's fluffy blonde hair was infringing the 'not-below-the-collar' regulations, the CO granted permission for two hours' grace to buy a hair-net. Barely pausing, she jumped on a bus to her Aunt Evie's, who lived near by. Aunt Evie took one look at her niece's excited, nervous pallor, banned her from returning to spend the night in a camp-bed, and that was the end of her association with the FANYs. Would she be shot at dawn for desertion? Unlikely. Next morning cousin Beryl dropped her at the railway station. She was still in uniform, and here the real difficulties started. A single ticket to London? Didn't she realise there was a state of emergency? No unauthorised travel was permitted to members of the services. She went to a nearby hotel to think things over. At that moment a young man climbed out of a large sports car and strolled into the bar looking for a cocktail. Verily took a calculated risk – 'Weren't you at school with my brother?' – and pulled it off.

Extraordinarily, it turned out that he had been and soon he had agreed to drive her to London, leaving the next morning. She took a room in the hotel and telephoned Donald. He was prepared, with the ring bought, the licence secured and honeymoon booked.

The next day her suave chauffeur arrived at the agreed hour. The sports car, it turned out, was entirely unreliable. Gasping, exploding and coughing smoke, it needed regular stops to replenish oil and have the engine tinkered with. At 8 o'clock that evening they arrived in Piccadilly in a cloud of blue fumes. '"Hallo, darling," said Donald, kissing me as though I had just got off a number 9 bus.'

The marriage would take place at two o'clock the following day. At the last minute Verily decided to telephone her parents and invite them. Donald, impoverished and far older than his bride-to-be, was not a popular choice, and the news didn't go down well with Mrs Bruce, who, having threatened to stop her daughter's pocket money, banged down the receiver. 'Yes, this was love all right,' concluded Verily.

And so, in August 1940, at Christ Church, Mayfair, as the Battle of Britain was getting under way, Verily Bruce became Verily Anderson. It was in every way a consummation:

That was when I looked back. Selfish, frivolous, and unreliable, I vowed to do better now that I had some real aim in life.

Their daughter Marian was to be born exactly nine months and three days later, closely followed by Rachel, Eddie, Janie and Alexandra. Not for a moment did Verily consider that her contribution as a FANY might have had more value to the war effort than cooking shepherd's pie for a Ministry official and having his babies. The possible penalties of her desertion from the army held no fears for her. Marriage and motherhood made sense of things. And it is reasonable to assume that countless wives would have viewed things in the same light. The Andersons honeymooned at a quaint Sussex inn, unruffled by fighter planes sparring in the blue skies above. Lounging in the pub garden, Verily had no qualms. Everything added up. Being a good wife was more than a subsidiary condition, it was a form of national service in itself. There was no irony in her emphatic defence of the married state:

If I can make you happy, you'll do your job at the Ministry better. Then we'll win the war.

As for the FANYs – they didn't really want her back, but to keep the bureaucrats happy she was required to produce a medical certificate stating that she was unfit for service. This was easily procured through a doctor friend of a friend, and the deed was done. Then as now, it helped to have influential contacts.

The Sad Atlantic

Helen Forrester and Harry O'Dwyer kept their engagement secret from their families. Harry's mother had still not forgiven him for abandoning his priestly vocation. And, despite the fact that the Forresters had fallen on hard times and were living in a slum, the class divisions ran deep. They retained their cultured accents. Harry was unquestionably 'beneath' Helen; also, he was a Catholic. Helen knew she would never gain her parents' approval of such a match. The couple decided to marry as soon as possible after she was twenty-one, once the little house Harry had bought was ready, and when their consent would no longer be required. Throughout spring 1940 they lived for their reunions. Harry's short spells on shore were times of joy and intimacy, as Harry coaxed and reassured his fearful young fiancée that she really was his girl, his one and only. For her part, she loved him with all her being.

But the fear never entirely left her. She knew that while he was at sea he was in constant danger. And in August 1940 she received the news that he was lost.

Cruelly, she only found out through the unluckiest of circumstances. Employed by a small social work charity in Bootle, Helen's job was to assist bereaved wives and the relatives of missing or drowned sailors claiming pensions. That morning there was the usual queue of widows in the waiting room, and Helen saw them one by one. Eventually it was the turn of an older woman, who explained her business; her son Harry, a merchant seaman, had gone missing with his ship in the Atlantic, and she now wished to make a claim so that at least she would benefit by his death. She gave her name as Mrs Maureen O'Dwyer.

I thought I would faint . . .

Helen quickly referred Mrs O'Dwyer to a colleague and fled to the building's basement.

In the clammy grime of a disused coal cellar, I stood shivering helplessly, so filled with shock that I hardly knew where I was.

Convulsed, but as yet dry-eyed, Helen was still just sufficiently composed to be sickened by the woman who could throw out her own son, yet still try to gain financially by his death. It seemed impossible to say or do anything that would make sense of her loss, or bring reconciliation. To have held out a hand to Mrs O'Dwyer would have seemed a betrayal, while to speak to her own parents would have subjected her to outright derision. How could she bear to have Harry scorned by them? He was a sailor, but he was the man she had loved. She stayed silent.

It took Helen superhuman efforts to contain the grief which now threatened to overwhelm her; unarticulated, it worked away like a poison, ravaging her from within. Ill health, hunger, parental neglect, poverty and fear had already wrought great damage; now the blow of Harry's death took away the one prospect of happiness in this lonely life. Out of her mind with sorrow, she sobbed through the night, her sister Fiona sleeping in tranquil contentment beside her. Walking home from work after dark, she cried in the blackout when nobody could see her tears. At her office, Helen realised she was not alone in her suffering. Death had come to Merseyside. Day after day she sat at her desk, working her way through the rows and rows of weeping wives clutching tear-stained children. Often it was her job to break the news to them. Sometimes a seaman would come to her, sobbing, sent ashore on compassionate leave to discover that his family had been killed in an air raid. Consumed by her own pain, the distress of these others was almost too great to bear. One dreadful Saturday Helen's controls collapsed: tears sprang to her eyes as she cried out, full of pity and anger, 'It's madness to send men to certain death like this!' Rage possessed her. What right did Harry have to die? Why had he left her? Why had he got himself killed? 'We could have been married by now.'

Part of Helen Forrester's terrible anger stemmed from the feeling that Harry's death had robbed her not just of love, but of the chance to escape from her home, and from her mother. Marrying Harry would have meant trading the thankless task of cleaning up after her own family for more of the same work – but at least under his roof it would have been done with love. Now, at the age of twenty-one, Helen saw her youth, her happiness stolen from her. She felt trapped for ever in her loneliness. 'I wanted to die.'

★

Between September 1939 and May 1943 over 30,000 Allied servicemen and merchant seamen would be engulfed by the grey waves of the Atlantic. Helen Forrester's premonition of Harry's horrible death, of his struggle and choking by icy water, was true for thousands of individuals, forgotten among the tally of losses. For the women of the Second World War, torpedoes were the intangible agents of grief and bereavement. But a few experienced them at first hand.

This is not primarily a book about heroines, but it is a book about women who rose to the demands of history, and in 1940 those demands were becoming increasingly extortionate. The story of Mary Cornish is only one example of an ordinary, frightened and unprepared woman who, at a time of extremity, responded gallantly to the calls of duty and responsibility.

As the danger of enemy attacks intensified, so did the importance of sending children to safety, and the government decided to extend its evacuation plans to enable school-age children to be received overseas as well as in far-flung areas of Britain. The Children's Overseas Reception Board ('CORB') was formed, and anxious parents applied by the thousand to send their children to safety in South Africa, Australia, Canada and the USA. Known as the 'seavacuees', the children would be travelling without their parents, under the care of appointed guardians.

The piano teacher Mary Cornish was one woman who volunteered to work in this capacity. Mary was now forty-one, an intelligent, confident, self-sufficient spinster; until the war her job, her friends and music had been her life. She volunteered; but the summons to sail to Canada was slow in coming. While waiting to depart, Mary spent the summer holiday haymaking and fruit-picking on a Sussex farm. Finally, in late August, her instructions arrived.

On Friday 13 September 1940 a convoy of ships including the SS *City of Benares* set sail from Liverpool with ninety excited child evacuees and a number of such escorts on board. It was crewed by British officers and lascar seamen. Mary, along with her allocated batch of girls, was familiar with the emergency drill. After their departure the children settled into enjoying themselves. There was delicious food to eat, and a party atmosphere; the girls had started a choir and were learning to sing 'In an English Country Garden' for their Canadian hosts. Four days out to sea the convoy of destroyers, required elsewhere, returned to British waters. The liner was now accompanied by a motley fleet of merchant ships, incapable of giving naval protection. A storm blew up, and that day a lot of the passengers were suffering from sea-sickness, but by evening the ship was tossing less, so after dinner Mary and two of the other escorts took a stroll on the deck. They were in good spirits, and Mary – perhaps with the girls' choir in mind – led the group singing Christmas carols and verses from 'Greensleeves'. At about 10 o'clock she decided to go below. It was then that the torpedo struck. Aboard U-48, Kapitänleutnant Heinrich Bleichrodt had no idea that he had fired it at a liner carrying children.

It took just fifteen minutes for the SS *City of Benares* to sink. The missile had ripped a giant hole in the stern. The U-boat also sank the two ships that flanked the *City of Benares*, and the rest of the small fleet dispersed to avoid being sunk in their turn.

The engines died, the ship filled with the acrid smell of cordite, alarm bells rang. The children got dressed and hurried to their muster stations. Mary knew it was her job to get her group of girls into a lifeboat, but when she tried to reach their quarters she found the corridor blocked by debris; lacerating her hands, she pushed a gap through the mound, struggled through and got help to pull the children out of their cabins and up on deck. The only soothing words she could find to say to them were: 'It's all right, it's only a torpedo.' The crew started loading children into the boats. Mary returned below to see if any had been overlooked, but an officer ordered her back on deck. Having now become separated from her group of girls, she was hastily told to join a boatload of thirty lascar crewmen, a couple of British officers and six small boys; she never saw the girls again.

A long night passed; the storm was rising. Mary – like the boys, many of whom were barefoot and in pyjamas – was inadequately dressed in a short-sleeved silk blouse, a skirt, a jacket, stockings and sandals. When dawn broke over grey foam-crested waves, the occupants of lifeboat number 12 realised they were alone in the middle of the Atlantic.

Meanwhile, in West Sussex, Mary Cornish's beloved younger sister Eileen Paterson and her husband received a letter from CORB informing them, as her next of kin, of the sinking of the *City of Benares*, explaining that Miss Cornish had not been reported rescued, and conveying the Board's 'very deep sympathy in your grievous loss'. Their daughter Elizabeth still remembers 'finding my mother weeping in my father's arms in the garage at the bottom of the garden . . . he was trying to comfort her'. Letters of sympathy poured into the Paterson family, who tried to take consolation in the thought of a valiant sister and aunt who had died carrying out her duty to the children in her care.

Far from any communication, the ordeal that played out on the cold waters of the Atlantic ocean is a tale of almost incredible endurance. The few British officers took charge, organising crew members to crank the propeller, rigging a sail and a tarpaulin to shelter the stern of the boat, distributing rations. The food they had was carefully eked out, as was the water, which was in much shorter supply. On two small beakers of water a day, everyone suffered from terrible thirst. It was cold too: September was not a time to be afloat on the Atlantic in an open boat dressed in cotton pyjamas. Mary, the only woman on board, now demonstrated unexpected fortitude, stamina and imagination. She herself was suffering as badly as the rest of them from thirst and exposure; in addition sanitary arrangements were a particular trial for her, since there was no possibility of concealing her occasional need to use the one and only bucket on board. But as day followed day, and their plight became worse, Mary's relationship with the six young boys became the key to their survival. They relied on her not only for her kindness – she would massage the circulation back into their frostbitten feet, wrapping anything she could find round them to ease the pain – but, crucially, for her ability to raise morale. At first, while the boys were still lively enough to believe they were having a great adventure, she got them singing. 'There'll Always be an England' and 'Run, Rabbit, Run' were favourites. She invented games and boosted their sense that they were brave and plucky. But before long they came to rely on her to distract them from their misery. When spirits dropped, it was Mary who rebuked them: 'Don't you realise that you're the heroes of a *real* adventure story? There isn't a boy in England who wouldn't give his eyes to be in your shoes! Did you ever hear of a hero who *snivelled*?' Something in the schoolboy psyche craved such reminders, and the schoolmistress in Mary understood this. From the depths, she dredged up memories of adventure tales like *The Thirty-Nine Steps* and *Bulldog Drummond*. Every night, before the children settled for a few hours' sleep, Mary's tales of Captain Drummond's exploits persuaded them to forget, for a little while, how hungry, thirsty, cold and cramped they were. Because her memory of the original stories was a little faulty, she embroidered. With his lean jaw and fearless demeanour, Captain Drummond soon found himself in danger from a Nazi spy ring, braving submarines, parachutes and fighter planes. There were hair-raising escapes and dramatic rescues from the edges of precipices. The boys loved it. Nothing else came near in giving them what they now most wanted: forgetfulness. 'Aunty, Aunty, please go on,' they begged, as each instalment came to an end. So, like all the best storytellers, she promised more for the next day.

On Sunday, after five days at sea, hopes of rescue suddenly soared when the crew sighted a steamer. Mary's petticoat was commandeered, and they ran it up the mast to signal distress. With wonderful certainty now, they watched as the outline of the steamer became more distinct and swung around, growing closer till they could see the sailors on board – only to turn to shocked dismay at the last moment as the vessel slowly and decisively resumed its course in the opposite direction. Later it appeared that the ship's skipper must have feared that the lifeboat was a German submarine decoy; this sometimes happened, luring unwary ships to their doom.

By now the occupants of lifeboat number 12 were near to exhaustion. With their water ration down to half a beaker a day, their lips and tongues were cracked and distended. On the eighth day everyone was becoming lethargic, and even Mary was too depleted to tell stories. Hopes were beginning to die; there had been disappointments and false alarms. So when one of the boys cried out 'There's an aeroplane!' nobody took much notice. But this time it wasn't a freak. The plane was a Sunderland, it had seen them, and a signal was immediately sent that it was going for help. Within an hour another Sunderland appeared and let down supplies. They were still feasting on tinned fruit when HMS *Anthony* was sighted. One by one, more dead than alive, the survivors were helped on to the rescue ship. Mary was almost past reason. They settled her in; her throat was so badly swollen she could barely eat, and she could not imbibe hot drinks. She was dazed, dizzy, couldn't stand and couldn't remember how to undress. She was obsessed with one thing: her responsibility towards the boys. What had happened to them, and were they all right?

Thirty-six hours later HMS *Anthony* docked in the Firth of Clyde. On 27 September, in their country home near Midhurst, the Patersons received a telegram. It read simply: MISS M C CORNISH SAFE AND WELL.

CORB looked after Mary when they arrived and brought her to a hotel, where WVS ladies arrived bearing clothes. Even in her confused state, she was aware that the garments were peculiarly ill-assorted: a pink petticoat, a purple dress, yellow gloves. Almost immediately she was surrounded by journalists desperate for her story. When they interviewed her, there was the shock of hearing that many of the children and most of her fellow escorts on board the *City of Benares* had not survived. She ate a little, slept a little, drank and drank again. A dozen times in the night she woke convulsed with fear lest the glass of water by her bed had been removed. Beneath her, lifeboat 12 seemed still to roll and pitch, heave and drop; as she dipped in and out of sleep, her only thought was 'the boys – were they all right?'

Two hundred and eighty-five people died after the torpedo hit the *City of Benares*. Seventy-seven of the ninety children on board drowned. From then on, parents who wanted to send their children to safety had to make their own arrangements, as the operations of CORB were suspended soon afterwards. This island was becoming an ever more dangerous place to live.

Battleground

On 1 August 1940 Hermann Göring, Commander-in-Chief of Hitler's air force, had outlined the aims of the Battle of Britain to his generals:

'The Führer has ordered me to crush Britain with my Luftwaffe. By means of hard blows I plan to have this enemy, who has already suffered a crushing moral defeat, down on his knees in the nearest future, so that an occupation of the island by our troops can proceed without any risk!'

Throughout that summer the blue skies of southern England were criss-crossed with smoke and fire from swarms of German bombers and Spitfires. Joan Tagg, aged fifteen at the time, remembers watching them from her garden in Kingston-on-Thames: 'They were over Kent I expect – but you can see for miles in the sky. I'd always been interested in aeroplanes, and there would be the fighters in the sky, with all their vapour trails. You can't imagine what it was like seeing all these planes looping the loop and doing figures of eight . . . every movement they made there was a vapour trail. It was just so exciting – like a cinema show really.' In London, Sheila Hails remembered the men on Primrose Hill who cashed in on this thrilling spectator sport by hiring out telescopes: 'Penny to see the Messerschmitts come down!'

In her diary on 16 August Virginia Woolf described the experience of being underneath during an air fight. She and her husband Leonard were in their Sussex garden: 'They came very close. We lay down under the tree. The sound was like someone sawing in the air just above us. We lay flat on our faces, hands behind head . . . Will it drop I asked? If so, we shall be broken together.' The following week an enemy plane flew over the Ouse water meadows beyond their garden, low enough for Virginia to distinguish the swastika on its tail, and was shot down by British fighters. 'They side slipped glided swooped and roared for about 5 minutes round the fallen plane as if identifying and making sure – then made off towards London . . . It wd have been a peaceful matter of fact death to be popped off on the terrace playing bowls this very fine cool sunny August evening.'

On the same day Frances Faviell and her fiancé, Richard Parker, were walking a bridle path on the Surrey downs near Guildford; for her, it was a week's break from months of FAP and refugee duties. The view from the Hog's Back was panoramic, with the land spread out below them like a map. Above, in the blue August sky, the unreal aeronautical displays held them spellbound – a bravura stunt show of twisting, turning, swooping, diving planes which from time to time shimmered to earth in a cascade of fire, concluding with the silent, releasing vision of a tiny parachute slipping gently towards the ground – 'like a toy umbrella preceding the final crash'. Frances shook herself as she recalled that what she was witnessing was 'the real thing ... WAR ... I was glad Richard was with me ... I thought then – nothing matters if you are with the person you want to be with.' The fights were ferocious and went on all that day. The planes had machine-guns. Richard suddenly dragged Frances into the shelter of some bushes as with a furious popping one enemy pilot swooped, firing directly at them, spattering bullets in all directions. They were unharmed, unnerved, but – in Frances's case – seething with rage and indignation. The anger increased that night as they were wakened by sirens. Fire bombs had been dropped near by. Richard led a party to extinguish them with sand and stirrup pumps, and Frances joined in, stumbling among the flames that had caught the heathland. Nearby Croydon appeared to be blazing. They stayed another day, watching more and more dogfights. One after another, planes plummeted to earth out of the clear sky; at night, again, the sirens, and the hornet-like drone of engines signalled air raids on London, some 30 miles away. The Blitz was beginning.

On the afternoon of 7 September Frances heard the sirens from her flat in Cheyne Place, but by early evening Chelsea still seemed to be clear of bombs. The sun set – but darkness didn't fall. Instead, a curious pale orange glow lit up the sky 'almost like sunrise'. London's docklands were on fire. Frances and Richard climbed up to the roof of her building and watched in stricken silence as the inferno devoured Rotherhithe, Limehouse, Wapping, Woolwich, Bermondsey, its flames fully visible 7 miles down river. All night the East End burned; 900 aircraft had attacked. From then on, for the next seventy-six nights (with only one exception, 2 November), the city was blitzed.

During the Battle of Britain, Virginia Woolf had written an essay entitled *Thoughts on Peace in an Air Raid*. The experiences of a myriad women during the next six months of German bombardment are worth looking at in the context of her reflections:

Up there in the sky young Englishmen and young German men are fighting each other. The defenders are men, the attackers are men. Arms are not given to Englishwomen either to fight the enemy or to defend herself. She must lie weaponless tonight. Yet if she believes that the fight going on up in the sky is a fight by the English to protect freedom, by the Germans to destroy freedom, she must fight, so far as she can, on the side of the English. How far can she fight for freedom without firearms? By making arms, or clothes, or food. But there is another way of fighting for freedom without arms; we can fight with the mind.

Virginia Woolf's essay pursues the notion that men's and women's deepest instincts prevail in times of war. The Second World War seemed to her an embodiment of 'the subconscious Hitlerism in the hearts of men . . . the desire for aggression; the desire to dominate and enslave'. Her theme is that, just as womankind is motivated at the deepest level by her maternal instinct, so man has been propelled since the dawn of time by the power of his aggressive desires, his love of military glory:

We must help the young Englishmen to root out from themselves the love of medals and decorations. We must create more honourable activities for those who try to conquer in themselves their fighting instinct, their sub-conscious Hitlerism. We must compensate the man for the loss of his gun.

One may not agree with Woolf's allocation of apparently stereo-typical sex characteristics. There are plenty of examples of timidity among men, and we hear much today about women's aggressive-ness. It may even seem surprising to hear Virginia Woolf, a childless feminist, refer to the maternal instinct as 'women's glory'. But one has to remember that seventy years ago in Britain the attributes she ascribes as being innate among men and women would have been entirely accepted – indeed taken for granted – not only by the vast majority of the population but also by her intellectual readers. And if the pre-war iconography of the maternal angel endures even for Virginia Woolf in Bloomsbury, how much more so for Clara Mil-burn in the Midlands, Nella Last in Barrow, the Noble family in Lewisham, the Chadwyck-Healeys in their Somerset gentlemen's residence? Looked at in the light of Woolf's dissection, women's experiences of, and writings about, the Blitz illustrate an extreme moment in history – a moment when the weaponless woman was completely at the mercy of men. But perhaps it was a moment, too, when women revealed how far the pre-war stereotype fell short. The men did not surrender their guns, and Woolf's hope that the mind would triumph was perhaps overly optimistic. But, in 1940 and '41, in fear of their lives, women demonstrated that they were cleverer, braver, angrier, more articulate, more enterprising, more robust and altogether more complex than even they themselves had ever guessed.

★

Charles Graves, the historian of the Women's Voluntary Service, saw the Blitz as the moment when the great organisation created by Lady Reading fulfilled its potential: 'Here at last was the emergency for which WVS was originally formed.' He quoted one of their volunteers who had narrowly escaped death after an explosion had flattened an entire terrace of houses – 'I'm so glad,' she said, 'now we've had a real bomb to show that we have not wasted time on our practices.' There were many more examples, such as the WVS canteen crew who sheltered under their vehicle while an aerodrome was being bombed, emerging 'dusty but undaunted' to serve hot drinks to the RAF; the fearless WVS bicycle messengers maintaining communications by pedal-power after an army telephone service was destroyed by a falling aircraft; or the indefatigable volunteer who from her own tiny kitchen fed a crowd of 1,200 bombed-out citizens in Barnes, west London. These dauntless ladies, who had once poured their surplus energies into baking macaroons for church teas, now gave their all to help casualties: distributing clothing, running Rest Centres for the homeless and support systems for ARP workers and, above all, serving tea and buns. 'Tea became the common healer in all our disaster,' wrote one reporter of the Blitz. It was served, not as before the war, in china cups with lemon, but watery and beige from an urn, in hefty mugs stained with tannin.

Most of the 'tea-ladies' didn't make the headlines. One who did – Yorkshire farmer's wife Eveline Cardwell – became a news sensation by single-handedly capturing a German airman who had baled out by parachute over her fields. She accosted the intruder, signed to him to put his hands in the air and surrender his pistol (which he did), before delivering him to the Local Defence Volunteers. (The incident may have provided the inspiration for the film version of Jan Struther's pre-war *Times* column *Mrs Miniver*. In the American movie,

Greer Garson finds a wounded German pilot in her back garden and gives him breakfast before, with superb cool, handing him over to the police.)

Heroines cheered everyone up, and Mrs Cardwell was promptly presented with the British Empire Medal amid a blaze of publicity, '*pour encourager les autres*'.

Throughout the Blitz, women plugged gaps left by absent men: as fire-watchers, ARP workers, first-aiders, ambulance drivers, police officers, messengers, transport, demolition and repair workers. At this point in the war there was, however, no question of women taking up arms against the invading enemy. Churchill was adamantly opposed to the idea of women with guns, which would have implied a failure on the part of his sex to protect them. The Blitz, however, overturned the rules obtaining to male chivalry. It exposed the idea that the 'weaker sex' could be protected by the 'stronger' as a cruel myth. Aerial bombardment does not discriminate. There were countless examples of husbands and so-called 'protectors', called to relatively safe postings in outlying counties, leaving wives and children vulnerable. Albert Powell from Lewisham was one, sent with the RAF to Yorkshire. 'I was left in London in the front line with three children,' recalled his wife, Margaret. The civilian death toll of women and children under sixteen was 33,135, 55 per cent of the total.

Phyllis Noble decided that the only way to get through being bombed was to live for the day. Lewisham, where the Noble family lived, was on the rat-run taken by German bombers coming in over the Kentish coast towards London; the train marshalling yards at nearby Hither Green station were a frequent target for their loads. However, the acute fear that Phyllis had felt a year earlier had abated, to be replaced by a spirit of adaptation to circumstances.

I suppose an average of seven hours out of every twenty-four is spent in shelters.

Suburban, secure, settled Londoners are on familiar terms with the wail of sirens, the crash of guns, the whine of bombs, the thud of explosions. 'Have you done the black-out?', 'Have you got your gas-mask?' take the place of pre-war remarks – 'Have you got your umbrella?', 'What about your hanky?'

Getting to work next day was a question of 'if' not 'when'. After a night huddled in the cramped Anderson shelter at the bottom of the garden Phyllis would set off for her job at the bank in Bishopsgate, vaguely optimistic that she would arrive sometime, somehow. As often as not this meant accepting a ride on the back of a lorry-load of cauliflowers or fish boxes – 'a far more interesting start to the day than being packed tight in the train'. You banged on the back of the driver's cab when you wanted it to stop. 'One never knows whether on arriving at work the bank will be still & standing or down to the ground.' Sometimes Phyllis travelled by a boat service that had been laid on to get city workers into town from Greenwich Pier; for miles, blackened carcasses along the river banks were all that was left of the once towering East End warehouses. By every route, smoking shells, ruined buildings and smashed glass, overlaid with serpentine coils of hosepipe, testified to the night's bomb damage. 'It was hard to believe that what I was seeing could be real. Yet, with a lump in my throat and tears welling in my eyes, I knew that it was.'

For some, the heartbreaking vision of their capital in flames was mingled with awe at the strange impersonal beauty of destruction. 'Magnificently terrifying,' was Madeleine Henrey's reaction. 'A lethal fairyland,' wrote another woman, describing the city bathed in the milky light of thousands of incendiary bombs.

Night after night the population of London adapted to the raids by becoming subterranean. In the city's basements and cellars they huddled, in back gardens they burrowed into their Anderson shelters, or squirmed beneath their table-top Morrisons. With the prospect of hours of danger, discomfort and sleeplessness ahead of them, the female shelterers went prepared with the essentials: money, door-keys, a torch and, of course, make-up. By now, objections to women wearing trousers were beginning to seem irrelevant; but *Woman's Own* readers were advised to purchase a dressing-gown with pockets capacious enough to carry an entire beauty kit: cleansing wipes, powder cream ('which in an instant takes off all the shine and leaves you matt and composed'), powder puff, smelling salts, sedative tablets, comb and lipstick. The message was 'Stay lovely.' Two young Bermondsey women made a pact that they would not be found dead with their hair in rollers. 'If the sirens went . . . we took the rollers out. And put them back in when the All Clear sounded. Sometimes this could happen as many as three times a night.'

Thousands perforce herded into the damp and insanitary public shelters, but even vaster numbers queued to descend into the Underground, thronging its stairs and platforms, seething and stinking. The character of life in each shelter often depended on the marshal running it. There were quiet shelters, drunk shelters, courting shelters, fighting shelters. The indefatigable Mass Observers reported on a woman running one section of a shelter at Stepney, holding forty people. Every day this energetic lady made it her business to take all their bedding home, hang it out to air and bring it back in the evening after dinner: 'I see to it all for 'em.' The neighbouring section was run by a firm-handed woman who took pride in keeping the peace: 'We ain't had no fights here, not on my platform.' Air-raid warden Barbara Nixon was a regular visitor to one cheerful shelter run by a Mrs Barker, who had carried her gramophone in. The noisier the raid, the louder the music, and everyone would join in uproarious choruses of 'Roll out the Barrel' till three or four in the morning. Since sleep was mostly impossible, singing offered a morale-boosting alternative. Fidgets and nerves were held at bay, too, by smoking and knitting, both staple activities for 1940s womankind. Prayers and psalms helped to calm the fearful. One woman nightly drank herself insensible on brandy. But Flo Mahony's brand of downbeat fatalism was a more typical response: 'I don't think we ever really realised the danger. I can't ever remember being afraid. They would say, "If there's a bomb that's got your name on it, you've had it," you know?'

Nevertheless, incoherent distress often took hold, as recorded by Mass Observers in a public shelter during the Blitz:

'I'm ill! I think I'm going to die!'

'If we ever live through this night, we have the Good God above to thank for it!'

'I don't know if there is one, or he shouldn't let us suffer like this.'

'I'm twenty-six. I'm more than half way to thirty! I wish I was dead!'

Such terror was not irrational. The death toll was already high, as we have seen, but the figure almost doubles if we include numbers of those wounded: 63,000 of them (48 per cent) were female. One woman had to be taken to hospital suffering from uncontrollable grief. Her husband, son, daughter and son-in-law had all been killed in one bombing raid. It was enough to drive anyone out of their mind.

While the bombers droned overhead a surreal parallel life co-existed above the huddled masses in the underground shelters. The grandes dames of society, evicted from their West End mansions, took refuge in the Dorchester. The writer Fiona MacCarthy, who had been an habituée of the hotel since childhood (it had been built, and was owned by her great-grandfather, Sir Robert McAlpine), explains:

The Dorchester was said to be impervious to bombs because of its re-inforced concrete structure. It was widely believed that any bomb that hit the building would just bounce off again.

Here, a life of smart dinners and cocktail parties continued side by side with the evacuated riff-raff (tarts, commercial gentlemen, off-duty airmen) who had made their way to its once-decorous corridors in search of an impregnable refuge. The ballroom was strewn with mattresses. One of those who moved in was Lady Diana Cooper, wife of Duff Cooper, the Minister of Information. Each night she descended, carrying her treasured diamond dol-phins, trembling diamond spray, £200 in cash, her passport and make-up essentials, to a cubicle in the subterranean Turkish bath and slept there (with the aid of a sleeping-pill) till the all-clear came at dawn. Then she returned to her roof-floor suite for another hour's doze if she could get it. Service remained prompt and cour-teous. The staff brought in early-morning tea and *The Times*; flowers and messages were delivered. She would breakfast in bed, deal with phone calls and write to her twelve-year-old son John Julius, who had been evacuated to Canada ('I wish, I wish I could see you. Send me all the snapshots you can of yourself, or I may not recognise you, darling, darling'). Then it was time to dress, and 'buzz off to the Ritz for a drink with one or more of the boys'. At the Dorchester, the Coopers' social life was on tap: everyone who was anyone was staying there. 'We semi-dress for dinner much more smartly than we would in days of peace.' Above the competi-tive din of the bombers, the Hyde Park guns and a cacophonous dance orchestra the Coopers and their friends dined in the luxury-liner restaurant, 'lulled by Chianti'.

The gaiety of London's night life defied the Blitz. 'Restaurants and dancing had all gone underground,' Verily Anderson recalled. The 400, the Florida and the Berkeley were humming. But in March 1941 eighty people dancing at the cavernous Café de Paris – thought to be safe, owing to its depth below Leicester Square – were killed by two 50K landmines which exploded on the dance floor. The band was playing 'Oh, Johnny! Oh, Johnny! How you can love!' For a second, as the bombs fell, the dancers stood immobilised; then crumpled, dead, in sprawled heaps. 'Snakehips' Johnson and his fellow musicians were among those killed by the blast. 'The best swing band in London gone,' mourned Joan Wyndham.

*

While London blazed, Mary Cornish lay in bed in a Lanarkshire nursing home. The overnight wonder of her rescue from Lifeboat 12 had started to be replaced in the papers by more pressing news. But the beauties of the Scottish scenery were restorative. Gradually, the sores on her mouth were starting to heal, and massage was helping her circulation to recover. Her sister Eileen, brother-in-law Ian and flatmate Mabel had all visited her and, fed on buttered egg, milky drinks, creamed cauliflower and chocolate pudding with cream, Mary was regaining weight and recovering in peace. In October she was able to write to her sister that she had slept 'straight through . . . with no horrid boats or other nightmares, which was marvellous'. The numbed exhaustion was giving way to a renewed appetite for life: 'Still more cheering, I'm not half so unintelligent, & perk up quite naturally from time to time . . . almost without effort!' Already Miss Cornish was focusing on a return to her teaching job at Wokingham, making her base with Ian and Eileen near Midhurst. There, in the Sussex countryside, she would gently regain her fitness working on the land for a local farmer. Elizabeth, her eight-year-old niece, remembers being warned off the subject of her Aunt Mary's terrible experiences: 'We were told we must be very quiet and not slam doors and not on any account to talk to her about what had happened, because almost all the girls she'd been looking after had been drowned. It had been a terrible shock to her.'

*In September 1940 Mary Cornish's story competed with
the air raids for front-page space.*

Tough, spirited and stoical, Mary Cornish herself was reluctant to indulge in recollections of her Atlantic ordeal. Later that year she told her story to the author of a short book about the *City of Benares*, but after that, for better or worse, she barely ever spoke of it again.

Taking It

Already, in a year of war, women had come a long way. In 1939 Frances Faviell had been painting flower pieces and portraits in Chelsea. In the autumn of 1940, during a heavy daylight raid, she and Richard Parker were married; they spent the first night of their wedded life putting out incendiaries. By November she was spending almost all of her time doling out soup to rescue workers, caring for refugees and – as a trained VAD – at her first aid post. Like many others, she was evolving.

One night of heavy air raids the trains weren't running on Frances's usual route home. The explosions seemed to have quieted down, so she walked home through a grid of residential streets. She was in uniform. In one of the side streets Frances passed a group of people beside a recently destroyed building; there seemed to be a crater in its basement, but it was mostly filled in with rubble. A voice called out to her, 'Nurse!' She stopped and went over. One of the people was a well-built woman, also in nurse's uniform, another was a doctor, the other two were wardens. She now became aware that there was a terrible sound coming from the depths of the crater, seemingly underground; dreadful screams could be heard issuing from a crevice among the debris: 'Someone was in mortal anguish down there.'

'What are your hip measurements?' said the large nurse. Frances was small and slender – 'thirty-four inches'. Her shoulders were the same. She would fit into the hole. They could lower her head-first into it to assist the man trapped below. The doctor now instructed her. She must remove her coat, and also her dress; the fabric might catch in parts of the unsafe debris and bring the whole thing down. First, dressed in her blouse and regulation voluminous black knickers, she must descend with a torch to see whether it was possible to administer morphia. There was barely an inch of leeway either side; she must keep her arms close to her sides, her body as rigid as possible, and grip the torch in her teeth. The two wardens now seized her by the thighs, and lowered her. From below came a long, ghastly, animal screaming. 'It was as if I was having a nightmare from which I would soon waken.'

The torch showed me that the debris lay over both arms and that the chest of the man trapped there was crushed into a bloody mess – great beams lay across the lower part of his body – and his face was so injured that it was difficult to distinguish the mouth from the rest of it – it all seemed one great gaping red mess.

Below, the hole was cavernous. Frances was able to remove the torch from her mouth and speak the soothing words she had been taught: 'Try to keep calm – we're working to get you out.' But the stench was almost overpowering, and she was afraid of being sick. They pulled her up. 'On my feet I felt violent nausea and vomited again and again.' Once the bout had passed, the doctor explained to her what she had to do next. He gave her a small bottle of chloroform and a cotton mask; being careful not to inhale it herself, she must apply it as close as possible to the man's nostrils – or what was left of them. They lowered her back into the hole, and she did as she had been told.

'Breathe deeply – can you?' A sound as from an animal – a grunt – came from the thing which had been a face. She held the pad firmly over him. 'Breathe deeply ... deeply ... deeply ...' There was a small convulsive movement of revulsion ... another fainter one – and then the sounds stopped.

There were other bodies in the hole; Frances couldn't tell how many, but she could see the grisly fragments. Near to passing out with the stench and the chloroform vapour, she called out to the waiting team, who pulled her back up, gagging and retching, to vomit repeatedly on the pavement. 'Thank you, nurse. You did very well,' said the doctor. It was enough; she had played her part, and it was time to go home. On the way back to Chelsea she stopped to vomit at intervals until she reached her door, where her devoted housekeeper, Mrs Freeth, was waiting up, and administered brandy and tea. Little by little the uncontrollable shivering died down, but nothing could erase the memories: 'I had never seen anything like that horror in the hole.'

The Blitz brought the atrocities of war into ghastly close-up. There were, in 1940, many men who recalled the 1914–18 slaughter. But far fewer women had had contact with the unspeakable carnage that can be inflicted by explosive projectiles. Frances Faviell seems to have been unusually unfortunate in this regard. Having studied anatomy at the Slade School of Art, she was sometimes sent out by her FAP Commandant to perform the nauseating task of piecing together bodies dismembered by blast, in preparation for burial. 'The stench was the worst thing about it'; that, and the problem of finding all the bits and making them fit. There were almost always too many limbs, and insufficient other members, and the injuries were unspeakable. Frances told of Connie, a warden friend of hers who had had to move a man's body with a chair leg driven right through it. The air-raid warden Barbara Nixon encountered the pitiable remains of a baby on the street after it had been blown through an upper window. It had burst open on striking the street. Images like this could never be forgotten. For Edith, an ambulance driver working in the 'bombers' corridor' at Gillingham in Kent, the trivial impressions stayed with her – like a woman's 'sensible shoes' protruding from a stretcher, or the purple coat of another woman found in the rubble of her bombed home; much later they located the victim's remains under the kitchen table. Edith had them wrapped in two army blankets and carried into the ambulance – she noticed how the dead woman's long, wavy brown hair hung over the edge of the stretcher. They took the pieces to the mortuary. The blankets were needed back, but had to be abandoned; they had been ruined by the tangle of pulped guts and crushed meat that had once been her vital organs. 'I could not stop retching.' In south-east London, newlywed Dianna Dobinson's flat was destroyed by a landmine dropped by parachute. The mines caused horrifying damage: 'people were just blown to pieces.' Dianna saw bits of bodies that had come to rest in the branches of trees, which themselves had been stripped of leaves. Later, carts arrived to gather up the grisly fragments and take them away. Seventeen-year-old Londoner Cora Styles soon became acclimatised to such sights: 'When I went to work in the mornings you'd see piles of brick rubble, perhaps with an arm sticking out or a leg – I got so that blood, guts and what have you didn't have much effect on me. I knew a man who would go round with a basket collecting the bits, trying to put them together. He picked up somebody's head and the eyes were open; it nearly landed him in the loony bin.'

Common as such gory sights became, they were not universal. But few were spared the brutal sight of homes, hearths, personal belongings, clothes, treasures and souvenirs indiscriminately wrecked and exposed by the bombs. Elizabeth Bowen emerged from an air-raid shelter to the sight of a gashed-open apartment block: 'Up there the sun strikes a mirror over a mantelpiece; shreds of a carpet sag out over the void.' One might see the cross-section of a bathroom, with a towel laid out ready on the tub waiting for its occupant, an assortment of stockings draped in a tree-top, remnants of dresses hooked over broken rafters, twisted light fittings at the bottom of the garden. Wedding presents, kitchen equipment, books lay scattered among the wreckage and matchwood.

Here, a woman might feel her very identity dismembered, as loved and cherished objects, things long desired and ill afforded, things hoarded, collected and enshrined were hurled from their alcoves, blasted from their cabinets and smashed to smithereens. Pre-war woman was equated and identified with the home. Part of her perceived task in life had been to embellish it, to beautify it. Hilde Marchant, a journalist who wrote an account of the Blitz in 1941, witnessed dispossessed and injured women in a hospital after their homes had been bombed:

They wanted to get back home, though their homes were damaged and broken . . . Though they were scarred, there was still that vivid picture of peace in their own kitchen. It is more than a sense of possession. It is more than just the female desire to protect the working husband. Home was something regular and real, home was the shape they had grown.

'When I saw my house with the roof off and the windows blown inside out, it drew me out by the roots,' said one of the women.

There must be no junk in the attic. For precautions to be taken see pp. 2 and 3.

Keeping calm and carrying on – an illustration from the Fire Party Handbook *showing how to put out incendiaries.*

From chintz curtains to quilts, tables to teacups, every eau-de-nil interior in the land was a temple to that revered household deity, the British wife. And now her ritual objects lay scattered, exposed, broken. Could she ever be the same again?

Resilience kicked in. When Hilde Marchant's own flat was bombed, she was able to reflect ruefully on the fate of her possessions. She had many books, but she had read them all. Her clothes had gone, but by good fortune she had gone out wearing her fur coat, so that at least was saved. Her cupboard full of clippings, photographs and souvenirs was to be regretted – 'but all that had been important was remembered'. She was able to retrieve only a sponge bag, a dressing gown, stockings, a blouse and a pair of shoes. As she packed them, she had an insight: 'Really, the essentials of living were very few.' Divested of all she held dear, all that had once contributed to her composite female identity, wartime woman was having to learn a new kind of survival.

As the bombs smashed up the fabric of everyday life, so notions of property morphed and at times dissolved altogether. The scattering of belongings could seem like a gift from the gods. A woman working as a driver in London regarded perishable and damaged goods as fair game. She was called to help out at a bomb site which had once been the premises of a beautician; among all the muck and muddle and smashed beams, the demolition men salvaged some 200 boxes of high-quality face powder, 'in good shades too'. They dug out the boxes with great eagerness, and it would have seemed churlish to refuse such largesse, just because the labels were stained.

Social distinctions seemed equally irrelevant under the falling masonry and shrapnel. Sheila Hails was coming home from a dinner party when a raid began. 'I took shelter under a porch, only to find there was already a man in this particular doorway; however we just crouched down and threw our arms around each other. At the time it just seemed ordinary . . . we sort of smiled at each other. He was a milkman I think.'

What did it feel like to be faced with extinction? A nurse who survived being buried alive recalled how she began, slowly, to suffocate. Realising her end was near, she put her trust in Christ. 'I was perfectly peaceful as I thought about death . . . [and] confident that very soon I would be in the presence of God.' When rescuers arrived, she felt they had cheated her of her heavenly salvation.

There are accounts, too, of a kind of euphoria experienced during air raids; it drew, perhaps, from that realisation noted by Hilde Marchant, that one could find happiness and meaning without the accretions of cutlery and furniture, and that just being alive was enough. Mass Observation interviewed a woman whose block was hit, with her underneath. Miraculously, this woman was almost unhurt, though the ceiling was collapsing above her. Streaked with plaster dust, she emerged into the street:

'I've been *bombed*!' I kept saying to myself . . . 'I've been *bombed*! *I've* been bombed – *me*!'

It seems a terrible thing to say, when many people must have been killed and injured last night; but never in my whole life have I experienced such *pure and flawless happiness*.

Some bomb victims managed to draw from even deeper within themselves, finding wells of self-belief that transcended the fear of death. As Barbara Cartland said, war could bring moments of wonder, even glory. She cited the example of a friend of hers who was buried under the ruins of her house for five hours, trapped by her legs. At first she felt terror, and desperation to get free. Time passed, and rescue didn't arrive.

Suddenly my brain seemed to clear, and I knew that it was all unimportant. It didn't matter – the shattered house, my imprisoned body – I was still there. I myself and alive, with a new sort of inward aliveness I can't explain. It seems ridiculous to say it, but I was happy – happier than I've ever been in my life before.

This woman seemed to be discovering autonomy for the first time. As they smashed up her home, was this sense of release, of 'inward aliveness', the truest kind of emancipation the bombs could bring?

Nights of Fire

Transcendent moments aside, there were few compensations for the danger and anxiety that were now an inevitable part of war on the home front. Everyday life for the majority of women was now becoming a question of endurance, of simply coping. As the Blitz became 'normal', the sense of shock abated, leaving them bored, passive, sickened, above all deeply tired.

Throughout autumn 1940 twenty-four-year-old Anne Popham was writing to her artist lover, Graham Bell, who was training with the RAF in Blackpool. Graham, alienated and lonely among his new colleagues, was hungry for details of their 'old' life, but that life had changed; destruction had visited.

In September Anne and her flatmate, Ruth, were bombed out of their Brunswick Square flat. They moved in with Anne's brother in Islington; meanwhile, Ruth's father was killed in a raid which destroyed the government office where he worked. Anne was an educated, aware young woman, but her letters aren't about the progress of the war, the fight against Nazism, or even her hopes for the future. They dwell instead on the minutiae of how, one at a time, she got through the difficult, dreary days, with an immediacy which helps to show what life must have been like for thousands of independent women at that time:

14th October 1940.

Darling – I must say I am having a terrible time. Bombs have been raining down ever since I got home at about quarter to eight. It is only 9 now, but it has been whizz whizz whizz all the time. Even I feel quite alarmed & unhappy for several moments at a time as I am all alone . . . I suppose there has been nothing very near, as the house has rattled only twice, but there must have been over 15 whistles, and there are several fires, the guns going whang all the time making the shutters shake.

23rd October.

My dearest darling Graham . . . I dismantled our little home with the aid of the boys . . . I managed to get everything out but the jam jars, one pot of my marrow jam without a lid, some shredded wheat, & the bookcases . . . I spent the rest of Sunday as you can imagine. Sweeping. Putting down carpets. Lifting heavy weights, arranging rooms etc etc . . . trudge off in the miserable rain with a dusty headache to the bank and to re-direct letters at the Post Office. Raiders overhead, shut . . . Rang Ruth . . . Her father's body hadn't yet been found, as more debris had fallen . . .

Ordered ½ ton of coke for the boiler 30/- down. Spent <u>hours</u> waiting in the Town Hall to register change of address &c . . . Came home & pushed furniture about again. Did a week's washing up . . . Lay down <u>utterly exhausted</u> to rest my aching back, meaning to write to you any minute. Tris [her brother] had to wake me up to get me to go to bed.

Darling I suppose you have made one of your vows not to write till you hear from me. I do hope you haven't. I depend on your being better than me & I'm sure your life is easier . . .

Very much love sweetheart.

The everyday misery of war came home to many that autumn. A year in, the gnawing fear and apprehension that had accompanied the prospect of invasion had receded, to be replaced by the sheer weary difficulty of putting up with things. In 1940 women's entire way of life was under aggressive assault. In the face of this, the average woman demonstrated the qualities of endurance and submission that had been bred into her sex over centuries. She was used to being a second-class citizen, used to being patient and passive. Seventy years ago most women felt that world events were something out of their control. War, and bombs, were foisted on them by men; they had no choice but to accept what they couldn't challenge. Conversations with women who lived through the Second World War run to a refrain of stoical acceptance:

'We all had miserable days . . . but we weren't allowed to be miserable. It was a case of 'Get on with it. You've made your bed, now lie on it.'

'We were much more accepting in those days. We didn't fight life like they do today.'

'You just got on with your life, like . . . You had to live through it, and if you survived, well, good luck to you.'

Living in Britain in 1940 meant enduring a barrage of hardships ranging from death, injury, bereavement, homelessness and poverty to lesser annoyances such as exhaustion, electricity cuts, high food prices, queues, shortages of eggs, kippers and Cutex nail varnish.

'You just grin and bear it – that's all you can do.'

But such passivity was being put to the test as never before. This last comment came from a woman who survived one of the most horrifying nights of the war, 14 November 1940, the date of the Coventry Blitz. The catastrophe visited upon this small city was the pattern for the subsequent bombings of other compact town centres – Southampton, Birmingham, Sheffield, Portsmouth, Leicester, Bristol, Clydeside – all of which had the heart knocked out of their close-knit communities. The German strategy was to set fire to the city centre with incendiaries. Thirty thousand of these were dropped on Coventry that night. Guided by the blaze, whose light could be seen from the south of England, heavy bombers then gutted what was left at a rate of at least one bomb every minute for over ten hours, pulverising the medieval centre, including Coventry's beautiful cathedral.

It is now estimated that up to a thousand people may have lost their lives that night; more than 1,200 were seriously wounded. In Coventry and Warwickshire hospital matron Joyce Burton and sister Emma Horne drew on all their reserves of courage and training to maintain morale and care not only for their existing patients but also for the numerous wounded and dying citizens brought in by ambulance during the course of that terrifying night. The sick were in danger from fire, flying glass and debris; the nurses had to move these people out of harm's way, placing them on mattresses under the beds and protecting them from flying fragments with bowls placed over their heads. They reassured and comforted them. Casualties were arriving every few minutes; often, they were firemen injured and burned by incendiaries, many with scalding shrapnel buried in their flesh. For the dying, morphia was administered. By a miracle, the nurses' home had just been completely evacuated, minutes before a high-explosive bomb reduced it to ruins. Bombs shattered the water mains, and nothing could be sterilised with boiling water; in the middle of the night the emergency generator failed, and doctors had to operate by battery lights. Smashed windows let in the chill winter air, and the dead lay among the dying. Without exception, everyone in that hospital worked through till the all-clear, and – that November night – every member of staff survived.

Joan Kelsall still lives in Coventry in a modest but cosy semi-detached house not far from the M6 motorway. In 1940 she was nineteen, living with her family near the city centre, with a good job working at the Scotch Wool and Hosiery store. Her memories of 14 November are more typical:

It was a bright moonlight night. The sirens went off. They'd been going off for quite a while. 'It can't be anything,' we thought. Then all of a sudden we heard this awful drone, so of course we just got straight out of the house into the shelter. And that bombing didn't stop till it got daylight. It was one continual drone, and bomp-bomp-bomp-bomp-bomp. But it never entered my head that I might die.

In the morning I got up, and the smell was dreadful – burning wood and everything – we were only ten minutes out of the town centre, and just up the road was the Daimler factory, which was a target. 'Well,' I said to Mother, 'I'll have to go to work,' not realising how bad it was, so I got my bike out and got as far as Bishop Street, and I couldn't get any further. There were firemen and hosepipes everywhere, and the wardens wouldn't let you through . . . It was then it dawned on me. The city was flattened – there was just nothing left. And I thought, 'Oh, I've lost me job.' So I came home. And the familiar area I'd grown up in had just all gone . . . But our house had been spared. There were people wandering around – and there was no water on, so they were all trying to get water from somewhere. They looked dazed. But they didn't moan a lot; you know, it was amazing how cheerful people were. I think they thought, you know, 'We've got to get on with it.' There was police and the WVS giving them assistance, with canteens and so on.

But I started to cry – 'I haven't got a job! I've lost me job!' I was only a teenager. And me mother was very cross. 'You've got your life,' she said. 'Don't worry about your job.'

The citizens of Coventry picked their way among the remains of their city, each with their own tragedy to deal with. Alma Merritt and her family broke out of their shelter; heat had warped the structure and they had to get free with a mallet. 'We came out to find our home had gone.' Twenty-one-year-old Alma went to her job at the Gas Department, but most of her office block was destroyed. 'I walked into the city centre. In the Cathedral the heaps of stones were still steaming. I don't remember eating at all that day.' Joyce Hoffman's family escaped from the cellar of their burning house and found safety in a public shelter. They emerged next day to find their home a shell, everything they possessed destroyed. 'All we had were the clothes we were wearing, and my mum and gran had their handbags.' The Wall family were forbidden from taking their dog Skip into the shelter by an over-zealous ARP; poor Skip was tied to a lamp-post outside, never to be seen again.

Eight miles away to the west, Clara Milburn arose after a sleepless night and listened to the radio reports of the destruction over breakfast. She had lain awake in the shelter, listening to the bombardment. The sound – 'like old sheets being ripped up' according to one woman quaking in her Stratford shelter – could be heard across the Midlands. 'I feel numb with the pain of it all,' wrote Mrs Milburn. Shocked and dispossessed people from the city were making their way to the country villages. Clara immediately offered up her spare rooms and donated rugs and deckchairs to the 'trekkers' who had straggled out to Balsall Common.

Atrocity on this scale left the habitually gentle sex struggling to express their sense of violation. Where a man might react to massacres inflicted by such raids through physical reprisals, women were often left helplessly venting their fear, grief and sense of wrong. 'I coped by getting angry,' says Joan Kelsall. 'You sort of think to yourself, "I'll get them," and that helps you through.'

Rage against all things German spilled out in some cases into an intensely 'unfeminine' hatred. Cora Styles was sixteen when a piece of red-hot shrapnel whistled three inches from her head and nearly killed her. To this day she feels Germans are the enemy. 'Perhaps this is a terrible thing to say, but I HATE the Germans. GOD, I hate the Germans. I said then, if I get my hands on a German I'll . . . I'll batter him with a saucepan!'

Marguerite Patten reserves her saucepans for the kitchen, but also still finds it hard to temper her profound sense of outrage:

People were terribly killed. I defy anybody not to feel hatred. My God, we thought, let us get up and at them . . . I agree with my husband who used to say, 'The only good German is a dead German.' Oh, yes, we DID hate them. And it wasn't hatred of the actual pilot who did it, it was hatred of the people who organised them . . . Oh, yes, definitely – we hated, hated, *hated* them.

Mrs Milburn went out into her garden and exterminated the pests, meting out a horrible revenge on the vermin that killed her vegetables:

I kill all the wireworms, calling them first Hitler, then Goering, Goebbels,

Ribbentrop and Himmler. One by one they are destroyed, having eaten the life out of some living thing, and so they pay the penalty.

A Bristol woman working in an aircraft factory told herself that every rivet she hammered into a Spitfire was another nail in Hitler's coffin; in one week she broke three hammers. In such reactions one can begin to see the breakdown and collapse of familiar models of womanhood. Tender-hearted passivity and stoicism had their limits; stress found outlets where it could.

*

Hatred, anger, aggression: by 1940 the stereotype of the soothing, neutral, deferential woman was starting to erode. The constant nearness of death awakened violent passions, emotional and physical.

The aphrodisiac effect of war on men has often been commented on, brought about by a combination of frustration, excitement and a subconscious desire, perhaps, to compensate for loss of life through the regenerative urge. But women were also touched with a heady mix of impulses: elation, tenderness, impetuosity, arousal. By the time the Blitz started Joan Wyndham had fallen decisively for gorgeous Rupert Darrow, who, with his dark hair, aquiline nose and all-over tan blended the looks of a Hebrew king and those of a Greek god ('bronzed all over . . . Oh boy, oh boy!'), though her decisiveness failed her when it came to losing her virginity. Rupert was very persuasive:

'Would you rather I raped you in the proper he-man fashion, or will you tell me when you're ready?'

'I'll let you know.'

. . . Inside me I could feel every moral code I had ever believed in since childhood begin to crumble away . . .

Eventually, following much discussion of cocks, orgasms and contraceptives, Joan made her decision sitting in an air-raid shelter with the London streets on fire around her. The flashes, booms and flaming skies had ignited her desires. 'The bombs are lovely, I think it is all thrilling,' she wrote in her diary. 'Nevertheless, as the opposite of death is life, I think I shall get seduced by Rupert tomorrow.' That night 430 people were killed, and 1,600 injured. The following day it was Sunday and Joan put on her best black-and-white checked trousers and went to church. Afterwards she went to Rupert's studio in Redcliffe Road and they had lunch. The hour was approaching. In the event, Joan's deflowering was an anti-climax, for her anyway: it combined unpleasant pain with a sense of disappointment and the absurdity of the whole thing. Afterwards, exhausted with stress and over-excitement, she slept through a heavy air raid. Two nights later Redcliffe Road was hit. Joan raced round, faint with fear. Number 34 had caught it. Partly crushed beneath blocks of collapsed wall, the very bed on which she had been seduced hung over the street, balanced precariously on the remains of Rupert's bedroom floor. Blindly she fled to search for him; could he have gone to her studio? There, propped on the landing, was a note from him, along with his guitar, his cat (in a basket) and his gas-mask. He had, it turned out, been saved by pure luck, having chosen the very moment when the bomb went off to go to the shelter and borrow sixpence for the gas meter. Days later, Joan was still delirious with relief at Rupert's narrow escape – 'It took that bomb on number 34 to make me realise how much I love him . . . this is the happiest time of my life.'

Mary Wesley's wartime novels such as *The Camomile Lawn* (1984) give form to her stated view that 'war is very erotic, people had love affairs they would not otherwise have had.' In 1940 the then Mary Swinfen, married to Charles Eady, 2nd Baron Swinfen, was doing just that with an exiled Czech politician, a British soldier and an attractive Jewish-French barrister who had escaped from the Nazi invasion of France. There were to be many others – pilots, paratroopers, officers, commandos, French, Poles, Americans, flames old and new. For women like Mary, with the audacity to disobey the rules, there seemed nothing to be lost. 'We had been brought up so repressed,' wrote Wesley. 'War freed us. We felt that if we didn't do it now, we might never get another chance.' Being a passive, docile instrument of men's desires was not Mary's style; the shriek of bombs released explosive energies in her.

With death raining down, sex was a way to challenge extinction. Phyllis Noble noticed that the Blitz had reinvigorated her parents' sex life – she could hardly fail to, walking in from work one day to find them making love in the sitting room armchair in broad daylight. In the London Underground shelters, one might catch an occasional glimpse of a couple having intercourse in the darker recesses beyond the tracks. 'I had seen a couple locked together during the most terrible bombing, absolutely oblivious of anything except each other,' remembered Frances Faviell. At moments of the most terrible bombing, expressing love physically was an act of defiance against the ruptured bones, the crushed guts – the living urgency of sex a kind of triumph over the gory imperatives of war. The available evidence suggests that fear, loss and destruction seem (to some extent) to have precipitated the sexual liberation of both men and women. Compared to the years before the war, in 1939–45 more women were having sex both before marriage and with men other than their husbands, more of them were contracting sexually transmitted diseases, more were using contraceptives, and women's knowledge of the facts of life increased. The divorce rate also increased at this time.

The extremes of *Blitzkrieg* exploded our cities, our factories and our infrastructure. Now, as violent death sabotaged family life, as everything dear and familiar to women was smashed to tatters and fragments, it was exploding the sexual contract.

4 'Ready to Win the War'

White Alert

The unwritten contract between men and women was questioned as never before in 1941. That year, British civilians continued to endure intense bombing raids, while their forces were beleaguered in the Balkans, North Africa and the Atlantic. It was during these dark days that people began to see that the war could not be won without the active involvement of women.

Most histories of the Second World War trace its narrative from conflict to conflict. The timeline of 1941 pinpoints naval losses, the escalating North African campaign, sea battles off Greece, the evacuation of Crete. This is history experienced by men. For most women it was a different story.

In the summer of 1941 Kaye Bastin's husband was thousands of miles away, and she was pregnant. Born Kathleen Emery in 1921, she, like so many girls of her generation, had grown up believing that she had no opportunities in the world. Though middle-class, her family had lost money in the Depression. One-time owners of a hotel outside Brighton, the Emerys were reduced to living in three rooms above a sweetshop. The best cards in Kaye's hand were her looks and her educated speaking voice. A personable blonde with a tidy taste in clothes, she was also intelligent and straightforward in manner. But she was forced to leave school at fourteen, and life lacked promise:

I had no ambitions. I just got on with what I had to do. I never thought I'd get married, because we hadn't any money.

Kaye got a job in the accountancy office of Plum & Roddis's department store in Brighton. On seventeen shillings a week she could afford to go dancing with a girlfriend, so long as she did her own dressmaking and never went to the hairdresser. Nothing in this limited life had given her any foretaste of the licence and self-determination that war would bring with it. That summer, from the window of her office overlooking the coast, Kaye was able to watch dogfights between German bombers and Spitfires launched from RAF Tangmere just twenty-five miles away. In August 100 Stukas dive-bombed the airbase, flattening it and killing twenty people. Brian Bastin, a ground-based engineer with the RAF, was one of those who had a narrow escape; that night he slept in the fields. A few months later Kaye and Brian met on the dance floor:

They had a 'Paul Jones' – you know, when the music stops the boys keep moving, and you get a change of partner. But Brian wasn't dancing, he was hiding behind a pillar – and he came forward and took me. And that's how I met my husband-to-be.

Afterwards, he asked if he could walk me home, and he saved my life. He had heard some German aircraft unloading their spare bombs. He grabbed me, and pushed me against the wall.

Kaye found Brian irresistible. Not only was he her saviour, but he also turned out to be musical and well educated. And as if that weren't enough, Brian Bastin had the dash and glamorous good looks of a young Clark Gable, pencil moustache and all. The pair got married in April 1941. Kaye was twenty.

The wedding was a very simple affair. I had a piece of nice blue material and a friend made up my dress for me, with a hat to match. And it was lovely, getting married.

Afterwards we were going to live in Rustington, near where Brian was stationed. Well, on our wedding night there was bombing. And we hadn't gone to the shelter – one didn't, always – and the ceiling fell in on our bed, the first night.

But then we were together, and we enjoyed being with each other so much, and that was the main thing.

The idyll was all too brief. Four months after Kaye's wedding, the RAF posted her perfect young husband to South Africa for pilot training; he was away for the birth of his daughter and was not to return for another three years.

*

War for the majority at home, like Kaye, meant waiting, enduring and more waiting. It meant managing, coping and doing without. At the lower end of the social scale, there might be considerable hardship, since ordinary soldiers were expected to support their wives out of their pay. Until 1944, the wife of a private with two children could receive as little as twenty-five shillings a week.* In 1941 shortages of food and consumer goods started to penetrate daily life. War was often dangerous and frightening – women were more likely to be the victims of domestic air raids than their menfolk, stationed abroad – but it was also depressing, gruelling and tedious.

Feeling useful was not enough; even vital functions like ARP work (one in six ARP wardens was female) were boring and wearisome, until an alert sounded. Keen to do her bit for the war effort, and lying that she was really eighteen, Pip Beck joined the ARP Report and Control Centre in Buckingham, where she soon became familiar with the various levels of alert: white for no enemy activity, yellow for 'a precautionary state', purple for 'prospect of enemy aircraft', and red for 'imminent attack: sirens to be sounded'. She was also trained to operate telephones and take important messages. 'We never had to put our skills to the test though.' The rota required her to show up once a week at the centre, but once there, there was little to do apart from gossip round the fire with the other wardens. Pip – mainly, at this time, preoccupied with her love life – did her embroidery, while Miss Southerden, her partner, knitted. They sipped Horlicks and ate biscuits. In two hours the phone rang three times – all 'purples'. The high point of Pip's ARP career was when a 'red' came through and Pip was allowed to sound the siren. 'No bombs fell though.'

Essentially – though this would soon change – most women were still passive: they were the bystanders, not the players; the victims, not the perpetrators.

In *The People's War* (1969), his comprehensive social history of the home front, Angus Calder describes the public mood at the beginning of 1941. Government directives to stay at home, wear white in the blackout, carry gas-masks, save for victory and so on were increasingly being shunned. The British were growing grumpy and dispirited. A year after the German invasion of northern Europe,

* The figure was then raised to sixty shillings – which was still under 50 per cent of the pay of a man working in a factory at that time.

fewer people in Britain were interested in the bigger picture of the war beyond our shores. Women in particular had little mental space to do other than carry on, as arduous day followed arduous day. A survey taken by Mass Observation at that time also showed that the people whose lives were most directly affected by bombs were those who were least interested in the macro events of the war.

Mass Observation offered the case-history of a sailor's wife in Plymouth who in March 1941 had been blitzed out of her home in a working-class area. This woman's husband was at sea. One of her three small children had been killed, another slightly injured, and she had no money. Before the family could even eat she had to find a feeding centre. Her next problem was shelter. The principal rest centre had been destroyed by bombs, so she made her way to another and left her children there, but more bureaucratic hurdles would have to be surmounted before she could find long-term accommodation. Then she had to get new ration books for her family and somehow find clothes for them. Next she had problems dealing with the dead child; the body had to be found, the death reported. And what about her belongings, now buried beneath rubble? She applied to the Assistance Board for compensation, to the Mayor's Relief Fund for a cash advance and to the local office for new identity cards. The children would need new gas-masks ... Small wonder if this grief-stricken young wife, with all the troubles of the world laden upon her narrow shoulders, took little interest in the Battle of Keren in Eritrea, despite its decisive impact on Mussolini's East African forces, or paused to consider the effect the Belgrade–Berlin negotiations might have on Hitler's advance in the Balkans.

Even if you weren't blitzed and bereaved, mundane things loomed large: 'Sometimes it is the small irritations of a war which irk the most,' remembered Helen Forrester. Barbara Cartland put in a plea for her kind: 'Women who once had six servants now cleaned and cooked and looked after their own children ... Try to run a home without saucepans, frying-pans, dishcloths, floorcloths, toilet paper, brushes, vim, fuel of any sort, and, of course, soap! We never had enough.'

Morale was low. As often as not in those dreary days, housewife Nella Last reached for the 'off' button – 'the wireless was dreadful.' Nella's diaries from the early months of that year give a picture of how cheerless and crushing life could be, as absences, shortages, unhappiness and fear worked their harm on her community. She wrote of her distress prompted by the sight of a young woman who came into her WVS Centre; this girl's soldier husband was going abroad for two years. 'Today her beauty was clouded and dimmed . . . My heart ached so for her, and for all the other unhappy girls like her.' A few days later she tells of an encounter with Ruth, another young friend; this time the topic was what to do if the Germans won. Women would be at obvious risk from the victors, but Ruth was calm. She always carried a razor-blade, and would not hesitate to open her veins 'if the worst came to the worst'. 'A shadow seemed to fall on my heart as fresh problems rose in my mind, and a pity for mothers of girls crowded out the feeling I always have for mothers of boys.' Musing, Nella got on with her tasks. But on 14 February Nella was worrying again, this time about famine: the men were too busy killing each other to farm, or fish – 'such senseless, useless waste . . . so wrong and twisted'.

*

In London that spring, there was at last a lull in the bombing. Frances Faviell (now Parker) went to the hairdresser to have her short unruly hair permed. There had been no call for perms during the worst of the bombing, for who would want to be caught with their hair stuck in a waving machine when the sirens went off? There were celebrations, too, when Anne, the daughter of Frances's upstairs neighbour Kathleen Marshman, married Cecil, a good-looking Canadian soldier. Then, just before Easter, Frances found that she was pregnant: no more FAP duties for her. 'Yes, we all felt cheerful!'

On 16 April Anne and Cecil returned from their honeymoon in the Midlands, radiant and in love. At nine o'clock that night – 'to our astonishment' – the sirens went.

That night 685 German bombers attacked London; as the furious noise doubled and redoubled the Parkers took shelter in the ground-floor dining room, which had one wall of reinforced concrete. Frances telephoned Kathleen upstairs, but she declined their offer of a safe corner; as for Anne and Cecil, the only place they wanted to be was their own bed upstairs. Bombs were raining down; flares and shells lit the sky. That night, one of the worst of the entire Blitz, over 1,000 people were killed. And at 11 p.m. a parachute mine reduced 33 Cheyne Place to an enormous pile of rubble and debris.

Underneath it, protected by their ferro-concrete wall, Richard, Frances, their unborn child and Vicki the dachshund survived. They were unhurt and they were homeless. But Kathleen and the newly-weds Anne and Cecil died sickeningly pointless deaths.

*

Barrow-in-Furness had so far been spared. Nella Last's reflections at this point in the war are worth quoting fully:

I'm tired to my soul-case tonight . . .

So much dying: family unity, peace to live one's own life, the ordinary decencies of everyday life, hopes and ambitions, aims and endeavours. It gives me a fear of the future sometimes, a fear of the aftermath of things, and a wonder about how all the boys and men that are left will begin again. Women are different – as long as there are babies to tend and care for and hungry, tired men to feed and tend, a woman will *be* a woman, and make a wee corner into a home. It's the men I think of.

Nella Last's view that tending, caring and feeding were women's natural role was one shared by the authorities. But there were still plenty of women who lacked hungry babies or weary husbands. Their capacities extended beyond the homely embellishment of wee corners. Over the course of the war women's responsibilities ranged from driving three-ton trucks to operating anti-aircraft batteries, from spying to code-breaking, from engineering to ship-building. And yet the conviction that 'a woman will *be* a woman' – that women were essentially handmaidens, auxiliaries, a back-up force – ran very deep.

Nella's own town was heavily bombed in May 1941. She and her husband cowered in the indoor shelter as plaster showered around them, thinking their last hour had come. After the all-clear she emerged to view the damage: 'My loved little house . . . will never be the same again.'

Red Alert

War has its own imperatives. It was beginning to dawn on the government that enormous numbers of servicemen who ought to be out there fighting for King and country were tied to desk jobs and petty duties. This posed a knotty problem.

The requirements of the army seemed bottomless. That year, the army was calling for another 1.75 million men. Meeting this demand meant raiding the factories for army recruits and yet, to equip this number of soldiers, the munitions industries would have to expand by an extra 1.5 million workers. The sums just didn't add up. Where were these recruits and workers to come from? The Minister of Labour, Ernest Bevin, was a keen advocate of the voluntary principle. But now, reluctantly, the government was forced to accept the only logical solution: women would have to make up the shortfall, and compulsion was the only answer.

This decision would quickly affect the lives of every available woman in the country between the ages of eighteen and fifty. Early in 1941 Bevin proposed to start the registration of women aged twenty and twenty-one, who, provided they were not pregnant and had no children under fourteen living at home, would be regarded as 'mobile' and eligible for direction into 'essential' work. By the end of the year women up to the age of thirty would be required to register.

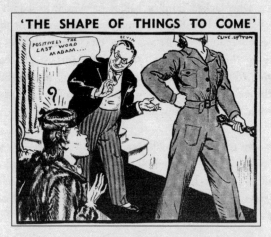

What, swap fur coats for overalls? Bevin's task is to persuade women to accept conscription.

Bevin's hand was forced to make this Essential Work Order, but his heart was not in the legislation, and he continued to appeal for volunteers. Uncertainty sharpened the inevitable controversy over women's conscription. 'We all feel very strongly,' wrote a soldier to the *Daily Sketch*, 'against the conscription of our wives and sweethearts, who are the very people we are fighting to protect from Nazism and all it stands for.' The Labour Party conference came down against the measures, with one MP claiming that servicemen felt 'tremendous resentment about the women left behind in the home being turned out to do tasks for which they were not fitted'. In any case, how could women be turned into industrial workers overnight? Serious social problems would surely result, wreaking havoc on our national life.

The controversy struck at the very heart of the relationship between the sexes. The effect of women's conscription on men in the services abroad was only part of it. The army had a sleazy reputation; parents, fearful that their daughters would be seen as 'camp followers', needed reassurances that their virtue would be carefully safeguarded. Images of housewife snipers and grannies with machine-guns haunted the public consciousness. Surely a woman couldn't be expected to kill Germans, like a man? To counter this, a clause was carefully drafted into the Act: 'No woman should be liable to make use of a lethal weapon unless she signifies in writing her willingness to undertake such service.' Feminists, meanwhile, welcomed the measures – women's energies had been wasted long enough; it was time to put them to work. But other worries surfaced. Would there be a conscience clause for pacifists? (There would.) Some concerns were the precursors of perennially familiar themes, such as: how would working wives cope with housework, shopping, children, elderly relatives? And after their taste of life in the services, would conscripted women willingly return to their primary job – in the home?

The outcome was perhaps predictable. Men were deeply conflicted about the necessity for women's conscription. There was essentially a lack of connection between the compelling need to oblige women to do war work and the deeply held view that women must stay at home to tend, feed and care. The only way to reconcile this contradiction was to offer reassurances. Women would not kill; they would not bear arms; they would not shoot down Germans in Spitfires, nor bomb German cities. Their job would be to make the bullets that were loaded into the guns for the men to fire, to fill the bombs with explosive, not to fire them or drop them.

Women were seen as subsidiary; they would 'free a man for the forces' by taking over the desk jobs and petty duties that prevented our brave boys from doing the work *they* were naturally suited for. Women were to be allowed to choose between industry and the auxiliary services. War bureaucracy offered them the same 'clean', 'feminine' and 'respectable' jobs that the pre-war business girls had enjoyed. And above all they would continue to tend, care and feed – as nurses, land girls, cooks, storewomen, orderlies and cleaners. Seamlessly, the authorities upheld the sexual status quo, while encouraging the notion that every woman could do her bit for King and country. Even when the need for women to work on anti-aircraft batteries became urgent (by 1942 there would be more women deployed on air defence than men) they retained their official 'non-combatant' status. The AA women were, however, permitted to die or be wounded alongside their male comrades, and frequently did. But they were not granted the same service medals as the men, and were paid a third less. The vocabulary of feminism was still largely conspicuous by its absence from all discussions of female participation.

On 18 December 1941 the National Service (No. 2) Act was passed, making conscription for women legal. Voluntarism was abandoned. It was now a matter of time before each and every 'mobile' woman in the country was called upon for war duties. When it came to the point, the government had little difficulty persuading the British people that women's conscription was a necessity. 'In the end . . . the operation went wonderfully smoothly,' remembered Mary Grieve, editor of *Woman* magazine. Everyone was happy – women too. Surveyed, 97 per cent of them agreed 'emphatically' that women should do war work.

By the end of that year, even before conscription started to take effect properly, there were just over 200,000 members of the three women's services, more than five times the number for 1939 (36,100). The figures would peak in 1943 at a total of nearly half a million. The total numbers of working women would also peak that year, at seven and a half million. Since the beginning of the war, an additional million and a half women had joined the 'essential' industries.

The effect of conscription on female morale was to raise their sense of self-worth immeasurably. Men were removed from all the jobs that women could do as well, and the only limit on a woman's contribution was her physical strength. The sacred myth of the housewifely angel as a full-time unpaid drudge was conclusively exposed by Bevin's new law. Soon after it was passed Edith Summerskill, the feminist and Labour MP, wrote in *The Fortnightly* magazine:

The periodic upheaval occasioned by war reveals that women have individualities of their own and are not merely adjuncts of men. They have aspirations and ambitions which become apparent in war time, because only then can they enjoy a real freedom to achieve at least some part of their heart's desire . . .

The freedom which women are enjoying today will spell the doom of home life as enjoyed by the male who is lord and master immediately he enters his own front door.

Many women now found that their wartime activities offered an emancipation unimagined by their mothers and, by halfway through the war, the occasional mutterings about female independence to be heard among the ranks in the late 1930s were becoming a chorus. 'Most of us felt that [conscription] was only right and were glad to be regarded as equally liable as men for the defence of our country,' was Frances Faviell's view. Mass Observation continued to harvest the views of women at this time. One of their interviewees was recorded rejoicing in her new-found liberty as a working woman: 'For a housewife who's been a cabbage for fifteen years, you feel you've got out of the cage and you're free . . . It's all so different, such a change from dusting. I think the war has made a lot of difference to housewives. I don't think they'll want to go back to the old narrow life.' Meanwhile Monica Littleboy's experiences in the Land Army, the WAAFs and the FANYs were transforming her from a shy teenager into a confident woman: 'I was never without somewhere to go or someone to escort me. I had come out of myself and lost much of my shyness. I could go anywhere, any place and find enjoyment.' The same loss of inhibition was echoed by a Mrs M. in the Midlands: 'The war changed everything. Until then I had led rather a sheltered life, but now I had to meet and mix with more people . . . The public houses were always so busy . . . it was so unusual to see women drinking. It just hadn't been done before.' These were new voices, speaking with a new confidence.

Young women like Phyllis Noble began to feel that a future beyond the home was a reality. In the autumn of 1941, thirsty for self-improvement and intellectual stimulus, she and her friend Emily Pluck ('Pluckie') started attending psychology evening classes at Morley College in Lambeth. Friends at Morley encouraged Phyllis's latent interest in feminism, and she and Pluckie joined a rally in Trafalgar Square, where Edith Summerskill and Nancy Astor spoke out in favour of equal compensation for women who had received war injuries. And their proto-feminist tendencies were stoked by attending Conway Hall meetings to hear speakers like Bevin's Labour Party colleague Mary Sutherland on the topic 'Women and the War'. In her diary, Phyllis recorded that she had found this talk enlightening, but questioned Sutherland's assertion that 'most marriages are happy'. 'I feel bound to disagree,' wrote this precocious nineteen-year-old. 'I think probably most couples jog along as best they can in their self-made rut.'

At Morley too they were taught by Amber Blanco White, who persuaded them to read feminist writers such as Vera Brittain and Winifred Holtby – they were 'models in whose footsteps we might follow'. With her gangly height and gappy teeth, Amber Blanco White was a woman of charm and vivacity, and she opened her students' eyes to the possibilities of sexual freedom for women. Before the First World War she had had a notorious affair with H. G. Wells and she revelled in introducing her psychology class to the delights of free love, advising them never to tell their husbands if they had a lover, and advocating sex before marriage as being good for mental health. She even acted out, in front of the entire class, how couples could get more fun out of their sex life by adopting unorthodox positions for intercourse. Phyllis and Pluckie came away from such sessions inspired with breakaway dreams. In the questioning intellectual climate of wartime London, freedom, modernity and equality of the sexes were surely now within their reach. A whole world of fascinating work and endeavour seemed attainable: 'uncertainty about the future made us more determined to squeeze what we could out of our wartime lives.'

At this point, peace still seemed very far away.

A Man's Job

Once Bevin introduced registration, individual women needed little encouragement to join the services. Conscription acted as a spur and a challenge. If you weren't part of it, you were losing out. A steady procession of young women set out to see for themselves how they could make a difference, to their country, to their own lives and, in some cases, to the course of history.

One of these young women was probationary teacher Dorothy ('Doffy') Brewer. Today, at over ninety, Doffy still possesses something of the shyness and gentility that she felt to be so cramping as a young girl growing up in suburban east London in the 1930s. Back in 1941 she was twenty-two, plagued with the feeling that she was missing all the fun. 'What was I doing? Nothing . . . If there was something that could be done, I wanted to be part of it.' Large numbers of Doffy's pupils had been evacuated, making her feel all the more pointless. She was well aware that teaching was a reserved occupation for all women over the age of twenty-five, but Bevin's new rules meant that from September this would be reduced to twenty. Her year's probation was due to be completed in August. Between resigning from her job and joining the army, she had barely a month. Doffy felt a bubble bursting in her brain. As she sat on the bus on her way to school one wet morning in June things came to a head. Outside, rain was coming down in sheets; she could barely see out of the bus windows. As ever, the local bore, Mr Harris, made straight for the empty seat beside her:

I thought: I'll join the Army if Mr Harris says . . .

'Flaming June, eh?' he remarked, as he thumped himself down.

That was it. Mr Harris had made my decision.

A BBC appeal calling for kine-theodolite operators attached to the Royal Artillery persuaded Doffy that she was a suitable candidate for the ATS: she had mathematical qualifications, good eyesight, good general health, love of open-air life, and she was five foot two in her heels. She posted her resignation letter to the Education Office, and on the way home went into the recruiting office and took the oath. There they told her, 'You'll be doing a man's job.' Her pay, however, would be two-thirds that of her male counterpart.

Kine-theodolites are subtle and complicated instruments that can not only photograph a target – an aeroplane, say – but also locate it in time. They can also calculate with accuracy the position of the shell-bursts fired by a gunner. But this important information could not be used in action, as the results took hours to produce. Instead its value was in training gun teams. The urgent need for operators meant that Doffy and her fellow ATS (none of whom had ever studied physics before, since few girls' schools included it on the curriculum) would be given just three weeks' training.

However, before she could learn to be a kine-theodolite operator she, along with thousands of other young women now recruiting, had to learn to survive in the army. In September 1941 Doffy Brewer was among 200 young women who arrived for training at Talavera Camp on Northampton racecourse. Two weeks later another 200 arrived. It was the same across the country, and the basic training routine was the same for all of them. 'If you survive it,' wrote Doffy, 'nothing in the way of discomfort, humiliation, culture-shock or fatigue that life can bring afterwards can be as bad.' For three weeks she and all the other 'rookies' were alternately bullied and shamed, crushed and abused.

The boot camp approach was quite deliberate, and completely impersonal. It started on day one, with latrine parade. Twenty-four girls with no notion of what to expect were quick-marched in groups of six to use the latrines, and given precisely one minute each, no more. This was followed by the issue of kit and bedding: khaki uniform ('not becoming'), stockings, winter woollens, nightwear, coat, overalls and underwear. Blankets and sheets. Ear plugs. Shoes, cleaning gear, tin mug and cutlery, toothbrush, hairbrush and mending kit – which immediately came in useful. The corporal handed out the next item with an order: 'Here's your brassière. Make it fit before morning parade tomorrow.' And finally, sanitary towels:

'These are issued every month. One packet, size two. If you want size one or three, you'll ask your corporal.'

We all nearly died of shame . . . Nobody talked about such things, openly.

However, Doffy and her comrades had a man to thank for this thoughtful provision. Sanitary towels were Lord Nuffield's contribution to the grateful Women's Services and would become known to many as 'Nuffield's nifties'.

Next, Doffy was given her ID disc. It was to be signed for, and never removed. That was followed with instructions on how to lace up shoes in the correct fashion.

We fell out, groaned our way into the hut, and folded our individuality into our suitcases, for the duration.

Next day was drill: more commands, square-bashing, parades. But it was in the canteen that Doffy's middle-class gentility came under worst assault. She learned to dread the foul-mouthed mockery aimed at her by the other girls, most of them Midlands lasses who had left their jobs as skivvies and housemaids to join the army. Their language was larded with obscenities; it seemed to Doffy that they took malign pleasure in finding disgusting interpretations for her every remark. 'It was sheer hell.'

Inspections, medicals and more inspections. Marching and manoeuvres. And scrubbing. The scrubbing was carried out, in long lines, on hands and knees, wearing indestructibly thick denim overalls. It took hours. The sergeant-major who came to inspect the work walked his muddy boots across the wet concrete floor that they had just scrubbed and told them to do it again. 'Some of the girls cried.' Everyone had blisters on hands and feet, everyone was suffering from the cold 6.30 a.m. starts, after uncomfortable nights on rough cotton sheets. The food was fit for pigs. 'Serve your country? Hold on to the thought, if you possibly can.'

By the second week the blisters were starting to heal, and Doffy had learned always to carry her own bath plug. She had also made friends with the only other girl not from the Midlands, and a simple intelligence test had given her the chance to shine. Then came the pep talk from the Regimental Sergeant-Major, the 'truly Great Man' of the camp. It was this that finally broke Doffy's spirit. Expecting yet another round of browbeating and bullying, she stood firm, only to find all her resolve undermined by the RSM's strategy of carefully calculated emotional sabotage. Instead of haranguing them, the Great Man made the new recruits feel *understood*. He knew, it seemed, just how they felt: 'I've been in the Army for twenty years . . . and I'll tell you this: I'm still homesick, and *I* want *my* mum!' Then he went in for the kill:

'There's nothing I'd like better than to be at home with her right now. But we're in the Army to fight Hitler. Remember Hitler? He's waiting for us. We're going to finish him together, you and me. We haven't got time for a few months to cry for mum.'

. . . I felt the warmth spread through me. I was lost. I belonged to something greater than myself. Love and loyalty . . . Alternate bullying and praise; pushing to the limit of endurance with threats and insults, then a kind word. I knew what they were doing. But it still worked. Only a broken spirit can love.

★

As male fitters and engineers left the factories and depots for training camps and battlefields, their places were filled by women like Doris Scorer.

Doris, a sunny-tempered, fashion-conscious teenager, was seventeen when war broke out; she and her widowed mother, a charlady, were living in Islington. She spent her days in the Canda Manufacturing Company – better known as C. & A.'s – off City Road, machining dresses. Work continued through the Blitz, the wail of sirens and the clatter of guns which interrupted production sending the girls scurrying for the basement. When the all-clear sounded it was back to loading bobbins on to the buttonhole machine, or working the pedals on the press stud machine. Nights, Doris and her mother spent in the public shelter, huddled in blankets, doing their best to sleep on the damp concrete floor. But the shelter saved their lives.

In common with thousands of other Londoners, they crawled out from the protecting earth one morning, as usual aching and longing for a cup of tea, and discovered the damage. The way into their street was barred by ropes. Mrs Scorer's tiny two-room flat was part of a house which now stood exposed to the elements, with daylight pouring through a huge crack running from top to bottom. Wardens had taken over the site:

'Sorry Missus, yer can't go in there.'

'But me 'ome's up there,' said Mother, looking distraught and pointing to the cracked and shattered upstairs windows.

Doris pleaded. She had to collect her work overall – for woe betide any employee who turned up at C. & A.'s without it – and they were allowed to dash in and get their things. Inside, everything was spattered with oily dirt. There was no time to wash or put on lipstick; they rescued the terrified cat and grabbed their birth certificates and a shoebox with their family photographs. 'We didn't take the family silver 'cos there wasn't any.' Then, leaving Mother to deal with compensation forms at the Town Hall, Doris hurried off to work.

Homeless now, they were effectively refugees. After one night lying on the floor of a reception centre off the New North Road with a huddle of tearful, bombed-out families, Mother decided to throw herself on the mercy of her sister Elsie at New Bradwell, near Wolverton, in Buckinghamshire. A telegram came by return: 'Come to us at once'. By the time they got off the train at Wolverton the next day they were exhausted.

We headed slowly for Auntie's house, our possessions in a battered old suitcase, our underwear and other garments tied up in a tablecloth with the ends knotted, gasmasks slung around our shoulders, while Mother had the cat under one arm.

Two bag ladies: forty years after they were bombed out, Doris White (née Scorer) did her own illustration of herself, her mum and the cat heading for Auntie's house.

Doris and her mother now became resident with Auntie Elsie, and life settled to 'a semblance of order'. Doris, who loved to sew, soon got work at a dress factory in Wolverton, and to her delight the same firm took Mother on as tea lady. Bert Alston was a good employer. Those were contented days; over 'Music While You Work' the machinists had lots to gossip about, whether it was boyfriends in the forces or the latest couple seen smooching in the cinema. But in 1941 all that came to an end.

A letter came for me, 'Please report to the works office'. It was for an interview for essential war work. I had the choice . . . join the Land Army (wot and leave me mum), clean out train boilers (a filthy job), be a porter on Bletchley railway station (mmmm), munitions worker (and blow meself up) or be an aircraft worker. Now that had appeal, that would surely suit my seven stone frame. Reluctantly I gave my notice in to Bert.

And so in 1941 Doris found herself, along with a host of women of all ages, kitted out in a denim boiler suit, hair neatly turbaned, 'ready to win the war'. As Fitter III, Grade 3, her job was as 'mate' to a man who was a Fitter Grade 1. The Wolverton Works was geared up to repair and maintain damaged aircraft. Doris was trained on the job by her mate, handing him five-eighth drills, fetching castle nuts and split pins, collecting blueprints. She soon graduated to the greater skill of drilling out 'skins' of aluminium used to patch the wings of shelled Typhoons, filing down the irregularities and holding rivets in place while her mate gunned them into the metal, sending a searing sensation into her fingers. Sometimes, if the rivets needing to be held in place were particularly large, her mate would do this job, while allowing her to do the gunning. The work required great skill and delicacy of touch. Doris's conscientious approach won her the confidence of her mate, and sometimes he would even send her to cut aluminium – 'not many were allowed to do this dangerous job.' When completed, each repaired aircraft went before an inspector, who examined it in detail while Fitter III and her mate stood by, anxious that their work had made the grade. The inspectors were gentlemen, and Doris held them in respect.

But, despite the large numbers of women now employed at the Wolverton Works (40 per cent of aircraft employees were women), it remained an uncompromisingly male environment – a place where

'bugger' and ''ell' punctuated every sentence, where burping and far-
ting were tolerated, where grown men behaved like ten-year-olds.
There was the anti-social man who ate raw onions for lunch, the
joker who jammed the drawer containing the girls' belongings by
driving a nail through the runner and the idiot who booby-trapped
the shelf where Doris kept her handbag: when she reached up for it
she was showered with nuts and bolts. The girls got their share of
taunts, caterwauls and wolf-whistles.

Nevertheless, Doris became fascinated by her work. It was absorbing, responsible and dangerous at times. She took pride in the finished
product and, above all, she knew it was important.

Cheap Wine, Pink Gin

In her time off Doris enjoyed the weekly dances at the Science and
Arts Institute in Wolverton. At these, she often noticed a group of
girls accompanied by officers gathered round a table in the corner:
'[They] looked immaculate and very stand-offish. *Their* nails were
like an advert for Cutex . . . they did not mix much.' Who were they?
The centre of code-breaking operations at Bletchley Park just six
miles away was shrouded in secrecy. Doris and her factory friends
speculated about what '*they*' did 'over there at the Park', but never
found out. 'It was very hush-hush. They kept to the Secrets Act as
they were supposed to, for as the posters said – "Careless talk costs
lives" and "Walls have ears".' Locally, the Bletchley girls were recognised as being a race apart, distinctive for their air of elegance and
education. Doris was in awe of their desk skills and evident intelligence. 'We could see that they came from good backgrounds, while
we were what was termed "born on the wrong doorstep" . . . They
were billeted in the better houses in Wolverton, some of these lucky
enough to have a bathroom, which was a rare feature in these times.'

Twenty-one-year-old Mavis Lever was one of them; she had
arrived at Bletchley Park in 1940. Mavis had discovered a passion for
Germany's language and literature while still at school in the 1930s
and was deep into her studies on German Romanticism at University
College London when war broke out. The college then evacuated to
Aberystwyth. At this point, despite her passion for Aryan culture,

Mavis decided that she didn't want to read German poetry in Wales with a war on. Her first thought was to take up nursing but, encouraged by her professors, she went for an interview at the Foreign Office.

First of all I thought I was going to be a spy; then I thought it was going to be a job in censorship. In fact we weren't allowed to be told what it was. We were just told it was very important. Initially I was at the Ministry of Economic Warfare opposite St James's Underground Station, checking commercial codes, finding out who was supplying certain important minerals to the Germans. Then in summer 1940 I moved to Bletchley.

Mavis herself would have agreed with Doris that girls like her were privileged:

We were paid £2 10s a week, a guinea of which had to go on one's billet. I lodged in a grocer's shop, which meant I had bacon for breakfast! Later I was moved to a manor house, where I was waited on by a manservant who produced spam on a silver salver – but then the manservant was called up . . .

Well I absolutely adored the job. I was under the code-breaker Dilly Knox – we were quite famous in Whitehall as 'Dilly's girls'. In fact everyone was in at the deep end. There was no book you could read about the history of code-breaking, and there was no professor to consult.

Today, Dillwyn Knox's contribution to the cracking of the Enigma code is recognised as having been crucial. Knox, an eminent papyrologist, had had a classical training and had studied literary papyri. He had the ability, and intuition, needed to recognise the metrical and rhythmic patterns of ancient poetry, and he brought these qualities to his cryptographic work. As Mavis explains, it was this approach that gave Knox the edge over a more mathematical system for code-breaking – and it was one that, with her literary background, she shared:

There are so many ways of setting an Enigma machine – millions and millions of them – that quite often the mathematically minded were reduced to questions of probability, as in 'What are the *chances* of getting this out?' But we just floundered in head-first and hoped for the best. One woman in my section dreamt the combination, and she turned out to be right! We worked by intuition, and strokes of imagination. But also, importantly, by psychology. For example, the Enigma machine has little windows, and you have to set the wheels to four different letters, and of course the operators were told to set them at random, but they never did. Instead they used dirty German four-letter words, or their girlfriends' names. Well, we quite often knew our operators. So instead of having to work out the probability of what the setting of the wheels would be, we knew they had a girlfriend called Rosa, and it would work out. And so we built up all kinds of little tricks. Maths doesn't really get you anywhere. It's really much more like a game of Scrabble. You've got to have inspired guesses. And really that is a female quality.

To give you an example: Keith Batey, my husband, had trained to be a mathematician; we met at Bletchley. And I remember one occasion when I was tackling something. Keith looked over my shoulder and he said, 'The chances of you getting that out are four million to one against you.' Well at coffee time I walked over to him, and with the greatest of pleasure I told him: 'That came out in five minutes.'

Mavis knew that her job was one of extreme importance but, ironically, it was rare that she was able to appreciate what a difference her work made.

You're only given a part of the message to decrypt, and then it's got to be translated and analysed, before they decide where it has to be sent on to: the Defence Ministry or the Admiralty or the Secret Service or what-have-you. There was the strict principle of 'need to know': you only knew what you genuinely *needed* to know, because if you're captured they'll learn the lot.

So we never knew what was going on in the bigger picture.

But there was one occasion when Dilly's girls got a real sense of how their work could change the course of history.

Early in 1941 conflict in the Balkans was hotting up; British convoys bearing forces were coming in from Alexandria to bolster Greek defences against the Axis, but first they would have to encounter the Italian navy. The sea engagements which followed, in March 1941, were crucially affected by the work of the women and men based in Buckinghamshire.

Soon after Mavis's arrival at Bletchley, Knox and the girls successfully broke the Italian naval Enigma. In principle this code was easier to crack than the German one, since the machine in use was more elementary. But because its message traffic was also far less busy, decoding it proved correspondingly challenging. There just wasn't much to go on. However, on 25 March Mavis and the team were able to decipher messages warning of an impending Italian naval operation in the eastern Mediterranean:

The one time when we really saw the bigger picture was when we got an Italian message that said 'Today Is The Day Minus 3'. So – what were the Italians going to do? You see, this was an occasion when you had to break the whole message in order to decipher it. And then it came out: it was the Battle of Matapan.

The next day two further messages came through. The urgency of their content prompted a 'jumbo rush', and Dilly, Mavis and her colleague Margaret Rock worked flat out decrypting them. The information pointed incontestably towards an imminent Italian naval thrust in the Aegean. With hindsight, it appears that Italian naval command underestimated British forces in the Mediterranean, believing them to have only one operational battleship. In reality they had three. Moreover, Commander-in-Chief of the Mediterranean fleet Andrew Cunningham was an expert in night-fighting. Based on the information he now received from Bletchley via the Admiralty, Admiral Cunningham deployed cruisers and air forces to the south of Crete. They torpedoed the Italian cruiser *Pola*. Back at Bletchley on the 27th, more decrypted messages showed that the Italians still thought the British fleet was in Alexandria. In this belief, they sent a squadron of cruisers and destroyers to rescue the *Pola* and were taken completely unawares when, acting on the intercepted intelligence, Cunningham's battle fleet ambushed them after dark off Cape Matapan on the Peloponnese. The British sank three cruisers and two destroyers. Three air crew were lost. Of the Italians, 2,400 sailors were killed, missing or captured.

Oh we celebrated that all right. Cunningham had gone to the exact spot where they were going to attack the convoys. And yes, we had a drink – amongst ourselves – and I remember we got hold of a very cheap bottle of wine, and wrote Matapan on the label, and then discovered of course that the cleaner would see it, so we had to take it off. One had to be terribly careful about the cleaners! What would they think when they read about

1. Two young women from the Worthing 'Blackout Corps' paint their local hospital windows.

2. Spirit of the Blitz: a West End hairdressing salon picks up where it left off – in an air-raid shelter.

3. Cross-section of a life: the bombs exposed and revealed women's interior-based existence as never before.

4. A cosy, if cramped, scene at Holborn station. No matter where, the 1940s mum always had something to knit. By the end of September 1940 over 170,000 Londoners were taking shelter in the city's Underground stations.

5. As the threat to Britain intensified, every mother had to choose between her children's safety and her maternal instincts.

7. Teenager Phyllis Noble, photographed at the time of Dunkirk, 1940.

6. and 8. Volunteers like Joan Wyndham (*above*, in uniform after she joined the WAAF in 1941) helped trained nurses to staff the first aid posts established across the city.

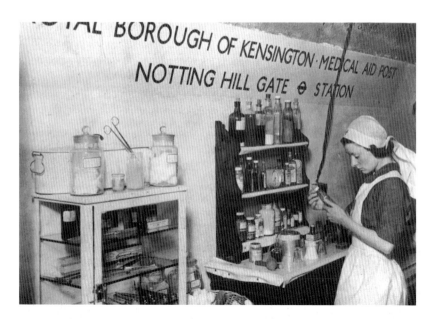

9. For women, joining up often meant carrying out domestic tasks in a military context. This Wren steward has a typically unglamorous job.

10. A London Labour Exchange, 1941. After women's conscription was introduced, recruitment figures increased more than tenfold.

11. The Navy, Army and Air Force Institutes, or NAAFI, which ran canteens and shops for the forces, was 'a forgotten army', largely staffed by women.

13. Barbara Cartland with her ATS hat on, plus lipstick.

12. Dorothy ('Doffy') Brewer went for training with the ATS in autumn 1941. 'If you survive it,' she wrote, 'nothing . . . that life can bring afterwards can be as bad.'

14. Unsuspecting ATS recruits arriving at Aldershot in 1941.

15. and 16. Two mothers, two wartime diarists: (*left*) Clara Milburn and her son Alan; (*right*) Nella Last and her son Cliff.

17. Women's Institute members bottling jams and jellies. The making of preserves exemplified the frugal ethos of the older generation.

18. In the Y-service WAAF Aileen ('Mike') Morris became expert at eavesdropping on enemy transmissions. Her intercepts were despatched to Bletchley Park for decoding.

19. 'Nobody ever blabbed'; like everybody else at Bletchley, code-breaker Mavis Lever was sworn to secrecy about her work.

20. The Decoding Room at Bletchley Park, nerve centre of wartime decryption.

Matapan in the paper, and then saw a bottle in the office waste paper basket with Matapan on the label? One had to think fast about that kind of thing.

Soon after we saw Cunningham on Pathé news, and we only wished we could have told our parents that it was all because of these messages we'd deciphered that he'd won the Battle of Matapan.

Later, Cunningham came down to congratulate us, and we all had drinks together. I think the Matapan business really was a high spot of my life – just knowing we had done something that was helpful. But so much had to be repressed and kept secret. I think that is probably the most extraordinary thing about Bletchley – there were about 10,000 people, not just at Bletchley itself, but the Y service people and so on who were doing the intercepting; they *all* knew this secret – and nobody ever blabbed.

The Italian navy was now in disarray, unable to intervene in the British retreat from Greece and Crete. Victory at Matapan was wisely attributed by the press to good air reconnaissance; thanksgiving services were held, and Admiral Cunningham hailed as unchallengeable master of the eastern Mediterranean. He was a fine naval commander, but it was only just that he thanked the women who had made his position possible. Mavis was not able to tell her own side of the story to a soul for another thirty years.

* * *

★

In her eighties, with many later achievements to her name, Mavis Batey (née Lever) is able to look back with satisfaction, aware that her intellect, her intuitive powers and her stamina have been acknowledged. She knows that her work and that of her colleagues, carried out in a chilly hut in Buckinghamshire, enabled men on destroyers in the stormy Aegean Sea to scramble bombers, fire torpedoes, drown enemies. The kind of historic actions which had Nella Last reaching for the 'off' button on her radio directly involved many remarkable women, whose contribution was not only important in itself, it changed their lives.

Yet, though crucial to its outcome, the Bletchley girls could only imagine what it was like to live through a battle. Nurses were among the few women who had close-up experience of war in all its frightening, sick, ugly reality. After her narrow escape from France in June 1940, QA Lorna Bradey might have been excused for deciding that

front-line nursing was not for her. On the contrary, her appetite for
adventure was undiminished: 'One felt a great urgency to get on
with the war – sitting at home was no good.'

She didn't sit at home for long. Lorna was ordered to join the medical team on board a hospital ship bound for Cape Town. She was
thrilled – 'tremendous excitement everywhere' – until she discovered that her job was to help care for a rabble of disorderly Australians,
most of them, it appeared, injured in street brawls. This 'loathsome
collection of men' were en route home to Australia. The plan was to
jettison their troublesome patients at Cape Town, but it was not to
be. Orders were now received that the ship must proceed to Suez,
where the men who had recovered would be required to join the
desert army against Rommel's advance. They had just forty-eight
hours before departure so, while the Aussies went on a drunken ram-
page, Lorna and the QAs took advantage of a wonderful welcome by
the Cape Town expat community. Then they were back on board for
another six weeks. Between theatre duties, deck tennis, bridge, boat
drill practice and her new boyfriend (this time, a handsome blue-eyed
first officer) the journey passed, but the rebellious Aussies were near
boiling point by the time they got to Suez. 'We were ordered to lock
our cabins at night.' When the troops were finally disembarked and
carried off in transports, 'a silent cheer of relief went up from all of
us . . . That was our first mission done.'

The hospital ship was Lorna's home for fourteen months. And she
was fulfilling an ambition: 'I would travel, see everything and have
plenty of fun.' Once rid of the Australian soldiers, life began to
resemble a cruise as the ship plied between Suez, Aden, the Cape and
Bombay; wherever they docked the QAs were welcomed with parties and dances. They ate delicious food, sampled South African
wines, bathed and went horse-riding. Folding hills, jacaranda trees,
blue bays and moonlit velvety nights completed the picture-postcard
quality of those unforgettable months in the southern hemisphere.

But this wasn't war. We itched to get back to work . . . 1941 was a bad year
for the Allies and we were destined to go into the teeth of the battle at sea.

From January 1941 the deep-water port of Tobruk, on the northern Libyan coast near the border with Egypt, had been in Allied
hands. From April, the troops there were besieged by Axis forces,

who finally retook this important base in December. During the siege, the Royal Navy provided vital support, bringing in supplies and fresh troops and ferrying out casualties. Lorna's ship was one of these, under orders to run between Alexandria and Tobruk.

We were to go to Tobruk at top speed – load the wounded from the Lighters and return, operating on the severe cases on the way down. So the 'Tobruk Splint' was born – a long plaster of Paris splint to immobilise the wounded and fractured limb until we could get them to base . . . We took great pride in the time it took us to load the patients and turn around. Tobruk harbour was a mass of wrecks and floating debris and made the entry most difficult. It was always made about 5.00 a.m. We would wait outside the harbour at night and go in . . . We would be well on our way back by 10.00 a.m.

At last we were being put to the test . . .

This was no Mediterranean cruise. As winter came on the weather grew cold, grey and stormy. Tobruk was running short of medical supplies, and many of the patients, who had been holding out there for months, were in a lamentable state with festering, gangrenous wounds. The run to Alexandria was fraught with danger. Their sister ship was torpedoed and sunk. Lorna's counterpart on this ship, the theatre sister, survived to tell a harrowing tale. The captain had given orders to abandon ship at the moment when the surgical team were in the middle of a serious abdominal operation. In dreadful haste they closed up the patient's wound, bound him to a stretcher and, holding on to it to the best of their ability, leaped into the sea. When she was picked up the sister still had her operating gown and gloves on, but the patient was never heard of again. Lorna and her medical team were working flat out. Everybody knew that the sea was full of enemies and that they were being 'watched'; constantly at the back of her mind was the thought that their ship could be next, and the tedious boat drills no longer seemed pointless. Caring for their patients and getting them to safety was paramount, but nursing through a force 8 storm was beset with difficulties. 'You can imagine taking off stinking plasters in a rough sea!' Lorna remembered having to break off in the middle of an operation and dash to the side of the ship to throw up. The best cure was pink gin and a slice of ham – apparently it worked.

Stocking Wars, Sex Wars

At home, though the Blitz had abated, a sense of urgency prevailed. Lord Beaverbrook, the Minister of Aircraft Production, wanted 2,782 new aircraft by December 1941, and it was accepted that women factory recruits like Doris Scorer in Wolverton were essential. For her part, she was starting to become familiar with wearing overalls and putting up with the bad language, sexism and tomfoolery of her male colleagues. She was now regularly working a twelve-hour day helping to get damaged aircraft flying again.

But she was eighteen and looking for fun too. Missing out on Friday night dances at the Institute was not an option, but the long hours presented a challenge to a dressy young woman like Doris with a taste for colour and sparkle. Lustrous locks were essential to distract from wartime shabbiness. The thing to do was to put your hair in curlers in the morning, anchoring them under your headscarf, wear stockings under your boiler suit for speed and carry a paper bag containing your dress and shoes into work. Then at the end of the day you nipped into the Ladies for a quick wash, curlers out and hair brushed. Time for some make-up: lavish lipstick was indispensable if one was to be attractive. Mascara came in solid cakes in a small plastic box. You spat in it to loosen the colorant, then rubbed in a little long-handled applicator brush. Next the dress came out of the paper bag to be slipped on and the trousers were discarded, silky stocking-clad toes reappearing in high heels; the final touch: a flower, or a diamanté hairslide clipped to the coiffure. Transformed, the girls pranced out of the works to stunned gasps from the male fitters: 'Bet there's not a virgin amongst yer,' muttered one.

Glamour was important to Doris. A townie born and bred, she felt out of place in rural Wolverton and missed the London shops, which had stocked fashionable styles influenced by movie stars like Veronica Lake or Rita Hayworth. Wedges or peep-toes with ankle-straps were the only smart way to totter: the higher the better if you were small, like Doris. But as rationing made itself felt, the Hollywood look got harder to maintain. Doris's ability with a needle helped her to keep up appearances on the clothes front, though like everyone she found the shortage of rubber, a vital component of elastic, awkward to say the least. A frequent wartime catastrophe was the sudden collapse of knickers in the most inopportune places, due to elastic- or button-failure. Accounts of this misfortune, which seems often to have been greeted with wolf-whistles and guffaws, recur with comical frequency in wartime memoirs. From Tottenham Court Road to Sheffield city centre, from Truro train station to the British Embassy in Cairo, women's dropped knickers littered the ground, to the appalled embarrassment of their owners, who were forced to step daintily out of them, before picking them up and stuffing them in their handbags. Doris never went anywhere without a small gold safetypin.

'Don't look now, old girl, but your undercarriage is coming down.'
Elasticated underwear often gave way due to the rubber shortage.
Her suave date has grown accustomed to RAF vocabulary.

Doris disregarded the older generation, who thought that to wear make-up was 'low' or 'fast'. Compared to the country bumpkins, city girls like her were big spenders on manicures, beauty products and permanent waves. More than anything she minded not being able to lay hands on the paints, powders and perfumes she craved. Magazines of the time encouraged women not to let themselves go in wartime. Beauty was a duty: 'No man wants to come home to a wife or sweetheart who shows in her face how much she has worried about him.'

So Doris slapped on Pond's Cold Cream by the potful until it became
scarce. But by 1941, despite the best efforts of the Board of Trade to
procure cosmetics (motivated by the belief that they were good for
feminine morale), the popularity of such products was contributing
to the shortages. Queues formed whenever news got out that a con-
signment had arrived from Coty or Max Factor. So how was a girl
like Doris to keep her pretty curls in place with Kirby grips and
Wave-Set virtually unobtainable? How was she to achieve that
dreamy gleam on the lids with no jewel-tinted eye-shadow? Along
with thousands like her, she learned all kinds of dodges. Sugar-water
did the job just as well as Wave-Set, it turned out, and Vaseline on the
lids made one look irresistible – 'or so we thought'. Doris and her
contemporaries learned to eke out their dwindling supplies, and to
adapt. A lipstick's final days could be prolonged by adding warmed
almond oil, or by melting it in an egg-cup over hot water. Bicarbo-
nate dusted under the armpits could substitute for deodorant,
shoe-polish could replace mascara, starch could be used instead of
face powder. Perfume, made with imported substances, was particularly hard to come by. Doris would have loved to dab Bourjois's
'Evening in Paris' or 'Ashes of Roses' behind her ears, but made do
with a sixpenny phial of Lily of the Valley or Violet Water dispensed
from a huge bottle at the chemist's.

Women in civilian jobs like Doris had far more scope to primp and
prettify than their sisters in the services. When Doffy Brewer left
home to do 'a man's job', and packed her individuality away in her
suitcase, she also packed up many accepted ideas about femininity.
Gone were modesty and maidenliness, personal vanity and refine-
ment. Barbara Cartland, a life-long champion of 'ladylike' values,
worried a great deal about the way the ATS appeared to be system-
atically eradicating femininity. The training programme seemed
geared to stripping out all that was 'soft, feminine and illogical' from
its impressionable young recruits. 'There were some appalling results
of intensive training and suppressed femininity,' she wrote, and
reported instances of ATS officers who were indistinguishable in
appearance from men. Underlying the prejudice against masculinity
in women was a fear, too, of female homosexuality, which remained,
in the 1940s, a topic both inflammatory and surrounded by ignorance. Away from home in an all-female environment, there was

more scope for 'pashes' and crushes to develop both into love and licence. One ATS officer who had been jumped on by her drunken corporal reported to her commanding officer that she had been subjected to a lesbian assault. 'What's that?' was the CO's bewildered reaction.

Where would it all end? Post-war, Barbara Cartland foresaw new battle lines being drawn up – 'I am convinced the next war will be a sex war!'

But Cartland observed that, 'thank goodness', feminine characteristics nearly always prevailed: 'the old Adam – or rather the old Eve – would out'. Like Nella Last, she held to the view that 'a woman will *be* a woman'. They were probably right. Evidence suggests that ATS girls clung tenaciously to the remnants of their femininity. In fact it was during her time in the army that Doffy Brewer used make-up and lipstick for the first time – she might have chosen a lovely new shade named 'Burnt Sugar', specially created, according to its manufacturers, to go with khaki. Certainly the propaganda needed women to believe that army life wasn't all ill-fitting underwear and swearing. Recruitment posters showed glamorous women, mascara'ed, groomed and shapely. As concessions to female vanity Jenny Nicholson, the author of an advice manual for servicewomen, recommended ATS recruits to pack pale-coloured nail varnish (dark shades were not permitted), nail varnish remover and a mirror. Nicholson also interviewed a male drill sergeant about his experiences with the rookies:

When I put them 'at ease' they giggle and chatter till I want to crown the lot of them . . . You have to be tough with them . . .

I'll say this, though, that although they don't take to discipline – they're more individualistic you know, and it's difficult to get them to stand still for any length of time – once they get the hang of it and start to take it seriously, they make a very nice job of it. I've found that the most feminine and attractive ones are the keenest square-bashers . . . They are vain enough to want to look their best doing everything.

In other words, the prettier the girl, the better the soldier. What could be more gratifying to male self-esteem, particularly as this sergeant seems to have seen his job as regimenting an unruly crowd of small children (for 'individualistic', read capricious, or disorderly)? Women were working to pack away their female identity and adapt to 'men's jobs'; but it seems that men were not yet ready to meet them halfway. Double standards prevailed: while every troop locker in the army had its display of Jane Russell and her thirty-eight inch bosom, commanding officers in the ATS rigorously banned even the most modestly clothed pin-ups of Clark Gable or Errol Flynn from the servicewomen's bedsides.

In fact, far from suppressing the female urge to beautify, war conditions seem to have raised the status of titivation to a fine art. Increasing shortages of dress fabrics, cosmetics and toiletries gave them rarity value, putting a premium on anything that could lend gloss to the drabness of a woman's wartime wardrobe. And that year, it became drabber still. On the morning of Whit Sunday 1941 the President of the Board of Trade announced on the wireless that clothes would be rationed, 'thereby ruining the Sunday-breakfast appetites of millions of women who regretted not having bought that little outfit they'd dithered about the other day', as Mollie Panter-Downes informed her New York readers. The first allocation was sixty-six coupons. Out of those, a woman set on a new outfit would have to surrender fourteen for an overcoat, eleven for a dress, five for a sweater, three for knickers and two for a pair of stockings – already, over half a twelvemonth's allocation blown. That left no room at all for impulse buys. The second issue of coupons was reduced to sixty, which had to last fifteen months, and by the end of the war the allowance was down to forty-one a year. Regrets aside, the public accepted the fairness of the new scheme and its importance in redirecting clothes-industry workers like Doris Scorer into the war factories.

After the introduction of clothes rationing everyone got cunning about recovering and refurbishing their existing wardrobes, though it wasn't exactly good for morale. Wearing patched, remodelled skirts, and pilled, frayed sweaters day in, day out was enough to get anyone down, but self-control faltered when it came to stockings. It was one thing to look shabby-chic in jerseys made from unpicked and reknitted wool, but how could any woman hold her head up high wearing baggy lisle hosiery the colour of dirty rainwater? And, like it or not, as skirt lengths rose in proportion to the availability of fabric, lower legs were now on view. Every woman's account of living through wartime reverts to the theme of stockings.

This was, of course, before the days of nylons, not to be seen in this country before 1942, when they were brought in by the Americans. After Leicester Square was hit by its first big air raid, clothes-conscious Madeleine Henrey, 'fearing a shortage', reacted by bulk-buying silk stockings. It was an act of foresight which paid off since her prime source of silk hosiery – the market barrows in Berwick Street – dried up completely soon after. Madeleine's war memoir gives the impression that London was swarming with women in perpetual anxious pursuit of these unobtainable items: 'Etam, where I used to buy my silk stockings . . . closed'; 'I was told to come back in three days' time'. The rare consignments of a few thousand pairs were 'sold within a few hours to women who had started to queue up when it was still dark in the morning'. If you could afford it, seedy men in bars were selling four-and-sixpenny pairs for seven-and-sixpence, but Madeleine probably couldn't. Too often, one could only dream of lovely legs. 'It's getting easy to recognise the haves and have-nots now – womenfolk I mean – by the wearing of silk stockings,' wrote Nella Last, who envied them such luxuries. 'There is such an *uplift* about seeing one's feet and legs so sleek and silky.'

But with silk in short supply or prohibitively expensive, sickly-yellow cotton lisle seemed like the only alternative. Hideous as these were, they were also impractical, according to Doffy Brewer. Less hard-wearing than silk, they needed frequent darning, and when washed could take up to four days to dry. Where keeping up appearances didn't matter, it was preferable to go about in socks, or bare-legged. Many women also tried substitutes: you could stain your legs with coffee, onion skins, wet sand, gravy browning or even potassium permanganate (if you could get it) and get a sister or friend to draw the 'clock' and obligatory seam up the back with eyebrow pencil. 'Silktona' marketed a leg make-up advertised as 'giving bare legs the elegance of sheer silk'. But endless worry surrounded the question of what to do if you worked in an office with a dress code. Phyllis Noble's job at the National Provincial Bank was still a Reserved Occupation (until 1943), and the outmoded standards expected of female employees hit her hard. Their vigilant female supervisor, Miss Challis (known as 'Auntie'), was adamant that bare legs were inadmissible, even in summer. 'No one dared defy Auntie's edict.' Phyllis decided to give Silktona a try. Applying the cream

evenly turned out to be a laborious procedure, as was drawing in the
seams and clocks, but in the end she felt proud of the result – 'the
illusion was completely convincing.' Unfortunately, she couldn't
resist letting a couple of her fellow clerks into the secret, and soon
the rumour that 'Miss Noble was *not* wearing stockings' was all over
the bank. Her legs became the irresistible focus of the male employees, who followed her, practically on hands and knees, gawping at
the backs of her calves. Despite this, Auntie and the authorities caved
in, and 'leggy nudity' was permitted, provided it was discreet.

For Helen Forrester in Liverpool, a deadlock over stockings was to
prove far more intractable, and also exposed the appallingly sexist
standards of the day. Heartbroken at the loss of her fiancé, Helen had
struggled on hungry, downcast and browbeaten through the winter
of 1940–41, still working for a pittance at the charity in Bootle. The
first glimmer of hope for her came in March 1941, when she was
interviewed for a post as a clerk in the Wages Department of the
Petroleum Board, a consortium of fuel companies (she was appointed,
she later discovered, because Mr Fox, the pudgy, pasty installation
manager, only ever picked pretty girls with nice legs). As Helen
started her new job she felt a cloud begin to lift. The other girls were
friendly, and the pay was £2 7s 6d a week; she bought a pair of much-
needed new shoes with high heels, with enough left over for some
morale-boosting dentistry – for these were still the days when the
poor paid a high price for toothache. Then in the first week of May
Liverpool was mercilessly bombed, with over 1,700 people killed and
76,000 left homeless. Without warning, Helen's mother decided to
move the family away from the blitzed area to a damp bungalow in
the suburb of Moreton on the other side of the Mersey, leaving her
– after fares were paid – with subsistence money. She was back where
she started. It was at this point that the Stocking War broke out.

Quite simply, Helen and her workmates could not afford stockings, so they went bare-legged. Helen would coat her legs with a
solution of tinted wash, cheaper than make-up, which proved adequate, though in cold weather the skin of her legs got badly chapped,
and she had to suffer the ribald remarks made by the male staff at the
Petroleum Board. For some time the girls' stockingless condition
went unnoticed by the unpleasant Mr Fox; his secretary, Miss
Hughes, was always immaculate in lisle. But one day an order was

issued. This indecency must end. The female employees were to cover their legs forthwith. Next morning two of the girls turned up in slacks. Outraged, Mr Fox retaliated by calling them into his office and threatening them with dismissal, from where they emerged in tears. Something about this injustice emboldened Helen. All her life she had been bullied at home; now here were the bullies again, this time taking over the office. 'Let's talk to Miss Hughes,' she suggested.

Miss Hughes couldn't advise them, however, she bravely promised to speak to Mr Fox. But here she hit a wall.

Written in stone, the edict came down once more. All ladies on the staff would in future wear stockings.

Back they went to Miss Hughes, this time with a stronger card in their hand. Trembling at her own audacity, Helen explained that, if the order was enforced, they would all have to resign, reserved occupations or no reserved occupations, and they would do so even if it meant signing up to the ATS. At least there they would be provided with stockings, however woolly and awful. Reluctantly, Miss Hughes agreed to try again, and returned saying that Mr Fox would see them in his office the next morning.

Helen felt 'caught between male pigheadedness and dire necessity'. She agreed to be spokeswoman for the group and mentally prepared herself for a future scouring pans in an army canteen.

The encounter was a collaborative triumph for the girls. Helen led the assault on Mr Fox. Initially he remained unmoved; if the girls weren't prepared to darn their hose he had no sympathy. Helen was outraged at this. She had spent hours of her life repairing ladders with a crochet hook, and pointed out that they were far too poor to waste good hosiery. But couldn't they wear slacks, which would be smart, and warm in winter? 'His mouth fell open. He was genuinely shocked. "Not in my office," he replied frigidly.'

Another girl, who had not up to then said a single word, suddenly spoke up. 'If you insist about stockings, we shall all have to find other jobs,' she said baldly.

There was a silence. All Mr Fox's male staff had been conscripted; he had things how he wanted them now. How on earth would he replace his entire female workforce? But the turning point came when this

same young woman advanced demurely towards Mr Fox with the
words, 'Our legs don't look too bad.'

As she spoke, she slightly raised the hem of her mid-length skirt
and extended a well-turned, evenly stained calf towards him:

'Oxo,' she announced simply.

Mr Fox was caught, and he knew it. It was he who had appointed his
female employees on the basis of their shapely legs. Snarling with
defeat, he dismissed them. They never heard another word and,
though daring to wear slacks was carrying liberty too far, they all
knew there would be no further objections to them going barelegged.
This they continued to do for the remainder of the war, in summer
and – sore, raw and bleeding with chilblains – in winter.

*

For thousands of women like Doris Scorer, Phyllis Noble and Helen
Forrester, lipstick shortages and stocking wars were in the fore-
ground of their lives. It was like some law of nature: the more war,
with its demands and privations, encroached on the attributes of
femininity, the more resourceful and ingenious women became in
expressing those attributes. Their self-respect as women was at stake.
Make-up and elastic shortages embarrassed and undermined them,
but they were possessed with an obstinate spirit. As one woman said,
'one needed that lipstick to show that one's flag was still flying'.
Female morale required beauty. Even if you were lonely, even if the
husbands and boyfriends you loved and wanted to please were on the
other side of the world, you curled your hair and went to the pub, or
the dance. It made the waiting and the enduring less punishing; it
made you feel better about yourself. So you put on your war paint
and set out to get a wink and a flattering comment from the fitters,
the foremen or even the patronising drill sergeant.

Hardly surprising, then, if things boiled over from time to time.

Newlywed Kaye Bastin was still waiting. Brian's family, who lived
near Henley, took her under their wing, and baby Anne was born late
in 1941. While she was still small they moved back to a flat in Brighton.
Here, Kaye made life work on her own terms. 'There were so many
like us . . . we just had to get on with life.' She had plenty of friends
and took Anne to the local mother and baby clinic. Her niece was

always willing to babysit if she wanted to go to the pub at the end of the road with her sister. Intermittently, letters arrived from Brian. 'He was having a good time in South Africa. He was a young man . . . I knew that he wasn't faithful, because he wrote and told me about his girlfriends. And in fact one of them got pregnant and had to have an abortion. Then there was another one, who conceived, but she didn't have it, because it was an ectopic pregnancy.'

Her husband's sexual transgressions were no worse than those of innumerable servicemen posted abroad. Though barely twenty-two, Kaye now drew upon a reserve of tolerance and broad-mindedness that would stand her in good stead for the rest of her life. She loved Brian, and she accepted his infidelities. 'I couldn't expect him to be faithful, because of being away for so long.' But Kaye wasn't prepared to be lonely either. 'There was an officer in the RAF, though I didn't actually sleep with him . . . and there was a New Zealander who took me out to dinner at the Bodega . . . And there was Jack – he was a warrant officer in the army; I met him in the pub, and when he was on leave he used to come and see me, and he did sleep with me. He hoped I would leave Brian. Well – I told Brian about mine, because he told me about his . . . But he was the first to stray.'

Honesty and goodwill on both sides rescued the Bastin marriage. 'I'm the sort of person who can take on these problems and deal with them,' she says today. 'The important thing is not to make a fuss about everything.' Unlike those of thousands of separated wives, Kaye's wartime marriage didn't end in divorce. In 1938 fewer than 10,000 divorce petitions had been filed, less than half by husbands. By 1945 the numbers would reach 25,000. Over half of these – 14,500 – were filed by husbands, of which about 10,150 (70 per cent) were on the grounds of adultery by their wives. Each case, in that torrent of petitions flooding the courts throughout the 1940s, told its own tale of loneliness, infidelity, adultery, betrayal. There was Mrs Louis, a Berkshire woman whose RAF husband came home on leave and, having peremptorily informed her that he would be divorcing her to marry someone else, not only sent a furniture van round to remove all the household goods, but had all the lights ripped out of their fittings. There was Elizabeth Jane Howard, who felt she had made a mistake from the outset when she married her husband, Peter Scott (son of the Arctic explorer), but despite many flagrant infidelities waited till the war was over before divorcing him: 'He was fourteen years older than me so it was not a success really from the start . . . but I felt I couldn't go while he was fighting the war.'

Margaret Perry, a Nottinghamshire nineteen-year-old, was another who married in haste in 1942; neither Margaret nor her new husband, Roy, had thought things through. Isolated in a miserable lodging in north London, Margaret soon fled back to stay with her mum in Nottingham and got a job in the city's chief department store; unknown to Roy she fell under the spell of a married RAF officer twice her age, who impressed her with his 'mature' ideas about politics and vegetarianism. Margaret, eager to learn but young and bewildered, was easy prey. Later she was conscripted into a munitions factory, where she became fascinated by her boss, Peter, a pacifist – also married. 'I began to worship [him] in a way that was not good for me. Roy and I began to quarrel violently.' By 1944 Roy could take no more of his young wife's infidelities 'of mind and body'. They parted. 'He'd had a very raw deal from me.'

Precipitate marriages followed by prolonged absence were putting unendurable strain on relationships. The Mass Observation diarist Shirley Goodhart recorded the distress of a friend whose husband had left her 'for another girl whom he met abroad. This separation is breaking up many marriages.' Shirley herself had married her doctor husband, Jack, early in 1941. Soon after that he was sent to India; she would not see him again for four years. Could their marriage survive?

Barbara Cartland worked as a welfare officer during the war. Her sympathies were with the women, but she was equally non-judgemental about the men:

I was often sorry for the 'bad' women . . . They started by not meaning any harm, just desiring a little change from the monotony of looking after their children, queuing for food and cleaning the house with no man to appreciate them or their cooking.

. . . and who should blame a man who is cooped up in camp all day or risking his life over Germany for smiling at a pretty girl when he's off duty? He is lonely, she is lonely, he smiles at her, she smiles back, and it's an introduction. It is bad luck that she is married, but he means no harm, nor does it cross her mind at first that she could ever be unfaithful to Bill overseas. When human nature takes its course and they fall in love, the home is broken and maybe another baby is on the way, there are plenty of people ready to say it is disgusting and disgraceful. But they hadn't meant to be like that, they hadn't really.

Before the war, the press had fed off the public's prurience about broken marriages. The 'bolter', or divorced woman, would have had to outface disapproval or even flee the country to escape guilt and disgrace. In 1941 things had changed; a woman on her own was less likely to be deterred from leaving her husband by the thought of becoming destitute. Probably, as an important part of the workforce, she would be able to support herself. Just as importantly, she would be less afraid of being judged; the Abdication crisis had nudged public opinion a step closer to leniency. But above all, everybody now knew what it felt like to be lonely, worried and frightened, and Barbara Cartland's compassionate lack of censure was a common reaction to the external pressures imposed by war. Self-righteous condemnation seemed unnecessarily cruel in a world of bombs and shortages.

Some of the stigma was lifting from divorce. Along with modesty and maidenliness, the winds of war were starting to blow away the injustices and misrepresentations that had clung for so long to the lone woman. The 'old, narrow life' was becoming broader. Though uncertain, a small flame had been kindled. Was it, perhaps, possible that the cage doors were indeed standing open – that one might emerge from the dusting and cooking and queuing, and step through to one's heart's desire? Official recognition that they were 'essential' gave a boost to jaded nerves, as women began to see that, after years of being cabbages, they were needed. And under the mantle of total war, everyone's desires and dreams seemed legitimate, not just men's.

Women in Uniform

Late in the year, the Wiltshire hedges were thick with haws and spindle-berries. The village pond froze solid and then thawed. At Ham Spray House, Frances Partridge and her small family kept as far as possible to the everyday routine. There were reviews to write, beehives to repair, a vegetable garden to cultivate. Frances's diary entry for 16 November 1941 recalled a contented day attending to her son and practising her violin:

R. said how happy he was, so did Burgo and so did I. When I wake these days, in spite of the war and our uneventful life, it is to a pleasurable antici-pation of minute things – the books I'm going to read, the letters the post will bring, the look of the outside world.

But invasion was still a fear. They hoarded their tinned food. Every evening at 9 p.m. – in common with families across the country – they huddled round the wireless for the news bulletin. In the desert Rommel's army was continuing to block the British offensive. The Germans were marching towards Moscow. In the month of November 11,000 Russians starved to death in Leningrad.

On 2 December Churchill outlined proposals for increasing the wartime workforce. Frances's husband, Ralph, would be affected by the call for men between forty and fifty-one to register for military service; he determined to testify as a Conscientious Objector. At the beginning of that month tension between Japan and America increased dramatically; in response to this threat Britain expanded its Eastern Fleet. Frances felt she was living through an earthquake; the ground she stood on, her familiar pleasures, her values and her deep personal happiness with Ralph seemed to be crumbling and giving way beneath her. On 7 December she wrote:

All the events of today have been blotted out by the evening's news. Japan has opened war on the U.S.A. with a bang, by an almighty raid on the American Naval and Air Base at Pearl Harbour. No ultimatum, no warning; the damage has been ghastly and casualties extremely heavy. Nothing could have been more unprovoked and utterly beastly.

The world now seemed to be engulfed in war.

But the cares and worries of everyday life still had the power to dominate larger concerns. These included, in her case , the departure of the Partridges' servant, Joan. When Joan's boyfriend was posted abroad she went to Frances, white-faced, to tell her, 'Mrs Partridge, I want to leave and do war work.' She had been to an aircraft factory in Newbury to see if they would take her on. Frances was aghast. Joan's misery was plain to see, and she felt powerless:

Of course it is the happiness of not one but hundreds of Joans and hundreds of Gunner Robinsons, thousands, millions I should say – of all nationalities – that is to be sacrificed in this awful pandemonium . . . We were both too upset to read.

But of course she was also only too aware of the effect Joan's departure would have on the Ham Spray household:

Our life gets more domestic and agricultural and when Joan goes it may get more so. If only I could cook!

After Joan left she did her best to learn, but there was also the housework. By Christmas Frances was finding that sweeping and dusting were an excellent antidote to cold. It also filled her with a 'glow of virtue', and even Ralph washed up and helped to bottle fruit. Her wartime diary reflects on the mindless physical energy it required to scrub the nursery floor, a task 'I can take no interest in'.

Frances had help from a succession of Joans and Alices and Mrs Ms throughout the war. They came and went intermittently, each time leaving her submerged in domesticity, wringing her hands at the lack of help, frustrated at the boredom of childcare and housework, and by her culinary shortcomings. The Joans and Alices meanwhile were volunteering or being conscripted into the factories, the forces, the farms and the forests.

As early as 1940 a book had appeared entitled *British Women at War* by Peggy Scott, which set out to celebrate women's contribution to the war effort. The tone of the book was whistle-while-you-work cheeriness, and its pages were peopled with non-complaining girl guide types who all set to work with a will:

The modern girl with her freedom, her independence, her disregard of public opinion, was vindicated at once in the new war. She fitted into the Navy, Army and Air Force as easily as she had done into a mixed bathing party.

But with the advent of conscription modern girls knew that they would no longer have the luxury of choosing between the services, and many decided to join up while they still could. So what were the factors influencing their decision?

★

For a surprising number it was the clothes. Few of them knew what to expect, so they judged on appearances. Christian Oldham, the convent-educated daughter of an admiral, had been to finishing school in France before the war and joined the Wrens in 1940. Years later, when she published an account of her time with the service, Christian couldn't decide what to call it, until she mentioned casually to her editor, 'You know, *I only joined for the hat.*' They both agreed it would make the perfect title.

Christian Oldham claims to have been 'hat-minded' from the age of three. At twenty she was even more susceptible to the flattering double-breasted tailored jacket, svelte skirt and pert tricorne hat that comprised the officers' uniform. Vera Laughton Mathews, Director of the Wrens, had commissioned the elite fashion designer Edward Molyneux to come up with the look. 'The effect was a winner,' according to Christian, and entirely accounted for the huge waiting list of applicants wishing to join:

The great thing was, of course, that the ATS and the WAAFs had these frightful belts which made their bottoms look enormous, whereas the Wrens had this nice straight uniform which concealed your worst points. Joining the Wrens was quite the most fashionable war work.

Admittedly, the ATS uniform lacked pulling power: in truth, a single-breasted, belted khaki jacket bulked out with cumbersome pleated pockets did nothing for one's figure. The WAAFs suffered from the same defect where pockets and belts were concerned, accentuating hips and bottoms. Fashionable or not, most recruits underwent a reality check once they'd signed up and been issued with their new uniform. An ATS recruit recalled that

[the uniform] fitted me about as well as a bell tent, trailing on the floor behind me while my hands groped in sleeves a foot too long. Evidently the army expected its women to be of Amazonian proportions. I was to find that the army had a genius for issuing absurd garments and expecting one to take them seriously.

The ATS recruit who sketched this 'kitting-out' session recalled:
'I do not know how the sizes were worked out, but they all had to be altered.'

And there were universal complaints about frumpy underwear: 'The knickers were long-legged ones: we called them "twilights" and "blackouts" – light blue in summer, darker, knitted ones in winter, plus vests and cotton bras.' One group of recruits fell about in hysterical merriment at the sight. 'Just imagine anyone thinking we would be seen dead in them!' They parcelled the woolly knickers up and sent them off to their aunts, an action they regretted in November, at a freezing station somewhere in the Hebrides.

Again and again women cite uniform as being the key factor in their choice of service. With her fearless look, sprightly smile and upright bearing, the image of a woman in collar, tie and a jaunty hat came to epitomise the British war effort. She radiated from thousands of recruitment posters, magazine covers and advertisements. A dazzling Wren exhorted the public to buy Kolynos toothpaste; three immaculately-coiffed servicewomen beamingly beseeched the public to invest in National Savings Certificates, while in an ad for sanitary protection two ATS girls were seen striding confidently to their duties: 'Women are winning the war – of Freedom!' ran the copy, which also included the useful reminder that 'Tampax takes up next to no kit room.' As a role model the woman in uniform was glamorous and gung-ho, willing and steadfast, stout-hearted and dedicated. But her unshakable direct gaze also called into question centuries of doe-eyed submission, replacing fuzzy sweetness, modesty and humility with an entirely new incarnation of womanhood. This was not the devil-may-care hoyden or flapper of the 1920s; nor did she have much in common with her 1930s successor, discreet and golden-voiced, whose sole aim was to marry the boss. This young woman was imbued with a higher purpose, she had a vision. For her, King and country came before hearth and home.

Not everyone welcomed this unfamiliar reversal. Clara Milburn and her husband were deeply shocked when they heard that Princess Elizabeth had joined the ATS: 'We did *not* approve.' Early on, the *Daily Mail* invited readers to send in their ideas for what they most hated about the war. 'Women in uniform' came top. Servicewomen had to contend with prejudice and intolerance. Often, women themselves were hostile to their own kind. Vera Roberts trained with the ATS at a base near Harrogate, a bastion of the Yorkshire bourgeoisie:

A lot of people had a real down on women like us in uniform . . . and the Harrogate ladies gave you a dirty look and just spat in front of you. They thought we were the lowest of the low – that we were common, I suppose. I've never forgotten that.

The implication was that a woman prepared to wear collars and ties and brass buttons – not to mention the horror of trousers – must be immoral. Men equated 'masculine' garments with the possession of masculine characteristics: as in 'she would immediately stride and shout and swear and drink'. There was the fear that such women might stray into male territory, and avail themselves of male liberties. It still wasn't thought proper for women to enter a pub, 'not if you were what was considered well brought-up. Only tarts did that!' The public – as here, interrogated by Mass Observation – viewed drinking servicewomen as sexually 'easy':

Those ATS girls were a disgrace. They come into this pub at night and line up against that wall. Soldiers give them drinks and when they're blind drunk they carry them out into the street. And we're paying public money for them too!

*'Time, gentlemen, please.' Women in uniform, and women in pubs.
What was the world coming to?*

Army girls in particular, perceived as lower class, were singled out for abuse: 'nothing but a league of amateur prostitutes', 'bloody whores the lot of them'. And the wits had a field day, attaching innuendoes to volunteer and conscript alike: the ATS were 'officers' groundsheets', while the WAAFs were 'pilots' cockpits'. If you joined the Land Army, it was 'Backs to the Land', or if you preferred the Naval Service, it was 'Up with the lark and to bed with a Wren.'

It would appear from this that much of the public found it hard to cope with the reinvention of womanhood through uniform. The look, the anonymity, the sense both of cohesiveness and confidence delivered too many mutinous messages. Joining up meant escape from controls and subjection, but it also meant laying yourself open to abuse and vulgarity. You couldn't win.

Or perhaps you could. In her account of life in the ATS, Hilary Wayne reflected that putting on uniform had a transformative effect.

I think we not only looked different, we felt different . . . I personally felt less self-conscious . . . The fact that we were all dressed exactly alike gave me the comfortable feeling that, whatever happened, I could not be conspicuous.

And it could be better than that: for its wearers, uniform served as a guarantee of respectability, inviolability almost. Drivers, for example, gave you lifts and bought you meals. 'I never had any trouble at all,' recalled a nurse who like many others regularly thumbed rides when she was in uniform. Eileen Rouse came back to her native Plymouth after six weeks' ATS training in Honiton, pleased as punch with her new clothes: 'Oh dear me, I thought I was the cat's whiskers with me shirt and me tie, and I don't mind telling you, me mum and dad was proud of me when I came home!' For Pat Bawland, a childhood of poverty, hunger and pawn shops had been followed by work as a lowly invoice typist on fifteen shillings a week. Putting on the uniform of the Wrens was for her a crowning achievement:

I'd always had hand-me-down clothes. When I actually was supplied with my uniform, it was wonderful – the quality of it!

Pat's time in the Wrens gave her a precious, and enduring, self-esteem:

Going in the Wrens changed me. I learned that, though you could be proud when you're wearing rags, you can do better when you're smart. And the beautiful lace-up shoes! – I polished them till they shone! I was the smartest one in our group. And being in uniform I became one of many the same. The only difference was in our speaking and our jobs, but we all sat down to the same meals. I didn't have to lie about my dinner. I didn't have to lie that I'd had breakfast. And I didn't have to think about pawn shops any more. I could live like a normal human being.

Few servicewomen seem to have had their new self-respect dented by the continued mutterings about immorality. The pride, esprit de corps and the sense that being in uniform gave, that one was part of something bigger than oneself, all contributed to the reality of wartime emancipation. Flo Mahony's feelings were typical of many:

In my uniform I was confident to go anywhere and do anything. It was quite different to being a civilian. In a way it was the making of me. Wearing a uniform, you felt part of something bigger. And you really felt you were *somebody*.

The Lowest Form of Life

The Women's Land Army was regarded by many as being at the bottom of the status pile; the clothes were inferior, and the work would ruin nicely kept hands. Even so it had special attractions. Some fearful recruits saw it as an escape from the bombing, others as offering a less regimented life with fewer brass buttons to polish.

Twenty-year-old Jean McFadyen from rural Argyllshire felt she was a nobody. Her decision to join the Women's Land Army was based on her humble view that this service was the right level for her. But she too was among the approximate 40 per cent of women who chose it because she actually liked the smart uniform:

I wouldn't have minded if I thought I could have got into the Wrens or the WAAFs, but I didn't want to go into the ATS. I didn't like the uniform! That horrible khaki!

So one day I was out walking through the central part of Edinburgh and I saw a cardboard cut-out of a girl in uniform. They were recruiting for the Women's Timber Corps. And when I saw the cut-out I thought, 'That's for me, that's the uniform I want'. So I went in and volunteered.

Till 1942, Jean's world had been confined to the sculleries and pantries of the lairds and moneyed individuals who employed her in Argyllshire and Edinburgh. Jim Park, her boyfriend, had worked in a biscuit factory but had been conscripted into the 51st Highland Division; the relationship had not developed as far as a commitment before he went abroad. Knowing that her own call-up was imminent, she was one of many who decided to leap before they were pushed.

The Timber Corps was a section of the Land Army. Jean was

handed a registration card; she still has it. It proclaims: 'You are now a Member of the Women's Land Army. Your Country Welcomes your Services.'

Peggy Scott described the Land Army girls in *British Women at War*. Scott presented a version of them as free spirits who preferred rosy cheeks and a windblown hairstyle to the buttoned-up presentation of the ATS. Cleaning out pigsties held no horrors for this type; her motherly instincts stood her in good stead caring for animals and milking cows, and the fresh air did wonders for her complexion. In the evenings there was time to take up water-colouring, and in spring to rhapsodise over the antics of newborn lambs. In reality the Land Army, especially the Timber Corps, was far from being a pastoral soft option.

Jean McFadyen was sent to a remote area of Aberdeenshire, where she was trained in the use of tools and the basics of forestry work, including axe-swinging. The girls were issued with work clothes – a greatcoat, bib-and-brace denim overalls, a mackintosh, Wellington boots and two pairs of thick woollen socks – all a far cry from the smart 'walking-out' uniform that had attracted Jean on the cardboard cut-out. 'The get-up did absolutely nothing for our vanity!' The girls lived in communal huts, working and eating together. Their diet, she recalls, was principally spam, and mince. They slept in rows 'army style', alternately head-to-toe. 'Your head would be at the bottom of the camp-bed with two pairs of feet on the beds either side of you. If you were caught moving your pillow up the other end you were in trouble . . . Lots of the girls cried themselves to sleep every night. We had blisters on our hands and feet.'

Once the training was over they were sent out to start their duties. Meeting Jean today, it is hard to imagine such a slight, bird-like woman undertaking such arduous work. Some of the girls worked in sawmills using chainsaws; but Jean was out felling, cross-cutting and snedding* the timber by hand.

In summertime we started very early, but in winter we didn't leave the camp till 8 in the morning. We had up to an hour's drive away from the camp on an open-topped lorry before we got to our place of work. The first winter I was there it was freezing, and when I came home I couldn't

* To sned: a pleasingly obscure word meaning to cut or lop off a branch: OED.

walk because my legs were rubbing against the damp denim. The next day I went to work wearing my pyjamas underneath my overalls! And that work was not easy. I had a sore back, sore legs, sore arms – and massive muscles!

Despite being skinny and barely five foot tall, Jean took her share of the weight, lifting whole felled trees and throwing them on to a stack taller than herself. It could take a dozen girls heaving together, always with two 'heavyweights' at either end, to get each trunk up on to the stack. They loaded the lorries, and two girls drove them to the station, where they were then unloaded on to the trains. Jean took her turn too with the sawmill teams – 'I was always scared I would lose my fingers . . . it was known to happen.'

Despite the hardship Jean never regretted her decision to join up:

The war opened up life for me. I escaped from my mother's eye. And I met people my own age, which I would not have done had the war not happened. I'd have probably gone on in service, and finished up an old maid.

For even in rural Aberdeenshire there were social compensations: on Friday nights the girls jumped off the lorry, fought for the bathroom, donned a dress, then walked three miles to the nearest village, where there were dances that lasted till one or two in the morning. By 1942 attractive men were in short supply – 'there were farmer boys, wee laddies . . . But we danced with each other mostly. There was always a live band with accordions and fiddles, for reels and Scottish dancing.' On Saturday afternoons they caught the bus into Aberdeen and went straight to the picture house. Jean's trips into the city, thronging with servicemen, gave her a taste of bustle and activity: 'it was a bit more fun, a bit more *life*, as it were' (though she still felt incapable of entering a pub – nice Scottish girls simply didn't). Jim, her boyfriend, was far away in North Africa with Monty's Eighth Army; she felt no obligation to hold every soldier or sailor at arm's length for the duration. 'I was not above a kiss or a cuddle, no, that was permissible! We had a life!'

Nevertheless, the girls scrambled every evening for the post to see if letters had arrived from their sweethearts. There'd be giggles at the acronyms on the backs of envelopes: HOLLAND, for 'Hope Our Love Lasts And Never Dies', or ITALY, for 'I Trust And Love You'.

It was Jim's mother, however, who contacted Jean to tell her that her son was missing after the Battle of El Alamein. Days of suspense followed, before she got the news that he had been captured by the Germans. 'It was horrible. But it was happening every day to somebody. Not that that helped.' Jim spent the three remaining years of the war suffering mistreatment and malnutrition in a POW camp in Yugoslavia. Jean kept in touch, but she had her life to get on with:

Ach, there were lots of good times. And it opened up my life. Mainly, it was the comradeship that made it. I worked with the same group for most of the time I was in the Corps, and I made great friends with them. We were all in the same boat.

Though her forestry work made a huge contribution to the war – providing everything from pit props to coffins, telegraph poles to armaments packaging, Jean was only marginally interested in the war effort:

I don't think we thought deeply about what we were doing or why we were doing it - we were just *doing* it! We were there to have fun.

But where the job made a real difference was in her own sense of self-worth. The war had turned her into a somebody:

The war changed my life completely. It gave me confidence. I know now that anything men can do, women can do better.

Kay Mellis was another young Scottish woman who left a life of narrow horizons and through war work discovered a new side to herself. She was billeted in a hostel with seven other Land Army girls, and conditions were as tough for her as for Jean McFadyen. The accommodation was in a courtyard harness-room with horses on one side, a braying donkey on the other and rats everywhere, which chewed their clothes. The work made no concessions to her youth or lack of strength:

We had to do whatever a man could do, there was no question. We thinned turnips with hoes – but the men used to always take the best hoes. And if your hoe was too big, it would rub between your forefinger and your thumb. Sugar beet we had to pull out by hand . . . We got sores, and calluses; you used lanolin to soothe them.

But three years of back-breaking farm work also boosted Kay's confidence in her abilities:

At the beginning we were told we were useless – coming from the town with our soft hands and posh Edinburgh way of talking. But I must admit that, when I could thin neeps a bit better, and lift tatties a bit better, it did make me feel really good. To think: 'Oh, I can do as good as you now.'

'Why does it always rain?' A Kentish land girl's view of cabbage-cutting. Here as elsewhere, there is no differentiation between men's and women's work.

Another propagandising publication about the Women's Land Army appeared in 1944. It was written by Vita Sackville-West, who, with her love of the land and keen appreciation of young women clad in boots and breeches, would appear to have been the perfect choice of author for such a work. Sackville-West's account of the WLA in Scotland complements Jean's and Kay's experiences, telling of 'townies' lifting potatoes, Scottish shepherdesses, the pleasures and perils of milking a cow and the satisfactions of rat-catching. And she described the life of the Timber Corps girls, romantically cut off from civilisation among the deer and the wild Highland scenery – 'Man's foolish war had penetrated even this.'

A less eulogising picture of the Land Army appeared after the war was over. Shirley Joseph described her 1946 memoir as 'an Unofficial Account'. In it she told of insanitary living conditions and lack of fresh food; of working seventy-hour weeks, with one week off a year. She told of dung-spreading, tractor-driving, ploughing, loading and five o'clock starts. 'I felt more tired at the end of the day than I had thought humanly possible' – and yet the farmer who employed her regarded her as a shirker. Surviving as a land girl required, in her view, robustness, genuine love of the country and lack of ambition. 'It is not necessary to be well educated or intelligent in the Land Army. In fact, the fewer brains and more brawn you have, the more the farmer likes you . . . Land girls are the lowest form of life in the eyes of many farmers.' Several other accounts confirm this picture: bullying farmers, misery and exhaustion. Monica Littleboy held out on a chicken farm in Norfolk for six months before quitting for the WAAFs. 'I was working with one man and a boy and thousands of chickens for company . . . the dust, confusion, dirt and noise had to be seen to be believed . . . at five o'clock I cycled back 4 miles . . . worn out and ready for bed.' The artist Mary Fedden chose the Land Army because she thought she would be safe from the bombs, but her Gloucestershire farm was close to an aircraft factory: 'we were bombed every night for a year . . . When the farmer was beastly to me I would go into the shed and sit among the calves, and cry,' she remembered.

But Shirley Joseph conceded that the experience had value. Communal living had made her broad-minded. The social mix encompassed girls from every conceivable walk of life and, exposed to all kinds of explicit narrations, she soon dropped her conventional outlook: 'If my mother could have overheard some of the conversations I listened to!' Like Jean McFadyen and Kay Mellis, she felt that her time with the Land Army had educated her, though she did not feel that the experience was likely to be of long-term value:

A girl can't milk a typewriter any more than she can drive a tractor for a dress shop . . .

It is true that she will see, in all probability, a new and different side of life. She will undoubtedly be a sounder judge of human nature. She will have learnt self-reliance and self-confidence; and never to take things at their face value . . .

But such knowledge and experience are not exclusive to those who serve in the Land Army. They can equally well be gained in any of the women's services.

Officers and Ladies

Shirley Joseph felt the main benefit of her time in the Land Army was its democratising effect, and many of her contemporaries would have agreed that social mobility increased during the war. Before the war, the distinctions between maid and mistress were set in stone. Patience Chadwyck-Healey would no more have chatted informally to Jean McFadyen, Pat Bawland or Flo Mahony than she would have fraternised with her mother's cook. Now in the FANYs Patience, and many like her in the other services, found herself not only polishing the same brass buttons and bashing the same squares as her social 'inferiors', but having to question her ingrained feudal assumptions:

During the war it was very interesting. One found oneself on an entirely new level of meeting people. I remember particularly one little person (well, she *was* a little person, actually), and I said something like: 'Where are you from?' and she had a slight accent of some sort, and she said 'Oh I was a parlour maid'. So I was quite interested, and I thought: 'This is some sort of revolution! Here we are sharing a dormitory together.'

And I learned how nice people like that were. One had never been able to talk to them before. But bit by bit talking to them became the norm. You know, we were all doing a job. In fact, they were very often better at the jobs we were asked to do – you know, when we were asked to clean the room or something.

And then eventually, when you became an officer, you also met women above you, who probably would never have crossed your social horizons – because perhaps they were qualified in business, for example. So one's rather narrow social circle was hugely expanded. Which was all for the good . . . It was a sudden jump – people who'd been miles apart *had* to come together and work together.

Patience's reflections certainly give an indication of social upheaval, though her observation that 'we' were just hopeless at cleaning out rooms compared to 'them' shows that there was still some way to go. The little parlour maid's accent was perhaps too much of a giveaway, just as Christian Oldham in the Wrens couldn't help noticing the unhygienic habits of some of her more 'interesting' dormitory-mates:

Some were wedded to their vests, which they had been wearing all day, keeping them on under pyjamas before they tucked down for the night. Putting your bra on outside your vest then of course comes naturally. The intermediate stage – washing – was passed over.

Christian, as in love with her morning bath as her dorm-mates were with their malodorous undergarments, found their BO offensive, though she tried to put it delicately:

The vest enthusiasts were rather more prone to this affliction than others.

Many accounts remark on how the 'lower orders' were also noticeably afflicted with bad language, crudity and vulgarity. But, quick to redress the balance on such observations, Christian commented that, overall, these were superficialities. Like Patience Chadwyck-Healey, she had grown up with narrow horizons and was glad of the opportunity to meet and mix with girls from across the social spectrum. Could 'the Colonel's lady and Judy O'Grady' ever be sisters? In Christian's friendships and working relationships there was one common factor – 'that was their integrity'. It had nothing to do with status, smelly vests or being 'born on the wrong doorstep'. 'I just realised that some people were true to their word and some were not.' But these ex-debutantes were speaking from a position of privilege. (Christian herself had secured her coveted post in the Wrens through the good offices of her grandmother, who played bridge with somebody who happened to be Vera Laughton Mathews's brother.) It cost them little to speak of settling down harmoniously with parlour maids. For Audrey Johnson, a lower-middle-class girl from Leicester, early days with the Wrens served only to remind her that she had joined the elite women's service:

Impeccable, well-to-do accents rang through the building. 'Marjorie was at school with you, I understand: and I believe you know the Somebody-hyphen-Somebodies.' 'Oh, you're Rosemary. Daddy told me to keep a lookout for you. He's at the Admiralty with your uncle.' Everybody seemed to know somebody of importance . . .

I knew no-one . . . I had a feeling that I must be the only girl who had left school at fourteen. But I was not going to mention that to anyone, and night school elocution lessons had helped a bit.

War undoubtedly threw up some strange bed-fellows; evacuated from Ilford to Wales between 1939 and 1942, middle-class teenager Nina Mabey had to adapt to some very different ways of life. She was billeted with a series of Welsh 'aunties' and 'uncles' who often seemed to come from another planet. One family seemed to her almost sub-human. They were curiously deformed, hardly spoke and kept the outside world at bay with permanently locked doors. Another of her hostesses expected Nina to wash and scrub the handkerchiefs her son sent home from college. Encrusted though they were with gluey mucus, she didn't feel able to refuse this hideous task. In Aberdare the house was full of black beetles and Mrs Jones served pilchards straight from the tin. Nina ate them, lukewarm, while her miner host Mr Jones stood naked in a zinc bath at the other end of the room, scrub-bing off the coal dust. One day she found Mrs Jones weeping in desperation after an avalanche of wet coal slurry, flowing off the slag heap behind the house, inundated the kitchen. Appalled at the mess, Nina found a shovel and wheelbarrow to help her clear it up, but Mrs Jones was distraught. 'It's not right you should do this kind of dirty work. It's not a job for an educated girl.' As well as accustoming her to 'other people's funny habits', these experiences awakened sixteen-year-old Nina's social conscience. Mr Jones often worked two shifts in twenty-four hours – 'doing his bit' for the war effort. 'What had his country ever done for him?' Wales, far from being a safe back-water, turned out to be a hotbed of fomenting socialism. Nina went to hear Aneurin Bevan speak, her teachers encouraged a burgeoning awareness of social injustice, and she developed 'a political allegiance that has informed my life'.

The melting-pot theory of war had an element of truth. WAAF Flo Mahony felt that the war had shifted her up the social scale. 'I think we've gone up a class. My family were certainly working-class, but I don't think I am now. I look on myself as middle-class.' Count-less recollections of joining the services tell of married and single, conscript and volunteer, bank clerk, shop assistant, chambermaid, schoolgirl, business girl, actress and debutante being thrown in together, emerging indistinguishable from each other in a democracy of coders, telegraphists, armourers and plotters, drivers, orderlies, gunnery and signals officers, and kine-theodolite operators.

But a closer reading of such accounts unearths as many instances of elitism and snobbery, charmed circles and special treatment, rank-pulling and system-working. Though not of their number, Mavis Lever was well aware that Bletchley Park was full of manicured deb-utantes whose daddies had pulled strings for them – 'No doubt about it, it was a good berth compared to working in a munitions factory.' Patience Chadwyck-Healey couldn't bear the way some of the grander girls got preferential treatment through their high-up connections: 'I became quite communistic in the end.' And accord-ing to Joan Wyndham, who had been called up to the WAAFs in 1941, officer rank could only be conferred if you were a bona fide lady: 'They look out for dirty nails, holes in stockings and try to find out if your mother was a char, and ask you trick questions to see if you say "toilet" or "pardon".' 'Toffs' were all too easy to spot. Ex-debutante Wren Fanny Gore Brown suffered from the coarse language in her 'Wrenery' at Dover, and the rough girls there stole her make-up. 'I was fair game because I talked different, didn't I?' And, as we have seen, middle-class Doffy Brewer's life was made a misery by the taunts of her working-class colleagues.

The fact was that uniform couldn't mask the all-too-obvious signs of caste, which every girl in the land knew how to spot. When Bar-bara Pym joined the Wrens she barely needed to glance at her fifty-odd fellow-trainees gathered at the training depot in order to conclude: 'I don't think there are really any of our kind of people, though there are one or two pleasant ones.' Though the Second World War exposed the classes to each other in an unprecedented way, it would take more than that to dislodge centuries of assumed superiority.

Tribal loyalties, tribal allegiances still held sway in the romantic arena too. A debutante in a munitions factory might experiment with egalitarianism by dating her proletarian work-mates, but the bottom line was that they smelled: 'I was used to dear darling upright people, straight from Eton into the Grenadiers.' Diana Barnato, who flew for the Air Transport Auxiliary, chose only to go out with fighter pilots and Guards officers – 'you didn't look at other regiments'. One well-educated Wren telegraphist was broad-minded enough to make friendships with the 'lower deck' and became deeply involved with a sailor. But she felt compelled to part with him on the grounds that he would never be able to provide for her or their children.

For women, the challenge would be to determine where their value lay in the new world which lay ahead. If a housemaid could work on a blood transfusion service, and a general's daughter could scrub out a latrine, what did that mean for their respective future identities? Would the housemaid be content to return to mopping floors or would she feel empowered to seek more fulfilling activities? Would the general's daughter recognise that her money and rank did not absolve her from menial tasks, and might she perhaps develop some fellow-feeling for the housemaid? The melting-pot would ignite change, but the revolution was still a long way off.

★

The story of Christian Oldham's life in the Wrens in 1942 unrolled against a backdrop of lamentable war news. The RAF suffered humiliating losses when two German battle cruisers based at Brest evaded Channel defences and broke through to the North Sea. In February disaster overtook Singapore with Britain's worst defeat of the Second World War. Eighty thousand troops were taken prisoner by the Japanese and endured the remainder of the war in deplorable misery, many of them tortured and starved. The Japanese marched on and took Rangoon. The war in the Atlantic continued to take a serious toll, while in the so-called 'Baedeker' raids the Luftwaffe blitzed some of Britain's most beautiful cities: Exeter, Canterbury, Norwich, Bath, York.

No publicity attended a secret meeting held 20 miles from Berlin in a sombre lakeside mansion next to the Wannsee. Here, in January 1942, fifteen representatives of the Nazi military and government sat around a conference table and hammered out the details of what could be done with many millions of assimilated and Eastern European Jews now under German control: the fateful 'Final Solution'.

At this time Christian Oldham, convent-educated, pretty and privileged, was starting out on an Officers' Training Course in a spirit of breezy optimism. Christian had no career ambitions. 'I had no idea what I thought I would do. At eighteen I was really useless and irresponsible and idiotic.' But she had joined the Wrens full of colourful aspirations. The lovely tricorne hat and couture uniform were foremost among these, closely followed by the vague notion that, having freed a sailor to join the fleet, she would

somehow find herself surrounded by clean-cut naval officers looking for romance.

Christian served her apprenticeship with a year's clerical work,
followed by another year running a degaussing* range at Tilbury.
The Officers' Training Course, based at Greenwich Palace, required
her to learn 'not only how to become an Officer but hopefully a
"lady" too.' Here the trainees were solemnly instructed about the
history, dignity and traditions of the Royal Navy, while attending
lectures on naval vocabulary, navigation, ciphering and plotting.
Wrens did not go to sea, nor were they offered the sailors' rum ration;
however they dined in the vast and lofty Painted Hall, and they were
encouraged to sing sea-shanties to get in the mood. At dinner the
napkins were of linen, the coffee was hot, and they were waited on
by faithful Wren stewards, whose job it was to serve, lay tables, valet
and scrub floors for the officers – no worries here about telling ladies
apart from the lower orders. In due course Christian qualified as a
plotting officer and was ordered to report to Plymouth. At last she
had her tricorne hat, and with it perched jauntily on her curls 'it was
headfirst into the unknown, and fingers crossed'.

At Plymouth, Christian was immediately given important duties.
She was placed in charge of one of four watches responsible for
receiving information from the operators at coastal radar stations,
who regularly reported the position of any shipping traffic that
appeared on their screens. Working shifts of fifteen hours in the
Operations Room, Christian learned fast, as she and her four Wren
ratings then plotted the movements in real time on to a map, so that
it could be seen and assessed at any given moment by the officer of
the day, by captains and visiting admirals. At the age of twenty-two
she now had the huge responsibility of recreating a moving panorama of the entire sea war as it unfolded in the North Atlantic, and
there was profound satisfaction in the realisation that she was up to it.
'I loved this job of keeping the picture bang up to date.' After two
days of this they had forty-eight hours off.

---

* Degaussing is work carried out to protect ships from magnetic mines, by neutral-
ising their magnetic fields. This is done by encircling the hull of the ship with a
conductor carrying electric currents. 'Luckily I was not expected to do anything
technical, but I would have to control all the processes of instrumentation for the
ships on the range.'

Constant contact with Naval and Coastal Command extended into the girls' off-duty time, and Plymouth life for the Wrens encompassed a round of parties, often on board ship. Glamorous officers now became a reality. Christian – as befitted an admiral's daughter – socialised with the *crème de la crème* of the naval hierarchy. The naval elite were the submarine crews, and the thought that many of her dancing partners were heroes who came from that 'unique and brave breed of man' brought a glow to her cheeks. Often, she and her friends would be asked to a party on a submarine. They had drinks on board in evening dress – 'space was at a premium and its tiny ward room was very cosy' – before repairing to the Moreland Links Hotel, 'where we danced the night away'. Love blossomed with Captain Lennox Napier, one of the more glamorous submariners, who already had a distinguished war record and had been decorated for his exploits minelaying and attacking German transports in the Mediterranean. But Lennox wouldn't commit. 'He would never have got engaged till after the war. He was a frightfully serious and successful sailor – sinking everything in the Med. An engagement would have been distracting for him – impossible to cope with.' They corresponded, and Christian tried to put marriage prospects with him out of her mind.

Towards the end of 1942 Christian was transferred to Belfast. Here the living was easy. All kinds of unobtainable goodies – or 'rabbits' as they were known – reached them from over the border. Off-duty, they took the train to neutral Dublin, ate themselves silly on steak and cream, and blew their pay packets on clothes and Christmas presents, which then had to be ingeniously smuggled back to Belfast. The work was similar. From her Operations Room in Belfast Castle she accurately tracked the merchant ships as they came up the Irish Sea from Liverpool and Glasgow, chivvied out to sea by their escort of corvettes like so many sheep herded by a collie dog. Early in 1943 the Battle of the Atlantic was reaching its low point. Shipping was protected by the RAF on one side of the ocean, and by the Royal Canadian Air Force on the other, but there was little that could be done to guard against the relentless U-boat wolf-packs lying in wait in the 'Black Hole' in between. The Wrens in Belfast Castle learned to dread the signal which alerted them to a U-boat sighting or attack.

In April 1943 the fleet destroyer HMS *Oribi* arrived in Belfast. The ship had suffered storm damage, and the crew – including Lieutenant John Lamb, its dashing first lieutenant – would be grounded for a fortnight while it was patched up at Harland & Wolfe's shipyard. No sooner had the *Oribi* docked than an invitation arrived at the Castle for a contingent of Wrens to gather in the ward room 'just as soon as the sun was over the yardarm'. Christian volunteered to join the party.

Well, John Lamb and I went out every night for ten days, and then we got engaged. One did everything very quickly – otherwise they'd simply be gone! There was a sort of stampede, a feeling that getting married was the only answer! We all got married in our twenties, and if you didn't you were on the shelf. As for Lennox, well, out of sight is out of mind I suppose . . . I was really rather hopeless.

I never really thought about a career as such. In any case, it didn't occur to me that anything one did during the war would have the slightest use after the war. Really, you felt safer if you'd snatched a man. Then at least you felt 'I've got some sort of future'.

Congratulations were offered to the engaged pair, and celebrations ensued. Got up in dinner jackets and evening dress, the Officers and Wrens quaffed copious cocktails, followed by steak and kidney pudding and plum duff, washed down with Dry Martinis and ending with port. Loyal toasts were drunk, before the company, extremely well-watered by now, launched into 'high jinks': wardroom polo, with a leftover potato as the ball; torpedoes – in which a midshipman was 'fired' tummy-down the length of the polished table at the target, which was the settee beyond; and obstacle races – making a circuit of the room on top of the furniture, without touching the deck. And more drinks all round.

War, and the Wrens, gave Christian Oldham what she sought, and what her upbringing had entitled her to: fun, posh clothes, servants, romance and silly sports; but they also expanded her capacities, tested her potential to its limits. Proficient, responsible and professional though she now was, Christian had grown up with a set of assumptions about woman's place in the world, assumptions which her wartime experiences were doing little to dislodge. Convinced that Lennox Napier wouldn't commit to an engagement, and that her spell with the Wrens could have no practical application in a peacetime future, she seized on the best offer of marriage that came her way. Christian wasn't one to, as it were, rock the boat. She continued to play a part in the jigsaw puzzle of war; but her talent for organisation, her brains and experience were stretched at that time in a way they never would be again.

Women Must Weep

The Wrens may have been the most fashionable of the women's services, but if you were looking for love nothing approached the WAAFs for ardent desires and heightened passions. Eighteen-year-old Pip Beck joined up with stars in her eyes, her patriotic motives mingling with romantic daydreams of the dashing aircrew she was likely to meet in the course of her new work. In August 1941 Pip left her home, her hairdressing job and her ARP duties in Buckingham behind, and with them her teenage dalliances. Norman, her sweet, serious Territorial boyfriend, had gone to India; he had asked her not to wait. Fancy-free, Pip arrived to take up her duties as a trainee Radio/Telephone Operator at RAF Waddington in Lincolnshire, the bomber base of 44 (Rhodesia) Squadron, so called after the large number of Rhodesian volunteers serving with it. As the van drew up the mere sight of a group of young sergeants set her pulse racing:

I knew from the brevets they wore that these were aircrew – the fabulous beings that I admired and hero-worshipped.

For a moment my heart beat a little faster and my imagination took wings – they were young gods and were all about me, though I was earthbound!

Tired after the long journey from her recruit base, Pip headed for the 'Waafery' hut and assembled her bed: like all service bedding it was made up of a stack of thin 'biscuits' that passed for a mattress, in sections, one on top of the other. Settling in, she was greeted by one of her fellow WAAFs: 'Hello – you just arrived? I've been here for a fortnight. I'm a parachute packer – what are you?' Their exchange was drowned out by a roar of engines. 'Ops tonight,' explained the parachute packer. 'This is a bomber station you know. You'll have a good time here. You can have a different boyfriend every night if you want to – it's wizzo!'

Pip's job as an R/T operator was to work two shifts totalling twelve hours each day in the watch office, with every third day off. Seated in front of a microphone and with earphones clamped to her head, she would be talking down the crews as they returned from raids. She learned to transmit and to log her R/T communications, to signal Morse code and to memorise the accepted ciphers: H-Harry, W-William, 'Niner' for nine to distinguish it from five, and so on. Soon the cramped watch office became her world and, though respect from aircrew could be grudging, the 'few' to whom our nation owed so much recognised that they themselves owed a debt to young women like Pip whose efforts kept them airborne. 'It was agreed that we applied ourselves to our job, and were really not too bad – it was even admitted that we brightened the place up – and of course, we made tea.'

Early in her time at Waddington, Pip got the chance – all too rare for girls working on the ground – to 'gain experience of their job from the air'. Today everyone flies, and it may be hard to imagine the intensity of excitement that Pip felt at her first time in an aircraft. Having signed the 'Blood Book' (exempting the RAF from any responsibility for killing her if the flight crashed), she was equipped with a parachute and climbed on board the Oxford with the squadron leader and his pupil-pilot. A short taxi down the runway, and they were aloft. Pip was entranced as the plane rose and the familiar airbase diminished into its surrounding fields, while the land below began to resemble a map. Up and up they flew through layers of clouds, until they entered the bright enchanted world of sunshine that lay above the cumulus. Nothing could ever compare with such heady excitement, and as Pip drank in the impressions she felt drugged with their sublimity. Before they descended, however, the squadron leader motioned Pip to change places with his pupil and put on the helmet. '"Now – you are going to fly the aircraft!" I was told.' Palpitating, she took the stick and, fearfully, effortfully, levelled out their descent as he instructed. Then, using the rudder-bar, she tried a banking manoeuvre, before once more straightening up. '"Ask permission to land."' Well, that she knew how to do. The squadron leader took over again, and soon they were approaching the runway.

Afterwards, when the euphoria had died down, she tried to weigh up her sensations. Normally terrified of heights, she was astonished to find herself unafraid. Above all, she reflected, that short hour in the air had given her a feeling of total liberty – 'the extraordinary sensation of being free of earth – of exploring this new dimension, the sky – and the immense freedom of space, sunlight, cloud . . . sixty minutes of wonders'.

Pip met airgunner Ron Atkinson at a dance in the sergeants' mess. Ron was twenty-one, tall, grey-eyed with dark hair and a youthful moustache. His teasing forthrightness disarmed her, as he explained that he had had a drink too many, but would call a halt if she agreed to dance with him. The band was beating as they whirled on to the thronging floor:

We fell in love – what else would we do?

Soon after Ron asked her to marry him. But Pip wasn't yet twenty; it was too soon to look to the future. She knew, too, how short the life expectancy was for aircrews. Overall in Bomber Command, 44 was third-highest in the roll call for casualties. She turned Ron down, and they quarrelled. Three days later she ran into him on her way to her shift. She recognised immediately from his battle-kit and the lucky charm dangling from his breast pocket that he was 'on' tonight. 'Phyl – I'm so glad to have seen you . . . Phone me tomorrow afternoon in the Mess – I must talk to you . . . Listen out for me tonight, won't you?' And he was off for briefing – the target was Le Havre.

Pip's shift took her right through till dawn. It was a long night. The hours dragged as Pip waited and watched. In breaks, she eased her cramped limbs on the flat roof adjoining the watch office. Nothing was visible as she stared into the starless sky across the blacked-out expanse of Lincolnshire farmland. Somewhere in that dark and limitless vault Ron's aircraft – 'H-Harry' – was still flying. 'Of course it was.' The mission was scheduled to return at 6 a.m. Towards dawn WAAFs and ground crew started to gather on the landing strip and on the control tower roof, watching out for the returning aircraft. One after another contact was made. Pip was logging, fighting her anxiety:

No H-Harry yet. I began to get a cold, shrinking feeling in the pit of my stomach . . .

By 8 a.m. they were all safely down – all except for H-Harry. Pip went off duty. As the new operators came on she hung back, willing his plane to appear, a spot in the white morning sky. But nothing. The tears came, and she ran for her billet. By afternoon all hope was gone.

Losing Ron at the age of eighteen was Pip's first experience of an air fatality. There would be many more. Though, as she herself said, 'one recovers quickly' at that age, she soon learned to live with sorrow. Working on a bomber base meant being in almost daily contact with the tragedy of young lives cut short. Pip Beck and her WAAF friends were giving their all professionally, but emotionally the constant presence of death drew on all their powers of female sympathy. 'Men must work and women must weep' ran the old song; but here at Waddington and at many other air bases, hospitals and service stations of all kinds across the country, women were working with barely time to wipe away the tears. And yet these girls' identification with everything healing, caring and nurturing could not be so lightly discarded. Every day they were subjected to the men's suffering. It plucked at their heart strings. One morning Pip observed a couple of aircrew limping back to their billet. One had his arm in a sling, another had his foot so heavily bandaged he could not walk without support. Indignant that they had not been provided with transport, she and her friend Rita impulsively sought out the men and offered to do what they could – 'perhaps we could help by doing the odd bit of ironing, mending or washing for them some time? . . . Removing the creases from a shirt seemed little enough to do after what I'd seen that morning.' Pip and Rita mothered their new friends Terry and Dick for a few weeks, until one morning the lads didn't come back.

In December the squadron's wing commander was shot down. 'We were all shocked by the news.' Not long after that Pip was on duty in control one night when a 'Darky' call came across the R/T. The codeword 'Darky' meant that an aircraft was lost or urgently needed help. Pip did her best to talk the Wimpy down, while the crash crew were put on immediate alert. As the plane wheeled around out of control the crew was able to communicate that one engine was unserviceable. Pip spoke to them again. This time the voice that replied was high-pitched and frantic. Seconds later the Wimpy appeared low over the airfield and crashed with a spurt of flame beyond the runway.

I felt shaken and sick. It had all happened in moments, and in that short space five young men had died in the smoking pyre of their aircraft; mine had been the last voice they had heard – would ever hear. I felt related to them in a strange hollow intimacy.

In April '42 six bombers from 44 Squadron took part in a daylight op over a diesel-engine factory at Augsburg. Pip knew all the pilots who took part in this fateful raid, but that day she was not on duty, so it was not till the following day that she heard of the dreadful toll it had taken. The entire camp was in shock: only one had returned safely:

Thirty-five men missing – thirty-five empty bunks, thirty-five empty places at table . . . Many of us wondered if it was worth it.*

Pip was far from being the only WAAF to lose her true love. One of the prettiest was eighteen-year-old Jean. Her boyfriend, Peter, was among the Rhodesian aircrew members. Jean had the sweetest singing voice too, and the other WAAFs would gather round the fire in the evenings as she crooned that year's hit love song, 'Not a Cloud in the Sky':

> I looked in your eyes
> And then at the skies
> Darling you know what I saw:
> Not a cloud in the sky,
> Not an ache in my heart,
> Not a cloud in the sky,
> For I knew you were mine
> Right from the start . . .

That spring Jean and Peter got married. Less than two months later he went on an op to Dusseldorf and didn't come back. After that, though nobody saw her cry, Jean's beautiful dark eyes took on the look of someone stunned. And she never sang again.

But Pip was in love once more. The Rhodesians at Waddington were

---

* Incredibly, one of the pilots had managed to crash-land and he and his crew survived. All were taken prisoner.

defiantly un-English, tough, bronzed and sexy, with informal manners and an air of having lived under wider horizons. Cecil was one of them, awaiting aircrew training. He had known Ron and comforted Pip after she lost him. At the next dance he singled her out, producing from somewhere a glass of champagne and sweeping her on to the floor amid a swirl of paper streamers and popping balloons. From then on, life became full of wonder. For her birthday he bought her a gold and turquoise ring, and the understanding grew between them that after the war they would be married. But Cecil's training included being posted on lengthy courses; when he was away, her world lost its lustre, and the weeks dragged by. She lived for the times they could spend together. Their snatched dates glowed in the memory: dreamlike evenings in the dark of a cinema or the cosy anonymity of a Lyons Corner House, precious hours rescued from an imploding world.

With Cecil away, Pip joined a choir formed by WAAFs and ground crew. With duties and choral rehearsals she was kept busy. A concert was arranged at the camp. Pip sang a solo of 'The Eriskay Love Lilt':

> When I'm lonely, dear white heart
> Black the night and wild the sea
> By love's light, my foot finds
> The old pathway to thee.

If only Cecil could have been there to hear her pour her love into the words. And then a letter arrived from him – he was about to go on leave. Overjoyed, Pip confided her excitement to Pattie, her motherly room-mate. Pattie listened in silence, before speaking:

'Pip – I can't stand it any longer, seeing you throw yourself away on him – I'm sorry to be the one to tell you, but you *have* to know – he is married.'

I stared dumbly at Pattie. 'It's not true,' I said. How could it be? 'It is,' she answered, more gently. 'My friend Marjorie works in Accounts, and she told me some time ago. He does have a wife . . . Oh Pip, I am sorry.'

How had he managed to deceive her? She wrote to him. There was no reply. Finally he arrived; one look told her it was true. 'I didn't want to lose you,' he said. He wouldn't take back his turquoise ring; she returned it to its box and put it away. 'The dream was over.'

Pip expected to feel heartbroken. It came as a surprise to experience, almost reluctantly, a different sensation – an unmistakable sense of freedom. 'How could it all disappear like morning mist on the airfield? Well, it had.'

And the death toll continued. One after another, friends, men she danced with, men she knew and other men she hardly knew at all set out and didn't come back. She and her friends went on with their work, but the sadness built up, and one day it tipped over. It was at evening choir practice, when Joan – one of the more elegant and composed among the WAAFs – suddenly fled from the room crying. Pip's best friend, Sally, ran out to comfort her, and soon they returned. But then it was her turn to collapse: 'tears began to trickle from Sally's face. She ran out.' Pip followed her, and after a few minutes with Sally weeping uncontrollably on her shoulder, they went back to the rehearsal. But before long Pip herself broke down:

A piercing sense of sadness flooded through me, causing my voice to break and my eyes to fill. Oh, God, what was the *matter* with us all! I too made for the corridor, where I sobbed my heart out.

It was an isolated collapse. Very soon after Pip's young spirits revived, as a new and heady relationship got under way with Mike, the Australian flying control officer – 'I was deeply attracted to him.'

For girls like Joan, Sally and Pip, war work in the WAAFs had an intoxicating, almost addictive quality. They were very young, very vulnerable; pitched out of their parental nests and left to fly on their own, they quickly discovered the euphoria of being airborne – literally, in Pip's case. Wings – whether throbbing skywards on course for Berlin or Dusseldorf or jauntily affixed above the left breast pocket of a tanned and weather-beaten pilot – had the power to seduce and mesmerise. And when they fell in love ('what else could we do?') that world above the clouds was their world too. Emotionally, the WAAFs shared the turbulence and the dives; they skimmed the rooftops and they crash-landed. But the freedom, too, was theirs – for a space.

Don't Die for Me

Some women, like Jean McFadyen, barely asked themselves what their war work was for. But most women in the forces accepted that their efforts were helping men to win the war by killing and hurting Britain's aggressors in every way possible. Conscription, however, forced people to examine their attitudes. And some women came to the conclusion that killing and hurting was antithetical to their most deeply held beliefs.

Frances Partridge's small corner of Wiltshire stayed true to the pacifist cause. From 1939 to 1945 Ham Spray was like a little fortress occupied by dissenters reading the *New Statesman*. In fact, Frances, at forty-one, was not at risk from conscription, and her five-year-old son was one of 9 million children under fourteen who the government considered needed their mothers. Nevertheless, her stance against the war was an articulate and representative one. State-endorsed murder filled her with horror, fear and disgust. She and Ralph firmly believed that wars never lead to peace, but only to the next war, and that the only lesson to be learned from winning one was that superior force brings victory. Despite her servant Joan's departure for the aircraft factory, Frances's mind was constantly occupied with the challenge to her own intellectual position:

As I clean basins, sweep stairs and dust tables, I often find my thoughts congealing into pacifist configurations, and wondering how so many intelligent people fail to accept the supporting arguments.

She argued and agonised about the morality of her convictions – it was wrong and horrible, she conceded, to require other women's sons to be killed in order to achieve a desirable life for oneself – but despite such qualms they were convictions that, throughout her long life, she never abandoned.

Sheila Hails was born in 1915 and has lived through almost a century of war. Another unrepentant pacifist, she now finds herself forced to accept that she has signed up to a lost cause. 'I'm still a pacifist, in my childish way, in fact I think I must almost have been born a pacifist, but pacifism never did win, never has won, never will win really.' Sheila, buoyed up by her father's support, was an eager intellectual who had come down from the north-east to take up a place at Newnham College, Cambridge. It opened up a whole new life to her – 'My world just exploded.' In 1940 she married her doctor boyfriend Philip Hugh-Jones and espoused pacifism with fervour:

I cannot believe that grown men should be trained to *kill* one another, and then be sent out to do it. And I'm very sceptical about the way we go on about our 'heroic' young men who go out to die for their country. I think – well, they are professional soldiers, they are trained to be brutal. They could have chosen to leave, but they didn't. So personally, I reserve judgement about our 'gallant heroes'.

I just find it quite unbelievable that governments think anything can be solved by war. There has *got* to be another way. But I've never been able to find out what that other way is.

Around her in 1941 and '42, other young women were 'enlisting like mad':

I thought at the time: I'm not going to do anything about it, so I didn't register, and I thought – when they get to me I'll make my stand, go to prison if need be! But by the time they tracked me down I was heavily pregnant.

Not all female conscientious objectors got off so lightly. Two hundred and fifty-seven such women were imprisoned during the Second World War. The first of these was a parlour maid from Newcastle-on-Tyne named Constance Bolam. As an 'absolutionist', she refused to undertake any kind of work that might release someone for active service. Her submission was treated with extraordinary contempt: 'You must recognise that we on the Tribunal have some common-sense, and you have none,' she was told. 'It is no good talking rubbish to us like that.' She was sentenced by the Newcastle magistrates to a month in Durham jail. The same chairman was quite public in his view that the women COs were bogus, that they were no better than deserters and had far less credibility than their male equivalents. There was abuse and scepticism about their claims. One woman was told she was a humbug. Another young woman – a hairdresser – must have doubted the seriousness of the cross-examining panel. Questioning her about her objection to taking life in any form, the panel pressed her: 'Cannot you take insect life?' 'No,' she replied. 'And you a hairdresser!' was the startling response.

Other women were mercilessly harried by the authorities. Alice Stubbings, a Staffordshire woman, was directed to work as a hospital cleaner but objected on grounds of conscience. The police pursued her, imposing fines which, when they were not paid, were commuted to three months in prison. A nineteen-year-old Quaker, Mary Cockroft, made a conscientious objection to working in industry as it would aid the killing. She was fined £10 and directed to do war work. When she refused to go, the fine was increased to £20, plus a two-month prison sentence.

It could reasonably be argued that, as pacifists, women are in no way distinct from men; certainly far more men were registered as COs, so it might appear that their consciences were more engaged than those of the women. But men had a great deal more to fear from active participation in the war, as well as a great deal more to object to. Thus, in a sense, the statement that a woman makes when she embraces pacifism is a stronger one than that of a man. The man who rejects war rejects the taking of human life, because he is personally implicated: in war he is expected to kill. But a woman has been exempted from the killing from the outset; society already regards her as fundamentally 'pacific'. So her rejection of war may well be something more profound, in that she challenges the entire framework of violence constructed by men around her. Her conscientious objection goes beyond the objection to taking life and enters a realm of dissension from all violence and hostility perpetrated on her behalf. Her very passivity and impotence against the killing rouses her to declare: 'Don't fight for me. Don't die for me. Don't treat me as a victim.'

Although only 1,072 women had appeared before tribunals by the end of the war, that figure bore little relation to the actual numbers of women COs. The Tribunals only saw women who had refused to work in a civil capacity; they didn't see the large numbers of others who objected to conscription in the forces but reluctantly caved in and agreed to work on the land, industry or civil defence. As with the Greenham Common Women's Peace Camp, started forty years later by thirty-six protesters and a few children, radicals prepared to stand up and be counted are always less numerous than inarticulate sympathisers. It took boldness to make a stand, and on the whole women were not used to behaving defiantly in public; the artist Mary Fedden felt herself to be a coward for not sticking her neck out. 'If I'd had the courage I think I'd have been a conscientious objector. But I was rather young . . . I went to court for several of my men friends and spoke up for them as conscientious objectors.'

Greenham Common's slogan was 'Not In Our Name' – again, a

direct challenge to the idea that men go off to fight on behalf of the women and children they leave behind, who owe them gratitude. Sheila Hails would certainly have agreed with the debunking of the gallant hero myth, just as Frances Partridge saw no reason to acquiesce with militarism just because it was the official line.

Frances's deeply held posture towards the war — and that of the many who held her views — still begs many questions. Her diary does not offer an alternative view of how the Nazis could be held at bay, nations protected, nor how militaristic governments could otherwise be discouraged than through armed resistance.

★

By 1943 the war had begun to seem interminable. From the time the Americans entered the war Churchill was never in doubt of an Allied victory. The Germans' disastrous campaign in Russia and the Allies' success at El Alamein and in East Africa increased this confidence; nevertheless the longed-for Second Front, designed to attack Hitler's Atlantic Wall on the north coast of France, still seemed impossibly distant. Day by day, it was still hard to endure the prolonged absence and heartache occasioned by the war. 'Cliff seems so far away,' wrote Nella Last in March, 'sometimes a sadness beyond tears wraps me round.' 'Three years today since Alan was made a prisoner of war — but it's no use moaning,' wrote Mrs Milburn sadly on 28 May.

Anne Popham's lover Graham had, despite her misgivings, joined the RAF as a trainee pilot. They corresponded with eager frequency, with Anne's letters full of heartening news and gossip about her London friends and her new day job on the picture desk at the Ministry of Information. At this time she dared to hope that, once his divorce came through, she and Graham might make a life together. In her fantasies they were gardener and housekeeper to the owners of some wealthy estate. 'I just wanted us to live together, somewhere.' Then in June 1942 the letters from Graham dried up. Concerns about their future as a couple had been replaced, for Anne, by concern for his safety. The ensuing months passed in a state of miserable uncertainty as to his whereabouts; all she knew was that he had been posted abroad for training — but where? Her plight, in those days before easy international communications, was all too common. Across the nation, women were living for letters:

22nd July

I am sitting by the gas fire . . . after the inevitable disappointment of homecoming. As I come in the gate I try to prevent myself thinking of the possibility of there being a letter, but I can never suppress a glimmer of excitement and hope which always turns to dullness as I open the door. But it can't be long now.

Please keep safe my sweetheart and remember you are the dearest thing in my world – I love you very much.

August 26th

Darling I still haven't had a word from you . . .

September 17th

I am all at sea – at this rate I don't know whether I should send you my love for your birthday or wish you a happy Christmas . . . I think of you and love you more and more.

In late September Anne finally got the news that Graham was safe in South Africa at an air school in the Cape. Early in '43 he was back in England. Graham's RAF pay now enabled him to employ a solicitor to start divorce proceedings with his estranged wife, naming Anne as co-respondent. All would soon be in place for them to marry. Over the next six months the letters track Anne's fluctuating hopes as he was posted from Yorkshire, to north Wales, to Nottinghamshire.

22nd April

Darling I suppose some sort of move is due again in your life. I only hope it will be southwards this time.

17th May

Is there any chance of you getting off . . .? Please let me know.

16th July

I think I will drop into my lonely bed now . . . I will get Saturday & Monday off & could add another day of my own & go up on Thursday night . . . Good night my dearest darling.

And then the letters stopped.

On the morning of 10 August she was in her office when the Ministry doorman called her and said, 'Somebody wants to see you.' It was Ruth, her flatmate, and she had a telegram. Graham's Wellington bomber had crash-landed at RAF Ossington in Nottinghamshire, killing the entire crew.

More than sixty-five years after that dreadful day, Anne tried to recapture what it felt like to be twenty-seven and to lose the dearest thing in her world:

It's very odd what one remembers and doesn't remember. I've blotted out the misery of it. It was too painful. I thought that's the end of everything I hoped for, the end of the world really. I remember thinking, I'm a widow . . .

But you had to face it I suppose. When someone dies, you have to look after yourself. And somehow, I don't know how, I really can't tell, but one just *had* to survive.

6   The Girl That Makes the Thing-ummy Bob

The Kitchen Front

Three years in, the war machine had become dictatorial. It commandeered everything that came its way, ruling, processing, shaping people's lives. Every day the newspaper headlines updated the campaign news with the latest from Japan, RAF sorties, new naval targets in the Atlantic, fighting in Russia, in the Philippines, in Burma and in North Africa. But the inner pages allowed no let-up. Advice alternated with directives, opinions with commands. March 1942: 250,000 20–21-year-olds will be directed to the ATS . . . clothing coupons will be cut . . . fines will be imposed on paper-wasters . . . soap flakes will go further if used to wash woollies in rain-water . . . the buffet at Euston station will cease to serve rolls with butter . . . Put your pennies in war savings, sow your peas now, recycle rubber, rear rabbits for food . . .

Rationing was no longer a novelty, it was a way of life. From onions to sanitary towels, toothpaste to toilet paper, there was no escaping from the urgent need to economise. Coffee, pepper, eggs, marmalade, mixing bowls, knitting needles, hats, hairgrips, shoes, elastic and a myriad of foods and commodities dependent on petrol, scarce raw materials, imports and labour were all now in short supply and getting scarcer, as were contraceptives, ping-pong balls and alcohol. Wedding rings were becoming hard to obtain. New mums hoarded nappies and safety pins. A convocation of women's magazine editresses was assembled to put the 'tragic' case of the large women in need of elastic corsets who had written to them in despair; sadly, the rubber shortage made their case hopeless. Goods were of poor quality: needles broke and saucepans dented. Anyone lucky enough to come by a bottle of sherry cherished it and laid it by for Christmas. Bananas, toffees, oranges and chocolate were becoming a distant memory for many children. And to a very large extent the

Coping in the kitchen: literally, a battle.

burden of coping with these shortages fell on women. Everyone agreed that women needed to join the services and the wartime workforce; nevertheless, the assumption continued unquestioned that it was a woman's job to feed everyone, to look after children and to care for the home.

Getting her family clothed, her housework and shopping done and meals on the table in the time left over from other duties drew on a high level of resourcefulness and ingenuity. Of these, meals took priority.

How laborious life was. Shopping for food had become a thankless chore requiring patience and stamina. Rage stirred in the heart of the housewife as she waited in the bus queues for the vehicles that would convey her to market, for to have the pick of the stalls she must push to be first on the bus. Each carried her shopping bag on her arm, for paper bags were wasteful and had been outlawed. But in Barrow-in-Furness, where once the countrywomen had set up their stalls of new-laid eggs and home-produced honey in the market square, Nella Last now lamented the sad change; the joyous scene of old was reduced to baskets of muddy cockles and a few warped beets, for which 'grim-faced women' queued and pushed. Vere Hodgson, a brisk middle-aged spinster living in Notting Hill Gate, recorded her pursuit of an onion: 'such a struggle'. When she finally got hold of one it was 'a victory indeed!' A great deal of agonising was expended on the question of how to get the best out of your ration book. Did you spread your custom round several shops to improve your chances of obtaining the sought-after lemons or eggs that you craved, or did you patronise one shopkeeper in the hope that he would put you first in line for two ounces of coffee or a quarter of sultanas when they came in?

Choice, where it existed, became ever more limited. Before the war you could have taken your pick from 350 varieties of biscuit, from Garibaldis to chocolate wafers. This had come down to twenty, most of them plain Maries. And in spring 1942 the white loaf disappeared.

Lord Woolton, the Minister of Food, headed an immensely successful propaganda campaign to persuade the population to eat within their means. With the emphasis on nutrition, the nation's health improved. The challenge now was not to combat hunger – there was generally enough food, of a kind that caused one WAAF to put on two stone during the course of the war – but to make oatmeal, parsnips, barley, spam, potatoes, potatoes and more potatoes taste appetising without the delicious but scarce ingredients required to ginger them up. Clever cooks eked them out with unrationed curry powder, Oxo, Daddies sauce or salad cream. Six ounces of salt cod mashed up with potatoes and Worcester sauce could make a nice fish paste – 'a nutritious picnic treat' according to one food writer. Substitution was the cook's key strategy: parsnips for bananas, milk and margarine for cream, dried egg for everything. Unrationed offal was put to good use. *Woman's Own* gave recipes for Brain Cakes and Brain Soufflé; the *Daily Express Wartime Cookery Book* offered Sheep's Head with Caper Sauce. But if you weren't adventurous enough for such exotica, food could seem unremittingly starchy and beige.

Nella Last was proud of her thrift. 'I cut my quarter of beef up small, and lightly fried it with a cut-up leek, added a carrot and a slice of turnip, diced, and simmered it all very slowly for two hours. Then I added sliced potatoes and seasoning, and cooked till all the liquid was absorbed. I had soaked dried peas in the pantry, so I added them with the potatoes; and if look and smell are anything to go by, it's a very good lunch,' she recorded in her diary in March 1942. But she felt she had to conceal her cheese-paring ways from her husband. Wars might rage and the roof might fall in, but Will Last's meals had to be on the table three times a day. With no milk to be had and sugar scarce, she thickened a water custard with corn-flour and sweetened it with honey. 'When I served the pudding, I said carelessly, "Oh, I've made clear honey sauce for a change." I know that one, he doesn't like economy dishes – if he realises they *are* economy dodges!'

Today many working women rely on ready meals to reduce the burden of food preparation. But, despite their availability in the 1940s, the Advice Division of the Ministry of Food discouraged the use of packets and tins, exhorting the housewife to draw on willpower and make stern resolutions, such as:

I shall use canned foods as little as possible, keeping them as an emergency supply.

I shall not grumble when the butcher does not have the particular joint I want; I shall take the next best thing and be thankful to get it.

The part played by the housewife in reducing consumption was fully recognised by the government, which expended much energy in persuading her to be frugal. Every effort was made to inject some fun into our stodgy and increasingly vegetable-based diet; jolly 'Dr Carrot' and hearty 'Potato Pete' appeared in recipe books and adver-tisements. 'Try cooking cabbage this way,' begged the literature, while competitions were mounted for the best wartime cake recipe – without sugar. Appeals and propaganda were effective (though was anyone fooled by recipes for 'mock apricot flan' made from carrots?), but the best persuaders were women themselves.

In 1942 the home economist Marguerite Eave married RAF gunnery officer Bob Patten. Due for call-up herself, Marguerite Patten resisted the pressure to volunteer for the WAAFs; in her pocket she had a letter from the Ministry of Food requesting her to assist their operation at a Food Advice Centre in the Cambridge area, a job which played to her extraordinary strengths both as cook and communicator. All big cities now had such centres. As soon as the wedding was over, she joined the all-female staff of organisers, dieticians and demonstrators to promote good wartime nutrition and economy among housewives:

As far as I know there was not a single man doing that job. Men weren't trained for it.

But what was so important about the Ministry of Food Advisers was that we didn't wait for people to come to us, we went to them. I remember that first Friday evening when I reported for duty in Cambridge I was told, 'Get your stall up early in the market square, Marguerite, because you'll want a good pitch.' 'The *market*?' I thought. Well, I'd never given a demonstration in a market before and I said so. 'Well now's your chance to begin,' I was told by the organiser very briskly.

But markets were just one way of reaching them. Many rural branches used mobile caravans that opened at the front, you see? – with a counter for demonstrations . . . and we got out to welfare clinics and the outpatients' departments of hospitals and so on.

These 'outreach' demonstrations gave Marguerite Patten a special insight into the housewife's wartime predicament:

What we found out was that the worst thing for the British was having to do without meat. The one thing the women always asked was, 'How long do we have to put up with this?' As a nation in those days we *loved* our Sunday roast, with plenty of meat, but just two vegetables: potatoes and cabbage. Or carrots, or Brussels sprouts, but never both together. But in wartime we had to do a complete change around and fill the plate with a selection of vegetables.

But you know those women were much more competent as cooks than they are today, because they had learned to cook watching their mother. They weren't experts, but they knew the basics. You could talk about a white sauce, or mashed potato, or tell them to do a roast, and they automatically understood.

'We never went without food, 'cause we had good mums, didn't we?' agrees onetime WAAF Flo Mahony. A generation of women who, like Nella Last, remembered the previous war had the resourcefulness to deal with shortages and they taught their daughters to be like them. Flo was brought up by her mother not to throw anything out. 'Our mums could make a piece of meat last for about three days, which today nobody could do, and they'd know what to do with the bones after that. If you had a war today people would starve.' Eileen Rouse says that her mum was the same. 'Oh, we managed, love. My mother was a very thrifty person; she could make our two ounces go round – well, you had to. My mum always used to get a bit of fat included with the meat from her ration so she could get some dripping. It wasn't a lot, but it helped the butter out, see? And I can honestly say that I don't ever remember being hungry.'

Clocking On

Where cookery was concerned, the nation's women had a deeply entrenched fund of know-how, adaptability and – at times – low cunning to see them through. It came from listening and sharing with each other, as women do, but it also came from their grandmothers and their great-grandmothers. Many of them simply knew, without really thinking about it, what to do with a carcase, how to make custard, chop suet, render dripping, bottle damsons, pickle beetroots. They went nutting, and blackberrying. To many, economising was nothing new, it was bred in the bone, and part of their identity.

What *was* new was combining being a thrifty housewife with a job in a factory sewing uniforms, or making aircraft, or barrage balloons, or munitions, or chemicals and explosives; trying to run a home while working on the buses; keeping up with the chores while clocking on as a post office worker, welder, engineer, or shipyard worker. By 1942 there were roughly three times as many women in work as there had been in 1939.

One of these was Zelma Katin. Zelma was married, forty years old with a fourteen-year-old schoolboy son and living in Sheffield. She had been attempting for years to get a job but, charring aside, there was nothing much available for an intelligent married woman. Then the war came, and suddenly she found she was wanted. It was a pity, she reflected, that this eagerness to enlist her services had only manifested itself in a time of mass destruction and loss of life; nevertheless she was willing to help the war effort and went down to the Labour Exchange. There she was asked, as a non-mobile woman, to choose between factory work or transport:

I thought of the heat, noise, electric light and airlessness of a munition factory and then I thought of the fresh air that blows from the Yorkshire moors across a tramcar platform in my city.

And so I became a clippie – a tram conductress.

The selection process for this job was a formality. The shortage of transport workers was by now so desperate that the Department would have given the work to a one-legged old age pensioner, but Zelma had to undergo a medical and a mental arithmetic test. By now she was starting to worry about how on earth she would cope with working a full week at the same time as looking after her house and her young lad. But when she asked whether it would be possible to work part-time, she had to endure a humiliating lecture from the patronising lady supervisor, who rebuffed her request in cut-glass accents. 'The country was at war, she said, it was my duty to accept the job that was offered me, and my boy was old enough to look after himself.'

In the event, Zelma was put on the early shift, starting before 5 in the morning, which theoretically left her free to do housework, shopping, and cooking from mid-afternoon, when she came off duty. In a letter to her husband, Louis, who had been called up to the army, she described her day.

The alarm went off at 3.30 a.m. By 4 she was up, washed and combed. Her shoes were polished and her uniform buttoned. At 4.25, having breakfasted on Weetabix and strong tea and packed a flask, a jam scone and a packet of cigarettes, she left the house. Her son was asleep, and the moon was still up. She travelled to the depot and clocked on at 4.45 a.m.; by 5 she was on board her electric tram where, for the next four and a half hours, with a small break for tea at 7, she was on her feet, seeing passengers off and on and collecting fares. Zelma noticed with amusement that the starting-out time of her passengers was in inverse proportion to their social class. The early birds were the 'proletarians' – factory hands in boiler suits; these were followed by neatly attired shop assistants, clerks and professional workers; next came the middle-aged men who employed them, sober-suited and well brushed. A second wave followed the first: the rank-and-file wives and mothers bearing shopping bags, seeking bargains at Woolworth's or at the grubby market, and finally the 'ladies of leisure', their perfume wafting past her as they alighted from the tram on their way to purchase 20-guinea frocks and silk stockings from hushed and hallowed down-town emporia. At 9.30 Zelma had precisely forty-eight minutes' break: time to queue in the canteen for a starchy meal, tea and a slice of parkin, eat it, dash to the toilet for a quick wash and brush-up, before another four hours on board her tram. Back to the depot by 2.45 p.m. to count her takings – she had sold 1,051 tickets – and clock off. Which left the remainder of the day to sort out some small difficulty with her son's school at the local Education Office, collect shoe repairs, do the shopping and stagger home by 4 . . . only to wake from her armchair with a start at 6. There was tea to prepare and eat, clearing up to do, a letter to write to her husband abroad, the beds to make and the floor to sweep. At dusk she retired, but first she set the alarm for the next day's early start.

*'Sorry – no more, Bert. And if I've gone to bed you'll find your supper in
the oven.' Married women doing jobs upset the pre-war status quo –
but by 1942 the clippie was becoming a familiar sight.*

Despite the precedent of the First World War, the sight of a woman taking tickets on a tram was a novelty. Zelma Katin found that her conductress's uniform gave off mixed messages of authority and immorality. Passengers looked askance at her sharing a friendly cigarette between runs with her driver; underlying their doubtful glances was the suspicion that she was 'up to no good' with him. From transport workers to technicians, females were popping up in unfamiliar guises everywhere. Mrs Milburn marvelled at the female telephone engineers who came to install a new extension. 'They were two girls! They did the job very well, too.'

The government had its work cut out to persuade women to take factory jobs. Propaganda and concerted recruitment campaigns such as the War Work Weeks in 1941 worked up to a point, but until conscription too many women didn't contemplate enrolling because they felt their jobs as housewives were full-time. The balancing act was an onerous one, as the writer Amabel Williams-Ellis discovered when she took on the task of researching their lives. She interviewed a Mrs Apperley, who was working eight-hour shifts and had 'nine at home to do for'; 'I get the worst of the house done before I come to work', but organising her weekly wash gave her headaches. This lady was coping, but Mass Observation reported on another who was quite incapable of making any dent in the mountains of ironing, unwashed dishes and children's mess that awaited her when she rushed home from her factory at lunchtime. Others collapsed under the pressure of the 'night-shift nightmare', sleep being sacrificed to work, childcare and keeping on top of the housework. Absenteeism often resulted from cases like this. Shopping, and the necessity of queuing for goods, also conflicted with work hours. Retailers proved inflexible; you could shop at lunchtime and skip lunch, break your journey home and gamble on the chance of getting what you needed at the end of the day, or join the endless lines of Saturday shoppers. If your ration books were registered at shops near your home, but you worked across town, what did you do? For others, it was child-care that created difficulties. Traditionally, grannies, aunties and neighbours had stepped in and taken up the burden of looking after the little ones, but now they themselves were often at work too. With a shortfall in nursery provision, it was often left to competent older daughters to take care of them. For example, Williams-Ellis reported the case of twelve-year-old Jeanie, who ran the home and looked after her younger siblings single-handed while all the grown women were at the factory.

'I don't see what business it is of yours if I want to look after my own child in my own way.' Despite expanding nursery provision, childcare still presented problems for working mothers.

Despite angry demonstrations by pram-pushing women staging 'Baby Riots' and demanding nursery provision, little sympathy was shown for these problems. As Penny Summerfield has convincingly argued,* schemes to help with childcare, shopping and meals were mostly a fudge: a papering-over of the wartime cracks. Officials, while urging women to adapt to the nation's needs by joining the workplace, seemed incapable of updating their own vision of the nation's mothers and wives. Aircraft parts and explosives had to be made, but tea also had to be on the table. Fear and conservatism prevailed, that women working in factories would bring about the collapse of home life. There was concern for the man coming home on leave to a cold hearth, unwashed dishes and even an empty bed.

* See Penny Summerfield, *Women Workers in the Second World War: Production and Patriarchy in Conflict* (1984)

This was not the cosy welcome he had pictured; where would it all end?

On the plus side, having a job was better than being unemployed, and work in the war factories was relatively well paid: better than the Land Army or the lower ranks of the services. Leaving aside the housebound wives of servicemen (some of whom found they could get paid for making aircraft components at home), the working classes found that having two or even three incomes was definitely an improvement on one, even if, as was the general case, the pay was 25 per cent less than that received by men for the same work.

Until 1942 Thelma Ryder lived at home in Plymouth and worked packing towels for the Initial Towel Company. But that year, when she was twenty-one, two things happened which took her out of her comfort zone. Bill, her fiancé, was on board HMS *Exeter* when the Japanese sank her in the Java Sea that February. With 800 other men, he was taken prisoner, but though he sent word to say that he was alive, the message never reached his mother, or Thelma. The Devonshire lilt in Thelma's voice becomes hesitant as she remembers. 'I just heard about the sinking on the wireless. We never heard anything else. It was hard to believe – unreal somehow. It sort of numbs you. But you just have to go on with your life, you know . . . and hope that he survives. I always felt he was there, though. Mum and I went to a spiritualist, and she said he was still alive, and that helped.'

But later that year Thelma herself was forced to confront a new life when she was conscripted into war work:

I was a proper Mummy's girl. I hadn't wanted to leave home. So I waited till they called me up, and then I was sent to Wellworthy's munitions factory in Lymington to make piston rings for aircraft. I was put into uniform – navy-blue overalls and hats, with a snood to stop your hair going into the machines. The first time I went home wearing my uniform Mum started crying; she said, 'I've never seen you in trousers before.'

But in fact work and being called up was what helped me most to deal with not knowing where Bill was. It was an old factory, very friendly. And I just used to sit at the machine and do the work. You had to do so many a day, and you were at the job up to twelve hours a day, for £3 a week. I didn't find it boring, I liked it. And it was something different I suppose.

Only trouble was, if you worked too fast bits of hot steel used to come flying out and stick in your eyes. There weren't any protective masks. You'd have to go up to first aid, and they'd get it out by putting drops in and with a magnet. But it only happened a couple of times because you got used to watching that the bits didn't go in your eyes.

Dangers of this kind beset the woman factory worker. In Yorkshire, Emily Jones's face was burned with slag, and slag got into Amy Brooke's ear. Joan Thorpe got her neck burned; Agnes Green had 'arc eye' (caused by intense flaming flashes in the welding shop – 'you feel as if your eyes are full of sand'), while all of their female workmates were suffering from excessive periods. This particular group of young Yorkshirewomen was conscripted in 1942 and drafted into welding work in two foundries in Huddersfield and Penistone. They had been trained for the job in Sheffield by an experienced woman welder, Valentine Pearson, who became their friend and mentor, and after they returned to their factories the group wrote letters to Valentine which, many years later, surfaced in the Mass Observation archive. An excerpt from Amy's letter to Valentine on 11 September 1942 gives a flavour of the girls' everyday life:

Glad to inform you that I am quite in order, I think I must have strained myself with lifting and I have done some this week . . . The rate fixer came up last Monday and what a bugger he is. I have been getting 160 plates out per day and now I have to get 205 plates out per day and I get 8/- per week extra. It's bleeding horse work, but it's not going to come off next week. Believe me, I have come home at 7.30 half dead. I have just washed me and looked at the evening paper and gone straight to bed, buggered.

On 21 September she wrote again:

My wrist to my elbow is all burned with Welding and it is burning like bleeding hell and as red as a beetroot, where I had hold of the shield in my left hand. I have just asked Eddie [a co-worker] what time we have some lunch and he said we only stop at two . . . so I said 'the hell I am having some bleeding lunch right now'. So I have put the pan on, we have a small secret gas ring in our department you see, so I am going to make good use of it.

If my letter seems all jumbled up you must excuse me because I have to keep breaking off, and doing a bit of work, to keep the production up, you know there's a war on.

Although Amy and her friends in Huddersfield had not chosen to become wartime welders, all of them had previously worked in factories. Rather less predictably, two volunteer factory workers who started training as machine operators in February 1942 were spinsters in their forties who came from well-off middle-class families. Elsie Whiteman and Kathleen Church-Bliss had met through their shared interest in the English Folk Dance Society, and in 1935 had moved into a half-timbered Surrey farmhouse together and started up a tea shop. It appears that their decision to work in a war factory was not only a patriotic one but also taken 'in a spirit of adventure'. Kathleen and Elsie were enterprising, public-spirited and educated – typical, in other words, of the great sisterhood of inter-war 'surplus women'; there was also something of the crusade in their decision to keep a joint diary of their experiences at Morrisons' No. 1 Factory in Croydon.

The pair started out with four months of training in which they learned tool-grinding, screw-cutting, lathing and scribing; they were taught to use gauges, trigonometry, and to be accurate within a thousandth of an inch. In June they arrived at Morrisons' to start work. Despite the 'hellish noise' and eleven-hour days, they soon settled in. Elsie discovered that she was making 'a small part of a Spitfire', while Kathleen was working on the aileron of a Wellington bomber – 'this gives a zest'. However the novelty soon wore off. Though some of their skilled operations required enormous concentration, too much of the work was mechanical:

'We nearly die of boredom. The hours drag interminably, the clock never advances and Sunday seems a long way off.

Fortunately, factory life had other compensations:

The only thing which quickens the pace at all are Rumpuses or Love. Love seems to have passed out of our lives . . . but Rumpuses crop up two or three times a week and do make a nice change.

Rumpuses included the horrible accident that befell Rachel, a turner at Morrisons', whose hair became entangled with a revolving rod protruding from one of the lathes; there was a terrible shriek, and she was found to have been half-scalped. It turned out that Rachel had obstinately refused to tie her hair up properly, but the row simmered on as she threatened to sue the management for negligence.

For Elsie and Kathleen, their world had narrowed to the confines of the factory; breaks and small comforts became all-important. They were plaintively indignant when management brought in an 'efficiency expert' to reorganise the tea room: he packed all the tables tightly together, altered everyone's 'special place' and had a wooden barrier put up to segregate the office staff eating area from that of the shop-floor workers. How mean to do such a thing, while at the same time refusing to provide the workers with stools to sit on because of the timber shortage. Occasionally the diarists raised their heads from the all-consuming job in hand to note greater events – 'At 9.0'c. this morning we heard the splendid news of the American landings in French North Africa' (8 November 1942) – but, not surprisingly, the majority of the entries are preoccupied with gossip, work, rumpuses, relationships with co-workers, food, physical discomfort, boredom and breaks. Yet very few of the nearly 2 million women who worked in the war industries recorded their daily lives in this way; Elsie and Kathleen's journal is a rare document.

'She's Most Important – in Her Way'

Women's presence in the war factories, as Elsie and Kathleen were all too aware, had become indispensable. Their diary was consciously written in part to give a voice to the million and a half women now spending their waking hours on the shop floor.

But from the male point of view, this presence was often jarring, incongruous and out of step with the sexual orthodoxy of the time. Their arrival caused consternation among male managers, who feared for their jobs and their virility. It became a matter of prime importance to them to maintain sexual discrimination in the workplace. To begin with, money spent on training women was looked on as money wasted, since it was taken for granted that the women would be going back to their homes and would not need special skills once the emergency was over. Women factory workers were persuaded by their anxious employers that they were not really the same as men. They were allocated 'easy', 'clean' tasks, more suited to semi-skilled workers and told it was for their own protection. Their work was presented to them as being an extension of familiar domestic skills that required patience and dexterity, like knitting or needlework. Among the Yorkshire welders, Enid Haley had been a seamstress who could do invisible mending; Agnes Helme had pre-war experience of decorating cakes. Both of these contributed to their skills with the welding rod. At the same time women workers were often manipulated by factory managers into working within semi-skilled 'ghettoes', redescribed as being appropriate to their sex, so as not to compete with the skilled male workers. Sometimes, too, women's work was sabotaged by male workers in the same factory. There were cases of women arriving to find their machines tampered with, their work undone.

The men's behaviour was often primitive and thoughtless. Factory work had an image problem; it was reputed to take mainly girls from the bottom of the social heap. Hardened male workers gazed in awe and wonder as the first female conscripts arrived, in trousers and nail-varnish. Were they ladies or whores? Did you show them respect, or did you rape them?

The Yorkshire welders endured annoyance from their male co-workers, who teased, snubbed and harassed them. Helena Marsh remembered how the charge hand would sneak into the welding booth where she was working and grope her; 'you daren't say a right lot'.

For many girls it took nerve to deal with the rough manners and coarse language of their fellow hands. 'My initiation into factory life was shattering,' recalled Rosemary Moonen, a peacetime hairdresser who found herself on the night shift producing assault barges and aeroplane wings, side by side with a crew of die-hard proletarians. On day one she was humiliatingly singled out by the foreman, who spotted that she was somewhat well-bred and reserved. Having allocated everyone else their tasks, he flung a broom at her with the words 'Take this! And sod around!', before walking off. Staunchly, Rosemary sat down and waited for him to return. A dreadful row then ensued as he accused her of neglect:

Summoning all my courage I retorted that until he had the decency to show me the job I had to do, presuming it *was* to help the war effort, I intended staying where I was. Somewhat taken aback he treated me to a stream of foul language calling me some of the filthiest names imaginable. I was so angry and disgusted by this time, that I brought up my hand and slapped him hard across the cheek.

The foreman apologised; Rosemary went home that night and wept bitterly. 'How was I ever going to stand the atmosphere?' But it wasn't just the men who gave her a tough time. Just as in the barracks, class wars were played out on the factory floor. And for Rosemary the hostility of her own sex was almost harder to deal with: caustic, foul-mouthed, uncouth women, who made it only too clear that she was not their sort, and not welcome. Margaret Perry was another conscript who worked in a Nottinghamshire factory making wire insulation for the Admiralty. She too found herself the butt of abuse and innuendo from her 'rock bottom' co-workers.

I'd been brought up in the same town but never quite got down to this level nor heard speech punctuated by so many colourful adjectives. I was under the impression that I had had a working-class upbringing but discovered that there were different categories of working-class.

In the war factories, as in the services, class distinctions were finely noted and observed. Here again, the notion that war was a great leveller is perhaps more rooted in fiction than fact. Few industrial workers in wartime had had more than an elementary school education, and literate women like Margaret Perry or genteel women like Rosemary Moonen were correspondingly conspicuous. Margaret did her best to blend in by adopting the vernacular. For Rosemary, things only improved when some new, 'better-class' girls – secretaries and shop-assistants – were taken on.

The welders seem not to have been afflicted by class differences. Amy Brooke and Emily Castle loved their jobs and took pride in their welding ability. Emily was even selected to train up a number of men at the Huddersfield Foundry. Despite, or because of, such aptitude, the women welders were paid less than their male colleagues. By January 1944 the average pay for women in metalwork and engineering was, at £3 10s, exactly half that of the male rate. 'They were jealous,' said Dorothy Roebuck, 'they didn't want us to be as good as them.'

After much lobbying, women welders were permitted entry to

the Amalgamated Engineering Union in 1943, but there was little solidarity with their male counterparts, who felt threatened by their incursion on to the shop floor. In fact, there was general reluctance by the women to join unions; workplace politics were seen as a male concern. Just as men felt that tough women in overalls doing a 'man's job' was a challenge to their masculinity, so women on the whole preferred to take the line of least resistance. There was a tacit acceptance on both sides that, after the war was over, when the fighter planes and tanks would no longer be required, Rosie the Riveter would return to being Rosie the housewife, cook and bottle-washer. Social structures in the 1940s had little room for working-class women to change their position in this respect. One investigation of attitudes among young women war workers showed that the average factory girl had little or no awareness of what she did as contributing to the war effort. According to the author of the research, this girl was half-hearted, self-centred, apathetic and unambitious for a career. 'I'll only be there till I marry' was, apparently, the underlying assumption of nearly all women factory workers.

Understandable, perhaps, that home seemed preferable, given the danger, boredom and oppression of factory work. It took Arthur Askey and Gracie Fields's famous popular song, 'The Girl That Makes the Thing-ummy Bob (That's Going to Win the War)' to remind the public that her insignificant part in a larger process would 'strike a blow for Britain'. Making a thing to drill a hole to hold a spring to drive a rod to turn a knob to work a thing-ummy bob might not seem heroic – 'especially when you don't know what it's for' – but the catchy lyrics helped give her a boost.

And there was another side to the story of the woman wartime worker: one that might have given credence to the worries of the moralists, who feared that such women, with money in their pockets, would take advantage of their new-found liberty. In their off-duty time the Yorkshire women welders let their hair down with abandon:

From Helena Marsh, March 1942

Violet and I are having a good time just now . . . We've gone to all dances and the places where one always gets merry, and have we been merry? I'll say we have.

From Violet Champion, 10 March 1942

We went to Joan's wedding last Saturday ... And, oh boy, did we have some fun. Helena had one over the eight and went flat out.

From Amy Brooke, July 1942

I went with Harry, the Air Force boy on Sunday ... We ... had a couple of drinks together and then I had a cuddly Woodly, very nice.*

From Amy Brooke, October 1942

I went to the Canteen Staff Dance on Saturday night. I had a real time and what do you think? I won the Spot Waltz Prize: a pair of Mauve Satin French Knickers and my partner won 60 Capstan Cigarettes. Just imagine the look on my face, when I opened my parcel to show him what I had won. I went crimson and did not know where to put myself. Ah ah, I bet you wish you had seen me ... I had a partner all night. I did enjoy myself.

Interviewed years later, one of the group – Joan Baines – recalled that in her view war time was 'a happy time because everybody ... were all right nice ... You used to have some fun.' Amabel Williams-Ellis's book about women in factories also points to the wealth of opportunities they offered for social life – particularly for the 'mobile' women transported to live in hostels. Sometimes there were up to a thousand girls living under one roof; carnivals would be organised, and dancing partners from local RAF or army camps brought in by the bus-load.

And if ever these young women felt deprived of boyfriends, from 1942 that lack was more than compensated for by the arrival in this country of the American forces.

Yanks

For Britain, 1942 was a low point in the war, dominated from the outset by the fall of Singapore. In the first half of that year, the conflict in the Pacific continued to swing in Japan's favour as they notched up victory after victory, and the entire eastern hemisphere seemed to be falling into Japanese hands. In North Africa, Rommel's Afrika Korps was battling to regain mastery. Meanwhile, the German army was

---

* But Amy's session with the Air Force boy sounds even nicer if pronounced with a Huddersfield accent, using the long 'u', as in 'coodly Woodly'.

pushing through Russia on its way to Stalingrad. But although the
Russian campaign had caused the blitzing of British cities to abate,
naval losses in the Atlantic remained severe. In Britain, the cry redoubled for a 'Second Front Now'; American leaders were pressing to
invade German-occupied Europe, and in August 1942 Churchill agreed
to mount the tragic Dieppe Raid, which resulted in 3,367 casualties.

But this deeply disheartening period coincided with events at
home that were more calculated to raise morale and revive jaded spirits, particularly for women:

One day . . . a gang of us heard a brass band playing 'Over There'. Yes, the
Yanks had come . . . They soon took over. They had bigger lorries, bigger
tanks, better uniforms, bigger mouths, and, rumour had it, bigger . . . !

Between then and D-day, a tidal wave of Americans, 2 million strong,
flowed through this country, some en route to far-flung battlefields,
others to stay. From Piccadilly Circus to Sutton Coldfield, from
Cotswold villages to city centres, you couldn't avoid them: the GIs
(so-called after the words 'Government Issue', which appeared on
their equipment) were everywhere. And after three years of bombs
and blackout, the Yanks' noisy, big-hearted, 'anything goes' sex
appeal was joyfully welcomed by many British women. But the
arrival of thousands of homesick 18–30-year-old men ('overpaid,
over-sexed and over here') also sent alarm bells ringing. The seduction techniques of the GIs were so proficient that a joke started to do
the rounds: 'Heard about the new utility knickers? One Yank – and
they're off.'

There was fear that the US bases would become hotbeds of vice,
attracting swarms of 'good-time girls'. Hastily, the WVS and the
churches set up over 200 'Welcome Clubs' to entertain the American
troops in a more seemly manner. Hostesses were hand-picked, and
dozens of young men from Idaho and Alabama found themselves
invited out to genteel Sunday afternoon tea-parties – though sometimes they had to bring their own food, as the English rations just
wouldn't stretch. The GIs were grateful; they were thousands of
miles from home, missing their Mom's pumpkin pie, yearning for
warm human contact in a chilly, grey island. That loneliness was
matched only by the British women's thirst for the transatlantic
glamour and luxury lifestyle they imported. When the GIs from

Steeple Morden 8th Air Force base returned the compliment and invited a contingent of locals to a Red-Cross-organised dance, the girls started out overwhelmed and baffled: what *was* this 'Jitterbug', 'with its collections of strange steps and athletic contortions'? But it was the Americans' epicurean largesse that left them gasping:

It was the food – Food with a capital F. That was the crowning glory of that first Red Cross dance.

Spread in front of them, on groaning tables, was potato salad, macaroni salad, cold meat, rolls, butter, pickles, chocolate cake . . . After three years of spam, potatoes and cabbage, the girls fell upon it and ate till they could eat no more.

And now, as it dawned on the affluent Americans how pinched and deprived life in Britain had become, they became ever more bounteous. Gifts flowed: chewing gum, cigarettes, flowers, cookies, candy and above all – dearer than gold itself – nylon stockings. With their menfolk on the other side of the world, exhausted with coping and fed up with shortages, British women were only too ready to be wooed with Hershey bars and Lucky Strikes. A girl with a generous GI boyfriend could really feel like a girl again. As Madeleine Henrey wrote:

They brought into our anxious lives a sudden exhilaration, the exciting feeling that we were still young and attractive and that it was tremendous fun for a young woman to be courted, however harmlessly, by quantities of generous, eager, film-star-ish young men . . . They introduced new topics of conversation, an awareness that life was not after all only tears and suffering. I felt myself, in common with the entire feminine population, vibrating to a new current in the spring air.

Our relationship with America has always been one of deep ambivalence: envy of its glamour and wealth, coupled with contempt for its perceived naivety; a fascination with its pioneering spirit, alongside mistrust of what may seem to us to be vulgarity and Philistinism. The new world feels patronised by the old, while the old feels left behind by the frenetic modernity of the new. The magnetism of Clark Gable's Rhett Butler was potent – *Gone with the Wind* ran for four years from 1940 to 1944 – yet the improbably named American divorcée Wallis Simpson, key player in the 1936 Abdication crisis, confirmed her country's slightly degraded image. Inevitably, all this and more entered the

sexual equation when the American army landed on these shores. In
Love, Sex and War 1939–1945, the author John Costello details many of
the infractions and incongruities that resulted from this sudden sexual
and cultural free-for-all. His book describes the willingness of British
girls to service the soldiers' needs in return for sweets and nylons; the
tricky misunderstandings that arose from the GIs' slangy advances
(was 'Hiya baby!' impudent over-familiarity or a friendly conversa-
tional gambit?); the random and frequent molestation and harassment
of servicewomen by American soldiers; outbreaks of domestic crime
and rape; infidelity; racism.

*'Don't forget, Beryl – the response is "Hiya, fellers!" and a sort of nonchalant wave
of the hand.' GIs and the communication problem, as depicted in* Punch, *1944.*

For along with tinned peaches and chocolate, the American army
imported its colour bar. English women didn't understand the rules.
When African American soldiers arrived in the small Glamorganshire
town of Porthcawl, the local girls were only too happy to go dancing
with them. Soon after, the whites arrived. Reacting with absolute
horror, they immediately instituted total segregation. Seventeen-
year-old Mona Janise was dismayed: 'Talk about sin in the Garden of

Eden, we thought we had done something wrong but didn't know what.' Around the same time Frances Partridge wrote in her war diary about a public relations exercise set up by American officers for the benefit of local English ladies, 'about how to treat the blacks' – all of whom carried knives, apparently, and would most certainly attempt to rape their daughters. The ladies were advised never to invite them into their houses, 'and above all never to treat them as human beings, because they were not'. Costello, however, suggests that – if British women had anything to fear – it was the predatory American soldier who, irrespective of his colour, refused to take 'no' for an answer.

On balance, the culture clash worked in favour of the resident women. Dolly Scannell, a married woman with a small child whose husband had been called up to the army, was grateful to be employed as secretary to a major at an American hospital base in Essex. Dolly, a fun-loving East Ender evacuee, was living near by with her sister Marjorie; her in-laws had also moved out of London, and her daughter Susan was in nursery school – leaving thirty-year-old Dolly to enjoy the freedom, general hilarity and perks of her new job. The GIs teased her and adored her; she was voted the girl 'with the most terrific gams' on camp, but turned down her prize: a weekend in Colchester with the GI of her choice. Once word got out about her 'gams' she had no peace – the soldiers found any excuse they could to come to her office and inspect her from the hemline down. 'I was secretly a little bit pleased and took to wearing nylons to enhance my prancing legs.' The stockings were, of course, one of the bonuses.

As Dolly worked for an officer she was collected every morning in a jeep, with a driver who would salute her as she greeted him. Delicious lunches were another benefit of the job. The typists ate with the officers; there was steak, and fruit. Dolly brought a large linen napkin from home and piled it full of oranges and pineapple slices for the children. From time to time they asked the army personnel back for tea and a game of cards; the 'amorous ones' were firmly discouraged and not asked again.

But later Dolly wondered whether she had missed out. Chores, children, a full-time job and a nun-like conscience about her husband Chas inhibited her from taking up the offers that came her way. One day a food parcel arrived for one of the US sergeants; it contained a wondrous cake:

It was covered with cherries, marzipan, nuts and angelica. The sight of it was enough to take one's breath away in those days of austerity. The Sergeant said, 'That's for you, Dorothy, if I can have a cup of coffee with you one day.' 'Indeed, you'd be very welcome any time,' I said delightedly. I took the cake home and watched the children's faces. The cake was as marvellous inside as it was out. I have never tasted anything like it and Marjorie said, 'What a generous man he must be, Dolly.'

The following night she was on her way to bed when she was disturbed by a clamour at the door. The sergeant was down below, bellowing for his coffee – 'You promised me,' he yelled. He wouldn't go away. Eventually she threatened him with the police, and he skulked off, muttering, 'Bloody dames, they're all the same, lead you on, take all you've got and give you nothing.' But it wasn't till the next day at work that Dolly finally realised that coffee wasn't all the sergeant had had in mind. He was still furious. '"When I gave you the cake . . . you said, *any time* it would be *your pleasure*." So he had been deceived by my polite expression.'

Another young GI took a different approach. He took Dolly aside and told her earnestly that being separated from his wife back home was 'affecting his health'. He had been to see the medical officer, who, he said, had advised him to form a liaison with Mrs Dolly Scannell, who for her part was separated from her husband. 'He thought it would be a good idea, not hurting anyone, if you and I could form some sort of association, and be faithful to each other.' Dolly sent him packing.

Her friend Maudie was more prepared to compromise. Maudie worked on an air force base and took it in turns to sleep with the pilots. She didn't regard it as infidelity; she loved her husband, and he loved her. But she also hated loneliness, and hated an empty bed. Sharing it kept her happy and contented; she took no risks and encouraged no delusions. 'Each resident knew that she was waiting for her husband,' recalled Dolly Scannell. 'What she offered them was a temporary haven and I believe she made life bearable for the pilots on their dangerous nightly missions over enemy territory.' Many like Maudie saw no harm in alleviating their loneliness and frustration, while comforting their American boyfriends.

Inevitably, many liaisons were also deeply romantic. The clean-cut, manly Yanks were the embodiment of Hollywood enchantment: those blurred idols that had kept British girls entranced in picture houses made flesh. In their arms one could be Veronica Lake, or Betty Grable. On summer evenings, Margaret Tapster used to dance to the sound of big bands with her beau, Sergeant Kurt Wagner; cheek-to-cheek, she caressed the collar of his costly, well-fitting uniform, breathed in his expensive aftershave and drank up his meaningless flattery, so voluptuous when spoken in a southern drawl: 'You have the cutest little ears honey, like pink seashells . . . Your hair smells like the jasmine flowers on our back porch.'

But in reality women like Margaret attracted the GIs for reasons other than their seashell ears. Compared to American women, the passive, weary British female often seemed pleasantly unchallenging. One grateful American man published an article in which he explained that he had chosen to marry an Englishwoman because of her submissiveness and eagerness to please:

While American women insist on a big share in the running of things, few European women want to be engineers, architects or bank presidents. They are mainly interested in the fundamental business of getting married, having children and making the best homes their means or conditions will allow. They feel they can attain their goals by being easy on the nerves of their menfolk.

So it was hardly surprising that love blossomed, many relationships fast developing into commitments. Starry-eyed eighteen- and twenty-year-old girls saw their dreams coming true. Not much older, the American soldiers, away from home on their first adventure, were looking for companionship, sex and the promise of domestic bliss which so many of these English girls seemed to offer. '[Eddie] told me he had gone back to the barracks that Saturday night and told his friends he had met the girl he was going to marry,' remembered Hilda, who had danced with Eddie once at her local American air base in Northamptonshire. They were married within three months. Ruth Patchen was working for anti-aircraft command in London when she met her future husband, Staff Sergeant Wendell Poore, on a bus. Wendell proposed a few months later; he couldn't afford a ring, so he pulled a picture of a diamond out of *Life* magazine and gave it to her. Despite family opposition, they started planning their wedding; when the war was over they would live in Cut Bank, Montana. Often, long and happy marriages were the outcome.

But reality caught up with some of these GI brides. Nineteen-year-old Mary Angove, who had volunteered for the ATS in 1940, was based at Seaton Barracks near Plymouth in 1942 when the Americans arrived. The first she saw of them was a soldier in a tin hat who looked like a German. That night the over-excited GIs rampaged around the camp, cursing, shouting and calling names at the girls through their blackouts. In light of what happened to Mary later, it seems these soldiers may have been a bad batch:

Probably they got a good dressing-down from their colonel in the morning. Luckily they left us alone after that . . . But I did date one or two of them. I met Kenneth one night when I stopped at the fish and chip shop in the village on my way back to camp. It was getting late; you had to be in at 10, otherwise you'd be put on a charge. Anyway, this Yank was in front of me, and he offered to get mine. So I said, yes thanks, and he walked me back to barracks and we made a date. But I didn't turn up.

But one morning I was off-duty, and I ran into him again. So then we went out for a while. It was on and off because we were in different places. But I ended up with marrying him . . . which was rather stupid of me. He was different then, obviously.

War had seemed to justify spontaneity. What place did caution have in a world where nothing could be anticipated? But by 1947 Mary had left her abusive and alcoholic husband and was back in Britain.

Heat and Sand

Nevertheless, Barbara Cartland would be among many who concluded that the Americans' presence added more than it subtracted from wartime Britain:

Believe me, I know what I am talking about when I say that the American airman and soldier is in general a well-behaved, decent-living, fine-principled boy. He is not sophisticated, he is not polished, he is very often adolescent in his outlook and knowledge, but his heart is all right.

As the tone of her remarks suggests, Cartland took a patrician and parental view of the GIs, but it was a forgiving one, and above all a deeply grateful one. The American soldiers' presence proclaimed the good faith of President Roosevelt who, together with Churchill, in February 1942, had established the Combined Chiefs of Staff to co-ordinate the Allies' war effort, 'and to provide for full British and American collaboration with the United Nations'. British people knew that the war could not be won without American help. And, failing an imminent Second Front in occupied Europe, that summer Roosevelt also reached agreement with the British chiefs of staff to mount Operation Torch, the landing of a combined force in French North Africa.

The backlash against Rommel was coordinated by troops on the ground in Libya, Morocco and Egypt. But from early in the war the island of Malta had been of key importance in controlling the sea route across the Mediterranean, vital to maintaining Axis supply lines. This Allied base was a thorn in the side of the German command: 'Without Malta the Axis will end by losing control of North Africa,' said Rommel. Throughout 1941 and the first half of 1942 the Luftwaffe bombed Malta remorselessly. Air raids were almost constant; the island was in a state of siege and in danger of starvation.

Corporal 'Mike' Morris's strong-minded and courageous approach to everything she did was never more in evidence than when she determined to go to Malta early in 1942. Mike's value as a fluent German-speaking member of the 'Y' Service had been proved during the Battle of Britain, intercepting transmissions between German bombers and their bases. But when bomber activity over Britain started to slacken, she took a new posting in Egypt, monitoring aerial threats to the troops in the desert. It was here in January 1942 that she received the news – which at first she took to be an error in decoding – that she had been awarded the MBE. It was a huge boost to her confidence. In February she marched off to see Group Captain Scott-Farnie of Special Signals Intelligence and explained to him that she *had* to go to Malta. As she saw it, the monitoring staff on the island were insufficient and under-trained in dealing with the quantity of radio/telephone message traffic from the numerous German bombers

now threatening it. There were QAs at the military hospital, but
there were no WAAFs working there, or any other servicewomen;
indeed women were now being evacuated from Malta. Mike knew
that she had better experience in this vital work than any of her male
colleagues. But Scott-Farnie did not see things her way. Her sex, in
his view, disqualified her. 'I'm sorry but it is out of the question,' he
said. And nothing she could say would persuade him.

I went on arguing but it was to no avail. Finally, choking with rage and
frustration, I picked up my heavy German dictionary and hurled it at him.
It missed, and that only made me even more angry, so I stormed out of the
office. If I did get killed, was that so serious? Was it not better that I, a
single girl, died, rather than a married man perhaps with children? The
all-important thing was that German R/T was being heard in Malta.

Later, however, she sought him out and apologised for her outburst.
But, having thought things over, Scott-Farnie too had been looking
for her. He had been to see the Commander-in-Chief, Sir Arthur Tedder, and Tedder, more enlightened, had given her his blessing to go.

Before departing, Mike went to see him. He was, she recognised,
most rare and unusual for a man. 'There was no quibbling about my
being a woman. He appreciated that I could do the job and there it
ended.' But with military terseness Tedder warned her that Malta
was now 'pretty uncomfortable . . . I hope you realise what you're
letting yourself in for?' Mike stressed that she felt she could help. As
she left, he called after her, 'Take your tin hat – you'll need it.'

Mike quickly discovered that Tedder's advice was in earnest. She
arrived in Malta on 13 February in the middle of a heavy air raid; the
flying-boat from Cairo was escorted by British fighters. Quickly, she
settled into her work; a receiving station had been set up at Kaura
Point to monitor transmissions from German bomber traffic based in
Sicily to the north. Soon after her arrival she was returning to her
hotel in the company of one of the airmen when they both confused
a Messerschmitt 109 flying low over the sea with a British fighter in
trouble. It was nearly a fatal mistake. The fighter aimed a volley of
machine-gun fire at them – '"Christ!" yelled the airman . . . "He's a
bloody Hun,"' as they hurled themselves flat on the ground behind a
wall. It missed them, and careered on, firing over the airfield. Shaken
and swearing, Mike's escort picked himself up and asked whether she

was all right. '"No, dammit, I'm not," I replied. "I've wrecked my stockings, and I've only got one more pair with me."'

Despite her concern for female accessories, Mike found she was accepted as 'a moderately decent type' and permitted to dine in the all-male mess. This also spared her the nightly journey – dodging bombs and shrapnel and picking her way across the rubble – from her safe lodgings in a labyrinth of tunnels for her evening meal at the hotel. The island was being pulverised – 'it was difficult to determine when one air-raid ceased and the next began' – though one that stuck in her mind was a direct hit on a neighbouring house. Mike and her hosts heard the occupant screaming in agony as the bombers droned overhead, followed by the chillingly sustained wail of a grief-stricken woman.

The gallantry of the airmen, ground crews and gun crews on Malta was extraordinary; equalled only by Mike's determination to use her skills to support their heroism. It was vital to glean any information possible about enemy movements. Under her guidance, Mike's Maltese unit was working unbelievably long hours to ensure round-the-clock monitoring; she and her German-speaking eavesdroppers could warn of impending attacks, advise on targets, alert fighters when they had been spotted, listen in on weather reports, determine the strength of enemy formations and contact threatened shipping convoys.

In the short time she spent in Malta, Mike Morris demonstrated – as she had during the Battle of Britain – a cool-headedness and intellectual grasp that materially aided that stricken island. But early in March Scott-Farnie told her that he wanted her back in Cairo; Messerschmitts were attacking our North African airfields and harbours, and the 8th Army in the desert needed all the support they could get. She agreed to leave on 9 March, her twenty-fourth birthday. After a farewell party she set out for Luqa airfield, joining a group of women and children who were being evacuated to Egypt. It was midnight, 'there was the usual raid in progress', and Mike and the evacuees embarked on two Wellingtons. They started to taxi along the blacked-out runway; suddenly without warning a third aircraft, about to take off, hurtled into one of the Wellingtons, instantly starting an inferno. The pilot of Mike's plane yelled at his passengers, 'For Chrissakes, get to hell out of here. There are mines on board that kite.'

There was no ladder. Clutching her briefcase ('filled with secret documents') Mike leapt for the ground; one of the aircrew grabbed her, shouting 'Move!' Ammunition was bursting past them; they dived for cover, face down, only to realise that they were underneath a petrol bowser. Seconds later the mines on the Wellington blew up, with a deafening explosion. The airman seized Mike's briefcase and rammed it forcefully on to the back of her head, just in time. He saved her life; heavy flying shrapnel drove deep scars into the leather. Her jaw was injured. Guided by the firework display, the German raiders were now having a field day over the airfield. When the din and chaos finally abated Mike and the airman staggered, covered in mud, to the control room, to be greeted with relief by the air officer. Mike's reaction was stoical: 'What a way for a girl to spend her birthday,' she grimaced. 'I really do think someone could have done better than this.'

A few days later she was on her way back to Cairo.

*

As WAAF Mike Morris resumed her interception work in North Africa, the SS *Highland Monarch* was embarking from Bristol destined for Cape Town. With the Mediterranean closed, this was the only route for services to reach the Middle East. On board were 5,000 troops and fourteen VAD nurses bound for Suez; one of these was twenty-two-year-old Helen Vlasto.

A startlingly pretty debutante, Helen was in the latest generation of an immensely rich Anglo-Greek banking dynasty; her father was a successful doctor. 'I was . . . not motivated in any particular direction,' recalled Helen; but her money, looks, charm and fluency in three languages would have qualified her as premium goods on the 1939 marriage market. A 'proper' education or job therefore wasn't thought necessary. Instead, by day she volunteered at the West London Hospital in Hammersmith, while by night she appeared in glimmering gowns at the West End hotels and grand houses of London's most glamorous hostesses: 'I felt I was living a double, and somewhat unworthy, life.'

When war was declared Helen applied to become a mobile VAD and in November 1940 was sent to Haslar Royal Naval Hospital near Portsmouth. Here she helped to set up the country's first blood bank. But six months in, despite putting her 'heart and soul' into this worthwhile project, Helen was engulfed by ennui. Longings for a boyfriend were beginning to surface:

'Oh my darling,' (I prayed inwardly to myself), 'do please manifest yourself. I need someone to love right this very minute.'
    And he did. Manifest himself, I mean!

The answer to her prayer appeared in the form of handsome surgeon Lieutenant Aidan Long, who joined the Transfusion Service as Medical Officer in March 1941. Aidan met her parents, and everything seemed just perfect until, with only twenty-four hours' warning, he was drafted to Iceland. They would not meet again for four years.

Aidan sent her a silver and pearl pin, and they wrote to each other. Helen continued to work in the transfusion unit, but she was impatient to return to hospital nursing, and there were rumours that she would be posted abroad. Eventually, in May 1942 Aidan was due back in England. He arrived on the 7th – but it was the very day that Helen's ship sailed: 'His bird had flown.'

As the *Highland Monarch* was tugged away from the dock the men on the decks were waving and singing 'Wish Me Luck as You Wave Me Goodbye'. Helen listened with a swelling heart. She found herself incapable of joining in, for yet again her feelings were overflowing into an involuntary prayer:

'Please, please, dear God, may it please You to spare as many of these fine men as is possible – under the circumstances that is – though obviously we've simply GOT to win this Middle East war.' And, selfishly, – 'Please, if it's at all possible, spare me to return safely home and find all well there.'

The *Highland Monarch* was two months at sea. Finally, on 26 July 1942, after travelling 15,000 miles, the troop ship's gangplanks were lowered in Suez.

Helen arrived at the 64th General Hospital, Alexandria, at a time when British fortunes in North Africa were at a low point. Rommel had inflicted heavy losses on British forces, and in June he had captured Tobruk. By early July Axis forces had pushed the British back to within 70 miles of Alexandria. The ensuing battle brought about 13,000 casualties, resulting in an uneasy stalemate, and the dismissal by Churchill of General Auchinleck. General Bernard Montgomery was now appointed to command the 8th Army.

The 64th was a base hospital designated for serious cases. Helen found the medical wards full of patients with dysentery, typhoid, sandfly fever and acute enteritis; there was also a serious epidemic of diphtheria. Many of the invalids had desert sores, caused by terrible swarms of flies that settled on and infected any exposed wound.

Hers was an orthopaedic ward; these patients, casualties of the Auchinleck retreat, seemed to have brought half the desert back with them. Sand was all-pervading. It got into the sheets, the dressings, into all the interstices of their bodies, between broken limbs and the plasters that encased them. No matter how often the nurses bathed their patients, yet more grit seemed to emanate from overlooked cracks and crannies. Soft-hearted as she was, Helen found it hard to stay detached from the often terrible plight of the men under her care. One of these was a jokey and stalwart Canadian Hurricane pilot, Mike Reece, who had been shot down; his burns were so dreadful that there was never any chance he would survive. It took an hour to change Mike's dressings, and his cheery, flirtatious courage so incapacitated her that she often had to flee to the basin in tears – 'I wasn't getting any better at it.' With his arms pinioned to his sides in bandages, he would blithely call on a mate in one of the neighbouring beds to drop something on the floor, so that the next passing nurse would have to bend over and pick it up, thus rousing the other patients to wolf-whistles at the sexily angled view of her bottom. Out of pity, Helen and the others never minded colluding in this simple diversion.

The night Mike died, she changed his drip and sat by his bed. He asked her to get his wallet out of the locker. She pulled out the photographs and held them up for him – his home, his parents, his beloved young brother – and talked about them for a long time. After he had gone she wrote to his parents, '[to] tell them how things had been with him, and how his thoughts and talk had been all of home'.

Montgomery was rallying his army. On 22 October, Helen had been on night duty. When she came off, she went to get some sleep, but had only managed an hour or two before she was called back on duty. Orders had arrived from General Headquarters in Cairo that morning that the 64th was to be converted into a casualty clearing station. The Allies were about to attack.

All that day preparations at the hospital were carried out 'in a state of awesome exhilaration'. The beds were remade with army blankets, vast drums were packed with dressings and taken to be sterilised, stretchers stacked, glucose drinks prepared, splints, bandages and medicines piled ready for use.

Montgomery attacked at 21.40 on a still and moonlit night. The roar of 800 guns broke the silence and marked the beginning of the Battle of Alamein.

It was a sound to chill the marrow in one's bones, and we hugged one another and held tightly to each other's hands, and a spine-chilling feeling came over us as we heard this great roar of gunfire, which lasted continuously for the first twenty minutes of the battle.

The sky to the west was like a gigantic firework display, lit by winking flashes all along the horizon, as the Eighth Army moved forward.

Casualties started to arrive before dawn on the 24th. Strapped in hasty bandages, grimy and encrusted in blood, they were sent from the first aid posts at the front, back to the 64th, where the staff did their best.

It was a night to remember for the rest of one's life . . .

Not for the first time . . . was I to sit at the side of a bed, mute and useless to the end, tormented by the knowledge that someone other than I should have been there at such a time.

The survivors turned to nurses like Helen for sympathy, skill and a listening ear. She heard of horrors: tank crews trapped in burning vehicles, dreadful maiming by mines, piles of bodies pulverised into the sand. In the ensuing days the stockpiled dressings began to run low; used ones were washed and rewashed by the nurses and laid out to bleach in the sun. Back in the fly-infested ward, Helen had to contain the urge to retch at the overpowering stench of burned, gangrenous flesh, while wounds daubed with gentian violet turned the mangled, blistered, bodies into macabre spectacles from some medieval picture of Hell. Bed bugs tortured nurses and patients alike. Helen sat through the desolate, homesick night duty on a stiff-backed chair draped with a white sheet, on which the insects could be easily spotted. 'If anyone were going to die, it would surely happen during those lonely hours.'

She saw it as her duty to give comfort where she could. As a woman, nursing made calls upon her that exceeded the confines of physical care. All too often an anxious man, fearfully mutilated, would call upon her to boost his male self-respect: 'What d'yer think the wife will say when she sees me looking like this? . . . Could yer fancy me, the way I am now? Be honest.' Nothing of this nature shocked Helen now. She was a woman; she was clean, fragrant, kind and pretty. And if he wanted a cuddle, if he needed a kiss, why deny it? Aidan was not forgotten, but these men needed succour of a kind that was in her power to offer. 'I gave many such kisses with all my heart, and found it no hardship to do. I reckoned it was all part of the service.'

Day and night, ambulances brought in more wounded. The nurses were working flat out, with wounds to dress, temperatures to take, pillows to plump, medicines to administer, every bed and every locker kept tidy for inspection. Twelve hours a day the hospital broadcast music programmes through the wards. As often as not it would be the bright tones of Vera Lynn singing 'It's a Lovely Day Tomorrow', or 'Yours Till the Stars Lose Their Glory' on *Forces Favourites*. And as fast as the patients in the 64th recovered, their places were refilled by casualties from the Desert Army's advance.

By early November the international newspapers on sale in the Alexandria streets were proclaiming: 'AFRIKA KORPS IN FULL RETREAT'. On 8 November Eisenhower's troops landed on the Moroccan and Algerian coast, as from its front page the *Egyptian Mail* shouted: 'ALLIES ATTACKING ON ALL FRONTS'.

★

On Remembrance Sunday Clara Milburn listened to the bulletin:

Sunday 8th November
    Great news today! American troops have landed in North Africa at several points . . .
    This is all very heartening . . . May we keep it up.

while the London diarist Vere Hodgson seized on a domestic simile to describe her excitement at the rush of events:

The Desert army is sweeping Rommel along the coast like dust before the broom.

Monday 9th saw the end of a long day at Morrisons' factory in Croydon. Kathleen Church-Bliss made a short entry in the diary she shared with her friend Elsie:

Monday 9th November

News still thrilling from Egypt and Africa . . .

Elsie's job is still taking all the vitality out of her and she comes back worn and white.

Frances Partridge hardly dared hope that now the tide might be turning. She reflected on events in an entry dated 11 November, twenty-four years after the Armistice that had ended the cruelty and slaughter of the previous war:

Prospects of peace suddenly loom closer. Next year perhaps? The agitation of the news has brought back the hateful waiting-room atmosphere; so far as mental or intellectual life exists the fire is nearly out, spiritual dust lies on everything and I sit gazing in front of me, wondering 'What next?'

On the 29th, cautious but still celebratory, Churchill broadcast to the nation: 'Two Sundays ago all the bells rang to celebrate the victory of our Desert Army at Alamein . . . We have been brought nearer to the frontiers of deliverance.' In Barrow-in-Furness Nella Last listened to him as she sat embroidering a cute face on to a stuffed rabbit, to be sold in aid of the WVS. But the uplift in Churchill's words failed to bear her along with it:

I listened to Churchill with a shadow on my heart . . . I thought of all the boys and men out East. How long will it be before they come home? It's bad enough for mothers – but what of the young wives? I felt my hands go clammy and damp, and I put my toy rabbit down. I looked at his foolish little face, such an odd weapon to be fighting with. I never thought my dollies and soft toys could be used in my war-time scheme of life.

For Nella, compassion got in the way of jubilation, and even hope. The war was far from over. What had this so-called victory achieved? Out there in the desert, many thousands had died horrible deaths in violent destruction wrought by angry men, their vandalism abetted by the women welders and machine operators and makers of ailerons and piston rings. Nella turned to her needlework. He was 'an odd weapon', the little rabbit; but making him was a task that spoke of gentleness, and peace, and motherly virtues. An act of generous creativity, it seemed one small, kind gift to offer to an afflicted world.

7   Sunny Intervals

No Tears Left

Any day, any time, tragedy could ambush you. Women in the forces were particularly exposed. WAAFs like R/T operator Pip Beck endured helplessly as the men they loved failed to return from missions. With the Battle of the Atlantic continuing to claim lives, Wrens who got romantically involved with naval servicemen often had to confront the loss of their boyfriends. Wren Pat Bawland watched in horror as a trainee Fleet Air Arm pilot nosedived into the runway at her Somerset base. He had married one of her fellow Wrens eight weeks earlier, and the girl was pregnant: 'I'll never forget seeing the searchlights at night trying to dig that plane out and get to his body.' Nobody was invulnerable. The North Africa campaign was bloody; in the Far East prisoners of war died by the thousand.

'Hearts do break,' remembered Bradford shop assistant Dorothy Griffiths. The staff of the branch of Marks and Spencer where she worked was fragmented by the war. Early on, one of her male colleagues had been shot down in the sea at Dunkirk. Ada, who worked with Dorothy in menswear, came from a family which seemed to have been singled out by a merciless fate. Her sister's fiancé had been drowned in a submarine; her brother Tommy had also been lost at sea. His wife Sally was helpless, distraught: '[she] had only lived for the time that Tommy would come home.' Then it was Ada's turn: she contracted TB and died at twenty-one. Not long afterwards, Dorothy herself was at work when she received a cablegram telling her of the death of her brother Neville on board his ship in the south Atlantic. 'I collapsed under the counter. I remember someone helping me upstairs to the rest room. I couldn't talk . . . They sent me home with one of the girls. I'd no tears left.' Later, she had to give comfort when Mollie, one of the other shop girls, got the news that she had dreaded. Her husband, who worked in bomb disposal, had been the victim of an explosion. 'There were no survivors. We were all devastated for Mollie.'

Today, Cora Williams (née Styles) lives alone in a spotless bunga-low near the Hampshire coast. Now in her late eighties, she's still full of fight, plain-spoken and secure in her opinions. She has learned that life is a battle.

Cora Styles was only fifteen when she met her fiancé Don John-ston at a dance hall in 1938, 'and by golly, couldn't he dance too!' Don joined the Royal Navy when war broke out, and in 1941 Cora left her office job at Ingersolls watch and clock factory in Clerkenwell to marry him. Her in-laws, whom she adored, were as happy as she was. 'It was a lovely old-fashioned wedding. Don looked so handsome in his uniform. To be together was all we wanted.' They started their married life in Londonderry, where Don's ship was based. She was happy in 'beautiful Ireland', and her young husband was everything to her: 'We were always laughing. Life was so good, you know – he was such fun. But it wasn't to be.'

Don's ship was on Atlantic convoys – '[He] was gone a couple of weeks, home a few days and then gone again.' Then they were recalled to the navy's main base at Chatham. Sadly, they missed see-ing Don's parents, who had sailed only two days earlier for America. 'We tried to resume a life.'

It never, never occurred to me that anything would happen to him. Never. Well, in May '42 Don was put on the aircraft carrier the *Avenger* as a stores rating. And then one night I was at my mother's, and he rang me there and he said 'I shan't be seeing you for a while.' Well of course he couldn't say anything more precise than that. And so I said OK.

It was at this point that Cora decided to volunteer for the Wrens:

They used to say 'Release a man for the sea.' I thought Don would be pleased, when he eventually knew . . .

Well, it turned out he was back on the convoys. The *Avenger* sailed from Scotland and took troops down to North Africa. And having left North Africa they were off the Portuguese coast and a U-boat came up at half past three in the morning and fired a torpedo and it went amidships and hit the bomb room. And the ship blew in half, and nearly 600 men were lost. And I think actually that most of them didn't know it happened. They must have been blown to hell.

But the first I knew of it was when I looked in the paper. They used to publish a list of ships that had gone down. And when I saw it I thought no – it can't possibly be, they must have made a mistake. I had had no telegram, so it could not be right.

Disbelieving, Cora waited. Soon after, a cable arrived from Don's parents, asking for news of him. She went down to the Naval Barracks Welfare section, and it was only then that she discovered what had happened:

It seems Don had never changed his next of kin when he married, so the telegram reporting him missing must have gone to his parents' old address, and I assumed it got lost, as they were in America.

When I left the barracks, I felt stunned, I just could not believe what I had been told . . . It was raining stair-rods. You've never seen rain like it, it was literally throwing it down from the heavens. My mind seemed to have gone blank, I hardly noticed how wet I was getting. I started counting the bricks in the six-foot wall I passed, which stretched back to the High Street. The most sad thing I then had to do was cable Don's parents: 'Missing. Presumed killed.'

I was in a bad state. One didn't have an understanding of what these men had gone through. They'd been blown apart. Years later I managed to get in contact with one of the survivors. He'd been on watch the night before, when they were coming out of the Med. And he saw the torpedo go past and hit the ship. And he said, 'It was the most terrible sight I've ever seen in my life, and it still lives with me today.'

Widowed at eighteen, Cora Johnston (as she was now) took stock of her situation. She was waiting to hear from the Wrens, and she had no more than £49 in the bank.

I sat down and thought about things. My parents wanted me to go home and live with them and I said, 'No, I'm going to stand on my own feet.' So I went to the Post Office and volunteered for a Christmas job.

However, the Christmas job defeated her. Weighed down by cumbersome parcels – many of them containing bleeding gifts of furred and feathered game sent by sporting Scots to their protein-starved southern relatives – she gave in her notice, exhausted.

But the Wrens were to prove a lifeline. 'On January 3rd they sent for me.'

Cora still had a long road to travel.

I'm someone who fights back. I've done it all my life. And I'm still doing it. I'm like a dog with a bone – I never ever give up.

But take it from me, you never get over it. The pain is there now, today – you never ever lose it. I still get upset. It'll stay with me until the day I die – but whether I shall ever meet him again I don't know.

*

Cora feels that her life has been 'a fight from the cradle to the grave – the latter being a way off yet! I think the war turned me from a silly lovesick girl into a strong woman.'

Her experience, and that in many other accounts of lives lived through the 1940s, suggests that by its midpoint the war was starting to have a transformative effect on the women of this country. The demure, retiring, unambitious young woman of 1938 had had some hard knocks. She had felt fear, smelled death in the Blitz, dealt with body parts, seen her possessions scattered and her home destroyed. She had been bombed, bullied by regimental sergeant-majors, burned by slag and blinded by hot steel. The hierarchies that had structured her everyday existence – class, culture and sexual divisions – were all being challenged. She had new skills, new responsibilities, while at the same time learning to live without much that, materially, she had taken for granted. Meanwhile, the men she loved were far away. At any time the news might come that they were wounded, imprisoned, disfigured or dead. But she was adapting, starting to become stronger, more independent, more reliant on her innate wits and abilities.

Ask any woman who lived through that time how she coped, and the chances are she will give the same simple, stoical answer: 'You just got on with it.'

*

A spotlight is all the brighter when the other lights are lowered. Perhaps living through those troubled, blacked-out times sharpened a sense of gratitude for moments of uncontaminated pleasure. And, too, the delight in nature and landscape; in affection and gratified desire; in food, sleep, laughter, dancing, art, a new hat or an afternoon at the pictures were in some measure enhanced by the constant reminders that love would pass and life was short. Perhaps they just had no tears left. How else to account for the curious statistic that emerged from a Blitz survey, that a fifth of women felt happy more often than before the war?

On 10 May 1942, the same day that three Royal Navy destroyers were torpedoed in the Mediterranean with over 100 lives lost, Nella Last and her husband packed a picnic of stewed prunes 'and a tiny piece of cake' and drove to Coniston Lake, their favourite beauty spot. After they'd eaten Nella napped in the car, then went for a stroll in the wood:

The fragrant larch boughs swung in the wind, but as I went deeper all was quiet and still, and the blue hyacinths shimmered in shafts of sunlight. Such peace, such beauty.

Doffy Brewer still remembers the rapture she felt when her work as a kine-theodolite operator took her to the deep west of Wales, where gunners were sent to train:

We were in Manorbier, which is a tiny village on the coast near the most beautiful countryside you've ever seen, with cliffs, and flowers. Oh, it was exquisite, it was absolutely lovely.

Our spirits used to go free, up on those cliffs. I learned to breathe, to be, to enjoy just being alive . . .

I used to lie down on those flowers and imagine all the plants that were there. I was enjoying myself in a way I'd never done before. I felt transformed.

And when she wasn't kitted out for an evening's dancing at the Institute, Doris Scorer's days off from the Wolverton Works often meant sunny afternoons at the 'bathings' – a stretch of the River Ouse on the town outskirts where teenagers like her met to sunbathe, splash and flirt. It was here that Doris first met Frank White – 'we were like soul mates'. Frank, though by origin a townie like her, knew the countryside like the back of his hand and, with Doris in her fancy shoes picking her way between the cowpats, the pair would roam the river meadows among the primroses, skimming stones and startling the water rats. Later in the year they gathered blackberries and investigated animal tracks in the snow. One evening they saw the Aurora Borealis. 'Happy days.'

For those like Nella, Doffy or Doris who weren't homeless,

maimed or bereaved, maintaining non-stop gloom was just too much effort. The human instinct for pleasure found outlets where it could. Nella was perhaps happiest when she felt she was using her house-wifely skills to greatest effect. At the end of an exhausting day unpicking a second-hand mattress, washing its cover and remodel-ling it into four smaller mattresses with the aid of half a dozen sugar sacks, she recorded: 'I think I'm the tiredest and happiest woman in Barrow tonight!' She had the capacity to find fulfilment in the small finite tasks of the home, each with its own sense of meaning, its own sense of completion. Christmas 1942 was a time of profound short-ages. Being able to poach some hard-won eggs and open a hoarded tin of apricots, to be served with 'cream' whisked up from powdered milk and water with a little sugar, gave Nella intense satisfaction. 'Never since the boys left home have I prepared Christmas Eve tea so happily.' And what joy she felt, opening her presents the next day, to find two pairs of silk knickers in a parcel from her daughter-in-law Edith, and a book of stamps from her young neighbour Margaret.

Small delights grew in proportion to their scarcity. At a time when eggs were almost non-existent Mary Fedden went to the grocer and managed to get two, one of which had a double yolk. 'We thought that was the luckiest thing that happened to us in the war.' Barbara Pym was even luckier; she got hold of a seven-pound jar of marma-lade: 'Not even love is so passionately longed for.' At the end of a day of black depression, missing her prisoner-of-war son, engulfed with uncertainty about the future, Clara Milburn found that going to church lifted her spirits. And later she went out into the garden, rejoiced quietly at the fading colours, took true pleasure in her new permanent wave and felt blessed by the regeneration of a damaged thumbnail that had finally ceased to be unsightly. What luck, too, to possess a wickerwork wheelbarrow, a sweet dog like Twink, friends and a home.

Hard work brought unexpected rewards. Susan Woolfit's war work as a member of the all-female crew of a narrow-boat plying the inland waterways of Britain gave her life new meaning; petty irrita-tions melted away in the face of an engrossing and physically demanding activity. Housework, queues, rations, responsibilities, keeping up appearances and the sheer ennui of war were replaced by thrilling excitement: 'I was enjoying every second of it.' She loved the boats themselves, their cosy cabins shared with congenial companions; she loved the still black nights on the canals, and the early mornings as the boats started up again, with the locks clanging and the water surging. Her work left her 'revitalised and vibrating with life and new hope'.

'You lived at that period from day to day,' says Cora Johnston. 'You had to because you would have gone under if you hadn't. Today was IT – because you never knew if the next day was going to be your last.' In some ways war made life less complicated. 'Why hesitate? Why defer?' was the insistent message that drummed through every disaster, every blow dealt by fate: 'Do it today. Do it now. Work – travel – experiment – enjoy – dance – love – live.'

Out of Bounds

Phyllis Noble longed for adventure. But, aged twenty-one, she felt trapped in a backwater. She had never in her life travelled more than 50 miles beyond London. Now, three and a half years after the declaration of war, she was still living under her parents' roof in Lewisham, still a wage-slave, still enduring the daily ordeal of travelling through bombed streets to her 'reserved occupation' in the foreign accounts section of the National Provincial Bank. 'That wretched bank. I'm so fed up with the endless routine work I could scream and scream every time I sit down at that hateful machine . . . It is high time I started making up my mind what I really want in life,' she confided to her diary, listing love, travel, a minimum of two babies and educational improvement ('there is so much I *want* to learn') as essential must-dos for the future.

Phyllis had had a grammar-school education and in autumn 1941 had enrolled with her friend Pluckie for evening classes at Morley College. She was naturally inquisitive and intellectual, and the classes had awakened in her radical ideas: socialism, internationalism, feminism. They also stimulated her thirst for travel and independence, and yet, beyond the nine-to-five treadmill, the future seemed only to offer a reprise of her mother's experience: housework, motherhood and drudgery.

This destiny seemed all the more preordained after she started going out with a friend of her brother, Andrew Cooper. Andrew had much to recommend him as a boyfriend. He was good-looking – blue-eyed with a silky mop of dark hair – besides being musical and a talented artist, and romance bloomed. Phyllis's parents approved of him too: they could see that his culture made him attractive to their daughter and, more importantly, he was safely and respectably employed. As a draughtsman with an engineering firm designing war weapons, Andrew was in a reserved occupation. The Nobles made him welcome for cocoa when he dropped in on his way back from Home Guard duty, or for tea on Sundays.

But despite, or because of, the settled nature of her relationship with Andrew, Phyllis now started to play a game of emotional roulette. How had she found herself living in a boring suburb, rooted in a boring job and all but engaged to her steady boyfriend, when around her the world was on fire? 'The dramatic events [of the war] served to increase my discontent with the dull part I was playing in them.' She knew she was flighty, bad and irresponsible but, like a gambler let loose in a casino, she couldn't stop herself: 'I was often uneasy about my capricious behaviour but unable to control it.'

It started with James, an intellectual Yorkshireman who worked at the bank. His good looks and dubious reputation both as a pacifist and a womaniser only enhanced his attraction. Pluckie too was besotted. With his misty eyes and searing intelligence he had both girls at his feet. Phyllis made a date with him to go second-hand book-shopping; the cover story failed to convince Andrew, who was openly jealous. But on this occasion her transgression went no further than an intense conversation in his Bloomsbury garret: 'I hugged my knees in delight at what still seemed to me this daringly unconventional act of being alone with a man in his bed-sitting room.' But that was all. Nevertheless, her susceptibility to stray bohemians continued to get the better of her.

Next was Don, an artist *manqué* who had worked at the bank: Phyllis and he had had a brief dalliance back in 1940, after which he had been called up by the RAF and sent for pilot training in Canada. Now, newly debonair and dashing, he reappeared on leave with the coveted wings gleaming on his breast pocket. When he also happened to mention that he had returned from Canada with no fewer than *eighteen* pairs of silk stockings in his suitcase, Phyllis was bowled over, but had to explain, very reluctantly, that she was about to leave for a

week's holiday in Wales with Andrew. She promised to telephone
Don as soon as she got back, fearing that in her absence he would find
another taker for the silk stockings. Meanwhile, she and Andrew
holidayed chastely with his grandparents in their seafront cottage,
and war seemed far away as they trekked the craggy hillsides of
Snowdonia and picnicked beside glittering waterfalls. 'By the end of
the week in such surroundings I was almost certain that Andrew was
to be my one true love.'

Almost certain. Back in London, she was straight on the phone to
Don. Don had given half the stockings to an ex-girlfriend, but spared
no expense to wine her, dine her and take her out to theatres. They
both knew that life was short in Bomber Command, and neither had
any qualms about dropping their commitments to enjoy a heady
whirl of pleasures. Youth would pass, the music would die, kisses
were there to be snatched. It was all over in a fortnight – but the
remaining stockings were hers.

Andrew, however, stayed loyal. By now he was 'almost a member
of the family'. He was virtually regarded by her parents as their future
son-in-law, and it became more and more difficult for Phyllis to
detach from him. Yet the inevitable culmination of the relationship
– marriage – was abhorrent to her. Five years earlier, in the pre-war
world, Phyllis's dilemma might not have been so acute. As with so
many young women, the war had thrown opportunities at her that,
in 1939, would have seemed out of reach. The uncertainty of war was
contagious. What law said that you had to marry a boyfriend because
your parents liked him? Who had ordained that one couldn't have a
bit of fun, play around, travel, experiment? The forces of convention
grabbed her and held her captive; breathless, she thrashed and writhed
for a little liberty, a little space:

I would not give up my freedom to go out with other men friends, such as
Don, which must have caused Andrew as much misery as my recurrent
attacks of discontent and despondency.

. . . I suddenly decided to break off from him. In a way, I still believed I
loved him, yet I knew I did not want to marry him and nor did I want to go
on as before.

Within a few weeks, circumstances were to drive her back. She discovered by chance that Andrew had fallen ill; he was in hospital with

suspected tuberculosis. Filled with remorse, she dashed to his bedside, and as soon as he recovered they were lovingly reunited. This time Phyllis dropped any inhibitions she may have clung to. She had long ago rejected the idea that virginity should be preserved until marriage; her future, she was convinced, held brighter dreams than just being a wife. And so the irrevocable step was taken one Sunday afternoon on the floor of his parents' sitting room while they were out. It was not a romantic setting: the pink and beige patterned carpet on which they embraced was curiously at odds with the brutal form of the iron Morrison shelter that dominated one side of the room. But she had no regrets. On the contrary, it was a coming-of-age, an awakening to the happy discovery of her own passionate nature.

March 8th 1942.

A new page for a new era – At last I've gone over the precipice!

It is certainly true that for many women the war years were dominated by exhaustion, worry, shortages, fear and broken hearts. But the hopelessness and unhappiness of war tend to eclipse the sunny intervals. Phyllis Noble's newfound physical infatuation with Andrew was of this kind: a series of tender, radiant vignettes that sit brightly beside the familiar monochrome home-front snapshots of food queues and factory lines. Desire had taken hold of them both. Now, whenever they could be together, they looked for privacy, a place to drain and exhaust their urgent appetites. After dusk, parks were good places; since the Blitz, the wrought-iron gates were no longer closed, and they would find a bench there under the majestic elm trees. At weekends the woods, with their undisturbed forests of deep bracken, were a bus ride away. Phyllis's cousin Nel, who took a warmly broad-minded attitude towards the young lovers, invited them to stay in her primitive cottage in Hertfordshire. There were enchanted nights with the owl hooting outside the bedroom window, candlelight illuminating their amorous exertions as they struggled to tear their clothes off and climb under the eiderdown. And a holiday in the West Country – despite the landlady who conformed to type by firmly allocating them separate bedrooms – offered the magical seclusion of empty moorland and sheltered hedgerows. They took bus rides to the coast and explored the cliff walks. In Dorset it was possible to buy cream cakes; they sat on the Cobb at Lyme Regis and devoured them, looking out to sea. At their lodgings they dined on hearty home-cooked fare, and ration books seemed to belong to a world they had left behind. Before bed they wandered again hand in hand between the high, violet-scented banks, and watched a spring moon rise over the darkening hedgerows.

*

Joan Wyndham's war was more crème de menthe and amphetamines than moorland hikes and cream teas. She was only nineteen when she qualified as a WAAF filter room plotter, too young and dizzy to have felt the pressure of home responsibilities. But war not only sharpened her appetite for excitement, drink, friends, men and fun, for a convent-educated virgin it offered unimaginable liberty to indulge them. And once she'd been relieved of her onerous chastity and acquired some contraceptive Volpar gels she launched into a free-spirited round of amorous adventures. In September 1942 Joan was posted to Inverness. That meant parting from Zoltan, her Hungarian lover in London, but she had few regrets, and shortly after arriving at the WAAF mess she had the complete low-down on all the available males within a 10-mile radius. There was Bomber Command HQ, and the Cameron Highlanders were the local regiment. Canadians were based in the area, and battleships arrived frequently. Even better, the Norwegian navy was much in evidence: 'they're gorgeous, sexy and very, very funny . . . they drink like fishes and take over the whole town'. But the hottest attraction, married though he was, was Lord Lovat,* who trained his commandos in the grounds of nearby Beaufort Castle: 'There is not a girl in our Mess who doesn't secretly lust after him – including me!' Great excitement, therefore, when the WAAFs got an invitation from the Royal Engineers to a dance at their mess, which was based at the castle. Unfortunately, his Lordship wasn't there. However, Joan danced with the next best, Lord Lovat's cousin Hamish. 'We got drunk together and I was on top form and happy as hell.'

For Joan, time off duty now meant dates at the castle to join Ham-

---

* Simon Fraser, 15th Lord Lovat, hero of the Dieppe Raid and later recipient of the Military Cross after his actions on Sword Beach during the Normandy invasion. He was also famed on that occasion for instructing his Scots piper to pipe the commandos ashore, in defiance of contrary orders.

ish in his aristocratic Highland activities. She accompanied him in borrowed brogues for shooting expeditions, admiring his 'jutting, compact Highland bottom' as he slaughtered the local wildlife and waited for him to make a pass at her. Up hill, down dale and through swamps they stalked deer and capercailzie, tummy-down in the heather: not Joan's idea of a good time until, flat on their faces in a bog one day, Hamish gasped, 'God, I want to rush madly to bed with you!' Hamish now offered a couple of days of bright lights in the big city, so Joan applied for 'forty-eight' and travelled to London at the earliest opportunity. With Hamish in his best Savile Row suit and Joan in her favourite little black dress, they hit the Bagatelle for cocktails – 'Three martinis later we were both floating' – followed by the Gargoyle for smoochy dancing, and then on to the 400 Club, with bowing waiters proffering brandy. As for sex, nothing was settled until they were in the taxi lurching back to Chelsea, whereupon he kissed her and popped the inevitable question: bed? Joan promptly caved in: 'I seem to find it awfully difficult to say no to a member of the aristocracy.' It had something to do with blue blood, she confessed. Sadly, the seduction scene was a disappointment: 'He was enormously heavy, and it was rather boring and seemed to go on for hours.' A streak of maudlin Catholicism inhibited poor Hamish from climaxing, and – explaining that he had to get to early Mass the next morning before catching his train – he declined to stay the night.

Onwards and upwards: in January 1943 Joan got news that gorgeous German Gerhardt, her first love, had returned from internment in Australia. They engineered a reunion in London, but this time Gerhardt seemed somehow 'old and rather grubby'. She rejected his offer of bed, but friendship was restored over a Soho pub crawl, ending at the Café Royal. Being a WAAF didn't mean putting all the old bohemian days behind her. Back in Inverness she surpassed herself at the St Valentine's dance with a combination of gin, rum, Algerian wine and Benzedrine. And life in the north of Scotland started to look up greatly with the arrival for refitting of the Norwegian ships, complete with mad, sexy, blue-eyed, blond Viking crew and limitless supplies of Aquavit. Joan fell for the first one to pick her up, Hans, who was six feet tall with 'the face of an angel'. At the May Day party he also proved to be 'a wizard dancer':

Dancing is the thing I like best in life . . . I danced with a narcissus between my teeth, and I can remember thinking – in the middle of a rumba – that I was so happy that I wanted to cry.

By 8 May she was writing in her diary:

Life is a dream of spring and fine weather, moonlit nights and beautiful young men . . .

and on the 18th:

I definitely love him.

Finding somewhere to go to bed together was a puzzle, until Joan got hold of WAAF insider information about a little hotel by Loch Ness, 'where everybody goes for their dirty weekends'. Hans proved sweet, handsome and somewhat inexperienced. They spent a wakeful night of passion; for him, at least, since Joan persisted in finding that the proceedings left her cold, physically if not emotionally. 'I felt nothing, except for love.'

Nevertheless it soon turned out that compatibility, sexual or otherwise, had nothing to do with it. Hans disapproved of Joan's habit of writing poetry; he also hated 'pansies', painters, and 'creeps who wear berets'. His idea of a nice normal woman was a cross between a blonde Vikingess ready to hike mountains and sail fjords and his mother, with a hearty meal of reindeer meat and cloudberry jam all ready for her son when he got in from skiing. This led Joan to wonder what could possibly be the attraction of such an uncultured outdoorsy Philistine:

Maybe this love of ours is just some kind of sick aberration only made possible by the war?

Maybe. Early in July Hans and the refurbished ships sailed for the Shetlands; Joan was posted to East Anglia for a refresher course, followed by a few free days in London: time for a riotous binge in the company of notorious beret-wearing bohemians Julian MacLaren Ross, Nina Hamnett, Tambimuttu, Ruthven Todd and Dylan Thomas. But the revels ended prematurely when the air-raid siren went off. The company piled into a taxi, with Joan squashed up against a lust-crazed Dylan; back at Ruthven's studio Joan was offered a mattress and

21. Dressed for the job, women shipyard workers manoeuvre a steel girder into position. Between 1939 and 1942 the numbers of women in the workplace tripled.

22. 'I felt that no one could possibly win the war without me!' In 1940 QA Lorna Bradey believed the world was at her feet. This later picture shows her in battledress, which replaced the impractical, but feminine, scarlet capes and white veils.

23. For Pip Beck, her job as an R/T operator at Bomber Command seemed the fulfilment of all her romantic dreams.

24. ATS kit inspection in a typical services dormitory. Note the 'biscuits', in three sections, laid out to form a mattress.

25. and 26. Jean McFadyen (*left*) was one of 6,000 members of the Timber Corps who worked in the forests year-round cutting timber for everything from pit props to coffins.

27. and 28. (*Left*) Land girl Kay Mellis from Edinburgh: 'I must admit that, when I could thin neeps a bit better, and lift tatties a bit better, it did make me feel really good.' (*Right*) Thinning turnips in the Lake District.

29. Images from the home front: a rumour has spread that this stall will be selling fish. A queue of hopeful housewives has formed, hours ahead.

30. Kerbside recycling, 1940s-style.

31. 'Half of the lawn will grow potatoes,' wrote Nella Last. Many housewives like her transformed their front gardens into vegetable plots.

32. Rag-and-bone women from a London branch of the WVS, collecting aluminium.

33. On VJ-day Helen Forrester (*back row, far right*) joined friends to celebrate. But her brave smile for the camera was a mask: she felt angry, lost and dreadfully alone.

34. Doris Scorer and her friends at the Works were bent on keeping up appearances: 'We always hoped to look like mannequins.'

35. 'Utility' styles skimped on details, eliminating cuffs, frills and fullness to save fabric.

36. As skirt lengths rose, legs became more visible, and the stocking shortage became ever more problematic. This model demonstrates one solution to faking the perfect 'seam'.

37. Christian Oldham chose to enlist in the Wrens because of the hat and the 'nice straight uniform' designed by Molyneux.

38. British girls were swept off their feet by the arrival of the sexy GIs. 'Heard about the new utility knickers? One Yank – and they're off.'

39. Verily Anderson with Marian and Rachel, 1945; childcare in wartime left her 'sapped' and wilting. Had fun become a thing of the past?

40. Not for all. Nightclubs and dance halls were humming throughout the war. Here, a black US serviceman in civvies teaches his partner to jitterbug.

'I had a simply wonderful leave – my heart was broken four times.'
Away from watchful parental eyes, many young women revelled in the
opportunity for off-duty romance.

a cupboard-sized room, where she took the precaution of wedging a chair under the door handle and tried to sleep as the bombs crashed outside. Impossible. Dylan was rattling at the makeshift lock, with cries of 'I want to fuck you! I want to fuck you!'

There were ominous thuds as Dylan hurled himself against the panelling. Thump went Dylan! Crump went the bombs! . . .

At last I heard Ruthven's voice firmly remonstrating, and finally the sounds of a heavy body being dragged reluctantly away.

I curled myself up under my greatcoat and slept like the dead.

*

Elizabeth Jane Howard was another hugely talented writer who confesses that her war was largely defined by men and sex. 'I do think people went to bed with each other much more easily,' she says today, 'very largely because it might be the last thing they did. It's probably Nature's way of preserving the human race.' Old age has given Jane Howard a kind of queenly assurance, as well as an unembarrassed honesty about her own youthful faults. In her autobiography *Slipstream*

(2002) Jane Howard describes herself as 'essentially immature . . . I'd succeeded in nothing . . .' She tells how she was turned down by the Wrens (who considered her under-qualified), and describes her unhappy marriage with Peter Scott. But in 1942 Jane became pregnant. As an important naval officer, Scott was allowed to have his wife billeted in a comfortable hotel close to his base, but he was out all day. 'I was homesick, and I didn't know what the hell to do with myself.' Pregnancy exempted her from war work. 'I read, I ran out of books, and I went for walks . . . I felt terribly sick. And the only thing to eat at this ghastly hotel was lobster. You try having lobster twice a day for three months when you're feeling rather queasy.' That winter she moved back to London. On 2 February 1943 – the day the Germans surrendered at Stalingrad – her daughter was prematurely born during an air raid.

But after a traumatic birth, Jane lacked maternal feelings for baby Nicola, who screamed, wouldn't feed and only compounded her sense of inadequacy. That summer she fell in love with Wayland Scott, her husband's brother. 'The first time he kissed me I discovered what physical desire meant . . . I was his first love as in a sense he was mine.' They cemented the guilt by sleeping together, then owning up to Peter. There was a terrible row, and Jane was carted off to stagnate at his naval base in Holyhead. But it was only a matter of time before the vacuum in her life was refilled. Threatened by boredom in Holyhead, she decided to put on a production of *The Importance of Being Earnest* with the navy, with Philip Lee, a handsome blond officer, playing Algernon to her Gwendoline. One winter afternoon they climbed Holyhead Mountain and made love among the crags. The affair continued after her return to London, where they borrowed a painter friend's studio for delicious, secret assignations. 'I don't think Pete ever knew about it.'

*

Meanwhile, Phyllis Noble still felt uncommitted, despite the physical bond that now held her to her lover. Her insistent sexual desire for Andrew seemed to point in the direction of commitment. Her parents liked him; her choice of boyfriend, if not her illicit sex life, had their blessing. But the war pushed in the opposite direction. Nursing, perhaps, would give her the chance to 'do her bit' while experiencing foreign parts. But in late 1942 the government was drawing ever more women into the conscription net, and, finally, Phyllis heard that she was to be released from the bank. However, conscription took little account of preferences; you had to go where you were needed, and the fear that she might be called up for the dreaded ATS made Phyllis consider, briefly, whether it would be best to avoid the whole thing by just going ahead and getting married. 'I knew Andrew was willing, and sometimes during our best moments together I thought I might be too. Then I would draw back – for, to me, marriage continued to seem like the end of the road.' And as the trap she most feared seemed to close on her, Phyllis blundered into yet another reckless relationship.

A good-looking redhead, with confidence bordering on arrogance, Stephen was another young man who had paid court to her at the bank, before disappearing – like Don – for overseas RAF training. That autumn he returned and quickly homed in on Phyllis. His glamour, domineering manner and well-travelled sophistication rendered her helpless, and she soon persuaded herself that it would be unkind not to 'help him enjoy his leave'. This didn't mean sleeping with him: 'Stephen was willing to accept that our relationship must for the time being remain platonic . . . Andrew remained my lover but had to put up with my temporary desertion each time Stephen appeared on leave.' Then in March 1943 Phyllis was accepted by the WAAF. She put herself down to train as a meteorological observer. Soon after, Stephen proposed to her and, swept off her feet, she accepted. That night she agonised about what she had done. This was a man she barely knew, had hardly kissed, felt no physical attraction for, and yet she could be pregnant by Andrew. Her family reacted with predictable horror, but Phyllis, now wearing a diamond and garnet cluster on her finger, was too deep in to backtrack. Circumstances came to her rescue, but the cost was high. Stephen's aircraft crashed. He survived, severely burned, after being pulled from the wreckage. When she visited him in hospital, he honourably suggested releasing her from the engagement, which initially she felt unable to agree to. 'But . . . whatever had drawn us together was waning.' They parted, and she returned the pretty ring, feeling she had learned a damaging lesson. Lovers were one thing, a husband was quite another.

*

Times were changing. For women in wartime, the wages of sin were often automatic dismissal, but no longer always automatic disgrace. Meanwhile, male attitudes remained predictably primitive. In time-honoured fashion, men continued to achieve a mental disconnect between their sexual and emotional needs. The pin-ups of bosomy Hollywood starlets and scantily clad cutie-pies adorning army accommodation and Spitfire fuselages played into a fantasy driven by lust and loneliness. So did 'Jane',★ the *Daily Mirror*'s famous curva-ceous cartoon blonde, credited with boosting troop morale every time her skirt got caught in a door or she lost her towel on the way to the shower. And if centre-fold girls didn't do enough to quench a man's libido, there were plenty of real-life vamps out there ready and waiting to do their bit. Servicemen away from home could take a 'pick'n'mix' approach to the locals, the amateur fun-lovers and the so-called 'good-time girls'. If you were in a hurry, or in transit, you consulted the graffiti on the toilet walls at barracks: 'Try Betty, she's easy' and so on. Ex-WAAF Joan Tagg remembers that when she was stationed at Oxford 'there was a girl there called the camp bicycle. I didn't know who she was, but all the boys there who needed her would have known.'

'Jane', with only a union flag to preserve her modesty.

★ Based on the real-life artists' model Christabel Leighton-Porter 1913-2000.

Where there are soldiers there are camp-followers. Wherever it might be, at home or abroad, the army attracted another, shadier army of women cashing in on a captive market and (in Britain) a law which turned a blind eye to the activities of street-walkers. The blackout favoured their dubious trade; in London they were dubbed the 'Piccadilly Commandos'. The numbers of such women reflected the increase in conscripts and, to the dismay of the health authorities, venereal infections showed a parallel proliferation. In the first two years of the war new cases of syphilis in men were up 113 per cent, in women 63 per cent. With the arrival of the GIs such diseases reached almost epidemic proportions. Outside Rainbow Corner – the American servicemen's club on the corner of Shaftesbury Avenue – the 'Commandos' were like bees round a honeypot; one US staff sergeant recalled how they swarmed round the darkened West End:

The girls were there – everywhere. They walked along Shaftesbury Avenue and past Rainbow Corner, pausing only when there was no policeman watching . . . At the underground entrance they were thickest, and as the evening grew dark, they shone torches on their ankles as they walked and bumped into the soldiers murmuring, 'Hello Yank', 'Hello Soldier', 'Hello Dearie!'

Apparently they often issued a supercharge of $5 – 'to pay for blackout curtains'. Sex was on the streets as never before. Less recognised is that some of these prostitutes were themselves servicewomen. Flo Mahony was a WAAF who shared her accommodation at her Swanage base with a pretty young woman named Phyllis, who regarded the nearby men's camp as a business opportunity:

She was a WAAF driver – a great friend of mine, and she had been a prostitute . . . Well, she would get dressed up and go off out at night. We covered for each other – and obviously we all guessed. She had red cami-knickers, she'd always got perfume and she'd always got talcum powder – things which were quite difficult for us to get. We never talked to her about it, but she went with servicemen I suppose. We all liked her, and she was no trouble to us.

The army was also a two-way traffic for sex workers: the services might offer an escape route to women trapped in a degraded profession – 'I've been working in London for years as a prostitute,' one of them confided to a fellow recruit, 'and I joined up to try to leave it all behind me.'

The Wages of Sin

Meanwhile, four years of war had not shifted men's deeply rooted presumptions as to what they felt owed by women. On the one hand, they wanted to go to bed with them. And men could be selfishly persuasive if they wanted sex with married women: 'A slice off a cut loaf ain't missed.' On the other hand, they wanted to be mummied, fed and looked after. They expected fidelity, modesty, domesticity and duty. Scattered over battle fronts from Mandalay to Mersa Matruh, husbands and boyfriends now nurtured the dream of coming home to find their domestic goddess fantasy intact. But things were changing. Disturbing clashes often resulted:

'How can I be sure she will be true?'

'Every time my husband comes home on leave I am terribly thrilled. But when we meet it is nothing but silly little squabbles.'

'My wife is working on a farm and I am in the Army . . . Each time I come home I see her being very friendly with the farm men. I feel angry and suspicious.'

'He asked me to clean his army boots for him.'

In 1939 there had been just under 10,000 divorce petitions. Now, not surprisingly, divorce rates surged. Women – and men – often embarked hastily and ignorantly on marriages which they then repented. But the millions of wives working in factories and army camps didn't have time to keep the home fires burning. The domestic goddess had hung up her apron and donned overalls or battle-dress. She was out earning good money and she was placing her duty to her country above her duty to her home. By 1945 that figure had increased to 27,000 petitions, 70 per cent of these on grounds of adultery. Had it not been for the conviction among many respectably brought-up girls that 'hanky-panky' was wrong there would surely have been many more.

But if innocence, trust and tradition got misplaced along the way, well, there were compensations. Making love in the crags or amid the bracken, dancing the rumba, spring nights and beautiful young men all helped to banish the miseries of war – and who would blame anyone for trying to do that?

*

Jane Howard's baby daughter Nicola had made an inauspicious start to life in 1943. Jane had endured a wearisome pregnancy and gave birth three weeks early after a long and agonising labour. In the following weeks she tried and failed to love the screaming little scrap who had cost her such pain and fatigue. 'I'd not wanted her enough and was no good as a mother.' She put her love affairs before her child at this time, and many years were to pass before her maternal feelings eventually matured.

Babies, however, were very much wanted by the powers that be. Before the war, there had been much wringing of hands over the decline of the birth rate in Britain. By 1939 it had dropped to below replacement levels, with 2 million fewer under-fourteens than in 1914, and a worsening situation developing by 1941. With worries about a shrinking and ageing population the correspondence columns of the press were deluged with anxious letters, of which the following are typical:

14 March 1942

Let us see a state-sponsored plan for the systematic increase of our population before it is too late.

9 October 1942

What are we doing about our . . . birth-rate, the increase of which must be considerably curtailed by the fact that innumerable husbands serving in the forces have been sent overseas for the duration of the war?

One explanation given for the statistics was that parents were too filled with gloom about the future to go forth and multiply. Mass Observation interviewed a young woman – a midwife – who angrily accused the authorities of trying to persuade women to breed more soldiers as cannon fodder: 'I think it's horrible. They don't want the babies for their own sakes at all, just for wars.' How-

ever, the 1943 figures, when they were published, showed an
unexpected turnaround. Nicola was one of 811,000 babies born in
the UK that year, a rise of 115,000 from 1941 figures. After that, the
figures continued to increase. The analysts breathed a sigh of relief.
It seemed that the practice and profession of motherhood would
not go into irreversible decline and that we would not, after all, be
overtaken by the fecund Germans. (When Naomi Mitchison's
daughter-in-law told her she was expecting a baby at this time,
Naomi's reaction was: 'It's one in the eye for Hitler.') An explanation for much of this boost was that large numbers of young people
born in the last, post-First World War baby boom were now reaching maturity. There was also the fact that 1939–40 had been a peak
year for marriages. However, included in that 1943 figure of 811,000
births were 53,000 babies who were illegitimate – a figure also set to
rise as the war progressed.

Behind the statistics lies a multitude of sad case histories. On 23
March 1943 Nella Last confided to her diary the upsetting tale she
had been told that day by a complete stranger at the WVS centre.
This woman had burst into tears without warning; Nella fetched her
a glass of water and listened while she unburdened herself: 'I feel I'm
going out of my mind with worry.' Her twenty-three-year-old
daughter, it appeared, was a married Wren, whose husband had been
a prisoner of war since Dunkirk. However the girl had no intention,
it seemed, of repining; she was always the life and soul of every party,
and it now transpired that she was five months pregnant. Between
sobs, the mother told Nella that she and her husband were being torn
apart by their daughter's predicament; the father, in a great rage,
accusing her of being a slut, with the mother inclining to believe her
daughter's tale: that she knew nothing of how this had happened and
must have been 'tight' at the time. Nella sat with her and did her best
to soothe her, but the poor woman was distraught.

Unmarried servicewomen who fell pregnant were duly noted on a
POR, or Personal Occurrence Report, then issued with 'Paragraph
11s' and dismissed from the force. In the WAAFs, for example, 'it
was a fate worse than death to get pregnant – you were out!' One
ATS officer posted to the Orkneys commented on the extreme
number of 'Para 11s' issued in her company – inevitable, she suggested, given that there were no fewer than 10,000 men on the island

in two ack-ack brigades. However it could be hard to tell if the girls were pregnant, as the ATS uniforms were oddly bulky and could hide a multitude of sins. One girl was heard screaming in her hut; she was packed off to hospital with a case of 'severe constipation', where it turned out that she was giving birth.

Far worse was the nightmare ordeal suffered by QA Lorna Bradey, who in 1942 was based in a Cairo hospital. While there she got a surprise message from an old nursing friend who had come down on leave from her hospital in Eritrea. 'Could I come at once to her hotel . . . urgent.' Lorna went down as soon as she was off duty and found her friend lying on the hotel bed, bleeding copiously. She had become pregnant by a very 'high-up' official and had travelled to Cairo for a backstreet abortion. To Lorna, who had studied midwifery, it was immediately plain that her friend could die at any moment and must be got to hospital. The friend begged her not to betray her secret, leaving Lorna no choice. She massaged her uterus, packed her out with towels, and obtained black-market antibiotics. 'Sepsis was the thing I feared most. I made her swallow a good handful of these.' Throughout the night Lorna sat with her, taking her weakening pulse, mopping up as coagulating blood and fragments of placenta came away from the welter of redness between her legs. At long last the antibiotics took hold, and the bleeding slowed. Lorna, having saved her friend's life, visited her over the next week as she improved, after which she returned to her unit – 'weak but alive' – and well enough to spin a tale about 'gippy tummy'. Despite Lorna's stupendous efforts, this friend broke off contact with her after the war. She knew too much.

Barbara Cartland stressed, however, that pregnant servicewomen like this were in a tiny minority. In her view, it was only surprising that there weren't more illegitimacies in the services, considering the danger and proximity that men and women underwent together.

Civilian women were often fair game for the soldiers. Seventeen-year-old Vivian Fisher's husband first deserted from the army and then walked out on her. Left on her own, Vivian took consolation in the arms of a soldier serving with the Royal Engineers; she had a baby girl by him, but he too beat a retreat. 'I was devastated . . . it took me a time to get over the hurt.' Her next baby, a boy, was born to Jimmy, an attractive GI who promised to marry her and take her back with him to America. She would have gone had her errant husband not returned unexpectedly. Another woman whose husband was abroad slept with a GI and got pregnant but decided her lover must not know, otherwise he would never let her go. Heartbroken, she finished with him, while suffering torments at the thought that she was also deceiving her absent husband.

Distance could cause terrible misunderstandings. A soldier based in Iraq went to his brigadier in great distress, having received the following cable from his wife: SON BORN BOTH DOING WELL LOVE MARY. He hadn't seen her for two years. The brigadier did his best to comfort the poor man, who departed – only to return shortly afterwards waving a letter which explained everything to his entire satisfaction. 'It's all right, sir, it's not her it's my *mother*. She's a widow. Must have been playing around with some man.'

The agony aunts did their best to respond to desperate women like this one who wrote in about their infidelities:

My husband is a prisoner of war, and I was dreadfully depressed and lonely until I met two allied officers who were very sweet to me. Now I realise that I am going to have a baby, and I don't know which is the father.

Do anything to avoid hurting your husband, advised *Woman's Own*.

Motherhood in wartime carried its own particular burdens. Pregnant mums (dubbed Woolton's 'preggies' from the minister's concern to distribute rations among the 'priority classes') didn't get extra clothing coupons. They were expected to let out their existing dresses to fit, though with their green ration books they were first in line for extra milk, meat, eggs and orange juice concentrate. Bombs were blamed for miscarriages; babies might be born in air-raid shelters or under tables in the blackout; traumatised and exhausted, their mothers often found their milk supply dried up.

If you took the decision to evacuate your children for their safety there was the pain of separation. But Madeleine Henrey and her husband decided to stick it out in London for the duration. Little Bobby, born in summer 1939, grew up to the sound of exploding bombs, and his loving parents, who had already had to take the dreadful decision to leave Madeleine's French mother behind in German-occupied Normandy, were reluctant to split up their family more than they had to. The Henreys had taken a small flat in the

Shepherd Market area of Mayfair; it was modern and solidly built. With a very young baby, Madeleine was not expected to take on war work; she spent her days wheeling the perambulator down the shrapnel-strewn pathways of Green Park, with Pouffy the Pekinese snuggled into Bobby's coverlet. She got reproachful looks from some of the local Londoners who thought her misguided for keeping the child in the city, 'but he grew plump and rosy-cheeked, oblivious of the thuds that woke us from time to time'. After a while the market costers and other shoppers got to know Bobby as 'the child who would not be evacuated' and treated him as a kind of mascot. When Robert Henrey returned from his office at the end of the day, he was often greeted by strangers giving him cheerful updates on his small son's progress.

Verily Bruce was another young mother who had no misgivings about her role in the war. In August 1940, when she married Donald and became Mrs Anderson, she reflected that she had now found her 'real aim in life'. She continued to harbour writing ambitions, but despite Donald's ministry post she was mostly kept too busy to fulfil them. Pregnant during the Blitz with the first of her five babies, she took up knitting 'tiny garments' and found the work so soothing that she was able to ignore the bombs. In spring 1941 Verily was awaiting the birth in a maternity home in Esher, in the next bed to Julie, a lively and loveable Cockney evacuee. Verily had Marian ten days after Julie's little boy James was born. The mum network quickly proved valuable for them both. Julie was lodging with a horrible landlady who made her wash the baby's nappies in a bucket in the yard; she was miserable. The Andersons had a spare room. Why shouldn't Julie and her baby move in with them?

'Oh, wouldn't it be lovely!' she said. And then she came back and said, 'I'm afraid I can't do it . . .' And I said, 'Oh, but it's all arranged, our babies are going to be brother and sister . . .' At which point she burst into tears and said, 'You see I'm not married.' 'Good heavens,' I said, 'that's nothing! All the more reason why you should come.' So she did, and she was absolutely wonderful, because I was very ill after the birth, and she just took over both babies until I was better and could help. And she could do the housework very much better than me!

By the time air raids on London resumed Verily had two small children. Three-year-old Marian found that the bombing provided a thrilling distraction from bed-time. As newborn Rachel slept beatifically in her cot she would bounce excitedly on her parents' bed listening to the bombs whistling over St John's Wood:

'One two three and a –'

'Bang!' she shouted with delight as the bomb exploded.

'More bangs?' she asked hopefully.

'Oh, the woos,' she said regretfully of the all-clear, knowing it meant she must return to bed.

Soon after, Verily and her two small daughters evacuated to Gloucestershire and set up home with a couple of friends who were there, working as land girls. Their husbands were abroad, and one of them had a young baby. Cockney Julie and little James joined them, and Donald came when he could. While her friends were out milking cows and lifting turnips, Verily took lodgers, did the cooking, looked after the dogs and ran a kind of women's baby co-operative for all four children.

Verily Anderson's memoir of her wartime experiences sits oddly beside the piles of books written by so many of her female contemporaries, with titles like *We All Wore Blue*, *A WAAF in Bomber Command* or *The Girls Behind the Guns*. The servicewomen write about uniforms and drill, camps and operations, romances and mess dances. In *Spam Tomorrow*, Verily – and she was typical of many thousands – writes about maternity wards and sick infants, orange juice and sweets, about threadworm, tonsillitis, cod-liver oil and the balloon and cracker shortage, and about how the only way to obtain a nursery fireguard was to salvage one from a bomb site. Babies had become her life. Even when a well-meaning friend persuaded her to take an evening out and go dancing at the Bagatelle she found she had lost the appetite for adult dissipations. Reluctantly she put on her best dress, donned false eyelashes and accepted a glass of champagne. It was no good. Her favourite club just seemed tatty, and the clientèle looked shallow and laughable capering around the room. 'We were . . . too sapped by the war and work and babies to do more than sit and wilt until the time was decent to go home.'

Under the Volcano

War and work and babies. Verily had a Cockney mother's help and a husband at home, but she still felt drained and exhausted.

War and men, war and sex, war and relationships. Negotiating a personal life while holding up a gruelling job proved formidable enough – all the more so for the many whose war work took them far from home, at times into the field of battle. In 1942–3 QA Lorna Bradey's career was to bring her up against some of the toughest challenges she had yet faced. She, and many women like her, endured the worst that battle zones could throw at her, proving the equal of men in stamina and courage.

Lorna's story, told thirty years after the war had ended, is not exceptional. Her experiences were typical ones for the indomitable nurses who staffed army hospitals in combat zones wherever they were needed, but they offer a vivid case history of the everyday stress, danger and brutally hard work that women like her encountered on active service abroad. At the same time, Lorna's account reminds us of the rapture, the thrills and the intensity bordering on hysteria that often accompanied the pressures. For Sister Bradey, those were days never to be forgotten.

Almost a year after Alamein, and with the Americans now firmly entrenched in the war, our enemies were beginning to take the defensive position. Early in July 1943 160,000 Allied soldiers landed in Sicily, taking the Italian and German divisions by surprise. From a British perspective, it was too early for a Second Front, and victory on the Italian mainland would re-establish Mediterranean dominance.

By November 1943 Lorna had already been working abroad for two and a half years with no break to return home. Now, as the 8th Army prepared to battle its way up the Italian peninsula, she and eighty of her fellow QAs were shipped from Tripoli in Libya to 'an unknown destination'. It wasn't hard to guess where: 'Sure enough we were dumped at Taranto.' From there they were taken to the small port of Barletta, further up the Adriatic coast from Bari.

'I would travel, see everything and have plenty of fun' had been Lorna's stated ambition since the start of the war. But the Italian seaside in November was not alluring: it was grey, rain-whipped, mosquito-infested and muddy. The girls' accommodation, in the form of Nissen huts, had yet to be built, so they were lodged in the unheated town museum, provided with only two primitive toilets for all of them: 'a nightmare'. A dreadful episode ensued when these toilets became totally blocked, and excreta overflowed down the museum stairs. The hygiene officer was summoned and ordered an eight-seater communal latrine to be constructed in the museum courtyard, with buckets. In the course of her duty Lorna saw suppurating wounds, amputations, burned-away faces, yet of all the experiences she underwent this was among the most traumatic. 'I never quite got over that – one's most private function in public. Women have other private functions to attend to monthly and the agony was awful.'

Nevertheless, the girls set out to enjoy themselves. The hospitable local bar-owners, Alvise and his wife Lilli, had access to black-market cheese, coffee and wines; Lorna and a group of nurses were invited back for mountainous bowls of spaghetti and tomato sauce, followed by a succulent roast, and torta, washed down with the local Spumante. Somehow they overcame the language problem and ended up dancing for hours. 'What fun we had.'

At the Barletta base hospital, casualties were coming in from the Allied advance, which that winter was grindingly slow, the Germans stubbornly giving ground. An estimated 60,000 Allied troops died in the eighteen months of that gruelling campaign. Lorna was seeing the fallout from the vicious and relentless fighting taking place at Salerno, Taranto and Bari. Convoys of wounded were arriving at all times of day and night.

I have . . . supervised and organised up to 88 operations in one day. The hope, agony and suffering on those faces spurred one on . . .

It was flat out – time was of the essence and we had no penicillin then. That was shortly to come. The impossible became possible, stretchers lined the corridors outside the theatre – life had to be saved . . . Very often we'd crawl off in the grey dawn to re-appear for duty the next day.

One pitch-dark night she stumbled while crossing the courtyard back to the huts and fell up to her waist in icy-cold liquid mud. 'I could not move, just sat there and cried with sheer exhaustion and helplessness . . . Momentarily I nearly broke. I was as near to hysteria as I've ever been.' An ambulance driver rescued her and took her back. Going to bed took ages. The temperatures were so icy that you had to bundle yourself up in layers of clothes before climbing under the blankets. Then no sooner were you dropping off than the knock on the door would come, and the cry, 'Convoy!'

You asked no questions – out into the night – hurry, hurry – men are dying.

It was Lorna's boast that, despite nursing under these conditions, she never neglected a patient.

But she also noted that the hardships were unfairly distributed between men and women. It wasn't just the toilets, though they were bad enough (and the Medical Corps were billeted comfortably in a hotel). Orderlies didn't always take kindly to being given instructions by a woman. One in particular consistently reacted to her commands with dumb insolence. It wasn't until she demonstrated her exceptional cool-headedness, resuscitating a dying patient in transit between theatre and ward, that this man got the message. '"My God," he said "that was wonderful – I will never question your authority again" and he never did, and became one of my great champions.'

At the other end of the scale was Charles, the senior surgeon, who relentlessly needled and patronised Lorna, bombarding her with crude jokes and insults. Only the support of her fellow staff made this endurable. Mutual respect was temporarily re-established when the two of them shared the agony of the most dangerous surgical operation either had ever witnessed. A German was admitted with a three-inch unexploded shell lying just beneath the outer membrane of his heart. He was alive, but removing the shell might cause it to explode, killing everyone. Despite this, it was decided to go ahead; Lorna would assist alongside the anaesthetist, and a disposal expert would be on hand to defuse the shell. Lorna's knees shook as she watched Charles make the incision and open the wound; she could see the shell as it had appeared in the X-ray, bulging just below the man's heart. With meticulous care Charles eased the tissue away to expose it; everyone knew his instruments might detonate it at any moment. He worked away until at last the shell was sufficiently revealed, then drew it deftly out and handed it to Lorna. 'He placed it on my outstretched hand. What a moment!' She passed it to the disposal officer, who calmly took it outside and slid it into a bucket of water, to be taken off and defused, two miles away. 'It was a miracle. The shell had in no way damaged the heart.' Charles turned to Lorna and said, 'Thank you, that was wonderful,' and she acknowledged his skill with newfound awe. Often, later, she would wonder whether the German ever realised that British medics had heroically risked their lives to save his. Unfortunately it wasn't long before Charles reverted to the uncouth rudeness that she'd become accustomed to.

In Italy Lorna Bradey's feelings ricocheted between the near hysteria induced by overwork and poor conditions, and elation at the good times. She was living at a peak of intensity. Henry, a boyfriend from the North African campaign, now showed up at Barletta. Off-duty she'd ride with him in his station wagon to secluded beaches, where they swam and ate picnics under the stars. Cut loose from pressures, these were magical interludes. White-crested breakers pounded the beach as they danced to Bing Crosby singing 'White Christmas' on Henry's old wind-up gramophone. The salt wind tousled his hair; there'd be bacon and eggs frying on a primus.

Neither of us expected it to last for ever ... We'd agreed to make no demands on one another, realising there was so much ahead and that we would be separated again and again.

In Henry's absence Lorna partied with the rest of them, taking the rough with the smooth. 'The tensions were terrific.' Once, an RAF officer who'd drunk too much vino tried to rape her. He'd ripped most of her clothes off and got his trousers open before she yelled at him that she would jump from the sixth floor if he went any further. Fortunately, the threat was enough to deter him. In March 1944 Vesuvius erupted. Over Bari the bright morning suddenly darkened as fragments of hot ash fell from the sky. Lorna and her pal Bobby took a week's leave and hitch-hiked to Sorrento. They saw the volcano smoking ominously across the blue bay, fiery lava still pouring out, mowing down the lemon groves in its path. They visited Pompeii, and Capri – a 'week of paradise' – and then it was back to Barletta. Convoys of wounded from the bloodbath at Monte Cassino were arriving every day. The week's leave was over. Lorna was now so exhausted it was as if she had never been away.

By this time, she and her comrades had become a tightly knit, extraordinarily efficient unit, and Lorna was proud of what they did. But the stress was wearing her down. One day the CO – 'a charming Irishman' – summoned her. With great tact and gentleness he questioned her about the demands of her job at Barletta:

Gradually the sluice gates opened and out it all came . . .

the hard grind, their accommodation, and above all the rudeness of Charles the Senior Surgeon . . .

I tried to be evasive – said he was a good surgeon etc. . . . [and] here was someone in authority being kind and understanding – I broke down – all the tensions released . . .
  He was astonished.

The colonel listened carefully. It was obvious that much of what Lorna was telling him was news, but his considered response, when it came, showed that he had been thinking about her needs. She was to be promoted to deputy matron at a 2,000-bed hospital in Andria, 10 miles away. In addition, her unstinting service was to be recognised by an official military accolade detailing her noteworthy conduct: she was to be 'Mentioned in Despatches'. The honour of this was not lost on Lorna. She had spent long enough with the army to know that normally this was an award conferred on soldiers for gallantry in the field. Why had she been singled out?

Did I really deserve it? What about all the others?

Lorna knew only too well the dedication of her fellow QAs and their stoical endurance.

He gave me a big hug. 'You represent all of them my dear.'

Worth Fighting For

At last, following the decrypting by Hut 8 at Bletchley of the U-boats' Enigma in December 1942, the Battle of the Atlantic was starting to go against the Germans. The French Resistance was gathering force. In Russia, Soviet forces were on the offensive, gaining ground around Stalingrad. The RAF were bombarding German cities.

By the KING'S Order the name of

Sister-Miss L.E. Bradey,
Queen Alexandra's Imperial Military Nursing Service,
was published in the London Gazette on
19 July, 1945,
as mentioned in a Despatch for distinguished service.
I am charged to record
His Majesty's high appreciation.

Secretary of State for War

Honoured for her distinguished service, Sister Lorna Bradey was
'Mentioned in Despatches'.

These dramatic developments had great significance for the war as a whole. But for many back in Britain catastrophes and explosions on distant oceans and in faraway cities were little more than background noise. In the summer of 1943 eighteen-year-old Nina Mabey, for all her newfound political awareness, was more preoccupied by her personal progress than by the prospect of a Second Front. That August she was on a Shropshire farm with her mother, cleaning out the pigsty, when the letter arrived informing her that she had won a scholarship to Somerville College Oxford. She went up to read French in October.

In the autumn of 1943, Oxford slept in a strange and timeless silence.

War had silenced the city's bells, making the spires seem more than usually dreamy and peaceful. Nina's life revolved around her academic work – she soon dropped French in favour of Politics, Philosophy and Economics – and abstract yearnings for romance.

Our war barely touched us.

Nina's entire adolescence had been played out with war as a background; she could barely recall a time when the blackout, rationing and war work had not been part of her everyday life. She helped with expected duties at her college, manning the stirrup-pump team with the rest and fire-watching on the roof of the Bodleian; but reading Wittgenstein, dances, skinny-dipping in the Cherwell, dons, dates and debates all held Nina Mabey in far greater thrall than events in the wider world.

For most women on the home front the war was more about deprivation and anxiety than bombs and battles. Shirley Goodhart wrote almost daily of her impatience for it all to end. Jack, her husband, had been away in India for over a year, and she longed for him daily, feeling 'miserable and husbandless'. The knowledge that Jack was safe, stationed with the Royal Army Medical Corps in India, helped, but only a bit, especially when she heard from him on leave in Kashmir.

It's a strange war that sends Jack almost to lead a life of very little work, good food, good pay and good holidays, and leaves me here to work hard and lead a drab wartime existence . . .

I don't want to have to sit all day in the office . . . and I'm suddenly desperately lonely and want my husband.

Britain was no longer in the front line, and the faraway fighting seemed only to intensify the frustration of life on the home front.

Margery Baines (née Berney) had married precipitately in 1940, and after a brief honeymoon her husband was posted abroad. Margery was far too impulsive and ambitious to endure the role of a Penelope, pining and lonely. 'By nature I was a leader.' Her high-octane manner secured her a place in an Officer Cadet Training Unit, but by late 1943 the army's brutality, pomposity and red tape were testing her loyalty to its limits. By then she had not only encountered the usual shocks attendant on army life – lice and fleas, filthy lavatories, stinking dormitories, bluebottle-infested kitchens, all 'terrifying to a young girl who has been sheltered from the realities of a classless society' – she had also run up against corrupt authority, inhumanity and victimisation. When her captain took a dislike to her and rejected her for a commission, Margery appealed and got the decision revoked. She was sent off to run a platoon in Aylesbury. But even now she was up against the inflexibility and mindless discipline of her commanding

officers. 'I believed [my girls] would work better if I could wring
certain advantages for them out of the rigid system. But I have to
confess that most of the time it was failure right down the line.'

In fact, Margery's time as a Welfare Officer with the ATS would
fuel her invincible determination to make something of herself, at
the same time as giving her invaluable lessons in overcoming defeat,
fighting for the underdog, and giving tireless consideration to those
under her command. The battles she would later undertake would
not involve guns or explosives, but, after the war, Margery's assertive
spirit and her army experiences would not go to waste.

*

Fears of invasion had receded. Despite continuing air raids, the full-
on Blitz seemed like history. Churchill had promised that – though
the end was not in sight – it was, inexorably, coming. Slowly but
surely the phrase 'after the war' began to be used with cautious optimism. 'People talk about the end of the war as though it were a
perfectly matter-of-fact objective on the horizon and not just a nice
pipe dream,' wrote Mollie Panter-Downes at this time.

Hopes for the future were surfacing, irrepressibly, breaking
through the gloom of everyday life.

Up in Kintyre, Naomi Mitchison took a robust attitude to present
hardships and directed her powers to improving the lot of local
women. Briskly, she set off to talk to the Scottish Education Department about getting adult women back into college after the war. 'I
am full of ideas about it.' Intelligent women were going to waste;
their unexpended energies could be harnessed for the good of the
community. Naomi herself was endlessly active on committees and
in meetings, working tirelessly to promote causes allied to post-war
reconstruction, such as a scheme for Scottish hydro-electricity.

But more usually, imagining a world beyond wartime involved
finding ways to make up for all the deprivations. Land girl Kay Mellis's dreams revolved around new clothes:

If you really wanted a dress, and you didn't have the coupons . . . well, I
used to think, you know, when the war's finished I'm going to buy material
and I'm going to make myself a new dress.

That was what we saw the future as being. A free life, being able to go into the shops and buy materials and make things, or buy a couple of pairs of shoes.

And my friend Connie – she was a great knitter. She was going to knit for Scotland, and I was going to sew for Scotland.

When they thought about their own role, most women focused on the fulfilment of domestic aspirations. Lovely breakfasts were what Clara Milburn missed: coffee, butter and marmalade, though above all she looked forward to her son Alan's return. After three years in the FANYs Patience Chadwyck-Healey, exhausted by the lack of privacy, yearned for a rural retreat. 'I just wanted to grow roses in a little cottage miles away on top of a hill somewhere – utter peace and flowers and relaxation – that was what I thought would be absolutely gorgeous.'

Thus, for most, the principal preoccupations were the traditionally feminine concerns of home and hearth. In 1944 the author Margaret Goldsmith set out to inquire on women's wartime state of mind. Many wives, she reported, 'are so homesick for their pre-war way of life that they seem to have created in their imagination a glowing fantasy of what this life was like. All the small yet grinding irritations of domesticity are forgotten.'

But what would the reality be in that longed-for home, in that imagined dream-time 'after the war'? The millions of women who had taken on war work or been conscripted knew that the world they'd grown up in would never be the same again. They would still be mothers, housewives, feeders, healers, carers and educators. But after so much sacrifice, they wanted to believe that life after the war would be better than what had gone before.

So when, on 2 December 1942, the liberal social reformer Sir William Beveridge published a report which promised a 'comprehensive policy of social progress', the women of Britain turned eagerly to its pages to discover what plans their leaders had to improve their lot. Was it possible that the government was starting to recognise that half the population of Britain lived lives of unaided struggle, and that there existed a genuine political will to assist and support their efforts?

That evening, Nella Last listened to Sir William broadcasting to the nation as he laid out a utopian vision. In the new, post-war world

Want, Disease, Ignorance, Squalor and Idleness would be regarded as the evils of a past age. He explained with care the workings of a contributory scheme which would supply a comprehensive safety net covering all eventualities, for the entire population. There would be Family Allowances, a National Health Service and National Assistance for the unemployed. The pioneering scheme offered everything from maternity grants to funeral grants, 'from the cradle to the grave'.

'Never since I first listened to a speaker on the air have I felt as interested as I was tonight by Sir William Beveridge,' reported Nella. His broadcast left her feeling profoundly hopeful about the future. The scheme would surely make a huge difference to women: 'It is they who bear the real burden of unemployment, sickness, child-bearing and rearing – and the ones who, up to now, have come off worst. There *should* be some all-in scheme.' As she wrote up her diary that night, Nella was struck by how Beveridge's proposals seemed in so many ways to chime with her own deepest aspirations. She recalled pre-war days when she would discuss social issues with her sons and their friends. Back then her proto-feminism had not gone down well: '[They] thought I was a visionary when I spoke of a scheme whereby women would perhaps get the consideration they deserved from the State.' But could this be her vision coming true?

Yes, war *could* change things for the better. Nella Last had no regrets about the pre-war days; she knew all about want, disease and squalor. There was dreadful poverty in Barrow during the Depression. Wages were so low that children in the town went barefoot; and they all had toothache, because their parents were too poor to send them to have their teeth pulled. Impetigo was rife – the kids were scabbed and raw from it. The husbands were tyrannical when it came to money. They spent their wages on cheap beer, yet held their wives to account for every penny.

It now dawned on Nella how selfish Will, her husband, could be, how he had never made provision for his dependants in the event of his death, or paid for insurance, or given her decent housekeeping money. And now here he was complaining that, under the new scheme, he would have to work till he dropped. Nella felt angry. She didn't want to be 'cared for' by her husband; she wanted to be appreciated and she wanted some understanding of how housewives like her were always on the sharp end when things got difficult. Will Last was simply unaware of what narrow margins his hard-worked wife survived on. Her husband's tight-fistedness left her having to subsidise the children's welfare with what she could save from the housekeeping. When sickness struck, or an operation had to be paid for, life became tough indeed. If implemented, Beveridge's proposals would sweep away all this hardship. From now on, something started to change in this fifty-two-year-old housewife from Barrow-in-Furness. Nella's Mass Observation diaries track a growing contempt for her husband, a rage at his dismissive attitude towards her and a gathering sense of her own value and talents. 'I'm beginning to see I'm a really clever woman in my own line, and not the "odd" or "uneducated" woman that I've had dinned into me,' she wrote.

The Beveridge Report sold over 600,000 copies. Mollie Panter-Downes reported to her New York readers that Londoners had queued up to buy the doorstop manual for two shillings, 'as though it were unrationed manna dropped from some heaven where the old bogey of financial want didn't exist'. These avid purchasers had read it with new optimism:

The plain British people, whose lives it will remodel, seem to feel that it is the most encouraging glimpse to date of a Britain that is worth fighting for.

For Nella Last, and for many others, the Report read as a manifesto for women, a true attempt to offer them a better future.

Though the Beveridge report continued to be kicked around parliament like a football for the remainder of the war, its huge popularity ensured that no government could now duck out of the post-war creation of a welfare state. Family allowances would become a reality; there would be a National Health Service. Hopes soared that scrimping and saving, drunk tyrannical husbands and scabby barefoot children with rotten teeth would all become distant memories. The bitter sacrifices of housewives across the nation had, it seemed, gained some official recognition at last.

8   Over There

A Song and a Cheer

By the fifth Christmas of the war, there was a depressing shortage of festive fare. 'No chance of chicken, turkey or goose,' wrote diarist Vere Hodgson. 'If we can get a little mutton that is the best we can hope for.' Coal was 'a worry'. But the embargo on bell-ringing was lifted, and Christmas Day passed without reports of enemy activity over Britain.

In Scotland Naomi Mitchison hung up garlands gathered from the woods and rejoiced in her ersatz Christmas pudding and tinned pears. There were even stockings for the children. In the afternoon Naomi organised a round of rampageous games, from 'The Farmer's in his Den' to 'In and Out the Dusty Bluebells'. But there weren't enough crackers to go round.

Wren Maureen Bolster, based at Southampton, wrote to her fiancé, Eric Wells, describing the revels at the sailors' mess: 'I must say I've had one of the best Christmases I've ever known.' On Christmas Eve the Wrens stumbled round with a torch being Father Christmas, distributing parcels. There were real eggs for breakfast, followed by carols at the mission. Dancing, drinking, community singing and egg-and-spoon races went on till three in the morning. In Inverness, Joan Wyndham and her fellow WAAFs spent Christmas night downing quantities of port and dancing with fighter pilots.

Nella Last wished her husband a happy Christmas. 'He scowled and muttered.' The sweet coupons were tight in his pocket, and it was clear that not so much as a sugar mouse was coming her way this festive season. Nevertheless she stuffed and roasted a corner of pork, found a dash of rum to liven up the sauce for her plum pudding and managed to rejoice at the sight of four late-blooming roses on her Christmas dinner table.

In Croydon, Elsie Whiteman was unwell, and her friend and flat-mate Kathleen Church-Bliss enjoyed a holiday from her work in

Morrisons No 1. Factory. In common with much of the nation, Elsie and Kathleen spent much of the day listening to the wireless, pausing especially for the King's broadcast to the nation at three o'clock. Clara Milburn went to church – it was packed – and later enjoyed a hoarded bottle of 1926 Graves. 'Grand!' Then she too sat down to hear His Majesty's message:

Some of you may hear me in your aircraft, on board your ships, or as you wait for battle in the jungles of the Pacific islands or on the Italian peaks. Some of you may listen to me as you rest from your work, or as you lie sick or wounded in hospital. To many of you, my words will come as you sit in the quiet of your homes. But, wherever you may be, to-day of all days in the year, your thoughts will be in distant places and your hearts with those you love. I hope that my words, spoken to them and to you, may be the bond that joins us all in company for a few moments on this Christmas Day.

As the notes of the National Anthem crackled across the airwaves, Mrs Milburn needed no reminding of absent loved ones:

All day long we think of Alan and long to have him here. Every hour of the day one wonders what he is doing. And will he be here next Christmas? May we all be here together.

Watching, waiting and praying were predominantly female activities; but in many cases women themselves were far from home. Mike Morris of the 'Y' Service, now based at Allied Supreme Headquarters in Algiers, had hoped to go home for Christmas after two years abroad. But the Italian invasion meant that her vital interception skills could not be spared. She was disappointed, but the festivities were infused with hope for the future. General Eisenhower was convinced that 1944 would see an Allied victory; 'his optimism was infectious'. And on Christmas Day 1943 there was work to do. Mike and her colleagues were frantically busy with preparations for Operation 'Shingle', the amphibious landings at Anzio, now planned for less than a month away.

*

Irrepressible, unprompted, hope for an end to the war was flickering into life. The enemy was being rolled back by a series of military successes. A huge boost to British morale came on Boxing Day, when the German warship *Scharnhorst* was sunk with the loss of 1,900 lives. Early in 1944 the news from the Eastern front continued to be encouraging to the Allies as the Red Army drove German troops backward across the Dnieper and towards the Polish border. German civilians suffered, too, from the successive assaults of the RAF throughout 1943 and 1944. Firestorms consumed German cities, and thousands died. The Italian campaign was hard-fought; on 22 January 37,000 US and British troops landed at Anzio, and the British press celebrated the lack of German opposition (prematurely, as it turned out). In the Pacific, American warships were making headway against Japan's expansion, though that nation's ferocious tenacity was to prove intractable over the coming year; meanwhile intrepid Indian, Gurkha and British forces in Burma were holding out in a terrible war of attrition. The tide would eventually turn against the Japanese, exhausted by disease and defenceless against British tanks. And though its exact location was a closely guarded secret, the entire British nation understood that a Second Front was in preparation. 'Some people think it will start in the Balkans, some favour Norway and few think we shall try through France,' wrote one anxious Mass Observation diarist. Many like her were restless and impatient, awaiting the onslaught that would, surely, mean the start of the endgame.

In this atmosphere of expectation and suspense, it was vital to keep morale high among the soldiers, some of whom had, by this time, been away from home for years. Many men who had embarked on troopships with a song and a cheer back in 1941 were, by 1944, battle-weary, despondent and desperately homesick. They missed domestic comforts, they missed female companionship, they missed their children, they missed the little *finesses* of everyday life that their wives, mothers and girlfriends could provide, and they missed their physical presence. Typically, soldier Peter Jackson wrote to his fiancée, Joan Tamlin:

I'm just living for the day when I can hold you in my arms forever . . . It's a heart aching experience, loving you like I do and being away from you.

Basil Dean, who set up ENSA (the Entertainments National Service Association, otherwise known as Every Night Something Awful) in 1939, persuaded the government to support his efforts in lightening the load of war workers and soldiers. Over the course of the war

ENSA mounted two and a half million performances, involving four out of five members of the entertainments profession in Britain. Women performers were hugely popular, adding a welcome touch of lipstick and femininity to the laddish environment of army camps and barracks. For some of these women, the experience of travelling to far-flung theatres of war and offering up their talents to the Allied cause was to prove profoundly life-changing.

*

For the soldiers who couldn't go home, home might travel to them. Women were its representatives.

Early in the new year of 1944, two women set sail from Liverpool. Joyce Grenfell had packed her trunk, said goodbye to her husband, Reggie, and now – as far as her loved ones were concerned, for her destination had to be kept secret – headed into the unknown. Joyce, a singer and comedienne, was possessed of a deep faith, an infectious zest for life and an infallible instinct for the ridiculous. Viola Tunnard, funny, quiet and clever, was her accompanist. By early February the pair had arrived in Algiers for the first stop of a thirteen-month tour that would take them to hospitals, army bases and far-flung military units in fourteen countries. Joyce both wrote home and kept a diary throughout, recording her observations with humour and compassion. That year of entertaining the troops was 'the time of my life'.

From the outset they were often giving three concerts a day. In Algiers she and Viola performed at Hospital No. 95, occupied by 2,500 men wounded in the desert war. They started out in orthopaedics; a piano was pushed into the centre of the ward. Before the concert Joyce chatted to the patients. 'There were two of the illest men I have ever seen I think. Just skulls but with living wide, very clear eyes.' Joyce apologised to them for the awkward positioning of the 'stage'. 'I said to the illest of the two very ill ones that I hoped he'd excuse my back when I had to turn it on him and he said he would if I'd excuse him for not being shaved. Oh, gosh.' Next day she discovered that he had not survived the night. 'I wish I could tell his family how he smiled and even sang with us the day before he died.' Over the next few days they worked their way round the huge hospital, adapting as well as possible to their improvised concert venues. Making music in tarpaulin marquees was challenging – 'their acoustic properties are exactly nil'. Despite this, they got the men joining in, fortissimo. Later they performed to sixteen eye patients. There was a shy boy who had lost his sight; Joyce noticed how his pals were endlessly gentle and caring towards this young soldier, looking after him 'with all the tenderness of mothers . . . They were happy when he was and exchanged looks . . . He sang with us; and he cried a little.' Next door Joyce met another man who had lost both eyes. 'He has reached the accepting stage and had a look of strange radiance.'

In March, Joyce and Viola moved on to Naples. The city was covered in pink volcano dust. Just to the north the battle for Cassino was raging, German forces holding on to their defences after the bombing of its famous monastery.

Monday, March 20th, 1944

Oh God, the sights I've seen today. We haven't *touched* the war till today. Bed after bed filled with mutilated men, heads, faces, bodies. It's the most inhuman, ghastly, bloody, hellish thing in the world . . . It was quite numbing.

Crowded out, the days whistled by: 'Tuesday Malta, Wednesday Cairo . . .' In early April they were in Baghdad, from where they were driven out to Kut, a sandy outpost, '115 miles from anywhere', to give a show in the local NAAFI to eighty English troops.

Friday, April 14th, 1944

Oh the desert! Oh the desert in heat! Oh the desert in heat and wind and dust!

. . . I do not like dust storms. Very depressing and poor for the morale. Felt far away from home and sanity and safety.

On the way back to Baghdad the dust blew up again, as hour after hour their jeep jolted across the mirage-strewn desert. Once, a camel train came into distant focus through the swirling sand. Soaking off the grime in two inches of cold water that evening, Joyce contemplated the (unfounded) rumour that Allied troops were already invading northern France. 'My heart sank like lead. Will we get home?'

Touring sprang surprises on them at every turn: in Maqil the piano had no A sharp, and its lid harboured an angry scorpion. Joyce recorded tussles with cockroaches, beetles, ants and fleas ('Flea won'), as well as seatless lavatories: 'my lav-life is of *great* importance to me. I'm affected here by having to do all from a stand or crouch position.' Their work continued to be emotionally harrowing; Joyce couldn't bear to sing songs like 'Someday' or 'All My Tomorrows' to dying men. But she was never in any doubt of its value. Time and again she and Viola were compensated by the men's laughter and the way music and comedy could make them forget. They talked to the men too – about 'home and ordinary things'. It was clear that they were needed. Men in hospital craved distraction – though perhaps not of the kind accidentally implied by the 'bounder' who introduced her and Viola as having arrived 'especially to entertain men in bed', at which a wag from the back of the ward piped up: 'Cor, they've laid that on now!'

Travel, too, had its own rewards. The pair had left for sunnier climes just before the Luftwaffe renewed their attacks on England in what became known as the Little Blitz, and Joyce appreciated her fortune in being far from home at that time. 'I'm so b---y lucky to be here doing this job and seeing this beautiful country, and being full of fruit and sun.' Over an exotic meal of chicken followed by pancakes filled with pineapple jam, Joyce admired a sunset sky full of flying storks.

Back home, everyone was obsessed with food. The scarcity of fruit in particular had become distressing. Joyce and Viola, meanwhile, were being driven up to a leave camp in the mountains above Beirut:

We kept passing open-fronted fruit shops with piles of glossy melons, more purple egg plants, baskets of tomatoes, strings of red peppers, fresh dates on their yellow stalks, lemons and oranges and candelabra bunches of bananas, both green and yellow.

After the drab greyness of home, the Middle East was bursting with colour: the intense green of heaps of tiny cucumbers, the yellow robes of Bedouins – 'no two alike' – the pink and white striped djellabas of little boys, the myriad hues of the Damascus bazaar.

Vera Lynn's travel experiences with ENSA lacked such picturesque qualities. The 'Forces' Sweetheart' contacted the organisation in spring 1944:

I phoned up their offices in Drury Lane and said I thought I ought to go out to sing for the boys themselves, rather than just stay at home. And at that time the Jap war was at its peak. So, when I phoned up they said, 'Where would you like to go?' And I said 'Well, I'd like to go where there isn't any entertainment.' So they said 'There's only one place that nobody's going to, and that's Burma.' And I said 'Okay, I'll go there.'

Vera had never been abroad before. She set out in a vast Sunderland cargo plane, with her accompanist, on the long journey east via Gibraltar, Cairo and Basra, arriving at the Bengali seaport of Chittagong, to find the decisive Battle of Kohima at its height. Three hundred miles up country, the Japanese army were attacking this small garrison of 1,500 men with 12,000 troops. Ferocious artillery fire deterred the initial assault, and a combination of British reinforcements, Japanese lack of supplies and sheer luck helped stave off the capture of this vital route to India. By June the Japanese were in retreat.

For Vera, the memories of those four months on the road are still fresh. The colonel at Chittagong saw her off with the present of a bottle of whisky: 'Medicinal purposes only, my dear – a chotapeg every night.' She didn't drink. But in every other way Vera took jungle life in her stride. Unfazed by the foreignness of everything, she preferred not to be singled out for star treatment, proudly adapting to the same accommodation, washing facilities and food as the army:

In the Far East I lived like the boys did – in a grass hut with buckets of water – one for toilet and one for washing. And you took whatever meals was offered you.

It's true you never quite knew what you were eating . . . I remember having plain boiled rice with a dollop of jam in the middle. And all the boys were looking as they went by to see if I was eating anything different to them, but I wasn't! There wasn't much else to give us, really, out there!

She resigned herself, too, when it came to appearances:

I couldn't use make-up at all – as soon as you put it on you would sweat it off. As long as I had lipstick: that was the important piece of make-up. As for my hair – well I had a perm, and of course there was no such thing as hairdressers abroad – so my hair went all fuzzy and curly. But I had no option – I just had to put it in a bucket of water and wash it and let it dry in the heat. They didn't have hairdryers out in the jungle!

But Vera was a celebrity, and as such she was accompanied by the gentlemen of the press. It was not her way to shrink from journalists. One tropical night, she sat with two of them outside the grass huts by a swirling river, protected from panthers, boa constrictors and the Japanese army by a barbed-wire palisade. The war correspondents, Dickie and Gerald, had failed to extract any form of sundowner from the mess that evening. That was when Vera remembered her bottle of Scotch:

I thought 'Right, I'll surprise them', and I went back to my grass hut and came out with this bottle of Canadian Club – and they couldn't believe their eyes. Well, there was nothing to dilute it with, so the three of us sat outside with this river going by and the hut behind and all these barbed wire railings, drinking neat Canadian Club. And then I staggered into my hut afterwards and got into my little bed, tucked all my netting around me, and sat and watched the bush rats running around the ceiling inside, like little squirrels with bushy tails.

Dickie set up a stunt that nearly landed her in trouble:

I didn't see action – I was billeted behind the lines. But Dickie Sharp wanted to go up the road to Kohima so he could record me singing with the sound of gunfire in the background. He said 'Are you game?' And I said – 'Yes, OK – all right.' But one of the commanders in charge of the station heard about it and said, 'No way, because if anything happens to Vera Lynn while she is under my protection, I'll be shot at dawn.'

Vera was indispensable. Her voice and her songs had – and have – a uniquely affecting and patriotic quality which touched her listeners' souls:

> These are the chains
> Nothing can break –
> There'll always be an England
> And England shall be free
> If England means as much to you
> As England means to me . . .

But she herself recognises that it was her very ordinariness that stole their hearts. In her nineties, this woman is still luminously beautiful, but the comfortable cardigan and clipped Cockney are the clues to Vera Lynn's sweetness and approachability. The lads of the West Kents and the Durham Light Infantry, killing and dying in a rat-infested wilderness strewn with human remains, recognised her as a symbol of the world they were fighting for:

I wasn't a soprano or an opera singer, and I wasn't a glamour girl. They knew I came from East Ham. I sounded just like one of them, just like the kind of girls they knew at home – an ordinary working-class girl. So they could connect with me, and I with them. I was singing to my own kind.

All of which made Vera the more personally affected by the terrible losses suffered in that punishing campaign. By the time the Japanese army was retreating, over 4,000 British and Indian troops were dead, missing or wounded. It was hard for her to bear.

It's one of the things you can't help thinking of: How many of these boys are going to get back home? Here they are, sitting, alive at the moment . . . clapping me for what I'm doing. At lunchtime there'd be that patch of grass – and it would be full of men who'd walked for miles, and they'd have been sitting there for hours, waiting, not just to hear me sing, but to see me singing.

And afterwards, when they get up off that grass, and pick up their rifles, and go back into the jungle – what then? There'd be an empty piece of grass at daybreak.

But the best thing was knowing that I was taking a little bit of home to them. One of the boys said to me once – 'England can't be that far away, because you're here.'

I could give them the feeling that they were just around the corner.

Dancing the Night Away

The vital contribution of wartime artistes like Joyce Grenfell and Vera Lynn has been much acknowledged. At home and abroad, they and many others, from conjurers to comedians, did their best to cheer, amuse and delight at a time of austerity, war-weariness and low spirits. Female performers had an incomparable glamour and allure that appealed to love-starved – and sex-starved – servicemen. At the famous Windmill Theatre ('We Never Closed') soubrette

Vera Lynn, the voice of the war.

Doris Barry and the other Windmill girls played to packed houses; the manager, Vivian Van Damm, persuaded his troupe to pose naked in 'tableaux vivants', as mermaids, or Britannia. The experience quickly disabused Doris of any romantic views she might have had of men – 'It wasn't very good to be up there on the stage with an audience full of men with raincoats across their knees, half of them playing with themselves.'

People in Britain were spending more money than ever before on pleasure; by 1944, 120 per cent more than in 1938. And where ENSA concerts were lacking, people flocked to the cinema, went dancing or made their own entertainment. Community singing flourished; pubs and air-raid shelters rang to the chorus of 'Roll Out the Barrel' or the endlessly popular ditty: 'Hitler has only got one ball. / The other is in the Albert Hall'. Theatre director Nancy Hewins took her all-women acting company on the road throughout the Second World War, putting on no fewer than 1,534 performances of thirty-three plays, of which half were by Shakespeare. The petrol shortage reduced the company to travel by horse and cart. They slept in barns or on floors.

When twenty-two-year-old Isa Barker was a land girl in rural East Lothian she discovered that her hostel was a mine of talent:

We found out that we had a couple of beautiful singers; and there was one girl who was very adept with poetry recitations, and could make people laugh. And I had been in a tap-dancing troupe for five or six years when I was younger.

Isa and her friends were persuaded by the Land Army rep to devise a show; for the next six months they staged the 'Revue by the Land-girls' weekly on Friday nights, in village halls round the district, with audiences from the local community. Their signature tune was:

> We're in the Land Army
> We think we'll all go barmy
> If this goes on for years and years and years . . .

With a ticket price of sixpence a head, plus raffle prizes donated by the local farmers – fresh eggs, butter and even a sucking pig – the event soon raised £300 for the Land Army Benevolent Fund. Today, the concerts remain the high spot of Isa's war:

We didn't get to bed till about two in the morning because of people enjoying themselves. And on Saturday mornings you'd get up and think 'Och, we've got to lift manure.' Well, we could hardly lift the fork, never mind the fork with the manure on it!

Meanwhile, hundreds of miles from the Scottish glens, London buzzed with life. Throughout the war the 400 Club and the Gargoyle did good business. The Ritz and the Berkeley were a whirl of fun, packed with couples in uniform and evening dress. ATS recruit Vera Roberts would catch a train from her Home Counties base to go dancing to Joe Loss and his orchestra at the Hammersmith Palais; it cost only sixpence if you were in uniform. 'We got up to quite a few tricks. I used to roll my hair up – then when I got to the dance I'd let it down. Once we were going to this dance in Croydon; I had this gold dress – so what I did was I put an elastic round my waist, and pulled it all up under my greatcoat. And when we got to the dance you let your dress down, took your coat off, and you were a civilian!' As another young woman remembered, 'If this is war, why am I enjoying it so much?'

For Helen Forrester in Liverpool, dancing helped to anaesthetise the pain of loss. Her fiancé, Harry O'Dwyer, had been killed in the Atlantic in August 1940. The ensuing emptiness in her heart continued to gnaw: 'As I lay in bed, I would still occasionally burst into tears.' But there was nobody she could tell.

All through the war, late at night, I danced. I danced with men from every nation in Europe, and they had one attitude in common; they never talked about what they would do after the war. Perhaps they accepted, what I feared, that they would be killed.

Defended though she was, new relationships slowly entered Helen's life. Through her job at the Liverpool Petroleum Board she met a onetime oil company employee, Eddie Parry, who was visiting his colleagues while on leave from Commando training. Eddie – tall, tough, fair and lean – had a reputation as a tearaway, a womaniser who went on pub crawls, swore and got drunk. But with Helen he was different: respectful and gallant. He walked her home one rainy night, and Helen realised she was struggling to conquer feelings that had lain dormant since Harry's death. After Eddie returned to his unit they corresponded. Helen was deeply attracted to him, and she also discovered that they had much in common: secret vulnerabilities, a capacity for endurance and a defiance of what life could throw at them. But she pulled back from making any gesture of commitment. Their letters kept her going, and, though they met whenever he had leave, she was clear-eyed about his shortcomings. Eddie was not husband material; moreover, as one of Churchill's crack raiders, he would inevitably be in the greatest danger once the Second Front got under way. He himself recognised that he was training to kill, or be killed.

So Helen did not feel she was betraying him when she made friends with Derek Hampson, a wounded bomber pilot whom she found weeping one evening on the rocky beach near Moreton. Tear-sodden though he was, Helen couldn't help noticing this young man's film-star good looks. He was blond, 'easily the most handsome man I had ever met . . . like . . . some beautiful gift of nature, a perfect Arab pony, for example.' They got talking; his voice, as it steadied, betraying his public-school education. It turned out that Derek had crash-landed his Lancaster, broken his thigh and was being nursed in a convalescent home for airmen in nearby Hoylake. The ordeal had shot his nerves to pieces, the last straw being the news that his best friend in the squadron had been posted abroad. Helen agreed to go to the cinema with him.

Once Derek's thigh healed, she discovered that he was also a wonderful dancing partner. Helen told him how she supplemented her meagre clerical income with dress-making, and he in turn revealed that before the war he had been in the rag trade. 'I sell clothes – ladies' dresses, mostly . . . [But] you absolutely must not tell anybody, particularly the RAF types. I would be ribbed to death, if they knew.' Even Helen's spiteful mother found Derek's good looks and educated manner irresistible.

By contrast with the electricity between her and Eddie, Helen felt no 'jump of desire' for this handsome, fashion-conscious young man. And gradually it dawned on her why. 'He was truly and faithfully in love with a man he had known since boyhood.' Homosexuality was illegal and punishable by up to two years' imprisonment, and Derek was terrified of exposure and blackmail; but Helen's sufferings had made her tolerant, and she felt pity for his vulnerability in the macho world of the squadron. Over time she persuaded him that he could trust her with the knowledge of this secret relationship, and in return she confided in him about her own sorrows and disappointments. And so, as they sat one sunny day on the sea wall at Moreton, looking out over the barbed wire at the blue ocean beyond, he turned to her and, with unconcealed embarrassment, suggested that they marry. Helen reacted more with surprise than shock – 'Derek!'

'Helen, it would offer some protection to my friend and me – having a woman in the house . . . Listen to what I have in mind. I would take you into the business with me, as an equal partner . . . you're good with clothes, and it's an interesting thing for a woman to be in . . .

Think about it . . . You'll have a good house, I promise you. And we'd never question your comings and goings – I mean, if you found, well – a lover.'

It was not out of anger or pique that Helen checked his flow:

'I couldn't, Derek. I just could not do it. I am a normal woman with a normal set of desires and hopes. I am just very, very tired at present; yet, sometime, I hope to marry.'

His face had fallen . . . I felt very sorry for him . . .

'Believe me, I understand your predicament. But I could not live such a lie. I just couldn't.'

In time, Derek returned to his squadron. Once a month he wrote to Helen, and she replied. As a bomber pilot it was his job to deliver heavy explosives to military targets. But they often missed, killing German civilians, and his sensitive nature rebelled against being the cause of so much suffering. Then the letters stopped. Eventually, an envelope addressed to her in unknown handwriting arrived from Yorkshire. It was Derek's mother, who had discovered Helen's letters in her son's belongings, returned to her after his death. He had been killed in action. For the bereaved lady it must have been some consolation to find that he had a girlfriend; but who would write to Derek's real lover? Meanwhile, to Helen, it seemed that whoever she allowed to get close to her was singled out for untimely death. 'I grieved . . . for the slaughter of my generation.'

The Secret Army

Helen Forrester was learning to live her life provisionally. There would be time enough – when the war ended, as it surely soon would – to determine what to be, who to marry. 'Like many other women I was waiting it out.'

Monica Littleboy was one of these. In the brief period in 1939 that she had known her boyfriend, George Symington, their romance had seemed to offer everything her young and passionate heart had ever dreamt of. But by 1944 she had not seen George for four and a half years. '[He] had gone to the Far East, for how long I did not know.' Monica had a spell in the WAAFs before opting to become an ambulance driver with the FANYs, attached to the Red Cross, where she was trained to drive and maintain a heavy vehicle, and to lift and carry stretchers. Posted to Dorset under Southern Command, she threw herself into her work and found temporary happiness with a gentle older officer who talked to her of marriage. 'He was posted elsewhere . . . We both knew that things were not to be.' When news finally reached her that George had been taken prisoner by the Japanese it intensified her memories of their love. 'I have realised that

George Symington is the only person I could really marry and be happy with,' she confided to her diary.

But he was so far away. At this time Monica's job gave meaning to her life. Her ambulance, her friendships in the FANY, above all the patients – from dysentery cases to plane crash survivors – were the here and now of her existence. 'I learnt more about human nature there than anywhere else.'

And now the time was approaching when the commitment of women like Monica would be put to the test. It is tempting to compare the slow accomplishment of the Allied invasion to a gestation; for women, a time of gathering readiness and anticipation in the hatching of a long-awaited outcome. Nature has fashioned our sex for patience; we know, too, that a long-prayed-for event may bring death, blood and a mother's tears. Mystery and fear, love and faith in the future: with victory at stake these preparations were, for many women in Britain, burdened with more hopes than any military campaign before or since.

Rumours were abroad from early spring that the Second Front was due. On 2 April a friend of Frances Partridge told her he had it on good authority that the invasion would be launched that very night. Frances lay sleepless for hours, listening to every aeroplane. By May the tension was palpable; everyone knew it was about to happen, but nobody knew when. Up in Scotland, Naomi Mitchison was consumed with anxiety: '[There is] this awful ache about the Second Front, the thing one wants and fears so terribly, that is at the back of one's thought all the time, like a wave, a tidal wave coming in from the horizon blotting out everything.' Trippers were banned from the coastal zone from East Anglia to Cornwall; its roads were clogged with an endless stream of military traffic. Sherman tanks were to be seen noisily negotiating the cobbled streets of medieval towns, and convoys of despatch riders roared on motorbikes from village to village. Verily Anderson, who had retreated to the country with her small children, confined them to the garden. The lanes were perilous, with tanks crunching indiscriminately into gateposts and gable ends. Two of the little ones nearly got pulverised in their pushchair when a convoy of armoured vehicles swept away the protecting wall beside them. When Vera Brittain went to her Hampshire cottage that spring she ran into ammunition dumps and transports concealed in leafy glades, where they could not be spotted by German reconnaissance aircraft. American soldiers were everywhere in the banned zone – 'a nuisance to anyone walking alone,' wrote Mass Observation diarist Shirley Goodhart, who worked in Salisbury.

Behind the scenes, women played their part in the preparation for this most audacious of campaigns. The routine of Doris Scorer's life in the Wolverton aircraft factory was disturbed when she and her workmates were unexpectedly taken off repairs and transferred to the woodwork shop. Rumours began to circulate that they were going to work on making gliders. 'We didn't have a clue what a glider was.' Doris and the girls weren't told, but the light aircraft they were making would be used to carry invading troops over the Channel to France. It was an exacting job, sawing the lengths of wood forming the wing struts to precise lengths, gluing them into the frame and securing them with tiny brass nails. The pace of work was fast and urgent. From Autumn 1943 the WVS were kept busy day and night providing food and hot tea for builders and engineers working on the construction of concrete caissons in the Thames estuary and at other significant ports. From 5 April 1944 a travel ban was imposed on everyone working at Bletchley Park. The women there worked flat out translating intercepts to locate the position of mines laid in the English Channel and decrypting German signals which confirmed that the enemy was being successfully misinformed about the intended landings. As an ULTRA code-breaker, Mavis Lever was able to reassure her superiors that German spies and reconnaissance had failed to spot the construction of the Mulberry harbours: 'They never once asked what was going on at Southampton or Portsmouth. We were much comforted to know that they *didn't* know about them. In a way, the questions the Germans didn't ask were as important as the things that they were asking. And we knew that they were keeping two Panzer divisions down at Calais, which was a great help.'

SOE agents in the field, preparing to assist operations behind enemy lines in France, were supported by the FANYs, who were kept busy sewing French tailors' labels into the clothes that would help to disguise them. It was also the job of the FANYs to offer agents the lethal 'L' tablet, to be taken if they were captured.

Making gliders in the Wolverton workshop: the tools and construction process are
evidence of Doris's memory for detail. But notice also her handbag under the
workbench, her hairnet and her heavily nailed clogs.

Senior Wren Christian Lamb (née Oldham) had been assigned to a
post in Whitehall under Admiral Mountbatten. Here she observed
the comings and goings of Winston Churchill and a number of scientific boffins. There was a 'sense of urgency in the atmosphere,
humming with activity', but it was not till years later that Christian
understood that these offices in Whitehall were the very heart of
Operation Overlord. It was here that the prefabricated floating 'Mulberry' harbours were devised; here that the PLUTO pipeline – to
run from the Isle of Wight to Cherbourg – was conceived, along
with the entire programme for the construction and concealment of
the caissons, breakwaters, pontoons and floating ramps which would
make the invasion feasible. Christian herself was sworn to the utmost
secrecy about her job. She was among the few who knew that the
landings would be on the Normandy coast. Working from large-
scale maps of France pinned up on her office wall, it was her task to

identify everything visible that could be seen from the bridge of an approaching invasion craft.

WAAF Edna Hodgson meanwhile had been allocated to the typing pool of General Eisenhower's HQ in Bushey Park. Edna had no knowledge of the invasion date. But, as the time got closer, her working hours were prolonged. She often arrived at 8.30 a.m. and worked through till the early hours of the next morning on lunch and a snack, surviving on three or four hours' sleep a night.

Some of the Wrens based in the south of England ports – like Maureen Bolster on HMS *Tormentor* in Southampton – were in on the most closely guarded secret in Britain's history. Maureen was a faithful correspondent to her beloved fiancé, Eric Wells, who was based in North Africa, but as the time got closer she could do no more than hint to him of her real forebodings:

1 May 1944

My dearest

The first of May – the first of May already. It can't be long now. I find it hard to take it in that England, my country, is on the verge of her greatest campaign of all time. It's too immense, too shattering.

I hardly dare think what it will mean, the lives that will be lost, the numbers of everything involved – ships, planes, armour, men. One waits impatiently, wanting to get the strain of waiting over yet dreading it . . .

Everyone is expectant, unsettled . . .

On his last leave before the invasion Eddie Parry returned to Moreton and looked up Helen Forrester before rejoining his Commando force. He would be in the forefront of the landings, and Helen tried not to think too hard about his prospects. Returning, Eddie missed the train. The May night was warm, and they walked to the Wirral bus stop together. At the foot of Bidston Hill he stopped, and there, under the starlit sky, asked Helen to marry him: 'after the war – when I've got started again'. It was the last thing she was expecting. Eddie, the foul-mouthed rascal, the tough adventurer; surely holy matrimony was the last thing on his mind? He folded her in his arms. 'I want to come back to you, Helen. Nobody else.' Her self-control crumbled. What did she want? A husband, yes. She knew that Eddie was not the conscientious, devoted type. But more than that, she realised she wanted *him*: 'desire shot through me'. Perhaps she was being too demanding. Perhaps it would be all right. He would be reckless, forgetful, he would not live up to her dreams – but he would not desert her. '"Yes," I said, and put my arms round his neck.' He kissed her solemnly and with passion. The night became cold. Eddie told Helen to go home, kissed her one more time and, without turning round, headed off to catch his bus.

Through May the sense of expectation intensified. Sylvia Kay, who worked General Eisenhower's private switchboard (known as the 'Red Board'), was told that she must prepare to move to an unknown destination. Next morning she and her colleagues were trucked to Cosham near Portsmouth. They were given tented accommodation and detailed to run the switchboard operation under canvas from a base in Cosham Forest; 'it was a sea of mud'. Just north of Portsmouth, at the operation's nerve centre of Fort Southwick, ATS volunteer Mary Macleod spent long days working in an underground cavern, typing out meticulous invasion plans, much of them in code. Meanwhile hundreds of firewomen joined their male counterparts to guard ammunition dumps.

Across the south of England, hospitals had been cleared of civilian patients prior to the invasion. Rows of beds now stood ominously empty. A young Irish nurse, Nancy O'Sullivan, based at a 1,000-bed hospital in Surrey, had been waiting for weeks. She and her colleagues scrubbed the wards and scrubbed them again. QA Maureen Gara was sent to East Anglia to prepare for D-day. There, she and her colleagues spent their spare time stitching together a huge red cross out of hessian, to serve as a ground marker for air crew, hostile or otherwise. Meanwhile, Monica Littleboy and her fellow ambulance-driving FANYs were posted to the Isle of Wight, where they prepared to be on the receiving end of many thousands of returning casualties.

On 24 May Elsie Whiteman came home from working in her components factory in Croydon and wrote up her diary: 'More hordes of bombers over this morning. The invasion seems very imminent and we hardly expect to get our Whitsun holiday.' But still nothing was announced. 'Friday 26th May. Everyone anxiously expecting the Second Front every day, but the weekend passed quietly.' The assault troops were given embarkation leave.

Twenty-eight-year-old Aileen Hawkins from Dorchester was an

ATS sergeant who as a girl had met the ageing Thomas Hardy in his home city. The courteous old poet had approved of her youthful verses; encouraged, she continued to write and publish poetry for the rest of her life. During the war Aileen married Bill, her pre-war sweetheart, now a Commando. As the day of the invasion approached she took time away from her anti-aircraft battery to say goodbye to him, knowing that these might be their last hours together:

> *End of D–Day Leave*
> Please, hold back the dawn, dear God
> I cannot bear to let him go,
> the world's a battle field out there
> big distant guns pepper the skies
> a wailing siren stabs the air.
> This moon-washed room our paradise
> where we have had such little time
> to share this precious love of ours.
> My gentle one – a soldier now –
> these years have left their mark on him,
> touching his war-wearied face
> I almost stare into his dreams . . .
> . . .
> The clock's long hand will point the hour
> the train will rattle from my view
> and I will be alone once more
> just longing for his love again.
> 'God', as he sleeps close to my heart,
> slowly the end of leave draws near.
> I cannot bear the time to part:
> 'Hold back the dawn another hour'.*

From 1 June all the Wrens had their shore leave cancelled. Phone calls were forbidden, and they were confined to barracks. 'We are gated,' wrote Maureen Bolster to Eric. She and her friend Rozelle Raynes were kept busy delivering extra ammunition and signals to

---

* Bill survived, picking up no fewer than twenty-one service medals. For twenty-one years after the war he and Aileen were employed as gardener and housekeeper by the concert pianist Sir Clifford Curzon at his home in Hampstead, until Bill's death in the 1960s. Aileen died in 2006.

the ships lying in wait. On 3 June, Maureen passed the soccer field and saw a mass of lads from the Commandos with their kit and tin hats resting in the sun. She was choked at the sight: 'They looked so young I could hardly bear it and tears ran down my cheeks.'

D-day had been scheduled for Monday 5 June. But on the 3rd Eisenhower and his generals reluctantly accepted that the weather forecasts they had been given made a provisional postponement necessary, and on Sunday the meteorological advisers were proved right as cloud and wind built up. On the Isle of Wight FANY Monica Littleboy and a friend bicycled out over the chalk downs to the west of the island and climbed up to Tennyson's monument, from where they looked down at the Armada-in-waiting, lying at anchor on the Solent. 'A glorious view from here all round, and here we proved that the shipping was even more intensified.'

Next morning, 'dull and windy', the FANYs were given a security lecture and warned that briefed personnel ('BPs') could be a risk if they were delirious while being carried as patients. 'Anything we heard we were to forget.' The typists working in the Fort Southwick caverns had been instructed to type out two sets of documents, one of which would be signed by the chiefs. The first set gave orders to postpone the invasion, the other set commanded it to go ahead. On the evening of Sunday 4 June, in conference with his colleagues and advisers, Eisenhower heard that the weather was due to improve on Monday afternoon, sufficiently for the armada to sail overnight. The decision was made.

On 5 June village streets and country lanes in the south of England fell eerily silent. That day the news came through that Rome had fallen to the Allies. Clara Milburn hung up the Union Jack in the orchard and felt cheered; a letter had arrived from Alan that morning. This success meant that the war was a step closer to ending, and he was a step nearer home.

The Smell of Death

On the morning of 6 June 1944 Verily Anderson and Julie, her Cockney mother's help, were tidying up the Gloucestershire cottage when their children came rushing in from the garden:

'Aeroplanes! Two tied together!' James cried.

'Huge,' said Marian.

The sky was vibrating with sound. We ran out on to the lawn. None of us had seen aeroplanes since we came to the Cotswolds. Now they moved in a continuous stream over us.

'They're towing gliders,' said Julie. 'James is right.'

'It's our invasion!' I said, jumping up and down. 'It can't be anything else. We've invaded France!'

There was no wireless in the cottage. They hurried across to their neighbour, the cowman's wife, who was listening to the live broadcast:

'Yes, It's the invasion all right,' she said. 'They've landed in Portugal. Hundreds of our poor boys killed.'

'Portugal?' I repeated.

'Some such name . . .'

'Could it be Normandy?' I suggested.

'Yes, Normandy. Same thing no doubt. They're all foreign places.'

All that day the planes streamed towards the coast, wing to wing, dropping an oily smoke screen as they went. Sheets hung out to dry that June morning were stained with black grease blown across by the gusty Channel breeze. Sheila Hails, marooned with her young baby in an isolated cottage near Lulworth on the Dorset coast, climbed the cliff that morning and saw an amazing sight:

I went up the grassy hill, and then I stood and blinked. There was an endless queue of ships sailing across the Channel. It was incredible, fantastic really, and I knew the invasion was happening.

That Tuesday Verily, Sheila and many thousands of others had to be content with newspapers, wireless broadcasts and prayers to compensate for the feelings of hope and helplessness that dominated everyone's waking hours. Yet again, it was woman's lot to be the one who watched, waited and prayed. Orderly queues formed to buy the evening editions, while others waited in line to give blood. The King addressed the nation. Mollie Panter-Downes tried to describe D-day to her New York readers. She sensed a mood of grim revenge among Londoners watching the fleets of aircraft roaring coastwards: 'Now they'll know how our boys felt on the beaches at Dunkirk.' But she also sensed a lack of connection between the heroism and suffering taking place 'over there' and the everyday mundanities she observed on the street: 'men and women going to the office, queuing up for fish, getting haircuts, and scrambling for lunch'. With her customary eye for minutiae, she noted the typists in their summer dresses going into Westminster Abbey to pray by the tomb of the Unknown Soldier – were *their* sweethearts sharing his fate? – the flower-sellers peddling patriotic buttonholes and the curious hush which descended on the city, '[like] a wet Sunday afternoon'.

For London-based Frenchwoman Madeleine Henrey the anxiety was unusually heightened. Might the invasion finally mean a reunion with her beloved mother? St Malo in 1940 had seen the little family wrenched apart from each other. Abandoned on the quayside, Madame Gal had been close to despair, convinced that the steamer on which Madeleine and her grandchild had sailed away had met with disaster until, eventually, a letter from Madeleine got through. Four years had passed, during which Madame Gal scraped a living with her needle, finding lodging with a humane widow based in Versailles and living for the day when they would all be together again in Normandy. But what had become of Madeleine's fairy-tale farmhouse, her little patch of heaven at Villers-sur-Mer? Situated just twenty miles to the east of Sword beach, it lay full in the path of the invasion. If it hadn't already been pillaged by the Germans, Madeleine was left to imagine how the Allies might vandalise what was left.

*

All around us the great armada was on the move . . .

wrote Wren stoker Rozelle Raynes, who was based at Southampton with her friend Maureen Bolster. For them, the thrill of being close to the action left them with indelible memories. Rozelle would have given anything to be setting out with those men. As it was, she had to be content with a smaller adventure. Three Wren stokers, including her, were summoned in the early hours to help rescue three landing craft that had broken down near the Needles. Being aboard her tug

steaming towards the Isle of Wight was the nearest she got to experiencing the invasion:

There were all the ships we knew so well . . . armed merchant cruisers, destroyers, minesweepers, corvettes, trawlers and ocean tugs, every one of them moving towards Normandy and a fate unknown.

At last the great day had come; the tension was broken, and the soldiers and sailors laughed and cheered as our little tug kept pace with them, clouds of rainbow-tinted spray breaking over her stubborn black bows. One man leaned over the stern of his landing craft as it gathered way and called out to us: 'You're the last bit of Old England we'll see for a while, girls, and you sure look worth fighting for!'

From the Isle of Wight, Monica Littleboy had a grandstand view of the immense fleet:

All day [the ships] went by, with never a stop and not more than 100 yards between each vessel . . . We knew this was no exercise . . . our hearts were with these men. The cold grey choppy sea and the strong wind that was blowing almost seemed as if it would tear the little barrage balloons away. There were tugs and tankers, masses of them, landing craft of every kind, all towing one another and bouncing about like peas on a drum. Thousand upon thousand. We could see the boats loaded with tanks and trucks and low in the water. Then came the troop ships, dwarfing everything else, solid, full, we knew of Canadians etc, men who had been to parties in this very house – personal friends. And we waved and cheered and knew that the great moment had come.

We climbed back to Tennyson's Monument again and there we saw them round the Needles. As far as the eye could see were ships, ships, ships, the horizon black with them whichever way you looked. A great armada that thrilled your very soul. And still that night after dark the lights on the ships were steadily going past . . . I slept fitfully and dreamed the whole night of only one thing, the invasion, and I knew before any radio announced it that we had our feet in France.

From then on, Monica had 'no time to think'. Within twenty-four hours casualties started to arrive on the island. Red Cross boats were ferrying patients day and night, with urgent cases dropped off at Yarmouth. Monica raced up and down to the quay, unloaded patients, reloaded them on to hospital ships and carried donors to give blood to those who vitally needed it. The sights were pitiful: burns, fractured skulls, shot-away faces. Some of the victims were mere boys, dazed with suffering.

At 8.30 p.m. on 6 June, the first, solitary patient appeared, covered in wet sand, in Nancy O'Sullivan's empty Surrey hospital. 'We devoured him.' And when she came back on duty next morning the wards were unrecognisable. Every bed and every corridor was filled with casualties: 'It was the real thing.' From then on she was working flat out to patch up the wounded as they arrived.

In Portsmouth, teenager Naina Cox was working in a big dry-cleaning firm that dealt with service uniforms; she had just completed a Red Cross course that spring. At 2 p.m. on D-day she was summoned by her commandant to come up to Queen Alexandra's Hospital and help with casualties. Quickly, she ran home to tell her mum, scrambled into her uniform and headed up the hill to the hospital. There she found the wards had run out of space; the corridors were lined with stretchers. As an inexperienced junior, Naina was given the job of cleaning up the patients. Many were bloody and grimy, but fear had also struck at their bowels, resulting in fouled bodies and garments. For several days Naina washed the excrement from hundreds of traumatised soldiers. '[They] were so completely exhausted they didn't care one jot what happened to them . . . As I worked . . . I was thinking, "How long will it go on? If I come tomorrow and the next day, will I still be doing this?"' But she barely hesitated when the sister asked her to perform the same task on the German prisoners' ward. In a stinking Nissen hut, the terrifying enemy lay festering and utterly demoralised: dirty, unwholesome and glazed with defeat. 'Some of them were only kids, they weren't really much older than me. One of the rules of the Red Cross is that you are there to help everybody. I'm glad I didn't refuse to help those men.'

During that terrible first week as the Allies battled to gain their foothold in France and German forces retaliated, planes were crashing on the Isle of Wight, and bodies were washed up on its pebbly shores. Sometimes Monica Littleboy accompanied stretcher cases across to the mainland hospital. 'I saw sights [there] which I hope I may, please God, never see again. They were burned so badly as to be unrecognisable, only the burning eyes could one see, and as we loaded our stretchers I could feel those eyes following me round the ward. I tried to smile at them; my smile was stiff and I felt sick and though I was so full of sorrow for them something inside me just seemed horror struck.'

Maureen Bolster was equally appalled when she met a shell-shocked lad just back from the fighting. He was trembling and could barely speak. 'Poor kid, all he could say was, "Make me forget it, please make me forget it. I've just got to." I felt quite sick with pity . . . What that kid had seen was beyond telling. For one thing he had seen his special pals blown to pieces.'

A soldier who must face fear and horror deals with it in a number of ways. Above all, he has been trained to obey orders, to kill or be killed. If he feels pity, tenderness or sensitivity to his fellow man, he must learn to suppress it in the interests of winning the war. He cultivates a veneer of brutality; he develops black humour, bravado, cynicism, impassivity. He forces himself to forget. Instilled from boyhood, such qualities are all part of growing up to be a man. By contrast, the reactions of Maureen Bolster, Monica Littleboy, Naina Cox and many other women show the vulnerability of women exposed to war's horrors. Pity, compassion and distress at the pointlessness of human suffering are the emotions of an entire sex unhardened to inhumanity; more than that, a sex as indoctrinated with susceptibility as men have been with their stiff upper lips.

It is impossible to say whether women are by nature more humane and tender-hearted than men. Probably they are not, but it is safe to say that mid-twentieth-century society assumed passivity in its women, just as it expected vigorous action of its men. Built into the 1941 National Service Act was the precondition that women would not make use of lethal weapons, would not kill. Aggression and heroism were left to men. But for many of those soldiers, D-day proved traumatic; seasick and terrified troops floundered up those beaches past the bodies of their drowned and dying comrades. And the wounded survivors of that bitter fight returned to have the unheroic shit swabbed off them by meek teenagers like Naina Cox.

*

That June, Helen Forrester was laid low by a bad bout of influenza, followed by the onset of rheumatism in her legs. For over a month she stayed in bed, sustained by letters from Eddie, who had survived the invasion. Written in haste from the battlefield, these were jokey and loving, soldierly and plainspoken. 'We'll get married next leave. Be ready.' With anguish he described how one of his oldest friends, hit by a sniper's bullet, had died in his arms. Slowly convalescing, Helen read the letters, waited and hoped, and – together with most of the population – listened to the BBC's nightly broadcasts. By mid-July, British and Canadian troops were attempting to strike to the east of Caen with a massed tank assault. But Operation Good-wood was a flawed campaign. Concealment had failed; the RAF had tried to bomb German defences to oblivion, but had aimed inac-curately. And commanders had not predicted the chaos that would ensue as too many troops attempted to cross too few bridges across the river Orne. Over two days the British and Canadians suffered 5,537 casualties.

By the third week of July Helen was recovering, though still weak. One rainy evening her father brought her the *Liverpool Echo* to read in bed. At the back of the paper she came to the public announcements. There was a more than usually long list of deaths.

Almost without thinking I ran my finger down the names.

And there it was.

'No,' I whispered. 'No! Not him!'

Had a malign fate selected her, vulnerable and demoralised as she already was, to be robbed of everyone she ever loved? What kind of punishment was this?

I could not speak, could not cry. I just wanted to die myself.

Compelled by an instinct stronger than her own wellbeing, Helen staggered into her clothes and lurched out into the rain. A strange momentum propelled her forward as, soaked to the skin, she strode insanely along the blacked-out lanes, through Meols, Hoylake, West Kirby, Caldy. '"Eddie," I cried, to the slashing, unheeding rain, "Eddie, darling."' Helpless grief tore at her. Some-how, she found the energy to stumble the 3 miles to the western vantage point of Caldy Hill. There she gasped and stopped, strain-ing into the dark obscurity of the Atlantic Ocean. In its depths lay Harry O'Dwyer's bones. In the blackness above, somewhere, Derek Hampson had met his fate. And in distant France, the war had killed another love. Now, among the shattered remains of all her hopes, Helen was left with just one: that for Eddie Parry it had been a quick death.

Mud and Warpaint

As the invading forces moved southwards and eastwards across France, the army relied on the kind of back-up that women were expected to give. Once the beachheads were established, it was possible for the FANYs to bring ambulances over to Normandy by landing craft. Wrens like Ena Howes, who had supervised the telephone exchange at Fort Southwick, had a role to play setting up communications. She and two others were shipped across to Arromanches and driven along bomb-cratered roads to their base in western Normandy, where they holed up in an empty medieval house and slept on the floor with their gas-masks as pillows. ATS girls were sent out to Normandy to run mobile army canteens. And WAAF nursing orderlies were put on board Dakotas and flown out to France to escort the wounded back to Britain, frequently under fire. For nurses were, as ever, vital.

Iris Ogilvie, a Welsh nursing sister with the RAF, aged twenty-nine, was among the first British women to land on the invasion beaches, just five days after D-day. Many years later Iris wrote a detailed account of her work setting up mobile field hospitals and helping to evacuate the injured. She had offered her services after her husband, Donald, a bomber pilot, had been killed over Holland in June 1943. 'I was devastated. He had died for his country and I didn't care what happened to me. I knew I wanted to make some contribution myself.' Initially, Iris was not made welcome. When the medical orderlies heard that she was to become one of their number, they reacted with unconcealed hostility: 'We don't want any b--- women in this outfit.' And the commanding officer of the unit was disbelieving. 'They're not going over, are they?' he asked as she and her friend Mollie set off for Normandy. He raised objections, telling them: 'We can't cater for you to have toilet facilities on your own.' Iris was not worried by such trivia.

On 8 June the nurses were briefed and handed their emergency packs: twenty-four hours' worth of rations, including chocolate, biscuits, compressed and ready-sweetened tea cubes, chewing-gum, a compass, four cigarettes and four sheets of toilet paper. Iris also brought with her a small waterproof bag for her Elizabeth Arden make-up. Like Vera Lynn, she was reluctant to be seen without her warpaint. 'I wasn't going to land in Normandy looking a sight! Bright red lipstick did wonders to pull one's face together.' On 12 June they stepped ashore on Juno beach. The beach-master gaped at the sight of the diminutive, fair-curled Iris appearing off the landing craft and said, 'Good God.' He escorted the sisters into the nearest underground shelter, and there the troops raised a welcoming cheer: 'Watch out, Adolf, you've had it now!' called out one.

Reunited with their colleagues, the nurses' work began. Casualties were patched up and accompanied to the makeshift landing strip to be evacuated on Dakotas which were being used as air ambulances. In the early days Iris and her team sent 1,023 cases back to England. The unit kept close to the advancing forces, following them to Cussy, near Bayeux, then eastwards to Camilly, and they were often in danger. Their convoy was attacked; shrapnel fell on their tarpaulins, and a damaged aircraft nearly crash-landed on the tents. While in Bayeux, press photographers persuaded Iris and Mollie to pose for propaganda images, neatly dressed in skirts, giggling over the latest frivolous hats in a Bayeux shop window. The picture was staged, for consumption by a public who wouldn't have relished the reality: tin hats, battledress trousers and the total exhaustion of nurses dressing burns, giving bedpans and tending injuries round the clock. Just 10 miles away the Battle of Caen was raging. Three days after the fall of Caen on 9 July Iris Ogilvie entered the city, where over a thousand people had been killed; 'the smell of death was everywhere'.

*

QA Joy Taverner was twenty-two years old when she too made the crossing from Portsmouth to Arromanches five days after D-day. She had been waiting for months to put her training into practice on the battlefield. Joy was a clever, self-sufficient, strong-willed young woman, but the experiences that war would throw at her over the next twelve months would test every fibre of her being.

The Taverners were a closely knit, talkative, working-class family, Irish by blood. Joy had grown up in the villagey atmosphere of Golborne Road, down the hill from Portobello market in west London. There her parents ran a successful newsagents and tobacconists shop. Her father – 'the guv'nor' – was a mason; Churchillian in his way, he would stand importantly at his shop-door, thumbs thrust into his waistcoat pockets, complete with fob watch and cigar. For Joy, it was a good Christian upbringing, a childhood surrounded with affection. Her mother kept house and cooked for the extended family of brothers, sisters, aunts, uncles and cousins who lived and worked there under one roof. From an early age Joy loved animals. There were chickens in the back yard, dogs and cats 'of every kind', mice in her pocket and, Joy's favourite, Marmaduke the lizard. Her ambition was to become a vet.

War broke out when she was seventeen, and those dreams had to be abandoned. Instead Joy trained to be a nurse at Hammersmith Hospital, working there throughout the Blitz. Twice the hospital was hit. In 1943 she joined the QAs. That winter, along with fifty other recruits, she was sent to Peebles near Edinburgh to be drilled for conditions on the battle front: cross-country runs and gate-vaulting were the order of the day, until the nurses were considered fit enough to work alongside Monty's boys. The QAs had officer status and had two pips on their shoulders.

In spring 1944 Joy was sent down to the Portsmouth area to await the invasion. Joy herself takes up the story:

Finally we were put on an LST* and tied up in the Solent for three days waiting for the Mulberry to be taken over and for troops to take over the beaches. Finally we went to the Mulberry and one of the trucks with all our kit and belongings went over the side into the sea!

Eventually we landed and were sniped at by Germans. One of our doctors was killed and an orderly was shot and we had to amputate his leg at the side of the road. We had to be careful because everywhere was mined. Notices ('Achtung Minen') were on the roadsides. Lots of dead bodies.

We went to St Lô and put tents up in a field as a front-line hospital. In the operating theatre for three days and nights – only having a few hours off. Polish men, Germans and Canadians came in – as well as our own troops. I

* Landing ship tank.

had only the clothes I stood up in so washed my underwear – wrapped them in tissue paper and dried them in the camp oven!

As military personnel, the QAs had to demonstrate that they could cope with battle conditions. They were under constant shelling. No special arrangements were made to accommodate the nurses, but the soldiers were tolerant and agreed to stand armed to protect them if they needed to relieve themselves in the middle of a field. Some of the matrons regarded it as a question of honour to be able to drink the men under the table. By now, the romantic grey and scarlet uniform had been replaced by khaki battledress; Joy's matron took it very much amiss when she heard that her nurses had been mistaken for ATS and insisted – absurdly, in Joy's view – that the nurses wear their scarlet capes over their khaki slacks.

With new cases being trucked in constantly, Joy and the other nurses were surviving on cups of tea and sheer adrenalin. The mud was indescribable. The new wonder drug, penicillin, had just come in, and was being used for the first time. In August, the two German Panzer armies were caught by the Allies in a pincer movement at the Falaise gap. Many of the forces drummed up by Hitler at this point in the war were unfit veterans, Poles, 'Osttruppen' recruited from Soviet prisoners of war or very young conscripts. Joy nursed them all, often having to comfort wounded German teenagers calling out for their mothers. Many of such cases had lost blood, but if there happened to be an SS officer on the ward, they could be brutal. Fearful that the donor blood might come from Jewish sources, the SS forbade transfusions. Joy, outraged, made use of her own officer status to overrule such inhumanities.

Later, she tried to capture her feelings in verse. The lines she wrote stress the frustration she felt as a nurse, constantly confronted with suffering and yet so often incapable of giving help:

> Day followed night and then another day
> Of mangled broken boys.
> Irish, Welsh and Scots
> Jerries, Poles and French –
> They cried in many tongues as needles long and sharp
> Advanced.
> Their blood ran very red and so they died.

Yet her uncomplicated faith in a loving God helped her endure the suffering she saw every day around her.

It was while Joy was on the road with the Allies that she fell in love. Captain Pip Knowles was a handsome surgeon doctor working in Joy's field hospital. He was captivated by her pretty looks and chatty manners. The intensity of their relationship mirrored the intensity of the work they were both doing; the physical demands of caring for hundreds of casualties called upon all their reserves, and, not surprisingly, the strain was sublimated into feverish levels of emotion – the more so, since this was forbidden territory. Pip Knowles was married, with a child. Joy's daughter now says that her mother's religion and respect for family meant that she would never have made any claims on her lover, but there is little doubt that this man was the 'big love'. When Captain Knowles was transferred to another hospital, Joy applied to go there too. The canny matron, rightly suspecting her young nurse of ulterior motives, turned Joy's request down. The lovers wrote instead and snatched time when they could. Sue, Joy's daughter, found the love letters after her mother's death but felt that they were too private to read. 'There are photos of them in a field, somewhere in Normandy. They look like blissful teenagers. She's got her arms round his neck . . . there's no doubt it was an intimate relationship.' But the odds were stacked heavily against Joy's affair with Pip Knowles. They parted, their great love derailed by a sense – on both sides, perhaps? – that it was sinful, illicit.

The Allies battled their way across northern Europe. News of the failed attempt to assassinate Hitler boosted morale; surely, now, the end must be near? At the end of July the American army began to sweep across northern France, and on 23 August Paris was captured. 3 September saw the liberation of Brussels and on the 4th British forces entered Antwerp. In the army's wake, military hospitals were set up. That autumn and winter Joy and her fellow nurses made their home in a converted convent in the small town of Eeklo, west of Antwerp. This, after living under canvas for months on end, was luxury. The nuns made them welcome. Belgium was a welcome respite from mud and horror. And it was while she was there that she literally bumped, in a snowstorm, into her future husband, Sergeant Ron Trindles.

In newly liberated Belgium there were pleasures for the taking.

Alcohol, clothes and perfume were plentiful, and the QAs were thrilled to rediscover their feminine side, shopping and partying. Joy at this time was on the rebound, and she had seen too much suffering to feel that life owed her anything. On the face of it Ron – good-looking and breezy, with a touch of the suave cavalier about him – seemed a good bet. He was a slick and able dancer, plus, he had no ties. And so they dated. As he twirled her around to the strains of Glen Miller, Joy failed to detect Ron's severe and meticulous side. When it became apparent that her superior officer rank meant that he couldn't go into her mess, she – unlike him – took it in her stride. For in reality, this was a man who cared deeply about rank and who, as a Supply Corps sergeant, liked everything in boxes. The army, with its rigour and clockwork precision, suited his character. From Joy's end of things, Ron was a nice man who owned a fast car and was 'a charming companion'. And now that the Allies seemed to be beating back the enemy, there was perhaps room to have a bit of fun, to take a glimpse into a happier future.

As it turned out, there was little time for dreaming, as the Germans counter-attacked against the Allied advance, taking advantage of their overstretched supply lines. In Eeklo, the QAs took in victims of the Ardennes Offensive, one of the bloodiest battles of the war, with over 47,000 Americans wounded, and 19,000 killed.

But nothing could have prepared Joy Taverner for the ordeal still to come, as she and her fellow nurses continued to support the army's inexorable advance into Germany.

9   No Real Victory

Dim-out

Brixton, south London, Friday 23 June 1944. For the last ten days, Miss Florence Speed, diarist, and author of *Blossoming Flowers* (1942), *Cinderella's Day Out* (1943) and *Exquisite Assignment* (1944), had found it hard to concentrate on writing her escapist romances for the women's light fiction market. Seven days after D-day, powerful explosions rocked south-east England. From launch sites in the Pas de Calais, the Germans had begun a bombardment which threatened to exceed the damage of the Blitz. South London lay directly in the path of these V1s, or 'pilotless planes' – soon to be christened buzz bombs or doodlebugs. Deafeningly noisy, the most sinister and impersonal aspect of Hitler's mystery weapon was the way that its engine noise cut out shortly before impact. Round the clock, for most of June, there were to be approximately a hundred of these deadly explosions every day.

Since the beginning, Florence had been keeping a tally of bomb raids, numbering each one. In the early hours of that Friday morning she was woken by the sound of sirens. She picked up her bedside diary, and started to document the raids as they happened:

0210 The last notes of the sirens woke me fifteen minutes ago. Since then three of the flying bombs – no four, another has just gone off, – have just exploded . . . *Raid 732*

A new type by the sound of them . . . one hardly hears them before they explode – It's gone off. Six in a quarter of an hour.

Seventh audible. Going to be a nasty night.

Gone off.

0225 Very nasty near one & one scarcely heard the thing before it was down. There's a 1000 lbs of explosive in each.

0555 All Clear going. In intervals of sleep counted 14 bomb crashes.

0655 Crump again but not so near.

0730 All clear

0755 Warning *Raid 755*. Crump . . .

Miss Speed got up and dressed. After breakfast she went shopping, but by 10 a.m. there had been another twenty raids. She got home and, with a rather shaky pen, recorded '*Raid 776*'.

1454 Siren. *Raid 777*

1501 Crump.

Nuisance, as I was typing.

But can't stay put under my great window. Ninety per cent of all air-raid casualties are due to flying glass.

1515 All clear.

1645 Sirens. *Raid 778* . . .

1740 Hearing another of the darned things coming . . . There was a terrific biff. The house shook . . . A great column of smoke was rising skywards from the direction of Camberwell . . .

1829 *Raid 779*. Oh! What a joyful life . . .

2055 Warning *Raid 780*

2100 A Crasher down already. Had been in bed only 40 minutes. Looks as if we're in for a good night again.

2130 All clear.

2155 *Raid 781* Had just dozed off & think I didn't hear them.

2332 All Clear.

Across the south-east of England it was the same story: sleepless nights, air-raid warnings, streets deep in debris and broken glass. 'London is in a chastened mood,' wrote Vere Hodgson, describing the apprehensive atmosphere that pervaded the capital:

Saturday 8th July

Buses half empty in the evening. Marked absence of people on the streets. Thousands have left, and many go early to the Shelters. Children have been going in hundreds.

A curious hush fell on the West End. The 'up-for-the-day class of woman' who used to visit London for a perm and a little light shopping had been frightened off. Night after night people slept in their clothes, prepared for the worst. Those who didn't flee the city retreated to the underground again. 'I don't like these Bombs nearly as much as I did the old ones,' one charlady was reported as saying. Unlike in the Blitz, these bombs fell in broad daylight. You might be on your way to work, or shopping; when you heard their sinister growl, you sprinted for safety. Tragedy became commonplace. Hospitals were bombed. A queue of mothers and children, bombed out of their homes, was waiting to be given clothing when another bomb fell on them. Another hit a Lyons Corner House crowded with lunchers. On 18th June 121 members of the congregation of the Guards Chapel, practically next door to Buckingham Palace, were killed, and seventy injured.

Churchill acted as far as possible to resist what Vere Hodgson called the 'Horrible Things'. Here the secret army of sentinels at Bletchley Park played their part. As code-breaker Mavis Lever remembered:

Doodle bugs were the worst, terrifying. Well, to start out, the flying bombs – which had engines that cut out at a certain distance – were hitting Central London. Though I didn't know it of course, I was passing information to the Germans through our double agents, who had to get them to believe that most of the stuff they were launching was hitting targets north of London. And that would persuade them to reduce the cut-out. So then they were all hitting South London. And my parents lived in Norbury in South London, and their terrace was hit, and a neighbour killed, as well as several people I knew there ... And I had no idea when I went home and it was bombed that it was anything to do with me! – that I had helped it happen by putting out double-crossing information.

By autumn 1944, with Germany appearing to be on the back foot, and the Allies making steady, if slow, progress across northern Europe, the V1 attacks represented a deeply depressing setback. But not everybody found them so.

In 1943 ATS kine-theodolite operator Doffy Brewer had been posted to a gunners' practice camp at Clacton-on-Sea, Essex. Valuable work, as it turned out, when the pilotless planes started to hit London. 'The world of AA was rejoicing ... At last, here was every gunner's dream.' All the rehearsals, the calculations and simulations were paying off. These targets moved at an undeviating height, on an undeviating course. Coastal guns in south-east England were – along with RAF fighters and the balloon barrage – the most effective defence against Hitler's terror weaponry. Doffy and her friends were 'in the thick of things', caught up in the general enthusiasm as the men they had helped to train brought down V1s by the thousand. 'Success was phenomenal. Never had such an AA operation worked so well.' More than half the V1s were brought down before they could reach their target.

The rejoicing was short-lived. In August Doffy's unit was summoned by 'the brass', and told with great solemnity and secrecy that British reconnaissance suspected a new weapon of being developed. It would be a long-distance rocket, capable of enormous destruction. The kine operators were to pack their bags. Based just outside Dover, their new job was to scan the skies for the giveaway smoke trail that would reveal the new rocket's launch site. The ATS girls moved into their seaside accommodation, which had a flat roof, with a panoramic view over the Channel. They shared out the watches, always on the alert, scanning the seaward horizon, on which Calais was distantly visible. At the sight of that tell-tale plume of smoke, they would call out 'Fireworks!' 'Big Ben' was the code name for an identifiable target that could be photographed. With luck, that would enable them to calculate with pinpoint accuracy the location of the launch pad. An immediate phone call to nearby RAF Manston would then give our bomber pilots the coordinates they needed to destroy the missile and the rocket site.

Three weeks later, Doffy was at home on leave with her parents in Romford when she read in the paper that an enemy bomber and its entire payload had crashed on to a gas main. According to the report, there had been a huge explosion and fearful casualties. 'I was sure. I was sure that this was it.' Next day the paper reported two more giant explosions. Two more heavily laden bombers had, apparently, crash-landed on to two more gas mains. Doffy was not fooled and, as soon as she could, hurried back to Dover. There she found the girls jubilant. One of them had seen it: gazing out eastwards, she had spotted the rocket's unmistakable smoke trace as it zig-zagged up from the horizon, not over the Pas de Calais but over Holland.

'If only we kine girls could have stopped them. It was a nightmare of frustration.' But the V2 rockets had transportable launching equipment and were fired from platforms that were virtually undetectable. There was something both fearful and arbitrary about them;

nobody could tell when or where they were about to land, and if you knew, you were probably dead already. The attacks persisted until March 1945.

'Horrible creatures are Germans,' reflected Clara Milburn.

*

With painful slowness, the enemy was being defeated; everyone knew that the war would be won: no, not by Christmas, but next year, sometime. The Home Guard was disbanded. In September 1944 blackout restrictions were relaxed: something of an anti-climax, as the country now adapted to the 'dim-out'. Civil defence outside London was becoming redundant. There were other straws in the wind. In November ice cream crept back on to the menu of some London restaurants for the first time since 1942. Occasional batches of oranges started to reappear in the shops, and as Christmas approached there was optimism about the turkey supply. But the word 'victory' rang a little hollow, as Allied troops in northern Europe and Italy failed to maintain the momentum of D-day. Over 1,000 British troops had been killed in the costly failure of Arnhem; 'We all thought the war was so nearly over and now we hear of such sacrifice of lives it makes me miserable,' wrote Mass Observation diarist Muriel Green. 'I suppose we are taking victory so much for granted it makes such disasters seem worse.' Twenty-three-year-old Muriel was working in a hostel for factory workers; over Christmas she noticed that the word 'victory' was used by few people in her hostel. Instead, they raised a glass to 'peace'. 'The war seems to have got to the stage where more fighting only seems waste . . . Fighting seems to spread fighting; there is no real victory.'

Swamped as she was by army bureaucracy, ATS officer Margery Baines also took a jaundiced view of the Allies' progress in Europe. Her own battles with authority were starting to invade her waking hours and affect her health. In 1944 Margery suffered a nervous breakdown. The Army's medical officers, with an infallible instinct for the illogical, pronounced that the only cure for Margery's ills was motherhood. Having added up one and one and made three, 'they discharged me and allowed my husband home on compassionate leave'. Self-evidently, no other feminine concerns could compete with the future of an infant. Once safely pregnant, it was back to civilian life, to queues and shortages. 'Like other Britons, I was now faced with the prospect of peace. And a sad business it was too.'

Knowing that peace was coming made women start to weigh up what it might hold in store for them. Maggie Joy Blunt, a single woman aged thirty-two, had been keeping a diary for Mass Observation since 1939. When younger, Maggie had aimed high, hoping to become an architect. When this ambition foundered she pursued journalism, but the war had intervened and since 1942 she had been working as a publicist for a light alloy aircraft firm. She continued to hope for marriage but was now wondering about the prospects of earning a living:

June 25th 1944

The question that is in everyone's mind is – what will post-war conditions be like? . . . It will be a ghastly scramble for work . . .

October 11th 1944

I read somewhere the view that the change from war to peace would be so gradual we should hardly notice it. It will not be anything definite and spectacular like Lights up, Bananas for all, unlimited fully fashioned silk stockings at 2/6d a pair and everyone with a job they like and able to afford their own plot and bungalow.

Most of the older generation just wanted to return to 'normal'. For them, 'normal' meant the same as before the war. Barbara Cartland questioned a middle-aged married friend who had spent her war earning good money in a factory: 'What are you going to do when the war is over?' This lady had no desire to go on with her job. 'Have a good spring clean,' was the reply. 'If you only knew how sick I am of coming home dead tired and staying up half the night to get the housework done and the clothes mended . . . It's home for me.' For this lady, the coming peace didn't hold out any more ambitious prospect than washing the curtains and turning out her cupboards. In summer 1944 some Mass Observation interviewers went to Gloucester and asked a group of working-class women what they hoped the next ten years of their lives would be like. The answers were vague: 'Don't know. Really I don't.' 'Well, it's all according.' 'I'm not good at answering questions.' Abstract aspirations had no place on these women's mental map.

Writing in 1953 (in *Lady into Woman*), Vera Brittain analysed the condition of a generation of housewives at the end of the Second World War. She felt that British women were very much to blame in their failure 'to be intelligent about the future'. Society had indoctrinated them, middle- and working-class alike – as she explained – with the idea that homes, husbands and children should be their prime concern. Total war had then anaesthetised what moral sense they might have left, bombing and bludgeoning them into submission and meekness. Life for the housewife had become a dreary round of food queues, rations and coupons. So steeped was she in ignorance of politics, so unintelligent about the future, that she herself had become part of the menace to civilisation.

Vera Brittain's scorn of the humble British housewife echoes and foreshadows the cry of feminists past and present, that women can and should have a special relationship with peace. As the bearers of the human race, all their instincts cried out against killing and destruction. And yet somehow, faced with war propaganda and with the difficulties of organising for peace, women had become dumbly acquiescent, resigned to their own incapacities.

It is easy to sympathise with Vera Brittain's anger at their apathy. How depressing it was always to be fobbed off with an apologetic 'I'm not interested in politics. Looking after the house and children takes up all my time.' If only women could be helped and encouraged to detach themselves from the 'tedious small-change of wartime existence' and engage with the world of politics and reform then world peace would surely be within the grasp of humankind?

In *Lady into Woman*, Brittain exhorts her sex to give their energies to what she calls a 'women's service for peace', while disparaging housework and childcare:

Not even two World Wars . . . had convinced some women that the duty of keeping their homes clean and their children tidy was small compared with the moral obligation to be intelligent about the future.

But for the majority at the time it wasn't easy. Domesticity was completely central to most women's lives. Feeding, tending and caring were the outward form of woman's life-giving instinct, her very social identity. The war-weary mother of seven waiting for lambs' hearts or an ounce of cheese, the suburban matron hoping for synthetic cream: both were in their own way doing what they could to improve their lot in difficult times, to nurture their dependents, to 'keep the home fires burning'. How could they raise their heads above the daily grind and find the mental freedom to challenge militarism? How could they muster the arguments needed to attack government spending on armaments and call for the money to be spent instead on education and health? In 1944, just surviving and looking after their families took most of the energy that women possessed. They were chronically tired. Working for peace could wait – till peace itself came.

The National Effort

'What would you be doing, if it wasn't for the war?' Doffy Brewer's friends would ask each other.

'Oh, I'd be . . .'

And we all stared at one another, trying to imagine what peacetime was like . . . It was like staring into empty space . . .

Our personal aims had gone grey. All the colours had faded away.

Meanwhile, they gritted their teeth, they dug for victory, they bathed in five inches of water with a line on the bath to show the fill-up limit, they lived off one tablet of soap a fortnight and wrote letters to their loved ones on both sides of the thin, fibrous wartime paper. They did without sweets, they did without petrol, their meals were dull and starchy. They made do and they mended. It was called the 'National Effort'.

With the end in sight, they may have nursed dreams of bananas for all, or cornucopias of silk stockings. 'I long for an excuse to wear nice clothes,' was the *cri de cœur* of diarist Shirley Goodhart. But five years of war had virtually killed consumerism.

In pre-war Britain, men worked, women shopped. Daily, wives like Nella Last buttoned up their coats and, basket on arm, trekked down the country's high streets, ticking off their lists. Butcher, baker, greengrocer, dairy. To the grocer's for biscuits, Quaker oats and tea-leaves; to the pharmacy for shampoo and liver salts; to the haberdasher's for knitting wool and darning needles. With the exception of more serious acquisitions – houses, cars and three-piece suites – purchasing was what women did: it was *who* they were. As principal home-maker, the housewife was assumed to take an acquisitive interest in curtains, candlesticks, clocks and curios. Intermittently, the desire for cosmetics, a ready-made hat or a spring outfit saw her on a day's outing to the city. The defining opening sequence of the classic wartime movie *Mrs Miniver* shows its heroine engaged in the most feminine activity its director could envisage. We see her hurrying for her train at the end of a shopping trip, laden with parcels, but delaying her return for one final extravagance: a frivolous beribboned hat decked with an artificial bird.

But the wartime economy decreed an end to such fripperies. Mrs Miniver's hat, so symbolic of pre-war indulgence, disappears into its lovely stripy box, never to be seen again. With her husband and son at risk, and raiders overhead, Kay Miniver has more serious concerns. But five years into the war, Mrs Miniver's contemporaries might also have paused to reflect on how the 'National Effort' had stripped them of their consumer status, only to replace it with a new source of thrifty pride. For this generation of women – ahead of their time in environmental terms – acquisition, sufficiency and waste had taken on new meanings.

In his comprehensive chronicle of the war years, *How We Lived Then – A History of Everyday Life during the Second World War*, the writer Norman Longmate demonstrates with immense detail the privations endured by the British public. What emerges from his book is that women were on the sharp end when it came to doing without and preventing waste.

Cooking and heating homes meant fuel economies; here, the housewife was the target of pleas to try hay-box cookery, to try out recipes for raw foods, and never to use the oven for one dish at a time. She was also beseeched to cut back on coal consumption, to lag doors and windows against draughts, to share firesides with neighbours, to bank up the fire overnight and to sift ashes for unused lumps of coal, or reconstitute them from a mixture of coal dust and earth. In the cold winters of the war the kitchens of the land were full of buckets containing strange mixtures: tea-leaves, conkers, old wallpaper, cotton-reels, potato peelings, meat gristle – anything that would burn. In cold weather you piled on clothes. When it came to baths, everyone was encouraged to stick to the five-inch guideline. Helped by their strenuous efforts, by 1944 households were using three-quarters less fuel than had been consumed in 1938.

Early in the war an order was made that no paper was to be thrown away. The habit of dropping litter in the streets was defunct. Households were encouraged to donate everything from newspapers to old love letters – minus the pink ribbons – to be made into cardboard for the packaging of war materials. Millions of unwanted books were donated to be pulped. Paper carriers and bags of every kind were banned outright; one smart lady who had forgotten her shopping basket was spotted walking down the Headrow in Leeds city centre nonchalantly swinging a lavatory brush from her finger. Women working in typing pools were told to reuse ribbons and to type 'single spacing only', while the fear of making a typing error was exacerbated by the worry of wasting paper. Their letters were sent in reused envelopes with gummed-on labels. The shortage of toilet paper – which, inevitably, affects women more than it does men – was universally depressing and undignified. And by the end of 1944 it was becoming hard to buy sanitary towels.

Restrictions on petrol left many a family reliant on pony-carriages, pedal-power and their feet. 'We were a lot fitter than people are today,' remembers one woman. Public transport employed large numbers of women 'clippies', drivers and porters. 'Is Your Journey Really Necessary?' ran the slogan, and nobody used their car on a whim. Many of the one in ten people who owned one laid it up on blocks for the duration. Frances Faviell bicycled daily through the traffic-free streets of London to her first aid post, with Vicki the dachshund perched in her butcher's basket on the front. If you were going somewhere, you always took someone with you, and hitch-hiking took off. 'Don't forget,' says ex-WAAF Joan Tagg, 'we could hitch-hike anywhere in the country, and if you were in uniform people would stop and pick you up. You just said 'London' and they'd take you if they were going that way.'

If you were young and setting up house, or bombed out, equipping your accommodation (whatever it might be) with furniture, linen, hardware, crockery and other essentials was difficult. If the teapot broke, you might be the lucky one in three who, in 1943, managed to find one in the shops. When household linen was rationed in

October 1942, it was simply assumed that the coupons would be allocated to the mother of the household. If you wanted a carpet, you paid a high price, or bartered; if you wanted a rug you made your own out of rags. Many regretted donating their aluminium kitchenware to the 1940 'Saucepans for Spitfires' appeal. Launched by WVS chieftainess Lady Reading, it had seemed at the time to offer a specially feminine kind of sacrifice: a home-front echo, perhaps, of that made by the heroic young fighter pilots.

For the houseproud woman, life was hard. Fly-papers, floor polish, matches, commercial detergents, black lead and cleaning fluids were in short supply. Such women had standards and, as usual, they improvised: with vinegar, salt and beeswax. Soap was rationed from 1942, and a cake of Palmolive became something to treasure, eked out to the last fragment. 'The public has been asked ... to try washing clothes in the peasant French manner, with wood ash and water instead of soap,' Mollie Panter-Downes wrote in *London War Notes*. The public to which she refers did not, evidently, include men.

There were salvage schemes, many of them organised by women. As self-appointed salvage stewards they all wore a special badge with an 'S', and there was a pecking-order running from chief steward, responsible for 12,000 houses, down to the strictly local monitor – 'Mrs Next-Door' – in charge of just eight neighbours. Housewives were urged not to throw away aluminium milk bottle tops or cans. Rubber could be recycled in tyre manufacture, or even to make jumping boots for paratroopers. Leftover bones gathered at 'bone drives' went to produce glue, used in ship-building and shell cases. Battledress fabric could be made from wool remnants, while the nation's pigs benefited from every scrap of food waste that could be collected.

Often, the ladies of the WVS were the heroines of such initiatives. Over cups of tea they gathered in church halls and outhouses, to dismantle used electric light bulbs and batteries. They pulled old tyres from ponds and pounced on the contents of office waste-paper baskets. That legendary character the rag-and-bone-man was, in wartime, as often as not, a rag-and-bone-woman from the WVS. The grandes dames of society played their part; following the example of Stella Reading, Lady Beit invited the beau monde to a Thrift and Salvage Exhibition held at her home in Belgrave Square.

ÜP HOUSEWIVES AND AT 'EM!"

Paper, metal, bones! Herbert Morrison's salvage campaign set out to make every housewife feel she could do her bit for victory.

As we have already seen, clothes rationing was one of the most depressing aspects of the war to women who loved to be pretty, but were forced, instead, to be patriotic. When it was introduced in 1941 the President of the Board of Trade told the nation: 'When you feel tired of your old clothes remember that by making them do you are contributing some part of an aeroplane, a gun or a tank.' It was hard, at times, as you patched your underwear or shivered in a threadbare pullover, to appreciate the relationship between your frayed exterior and, say, the victory of El Alamein. The 1938 generation were already accustomed to shopping for quality not quantity; the throwing-away of clothes and purchasing of wear-it-once items were not part of the mid-twentieth-century female mentality. This made it easier to take a long hard look at your coupons, save them – often for months – buy the best quality you could afford and make it last, while doing your best to persuade yourself that it was smart to be shabby. Skill with a needle paid off, if you could find one to buy. Most women still made their own clothes; it was also a time when every daughter learned at her mother's knee how to knit, darn and take up a hem. Sheets, curtains, blackout material, parachute silk, butter-muslin, coffin-linings were converted into pinafores, blouses, bras and skirts. Constance Galilee obtained an army surplus blanket for just £1, dyed it and made a 'surprisingly dashing' winter coat. When Dilys Ormston's coat got shabby, she 'turned' it, which meant unpicking the lining, washing it, then taking the entire garment apart, seam by seam, and sewing it back together again inside out, before replacing the lining: 'almost as good as new'. Worn-out jerseys were unravelled. The wool was steamed to take out the kinks and reknitted into new jerseys. Women trimmed, dyed and remodelled their old dresses, attended WVS-run clothing exchanges, foraged at jumble sales or bought 'Utility', the guarantee of unadorned, cheap affordability. 'I've hardly anything respectable left to wear in bed,' bemoaned diarist Shirley Goodhart. Suppose she was bombed out at night? 'My stockings have just given out too. I was hoping that they would just last until I considered it warm enough to go without, but they haven't.'

Wedding dresses were handed down from bride to bride. The thoughtful Barbara Cartland started a pooling scheme for women to have their dreamed-of fairy-tale white wedding, coupons or no coupons. Over a thousand such gowns did the rounds of countless more girls – each of them cleaned, ironed and packed by Barbara; 'We got heartily sick of wedding dresses in my house before I had finished . . . The brides, however, were pathetically grateful.' But their guests were less than glamorous. One diarist described a February wedding party gathered in a chilly hotel reception room, all huddled in 'drab and rather cheap fur coats'. The guests' buttonholes might have been assembled out of garden flowers and carrot tops, the magnificent iced cake a sham, made from cardboard to conform with 'The Sugar (Restriction of Use) Order, 1940'.

Today's footwear obsessive would shrink at the reality that faced the seeker-out of ladies' shoes in 1944. Supply was so short that she might have to queue for the right to join a shoe queue. Cobblers were kept in business repairing and resoling, often with wood instead of leather, since hide was in short supply.

Unsurprisingly, the burden of child- and babycare fell entirely on mothers. The green ration book entitled them to jump queues and receive cut-price milk and orange juice. But once the baby came the mother had the additional headache of equipping her newborn. Nappies, cots and cot mattresses, baby baths, prams and pushchairs, even potties were all hard to come by. Toys and Christmas decorations were improvised from buttons, cotton reels, rags, pipe-cleaners. Clothing growing children was a struggle. Here as elsewhere, hand-me-downs and swap-schemes took the place of brand new. Some mothers agonised about their children's deprivations, from sweets to birthday candles, but most of the kids were resigned. They knew no other way.

Rationing had brought with it a low-protein, low-fat diet; healthy, if boring. Looking for ways to liven up family meals, the nation's cooks (i.e. women) turned to non-imported, locally grown, off-ration sources of food. They uprooted their bedding fuchsias from the front garden and replaced them with cabbages and beans. The 'Grow More Food' campaign brought neighbours together, exchanging recipes and gardening hints. Fridges were owned by few, so bottling, preserving and jam-making dealt with gluts; Phyllis Noble's mum spent much time giving away her surpluses of marrows and mushrooms. Subsistence smallholding flourished as many of these growers also started to keep hens, ducks, rabbits, goats, pigs and bees. Frances Partridge was one who, in March 1942, took delivery of 'two good little pigs ... dear little grunters with soulful eyes'. Seven months later the grunters, now vast, were 'executed'. The Partridges sat up till midnight making brawn out of the entrails and trotters ('everything except the squeal', as people said), stirring them in a cauldron 'like the witches in Macbeth'. The hard work was rewarded with pork, ham and bacon. The woods and hedgerows, too, were a glorious source of free food. In September 1943 Florence Speed went nutting in Effingham, and 'came home ... with eight pounds of blackberries not having seen a single nut! Lovely smell of jam-making.' For Sheila Hails, foraging took on a different meaning after D-day, when a torpedoed American ship yielded a rich haul on Lulworth Cove: 'An amazing amount of stuff was washed up; there were crates, broken or lying around on the beach. One was full of grapefruit, and another had instant coffee. It was wonderful! And we had a crate of ship's biscuits which kept us going for ages ... But awful that all those people drowned.'

It took the war for Nella Last, and thousands of other women like her, to realise 'what a knack of dodging and cooking and managing I possess, and my careful economies are things to pass on, not hide as I used to'. Mixing up hen food, extracting the maximum goodness from a bone of mutton, stuffing a toy rabbit with leftover scraps of winceyette, hoarding bottles of fruit were sources of great pride, to them and to their daughters: 'Our mums could cook, they could sew, they could do *anything*. They *had* to!' says ex-WAAF Joan Tagg. '*Nothing* was wasted.'

Never since the war has Britain been so sustainable, so prudent and thrifty, so community-minded, so self-sufficient – or so green.

Bombs, and the immensely real threat to the lives of loved ones abroad, gave an urgency to measures which women at home could perceive as making a real difference. Contemplating the bottled raspberries on their larder shelves, or wearing their refashioned coats made from army blankets, Nella and all those other women gained a sense of value, a satisfying awareness that their contribution had tangible meaning. And, somewhere inside themselves, they knew that the Spitfire pilots and tank crews had much to thank them for.

Back-room Girls

Scaling down on consumption is not a heroic or courageous activity. Heroism was for men. The majority of home-front women in the Second World War gratefully fell back on the more prosaic virtues of frugality and good housewifery. As we have seen, woman's function as auxiliary, provider of tea-and-sympathy and generalised faithful sidekick extended across the fields, the factories and the forces. For every fighter pilot, paratrooper, submariner or commando, there were legions of women drivers, technicians, cooks, censors, plotters, administrators, wireless operators, coders, interpreters, clerks, PAs, typists, telephonists and secretaries. One of them was Margaret Herbertson.

Fifty years after the war was over, Margaret decided to respond to a wartime friend who suggested she write a record of their work as 'back-room girls' in the FANYs. Both of them had been struck that, while much had been written about their glamorous fellow FANYs who had been parachuted behind enemy lines into occupied France, enduring, in some cases, capture, imprisonment and death in concentration camps, nothing had been said about the auxiliaries who worked behind the scenes. And yet the Special Operations Executive (SOE) was hugely dependent on their work giving aid to resistance movements and launching missions into occupied territory. As educated women from privileged backgrounds, Margaret and her friend had joined the FANYs because of its reputation as an elite volunteer service. Though nominally under the umbrella of the ATS, the FANYs had little to do with that branch of the forces, which was perceived as largely plebeian. Instead, the FANYs' semi-autonomy made it adaptable to a wide range of purposes. Thus during the Second World War the SOE deployed a large number of its clever, confident, hard-working young volunteers both as agents in the field and as coders, wireless operators or signal planners. Between 1942 and 1944 over a hundred FANYs – most of them bright girls under the age of twenty-two – were trained by SOE and posted to the Mediterranean.

At twenty-one Margaret Herbertson was a gifted, practical but, in her own words, 'terribly naive' young woman. She joined SOE as a coder in late 1943. In London, she was trained in the complexities of communicating between base stations and agents in the field, using coding systems considered unbreakable, and she was told how to use bluffs, or 'checks', to confuse the enemy. Once she had been briefed on the clandestine nature of her work and inoculated against yellow fever, she was sent to Cairo, and thence in June 1944 to Italy – on the very day before Rome fell to the Allies. Based near Bari, her first task was to participate in a complex signals deception, designed to persuade the enemy that Marshal Tito of Yugoslavia and his HQ were still in Bosnia, when in fact they had decamped to the Croatian island of Vis. An operator was despatched to a partisan base in Bosnia, from where a two-way signals traffic was set up. '[We] were required to encode quantities of bogus messages . . . I seem to remember that this included nursery rhymes.' The operation worked, successfully decoying hostile aircraft to the site of the false transmissions. Meanwhile, there was the added glamour of contact with field officers in the Balkans, some of whom sent coded flirtatious messages to the Bari FANYs, or 'dolls'; from time to time they arrived in person, with tales of their manly exploits. For Margaret, these secret activities resembled life in a thriller.

In autumn 1944 Margaret joined the staff of 'I' branch: the Intelligence Department. Here, her new responsibilities were to learn everything she could about the location and intentions of the German forces. In addition, she was expected to conduct thorough research – garnered via reconnaissance and agents' reports – into the terrain occupied by the enemy: its topography, politics and indigenous dynamics. This vital information was distilled daily into a fifteen-minute 'situation report'. Such was Margaret's responsibility in this process that her superior proposed that she be awarded a commission. But this was turned down 'on account of my age . . . The disparity of treatment accorded to women, as opposed to men, still required the shake-up it was to receive in the next generation but one,' she wrote philosophically. Eventually, Margaret herself was required to make the daily presentation, and after this the 'brass' caved in, and the commission was forthcoming:

On 8 November I became an Ensign and an intelligence officer. Some wag in the HQ coined the phrase 'The nearest thing to an intelligent FANY'. It was mildly irritating, but perhaps better than being called a 'doll'.

The front line was moving slowly and painfully northwards up the Italian peninsula. The FANYs remained at their base at Bari, with occasional exciting forays on leave to Rome and Florence, where they (respectively) attended Mass with the Pope and bought silk underclothes. Then in March 1945 Margaret's unit was flown in a Dakota up to Siena. 'The impact of my first sight of this delectable place was one that has never left me . . . Buildings reflected a pink light which was quite unforgettable, turning everything into shades of terracotta.' The girls strolled around the medieval centre, 'quite stunned by the beauty around us'. Their accommodation was in a gracious eighteenth-century villa across the valley from Siena; Margaret's annexe was named *Paradiso*. Evenings at that Tuscan villa were enchanted, with the sound of the city's bells tolling down the valley, and fireflies darting in the lengthening shade.

On the walls of another requisitioned Palazzo, they affixed their huge campaign maps, studded with myriad coloured pins and flags to display enemy formations, Partisan units and SOE missions. The task that lay ahead was to mobilise the Partisans for a planned offensive which would drive the Germans out of Italy. Weaponry was being

dropped for use by their units, and over 200 agents were working
behind enemy lines. The Intelligence traffic meant a constant flow of
signals from field to base, a large portion of which was deciphered,
interpreted and communicated by the SOE FANYs. Sixty-five years
later, Margaret still recalls the details of her daily life in Siena:

I concocted my reports in the evening, but if anything came up in the
morning, they had to be changed. So I kept my wireless beside my bed, and
also some notepaper. And most days I would wake up before 6, and I'd be
lying there in my indestructible stripy army pyjamas – much too small for
me (all the big sizes had gone) – propped up in my camp bed, listening in to
what the Germans had to say, and taking notes.

She often worked ten-hour days.

My job was to tell the people with whom I was working where the Germans were, and where they were moving to. But of course the Germans
never said 'We are moving to so-and-so . . .' You had to piece it together.
So if for example they said they were 'fighting valiantly' for a village,
which was north of the village they had been 'fighting valiantly' for the day
before, that meant they were moving north. Then we also had people on
the ground reporting on the German movements, who could recognise
their vehicles. And they might report that certain vehicles were moving
west . . . and one had to judge whether it was safe to drop someone there.
Anyway, it was a jigsaw puzzle . . .
   Well then I'd get up. We had no baths (we had to go into town twice a
week for a bath). Breakfast was tea and British Army bread, and fig jam. We
didn't eat off the country at all because the Italians were almost starving . . .
And then the trucks came to take us into Siena to the Headquarters.
   And then at 10 past 8 all the officers of the Headquarters would come
along for a 'sit rep', and you had to tell them what had been happening both
to our own troops, and the Germans, during the past twenty-four hours.

As an Intelligence officer during the final dramatic phase of the war
in Italy, Margaret was party to some of the most fascinating intrigues
of that campaign. Her field contacts included daring secret agents
like Dick Mallaby and Massimo Salvadori. Mallaby was parachuted
into northern Italy and captured by Fascists, but secured an interview
with the acting military commander of Italy, the German General
Wolff, which encouraged him to start talks with the Allies about a

German surrender. Salvadori had been dropped into occupied Milan in February 1945, where with false documents he passed himself off as a civilian, while acting as under-cover head of the SOE missions in Lombardy and liaising with Partisans and the regular forces.

After the winter attrition, pressure was building against the Axis. In bed, or travelling in the truck to the mess, Margaret was rarely without her earphones, her wireless tuned to the broadcasts from the *Oberkommando der Wehrmacht*. 'The enemy was in retreat. It was tremendously exciting.' On 9 April the German lines were subjected to a massive aerial and artillery bombardment. Two days later all Allied forces in Italy – including the SOE FANYs – received a special order from Field Marshal Alexander. 'Final victory is near,' he wrote, continuing with an exhortation 'to play our decisive part'. The Partisan wires were humming with traffic from the north. All leave was cancelled, and the FANY operators and coders were at full stretch, straining every nerve to interpret the incoming flow of messages. International armies were converging on Bologna, the gateway to the north. With the Germans in retreat Massimo Salvadori was instrumental in the uprisings of the northern cities, and the taking of German and Fascist prisoners.

On 28 April, a FANY wireless operator at HQ received an unambiguous signal from the field:

MUSSOLINI KILLED TODAY

and on the 29th the German chiefs in Italy signed an unconditional surrender at Caserta, with a ceasefire to take effect at midday on 2 May. Exhausted and dazed, the FANYs had worked themselves out of a job: 'there was no longer an enemy'.

Until Belsen

While Margaret Herbertson was spending her waking hours tracking the German retreat in Italy, QA Joy Taverner was still nursing in Eeklo in Belgium. In March 1945 the Allies crossed the Rhine; the army moved on, and life in the Belgian convent settled down somewhat.

It was in mid-April that Joy received the orders that would change her life for ever. She and a group of her fellow nurses were told to pack their things: they were to be taken into Germany to set up a field hospital. They were given no other information, before being taken to Celles airport, loaded on to a Dakota and flown north-east over Lower Saxony. It was the first time Joy had ever been in an aeroplane: 'a frightening experience'. They landed near Bergen and were piled on to an army truck. It was 17 April 1945, just two days after the British 11th Armoured Division's eastward advance had brought it to the gates of the Bergen-Belsen concentration camp. A British reporter, Richard Dimbleby, accompanied the troops, and famously told BBC listeners what he saw there:

In the shade of some trees lay a great collection of bodies. I walked about them trying to count, there were perhaps 150 of them flung down on each other, all naked, all so thin that their yellow skin glistened like stretched rubber on their bones. Some of the poor starved creatures whose bodies were there looked so utterly unreal and inhuman that I could have imagined that they had never lived at all. They were like polished skeletons . . .

It was Dimbleby's job to give a voice to the suffering, to try to make sense out of the senseless. But talkative, Irish, plain-speaking Joy, who had arrived two days earlier, was left incoherent, speechless with horror and incapable of describing what she found until forty years later. She was just twenty years old. 'My faith deserted me after that terrible experience and I have never regained it.'

The nurses of 29th General Hospital had a job to do and they did it. As soon as they could, they set up their tented hospital. Blankets, clothes and supplies were requisitioned from local shops. The sister collected the starving babies, put them under cover and tried to feed and revive them. Belsen was huge. Ten thousand bodies were lying there unburied, but up to thirty thousand prisoners were still alive when the camp was liberated. Bodies that showed any signs of life at all were collected on stretchers. The prisoners were starved, lice-ridden and suffering from cholera, dysentery, typhus and typhoid fever. Every day people died. The nurses put a board up outside their makeshift hospital and wrote on it the numbers of bodies to be collected and taken for burial in mass graves by German POWs. As a nurse, Joy was appalled at the Germans' disrespectful treatment of the dead. Uncovered corpses were being thrown into the graves, bulldozed and dismembered. At her instigation, lengths of fabric were acquired, and the dead were decently wrapped. 'Our Padre would go along and pray over each truck load.'

*This sketch of a concentration camp survivor was made by
Eric Taylor, a serving British soldier.*

The stench of excrement, death and burning bodies was excruciating; Joy would never forget it. She stayed at Belsen for nine agonising weeks. Before returning to England, she was taken for decontamination. Every inch of her was sprayed with DDT: 'It was in her ears, in her knickers, in her bra. And her family home was visited: they had to be warned about the lice she might be carrying, and what precautions they had to take.' But nothing could ever purge her of the memories, which were to give her nightmares for the next ten years:

We had no-one to talk to – we just had to keep going. Two of our sisters started drinking heavily and were sent home. I don't really know how we survived – we all supported each other and cried every night with our arms around each other . . .

We had been through the war but this was something so terrible that it took some time for us to come to terms with what we saw . . .

I cannot really write about everything that happened there. I have tried over the years to forgive the horrors . . .

Joy's daughter Sue believes her mother's inability to talk about Belsen was in itself a manifestation of the trauma she had experienced. But, unknown to Sue till later, Joy *had* found an outlet. Soon after her return from Germany, she sat down and struggled to find the words to describe what she had been through. The resulting poem, 'Until Belsen', is an attempt to express her sense of powerlessness and inadequacy, faced with perhaps the twentieth century's most inexpressible horror:

> *Until Belsen*
> We thought we had seen it all
>
> Our cheeks bloomed like peaches,
> Bright eyes, quick light movement.
> Flashes of scarlet, snow white caps
>
> We thought we had seen it all.
>
> The London Blitz, bombs, fires, headless corpses,
> Screaming children: Yankee Doodle Dandy!
>
> We thought we had seen it all.
>
> Scabies, Lice, and Impetigo, T.B., Polio
> And unmentionable V.D.
>
> We thought we had seen it all . . .
>
> Our souls sank deep and deeper still,
> Until with nowhere else to go, soft hearts
> Hardened and cocooned themselves.
> Laughter broke like glass over fields and orchards
> And from tent to tent.
> We tried; we really tried, but some they died.
>
> We thought we had seen it all.

Until Belsen.

There are no words to speak.
We hid within our souls, deep and silent.
We clung together trying to understand,
The smell pervaded the mind and the sights and sounds
Reached those souls buried deep within and for so long
Encased in rock.
Bitter scalding tears melted the rock
Our hearts were broken.

We had seen it all.

After she wrote that poem, Joy believed her heart would never mend.

★

Maggie Joy Blunt could hardly remember having seen such a beautiful spring. As the month of April drew to a close the suburban streets of her home town – Slough, in Berkshire – gloried in an early burst of lilac and wallflowers:

Last week 70° in the shade, everyone in summer frocks & without stockings, trees in leaf everywhere almost overnight . . . It has been wonderful, beyond describing . . .

'God is pleased,' said N, 'that we are freeing the concentration camps in Germany.'

As the news from the camps was released piecemeal over the ensuing weeks, it sent out a sickening shockwave, a sense of anger and shame for humankind. Photographs and newsreel footage gave the horror a hitherto unparalleled immediacy. Anne Popham's job in the Photograph Division of the Ministry of Information put her in the front line when the pictures started to come in. The girl at the next desk to hers was sorting them out. 'Hundreds of them were arriving. Some of them had to be censored – they were too nasty to be exhibited. I knew that concentration camps existed. But they were so much worse than anyone could possibly have imagined. I hadn't realised the people there were starved to death.' Maggie Joy Blunt was equally appalled: 'One suspected the Nazis of a certain amount of brutality & sadism, but not on this scale involving the death by starvation & deliberate degradation of 1000's & 1000's of men, women & children – the children worst of all.'

Joan Wyndham's party spirits were utterly quenched by the cruelty. Horrible doubts set in, about the religion she had grown up with:

18th April

Spent a Benzedrine-ridden night crying for the suffering of the children, and railing against God for allowing such torture . . .

My mind lately has been in a state of turmoil. I just don't know whether I believe any more or not. It is the first time that doubts have ever entered my mind, but I think I'd rather have an imperfect God than none at all, and no meaning to anything.

Clara Milburn listened to the broadcast describing the liberation of Buchenwald camp with disgust and outrage. 'Oh, these evil Germans! And those poor, poor souls.' Clara, a fervent patriot, had believed throughout in the righteousness of the cause. For her, the revelations of the concentration camps reinforced an implacable morality: 'How can one forgive such horrible deeds – or even forget them! We must *not* forget.' Vere Hodgson shared her anger. The Germans had described themselves as a Master Race. That claim now rang hollow. She had seen the *Sunday Pictorial* photographs which showed the unrepentant, smug faces of Belsen's women warders. 'They have no public conscience.'

Others reacted more with sorrow than outrage. Naomi Mitchison had witnessed political oppression in Austria and had tried to tell the world back in 1936, but nobody would listen. 'What was wrong with the German soul?' she now pondered. Sheila Hails, a pacifist, felt a bitter anger at the short-sightedness of government. 'I saw the films, and just felt utter horror. The British government had known about these camps for a long time, and they didn't do *anything* – all through the rise of Hitler.' Frances Partridge, as usual, explored her feelings in her diary. The gloriously unseasonable weather had prompted the Partridge family to pack a picnic and go bathing at a nearby mill-pool; but the monstrous images that Frances had seen in her morning paper imprinted themselves on her brain and wouldn't go away: 'a lorry stacked with naked corpses; others in the last stages of emaciation . . . in ghastly rows, waiting to be buried . . . They haunted me all day.'

Ralph and Burgo bathed. Frances sat by the millrace, racked with grief and anguish about humanity. The sanity of the world seemed to have received 'a fatal blow . . . I can't stop thinking of it and all it implies.'

Thelma Ryder's concerns were more material. Still working at her aircraft components factory in Lymington, she went to see the newsreel in her time off:

It was terrible – all those bodies piled up. But the German people must have known those things were happening. How could you not know? It must have been a hell of a smell around, you know?

Oh, God, I think it's terrible. Fancy treating people like that!

This Incredible Moment

The shockwave that convulsed Joy Taverner, Anne Popham, Frances Partridge and Thelma Ryder was just as seismic in its impact on their male counterparts. In the camps, babies and small children had been murdered; women and men alike had laboured, starved and died. In their crimes, the murderers – of both sexes – had not differentiated. Horror-struck, the public were united in their abhorrence of the atrocious regime which had perpetrated them. The Nazis' contempt for human values prompted a humanitarian consensus: such evil must never be forgotten or ever allowed to happen again.

For nearly six long years, the anti-Fascist banner had rallied diverse nations, from Britain to the Soviet Union. As their victory approached, and in the face of the Holocaust, it may have seemed – briefly – that the age-old sexual conflict could also be dispelled. The images of indiscriminate truckloads of corpses were a *memento mori* from a horror film. The pictures projected across cinema screens worldwide reminded audiences everywhere of their common vulnerability and humanity: '. . . composed like them / Of Eros and of dust'. The lines are W. H. Auden's, written in 1939, before he had known about Belsen:

> There is no such thing as the State
> And no one exists alone;
> Hunger allows no choice
> To the citizen or the police;
> We must love one another or die.

Whether politically or from either side of the gender fence, the
desire to be seen first and foremost as human was one to affirm,
surely?

In his history of the twentieth century, *The Age of Extremes* (1994),
Eric Hobsbawm dissects the international consensus against Fascism:
'[It] succeeded in uniting an extraordinary range of forces. What is
more, this unity was not negative but positive and, in certain respects,
lasting.' His historical hindsight, however, does not provide
Hobsbawm with much in the way of optimism:

As soon as there was no longer a fascism to unite against, capitalism and
communism once again got ready to face each other as one another's mortal
enemies.

In the new era, nations which had transcended their differences in the
face of a common evil would later revert to suspicion and hostility.
And, as we shall see, the relationship between men and women would
also relapse after the war, becoming troubled and unbalanced.

In 2003 Joy Taverner's grand-daughter-in-law asked her for her
memories. It was still hard for Joy to talk about Belsen, still hard to
come to terms with what she had witnessed there:

Whoever created us humans made some awful mistakes. I only hope that in
the future the world will become a more peaceful and friendly place.

*

By the end of April the European war was moving with dizzying
speed to its conclusion. At home, the sirens were quiet, and the public were told that they need no longer put up any form of blackout.
Mussolini's grisly end was succeeded with news that the Russian and
American armies had met; Berlin was encircled. What did it all
mean? Maggie Joy Blunt was appalled by the treatment meted out to
the Duce and his mistress, Clara Petacci, whose corpses had been
strung up and abused. '[I feel] shocked and depressed. Spitting on the
bodies . . . seems childish and barbarous.' But her low-spiritedness
was short-lived. Having spent the weekend spring-cleaning her living room, she was delighted with its brilliance and beauty. Her
beloved cat Dinah had had a new litter of three kittens. And on
Tuesday 1 May things definitely seemed to be looking up when the

office canteen served ice cream – 'the first time for 2 or is it 3 years?' But the overriding topic at work was: what would happen to Hitler? 'We wait, wondering whether Hitler is raving as they say, or dying, or dead, or will commit suicide, or be captured & tried and shot, and what his henchmen are doing & feeling.' In the office Maggie's female colleagues were discussing what should be done to war criminals. A Jewish woman proposed having Hitler's eyes put out with knitting needles. Next morning 1½ inch headlines on the front pages proclaimed: 'HITLER DEAD'. The following day reports came through of the surrender of the German armies in Italy. 'One can hardly keep pace with the news.'

As one by one the armies of Europe decelerated and inched to a halt, Britain's sunny skies clouded over. The temperature dropped, a bitter wind started to blow, and by 1 May the country was 'back to winter'. To make matters worse, Maggie's ears had started to exude a repulsive discharge which defied diagnosis. In the face of a chilling, sleety blast she trudged to the doctor, who confessed himself baffled, but prescribed an ointment to be applied regularly. Maggie felt 'like a leper' and anticipated spending the victory holiday with her cats, in self-imposed seclusion. And thus it was that on the evening of Friday 4 May she found herself in bed, mopping her ears with cotton wool and listening to the radio news announcing that the German forces in northwestern Europe had surrendered to General Montgomery.

It was the end of the war in Europe. But, showing a curious wariness and pusillanimity, no fanfares were trumpeted or flags flown for another three days, as the public awaited their leaders' permission for the long-awaited holiday to celebrate Victory in Europe. Announcements were withheld at the insistence of the Russian leadership, who did not want VE-day proclaimed until the Germans had also made their surrender to Marshal Zhukov. Across the land tempers were on edge, moods swinging between depression and high spirits. Everyone felt exhausted and nervous. When would it be? Sunday? Next week? June?

Maggie Joy Blunt, however, didn't wait for the officials to negotiate the formalities. It was a cold, wet evening, and the inflammation in her ears was bad, so she went to bed and ate a modest supper off a tray: lettuce, radish and beetroot salad, brown bread with a scrape of butter and honey, a glass of milk and, that rarity, an orange. Downstairs she had the radio switched on; she could attend to her suppurating ears while listening to the historic bulletins on her bedroom speaker:

[I am] listening now to the repeat broadcast of Gen. Montgomery from Germany this afternoon. My emotions at this moment are indescribable. Enormous pride in the fact that I am British — Pride, wonder, excitement. 'Tomorrow morning at 8am the war in Europe will be over . . .' I can't be bothered to go downstairs & turn off the radio. I shall leave it on till midnight . . . The war in Europe is over . . . This is a tremendous moment.

The war is over . . . I cry a little. I think of my dearest friends, my stepmother, my brother in Egypt, of those over in the fighting services I have known. And I wish I had taken a more active part; it is too late now. But it is not too late to take part in the new fight ahead.

What sort of fight did Maggie envisage? In the case of this particular educated woman, her late-night thoughts moved seamlessly to consideration of a new political landscape, which for her meant a Labour government:

I believe with the utmost optimism, faith, hope & joy that we can have our better world . . . yes, that we can have it if we know clearly what we want & fight for it.

But it was getting late, and the weary voice coming through the speaker penetrated her utopian musings, reminding her of the extraordinary times that she and millions more like her were living through:

Midnight news now being read — the announcer sounds tired. Pockets of German resistance still remain . . .

I have been down and turned off the radio. For once I waited to hear the whole of the National Anthem, moved suddenly again to tears by this historic, this incredible moment. I stood with my hand on the radio switch listening to the National Anthem and to the voices of a thousand, thousand ghosts. They came over the air into that unlit, silent room, I swear it . . .

It's time I tried to sleep. One of the cats is outside my window waiting to be let in . . .

Tomorrow & tomorrow & tomorrow stretch before me. Infinitely more full of promise and interest than the war years have been. I feel that new &

exciting events await me ... the atmosphere is charged with a sense of release and potentiality.

And the bottom sheet, in an exceedingly frail condition from old age & much hard wear is now torn beyond hope of redemption.

I am sick to death of patching worn linen.

A Brief Period of Rejoicing

When the news came through to her mess, Mary Angove let rip with an ear-splitting yodel: 'YOOOO-HOOOO!!! – And I put my head round the Mess door, and I said to my Commandant, "The war with Germany's over!" – "Well," he said, "I thought it must be something like that."'

On VE-day the ATS, in common with the rest of the country, were off duty. Mary and her friends went down to the pub in Devizes for 'a few drinkies', followed by a greasy fry-up and an evening at the pictures.

Verily Anderson and her two little girls were staying with her parents at their Sussex village rectory, yearning for the war to end so she could start her married life with Donald again. And then suddenly, on Marian's fourth birthday, it did end:

'Marian,' I said, 'you must remember this all your life. It's history.'

They rummaged in a drawer for paper flags and carried them up the drive to deck the trees by the road. Warm weather had returned, and the village was planning high jinks for all on the green, but at heart Verily felt she was a Londoner. '"I know where I'd like to be tomorrow," I said wistfully.' On 8 May she resigned herself to getting the children ready for the afternoon's festivities in ironed frocks, adorning their little heads with red, white and blue ribbons. Mrs Bruce stopped her daughter as she was gathering up her own clean clothes. '"If you run," she said, "you'll just catch the next bus into Eastbourne, and then the train. I'll look after the children."' Verily didn't wait to be persuaded; by three o'clock, waiting for her connection at Eastbourne, she was listening to Churchill's victory speech relayed on the station's loudspeakers:

The German war is therefore at an end . . . The evil-doers . . . are now prostrate before us. Our gratitude to our splendid Allies goes forth from all our hearts in this island and throughout the British Empire.

We may allow ourselves a brief period of rejoicing . . . Advance, Britannia! Long live the cause of freedom! God save the King!

London-bound, Verily gazed out at the farms and villages and, as she drew closer to the capital, the suburban terraces of England in Maytime:

There was not a house in town or country without its flag flying for the day. Rural cottages, great Victorian villas, rows of railway-side tenements, however battered they or their surroundings, all had their flags.

Verily stepped off her train into a city in holiday mood.

Looking on, Mollie Panter-Downes felt as if the population had all set forth for a huge one-off family picnic. At the heart of her description of how London spent that unforgettable day floats a beguilingly festive image: the girls. Released from their imprisoning offices, 'the girls' were like flocks of 'twittering, gaily plumaged cockney birds', dazzlingly pretty, charmingly colourful, dressed for summer, cornflowers and poppies poking from their curls.

They wore red-white-and-blue ribbons around their narrow waists. Some of them even tied ribbons around their bare ankles. Strolling with their uniformed boys, arms candidly about each other, they provided a constant, gay, simple marginal decoration to the big, solemn moments of the day.

To many eyes, this was the expression of victory. The dark days were over. Bright colours, pretty things, and femininity would replace the sombre colours of war: khaki, dinge and blackout. Frivolity, floral frocks and youthful pleasures would return to the land.

Marguerite Patten's mother, like Verily's, seems also to have felt that this was a day when the younger generation should experience the celebrations. Marguerite's husband, Bob, was in the Middle East. Since 1943 she had found her niche broadcasting from the BBC's 'Kitchen Front' and was now sharing a home in Barnet, north London, with her younger sister Elizabeth, her small baby and their mother.

And my mother said 'You two girls ought to go to London to celebrate – I can look after the baby.' So off we went. And I can't even begin to tell you how we felt then.

Marguerite is well into her nineties. But her face still lights up at the memories:

Victory! We couldn't, *couldn't* believe it really had come. It was wonderful . . . The sheer joyousness of that day! I kissed more people that day than I kissed in my entire life. We danced, and we sang . . . and of course we all got as near to Buckingham Palace as we possibly could. You can't exaggerate the joy of that day. And we could go home in the dark and not worry about an air raid! And people could leave their curtains undrawn! No, the feeling of joy on that day was something to remember the whole of your life.

'A magic night' was how another young woman, Joan Styan, remembered the celebrations years later. For her the whole day was one of impassioned emotion and exhilaration, with an overpowering sense of being free again. She and her mum fought their way through the jubilant crowds to Buckingham Palace and sang along to the Vera Lynn favourites while waiting to see the royal family appear on the balcony. Vere Hodgson recorded in her diary that she and her friend Kit had been lucky enough to get into St Paul's Cathedral for a service of thanksgiving. They picnicked by the Thames – 'carefree after so many years of anxiety'. Like thousands of others, factory worker Olive Cox and her boyfriend were given a day off from the production line. They took the train from Chelmsford to London and wove their way through the City bomb sites till they got to Trafalgar Square, where they joined a crocodile of revellers dancing down Whitehall. There seemed no point in going home. Big Ben chimed midnight, and they lay down on the grass in Green Park and slept till dawn.

Across the country church bells pealed, town bands played, bunting fluttered from lamp-posts. Overflowing pubs, squares and streets stopped the traffic for a nationwide holiday, gramophones were set up at street corners and radios blared out dance music. Teenager Anne Thompson stayed out till three in the morning conga-ing down the Bedford River embankment. In Oxford twenty-year-old student Nina Mabey fell into the arms of another undergraduate who had joined the crazy crowds and promptly fell in love with him. Like many others, Sheffield housewife Edie Rutherford broke open the supply of gastronomic delicacies which she had hoarded for precisely this occasion; she and her husband feasted on asparagus tips and tinned tomatoes. Muriel Green got drunk on old sherry and Pommia: 'the strongest drink I know'.

Joan Wyndham headed for her mother's flat in Chelsea. For lunch there was tinned fruit salad washed down with gin, then they braved the West End. Caught up in a forest of crowds, Joan found herself swayed between a troupe of Polish airmen and the mighty herd, all chanting 'Bless 'em all, bless 'em all / The long and the short and the tall'. She lost her shoe dancing, her stockings were in ribbons. Suddenly, there was Winston Churchill on the balcony of the Ministry of Health, making the V sign, and roaring out: 'Were we downhearted?'

And we all yelled, 'No!' Then we sang 'Land of Hope and Glory' and I think we all cried – I certainly did. It was one of the most exciting moments of my life.

With the public rejoicing came private mourning, for the destruction of homes and belongings, for the theft of six years of youth, for relatives, friends and lovers who were not alive to see the peace. One young woman would never forget standing motionless amid a frenzied crowd, haunted by the thought of her brother, who remained 'Missing in Action'. For her and her mother, the war would never truly end. Another woman learned that day that her injured husband, in hospital, would live. Late into the evening she sat on the wall in front of her bomb-damaged house, watching as the newly lit lights streamed into the street, thinking of the many lives that had been lost. At last she went back inside; her two young boys were in bed. She stood and looked at their sleeping faces: '[their] lives lay before them in a world at peace'.

But for those excluded from the celebrations by geography, VE-day struck a bittersweet note. Too many people were still separated from those they loved. Soldiers like Jack Clark, who in May 1945 was moving into Germany with the British Liberation Army, felt curiously removed from their own victory. 'It may sound funny,' he mused in a letter home, 'but it didn't somehow make much impression on us when we first heard the capitulation ... we didn't take much notice but just went on cleaning our Carrier!' The fact was, that Jack's heart was in Rishton, Lancashire, with Olive, his wife:

Whenever I think of Home now I vision you with your loving arms outstretched to hold me closely . . . us walking hand in hand together and your
Love mirrored in your eyes when we kissed in the moonlight – the tender
loveliness and glorious womanhood of your beauty and the sense of com-
pleteness which only exists when we are together . . . My life is built around
the promise of our future together.

I'm watching the days and hours tick by.

For Jack, and for countless men like him, the promise of home was
the promise of womanly consolations. Olive, for her part, wrote
back to her husband, painting a picture of enchanting domesticity.
Baby David, born in December 1944, was growing apace: 'he is just
like a jack-in-the-box'. On VE-day the baby clinic was closed, so
Olive couldn't get him weighed, but she and her mum treated themselves to an extra 'cuppa', cleaned the house and put out the coloured
bunting. Somebody had just given her new pillow-slips, and she had
done 'a big wash'.

But it wasn't just the men stationed overseas who felt fractured and
incomplete when the European war came to an end. By 1945 QA
Lorna Bradey had been abroad for four years. By then she was desperately homesick: 'God how I longed to see my family. I ached to
talk to them.' Home leave was allocated by lottery, but her turn
never came round: 'I can remember the anguish and disappointment
each time the names were announced. I swallowed another lump in
my throat; perhaps next time.' She was in Genoa, on the point of setting up a new hospital with her beloved medical team, when orders
to go home finally materialised in June 1945:

I had always imagined the moment, the excitement, but it was not there. I
panicked. These had become my people. I didn't want to go. How could I
transmit all this to the folks at home? The gap, four and a half years, had
been too long. They wouldn't know what I was talking about, they had
shared nothing of what I'd been through . . . I dreaded the moment of farewell and left Genoa in tears with all my friends gathered around.

A week later she set sail from Naples, 'drained of all emotion'.

After the German withdrawal from northern Italy, Margaret Herbertson remained stationed near Siena with the SOE FANYs. All of
them chafed at the excessive formality of the thanksgiving parade

laid on to celebrate the 8 May victory. There was hymn-singing, to the accompaniment of a discordant piano, and the girls sweltered in their winter uniforms. 'The ceremony did not appear particularly joyful. I heard one senior officer remark, "You'd think we'd lost the war, and not won it."' Perhaps this was owing to the casualties they'd experienced at close quarters. For Margaret, the death of one of her closest colleagues soured the occasion. Captain Pat Riley had been killed only days before the end of hostilities, when his plane hit a mountain in the fog. Another friend, Francine Agazarian, had recently received news of her husband, an SOE espionage agent who had been captured in France. The Gestapo had hanged him at Flossenberg concentration camp. Margaret looked on helplessly as poor Francine, broken-hearted, trailed around the paths of their Sienese villa, her futile unhappy kicks sending the gravel flying. For too many, the victory was a hollow one.

Widowed at the age of eighteen when her young husband Don was torpedoed in the Atlantic, Cora Johnston had joined the Wrens early in 1943, working as a form-filler in the certificate office. It was a period of hard work and relative stability for her. 'God was very good to me. He gave me a wicked sense of humour that has seen me through some terrible, terrible times. I could see the funny side of everything.' But the shock of Don's dreadful death was to exact a grim toll. A year later Cora broke down completely:

I was crying all day, I was in a terrible state. Everything had caught up with me: the raids and everything that I'd been through had knocked me for six. And on the day that war was declared over I was invalided out of the Wrens. And there they all were, dancing in the streets, and there I was looking as though I'd come out of Belsen – black eyes, and *so* thin. And it took me two years to get over it.

For many, uncertainty and anxiety about loved ones in the Pacific continued to gnaw. Monica Littleboy had never forgotten George Symington. Memories of the irresistible young man who had first won her love back in 1939 still tugged at her, and she felt an overpowering sadness for him. 'No one had heard news of him for so long. Was he still alive? There seemed no prospect of an end to the war in the Far East.' Thelma Ryder didn't have the heart to celebrate VE-day. 'The Far East was still on, and I had had no news of Bill since

1942.' He had been on board HMS *Exeter* when the Japanese sank her in the Java Sea. Was it fair to expect Thelma to wait for somebody who might never come home? 'Well, I did find another chap towards the end of the war.' But in 1945 a telegram at last got through to his family that he had been captured; it included the words 'Inform Thelma'. Knowing that he still loved her sent the old feelings rushing back: 'I was over the moon when I heard.' But now she had an indeterminate wait ahead of her.

The diarist Shirley Goodhart had been feeling increasingly restless. Jack, her husband, who was stationed in India as a doctor with the Royal Army Medical Corps, had written to her in April to say that his service required him to spend a total of three years and eight months in his posting. 'That means we shall have another 18 months apart.' The rejoicing around her did nothing to quell Shirley's mounting depression, but vigorous housework seemed to help. 'I spent most of the morning scrubbing and polishing and had no time to feel miserable.' On VE-day she joined forces with Nan, a girlfriend in London. Neither was in the mood for dancing and drinking, so they avoided the West End. Instead they visited another friend, Adrian, who was wounded in hospital, gave him an outing in his wheelchair and enjoyed the kind of palmy relaxed day that they would have taken for granted before the war: '[We] sat out of doors enjoying non-hospital, non-canteen food, and warm weather, and each other's company. We talked lightly, about books, about people, and a little bit about VE-day ... On our way home Nan and I decided that we couldn't have chosen a better way of celebrating.'

The Right Telegram

For those whose menfolk had been imprisoned in Germany, however, the long wait was at last over: the time had come for happy arrivals, glad reunions, heralded across the land by telegrams. Those faded slips of paper, franked and signed, with their abbreviated, pasted-on communications are still preserved among treasured letters: HOME SATURDAY STOP MEET ME STOP.

On VE-day Jack Milburn was in bed running a slight temperature. Clara left him there and mounted her bicycle to fetch bread from the village. The day was spent intermittently listening to the broadcasts from London, including the weather forecast, suspended for the last five and a half years. But it was impossible not to keep thinking of Alan: 'He will be here soon.' The Union Jack was hoisted on its pole in her front garden. His room was ready.

Wednesday 9th May

A Day of Days!

This morning at 9.15 the telephone rang and a voice said: 'I've got a very nice telegram for you. You are Milburn, Burleigh, Balsall Common 29?'

'Yes,' I said.

The voice said: 'This is the telegram. "Arrived safely. Coming soon. Alan".'

Clara was bursting as she called out to her husband, 'We've got the right telegram at last!' Upstairs she ran, and there, together with their devoted maidservant Kate, the Milburns gave themselves over to pure happiness:

And then all three of us, Jack in bed, Kate nearby and myself all choky, shed a tear or two. We were living again, after five-and-a-half years!

Two hours later the telephone rang again. The operator put through a long-distance call:

'Is that Burleigh, Balsall Common?'

'Yes! Is that Alan?' I said.

'Yes.'

And then I said: 'Oh, bless you, my darling.'

All evening they waited and at last, tired out with the emotions of the day, Clara went to bed – only to be woken by the telephone yet again. The clock showed nearly midnight. Alan had arrived at Leamington station, a drive of nine miles. It was a warm night; she climbed quickly into her clothes, ran down and started up the car; the roads were empty until she reached the town, where crowds were still milling, and she had to sound the horn to clear a way. There in front of the railway station two figures were visible in the lamplight, one in blue, one wearing a khaki beret. For a moment she mistook him, until the man in the khaki beret strode to the car –

'Is it Ma?'

– and then they were in each other's arms.

Mrs Milburn's wartime diary ends two days later on 12 May. The victory that had brought her son back to her had made her life complete; there was nothing more to say, for her cup was full. After Dunkirk there had been seven weeks of numbing anxiety. Since then, for five years, her daily life had been permeated with an all-consuming uncertainty and a constant longing for his letters. She had drawn on all her stoicism and patriotism to keep her spirits afloat, to endure the absence of everything that made her a mother. Being needed by Alan had made sense of her life. 'How I have longed to have the little toffee tin of grey trouser buttons out again all these long five years . . . The long, bad years of war begin to fade a little as Alan's voice is heard . . . and the house is once more a real home.'

With him in it, how happy she was. There was mending to be done.

Patrick Campbell-Preston and his young wife Frances had been married for just nine months, following a whirlwind engagement, before he too was captured at Dunkirk. By 1945 he was being held in Oflag IV-C (aka Colditz), the high-security prison for officers regarded as escape risks. Frances wrote to him weekly with bulletins of her life at the tiny cottage she had found in Berkshire for herself and their little girl, Mary-Ann. The month before Patrick's return was 'gruelling'. Which army would reach Colditz first? What if the Nazis shot everyone in a final mad gesture? Frances was a nervous wreck – 'every telephone call was torture' – and she drifted ghostlike round the cottage for days, listening to every radio bulletin. When the news of the liberation of Oflag IV-C came out a couple of weeks before VE-day, Frances let out 'a bellow like a mad bull'. But a week then passed without further news before the 1 a.m. phone call announcing that Patrick had landed at a military aerodrome near Beaconsfield. Laughing, crying, Frances was unable to believe the truth of his return. But then there he was, thin and weak and more handsome than ever. For two whole days he and Frances caught up. There was five-year-old Mary-Ann, whom he had never laid eyes on, to get to know. And there was a torrent of talk:

This was the only time Patrick ever talked of his experiences. After that he never referred to them again. It was like lancing a colossal boil, after which the wound was sealed and healed.

Jean McFadyen was still working for the Timber Corps when the war came to an end. The end-of-war celebrations meant release for her boyfriend Jim, who since 1942 had been held in a German POW camp in Yugoslavia. During his captivity correspondence between them had been intermittent. 'I just couldn't believe it when it came to an end.' Jim had suffered appallingly. When the Germans realised that their bases in Yugoslavia were threatened by the Red Army they pulled out rapidly, leaving prisoners like Jim to their fate. Jean remembers Jim telling her how the men went mad, scavenging for food. Eventually they were found and flown back: the first time he'd ever been in an aeroplane.

I got a telegram from his mother to tell me he was being trained up to Edinburgh. I couldn't come straight away, because I had to apply for leave; then I travelled down to Edinburgh. And he came to meet me off the train, wearing a suit of his father's that didn't fit him because he was so thin – suffering badly from malnutrition. There was a big difference in his appearance. But I recognised him.

To be honest I can't really talk about it . . . It was such a happy time. Just such a relief . . . Everything was over. The war was finished.

*

Demobilisation was a piecemeal process, and the conscripts and volunteers awaited so eagerly by their womenfolk returned to Britain only when they were authorised to do so. Doris Scorer's boyfriend, Frank White, had volunteered for a three-year stint in the navy in 1943. Nothing she could say would dissuade him, and he left her in tears, with the words 'Don't wait for me'. But as time went by she missed him more and more. Their romantic canal walks, and Frank's passion for the natural history of the Buckinghamshire countryside, passed into nostalgic memory – those happy days nutting in the copses, peering at the diadem spiders spinning their webs among the blackberries, secret kisses behind violet-scented banks. 'He seemed so far away, when would he come home?' She sent him airgraphs, and tracked the movement of his ship, the destroyer *Exmoor*, in the eastern Mediterranean. In February 1945 Doris found a column inch in the newspaper, describing how crew from the *Exmoor* had overpowered a German raiding party on the Dodecanese island of Nisiros, killing eight and taking thirty prisoners. She bubbled over with pride.

Back at the Wolverton aircraft factory, Doris was temporarily assigned to a desk job. She quickly discovered that, far from being a task requiring awe-inspiring skill, the checking of invoices was undemanding work. It gave her a vision of a better future. They did invoices at Bletchley Park, didn't they? Doris went out and bought herself a dictionary: 'I was going to conquer the world.' If she learned to spell, and picked up shorthand, surely she could compete with those rarefied beings 'over there at the Park'. But two weeks later she was put back on piecework.

Doris's war ended when her aircraft woodwork shop was abruptly stood down. With nothing to do, the girls were first put to work on their knees scrubbing the steps up to the manager's office; then they were retrained as French polishers. She finished her Works career rubbing linseed oil into lavatory seats.

Then came the telegram: BE HOME FRIDAY NIGHT STOP MEET ME STOP. Doris shared her good news with everyone who would listen. Friday came. She washed her hair, sluiced her armpits – 'no bathrooms for us' – made up carefully and dabbed her best perfume, Bourjois's 'Evening in Paris', behind her ears. She sewed up a ladder in her stockings and put it to the inside, hoping it wouldn't show, then made her way to the station wearing a pale-blue dress with a flattering ruched front. A cloud of smoke announced the chugging arrival of the train. 'Wolverton! Wolverton!' called out the woman porter.

Was he on this one? There was someone struggling with a kit-bag, holdall and parcels, a tall figure in black . . . a face tanned from the Mediterranean sun, eyes bluer than ever. It was *him*.

Later, an acquaintance of Doris who witnessed their rapturous reunion told her: 'Ooh, it was *lovely*.'

Chief Petty Officer White and Doris Scorer were married by special licence during his leave. But no sooner was the fortnight over than Frank had to head back to Chatham to complete his service commitment. With a year of that still to run, twenty-one-year-old Doris had her navy wife's pay book to live on, and a run-down rented house to get into shape. Until his return, she was on her own.

Frank was to prove a caring but conventional husband. 'Hubby', as she called him, was hard-working and over time scaled the job ladder to become a teacher and lecturer, but his expectations of his wife – that she would stay at home, and that meals would be on the table at a set hour – did not evolve along with his career. That urge to win the war and conquer the world stayed with Doris, however, as did the allure of putting pen to paper. Thirty years later, the Wolverton housewife wrote and published a memoir of the war years, in which her own experiences were centre-stage; its triumphant title: *D for Doris, V for Victory*.

As the homecomings began, parties were laid on for the returning servicemen. In Liverpool, as elsewhere in the country, communities welcomed them back with slap-up feasts. There was great baking and cutting of sandwiches. Helen Forrester couldn't help but feel bitter envy at the sight of happy wives, equipped with pails of whitewash, chalking the house walls with their husbands' names: WELCOME HOME JOEY. WELCOME HOME GEORGE. Harry O'Dwyer was one of 30,248 merchant seamen who would never come home to her. Eddie Parry was one of the 264,443 British servicemen who would never come home either. It struck her then that nobody ever painted messages for 'the Marys, Margarets, Dorothys and Ellens, who also served'.

It was still a popular idea that women did not need things. They could make do. They could manage without, even without welcomes.

In fact, many Marys, Ellens and Dorothys spent the next couple of months, or more, feeling jaded and impatient. WAAF driver Flo Mahony was in north Wales for the victory celebrations. There were, she recalls, some small bonfires. But more memorable to her is the sense of uncertainty and resentment:

None of us knew how much longer we were going to be in the Air Force, or when we were going to get out. The war basically stopped. There was no more wartime flying. And so air crew were redundant and they didn't know what to do with them. So they sent them to the Motor Transport section and told them to go and be drivers – and of course that was our job. So there was quite a bit of resentment of these air crew. And a lot of people were at the end of their tether and were quick to flare up, and there were lots of frictions.

Everybody was given a demobilisation number. When your number came up, you went to the Demob Centre and were sent home. Flo Mahony's friend Joan Tagg, a wireless operator, had joined the service later than she had, so didn't expect to be released as early. But the great pride she had taken in this important and highly graded job suffered a mortifying blow when, in the summer of 1945, it was stopped overnight, and she was posted to Gloucester to do number-crunching in the Records Office:

The men were coming back, and the men automatically took over our jobs. We weren't wanted . . . And this was the worst possible posting they could give me because it was clerical. Also, when they posted me as a clerk they wanted me to remuster, which meant going back two grades. I had loved being a wireless op, and I was absolutely livid.

Men and women alike chafed at the tin-pot bureaucracy and officiousness that now prevailed. 'The day war ended they started the spit-and-polish,' says Joan. Flo agrees: 'The Air Force was known for being relaxed compared to the army. But now there were so many people sitting about with not enough to do, and suddenly, you had to go on church parade, you had to do this, you had to do that. You had to be properly dressed. And they started making us do drill all over again.' There was work, but it seemed to have no purpose. Idle servicewomen – and men – were encouraged to attend EVT (Educational and Vocational Training) classes to prepare them for civilian life. A future as a shorthand typist or counter clerk beckoned.

Still in Italy with the FANYs, Margaret Herbertson took up the offer of a job as 'FANY Education Officer'. She too remembered the early days of peace as having an anti-climactic quality. The flow of signals had completely dried up, leaving coders and intelligence officers like her with nothing to do. 'We all felt quite dazed. The war, for many of us, had lasted for over a quarter of our lives. I spent a day tearing up papers.' The War Room, with its atmosphere of feverish urgency, its charts and diagrams, had been dismantled. As far as getting home was concerned, priority went to servicemen who had spent far longer abroad than the girls. Some of the FANYs immediately volunteered for the Far East. Others just applied for leave and went on sightseeing tours round Tuscany.

Ironically for her new appointment, Margaret had herself opted out of education when she first decided to join the war effort back in 1939. But, untaught though she was, her superiors put her in charge of batches of FANYs who came seeking instruction in English Literature, Current Affairs, Needlework, Art History, Italian and so on. Hastily, she assembled a rag-bag of tutors, including nuns, librarians and miscellaneous semi-qualified colleagues, and together with them devised a reasonable programme, which included educational outings. These last were fraught with peril. Every bridge in central Italy had been blown up by the retreating German army, and an improving day out to admire Quattrocento frescoes in the hilltop town of San Gimignano involved a spine-chilling detour up a zig-zagging 1 in 10 gradient. The road was barely wide enough for the three-ton truck, and the girls closed their eyes, clinging to the sides of the vehicle and praying. Undaunted, in June Margaret organised a cultural trip to Venice: getting there took fourteen hours across mountain passes, negotiating pontoons and carrying their own tinned provisions – but no tin-opener.

By July arrangements were under way to send the FANYs back to England. Margaret had the job of processing despatch of their luggage, and ticking innumerable boxes relating to the hand-in of their uniforms: 952 small sleeve buttons, 310 tunic buttons, et cetera, et cetera. On 11 August 1945 she and her group of eleven girls piled their cases on to two army trucks and said goodbye to Siena. '[It] has continued to tug at my heart.'

Then followed an experience which would be shared by returning personnel worldwide. Transit camps had all of the discomforts of barracks and billets, but none of their well-worn cosiness. Add to that the daily frustration of petty-fogging army bureaucracy and the intense heat of a Neapolitan August, and it was unsurprising that morale became low after three weeks not knowing when shipment would happen. Several of the FANYs became ill. At last, on 3 September, they embarked on the *Franconia*, ten of them sharing an airless cabin. On board were thousands of troops, and an apprehensive huddle of young women – Italians, Yugoslavs and Greeks – who were being sent to England: a shipment of foreign brides. 'The weather, at first hot and sunny, grew grey and overcast as we sailed north west towards the Irish Sea.'

QA Lorna Bradey arrived home in Bedford to an ecstatic welcome from her family. But after the brilliant colours of Genoa and Naples, everything looked shabby and diminished. And just as she had feared, things at home were very different. Lorna and her sister had always shared an unstrained intimacy; but when she opened her trunk, she found to her fury that her sister had 'borrowed' all her clothes. It took a while to appreciate that the family had been struggling for years to scrape by. Her mother – always selfless, never petty – said nothing as her hungry daughter polished off the week's butter ration at one sitting. But the first question on everyone's lips was, did she have any coupons to spare? 'No, was the firm answer.' She would have to go out, join a queue and get some. After Italy, home was all a dreadful anti-climax.

I tried to get into the pattern of life – but I was lost. We had nothing personal to say to one another. If I talked about my experiences they were politely interested. They just did not understand.

Tomorrow's Clear Blue Skies

For many, the weeks following the celebrations felt haphazard, disorienting. There was peace – but it was not peaceful. The final thrust of the Allied victory in Europe, and Germany's last ghastly spasms, had subsided. But the after-shocks reverberated: there were journeys, telegrams, arrivals, departures, greetings, upheavals, reunions. There were marriages, and divorces. There was grief, mourning and fear about the future. So many people's lives were still precarious, unsettled, subject to the agitating inconsistencies of authorities and politicians. Children had to be returned to their parents, sons to their mothers, husbands to their wives. In the longer term houses needed to be built and jobs found. In Europe the infrastructure was collapsing; populations were starving. And as the war in the Far East still dragged on, there was another great exodus of soldiers on their way to the battlefields of Burma, Malaya and Java.

It was hard, in those days, to feel any faith in the promise held out by Vera Lynn's heartfelt rendition of the Irving Berlin lyric, 'It's a Lovely Day Tomorrow . . . '. On 23 May, a fortnight after VE-day, Churchill's Coalition government was disbanded. A General Election was called for 5 July.

What kind of world did women want? On the whole, nothing too radical. There is little evidence that Britain's women were emerging from the Second World War with plans for a feminist revolution or a Utopia. Working on Sheffield's city trams as a 'clippie' during the war, Zelma Katin had become known as the 'Red Conductress'; throughout, she had made her voice heard at meetings of the Transport Workers' Union. She made common cause with the workers, moved to solidarity with them by the injustices she saw regarding pay and hours, and displaying an admirable stamina on committees. When hostilities ended she felt grateful for all the insights her contact with the proletariat had given her and looked ahead to a brave new world. But more than a new world, Zelma just wanted a rest:

I will confess that I am thinking not only of a future for humanity but a future for myself. I want to lie in bed until eight o'clock, to eat a meal slowly, to sweep the floors when they are dirty, to sit in front of the fire, to walk on the hills, to go shopping of an afternoon, to gossip at odd minutes . . .

'And is this – THIS – your brave new world?' you ask.

Yes; just at this moment, when I'm hurrying to catch my bus for the evening shift, it is.

There were exceptions. Naomi Mitchison's socialism had remained intact throughout the war: 'I doubt if anything short of revolution is going to give the country folk the kick in the pants which they definitely want, or rather need.' Vera Brittain had spent a lifetime espousing both feminism and pacifism, which to her were two sides of the same coin. She had not hesitated to attack the leadership of Winston Churchill, continued to press for women's equal participation in public life and found in her husband's candidacy for the Labour Party a further cause to back. Left-wing women like this had plenty to vote for, a world to be conquered.

After the First World War women's history had turned a corner. In 1918 the vote had been granted to property-owning women over the age of thirty, followed by the full vote in 1928. But there was no comparable prize for women in 1945. After six long years of home-front survival Nella Last, and thousands more like her, were deeply tired. On VE-day Nella felt 'like death warmed up'. It was a sensation that could only be alleviated by restorative contact with nature. Coniston Lake worked its usual magic:

It was a heavy, sultry day, but odd shafts of sunlight made long spears of sparkling silver on the ruffled water, and the scent of the leafing trees, of damp earth and moss, lay over all like a blessing.

Nella decided to vote Conservative. 'I don't like co-ops and combines, I hate controls and if . . . they *are* necessary from the economic point of view, I don't want them so obvious and throat-cramming.' For so many women like Nella, her home was her area of control. That May, the Lasts finally got workmen in to refurbish their bomb-damaged house. Carpets were relaid, electrical fittings rewired, and the pelmets were replaced over the windows:

By 4.30, all was straight, and the air-raid damage, the shelter and the blackout curtains over my lovely big windows seemed a nightmare that had passed and left no trace.

In 1945, the average British housewife cared less about broader issues and a great deal more about the roof over her head, about queues and food shortages. These had got so bad by the end of the war that one of them, fifty-year-old Irene Lovelock, decided to found the British Housewives' League.

In June 1945 something inside Mrs Lovelock snapped. The wife of a Surrey vicar, she returned home in a state of rage after spending a long morning queuing for food in the pouring rain; her fellow queuers included grandmothers and women with small babies in prams. She marched into the house and, though she had no experience of leading public meetings, told her husband she wanted to borrow the parish hall. There she took the platform and soon found herself waxing eloquent on the subject of queues and malevolent shopkeepers. Realising that she had tapped into a profound well of resentment, she then wrote to the local paper and got a huge response. The movement snowballed, and in July Mrs Lovelock became chairman of the BHL Committee, heading up a campaign to improve the lot of housewives and their families. In the early days there were only a few hundred members, whose principal targets were the manipulative shopkeepers who expected women to wait, often for an hour, until they were ready to open the shop. Provisions were then issued to the front of the line until – often within half an hour of opening – they cried out 'No more' and banged down the shutters. This happened all too often – particularly, it seemed, in the case of fishmongers. But the League grew; in August it held its first London meeting and, as shortages became harder to tolerate in the post-war period, so the BHL increased its active membership by thousands, who called upon politicians to attend with urgency to the things that women *really* cared about. Tradesmen's deliveries should be resumed at the earliest opportunity. Queues should be eliminated. Housewives had worked their fingers to the bone for nearly six long years, running their houses without help, clothing their families, battling with the mending. Among the League's stated aims were 'an ample supply of good food at a reasonable price' and 'the abolition of rationing and coupons ... These are a threat to the freedom of the home'. Some branches even swore an oath not to buy expensive imported fruit like pineapples or tangerines.

Enraged by obstructive fishmongers, middle-class women banded together to voice their frustration.

Mrs Lovelock and her League offer a fascinating case of the contra-
dictory impulses that swayed women in the 1940s. Here we have a
vigorous, independent-minded female activist, determined to mobilise women and make their voices heard in public. Her movement,
with its parades and demonstrations, almost certainly drew inspiration from the tactics of the Suffragettes a generation earlier. But its
aims, to begin with, were confined to getting butchers' deliveries up
and running and preventing exploitation by fishmongers. For Irene
Lovelock's world view, like those of many thousands like her, was
unquestioningly traditional. A mother of three and pillar of her local
church, she would have accepted the biblical portrayal of the virtu-
ous wife: 'for her price is far above rubies . . . She riseth also while it
is yet night, and giveth meat to her household . . . Her children arise
up and call her blessed.' Her wifely identity was bred in the bone.

The League, while stoutly maintaining that it was non-affiliated,
drew its membership from the conservative middle-class. Because of
this, it was infiltrated and identified with the doctrinaire right wing
of the Tory Party, who feared and resisted socialism in all its guises.
Rationing, and controls, came under that heading. Soon the BHL's
crusading protest on behalf of the housewife began to look like big-
oted and reactionary extremism. The press reported scuffles and
disturbances at BHL gatherings. Labour politicians took advantage
of the mixed messages to discredit the housewives' cause as propaganda, denouncing these 'middle class women' for stirring up unrest
and disaffection with their policies. Women's primary interests –
home and family – fell victim to dissent, and before long the
protesters were regarded as a parochial, if strident, minority.

It is hard not to feel some sympathy for Irene Lovelock and her
tribe of honourably intentioned mothers and grannies. For six years
they had meekly accepted the need for every aspect of their lives to
be regulated by the state, and now their patience was wearing thin.
With supply problems becoming ever worse, worry about food was
even more intense in the post-war period than it had been during the
years of conflict. Bread rationing, introduced in June 1946, was the
last straw. But another whole six years would pass before queuing for
brisket would become a memory.

★

Shirley Goodhart's Mass Observation diary provides an insight into the way intelligent women thought about politics in the weeks immediately after the war. A conversation Shirley had with her mother shortly after VE-day shows them both thoroughly engaged with the question of their future government, but it also shows a generational divide:

May 20th 1945

Mother and I sat up till midnight talking politics . . . Of Attlee: 'I used not to like him, but I am changing my opinion and I think that he will be our next Prime Minister . . .'

I have said that I expect the General election to bring a Labour government with either Attlee or Bevin as Prime Minister. If Mother were free, I believe that she would vote Labour, but for my father's sake I expect that she will vote Conservative. He always has been Conservative and is too old to change. Thank goodness she expects me to vote Labour! My parents-in-law would be horrified and to avoid arguments I shall have to be quite dumb about politics when I see them in the summer.

On 5 July the British electorate voted; the results were delayed three weeks until the 26th, because postal votes had to be gathered from servicemen and women still stationed abroad. Opinion polls which indicated a swing to Labour were generally disregarded, and few doubted that Churchill would gain a majority.

The Oxford student Nina Mabey had decided to join the Labour campaign. Already this vibrant, clever young woman had broken loose from her parents' right-wing political opinions, which to her seemed inexplicable. Nina felt unaccountably lucky to have got a place at a top-class university. At Somerville College, where she was reading Politics, Philosophy and Economics, she had given the matter much thought. It would be a betrayal, in her view, to use her classy college education to fast-track her way into the privileged ranks. Enthusiastically, she had joined the Labour Club. 'Our duty was to make sure, when the war ended, that a new, happier, more generous society would take the place of the bad, old, selfish one.' And this was the line she had argued, vehemently, one evening in 1944, with another undergraduate in her year-group who, she discovered, was steering an opposite course by joining the Conservatives. The young woman in question was chemistry student Margaret Roberts, later to become

Margaret Thatcher. She was 'a plump, neat, solemn girl with rosy cheeks and fairish hair curled flat to her head who spoke as if she had just emerged from an elocution lesson.' Though Nina felt her idealistic arguments to be compelling, she became aware after a while that they were not getting through. So she changed her tack. How on earth could one want to be associated with such a stuffy institution as the Conservative Club, when the Labour affiliates were all so much more fun? All the *really* interesting people were members.

Margaret smiled, her pretty china doll's smile. Of course, she admitted, the Labour Club was, just at the moment, more *fashionable* – a deadly word that immediately reduced my pretensions – but that, in a way, unintentionally suited her purposes. Unlike me, she was not 'playing' at politics. She meant to get into Parliament and there was more chance of being noticed in the Conservative Club just because some of the members were a bit stodgy.

By the summer of 1945, however, Nina and her 'fashionable' friends were electioneering in earnest. The Labour manifesto, entitled *Let Us Face the Future*, promised the Dunkirk spirit applied to the tasks of peace. 'The whole Labour movement was riding on a high tide of hope.' Nina and a group of Socialist activists from Oxford decamped to nearby Reading and threw their energies into Ian Mikardo's campaign. Mikardo, a prominent advocate of nationalisation and the extension of wartime controls, was hoping to overturn a safe Conservative majority of 4,591. The students were swept up in an atmosphere of feverish political excitement. In bus queues, in pubs and on the streets Nina sensed that the British people truly wanted change; from demobbed soldiers to grandmothers with shopping baskets there was, she felt, a groundswell of longing to make the world anew. Things could be different. There could be a free, equal society. They pounded the streets, knocked on endless doors and chanted their new campaign song: 'Vote, vote, vote for Mr Mikardo, chuck old Churchill in the sea.' Nina stood on a soapbox on a corner fighting to make her voice heard above the lively crowds. Her feet were blistered and her throat was sore. She lived for a week off marmalade sandwiches.

Naomi Mitchison had mixed feelings when she heard that her husband, Dick, had been offered the Labour candidacy of the marginal seat of Kettering. As a candidate's wife she worried about looking the part and felt she ought to acquire some stockings. But Naomi was essentially a bohemian and drew the line at wearing a hat. While Dick played by the rules in a city suit, his loyal wife supported him in gipsy glad rags, 'eating chips out of a bag'. For his sake she canvassed, addressed envelopes and made speeches at street corners, but her heart was not in it. She preferred to spend time in Scotland, dealing with the practical needs of her estate, and writing. 'They [Dick's campaign force] don't recognise that a wife has any job apart from her husband. Nor does Dick really recognise this farm. And never has recognised that writing is anything but a spare time occupation. I suppose the next generation will be better,' she wrote sadly.

But Naomi had no doubt that this election was of supreme importance. Everyone knew that a massive task lay ahead. Britain was still living with the legacy of the 1930s Depression: child poverty, slums, ill health and the spectre of unemployment loomed. War or no war, nobody had forgotten the Jarrow marches. The country owed £3.5 billion. Bombs had destroyed or damaged three-quarters of a million houses; willow herb flourished in the craters where buildings once stood. The streets were full of rubble, the roads potholed, trees and public spaces neglected. The houses that remained needed paint and repair work. All the park railings had been removed and replaced with barbed wire or nothing at all. Trains were late and slow, and there was little in the shops.

Rations continued short. Nella Last couldn't get any bacon; people in Barrow were having to wait a fortnight for sugar, and there were queues everywhere, she reported, 'for wedge-heeled shoes, pork-pies, fish, bread and cakes, tomatoes'. In Slough, Maggie Joy Blunt complained of the unvarying diet on offer where she worked: 'We have had nothing but cabbage on the menu in the canteen for weeks and weeks.' Barbara Pym often felt close to tears when, after waiting for ages, buses failed to stop because they were too full. Queues were so bad that she often decided to go without things rather than join them. She was bad-tempered and irritable, and her nerves felt frazzled.

This sensation was shared by many. Mary Wesley remarked on a generalised feeling of 'sadness and emptiness'. In Paris, the British Ambassador's wife, Diana Cooper, was 'overcome . . . with the miseries, the senselessness, the dreadful loss'. People laughed when the radio comedian Robb Wilton seemed to catch the national mood, joking about his wife's gloomy reaction to VE-day: 'Well, there's nothing to look forward to now. There was always the All Clear.' But it was close to the truth.

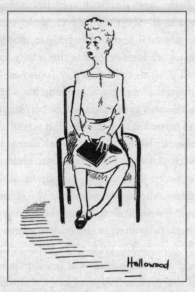

'By the way, dear, did anything come of all that election fuss we had a fortnight ago?' To many women, post-war politics seemed irrelevant to their dreary, everyday lives.

The middle-aged novelist Ursula Bloom felt badly let down by the peace, which seemed to have little to offer women of her class and generation. Ursula was fifty-three, and came from solid patriotic middle-class stock. Her parents had gone without to bring her up nicely; she had always supported herself, had maintained standards by sheer hard work and had married a naval commander. At the end of the war she felt she deserved some respite from all the penny-pinching and self-denial, and she yearned to eat steak. 'I'm growing very old, I thought, because after all I'm not even glad that the war is over. Apathetic.' Now Ursula couldn't get decent meat or a live-in maid for love or money. Above all she felt enraged and compromised by the black market in hard-to-obtain goods and luxuries. Even reputedly high-minded pillars of society cheated and lied to get whisky, nylons, eggs, petrol coupons or – her personal undoing – digestive biscuits. 'I wanted to rejoice,' she wrote, '[but] rejoicing did not come.'

And now, in the summer of 1945, Ursula looked on with mounting disquiet as the election campaign proceeded to confirm all her worst fears. She predicted class warfare, culminating in revolution. The nation seemed to be turning its back on Churchill, though he had saved the world for them. She caught a glimpse of the old man in his car looking pale, weary and shrunken, 'making the V sign which was already very out of date'. Nobody was cheering him. Fearful for the outcome, Ursula offered her modest services to the Tories but shrank at the sight of the sullen young men from the opposition staking out the Conservative committee rooms. With their shabby clothes and aggressive postures, they seemed hostile and full of rage. '"Vote Labour. Vote Labour. Vote Labour," they muttered.' Nevertheless, Ursula set out in a spirit of patriotism. Canvassing round Chelsea, she knocked on the door of a surly woman who told her she wanted a new government because she couldn't get rusks for her baby. Ursula, a practical woman, brightly suggested that she bake bread crusts in the oven. It had worked for her when her own son was little. But her well-meaning advice was met with black looks.

'Think I have time for that?' she challenged. 'Besides, the little bastard isn't worth it.' . . . She was furious with me for being kind. 'The likes of you have never had to work,' she said, and went away growling: 'Vote Labour. Vote Labour. Vote Labour.'

What kind of a fair world was this, reflected Ursula. Surely this was no way to help one another? On another doorstep she tried to explain to an unwelcoming woman that the rich were bled so dry by taxation that they could pay no more. There were no rich people left. Her own earnings, Ursula admitted, were ravaged by the taxman at up to twelve shillings in the pound, which went to support individuals like her. 'More fool you!' came the tart rejoinder. It was all utterly discouraging.

In Reading on election results night Ian Mikardo invited all his volunteers and supporters to a party and rewarded them with large quantities of whisky. Everyone got roaring drunk. But Nina Mabey couldn't be there. It was the height of summer, and in the Shropshire village where her mother was now based she was needed to help with mail deliveries while the postman got his harvest in. And so she heard the news as she pushed her bike up the hills and freewheeled down the vales of the Welsh borderlands, her letters and parcels in her basket. After the three-week wait, the results were announced in a cascade of hourly bulletins. Farmhouses and cottages alike had their windows open; from inside, she could hear the election results being broadcast across the valleys and pastures:

'Labour gain,' the wireless said. 'Labour gain, Labour gain . . .'

Nina could barely prevent a foolish grin from breaking across her face at every halt on her route, hardly stop herself from asking the farmers and smallholders she met what way they had voted. In any case, this Montgomeryshire constituency was true Liberal heartland, its outstanding MP Clement Davies the leader of his party.

Later that day she got the full picture. It had been a Labour landslide; the party had won an effective majority of 146 seats over all other parties combined. Ian Mikardo had gloriously justified all their efforts in Reading by bringing in a majority of 6,390 over his opponents. The Tories were wiped out. That evening Nina stood in Montgomery's market square and listened to Clement Davies's victory speech, in which he generously conceded to Labour's spectacular win. He spoke passionately of tolerance and goodness, wisdom and hard work. She was immeasurably touched:

Tears of joy ran down my face. It was all coming to pass. The new world, the new day, was dawning.

For Nina, the promise of clear blue skies was being fulfilled.

Naomi Mitchison had come down to Kettering for the count. Dick Mitchison won his seat with an impressive majority, and his wife and supporters were euphoric. As the scale of the Labour victory became apparent, Naomi grabbed a couple of gladioli from a vase on impulse and stuck them in her hair.

Some Tories, like Virginia Graham, tried to see the funny side. 'We went to the Ivy on Election Night so we all felt a bit giggly,' she wrote to Joyce Grenfell, now back from the Middle East. But the fun of addressing her chums as 'Comrade' suddenly started to fall flat. 'I suppose that if the tumbrils are coming they make so much less noise than bombs we can't treat them seriously.' Others were less amused.

The Conservative Member for Barrow-in-Furness had lost by 12,000 votes. Nella Last called in at the WVS; her organiser, Mrs Lord, was distracted with anxiety. No doubt about it, trouble was in store. There would certainly be civil uprising and riots now that the 'soldier vote' had trounced the 'Tory dog'. Mrs Lord's trembly voice rose in hysteria. Nella gave her two aspirins washed down with a little sherry in a medicine glass.

Ursula Bloom felt full of dread. She feared for her country which was now going to be led by inexperienced politicians. State controls would foster inertia in men's souls. And what presumption to treat her class as idle parasites. In particular, she felt affronted by the implication that she herself was a lady of leisure. She had worked hard all her life. It enraged her. To her, the 'new world' coming into being felt full of loathing and envy, and it was a world which she now had to grow old in.

The revolution had begun.

Little Boy and Fat Man

Politics were swept off the front pages thirteen days after the Attlee victory, when the morning papers carried news of the atomic bomb which had been dropped on Japan from those deceiving blue skies. A 'RAIN OF RUIN' had descended from the air, reported *The Times* on 7 August. Next day the *Daily Mail* told readers: 'Hiroshima, Japanese city of 300,000 people, ceased to exist at 9.15 a.m. on Monday morning . . . While going about its business in the sunshine of a hot summer's day, it vanished in a huge ball of fire and a cloud of boiling smoke.' Three ladies from Southampton promptly penned a deeply felt outburst to the editor of *The Times*:

Sir, – The use of the atomic bomb on Japan must surely appal anybody whose natural feelings have not been entirely blunted by the years of war . . .

The argument that war can be ended by increasing the destructiveness of weapons has been shown again and again to be fallacious . . . It is for people everywhere to say: 'This shall not be.'

Yours, &c., VIVIEN CUTTING; MAVIS EURICH; OLIVE C. SAMPSON.

'It's a new kind of bomb, darling, for the benefit of mankind.'
How could one explain the atom bomb to the next generation?
What kind of world were they growing up in?

Their heartfelt letter was published on 10 August, the same day that the paper carried a shorter report of the follow-up attack: 'ATOM BOMB ON NAGASAKI – SECOND CITY HIT'. The Americans had code-named their two nuclear bombs Fat Man and Little Boy; those who developed these unknowably destructive weapons did not, it seems, consider that they might possess any feminine attributes. On 14 August the Japanese surrendered.

Thelma Ryder felt nothing but relief. The war was really over now, and Bill would be released.

I thought it was wonderful really, because we'd had enough of war. I thought – anything that will end any war, anywhere . . . After all, they'd asked for it hadn't they? – you know, what with the terrible things they'd done. I know it was horrible for them, but it had been horrible for us too.

Many felt the same. 'At last, at long last! The day we have waited for nearly six long years has come round,' wrote MO diarist Muriel Green. On Wednesday 15 August the flags and bunting came back out again, and happy crowds gathered in front of Buckingham Palace. The royal family made more balcony appearances, and more fireworks were let off down the Mall. There were bonfires, parades and street parties. Children were treated to unforgettable spreads: jellies, hot dogs and cakes. Eileen Jones, a twenty-three-year-old munitions worker in Eccles, Lancashire, celebrated by quitting her job. Her brother Albert had spent three years as a POW in the Far East. After five years of twelve-hour shifts drilling parts for submarines on inadequate pay, she'd had enough. Albert would be freed now, so she walked out, rejoicing.

But the obscene destruction caused by the atom bomb made it hard for many others to replicate the enthusiasm they had felt three months earlier on VE-day. One despairing woman took to her bed for a fortnight, and a respondent to Mass Observation wrote: 'It casts a gloom over everything, and its terrifying possibilities make nothing worth while doing.' Ursula Bloom spent the morning of VJ-day rushing round Chelsea trying to buy enough bread to see her household through the holiday period. The shops were all shutting, with no information as to when they would reopen. Ursula was slipping ever deeper into a mood of profound gloom and fear about the future. Would mankind never learn? 'Fear rose like a flagrant weed in our hearts. This was not victory!' Nella Last felt the same. 'Tonight I thought of the dreadful new bomb – we will always live in the shadow of fear now ... I've a deep sadness over my mind and heart like a shadow, instead of joy the war has ended.' Frances Partridge, who had felt a quiet elation after VE-day ('surely it's only logical that pacifists – of all people – should rejoice in the return to Peace?') felt sickened when she read an account of the after-effects of the atomic bombs. Victims unhurt at the time of the explosion were falling sick, with bleeding, rotting flesh and nausea, followed inevitably by lingering death. What kind of world was her child growing up in? He was only ten ...

I thought with despair of poor Burgo, now so full of zest for life and unaware of its horrors. My own instincts lead me to love life, but as I read on, a desire welled up in me to be dead and out of this hateful, revolting, mad world.

Shortly after the bomb was dropped, the *Daily Mail* columnist

Ann Temple offered a 'Woman's-eye view' of the new atomic age. Reactions to the cataclysm were, she argued, split along the lines of the conventional sexual divide: the male, as a natural hunter and killer, looked on with awe and exultation; the female, at heart a pre-server, begetter and guardian of life, felt a deep fear. But women were also endowed with great intelligence and wisdom. Our nation would be short-sighted indeed if it failed to deploy these character-istics. In 1945, women's increasing empowerment and influence gave only grounds for optimism. Today, the town council; tomorrow, who knows, the United Nations? Yes, women could save the world.

And yet the deeply embedded consensus that women's proper destiny was wifehood and motherhood continued to block the way ahead. Churchill's coalition had held out against all attempts by the female labour force to achieve equal pay with men. And when the scale of the British post-war economic calamity became apparent – for with the American lend-lease arrangement termi-nated the country was running on empty – the political patriarchy was in no mood to embrace sex equality in the workplace or any-where else.

Haunted

On VJ-day Lorna Bradey was invited to a celebratory party in her home town of Bedford. A huge bonfire was lit. Lorna gazed into its flames, absorbed by her private memories. Over five years of war, she felt she had lived volumes. 1940: Dunkirk – fleeing from the German invaders down the crowded highways of northern France as bullets sprayed the roof of their ambulance – Messerschmitts dive-bombing the decks of their fleeing vessel; 1941: the tropics, blue bays and jacaranda trees – Tobruk harbour, and the dawn escape across grey, foam-flecked seas back to Alexandria; 1942: Cairo and the desert, the background to a horrifying drama as she saved the life of her friend, bleeding to death after a backstreet abortion; 1943: Italy, the high emotions of the operating theatre at Barletta: amputations, burned-away faces – the parties, the kisses, dancing with Henry on the Adriatic shore; 1944: Mount Vesuvius erupting, Capri . . .

I seemed to be standing on the outside looking in.

In August 1945 Lorna felt like a spectre at the feast.

For Phyllis Noble the end of the war brought on an overwhelming existential melancholy. For two years she had been working as a meteorological observer in the WAAFs, during which time she became romantically entangled with a handsome navigator named Adam Wild. As ever, Phyllis was at the mercy of her emotions. Her love affairs were in a complete mess. She loved Adam and was sleeping with him, but Adam didn't love her; meanwhile Philip Horne, a married officer at her Norfolk base, had declared his passion for her: 'Forget that twerp Wild and marry me – when I'm free, that is!' At the same time she continued to be haunted by the memory of her relationship with her earlier sweetheart, Andrew Cooper, to whom she had lost her virginity back in 1942. She knew Andrew still held a torch for her. In light of her other failed romances, she now hoped they might be able to pick up where they had left off.

But her hopes for a renewal were to be dashed. After VJ-day they met. It emerged that during the time they had been apart Andrew too had had one or two light-hearted relationships. Whether they were physical ones she did not inquire, but surmised that they probably were. In any case, they were both adults now, what was to be lost by being open about such things? So she told him about Adam Wild.

It was a mistake. Andrew reacted with resentment and dismay. 'He had remained faithful to me and, in spite of everything, had hoped and believed that I would have remained faithful too.' Later, she received a letter from him, telling her that she was vain, empty and superficial – a 'despicable creature' – and breaking it off for good.

Phyllis now felt utterly drained. The dislocations of war, her turbulent passions and her own lack of a personal compass had beached her. Dispersals of friends and family were upsetting; in 1944 a V1 had hit Lampmead Road, where her beloved grandparents lived. Though the poor old couple survived, their cosy home had been destroyed, aspidistras, ornaments and all: 'It was the end of an era.' The damaged remnants were carried on a handcart round to Uncle Len's, and Gran and Granddad sadly took up residence in a top-floor flat with no garden. Phyllis watched their decline with pity and dismay.

I fell into a mood of trepidation and gloom. I had recurrent nightmares about death, represented by skeletons and threatening people in black, and with so many people moving out of my life I felt bereft and uncertain about the future.

Peace, far from offering a new start, had slammed the door in her face.

Helen Forrester too felt that life had been merciless to her, but on VJ-day she celebrated with the rest. The office workers at the Liverpool Petroleum Board were given a holiday, and Helen joined five of her single girlfriends. They smartened up – as well as they could, in their threadbare dresses and heavy utility shoes – and went out for a day's fun. Along the way they found a friendly demobbed soldier to join their gang, and someone suggested having their picture taken. The soldier was just for show, unclaimed. Two of the girls were 'fancy-free', and two engaged. Another had lost the man she loved. Nobody except Helen was in mourning for two dead lovers. Later, the picture seemed to encapsulate that time when, after enduring six sad, bitter and laborious years, the wartime generation of women stood – wearing bright, forced smiles – on the threshold of a new world.

I smiled for the photographer, but I remember that I wanted to scream at the unfairness of life.

Surrounded as she was, Helen felt angry, lost and dreadfully alone.

★

There were 60,000 British POWs held in Japan, and by the beginning of September 1945 news began to filter through from officials that the camps were being cleared and the prisoners evacuated. By now it was also known that many of them had been brutally treated. Was George Symington one of them? Monica Littleboy's memories of her tall, slim, handsome boyfriend with his cultured manners and easy charm seemed so long ago; 1939 was a world away. In 1945 Monica was starting a new life; she left the FANYs, went to London, secured a promising job as a programme assistant with the BBC and began dating a confident, attractive man who also worked in radio. Then, one evening in the autumn of 1945, the telephone rang at her digs.

The operator put through a call from Southampton Docks. Disbelievingly, she heard the voice of George Symington:

It was as if a life had suddenly come back from the dead . . . a voice from the past . . .

George wanted them to meet. Monica now found herself struggling with a mixture of emotions: curiosity, tenderness, unease. Full of misgivings, unprepared, she agreed to see him.

He arrived in a taxi, with kit bag and all . . . He stood there. I couldn't believe my eyes. This was not the young man I had known. I was stunned. Misshapen, pitted, scarred. Only the eyes were the same.

I looked at this hulk of humanity and my heart bled.

Somewhere inside this wasted frame was the man she loved. Pity flooded her; pity born out of the past, fed by memories. It was a pity that would change the course of her life.

Thelma Ryder was luckier when Bill got back from Japan. She saw and was shocked by the cinema newsreels which showed the men's condition – 'It was terrible to see them, you know, their thin bodies and their bones showing through' – but she was spared the immediate sight of her fiancé, who had been starved and on his release weighed barely seven stone. Bill was restored to health over several months before setting out on the long sea voyage that would take him home, at last, to Plymouth:

He didn't get home till Christmas 1945.

I went up to the station to meet him. Well they told me the train was coming in on one platform and I was waiting there, but it came in on a different one. And there was me galloping up the platform – and Bill was with his mates. And they said to him 'Look, there's Thelma coming – look at her – she's like a racehorse!' I couldn't get there quick enough.

There is wistful affection in Thelma's voice as she remembers their reunion:

Yes, I recognised him. Even though his hair was cropped short – they had to keep shaving it off because of the lice and all that, you know. And then I got on the lorry that they sent for them and went up to the barracks with him. And then he came home to my place to stay.

But you know I never heard him complain. He'd say, 'They were only doing their job, like we were.' Bill was never bitter; he never bore any malice. But I said, 'Well, we never treated our prisoners like they treated you.'

And he was just lovely . . . We were married in 1946, and we were happy for twenty-nine years.

Demob

When the war ended Shirley Goodhart left her post with an aeronautical engineering company and moved in with her mother-in-law in Blackburn. In autumn 1945 all her thoughts revolved around the return of her husband, Jack, who was still in India with the Royal Army Medical Corps. She longed to have a 'normal' family life, and at twenty-eight was increasingly desperate to start a family.

December 31st 1945
  Found myself dreaming of 1946 and Jack . . .

On New Year's Day 1946, filling in the heading for her new Diary (Mass Observation requested its contributors to give minimal personal information), Shirley found herself wondering what to put under 'occupation'. For four years she had written 'aerodynamist'. And now?

'Nil' sounds as though I am idle, which is far from the case. 'Honorary Housekeeper' was the best suggestion, or 'Honorary Mother's Help'!

The following afternoon she helped out a busy friend by taking her baby to be weighed at the clinic:

Felt most maternal, so much so that I nearly cried when I saw a reflection of myself and the pram in a shop window.

Jack was lobbying hard to be demobbed. On 5 January Shirley got a letter from him to say that he was applying for compassionate leave 'because we want children'. She tried not to speculate about his return. Finally in mid-February a telegram reached her: COMING HOME STOP WRITING. She was now full of hope that he would be back by mid-March:

I just can't believe that he is really on his way home – and won't be able to believe it until I see him. I live from post to post. What will tomorrow morning's letter bring?

Shirley had overestimated. Two days later the telephone rang:

I heard Jack's voice. He had just arrived in London, having flown home. I still won't really believe it until I see him, which won't be before tomorrow afternoon.

February 21st

Jack phoned me from Preston when he changed trains, and I went to Blackburn to meet him. He looked just the same, except that he is browner than I have ever seen him. We met just as though he had only been away for a few days. I had been pretty confident before, but now I am quite sure that we are not going to have to make any difficult adjustments after our three years' separation. Very soon we shall have forgotten all about those three years.

February 22nd

It's so nice to have Jack to cook for, and to eat meals with someone who has a good appetite . . .

Twice today I've tried to read the paper . . . but Jack is far too disturbing.

February 23rd

Jack and I are just about deciding that it is really true that he is home, and not merely a dream. It really is quite as wonderful as we had ever imagined.

All the satisfactions of peace are present in the picture of the Goodharts' happy and apparently seamless reunion: Shirley's diary conveys her profound pleasure at their easy compatibility and harmonious domesticity. This was, surely, how it was meant to be.

Shirley Goodhart was one among millions of women who welcomed their loved ones home over the course of the long, slow demobilising process, in many cases after four or even five years of absence. A whole six years had gone by since the outbreak of war. But whereas in peacetime six years may slide imperceptibly one into the other, so that the minute, cumulative differences wrought by time blend, barely noticed, into a person's overall appearance, war had altered many of its victims almost beyond recognition. Physically, the greying hairs, the crow's feet, the thinning skin and in many cases the injuries and illnesses told their own tale. Some were thinner, others were fatter. Sallow city-dwellers had been transformed into sunburned plough girls with calloused hands. But the turbulent times had made an even more profound mark on attitudes, beliefs, hopes and assumptions. Whatever their wartime experiences, few had emerged unscathed — but many felt that they were entering the next period of peace as, essentially, different individuals from the ones they had been when the last peace came to an end in 1939.

Britain's wartime women had changed from occupying the passenger seat to driving the car. And that made them feel a new sense of power. Ex-FANY Margaret Herbertson speaks for all of them:

We weren't so naive. No doubt about that at all. The great thing is, we grew up. We'd met a lot of people and could size up people much more. We'd stretched our minds a good deal I think, and we'd learnt a lot . . .

— which was surely an understatement.

Mike Morris could intercept messages from enemy aircraft, Mavis Lever could crack their codes, Doffy Brewer could calculate how to train guns on missiles, Doris Scorer could repair the wings of Typhoons, Pip Beck could talk down an air crew, Christian Oldham could track the courses of battleships across the Atlantic, Flo Mahony could drive a six-ton truck, Jean McFadyen could fell a fifty-foot tree, Frances Faviell could bring relief to pulverised victims in blitzed craters, Lorna Bradey could work round the clock saving lives, Joy Taverner could endure the concentration camps. Other women could weld the hulls of destroyers, fly Spitfires to their appointed aerodromes, help gun down Messerschmitts, rescue the crews from burning planes, train submarine crews to fire torpedoes, even operate behind enemy lines in occupied France. Countless more women contributed by taking on the jobs that the men had left behind: in transport, in shops, in factories, in hospitals, schools, ministries and offices across the country. Unheroically, but stoically, innumerable women had over the years endured the loss of their homes, coped with shortages, brought up their children without help, volunteered their time and energy to the war effort. Emotionally, too, the war had made many claims. Loneliness, anxiety, fear, grief and horror had invaded their tranquil world. In war, many of them had indeed 'learnt a lot', including that there was more to life than domesticity.

Innumerable hopes were now pinned on the ability of our leaders to make the world anew. The great powers regrouped after the Potsdam Conference, the first General Assembly of the United Nations gathered in London, Attlee's Labour government set out to reinvent the British nation, and slowly but surely the army was demobilising. Between them, what kind of future would they make for those millions of women, weary of war, but filled, nevertheless, with hope, and the knowledge of their own powers?

★

'The rejoicing had gone sour on us before it ever began,' recalled Ursula Bloom. She was writing of the devastation of the Japanese cities by two atomic bombs. For many, their ominous destructive power drained all the pleasure from victory. Commitment, promises and plans for long-term happiness seemed less relevant in a world that held such deadly scientific horrors.

Then, on 19 August 1945, with the shocking news of the bombs only just sinking in, President Truman announced the peremptory termination of the lend-lease agreement which since 1941 had kept the British war effort afloat. Officials were sent to Washington to try to persuade the American Treasury – hostile as it was to Britain's new 'Socialist' government – to loan £3.75 billion. The country was in debt as never before. *Woman's Own* columnist Rosita Forbes gave her readers a pep-talk about the deficit: 'Governing is only housekeeping on a bigger scale. Had you thought of that? If every week you spent more than the entire family pay-roll, you'd soon be in a fine mess, wouldn't you? England is in exactly the same state as the housewife going out on Saturday evening with her shopping bag and a good part of the weekly wages in her purse. For no country can spend more than it earns ... We can't just pick money like blackberries off the hedge.'

Meanwhile, in the corridors of Westminster, grand plans were taking shape for post-war reconstruction. Public appropriation of large portions of the British economy were one aspect of the Socialist dream. The other was the Welfare State. In March 1946 the Minister of Health and Housing, Aneurin Bevan, placed his National Health Service Bill before Parliament, while Ellen Wilkinson was working to realise the dream of free secondary education for all, as laid out in 'Rab' Butler's 1944 Education Act.

But the first hurdle to be overcome was demobilisation. Five million men and women reported to their demob centres, pocketed their service gratuity and clothes coupons or, in the case of the men, joined a queue at the clothing depot. Half a million of that number being sent back to 'Civvy Street' were servicewomen. Some of the first to qualify for release were married ATS women. Even those who weren't yet married jumped at the chance of skipping ahead of the queue. One uniformed bride-to-be announced: 'I'm going to make out my application form before the wedding, then dash up the aisle, out of the church, and drop it in the nearest letter-box!' But the majority had to wait their turn, and, from June 1945, the whole vast unwieldy process would take an interminable eighteen months.

Nurse Helen Vlasto had returned from Egypt in summer 1944. She was not released from her service as a VAD attached to the Royal Navy until spring 1946. She spent that year and a half based near Portsmouth, at the Haslar Royal Naval Hospital.

At Haslar, the main operating theatres were situated deep underground. Staffed largely by VADs like Helen, these gloomy, airless caverns were her workplace until she was demobilised. Here, masked and gowned, the nurses spent their working hours like troglodytes. Off-duty in the warmer months, they scampered for freedom on to the beach, gasping for air. But all too often in cold weather the girls huddled round the upright iron stove in the VAD mess, with letters to write, darning to do. Helen never forgot the fetid stench of those cellars, which reeked of Ronuked linoleum, stale cigarette smoke, malodorous girls and over-boiled vegetables. When Helen looked at her pasty face in the mirror, she felt she had crawled from under a stone.

Slowly, the medical services were going into reverse, moving an inch at a time into the post-war phase. In the autumn of 1945 enormous numbers of sisters and nurses were still abroad, attached to units awaiting demobilisation. With casualties due to return, military hospitals like Haslar took on clearance duties to relieve the imminent pressure on short-staffed civilian hospitals. For Helen Vlasto, this meant long hours in theatre getting through a backlog of non-urgent operations: hernias, tonsillectomies and haemorrhoids. It was not fulfilling work.

She felt moody and impatient: 'We were all on a treadmill until we were released, and there was nothing we could do but keep on treading.' Now, as the war wound down, her usefulness seemed to have expired. Memories of her debutante days – glittering hotels, swooning music and banked-up flowers – tugged at her. She was possessed by a craving for bright lights and luxury and jumped at any excuse to rush to London. Though they were faithfully corresponding, her long-distance romance with Surgeon Lieutenant Aidan Long, still out in the Far East, went on hold. Any boyfriend back from the various theatres of war would do, so long as he offered access to a touch of expensive, 'pre-war' living. Once up in town, Helen would slip into a gown, comb out her curls and do what she could to brighten her pallor with a touch of Coty. Then it was time to sink into the enchanted atmosphere of the Berkeley or the Mayfair; a spin of the revolving doors, and she was back 'in Fairyland', where piled carpets, the softness of silk-shaded lights and even the cosy ladies' powder room created a heavenly retreat – 'balm to my soul'. Helen's 'hotel' phase did much to compensate for a nagging sense that time was passing, that she faced an empty future with no idea how to fill it and felt she had no practical qualifications for a career in 'Civvy Street'. Had she wasted six years of her life?

Women's memoirs of the immediate post-war period demonstrate very clearly that feelings of isolation, nostalgia and apprehensiveness had begun to replace end-of-war euphoria. The urgent work that had given their lives value and meaning had been removed; with it had been extinguished what Nella Last described as 'the white flame' driving all their efforts: the desire for peace. But now that it had come, was that peace – with all its tantalising, indefinable promises of security and contentment – just a mirage?

A wintry light filtered through the uncurtained panes of the Cadogan Street bedsit. Ex-Flight Officer Wyndham woke to the sound of her landlord's sewing machine whirring gently and the distant thrum of London traffic. Shivering, she climbed out of bed and lit the gas fire, but the bathroom down the passage was freezing. Crouching on the hearth, she removed the wire pipe cleaners that served as crimpers in her hair and styled her dark curls, before repairing the ravages with Max Factor and Yardley's Cherry. 'Now I was ready to face the world.'

After four years as a WAAF, Joan was completely free. During her last few months in the service the array of choices before her seemed like an irresistible menu for the future. She might become a teacher;

or maybe let her legs get hairy, grow an earnest fringe and go to Oxford. Another scenario was to get a job selling clothes at Jaeger. If that failed, she and her girlfriend Oscar planned to start up a hamburger café. Then there was her thrilling new boyfriend, Kit Latimer; with him, finally, she had experienced 'the big O', and from then on their sex life had gone from strength to strength. Maybe they would get married and have babies (but what about the fact that he was penniless?). Life seemed to spread out its delicacies before her: countries she'd never seen, books she'd never read, people she'd never met, new loves. She wanted to devour everything, 'with such an acute and all-consuming appetite that it gives me a dry mouth, a tingling tongue and a pain in the side of my head'.

Two months later she was living in a room in Chelsea that cost £2 a week, with a battered gramophone, a stack of Fats Waller records, a dilapidated divan and her WAAF uniform dyed forest green. She had her £60 service gratuity, which would pay for the room till the following summer, but nothing to live on. Her only saleable skills were top-speed radar-plotting and commanding parade-ground drill: 'not much bloody use to me now'.

What to do with my day, jobless and faced by the awesome prospect of endless leave? I was beginning to realise that now I was no longer in the WAAF I would have to recreate my world from scratch every morning.

I hadn't realised I was going to feel so lonely, with no one to laugh or gossip with, no focus to my life.

Money was the first priority. Joan decided against breaking into her £60, which was earmarked for the rent. She piled her old ballet books into a suitcase and set off for the Charing Cross Road second-hand bookshops; a couple of hours later, with twelve crisp pound notes carefully hidden away, Joan was on her way to the White City dog-racing track. There *was* one useful skill she had acquired during her years in the Air Force . . .

Helen Vlasto was twenty-five in 1945; Joan Wyndham was twenty-two. For them, and many thousands like them, their time doing war work had moulded and fashioned the people they now were. For four or five years in many cases, their lives had had a structure imposed by authority. It was constantly impressed upon them that they were wanted and needed. Wren telegraphist Anne Glynn-Jones recalled 'the feeling that you were doing a real job, a job that mattered, that took quite a bit of skill – I loved it'. Flo Mahony thrived off it. 'Some people didn't like regimentation, but I did – absolutely loved it. You just felt all the time that you were doing a worthwhile job.' For Flo, her WAAF friendships, and the sense of purpose the service gave her, would remain for ever.

And now, with peace, came the dismantling of the entire apparatus that had given meaning to these women's lives. 'Every week now people were leaving. An edifice seemed to be crumbling,' remembered WAAF Pip Beck. Stoker Wren Rozelle Raynes spent the final days before Christmas 1945 in a state of nightmarish torment. For two and a half years her life had consisted of 'a happy whirl of nautical activities . . . unimagined maritime bliss'. Now, at the age of nineteen, her world was being pulled from beneath her. She spring-cleaned her office, went for a demob medical inspection, attended her last pay-muster and packed. At midday on 22 December 1945 she was summoned before the commander to say goodbye:

I had managed to get through the previous two days in a numbed sort of misery, but suddenly I felt I could bear it no longer . . . I . . . lost all control, and bursting into floods of tears ran blindly from his office.

Wren Rozelle Raynes sketched herself setting out to seek her post-war fortune far from her beloved Portsmouth.

Running on Empty

But Jean McFadyen was only too happy to find, in the autumn of 1945, that her services were no longer required. After three years of sweat, toil, blisters, backache, chafing, chilblains and freezing Aberdeenshire winters in the Timber Corps anything seemed preferable. With Jim recovered from his ordeal in the prison camp, they decided to get married at the earliest opportunity:

There was no question of a big church wedding or anything like that – it couldn't be done in the time allotted, and we couldn't have spent the money on it. Plus, everything was still on the ration.

We got married Christmas Eve 1945. It wasn't a white wedding – and I didn't have a long dress either. But it was a happy day, and we even had a dance! Jim had put quite a bit of weight back on by then; he looked much more like himself.

He was given his old job back – it was in a biscuit factory. At that time whatever a man was working at before he went away to the army, they had to keep that employment open. I didn't work – it wasn't thought seemly for married women, and men didn't like it if they did.

But of course we had no house. We got married without even giving a thought to where we were going to live or anything like that. We lived with Jim's mother and father. And I kept talking to Jim about getting a job, but it was 'Oh, no, no, no – I'll keep my wife.' He just didn't want me to. Very, *very* few of the men did at that time. I'd proved I *could* work, but 'No'. And – two women in a house . . . and it was not a big house either . . . And though I got on very well with his mother – we shared the housework – there were stresses. And I used to scan the paper every night for the hope that there might be somebody with a room to let somewhere so that we could move out and get a place of our own, but nothing ever appeared.

In March 1945 the Coalition White Paper had estimated that, in order for every family unit that wanted a home to have one, 750,000 new houses would have to be built. Until they were, a great many young men and women like Jean and Jim had no choice but to start their married lives crammed in with their in-laws. Domestic life became ever more stressful as a result. Meanwhile, there was nothing to do but pore over the small ads and importune the Council.

When Joan and Les Kelsall tried to set up home in Coventry their future looked very bleak. A total of nearly 4,500 homes had been destroyed in the November 1940 and April 1941 raids on that city. It didn't help that Joan, during a wait of over three years for her absent fiancé, had carved out an independent existence for herself. War had brought her a responsible WAAF posting in the Royal Observer Corps and a promising new romance which might have led to marriage – had she not already had Les's ring on her finger. In 1944, when Les finally came home, they married straight away. Joan became pregnant early in 1945 and was dismissed from the WAAFs – 'they more or less sacked me' – and their daughter Sue was born in November 1945. There was no question of being able to find a home of their own; instead, they lived with Joan's widowed father:

You just couldn't get a house, and my brother lived at home, so I had three men – and a baby – to look after and cook for, and no mum. It got pretty tense and difficult sometimes, because they didn't all get on, and I was sort of piggy-in-the-middle.

Les himself had spent three years as a naval signalman. While docked in Malta his ship had been the target of a Luftwaffe raid; there were terrible casualties, and Les was lucky to get away with shrapnel wounds in his leg.

I think the war affected a lot of men and they soon flared up when things weren't right – a lot of it was due to what they'd gone through. Les said, 'I've seen enough dead bodies, I don't want to see any more.' And I felt outnumbered. I'd been on my own and grown up; I'd turned twenty-one. And I didn't like having to give up the independence that I'd had, having to consider other people besides myself. And so we argued.

And my father always seemed to be telling me what to do if the baby cried . . . and that caused problems.

Well then we moved in with Les's parents and lived with them until my daughter was two . . . and then we had a *dreadful* row with his parents. And Les said 'Right, I'm going to get us somewhere to live.' And his father said, '*You'll* never get anywhere,' he said. 'Your head's too big,' he said. 'They wouldn't get a hat to fit you!' I've never forgotten that!

So Les said to me, 'Get Sue ready,' he said, 'you're coming down to the Council with me.' So we went down to the Council, and, oh dear, I was that embarrassed, there he was banging the counter . . . He said 'I've served this country,' he said, 'and there's *nothing* for us to come back to'. And in the end, we ended up with a prefab.

We lived there for seven years. When we moved in all we'd got was a cot, a pram, a bed and two hard chairs and a couple of cushions. It felt like a proper bungalow – the rooms were quite big. And it was modern – we weren't used to having a tank full of hot water! And it had a well-equipped kitchen, bathroom, flushing toilet and a garden. And it was a lovely home. Everybody knew everybody else, and we were all more or less the same age – with children too – and if your children were ill there was always somebody knocking on the door to see if you wanted something from the shops . . . I really loved it. I cried when we left.

For many women like this, the yearning for a home was more than the simple wish for privacy. Home was *who they were*, their creative power-base, a projection of their very identity. 'Four walls and a roof is the height of my ambition,' said one Mass Observation respondent.

'Well, were you or were you NOT the young couple advertising for a roof to put over their heads?' A roof and four walls in 1946? Dream on . . .

The Kelsalls were lucky. Many people who had become unhappily dependent on relatives or friends for accommodation jumped on the squatting bandwagon that started to gather pace in the summer of 1946. The authorities took a compassionate view, turning a blind eye to the trespasses of families who set up home with chemical toilets and orange boxes in disused service camps across the country. They were somewhat less benevolent in the case of a mass squat organised by the British Communist Party, which persuaded dozens of families to take over a block of unoccupied luxury flats in Kensington. The journalist Mollie Panter-Downes managed to gain entry and gave a sympathetic account of the squatters' predicament. One couple had come from sharing just two rooms with three other couples. It was eighteen months since the man had been demobbed, and in all that time he hadn't been able to sleep with his wife, because the four husbands all slept together in one room, the four wives and all their kids in the other.

She also interviewed Mrs Price, a happy young woman who had nested in the block and showed Panter-Downes round her new home with pride '"This is my airing-cupboard!" she cried, flinging open a door. "Isn't it lovely and handy? And this is my larder."'

Mrs Price had put a mattress on a trunk and covered it with a blue tablecloth to make a sofa.

We sat down on it to talk . . . 'We've been living with my mother-in-law, and it was such a squash I couldn't keep Baby with me. Oh I was miserable . . . I can't believe we're here, with a place of our own at last . . .

'I don't care what anybody says about the Communists, they do know how to get things done.'

Twelve days later the local authorities disconnected the services, and the squatters were evicted. The Communist ringleaders were found guilty but treated with leniency; everyone agreed that the circumstances that had driven them to break the law were extremely provocative.

* ✱

Nella Last was open-eyed about the problems Britain now faced – the housing shortage, unemployment, trade deficits, debt, the black market: 'will we ever get straightened out?'

I'm war weary and a bit debilitated. Certainly things have rather got me down lately, try as I may . . . Little things annoy me. My worries go to bed with me, sleep lightly, wake at a touch and are ready when I rise to keep pace with me all day. In spite of all my gay chatter and nonsense, I have no one with whom to talk things over.

Will Last had never been much of a communicator. After tea Nella would take her sewing on her lap, but the long evenings passed with barely a grunt, or just an indifferent 'Oh' from his armchair. If he did speak, it was to grumble and mutter till Nella felt she could scream with rage. These days, she no longer tolerated his querulous, dominating behaviour. 'I'm not the sweet woman I used to be.' Now everywhere Nella looked she saw disappointment: demobilisation was so slow, adjusting to the new world was hard for everybody, and winter loomed. At fifty-four, she found it hard to mask the feeling that she had been robbed of six years which would never come back.

'The new world was hard on the older woman,' recalled Ursula Bloom, who was also fifty-four. Compared to Nella, Ursula Bloom was among the privileged. She found it difficult coming to terms with the manifestations of socialism: industrial disputes and the fact that live-in maids had gone with the wind. Quite apart from the burdens of housework that that imposed, the middle-class's servant shortage had encouraged a wave of burglaries, according to Mollie Panter-Downes. All too often, the hapless householder returned from a trip to the cinema to find her unguarded home turned upside down, with not only her valuables stolen, but also all her irreplaceable essentials: clothes, bath towels, lipstick, gin and the closely hoarded contents of her pantry – tinned sardines, packets of tea and pots of marmalade.

Ursula Bloom also felt alienated by new trends. Young people were dancing a strange dance called 'Boogie-Woogie': 'I don't understand it, and often ask myself, is it mad or isn't it? ... I did not understand the modern dancing and the music.' The writer Angela du Maurier was another middle-aged woman who was finding it hard to adjust. She had just passed forty in 1945, but her infrequent visits to London prompted lamentations at the passing of the world of her youth. With the threat of bombing gone, the city's appearance of gallantry had been replaced with shabbiness and 'gone-to-seediness'. The sight of terraces of dilapidated houses depressed her terribly, but more than that she deplored the shift towards slipshod, permissive behaviour. 'It is not the face of London that has changed, it is its manner.' An avid ballet-goer, Angela donned her best evening frock for the 1946 first night of *The Sleeping Beauty*, only to find that the rest of the audience hadn't bothered to 'dress'. There were women in mackintoshes, woolly jumpers and hats, carrying shopping bags which they hid under their seats. They had arrived – horrors – by tube. 'I disapprove of the laxity with which post-war men and women take their pleasures.'

But Nella Last, Ursula Bloom and Angela du Maurier would have made common cause over the continuing shortages. Rationing was as stringent as ever; day after day, the majority of women's lives were dragged down by the persistent quest for hard-to-find foodstuffs and commodities. At the beginning of 1946 the fat ration was cut, dried eggs – so horrid yet so necessary – were removed from the national menu, and the threat of bread rationing loomed like an impending disaster.

The diarist Maggie Joy Blunt measured out her life by the meals she cooked, the cosmetics she could obtain, above all (for like many she was a heavy smoker) by the cigarette shortage. Thoughts of meat and menus troubled her sleep. With just '2 small bones' left from her weekend joint, she 'lay awake a long time last night, wondering what I could do with bone stock – still don't know.' Swansdown powder puffs, so painfully rare back in 1939, had, greatly to her relief, re-appeared at Harrods, but her hairdresser was preoccupied by the shortage of wholesale supplies, in particular rubber tubing needed for sprays. Occasional bananas and oranges were to be seen in the shops – no sooner spotted than pounced upon – but it was impossible to get Sylko sewing thread. With what she had left, Maggie spent an entire weekend repairing those worn-out sheets whose condition had so vexed her on the eve of VE-day.

In January 1946 the *Daily Herald* asked its female readers what their chief domestic concerns were. Food came an easy top, followed by household goods, chiefly bed-linen, table linen and towels. Clothes came last – 'the other things were more vital'.

Nevertheless, Mary Manton wrote a description in a newspaper of an experience familiar to thousands, entitled 'This Desperate Business of Hunting for Shoes'. She set out in the early morning in search of plain black walking shoes. Seven shops and five hours later she returned home empty-handed.

Sylvia Duncan was another 'housewife' who early in 1946 gave her side of the story to a daily paper. The hardship had finally got to the vast numbers of women like her, she said. Housewives still outnumbered full-time female workers in industry, the armed forces and civil defence combined by a million and a half (8,770,000, compared to 7,250,000). 'We have lost the love of our job,' wrote Mrs Duncan. 'There is no pleasure in it any more.' She told of self-denial and sacrifice. 'Very few of us feel really fit these days . . . We take a back seat, and our wants are neglected . . . We are the poor donkeys who can always carry an extra burden.' 'E', writing to the *Daily Mail*, felt utterly exhausted: 'I have no patience with the children, I don't enjoy anything, don't laugh at anything – in general, life is all wrong.'

Nella Last tried to identify what it was that had robbed her own life of meaning. The 'fun and laughter' which had sustained her even in the darkest days of the war had gone. And with them had gone the hope. Like the younger servicewomen, Nella's wartime activities with the WVS had given her a sense of purpose. Working for a common cause and looking ahead to peacetime had motivated everybody. 'I want to feel I am helping, in however small a way. I want the laughter and fellowship of the war years.' She was still young enough for the years ahead to yawn like a void. But what work was there for a housewife in her mid-fifties?

*

During wartime the numbers of women working had peaked at nearly 8 million; within a year of VE-day, that number had fallen by 2 million. Demobilised men were entitled to request a return to their old job, whether on the production line or on the buses. For the women who had plugged the gap, that meant a hasty retreat. 'There is not room for them all, especially the women,' the *Daily Mail* told its readers.

But the 'ghastly scramble' that diarist Maggie Joy Blunt had predicted back in 1944 was not as bad as its equivalent in 1919. Indeed, shortages in the post-war labour force impelled the government to launch a desperate recruitment drive aimed at luring women back into the workplace. A glance at some of the individual cases underlying the statistics does give a sense that women had a measure of choice when it came to their post-war careers. Helen Forrester put her devastated love-life behind her and sat down in front of the *Liverpool Echo* classifieds. 'Firms that had closed for the duration or who had gone over to war work, now re-opened, like crocuses in the sun,' she wrote. On the evening of VJ-day Helen answered every single advertisement that offered a secretarial post and accepted a well-paid job working for an electrical engineer. It was the first step on her ladder to freedom from the grind and grief of her war years, the first step to an entirely different life.

Ex-servicewomen found the adjustment harder than their home-based sisters. Going back into the workaday civilian world felt both unsettling and banal. Flo Mahony was demobilised in 1946; she was twenty-four and decided to return to her job in the offices of the Wandsworth Gas Company, where she'd worked before the war. It was mortifying:

In the air force you'd been a part of Something; you felt you were Somebody. And then there you were – just a clerk going to the office – back in a slot. That was quite difficult to cope with. I remember finding myself swearing at one of the typewriters, saying 'The bloody thing's U/S!'* In the Service you could get away with that sort of language, but in an office it just wasn't expected of you. You had to adjust, go back to being the person you'd been before . . . I think I lost a lot of the assurance I'd had in the Service. And I felt quite a resentment at some of the other women in the office who hadn't gone away – I found them quite irritating and smug.

I worked till I got married. I think we almost slotted back into our mothers' shoes when we came out of the Service. We took it for granted that women don't go to work when they're married.

VAD Helen Vlasto was due to be released from her duties with the Royal Navy in April 1946. As the date grew closer, it dawned on her how well she had been looked after for five years. Since 1940 she had been fed and housed. A vast bureaucracy had smoothed her way with ration cards and travel warrants. She had been carried on ships across the world, protected and privileged. Now, at the age of twenty-six, she was about to be at the mercy of 'the cruel world outside'. Before the war, Helen's experience of that 'cruel world' had been limited to the ballrooms and nightclubs frequented by her wealthy, socialite contemporaries. War had broken out when she was nineteen, too young in her case to have embarked on a career.

---

* Service abbreviation for 'Unserviceable'.

Helen felt an unspecified determination to 'get going and strike out on my own'. But doing what? 'I now knew for certain that I could never happily return to the leisured social life of pre-war days – but this was probably a thing of the past in any case.' When the last day came she felt frightened and tearful.

Back with her family, and all too aware of her limited qualifications, she resorted to scanning the Situations Vacant columns in *The Times*.

As soon as she saw the notice advertising traineeships for air hostesses, Helen knew that this was the job for her. In February 1946 civilian flights to Europe were just starting to resume, flying out of RAF Northolt and Croydon aerodromes under the banner of British European Airways. The airline industry was in its infancy, still intensely glamorous; most passengers were politicians, wealthy celebrities or royalty. Being an air hostess meant being the envy of your friends: 'It was thought to be the next best thing to being a film star or a model.' Helen applied at once and was invited for interview along with a crowd of stunningly attractive other hopefuls. And now her pretty face, her grooming and above all her dim, distant debutante training came to her aid, as she remembered the proper way to enter a room, closing the door behind her without turning her back on the row of waiting interlocutors, and discreetly flattering these important gentlemen with demure upward glances and a demonstration of her excellent French. Half an hour later the traineeship was hers:

I left the room feeling myself already not only figuratively, but literally in the clouds.

By a combination of luck, looks and class clout, Helen Vlasto now found herself pursuing a career that made sense not only of her time as a nurse, but also of her privileged background. Undoubtedly, being very pretty was an important qualification. She was now trained in the glories of being a high-flying waitress: 'how to serve portions of food delicately . . . whilst at the same time proffering the platter reverently to the left-hand side and slightly forward of the customer'. Soon she and her fellow trainees were being sent out on 'hops' to Paris, Brussels and Amsterdam, and longer flights to Madrid, Oslo and Berlin. There were passengers to usher to their places, polite announcements to make, drinks to serve, babies to cuddle, flowers to arrange, and always the importance of appearing neat and smiling in her ex-naval uniform (with the service stripes unpicked). In the gaps, she raced up and down to the West End for romantic rendezvous with Aidan Long, newly back from the East and now hunting for a medical post in London. No job could have been more fitted to a young woman whose pre-war life had designed her to be a social ornament. The days in Alexandria – the stench and the sand, the burned flesh and the blistered bodies – were fading. The war seemed to have happened in a time-warp; her new, peacetime world a revamped version of the old one.

'Tighten your belts everybody, please – we're approaching Great Britain.'
A neatly buttoned air hostess reminds her passengers that they will shortly be landing in the land of austerity. Punch, August 1948.

*

Joan Wyndham put £5 on an outsider in the 7.30 at White City. Jumping up and down and yelling her head off, she watched it nudge ahead of the favourite and win her £200.

Lurching from feast to famine, the course of Joan's post-war career was to prove correspondingly unstable and mercurial. Kit Latimer, her RAF boyfriend, showed up on leave, and they had a wonderful time both in bed and out, dancing round the bedsit to Fats Waller. After he departed money started to run short again. For £2 a week she marked time working for Ralph, an old pal in Fulham who made plastic ornaments for fish tanks, then moved on, this time stepping into the breach for a couple who ran a somewhat dubious hotel in a bohemian area of west London. Joan was employed to run it while the owners were off doing something illegal in Switzerland. Shortages and rationing contributed to the difficulties of hotel-keeping; with laundry services erratic, she ironed the sheets as they were, on the bed. The hotel offered an austerity breakfast: burned toast and dyed pink fishcakes which nobody would eat. But Joan was happy. She was working, and she was with people.

Sadly, it all came to an abrupt end when bailiffs appeared on the doorstep and announced that they had come to take away the furniture. Nothing Joan could say would dissuade them, and, fearing that she would be blamed by her employers, she decided to close down the hotel. It was back to the Cadogan Street bedsit, and pining for Kit. Soon after, that relationship too bit the dust. He wrote, confessing that he had never had such wonderful sex in his life as he had had with her, but had met another WAAF and was going to marry her:

He felt I was some kind of witch who had him under her spell . . . and was settling for a safe, cosy alternative. I nearly went mad with grief, and spent my time either crying or writing him long letters which were never answered. I had never felt so lonely in my life.

A Pearl of a Wife

Surrounded with small children, Verily Anderson was almost never lonely. The days before marriage and babies, when she was 'nothing but a nothing' had long gone. As a wife and mother, her life was focused. But Donald, her husband, was bogged down with Ministry work in London. Stranded in Sussex with the children, she missed him and yearned for the time when they could have a family home. Their infrequent days in the city together were spent house-hunting, to no avail, since everything vacant had been let, and, with house prices inflated by up to four times their 1939 price, a purchase was beyond their means. Verily's mother, unutterably generous, came to their rescue. "'I know what we'll do," she said . . . "I'll buy a house, and you can be my tenants.'"

Verily bicycled round west London looking for somewhere to buy; at last she happened upon 43 Edwardes Square. The house's stucco was grimy and peeling, and several windows were broken, but it was on the south side, its elegant cast-iron balcony giving on to the stately plane trees of the square, and its neglected rear garden filled with sun and straggling briar roses. For Verily, it was instant love – but first Donald had to see it. They arranged to meet the following day at the house agents', at a time when Donald could get free between meetings. Next morning Verily returned to inspect it again. This time there were competitors looking round the premises. She leapt on her bicycle and pedalled like fury up to the agency in Kensington High Street: 'every second counted'. She ran into the office only to find a third party, a well-corseted lady in smart gloves and high-heeled shoes, engaged in negotiations for Number 43. As soon as the smart-gloved lady had left the office Verily made frantic inquiries about her. Yes, she had made an offer, subject to a surveyor's report, and no, it had not yet been accepted. At this moment Donald walked in. Twenty dramatic minutes later the house was theirs. Mrs Bruce had agreed on the price, the War Damages Commission would pay a proportion of the repairs, they needn't bother with a surveyor's report, and the owner in Cornwall had accepted their offer, at long distance.

The war was over for us. I took the key again and held it in my hand.

The smart-gloved lady in high heels returned to make arrangements for her surveyor to view the house, only to find herself pre-empted.

Verily bought herself a sandwich and headed for Kensington Gardens. The traders around Earls Court Road were friendly and called her 'Dearie'. This was where she would come for the rations, she thought. Little Marion and Rachel would peep over the counter. With luck, there would soon be somebody else with rosy cheeks in a pram outside. The unloved roses would bloom in their garden.

I could almost see the family sitting round the table in our kitchen-dining-room. Two, three, four children, perhaps more, beating spoons and with gravy on their mouths. Donald presiding, and myself bringing the pudding from the cooking end. This was how home should be.

★

How perfectly Verily Anderson conjures up the post-war idyll, in just a few sentences picturing the happy home for which a nation had fought and laboured – men and women alike. Here in the west of London, six years of gruelling anxiety and physical hardship would be rewarded by the bounty of peace: the fecund womb and the over-flowing table; the benign authority of the husband, the sweet complaisance of the wife. At 43 Edwardes Square, God's in His heaven, all's right with the world.

A roof over one's head, domestic contentment and a placid, indus-trious wife didn't seem too much to ask after six years of tribulation. So much so, that the average man in 1945 simply took the entire pack-age for granted, as a contemporary humorous song lyric illustrates:

> 'Good morning, my sweet',
> I say to my Brenda,
> She cares for my home
> And I'd die to defend her.
> She mends my old vests
> And she takes out the pup
> And she sees to the kids
> Now that Nanny's called up
> She checks up the laundry
> And flatters the cook
> Then she goes to the library
> And gets me a book
> Her housekeeping money
> Is twelve bob in credit
> That ration book form is OK
> For she's read it . . .
> She's a pearl of a wife
> No man could have better
> So I kiss her good morning
> And then I forget her.

But forgetting her was becoming less acceptable. The war had raised questions about woman's role that could no longer be ignored, even in the popular press, which found it could sell copies on the 'Future of Woman' controversy.

In December 1945 the *Daily Sketch* decided to air the debate – on one side, the 'pearl of a wife' model:

Surely every married woman today is longing for the time when she can re-establish her home on pre-war standards, and is looking forward to this rather than to sitting behind an office desk, driving a lorry or plotting a plane's course?

on the other, the responsible, brave, intelligent woman who, having demonstrated her value and energy, was now poised to make her mark on the nation:

We have taken off our hats to them during the war – let us keep them off now in anticipation of the time when we can erect a monument to the first woman Premier who leads this country to a new standard of prosperity and announces that the peace of the world will never be shattered as long as we have an all-woman Cabinet.

The *Sketch*'s editors invited their readers to vote on the debate. The headline in their Saturday edition read 'CAREERS and the WOMAN: The Voice of 1945 Says Home is Best'. The readership's vote was conclusive:

%age who think that women cannot or should not combine marriage and a career:	77.2%
%age who think that women carrying on jobs after marriage is a good thing in itself:	12.3%
%age who say 'Let them choose':	10.5%

– all of which appears to confirm, empirically, what the historian Harold L. Smith has argued, using a compelling line-up of statistics and evidence, that a high proportion of the women who had worked during the war were sick and tired of it, and that they nurtured a nostalgic longing to recreate their pre-war lives in the home.

One of these was Dolly Scannell. In spring 1945 Dolly gave notice to the major at her American hospital base near Colchester. 'Now that we were winning the war I decided it could manage very nicely without me.' She was the mother of a six-year-old daughter, and the forces had no claim on her; the job had been a wartime fill-in, until she could resume her natural and normal destiny as a housewife. She and little Susan packed their bags, said their goodbyes and boarded a train for Liverpool Street; it was back to the East End, back to join the closed-in ranks of the housebound. Dolly's husband, Chas, was still with the army in northern Italy but was due home soon after VE-day. They would be a family once more.

Dolly was uncertain what to expect; Chas had been away for over three years. At this time women's magazines cautiously urged their readers to make allowances for their returning men. 'Don't expect to pick up the threads just where you dropped them,' wrote one psychologist, suggesting that wives would have to 'court' their husbands all over again.

So Dolly planned an affectionate welcome for her husband. She had stretched the rations and, on the day, she had a nice piece of meat ready for his homecoming meal. Little Susan was playing in the street with her friends but was persuaded to come in and put on her best clothes to meet the daddy she barely knew. Clean and ready, mother and daughter sat and waited, but Chas didn't appear. The child fidgeted, and an hour passed. Well, he would surely come tomorrow . . . They changed back into their everyday clothes, Susan happily rejoined her playmates, and Dolly, understandably irritated, returned to her chores. When the children knocked on the door for the fourth time to pester her for attention, she flung it open bad-temperedly with a 'Well, and what is it now?' – 'And there was Chas.'

Chas himself was not in the best of moods. What had taken her so long? And who was the dirty child in a green coat playing mud pies in the gutter? Not his daughter, surely? Dolly persuaded Susan to be kissed, before marching her off to the bathroom. But the child's bedtime presented a problem. For nearly four years Susan and Dolly had shared a bed, snuggling up to each other through the air raids, maternal cuddles taking the place of conjugal caresses. There was only one bedroom, and the child eyed her new, single bed in the corner with aversion. 'Is he going to sleep here then?' she asked, horrified. Dolly did her best to persuade her that it was temporary, and kissed her goodnight.

Slipping into her most glamorous brocade housecoat, Dolly went downstairs. After a shaky start, maybe Chas would mellow by the light of a flickering fire. She coaxed the coals alight and waited for him to make the first, amorous move. But something seemed to be preoccupying him; could it be that he felt shy after all these years? Dolly hoped that the dancing glow was heightening her attractions, but Chas suddenly switched on the light. There was something combative about his posture, and his voice, as he turned towards her, saying, 'Now I'll see the books,' and it took Dolly a moment to realise that he was demanding to see her household accounts.

I was furious, all my loving, welcoming mood evaporated. Everything had gone wrong, I was sure it wasn't my fault, and thus ensued, on our first meeting after the toil, stress and misery of the war, a fierce argument.

As an example of how the war had driven the sexes apart, Chas Scannell's homecoming gives a taste. His time with the army had turned him – and many others – into a stranger. He bossed his family about as though they were insubordinate rookies. Dolly felt rejected and self-righteous. Chas, for his part, was fearful that the war had let his independent-minded wife off the leash, and that unless he staked his claim as man of the house from the moment of his return he would become a second-class citizen under his own roof. In Chas's eyes, being anything less than dominant and masterful would be a betrayal of his manhood.

Unfortunately, his manhood was doomed to disappointment, that night anyway. More or less reconciled, the Scannells went to bed. Tenderly, Chas reached out an affectionate arm to draw Dolly to him. As he did so – 'a little voice came from the corner, "Can I come in your bed, Mummy?"' Dolly's maternal heart softened; she understood that to the child her father seemed an interloper. She was about to gather her up, but Chas intervened with a sharp authority in his voice: 'No, you cannot, just close your eyes and go to sleep.' Tears were the result.

Recent books by Julie Summers and Alan Allport* have combed the sources for similar tales of woe and incompatibility. Both books demonstrate how the war had derailed relationships, with stories of

* Julie Summers, *Stranger in the House*; Alan Allport, *Demobbed: Coming Home after the Second World War* (2009).

resentment, disillusion, dysfunction, exclusion and anti-climax on both sides. From men:

'Probably, "When I was in Peshawar in '43" is just as boring to my relations as their accounts of shopping trials are to me.'

'There seems to be nothing but the dull prospect of a pre-fab, raising the family, the 8.30 up and the 5.15 down . . . the prospect appals me.'

And from women:

'We were two different people, so much had happened in those years apart.'

'When their war ended, our war began.'

Desert Rat Charles Hopkinson walked through the door of his home after four and a half years abroad. The conversation went like this: 'Hello, Muriel, how are you?' 'Oh, Charles, I am fine. How are you?'

Thousands of married couples were trying to rebuild their lives, but they were strangers.

Divided We Fall

Once demobbed, Chas Scannell found work with a dockland ship-ping company; thankfully, he quickly lost interest in the household accounts. The Scannells were saving to repair and modernise their Ilford home, and by 1946 Dolly was pregnant again. She was broody and quiescent; nothing surfaced to upset the gentle routine of her days. Susan was at school, and she made sure that Chas's meals were always on the table when he got home from work. The baby boom was approaching a crescendo, and their son William was one of the 891,920 babies born in Britain that year; Dolly felt she should be counting her blessings:

The war was over, my husband was safe home again, I had a son and a daughter, a house with a garden, a husband with a job he liked. What more can a woman desire?

But perhaps she missed the friendships and flirtations, or even the dynamic efficiency, of her American army camp in 1943?

I was restless. I didn't know why. I didn't know what I wanted.

Already, the post-war idyll was showing signs of strain. Cookery expert Marguerite Patten's constant contact with housewives gave her an insight into their conflicting motives and influences:

A lot of women were glad to be housewives again. They said, 'Oh, how lovely to go back home, *oh*, I don't have to get up so early in the morning, *oh*, I don't have to spend time with those tiresome people in the factory, and I don't have to get dirty doing all that work, *oh*, what a relief!' But then when it happened they weren't so sure.

Others weren't glad: for example, they hadn't got their own money. They didn't like having to ask when they wanted a new pair of shoes, you know, 'Can you let me have the money?' And they missed the excitement, they missed the number of people they met; they wanted to go out, and they felt very closed in by the four walls of home.

There were very mixed feelings among women.

How could Dolly Scannell explain, without seeming ungrateful, her bouts of irritability at Chas's childishness? He would come home late and blame her for the spoiled dinner and grumble when his tea wasn't how he liked it. One day as he sat at breakfast whining about how the rinds hadn't been cut off his bacon, it all got the better of her; she seized a dinner plate from the sideboard and smashed it over his head. But Chas was completely unrepentant; with 'a look of fiendish hate' he grabbed a cut-glass bowl and hurled it at his wife with all his might. It missed and shattered into shards beyond the kitchen door, through which it had pierced a jagged aperture. Shaking, shocked, the Scannells faced each other across the debris of their kitchen. In the ten years since they had been married, Dolly had been through the Blitz, and Chas had survived the desert war and the Italian campaign; but never before had a domestic row come so close to physical injury:

We both knew 'what might have been' . . . I knew then, that although Chas and I could argue happily until the cows came home, I must never ever lay my hands on his person again, however lightly, for both our sakes!

*

Dolly Scannell took responsibility for, as she saw it, stepping out of line. She saw the dinner-plate incident as a wifely transgression, and

41. Anne Popham and Graham Bell in his RAF uniform. 'You are the dearest thing in my world,' she wrote to him.

42. Schoolgirl Nina Mabey grew up to become Nina Bawden, well-known author of *Carrie's War*, which was based on her experiences as an evacuee.

43. SOE coder Margaret Herbertson both experienced and contributed to the Allied victory in Italy in 1945.

44. Women welders were beset with danger from flying slag, burns and 'arc eye', partly because they often chose style over safety.

45. How to stay in fashion while fitting the caterpillar track to a tank.

46. 'Mummy's girl' Thelma Ryder was sent away from home to work twelve hours a day making piston rings for aircraft.

47. Joyce Grenfell and her accompanist, Viola Tunnard, arriving in Baghdad, 1944.

48. Vera Lynn in the Far East, 1944. 'I was an ordinary working-class girl. I was singing to my own kind.'

49. Backstage at ENSA HQ.

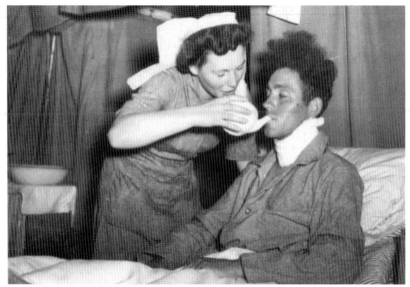

50. A QA tending a wounded soldier in an Italian field hospital.

51. QA Iris Ogilvie and a fellow nurse staging an upbeat publicity shot in front of a Bayeux hat shop, shortly after the Normandy landings.

52. QA Joy Taverner never questioned her early faith – 'until Belsen'.

53. The war is over. A WAAF returns home.

54. Celebrating VJ-day in Aberdeen.

55. Christmas 1946: GI brides and their babies await passage to their new homes.

56. Happy holidays in the long, hot, post-war summer of 1947.

52. QA Joy Taverner never questioned her early faith – 'until Belsen'.

53. The war is over. A WAAF returns home.

54. Celebrating VJ-day in Aberdeen.

55. Christmas 1946: GI brides and their babies await passage to their new homes.

56. Happy holidays in the long, hot, post-war summer of 1947.

57. and 58. (*Left*) Frances Faviell; (*right*) an old woman shovelling debris in the Russian Zone of Berlin. Faviell and her husband lived in the traumatised German capital from 1946 until 1949. She described 'the grim streets with their huge mountains of rubble and mile upon mile of yawning open ruins'.

60. The harvest of peace, July 1948: the inauguration of the National Health Service.

59. Vicar's wife and activist Irene Lovelock (*centre*), flanked by two other leaders of the British Housewives' League.

61. Happy ever after? Helen Vlasto's wedding day, 28 November 1946.

62. Peter and Phyllis Willmott in 1948, at the start of their forty-two-year marriage.

63. Laura Jesson chooses home and hearth in Noël Coward's *Brief Encounter*.

felt only pity for Chas over his uncontrolled act of violence with the cut-glass bowl. There was a sexual deal at stake. Men were entitled to their anger over uncalled-for bacon rinds. Women were supposed to be modest and compliant.

The apparent collapse of the deal made for good journalism. Ann Temple's finger was on the pulse; heading her *Daily Mail* column 'IS MODESTY NOW OUT OF DATE?', she stirred up a reader controversy around a topic that clearly pushed a number of sensitive buttons. Had the war turned women into insubordinate hussies, smoking and swearing? What did men want? Female readers writing in to the *Daily Mail* took the view that men preferred modest women. The Cheshire mother of two adult sons wrote to say that her boys enjoyed the company of modern girls 'with a real kick', but that both were resolutely 'pre-war' when it came to looking for brides: 'They are both firmly determined to choose old-fashioned girls with old-fashioned virtues for their wives.' Another correspondent asserted simply that 'An immodest woman is handicapped both in her personal and business relationships with men.' Only one woman disagreed: 'Modesty has to be out of date. How can a girl keep a modest manner when she has to maintain military discipline, or obey it . . . Think how in the last five years we have all been herded like cattle, crammed into rooms, houses, hostels, barracks, shelters . . . No privacy, no leisure, and no soap.' But far more typical was Rose, from Durham, who expressed the view that 'Most men like to draw out a woman's charms, not have them thrown at them.' Or dinner plates, one might add.

Rose from Durham was speaking for a widely held view, shared by the self-help guru Kenneth Howard (author of *Sex Problems of the Returning Soldier*, 1945), who had no qualms when it came to defining respective sex roles. Husbands, Howard explained, were expected to be chivalrous, masterful and reliable. It was their responsibility to earn a living and make tough decisions.

But in the normal household the woman's job is primarily a dependent one, and it is right that it should be so . . . Her role is not primarily to go out and struggle with the world. She is not fitted emotionally or physically to do so . . . Her greatest asset is her weakness and her capacity for love.

It is hard not to wonder where Mr Howard had been during the previous six years, while thousands of women were demonstrating their strength and competently struggling with a world full of danger and hostility. His sympathies are clearly with the scattered armies of men, for each of whom home was a rose-tinted memory; when he got back, "er indoors', presiding goddess of the hearth, would be there to meet him, the eternal feminine, surrounded by adorable clamorous children, bringing the pudding in from the cooking end. 'He has been dreaming of his home and his wife, and looking forward all the time to getting back to things as they were when he left home . . . What he really wants is for things not to have changed at all.'

And yet after the war the sexes were still poles apart, seeing each other, more than ever, through a distorting mirror. All too often, the man's dream of home and wife was a fantasy. Justifiably, Kenneth Howard tried to warn his readers how false this picture could be:

He conveniently forgets, for example, his wife's irritating habit of having meals always ten minutes late; he forgets that the garden badly needs new fencing. To him it all seems like a perfect paradise.

He also pointed out that their wives, when they got home, would not be how they imagined them. They might be fatter, or thinner, with more wrinkles, and rationing would have played havoc with their wardrobe.

Howard also made an apt observation about war when he declared that 'it is impossible to tell men to go and kill an enemy and risk their lives in doing it, and expect them at the same time all to be honest, chaste, kind and unselfish all the time'.

For the 'perfect paradise' was tainted, too, by sin and betrayal.

*

Though marriage in 1945 was a far more durable institution than it is today, the war placed unprecedented strain on it. At 47,041 the 1947 divorce figures had nearly doubled in just two years.*

Too many unions cracked under the strain of long absence, estrangement and, all too often, infidelity. There is no way of knowing how prevalent wartime adultery was, though there does seem to have been a general rise in illegitimacy and in bigamy cases. Reac-

---

* Contemporary figures offer a little perspective on those of sixty years ago. In 2008 132,562 couples got divorced in England and Wales.

tions of returning British servicemen to their wives' infidelity ranged from the big-hearted tolerance of Greg James, who smilingly accommodated two little cuckoos smuggled by his wife Lilian into the family nest during his absence in the Far East, to the murderous rage of Private Reginald Keymer, who strangled his adulterous wife in a fit of jealousy. Keymer was acquitted. This was far from being the only case of wife-killing by ex-servicemen; the Sunday papers greedily lapped up the lurid details, as tragedies piled up. Sergeant Albert Nettleton was given five years' penal servitude for beating his wife, Ivy, to death with the iron. Father of four Private Cyril Patmore was also found guilty of manslaughter after stabbing his wife Kathleen to death on 4 August 1945; he escaped the death penalty after Kathleen's adultery was cited as provocation. But on 28 May 1946 ex-serviceman Leonard Holmes was hanged after striking his wife Peggy on the head with a coal hammer, then, seeing that she was still alive, strangling her.

Such sordid incidents have happened throughout history, but placed in the post-war context they acquire more than usually troubling overtones of dissociation and misogyny.

For the waiting wife, the fantasy of a perfect husband was often just as illusory. One of the few things that had kept Margery Baines going during the bureaucratic travails of 1943 and 1944 was the thought that her absent husband, William, would admire her fortitude. She equated success as an army officer with success, in his eyes, as a woman. 'I had to do well to please him.' Margery's ordeal in the ATS had left her in full retreat from all her bright dreams of leadership, and, after her breakdown in 1944, she felt like a failure on every front, with nothing to show for her efforts, her ambitions. There had to be something she could do. Becoming a mother had the merit of conforming to expectations. If she couldn't run a platoon, then perhaps she ought to be focusing on what women were supposed to do and run a family instead.

Misfortunes now accumulated. Margery found herself pregnant with twins; they were born in 1946, but one of the two babies was stillborn. Three weeks after her confinement, while she was still adjusting to the loss of her daughter, Major William Baines abandoned his wife for another woman. Since their marriage in 1940 they had spent barely a year together.

At thirty-one when I was suddenly left with a baby of three weeks, and the world to face, I saw only finality and despair.

Utterly humiliated, Margery felt that she had failed as a woman. Mysteriously, the sun continued to rise each day, and baby Gillian continued to breathe and sleep, but the collapse of Margery's marriage caused her to feel annihilated. If she wasn't a wife, she was nobody. To be somebody meant that William had to recognise her qualities. 'Why hadn't my *husband* seen them if they existed?' Margery now channelled what was left of her self-belief into supporting her baby; as a single, husbandless mother, she was the victim of society's hostility towards the scorned and spurned wife. She felt like an 'odd woman' – an outcast and a freak.

The divorce figures in 1947 were tangible evidence of the mismatch between fantasy and reality; but innumerable unmarried women also succumbed to the emotional aftershock of war. The carefully controlled morals of generations of young women had been scrambled and derailed by wartime freedoms. More affecting than statistics are the repeated appeals sent by married and unmarried alike to the magazine problem pages. Here is just a handful, from the many hundreds sent to Leonora Eyles, Evelyn Home, Mary Grant and their ilk:

I am going to have an illegitimate child, and I am afraid its father was a young Allied soldier whom my family liked and trusted as a son. I have now discovered that he was married all the time.

I am ashamed to say that I have fallen in love with a new clerk in our firm. I am ashamed because I am already engaged to a boy in the Forces overseas.

I am engaged to a boy I love very much. Since he has been away, though, I have been going out with an Allied soldier. I am now expecting a baby by him . . . What am I to tell my fiancé?

The need was great, and the agony aunts did their best; the Marriage Guidance Council, first formed in 1938, now came into its own. Between 1943 and 1948 the volunteer counsellors in their small London office helped over 8,000 clients who were trying to unravel their matrimonial tangles.

A great amount of breast-beating and soul-searching ensued about the future of the family – and civilisation itself. Government and the church wrung their collective hands over the nation's moral laxity and the spread of immorality. For hundreds and hundreds of years, men and women had thought they knew where they stood. Had the war dealt that certainty a death-blow?

A la Recherche

From the evidence, both sexes still looked to an idealised past, hankering after a half-remembered world of grace and gallantry, of clinging subordination and virile authority.

But could it ever return? Had too much changed? To many women, the world of 1946 was an alarming and dangerous one, one which was fast eroding their sense of who they were. Hardship and worry were their daily lot, relationships were being tested as never before, the institution of marriage appeared to be spiralling helplessly into crisis, their homes, their roles, their sense of meaning, their whole world seemed to have been exploded. Life was 'all wrong'.

They longed above all to rebuild the remembered past amid the wreckage of the present – in the case of Madeleine Henrey and her mother, almost literally.

Shortly after the liberation of France, Madame Gal decided that the time had come to retrace her steps from Paris to the farm in Normandy that she had shared with her daughter Madeleine, her English son-in-law and Bobby, her baby grandson. The region was still littered with the charred traces of battle, and it was a difficult journey. Mme Gal walked into the house and nearly fainted from the stench that met her nostrils; the rooms had been vandalised and stripped of their contents. Cobwebs were everywhere. Ripped-out pages from Madeleine's copy of the New Testament, desecrated with human faeces, lay in festering heaps in the downstairs closet. 'What barbarians had passed this way?' Gradually, she pieced together what had happened; Germans and local looters between them had defiled her daughter's property and stolen every stick.

Patiently and courageously, Mme Gal set about the slow task of cleaning the farmhouse. Every day that passed she made a little progress; in the evenings she knitted a patchwork quilt from scraps of wool and wrote to her daughter in England. VE-day came and went; Madeleine herself was still unqualified for a travel permit, but whatever she could afford in the way of tea-leaves, soap or chocolate she sent to her mother. Neighbours brought eggs and butter. In anticipation of autumn Mme Gal made jam from the fruits of summer, gathered faggots from the wood and stored charcoal for the stove. At last, in September 1945, Madeleine's papers came through. Torn between anguish at leaving her husband and six-year-old Bobby and the joyful prospect of a long-awaited reunion with her mother, she set off for France.

Madeleine would have to travel to Villers-sur-Mer via Paris. She took with her as much food and clothing as she could carry. Victoria Station was a seething Babel of foreign servicemen and charging porters; the train reached Newhaven at midnight. On the channel steamer Madeleine shared a cabin with a young Englishwoman travelling back to be with her French engineer husband. They talked of living through the air raids, and of the occupation. It was a squally crossing. The arrival at Dieppe next morning brought back memories of the 1942 raid: 'The vessel cut through the swell towards the land where men fell that it should be liberated . . . In a few moments I would once again step on French soil.' After endless formalities, Madeleine was able to board the Paris locomotive – 'had it been chased by Spitfires?' As they chugged out of Dieppe she caught glimpses of destruction: a half-sunken vessel emerging from the low tide, bombed pillboxes and blockhouses. The train gathered pace through a countryside blitzed and scarred: roofless station buildings, twisted girders replaced by Bailey bridges, blasted track. At last, a magical sunset view of the Eiffel Tower, untouched in its glory, and they were in the capital.

Three days later, after ingenious machinations with the British Embassy had secured her a lift by road as far as Lisieux, Madeleine was on her way down the long poplar-lined arteries of France; speeding by the half-concealed wreckage of Tiger tanks rusting in ditches, the broken fuselage of a fighter impaled on the apex of a shattered farmhouse, two incinerated military trucks concertinaed into a burned-out tree trunk and an occasional destroyed aerodrome. Lisieux, when she arrived, was whitened rubble. From there she was collected by a neighbour from their village.

We drove rapidly across the plateau by way of Blonville, and as we approached . . . I felt my heart thumping against my ribs. I was longing to catch sight of my own land.

My mother stood framed in the entrance of the half-timbered house . . . I ran into [her] arms.

That evening Madeleine and her mother walked together through the ripening orchards and out on to the high ground with its panorama over the Le Havre estuary. Here in June 1940 she and Robert had watched the invading Germans dropping bombs on the port, the day before their flight to England.

What bitter, poignant memories were revived by the sight of this orchard, where [the] cows moved gracefully in the long grass, and where the hedges were filled with ripening hazel-nuts. The red autumn sun was breaking through the haze, and all was peace and content.

So much had passed, so little had changed.

But now there was work to be done. Madeleine became busy; she organised carpenters to do repairs and decorators to restore colour and brilliance to the house. She had the furnace overhauled and the windows reglazed; she begged and bartered for furniture and bedding; she dug the garden and got the cattle pond cleaned.

As the year wound to a close Madeleine cut holly boughs, shook the icicles off them and carried them into the house for Christmas; her clogs clattered on the clean stone flags. Madame Gal was warm by the fireplace, tending a cafetière perched in its embers. The house smelled of lavender, burning logs, toast and coffee. Here, together, she mused, the two of them, mother and daughter, had wrought a miracle rebirth, an apotheosis of all that was womanly, maternal and good. The rescue of her farm from the spoilers and wreckers was an act of female creation. 'The war was over and I had lived to see my farm handed back to me. Dreamily I thought about the future.'

I still felt a young enough woman to brave new ventures . . . Life had so many beautiful experiences to offer . . . I was thankful for my femininity . . . How would the next so important phase of my womanhood work out?

Down by the shore, the village church bells chimed the angelus.

For Madeleine, the war was truly over.

'A Fine Type of British Girl'

London, April 1946. On a sunny afternoon the romantic fiction author Miss Florence Speed strolled from her home in Brixton to Kennington Park and sat down on a bench in the walled garden to read her book and enjoy the daffodils. A group of small children were playing like puppies under the plane trees, yelping with happy laughter. Bees buzzed. On a day like this, the terrifying, deafening doodlebug raids which almost two years earlier had wrecked her sleep, night after night, seemed a distant memory. There was surely no more perfect way to relish the return of peace than to soak up the sunshine in a London park.

But Florence had barely read a couple of pages when a middle-aged lady arrived, sat down heavily on the seat beside her and started to grumble. This person was seething with indignation about the world. 'Disgusting,' she said, indicating the happy band of youngsters, 'that children are allowed in here. They're so noisy and destroy everything.' And she spewed out a catalogue of complaints, starting with a description of a recent bout of 'flu from which she was recovering, proceeding on to her high blood pressure and thence moving into a litany of the various things of which she currently disapproved, including the government, Mr Bevan, food shortages, children in general and the young women of today. She also took a low view of America – 'a horrible, dirty' place, in her opinion. 'It's a nice country – to get out of,' she declared. 'The GI brides are in for an eye opener.'

*

Three months earlier, on the evening of Tuesday 8 January, a mob of those reprehensible young women had besieged the building on the corner of Shaftesbury Avenue known as 'Rainbow Corner', screaming and weeping, as a little bit of the USA in London shut up shop for the last time. Since November 1942, the club had entertained 18 million American servicemen. Now, with the GIs heading for home, there was to be a final dance: the last jives would be jived, and the last jitterbugs jitterbugged. Eleanor Roosevelt, Anthony Eden and a starry line-up of performers were invited to attend. But the crowd was so dense outside that officials had to force a passage for the celebrities to enter. Many members of the public had climbed on to windowsills and lamp-posts to get a better view of the floodlit entrance. Traffic had to be diverted. A swarm of servicemen, policemen, hysterical girlfriends, passers-by and 'Piccadilly Commandos' became locked in a seething mêlée that see-sawed back and forth outside the club; fights broke out, and one woman fainted. The planned finale, with a band playing in the street, had to be abandoned; instead, they struck up their patriotic tunes, 'Auld Lang Syne' and 'The Star-spangled Banner', from the safety of a balcony. There were frantic goodbyes; many broke down. At midnight an American soldier came out and concluded the proceedings by nailing a board to the doors which for three years had never closed. It read:

OUT OF BOUNDS TO
TROOPS

The emotion surrounding Rainbow Corner's final hours is evidence of the place that 2 million young Americans now held in many British women's hearts. Despite the culture clash, and for all their brashness, impudence and noisy lust, the sexy, well-heeled, smart-uniformed GIs had marched straight into the affections of innumerable British women. More than 100,000 of these had married their American sweethearts. Witnessing their forced departure was an occasion for mass heartbreak; but, nothing daunted, the GI brides were determined to follow soon after.

From early after the end of the war – October 1945 – British brides of US servicemen had been clamouring to be reunited with their departing husbands. But priority had to go to demobilising the men first; the wives could follow when there was spare shipping capacity. This didn't go down well. Thousands of frantic brides from Wales, Scotland and the north of England travelled to London to demonstrate in Westminster. Many were heavily pregnant or with small babies, arm-in-arm, chanting 'Yankee Doodle Dandy' and 'We Want Boats!' There was hysteria, and fights broke out on the steps with policemen.

*'Goodbye, Piccadilly . . .': Rainbow Corner, the US servicemen's club, closed its
doors for the last time on 8 January 1946.*

Getting the war brides resettled with their new husbands in America and Canada was one of the challenges faced by authorities attempting to reorder post-war society. It was a bureaucratic swamp, involving visas, immigration laws and transport quotas. Every war bride had to demonstrate that she had the right documentation, and enough money to cover her railroad ticket. Then she – and her baby if she had one (and many did) – had to be processed through an ex-military camp at Tidworth near Southampton, where each woman was required to strip and line up to have a torch shone between her legs to check for VD. If she passed this humiliating medical examination she would be permitted to embark for the New World.

At last, on 26 January 1946, the SS *Argentina* set sail from Southampton. It was followed on 5 February by the *Queen Mary*; Victoria Stevenson, a reporter with *Woman's Own*, joined 2,000 young 'Pilgrim Mothers' (as the press named them) and 600 babies, packed on board like sardines: a veritable floating nursery. 'Many of the girls had never been to sea before,' Stevenson told her readers, and went on to paint a heart-warming picture of ship life for the happy brides, who included a nurse, a dress designer, a psychology student, a riveter and an ex-clippie. The American government official chosen to accompany them described them as 'a fine type of British girl'. Stevenson went to see a cheery crowd of young women in an eight-berth cabin, 'creaming their faces and curling their hair':

Occasionally a tear was dabbed away as they spoke of partings with their home folk, then a love-letter or a photo of their new home would be produced, and their thoughts raced ahead to the man they each loved and for whose sake they had uprooted themselves.

Knowing how many more brides were due to follow in their footsteps, *Woman's Own* went out of its way to present an upbeat picture of what had been dubbed the 'Diaper Run'. There were descriptions of the jolly laundry rooms, frequented by busy throngs of women wringing nappies or getting their babies' clothes aired. Fatherly stewards helped out with feeding bottles, resident Red Cross workers were on hand to help with all queries; sing-songs, religious services and instructive talks about America were organised. But Elizabeth Jane Howard, who was not a war bride, but had boarded the *Aquitania* with her British husband in spring 1946 along with 400 of them bound for Halifax, Nova Scotia, saw no cause to be upbeat:

It was the worst crossing, according to the captain, that they'd had for thirty years. And everybody was tremendously sick – except me.

And all those girls – I can't tell you what they were like! They were a huge collection of 'no oil paintings'. They were mostly working-class girls, and they all looked battered, flabby, sleazy, and older than they were, caused, I suppose, by years of rotten food and bad lights. And they were met at the other end – vociferously – by either their bridegrooms or husbands as the case might be.

And I just remember thinking how drab they all looked. I just remember thinking 'Goodness, how can anybody want to marry you?'

She herself was a statuesque beauty. But in 1945 Jane, desirable as she was, had had another love affair, followed by a couple of near misses. She was dependent on Peter, however, and was too frightened to take any action that would further jeopardise their shaky union. When her husband asked her to join him on his transatlantic journey, 'I could think of no valid excuse for not going.'

With its freight of brides and babies, the *Queen Mary* sailed up the ice-strewn Hudson River and neared Manhattan. *Woman's Own* again:

These British wives have the pluck and spirit of adventure of the old pioneers, only they go to no strange land fraught with unknown perils, they go to the friendly peoples of the great American Democracy, to forge yet another link between the two English-speaking nations.

When she first met Kenneth Davis outside a fish and chip shop near Seaton Barracks in 1942, ATS girl Mary Angove hadn't given much thought to forging international links. An on-off relationship with the attractive Yank ensued, ending with marriage in March 1945. Six months later Kenneth was shipped back home to Washington, DC. Mary was one of the 2,000 who crossed the Atlantic on the *Queen Mary* in February 1946:

Kenneth was probably affected by the war, because he became alcoholic.

I wasn't over there long. Actually, I left him three times.

The first time was when I was working at 'Fanny Farmer's Candy Store' in Washington, DC. I came back home one day, and he was in the bedroom with this girl. Well, I wasn't the sort of person to make a big hoo-ha about that, but he smacked me one – so that was that.

But then the next thing, there he was ringing up and saying he worshipped the ground I walked on and apologising, blah blah blah. So back goes Muggins.

The second time I was getting ready to go to the cinema with a neighbour. Suddenly he wopped me up against the wall; I ran next door across to her flat, and he sat outside watching our door. Finally he went off. I got back into our flat and found he'd taken my clothes and my passport. Next day I went to the British Embassy. They said, 'What do you want to do?' I said, 'I want to go to New York.' I just wanted to get away from him. I was really afraid of him, he was a barber and he had razors didn't he? They helped me to get a job in New York as a waitress. Then somebody told Kenneth where I was. So of course he comes up, and he's all over me . . . So back goes Muggins . . .

Then it was all right for a while. And then he came in one night, and said he was going to hit me. So I stood there and I said, 'Go on then, hit me.' So he did. Well that did it, I thought, 'Right, I'm off.' My sister-in-law lent me $25, and I went back to New York. This time I thought, 'Nobody's going to know where I am.' I got a job looking after two little girls not far from Central Park. Then I realised I wouldn't get paid till the end of the month. So I pawned my engagement ring. It was then I found out I was pregnant.

So I thought, 'Right, this child's going to be born British.' So I worked there and I made enough money to come home on the *Queen Elizabeth*. When I got home at the beginning of 1947 I had £12 and the clothes I stood up in. I never even let him know I had a child. You know, the Lord did look after me!

An altogether happier – and probably more typical – experience was that of Peggy Biggs. Peggy came from a tolerant bourgeois home in Marlborough, Wiltshire; she worked as a teacher and met the newly landed Lieutenant David Wharton in the summer of 1943 at a WVS dance in Marlborough Town Hall. They married early in 1944. For nearly two years, from D-day until she too travelled to America on board the *Queen Mary* in February 1946, they were separated. She would never forget her arrival in icy New York that Sunday morning:

We were all on deck to see New York's celebrated Skyline and Miss Liberty lifting her lamp beside the Golden Door. In our threadbare wartime British 'utility' coats we shivered in the bitter wind.

Peggy caught her breath at the sight of David waiting among the crowds, far below her on the dock. Where was the tall man she remembered, so good-looking and suave in his brand new, clean-cut officer garb? There he was in unglamorous civvies and a hat – the first time she had seen him out of uniform. Then he was with her, and soon she was caught up in the bewildering circuit of David's well-meaning but inquisitive relatives, all of whom flocked to view the new bride.

I was regarded as something of an oddity with my pronounced accent and typically English looks ... I was interviewed by newspaper reporters ... and generally made much of ... I was then faced with the task of getting down to daily life in a strange country with little money to spend and many lonely hours to face.

Peggy was a prudent, realistic person; 'any lingering feeling of wishing that I could live once more in England is dispelled by the knowledge that one can never go back'. Her marriage endured. David's culture and education were similar to hers, and, despite missing 'the BBC, British newspapers, tea properly made, fields and downs of the Wiltshire countryside, and even the English weather', she brought up a family, made a life for herself in New Jersey and in 1952 took American citizenship. She recognised, too, that America offered her material comfort at a level that she could never have enjoyed in the country of her birth.

The brides who left Britain had spent six years surviving on potatoes, carrots, spam and that inexpressibly horrible South African tinned fish that smelled of cat-food: snoek. Here in the land of steak and steaming hot dogs the comparison was glaring. Elizabeth Jane Howard's account of arrival in New York paints a picture of untrammelled luxury:

The *food*! I was ill in a minute, I couldn't cope with it at all. When you ordered a boiled egg for breakfast *two* boiled eggs came, and you thought, 'I just *can't* waste this egg!'

And what was so extraordinary was this city, all lit up. We'd been used to being in the dark for six years. And the lights were just absolutely dazzling and overwhelming and marvellous.

American excess took some getting used to. Buildings reached to the sky, hats were ten-gallon, there were traffic jams. People thought nothing of jumping into cars to drive forty, or even fifty miles. As one ex-Wren bride recalled:

I truly gorged myself with my eyes and my stomach. I learned to eat hamburgers, hot dogs, steaks and banana splits, with no worries about calories or cholesterol . . .

– and yet when you wanted a nice cup of tea all you got was a cup of hot water containing a little soggy bag full of brown dust.

Let loose on the sidewalks of Manhattan with her husband's dollars burning a hole in her handbag, Elizabeth Jane Howard went on a never-to-be-forgotten end-of-the-war spending spree:

I went shopping. It was dreadful, I'm really ashamed of myself. I spent all Peter's money. I bought my daughter two years' worth of clothes – marvellous American dresses. I bought coats and jerseys and cigars for my father. I had written down all my friends' sizes in shoes and clothes and I bought everybody nylon stockings which were absolutely like gold dust. When I got off the *Queen Mary* coming back the Customs man asked me, 'Do you always travel with four dozen pairs of nylon stockings?' and I said 'Yes.'

I had a whale of a time, I was so excited. I've always adored shopping. But it was wonderful, just absolutely, staggeringly exciting.

Between the extremes of madcap extravagance and borrowing $25 to get home lay a multitude of variations on the GI bride theme, from seasickness to homesickness, culture shock to racial prejudice, isolation to the language problem. Trams were streetcars, good girls didn't jaywalk, you said 'tomayta' not 'tomartoe'.

Setting transatlantic true love back on its course became a long-running and highly charged story in the media, which ran it over months, with the emotional travails, the shipment and reception of GI brides fed regularly to a public hungry for romance. Newspaper editors knew instinctively that the story of the 'Pilgrim Mothers' braving the oceans and mountains to follow the dictates of the heart touched something profound in the post-war breast. Perhaps this was because the GI bride appeared, on the face of it, to be 'having it all'. Adventure, enterprise and courage were hers, as she set forth to conquer the New World. The legacy of war would be, for her, a brand-new start and fresh challenges. She would be Scarlett O'Hara, Laura Ingalls Wilder. But – she would never forsake her birthright as a wife and mother. She had uprooted herself to become, not an adventuress, but an American housewife.

Our Mothers' Shoes

LAURA: Fred – Fred – dear Fred . . . I don't want you to be hurt. You see, we are a happily married couple, and must never forget that. This is my home . . . You are my husband – and my children are upstairs in bed. I am a happily married woman – or rather, I was, until a few weeks ago.

The brittle, refined voice is Celia Johnson's; the role, Laura Jesson in the 1945 hit movie *Brief Encounter*, screenplay by Noël Coward. In the film the violent passions of Laura's relationship with a married man – played out amid the roaring, whistling voids of a busy provincial railway station – bring her to the edge of suicide until, to the dying strains of Rachmaninoff's 2nd Piano Concerto, she accepts the imperatives of her marriage.

Watching, many members of the film's audience would have

experienced Laura's conflict as their own: women whose horizons the war had broadened, who ached to follow their star, but who dared not. Before the credits roll, Fred, simple, good and perhaps more understanding than his wife suspects, puts his crossword aside and folds her in his arms. Laura has pulled back from the brink, the danger is past. Her husband is not sexy or desirable, but he will protect her now, and she will stay safely in their chintzy home until the threat fades into a dim memory. *Brief Encounter* was notionally set in late 1938, and it is surely not far-fetched to suggest that its 1945 audience responded as powerfully to the movie's message of a return to a 'pre-war' type of peace and tranquillity as they did to the intense, near-tragic sentiments of the star-crossed lovers. In this way, *Brief Encounter* is a perfect evocation of the repressed emotional undercurrents of post-war Britain: there will be no more bombs, no more sirens, no more running away. Stay at home, urged the movie. Home is best. National trauma will be resolved by a reversion to rooted tradition, in which the sexes know their place, and two children, a girl and a boy, lie trustingly upstairs in bed. It was a potent message that would resonate powerfully for the female movie-goer of 1945. The likelihood was that she had left home and experienced a far wider world than the house-bound generation she had left behind in 1938. But was it the right decision to go back? Laura Jesson, and many of her real-life counterparts in 1945, would have to live with that question to the end of their lives.

Immediate post-war Britain was not a showcase for emancipation. Was it inertia, fear of the unknown, diffidence, modesty or just an instinct of self-preservation that deterred so many women of this generation from marching straight out through the door that their wartime experiences had opened for them? Or was it, quite simply, the demands of their men?

War had given men an uncomplicated brief: to defend, and to kill. Peace had taken it away from them. Exhausted, and deprived of his gun, his military status and his urgent mission, the demobbed soldier felt inessential, irrelevant and under-appreciated. One 8th Army driver got home to his empty London home to find a note on the kitchen table from his absent wife: 'Pilchards in the larder if you feel peckish. Joan.'

Here I was, in one of the greatest cities in the world, yet lonelier than in the middle of the desert . . . Somehow, something seemed to be wrong.

The male ego craved more than that. He – they – had won a victory. Yet many, like this man, came home almost unable to express how damaged, defeated and lost they now felt. One psychologist writing about men and warfare in 1945 put it into words:

In war they served their country; in peace they are needed no longer . . . men will not spring to attention when they pass. Words of command perish on their lips unuttered. The great days have passed like a dream; yet all their lives they will try to live in this dream.

Few women were so uncharitable as to walk out leaving a tin of pilchards for their returning husbands. As a generation they had been conditioned to minister to the male. They could help alleviate his loneliness, and his sense of irrelevance. And so they stayed – where they were most needed, forsaking their own aspirations, and paying the price of love.

*

In the spring of 1946 Nina Mabey was riding the crest of a wave. Her talents, her mind and her friendships had all been broadened by the independence that the war years had thrust on her, as an evacuee, as a college student and as a political campaigner in the 1945 election. In her last year at Oxford, Nina's Uncle Stanley gave her a portable typewriter. She had her first story published, and made up her mind to become a foreign correspondent. Shortly before taking her finals she was offered a launch-pad job as junior reporter on the *Manchester Evening News*.

She didn't take it. Instead, Nina became engaged to Harry Bawden, a demobbed airman a good deal older than her, whom she met when he returned after the war to take up his place at the university. They married soon after her graduation, when she was just twenty-one, in the autumn of 1946.

He took it for granted that we would live in London and I gave up what had been my ambition since the day Uncle Stanley gave me the typewriter without a second's thought . . . I felt, deep down, that I was still only a frivolous schoolgirl . . .

Being a foreign correspondent did not seem to fit with being married.

Nina was caught unawares by the wifely duties now expected of her: shopping and cooking; toast was about her limit. Tentatively, she applied for a job as deputy editor on an industrial magazine and was offered it. The salary, £900 a year, 'was £300 more than Harry was getting'. Worried that her mature husband would feel threatened by the earning capacity of his 'schoolgirl' wife, she went and sat in a news cinema in Oxford Street to think it over. Rising to leave after the newsreel was over, Nina felt groggy and fainted. She was pregnant. 'Harry was pleased . . . I turned down the job.' They couldn't afford a nanny on Harry's salary, so Nina would have to be a full-time mother. She lacked the courage to tell him what she would have been earning.

Or take the case of senior Wren Christian Lamb, née Oldham, who 'only joined for the hat'. She had married her lieutenant late in 1943, but played her part in the planning of Operation Overlord, and until after VE-day continued to contribute as a working Wren. But in 1945 a dream came true for her husband, John Lamb, when he was given his own ship, HMS *Broadway*, to command. With the competition so unfairly weighted against her, Christian resorted to 'feminine' wiles:

I realised I had to take second place after that and must do something to regain my position. It seemed a convenient moment to announce that I was going to have a baby.

Christian now jettisoned all prospects of a career in favour of 'a life-long commitment to being a sailor's wife'. Not that she had many practical qualifications in that field for, like Nina, Christian could barely boil an egg. Towards the end of 1945 John Lamb summoned his wife and new-born daughter to Gibraltar, from where he whisked them off on the next leg of their travels. 'I never stopped following the Fleet after that.' As a wife, Christian learned on the job and now thinks her wartime competence eased the transfer to full-time motherhood and home-making, both on ship and shore. She gave this new task all the enthusiasm she had given the old. At over ninety her gaiety and mental grip still make it easy to understand how attractive Christian must have been as a young woman. She loved travelling, found her new family adorable and relished the challenge of coping with their demands – from surviving a six-week journey to Singapore with three under-fives in a two-berth cabin to dealing with sickness caused by bad porridge in the middle of the Red Sea. 'It was great, great fun. I loved every minute of it.'

Patience Chadwyck-Healey was another who slotted effortlessly back into the pre-war template laid down for young ladies of her class. Patience had been brought up by nannies and nursemaids and given a cursory education. Her mother's principal activity was good works in the village; ambition was discouraged, and her life revolved around hunt balls and deb dances: in other words, the marriage market. Her wartime career in the FANYs, driving ambulances and staff cars, with responsibilities in the Blood Transfusion Service and the Bomb Disposal Unit ('all marvellously worthwhile') came to an end when she was demobbed in October 1945:

Well, I'd been very happy right up to the last days of my service. I thought I would miss the FANYs frightfully, but in fact I didn't. Actually, not being there was absolute bliss. And in '46 I began to think 'Now what can I do?'

Patience went to stay as a long-term guest with a friend in Suffolk. To get through the days she took up the offer of unpaid work on a local smallholding, feeding chickens and hoeing beetroot. But in the evenings she scrubbed the dirt from her fingernails and joined the family's social life:

During that time people were just getting back to what life had been like in the old days. Well, Suffolk was quite a social county, and it was starting to get back into its party-going mood, and there was Newmarket races, and drinks parties. And we used to gossip about this rather nice local family, named Maxwell . . . And it was there, you see, in the summer of '46, that I met my husband. So that was absolutely splendid.

Peter Maxwell was a regular who had served in North Africa and Burma in the Highland Light Infantry. Patience was twenty-six, and her parents had no difficulty in accepting her soldier fiancé, who came from a family of famous rifle shots and passed all the social tests. They were married at St Paul's, Knightsbridge, on 30 November 1946 and honeymooned in Sussex with a week's horse-riding. Two sons were born in the first three years of marriage; two daughters followed. Like

Christian Lamb, Patience had no doubts or hesitations. The surrender of her independence came as a welcome relief, not a sacrifice. In truth, Patience's entire upbringing had prepared her for this:

I was very happy to be an army wife, a camp follower. Peter always came first for me. And I was happy to be told what to do instead of having to think things out for myself . . . I never had a job again after I was married.

Frances Campbell-Preston was another military wife whose post-war life was determined by her husband's career postings. Soon after his release from Colditz Patrick was sent to Greece; Frances made strenuous efforts to join him there, only to find he had been reassigned to Staff College at Camberley. The subsequent life of a camp-follower was to take Frances and her family to Scotland, then with the Army of Occupation to Duisberg, Berlin and Hamburg. The merry-go-round only stopped when Patrick's health broke down.*

Tagging along in the wake of an ambitious ship's captain or glamorous professional soldier gave these women what they wanted from life. All three of them married husbands who came with important military trappings, who felt entitled to call on their wives to dance attendance on them. The women did so happily, and, given the shaping of their formative years, it would be unfair to expect otherwise. But talk about marriage to women – of any class – born in the 1920s, and there is a strong likelihood that they will adopt the same unfaltering posture towards their life choices:

Pip Beck, ex-WAAF R/T operator in Bomber Command: 'Being a mum and a wife was all I thought about at the time. That's what I was, so that's what I wanted to be. I didn't look beyond. I was quite happy with it.'

Cora Johnston, née Styles, ex-Wren: 'I remarried, and to begin with I was happy as a mum and housewife. I was houseproud. In those days after the war it took a long time to pull life back up again. You never thought about tomorrow or the next day. You just got on with it.'

Flo Mahony, ex-WAAF driver: 'We just slotted back into our mothers' shoes at that time. Women didn't go to work when they were married like they do today.'

---

* He died in 1960 of a heart attack, aged forty-nine. Frances went on to serve as lady-in-waiting to HM the Queen Mother for nearly forty years.

Eileen Morgan, née Rouse – ex Regimental Quartermaster Sergeant in the ATS: 'I loved my time in the service, but to me getting married was starting again. It was another adventure. It was all new to me. I was my own boss, I could do as I liked, make my own decisions, rather than receiving orders. I had a baby, settled in, and made my own life. I had no regrets.'

The Wifely Thing

Fear, lack of education, hardship, loneliness and social expectation all combined at this time to propel women back into their pre-war identity. They sought the kind of approval in the eyes of men that wifehood and motherhood could guarantee.

Like so many, Margery Baines had turned her back on her ambitions. She did as she was told and had a baby, hoping to please her husband by conforming. If her husband had stayed, Margery's story might have been different. But in abandoning her William Baines broke all the rules. In turn, she reinvented herself. Becoming a successful businesswoman was her survival strategy, and her salvation; it was also her rebuke to the limitations of a society which could only understand women as incarnations of the Madonna: passive, gentle and stoical. But when in 1946 Margery Baines turned her life around, she was motivated not by the attractions of power or making millions, but simply by the need to feed herself and her baby daughter. She really had no choice.

In her autobiography, Margery wrote that having a child forced her to 'think big'. In 1946 she was living in a small flat in Portsmouth. Although at this time she had no qualifications beyond the shorthand and typing skills which had earned her a modest, living-at-home salary in her twenties, she knew she had to earn 'a man's salary' to afford to go out to work and pay for a nanny. She started out taking in typing, but it didn't bring in the £15 a week she needed. So with £50 borrowed from her father she opened a one-woman typing agency from a tiny rented room, 8 feet by 10 feet, in Mayfair. Eventually this would become the famous Brook Street Bureau, the first employment agency (in 1965) to be listed on the Stock Exchange. But in 1946, starting it up meant the anguish of leaving her daughter Gillian with the nanny from Monday to Friday and commuting weekly to London.

The need to build up something for her future made it necessary. This is the dilemma of every working mother.

These were days of constant worry and struggle, of twenty-hour-days sustained by strong black coffee, of rush orders, of post-war lack of equipment, of feast but – more often – of famine. Margery collapsed, and her little business went down with her. 'I started again.' This time Margery conceived the idea of sending out temporary secretaries and quickly landed a contract with the Monsanto Chemical Company. It was a turning point. Soon Margery was run off her feet, doubling as telephonist and receptionist, or office-girl and emergency temp. She applied the attention to detail, learned in her days as an army officer, to her staffing. Nobody was taken on to her books without being tested. She was thorough and stuck to her targets. The business expanded, she was able to advertise, and Brook Street started to place permanent staff as well as temps; this was another milestone. Though her business instincts were uninformed, they were sound; she kept her overheads low, concentrated on running things well and was soon making a surprising profit, most of which she ploughed back into the company.

As the money flowed, Margery rediscovered a new and bubbling confidence. 'For the first time in my life I had found a job with scope for my energy and imagination.' It was a joy to succeed, to support herself and to repay her father. After the years of toil and deprivation, she holidayed in the south of France with a girlfriend: 'This was the first patch of gaiety I can remember since the break-up of my marriage and I was more than ready for it.' But the real reward came when she went shopping with Gillian and, without flinching, spent forty guineas on a hand-embroidered pink crêpe-de-chine dress and matching coat for the two-year-old child: 'the best London had to offer'. To be able, at that time of austerity, to exhibit her pretty little daughter, enchanting in pink and blue forget-me-nots, was the summit of Margery's ambitions. Through Gillian, Margery could again feel like a good mother, a 'real' woman.

It was . . . a joyous splurge of money I had earned on the person I loved best in the world. And nothing I have bought before or since has ever matched up to it . . .

To walk my daughter out in all her finery enabled me to hold my head high.

Margery was able to put her broken marriage behind her and rediscover wells of energy. She applied the techniques and insights into people that she had learned in her army days to her business, and the Brook Street Bureau prospered. The pre-war ideal typist had been a combination of waitress, handmaid and dogsbody, underpaid and undervalued. The Brook Street secretary had progressed from those days. In describing her modern ideal, Margery still held up the girl who 'anticipates a man's moods . . . she must be there when he wants her.' But she also stressed that it was a two-way traffic:

Personal consideration is everything in business. And a wise employer recognises that he should start his day by having a few minutes of personal chat with his secretary. He should ask after her boyfriend, or husband and children . . . If he strides into the office saying – 'Take a letter, Miss Jones' – then she says to herself – 'What am I, a machine?'

'Regard me as a feminist, not a suffragette, because I adore men,' she would later write in her autobiography. Margery's struggle, and her success, were played out against a backdrop of inequality and male condescension. '"Well, well," they would grin, "so the little lady's a tycoon. And how do you shape up with a pan of bacon and eggs?"' Inevitably, Margery rose to such baits. But more often she made allowances, taking care not to wound male dignity, nor did she turn herself into a champion for women's rights. In this she was very much of her time.

In 1948 Margery met a young barrister named Eric Hurst, and that year they were married; Eric, a balanced and intelligent man, supported his mercurial wife for many years. Margery would become a millionairess. But her second marriage, too, would finish in the divorce courts.

*

For all too many of the women in this narrative, a happy-ever-after ending was to prove elusive.

WAAF Pip Beck was demobbed in January 1946 and married her

boyfriend Leo Brimson ('Brim') that summer; she was three months pregnant by then. Despite parental disapproval Pip had seen enough 'immorality' during the war to revise her views of what was morally reprehensible. In her eighty-seventh year, Pip – her witchy, roughly braided hair still black, her former beauty still discernible – has no qualms talking about her youthful lapses; she has shed conventionality. It is early afternoon, and she has come downstairs, unkempt in a pink towelling dressing-gown. 'One saw so much of it – girls getting "into trouble", as we put it, and being chucked out of the services. They weren't "bad girls", they were just unfortunate. I got more tolerant. My mother minded, but I didn't; it was what I wanted. I was happy.'

But the Brimsons' early married life was difficult. The agonies and ecstasies of Pip's days in Bomber Command were behind her now: those fearful nights waiting for a mission to return, the heady wonder of flight, the all-too-brief lives and loves. The RAF wouldn't release Brim, permitting him only short leaves for his wedding and the birth of his son. Pip stayed with her parents above their shop in Buckingham, hauling the pram up and down stairs. The baby cried ceaselessly, and she was permanently exhausted. Brim wasn't there for her. 'My mother's post-war life was an anti-climax,' their son Peter remembers. 'For many years my father squashed her and treated her contemptuously.' Brim, a clever but unimaginative man, failed to appreciate his wife's love of poetry or take seriously her secret passion for writing. 'She was under his thumb. With her it was always, "Brim says . . ." or "Brim thinks . . ."'

After Cora Johnston's husband was torpedoed on his ship she got a life-saving posting in the Wrens. Struggling to salvage a future from the ruins, Cora fell under the spell of John Williams, her handsome office chief. He took her out, flattered her, and when he was posted to North Africa with the navy they corresponded. But even that wasn't enough to ward off the nervous breakdown which caught up with her at the end of the war. She was still only twenty-three. 'I didn't really know him all that well . . . I think the fact that I was deeply depressed and needed somebody may have had something to do with it.' In November 1945 they married – 'at that point I didn't know what a monster he was'. But over time the 'real' John emerged. He was caught fiddling naval accounts, became alcoholic and used physical threats to control Cora. Later there were repeated infidelities. Cora kept her head down, brought up two children and finally left him – in 1989.

In the summer following her return from Germany, Joy Taverner married Sergeant Ron Trindles. During her first year as his wife, Joy also began to find out what the man she had married was really like. And he was not, as it soon emerged, someone with whom she could share the trauma of her time in Belsen. The newly wed Trindles, like Pip Brimson, moved in upstairs above her family's tobacconist shop in west London. Joy now realised, in that confined space, that she and Ron were incompatible. Their whirlwind romance in Belgium in the early months of 1945 seemed impossibly distant. His charm and well-bred allure seemed all to have been a front. Joy – articulate, capable and imaginative – had married a man who appeared to have no interest in her, nor any initiative when it came to forging a career. In addition, his family from Northamptonshire turned out to be homespun and unsophisticated. Joy took on work to support him, but then she became pregnant. Their first child, Sue, was born in November 1946, by which time Joy was at the end of her tether. She told her mother she wanted to leave her husband. But there was to be no chink of support from that quarter. 'You've made your bed,' said Mrs Taverner, 'and you lie on it. There's never been a divorce in our family. That's not what this family does.' Joy caved in to circumstances. Ron got a passable, but badly paid job in an insurance company. She looked after her baby, cooked, and – in Sue's words – 'tried to do the wifely thing', but, defying convention, went back to work as a nurse as soon as she could. For Joy, marriage never delivered; her animals meant more to her. She had witnessed what men were capable of, and it is perhaps unsurprising that she remained sceptical of their worth. 'Men are what women marry,' she wrote once, in an angry diatribe entitled 'Useless Creation Man': 'they have two feet, two hands, and sometimes two women, but never more than one shilling or one idea at the same time . . . Making a husband out of a man . . . requires science, common sense, hope, and charity – mostly charity.'

In the end it was Ron who left. Unhappy but stoical, still haunted by the ghosts of Belsen, Joy shared her life with his for the best part of thirty years.

In the autumn of 1945, when Monica Littleboy encountered

George Symington after his return from Japan, her heart bled for the wreck that he had become: 'Misshapen, pitted, scarred . . . This was not the young man I had known.' But trauma and hardship had not changed George's feelings for her. These had kept him going and given him hope during his imprisonment; he persisted in seeking to revive their relationship. Gradually, compassion for his plight, and the rekindled flame of their old love displaced Monica's initial shock and disbelief. And she soon found that those emotions shackled her to him as securely as if they had never been apart. Becoming wife to a man whose health and mental wellbeing had been eroded by war was not how Monica had once envisaged her future, but their past passion now exerted an inescapable pull. Did she feel a pang at the loss of her new boyfriend, her job at the BBC? Would she regret agreeing to marry him? When the time came she realised that they were bound together not only by love, but by George's need, and her capacity to help him.

Here was the challenge given to me for peace time. Could I meet it . . . ? Could I keep this man alive and help him get back into his life again . . . ? The toughness I had acquired would be all his, the humanity he had so lacked in the war I had in full measure . . . I had not seen and done all that I had for nothing.

She laid her misgivings aside, said 'yes', and two months later they were married.

Almost immediately Monica realised how inadequate she was to her self-imposed task. George Symington had been offered a job with British Petroleum; she, as the conventional wife, would keep house, and they were lucky to find a one-room flatlet in central London. But George's ordeal as a prisoner-of-war had left him physically and mentally depleted. He had been starved and could not eat properly; was dizzy and uncoordinated. His emotions were chaotic and he would sometimes break down in tears impulsively. He suffered from intermittent but severe bouts of malaria, and when BP posted him to Iran for six months his health took a frightening dive. Left behind in England, Monica both feared for him, and missed him more than she could possibly have imagined. On his return she needed to draw on all her inner resources to care for him. There were times in those early days when she could not help contemplating what life might have been if George had been a well man:

My mind kept returning to my handsome, healthy boyfriends whom I had left behind. I was miserable [but] the warmth of my husband shone through from underneath and gave me courage to continue.

Time, and Monica's patient and practical approach gradually helped George to heal. Many years later Monica described herself as 'a very ordinary woman whose life was radically changed by the war'. In 1939 she had been 'Miss Average': middle-class, under-educated, lacking drive and looking no further than a qualification as a beautician. War had transformed her, giving her strength, confidence, patience, endurance and an overriding humanity.

Monica Symington was a woman who – like so many of her generation – expected little more from life than marriage and its natural by-products: a house, and a family. But Monica's marriage presented her with an unusually daunting challenge. Peace had no grand project to offer her, other than this: 'Could I keep this man alive and help him get back into his life again . . . ?' Returning him to normality was the goal to which she targeted her energies, and the achievement of George's renewal, through her dedication to him, was to give her own life happiness and meaning. Her story demonstrates the reconstructive power of love and compassion. And her rewards were their daughter, born in 1951, George's gratitude and steadily improving health, and the crowning success of his career as consultant to the House of Lords on energy, which were to bring his wife consolations and undreamt-of status and security.

Out of Uniform

Phyllis Noble was blessed with a string of handsome, healthy boyfriends. But marriage was not on her agenda in 1946. All her life Phyllis had wanted to travel; this desire had come before marriage, career, love or intellectual fulfilment. As a humble clerical employee, back in 1940, she had been struck with panic at the prospect – common to working-class girls like her – of a future confined to this island: 'Suppose I *do* just stick in England all my life? Suppose I do develop into yet another suburban matron . . .! What a bloody, damnable, awful, awful, awful thought!'

Though the war had failed her in this respect, as a WAAF she had at least got away from home. She felt she had come of age. But Phyllis's autonomy at this time had been bought at a high price. She had reached the end of the line with an assortment of experimental boyfriends, while Andrew, to whom she had lost her virginity, and whom she had always assumed would be there for her, called time on the relationship. With her love life lying broken in pieces around her, she sank into a profound depression. In the spring of 1946 Phyllis suffered a sudden and frightening physical collapse and was rushed into hospital with aggressive peritonitis. The doctors told her mother she was unlikely to survive. Six months later she was released, several stone lighter, but glad to be alive. Something told her that she would never be the same again. Was this the end of her youth? Had the war, which had given her so many varied and highly charged experiences, also robbed her of her own springtime?

In December 1946 Phyllis took her own first, shaky steps on the road to personal reinvention by undertaking her demobilisation formalities. There could be no new start until she was released from the WAAF. During her lengthy sick leave, she had been notionally 'posted' to a new station. She had to travel there and spend a miserable forty-eight hours unpicking her service identity: handing in kit, form-filling and reporting to the RAF medical officer. Then she was on the train back to London:

I had shed being a WAAF, along with the uniform, like an old skin I no longer needed. Whatever lay ahead, I felt that at last I was closer to a new beginning . . .

I had made up my mind that I was not going back to the kind of boring office life I had formerly known.

In 1941, Phyllis had been a bank clerk at the National Provincial Bank in Bishopsgate. Now, with social reformers around her seeking to reconstruct society from the war's ashes, it seemed to Phyllis Noble — and probably to innumerable twenty-four-year-olds like her — that her future was inextricably linked to the improvement of the post-war world. And after six months of hospitalisation, she also felt that she had a debt to repay. Secretly, she had begun to dream of becoming a doctor, which would mean another six years of study. Thus it was that early in January 1947 Phyllis set off, in a spirit of gratitude and civic idealism, to a government post-war advice centre in Tavistock Square.

The youngish adviser was kind and courteous. But, pressed to specify what kind of a future she had in mind, Phyllis's nerve failed her. The goal seemed impossibly distant and unrealistic. '"Well," I said cautiously, "I'm not really sure, but I don't want to work in an office, and I'd like to do something really worthwhile." "You mean like social work?" the youngish man asked. I grasped at the straw: "Yes. Well, that sort of thing."' Promptly, she was given forms to fill in and instructed to attend for interview in a fortnight's time, at the end of January.

And thus the map was laid down for a career path that, despite some deviations, would eventually bring her to authorship and academic recognition in the field of social sciences. The working-class girl from south London was to achieve social mobility in a way that, before the war, she could barely have imagined.

*

In 1946 more than twice as many passports were issued in the United Kingdom as ten years earlier: nearly 430,000. 'My generation was very much freer,' remembered pacifist Sheila Hails:

Very soon after the war [my husband and I] stayed on the Costa Brava, in a little pub, right on the beach. It was empty, almost desolate. There was a rough road to get there – you sent up clouds of dust. Today it's one of these seething holiday towns. But then there were only two other people there, and the people came out from the village and they danced on the beach! It was a wonderful place.

Frances Partridge was another pacifist who, as soon as possible after the war, opted to travel to a country untouched by conflict. In summer 1946 she and Ralph went with friends to Switzerland, where they found themselves welcomed with such forgotten luxuries as coupon-free bananas and croissants spread with lashings of butter and cherry jam, washed down with aromatic coffee. Learning more about the wartime work of the Red Cross, the Partridges delighted in the Swiss qualities of non-belligerence, humanity and civilisation, proof to Frances that the world could be a happy, benign place. 'How clean everything was!' she marvelled. 'Three weeks' bliss'.

Vera Lynn also had the opportunity to travel in Europe shortly after the war; she toured northern Europe and Scandinavia, performing live to audiences who during the war had secretly – on penalty of death – listened to her BBC broadcasts on radio sets hidden in cellars and hayricks. Vera was astonished not only by the warm welcome she received but also at how well the occupied countries were surviving:

The food! I remember my husband, my pianist and I, were in the hotel in Denmark, and they said 'Would you like some duck?' So we said 'Yes, that would be lovely.' Well, two ducks came on a platter! I said, 'Is that just for us, there's only three of us?' We couldn't believe our eyes! I thought – an occupied country can manage this! It was wonderful.

Such pleasures and material comforts made 'abroad' a tempting alternative to home and austerity.

WAAF Mike Morris was in Cairo when the war ended, still fancy-free and enjoying, more or less, an extended holiday. She was in no hurry to return to Berkshire, and – as her letters home and her 1946 diary chronicle – spent the next year making the most of the relaxations and privileges afforded to colonial expatriates in that seductive city. Mike's days were taken up with dress fittings, having her hair done at Georges' salon, shopping, sunbathing, playing tennis and enjoying the opera and theatre. As a high-ranking officer she frequented the Imperiale, the Medusa Bar, the Nile Club, the Gezira, and the Auberge des Pyramides and seems to have consumed copious rounds of drinks in all of them. In March she fitted in a short break in Italy to see Max, a boyfriend based in Positano, also making time for a shopping excursion to Rome for hats, jewellery and a fur coat. Romantically, she had no ties, nobody to answer to except herself. She conducted an enjoyable if risky balancing act between Max, James and the American Harald, all of whom were courting her, while she toyed, undecided as to which, if any, of them to marry.

Mike was reluctant to be tied down and equally reluctant to return home. Nevertheless, she bore her family's hardships in mind. They were so short of everything. She made a point of posting parcels of luxuries – easily available to her through the NAAFI, bazaar or black market – back to Berkshire:

I'm worried to see you had a further cut in fats – I'll buy some tins in town. I know the beef dripping was acceptable. I won't send butter, it's buffalo juice and horrid! If I see any really nice material I'll buy it for curtains and send it home on duty-free label. Measure up your and Daddy's room including bedspread.

If you want anything – Yardley, Lizzy Arden or Helena Rubinstein, it's only two-thirds of the price out here.

But at last the time came when she could remain no longer. 'My darling dearest,' she wrote to her mother on 25 May 1946: 'They say to say goodbye is to die a little . . . to-day I think I have died quite a lot. I have worked my last day as a WAAF intelligence officer . . . after nearly seven years it cannot help but hurt a little.'

There were farewell noggins all round before she embarked in June from Port Said on HMT *Corfu*. On the 14th they passed Gibraltar: 'Dear Mediterranean, I hope I'll see you again soon. I love your blue seas and skies so very much. Somehow, I feel very depressed. This awful feeling of "¿donde vamos?"' Two days later the ship docked in Southampton. She had missed the 6 June Victory celebrations by ten days, and disembarked in pouring rain to a country suffering from anti-climax. The euphoria of reunion with her beloved mother soon wore off; downpour was followed by a chill drizzle, 'very weary & oh, so cold', and her aloof father welcomed her in like manner, 'with a snarl'. By 21 June disappointment had set in, and she was utterly depressed:

Between you and me Diary – a Goddamn fool to leave Waaf-ing in Cairo for this.

Soon after, the entries thin out. In her own word, Mike 'mooched' – did nothing. Her main preoccupations during the early autumn of 1946 were her restless romance with Max, which she attempted to combine with the newer attentions of Geoffrey, and her application to work with the German Control Commission. At last in November her marching orders came through; by the end of the month she was only too happy to find her feet again in the Intelligence Division of the GCC at Herford in north-west Germany, followed soon after by a posting to Berlin.

Independence, worth, usefulness and the knowledge that her initiative and expertise in the German language were being recognised set Mike Morris back on course for a fruitful expatriate career in corporate welfare and personnel over the next twelve years. But the love affairs fizzled out. When Mike eventually married a divorced colonial officer in 1958 she gave up work and started to collect antique furniture. In later life she also took up ikebana (Japanese flower arranging) and became proficient enough in that art to offer demonstrations through the National Association of Flower Arrangers.

Vanquished

In November 1945 Anne Popham boarded a Dakota bound for Bünde, Westphalia, in northern Germany. Three long years had passed since Graham Bell's bomber had fallen out of the sky over Nottinghamshire. Time had eased the sharpest pain, but nobody had replaced Graham in Anne's heart. She forced herself to resume a normal life, accepting invitations among the cultured milieux in which she had previously moved. And it was at one of these post-war parties that a foppish young man approached her to see whether she would be interested in helping the work of the Monuments, Fine Arts and Archives Branch, which had been delegated to help restore the dispersed art treasures of Germany to their proper places, under the aegis of the Control Commission. As a German-speaker and former Courtauld graduate, Anne was ideally qualified.

Well, I thought I'd love to have this job. I was concerned about all the bombing and the destruction and the horror and the moving about of pictures and so forth. And I knew I had something of use and value to offer. I agreed to do it.

And so, late in 1945 – at a time when most Englishwomen, despite victory, were largely feeling crushed by unprecedented post-war gloom and hardship – Anne Popham found herself on a springboard to authority and future recognition. In post-war Germany she gave the best of herself, working to her strengths and finding in the meticulous task that now faced her a means of recovery, almost a salvation. Anne was given the rank of major, and based at headquarters in Bünde. The task of the five British zone regions was to reinstate the scattered or stolen contents of museums, churches and collections, to prevent the army's misuse and abuse of architectural gems and to implement reconstruction. Anne's job was to coordinate them. Her diary-cum-logbook of this work is a chronicle of frustrations and hindrances in the face of bureaucracy, broken-down phone lines and car engine failure. A few excerpts give a flavour of her busy working life in Bünde:

7th November 1945

Spent a lot of this afternoon trying to get through to Hamburg. Finally despaired & decided to wait till morning.

5th December 1945

Priority 1 call from Berlin. Public Safety have found a collection of pictures & require a monuments officer to inspect them immediately as it is a question of making an arrest.

8th December 1945

Chapter of accidents culminating in abandoning the Mercedes on the autobahn at 9pm . . . given a lift to Bünde, arriving 12 midnight.

Off-duty, Major Anne relaxed her business-like efficiency. Gone were the days when it was thought unseemly for women to drink alongside men. The mess was immensely sociable, and Steinhäger gin was twopence a glass:

One would go there before dinner and have one – and perhaps two, then a bottle of wine with dinner, followed by coffee and brandy. And sometimes the next day one would be pretty sorry for it . . . And then we used to go to Officers' clubs and go dancing.

Sometimes, things got out of hand:

Once when we were on a field trip we caught sight – through a window – of a very nice sofa, which we thought would be just right for our mess. And our charming Dutch padre, who was the ringleader, persuaded us to steal it. We got it into the car and drove it back to Bünde.

Together, work, fun, friendships and distance from England were healing the wounds. An awareness was growing in Anne, of her own worth: 'Until then I'd always assumed that everybody else knew best, but in Germany I realised that I was much better at a lot of things than other people, and that in some cases *I* knew best. I knew I was good at my job, and I felt valued and recognised too.' Anne was thirty now. She felt it unlikely that she would meet anyone to replace Graham, but she was convinced that, despite being a single woman, her work and life had significance.

The heartbreak had receded, the bad days were melting into the past. And if Anne needed any further reminder that life could be a lot worse, she had only to step outside the undamaged military enclave in which her Bünde HQ was situated:

I went to Hamburg. It was destroyed – absolutely flattened, worse than Berlin. Acres of debris. And you sometimes saw somebody sort of creeping out of a hole – appearing like some phantom from the vast wasteland of rubble. It was a terrifying sight – how had these people not been killed? How did they even exist? They'd certainly got it as bad as we had, if not worse. This was far worse than England . . . I was glad the war was over, but I didn't feel any sense of glory at all.

Confronted by such evident suffering, the triumphalism of the victor seemed an alien emotion – at least to this particular young woman. Anne couldn't comprehend her male colleagues' punitive attitude to the Germans. Her fellow officers seemed filled with anger. One day she invited Graf Metternich, the German Director of Monuments and Fine Arts, 'not a Nazi, but a very civilised, educated man', to discuss their mutual concerns. Later, she dined with the Graf in the British officers' mess and was dismayed to see a contingent rise and leave the room in protest at his presence. On another occasion, she was travelling with one of her colleagues when a German pedestrian accidentally collided with her on a railway platform. Her colleague flew into a rage with the man, abusing him roundly for not treating the Fräulein Major with proper respect. Anne conceded that the men had, perhaps, more reason to feel anger against the enemy: 'They'd been through the war in a way that I hadn't – though goodness knows us civilians got it almost as badly.' But to her it seemed so unnecessary, with the German nation on its knees, for these male officers to keep on kicking their victims, as if to continue proving that they were top dog. Despite a visit to Belsen, all Anne's instincts tended towards mercy and reconciliation with their one-time enemies.

When QA Lorna Bradey was posted to Germany in 1947, she too felt dazed by the level of suffering and humiliation she encountered. Lorna was sent to the British Military Hospital at Wuppertal.

The stench of decay as we drove through the town was unimaginable. With dismay I saw total destruction around ... I could read the hate on the people's white drawn faces. Some spat at us.

As winter approached hunger eclipsed every other need:

The Germans would do anything for food and stealing was rife ... The shops were boarded up and empty; only the ruins and dejected people creeping about ... One felt helpless – the conquered race.

Later, posted to another military hospital at Spandau outside Berlin, Lorna herself went hungry after the Soviet powers severed communications into the city. British, French and Americans organising the Berlin airlift ('Operation Victuals') were drawn together in adversity. Staff and patients alike kept warm by burning scavenged firewood, and food was short. The hospital admitted all patients except Russians. For Lorna, it was 'a strangely happy time', when, undeterred by international tensions, the nurses' off-duty hours were spent dancing at the French club at Lake Wannsee – 'tightening our belts'.

Humanity is not exclusive to women, nor were they all insensible to the sweet taste of victory. But the artist Frances Faviell was another young woman, like Lorna Bradey and Anne Popham, whose time in post-war Germany caused her to ponder the relationship between victor and vanquished, as well as between men and women. Frances had experienced the worst that the London Blitz could throw at her; being lowered into a bomb crater to bring help to a horribly mutilated victim was an experience that remained indelibly engraved on her memory. And she and her husband, Richard, had nearly been buried alive under the ruins of their flat. In 1941 their son John was born. Now, in the autumn of 1946, the Parker family decamped to Berlin.

Eighteen months earlier, in April 1945, Berlin had been pounded by Russian bombs. Civilians who tried to surrender or escape from inevitable doom were rounded up by the SS and hanged from lamp-posts. The Russian army entered the city. Out of control, its soldiers looted every item of property they could lay hands on, then, like animals, rampaged through the streets looking for women. It is estimated that up to 130,000 women were raped in Berlin in 1945. Frances had last visited Germany's capital in 1938. Half of it now lay in dust:

The complete and utter devastation of Berlin had shaken me profoundly. Nothing . . . had prepared one for the dead horror of this city.

In 1946, Richard Parker's job was to assist in implementing reconstruction and reparations in the British zone; meanwhile, Frances helped out at the improvised school set up for the children of the occupying troops. She employed an attractive but reserved young German woman named Lotte to look after five-year-old John in her absence. One afternoon she returned to find Lotte reading aloud to the little boy, who was miserable with a heavy cold. Touched by the young woman's intimate heed for him, Frances made an effort to draw her into conversation. What had it been like, she asked Lotte, that April, before the capitulation? 'For answer she fetched her diary for the months of April and May 1945.'

Frances sat down to read. The pages covered the dreadful final days of the Reich, that time of rumours, broadcasts and aching fear, when the people of Berlin began to realise that the war would be lost. Lotte described how she had hidden in a dark cellar, listening to the awful bombardment, emerging only to forage for food. Horrors piled up. The soldiers – 'filthy Mongol troops' – were more like murderers and bandits than military men. Filled with rage and malevolence against the German race, they had found Lotte and raped her, 'not once . . . but time after time'. She was one among the thousands of women, from young girls to grandmothers, who were seized and drunkenly forced into sex:

women with their children clinging in terror to their skirts, and young women held by one man while another took his pleasure . . . Every date and detail was set down in pencil – she had written it by the light of her torch.

It was one of the most horrible documents I had ever read, and I felt icy cold as I put it down.

A barrier broken between them, Frances now persuaded Lotte to talk more about her brutal ordeal. Further horrors emerged; she trembled violently and went white. Time would surely dull the pain, suggested Frances, even if it could never erase the experience. There was a chilling dignity in Lotte's reply: 'What does it matter what happened to me – we have lost the war!'

Lotte's brief story, which first appeared in print in Frances Faviell's 1954 memoir about her time in Berlin, offers a glimpse of the dreadful sufferings of Germany's female civilians. The following year the world was presented with a fuller female perspective on the sack of the city, when *A Woman in Berlin*, the anonymous diary of a woman journalist, covering the same period from April to June 1945, was first published in Britain. The diarist, an educated and liberal thirty-four-year-old, reflected on the collapse of Nazism as Zhukov's army rolled towards the capital:

These days I keep noticing how my feelings towards men – and the feelings of all the other women – are changing. We feel sorry for them; they seem so miserable and powerless. The weaker sex. Deep down we women are experiencing a kind of collective disappointment. The Nazi world – ruled by men, glorifying the strong man – is beginning to crumble, and with it the myth of 'Man'. In earlier wars men could claim that the privilege of killing and being killed for the fatherland was theirs and theirs alone. Today, we women, too, have a share. That has transformed us, emboldened us. Among the many defeats at the end of this war is the defeat of the male sex.

This German woman, experiencing the collapse of the Nazi edifice at first hand, put into words a deep truth about the wider world of men. They were addicted to control and domination, enslaved to the wielding of weapons; as Virginia Woolf had written, there was 'a subconscious Hitlerism in the hearts of men'. Without their guns and jackboots, they were left impotent and emasculated, supplicants and beggars.

But if she hoped that the demise of Nazism also spelled an end to male brutality, disillusionment was to be rapid. The day after she wrote that entry the Russians arrived in Berlin. Two soldiers lay in wait for her, tore off her underclothes, and forced her to the ground. Over the next two months there would be more; she only survived to tell the tale through a combination of astuteness, luck and intelligent instinct.

Thus, as this diary shows and as the appalled and awestruck Frances Parker discovered from Lotte's trembling confession, the onslaught of the victorious nations was accompanied by a wave of unprecedented violence against women. It was as if the war's calamitous endgame demanded a reassertion by men of their former ascendancy, an implacable conquest by the phallus. Lest war prove too liberating, too emancipating for women, they must be suppressed, subjugated and quelled to the last gasp.

Berlin *in extremis* illustrates the destruction of a male paradigm, as the German Reich imploded; but it also exposes with horrifying clarity the regeneration of violence, brutality and cruelty among men hell-bent on regaining sexual control. In Germany, the publication of the anonymous woman's diary would prove controversial in a nation deeply disturbed by the rapes. The book was denounced as a slur on German womankind; their men felt compromised and shamed, and the subject of the mass rapes remained largely taboo. Male authority was to rest largely unchallenged until another generation of women took their protest on to the streets twenty-five years later.

★

The temperature was dropping. By the time Phyllis Noble returned to have her social work interview at the end of January, Tavistock Square was covered in a blanket of snow. It was the beginning of Britain's worst winter in over fifty years.

Across the country the freeze had set in, a relentless north-east wind was blowing, and blizzards were making headlines: 'MORE CONTINUOUS SNOW; UNBROKEN FROST – COLDEST FEBRUARY DAY FOR YEARS; COLD SPELL TO CONTINUE – FIFTEEN DAYS WITHOUT SUNSHINE'. The sea froze at Margate and icebergs were seen off the Norfolk coast. As if austerity hadn't taken a severe enough toll on the country already, Britain now had to face serious crises in transport, fuel and food supply.

Maggie Joy Blunt went shopping in Windsor: 'it was really frightful, just made you want to curl up & die'. Back in her cottage in Slough, she relit the kitchen fire and started to thaw out, but decided not to take her coat off.

'Well, what's the decision – a fire now, or plum jam next summer?'
Winter 1947: a new ice age.

February 1st 1947

In the bedroom . . . the water in washstand jug has frozen solid, right to the bottom.

I am wearing thick woollen vest, rubber roll-on, wool pantees, stockings, thick long-sleeved wool sweater, slacks, jackets, scarf & 2 pairs woollen socks – & am just about comfortable.

February 24th

Last night the coldest we've had – I could feel my nose freezing in bed.

Though the miners went into overdrive to produce more fuel, frozen pitheads and disrupted coal distribution affected supply. Restrictions were enforced and hardship stories abounded; the nation shivered as electricity was cut off for five hours in every twenty-four, and it began to feel like a return to the blackout. Radio programmes were suspended, newspapers reduced in size, and people had to go for brisk walks, stand about in shops or go to bed in order not to freeze. Upper-class families who felt kitchen life to be beneath their dignity were forced to swallow their pride; it was the only warm room in the house. The government applied a stern utility ethos to consumption regarded as wasteful. Bakers were prohibited from making jam puffs; anyone wanting a wedding cake must apply for a permit. For families with babies washing and drying nappies was a nightmare, but there was an unexpected dimension to the crisis when thousands of them found that their newborn infants could not be christened, and would have to wait, nameless, until the snow thawed around cut-off churches. The *Daily Mirror* offered suggestions for do-it-yourself baptisms, but advised 'if you are in doubt, send for the parson'.

Margaret Herbertson, who had pursued her dream of an Oxford education once the war was over, was there studying for a Diploma in Social Studies that winter. Getting to lectures down the Iffley Road was fraught with peril, as her bicycle skidded and she lived in fear of falling off in the path of an oncoming bus.

I used to walk down to the Bodleian Library to keep warm. But everyone had had the same idea, and there weren't enough chairs, so I used to sit on the floor and work.

The Thames iced up, and Port Meadow flooded and then froze, so people skated. It was very picturesque – but it was hellish actually.

Thrifty Nella Last reverted straight back into wartime mode and took to cooking all her husband's meals on the hob of the dining-room fire. News of the electricity cuts made her all the more determined to bake and hoard what she could. On the night of 26 February she lay awake and listened to 'the heavy swish of snow'. In the morning drifts lay mounded up to the top of the garden fence at 9 Ilkley Road. Will Last took the broom and shovel to dig his way out to the bus stop. On 7 March another storm came in. It froze. A week later there were yet more heavy falls on top of the packed ice. Down town, cold, angry women stood in queues in inadequate footwear.

Maggie Joy Blunt struggled to be thankful for her warm clothes and rubber bootees, but she was not alone in finding the winter of 1947 the most trying time in living memory. 'Grumbles on every side,' she wrote in her diary. 'A bitter time & with the bad weather, to many it seems "worse than the war".'

★

Frances Faviell's account of that winter in Berlin makes British hardship seem light by comparison. Despite the non-fraternisation rules imposed on the British, she was in a position both to observe and alleviate the dreadful sufferings of Germany's defeated capital.

Berliners told each other that the Russians had brought their Siberian winter with them. 'One went to bed with the two words, Cold, Hunger, ringing in one's ears, and awoke to them again in the morning.' Frances saw children tearing at each other, fighting for the scraps in Allied dustbins, their limbs chapped and chilblained. The city was horrified to hear of a train arriving at the British zonal frontier carrying sixteen corpses. They were German people being repatriated from Poland who had died of cold en route. The only currency that would purchase food was cigarettes, and there was only one way – for a young or pretty woman – to earn cigarettes.

The British, Russian and American occupiers had their own supplies, and seemed to feel no scruples about giving lavish dances and dinners. Frances felt agonised by the uninhibited consumption that went on at such events. Wasn't there something hideous about putting on evening dress and dinner suits to attend them in a city that was starving? One night, when the temperature was at nearly its lowest point that winter, the Russians invited representatives of all the other powers to a ball in the Allied Control Administration building. Bands played; there were mountains of food and endless drink, served by ranks of young German waitresses in white cotton gloves. The glittering rooms were filled with banks of hothouse flowers. Frances looked around her, staggered. How could she dance, knowing that the cost of the flowers alone would have fed the waitresses and all their families? Just the fuel needed to grow those perfumed lilies could have saved hundreds of lives. In the early hours Richard and Frances escaped. Outside in the biting cold an ancient man with a piece of sacking tied round his head was stumbling around looking for discarded cigarette butts, the image of loss. 'The snow gave an air of death to everything, as if the ball, still going on in the brilliantly lighted building, was a pavane for the dead of this ghost-haunted city.'

Next morning, walking in the Grunewald, Frances found a frozen body under a bush, dark-blue in colour, and absolutely stiff. By 6 January the thermometer had dropped again to minus thirty-six degrees

Celsius. Daily, corpses of frozen children were being brought into the Kinderklinik. The non-fraternisation rules were relaxed where children were concerned, and Frances visited the clinic to see for herself. The doctors there were desperate for penicillin, bandages, clothes and blankets for the children. Frances did what she could, writing to the *Daily Telegraph* appealing for help, and was moved at the generosity of hundreds of British women who responded with parcels of baby clothes and other supplies. At home too, nobody was turned away without a piece of bread and a cup of the soup that Lotte now kept permanently simmering on the stove. But despair ate at her:

Death, death, death! It was nothing else. I hated the snow. It carried for me the dirge of all that is gay, coloured and vital. It brought in its white shroud the winding sheet for thousands that winter. I wanted to go home – back to London – it was almost as cold there, but people were not dying of hunger.

Frances Faviell learned much during her time in Berlin. In her memoir of that period she wrote about the terrible face of defeat, about the responsibilities that victory brought with it, and about our common humanity. Her determination to persist in befriending the ruined Germans also brought her up against some deeply uncomfortable truths regarding sex roles in the shattered Nazi state. Frances had become close to a Berlin family named the Altmanns. Frau Altmann, deeply religious and conventional, was principally concerned for her menfolk: of her two sons one was missing in Russia after Stalingrad, the other was a wastrel who had switched allegiance from the Hitler Youth to the Communists. Once prosperous, their stocks and shares had all gone, and her frail and elderly husband could no longer work.

The couple now unwittingly owed their lives to their daughters. The elder one, Ursula, brought in money and food through prostitution and the black market; she too had been raped by the Russians. Lilli, the younger, was a ballerina at the Staatsoper. But in the depths of January Herr Altmann died of cold and heart failure. Frau Altmann, numbed with grief, could not see that her daughters were also vulnerable. As young women their duty, in her eyes, was to their father and brothers. 'German women are brought up to worship the male members of the family.' In Frau Altmann's world, no man ever helped in the house, and he had the first call on every comfort. She fatally neglected her daughters, failing to notice their hollow-eyed hunger, unobservant of Lilli's pallor and ill-health. And soon after the death of her father, Lilli too died, weak and starving as she was, from a botched abortion; the father of her unborn child had been a Russian officer.

Frances pondered the need of German women to hero-worship the supreme male. Wasn't it a short but inevitable step for pre-war hausfraus like Frau Altmann - who unhesitatingly deferred to and idolised their menfolk – into the condoning of Nazism? Women who believed that their role was to be abject and submissive must surely share the responsibility for Fascism. She also noted – in Lotte and her other servant Gisela – an unquestioning observance of authority that unnerved her. Lotte's comment on the hanging of the Nazi war criminals absolved them of responsibility: 'The men had only been doing what they had been ordered to do,' she said. Lotte, like all Germans under instruction, carried out her orders to the letter. It amounted to a pitiless streak.

In addition, Frances's rescue missions – sometimes bringing home filthy, sick and lousy vagrants – were not popular with her squeamish, house-proud maids. She found their disgust disturbing. Had this passion for cleansing led to Belsen, to Buchenwald? Had the women of this country recognised, in Hitler's potent leadership, a form of domination that answered some very basic psychic needs: purity, obedience and sexual subordination? But when Frances sought answers it was male conditioning that stared her in the face, irrespective of nationality. The window of her apartment block overlooked a bomb site. Eight young boys, including John, her little son, were playing there:

Bang! Bang! Bang! they were shouting as they took aim at each other, and one after another would fall to the ground and feign death. Useless to take away the pistols – they found more, and the endless battles went on – every day our block echoed to the Bang! Bang! Bang! and their shouts. Any kind of toy weapons were forbidden by the Allies to the German children who looked on in envy and admiration at the British ones. I felt sick suddenly.

Hate, and the urge to kill or destroy, it seemed to her, were born not out of allegiance to union flags, hammers and sickles or swastikas, but out of the profoundest depths of male identity. Man's fundamental need for a weapon seemed ineradicable. Had she lived, Virginia Woolf's hopes that 'Hitlerism' might be conquered if man could be 'compensated for the loss of his gun' would have been disappointed, just as the anonymous woman journalist who believed she was seeing the Nazi myth crumble - and with it the 'myth of "Man"' - might well have joined Frances Parker in feeling sickened at the spectacle of a new generation of violence playing among the ruins.

In Berlin, in 1947, what possible hope could one feel for the future?

13　There'll Be Bluebirds

Flower Women

Will women ever be satisfied? Will a day come when there is no con-flict for us between our ambitions and our nesting instincts? Must choice always mean sacrifice? The women who lived through the decade covered by this book learned the hardest lessons of history about strength, self-determination, sacrifice and freedom. Women had proved to themselves that they possessed equal competence with men. If only to themselves, they had exploded the inequality myth. But after six tumultuous years, the desire to retreat from the fight was often stronger than the urge to press unpalatable claims. They wanted a quiet life.

'I'm not clever beyond homely things,' wrote Nella Last in her October 1947 diary, 'but if I'd not the delight in a well-cooked and -served meal, and well-kept house and my odds and ends of sewing, I would have nothing to make me happy at all now.' On the 28th she noted:

My husband says sometimes how lucky he is because I'm always 'serene and calm' and 'there's always home, thank God'.

The dollies and soft toys she made gave her intense joy.

If peace, for women like her, meant sewing stuffed rabbits by a cosy fireside, the spreading of a clean tablecloth and a husband's grat-itude, then surely they had earned it.

★

While Britain did its best to keep warm during the freezing winter of 1947, the Royal Family were visiting South Africa; the newspapers gave their trip exhaustive coverage. Back home, the March thaw brought with it catastrophic floods. Crops, vehicles, pets and ration books were washed away when rivers across the country burst their banks. With the waters lapping around their sitting-room suites and kitchen cupboards, East Enders teamed up 'in the spirit of the Blitz' to rescue furniture and belongings from ground floors.

But floods and austerity hadn't quenched our appetite for hearing about the lifestyles of the ruling class. Mary Grieve, the editor of *Woman* magazine, knew that her readership was in thrall to the House of Windsor and its doings: 'In the late forties the devotion to the Throne . . . built up into a fever of intensity.' Six years of hardship unleashed pent-up longings for an infusion of glamour into our grey lives. Tiaras, ostrich feathers and a hint of royal romance tapped into the yearnings of a public starved of dreams, and nostalgic for a time when the world had seemed a safer place. Princesses on horseback and kings on thrones represented a fast-disappearing world of order, security and Empire.

On 10 July suggestions of wedding bells became a delicious certainty when Princess Elizabeth's betrothal to Lieutenant Philip Mountbatten was announced by the Palace. 'Enthusiasm and affection boiled over,' wrote Mary Grieve. 'In 1947 the country needed something to rejoice about,' and next day thousands waited all afternoon outside Buckingham Palace for the young couple to emerge on to the balcony.

Clement Attlee's post-war government had embarked on an ambitious programme of reconstruction, social welfare and redistribution. There was no doubt in the minds of either the middle classes or the rich that their comforts were being eroded not just by strikes, power cuts and burst pipes, but by Labour's fiscal policies, designed to penalise the wealthy at rates of up to 95 per cent. 'The rich could not pay more, because with the present taxation no rich were left,' moaned Ursula Bloom.

But who would have guessed that the upper classes were feeling the pinch? In 1947, when Buckingham Palace announced that presentations were to be revived after the wartime suspension, no fewer than 20,000 debutantes were awaiting the summons to curtsey to their Majesties. Frances Campbell-Preston's family held an austerity dance for her sister Laura. Her father got in cider cup from the local pub landlord ('I told him to put in very little gin'), someone, somehow, found enough sugar to whip up cakes, and armfuls of flowers were brought in from the garden. Though guests came in dresses run up from muslin curtains it was a huge success, with Princess Elizabeth herself leading the conga.

'The war certainly taught us to improvise,' recalled Barbara Cartland in her memoir *The Years of Opportunity*. Her own experience in recycling wedding dresses for Service brides served her well when her daughter Raine was due to be presented at Court in spring 1947. Typically, she managed to lay hands on a vintage Molyneux frock for this occasion. But Raine had a whole season of balls ahead of her, and Barbara was determined that her daughter should star. Undeterred by the impossibility of buying large quantities of fabric in Britain, Barbara holidayed in Switzerland ahead of the Queen Charlotte Ball and managed to bring back several bolts of white tulle, which she had made up into a spectacular full-skirted gown in the style of the French Empress Eugénie. A blue taffeta dress, bought for £3 from a school friend and embellished by her mother with a deep hem of velvet and off-coupon artificial flowers, also earned her rapturous compliments.

Indeed, anyone who had hoped that the war would, overnight, level out our caste system had not reckoned with those centuries of entrenched privilege. Memories of desert warfare, death camps and troop ships were banished by nurses and FANYs alike; there were those among them who retreated to the shires, changed each evening into low-cut dresses and jewels, to be waited on by liveried footmen. 'Allowing for the general impoverishment,' commented George Orwell in 1946, 'the upper classes are still living their accustomed life.'

*

Britain had voted in a Labour government, but it seemed, by tacit consensus, that even under socialism the rich man – and woman – would remain in her castle, the poor woman at her kitchen sink. After such a war, who wanted revolution? In 1948 the sociologist Pearl Jephcott interviewed a sample of young, single, northern, working-class girls about their aspirations:

Q. Do you think a lot about any one thing today?
A. Yes, getting married.

Jephcott's conclusions were unedifying:

The majority regard 23 or 24 as zero hour as far as matrimony is concerned . . .

Practically every girl says that she will want to give up her job when she gets married.

On the whole work appears to call forth no strong emotions, only a feeling of relief at the end of the day, when you are rid of it and free to do what you like . . . They seem to have few ambitions which relate to their work.

Jephcott's study concluded that what changes there were, were subtle and small. Anyone who had expected, or feared, that the war would ignite a feminist revolution could be comforted by the thought that the nation's women were not about to mount the barricades.

Almost two years after its end, Nella Last began to assess what 'coming through' the war meant for women like her. She would have agreed with Pearl Jephcott that what changes there were were modest ones. For example, it was now more acceptable for women to brave the world on their own. Nella thought back to when her old Aunt Sarah, who had been widowed, had decided she wanted to live alone and refused a home with her relatives. There had been amazed shock in the family – it was just unthinkable, in those days, for a woman to set herself up independently. Today, such an attitude seemed archaic. 'Everyone asks more of life and that they should be let to work out things for themselves.'

In May 1947, in fulfilment of her own words, Nella planned a holiday – by herself. She would visit her son and daughter-in-law in Northern Ireland. Her husband would not be left to fend alone though; Aunt Eliza would cook Will Last's lunches while she was away and feed the cat. Will refused to make any contribution towards her jaunt, so Nella applied for a travel permit and withdrew £10 from her bank. The journey involved a train to Liverpool, connection to Speke airport, and a flight – her first – to Belfast.

My extra holiday is my own affair. When I felt the surge of joy run through my veins, I thought surprisedly that I'm not as old as I thought, that it's rather the monotony of my life that tires and ages me.

Afterwards 'I couldn't have had a better break,' was the verdict.

Monotony, austerity and stewed whalemeat continued to be everyday realities in 1947, but a nation of war-weary women had begun to feel, like Nella Last, that they had earned a little pleasure. The continued threat of economic strictures hung over the nation, but after six years of nervous tension, trauma and hardship it was time to slow down, to step off the treadmill. In compensation for the brutal winter, the summer of 1947 was long and hot, a time conducive to leisure and relaxation.

I am having a deliberately, deliciously idle afternoon on my bed. Weather is perfect; wonderful, brilliant, golden days. Why can't our summers *always* be like this?

wrote Maggie Joy Blunt on 13 August. And on the 17th:

'The crisis – where is the crisis?' asks the *Observer*. 'With Parliament dispersed, Ministers going on holiday – and the country bathed in a drowse of August sunshine . . .' Why should I worry about a crisis?

On a sunny August day all Maggie – and thousands like her – wanted was to be able to pause, forget and, as far as possible, bring back those happy remembered days before the bombs and sirens shattered their peace for ever.

Legislation had been introduced entitling workers to an annual paid holiday, and most of them took it that year in Britain, whether hiking in the fells or staying in a Blackpool boarding house, or at a Pontin's, Warners or Butlins holiday camp in the popular resorts of Skegness, Pwllheli or Hayling Island. The holiday-camp phenomenon was huge. One young working girl who went with her family to a Warners camp at this time recalled the mounting excitement as the family journeyed from Leicester, via Victoria Station (crammed with holiday-makers heading south) to Hayling Island. For this fifteen-year-old every detail remained impressed on her memory, from the orderly flower-beds, to the bottle-green chalets with their white window-frames, to the cheery waitresses. After long, happy days on the beach, you could take part in obstacle races, donkey derbys, fancy-dress and knobbly-knees competitions or the drag contest held on 'Topsy Turvy night' – it was all 'clean fun'. The evening's entertainment ended with the singing of 'Goodnight Campers' to the tune of 'Goodnight Sweetheart'. 'We had not had so much fun for years.'

At the other end of the social scale Glyndebourne, the originator (in 1934) of the 'country-house opera', was back in production by the summer of 1947 after a wartime interval when its stately interiors were made over to evacuees. Now Victoria Station also offered the spectacle – at 2.45 in the afternoon – of a host of opera-lovers board-ing the Eastbourne train in full-length evening dress and mink stoles rescued from their wartime mothballs. The hit of the season was the lustrous contralto Kathleen Ferrier, in Grecian tunic and bay leaves, singing the title role in Gluck's *Orfeo*. Audiences were offered a spe-cial cocktail named after her, a hideous-sounding concoction of crème de menthe, brandy and lime juice. All was not austerity.

And there were other signs of a returning light-heartedness, even at this time of generalised hardship. On 28 August the *Daily Graphic* sent its female staff out on an assignment headlined 'WOMEN WITH THEIR EYES OPEN', to report on whatever they saw that raised their spirits:

– the nonchalant way people eat peaches at five for a shilling as if they had never been a luxury . . .

 – a glimpse of the screen star Margot Grahame wearing earrings orna-mented with her initials . . .

 – the Oxford-street fashion parade of gay summer dresses and smart shoes that was a triumph over austerity. Nearly all the girls had longer skirts – about two inches below the knee. Very attractive.

*

Two whole inches below the knee? Could it be that those fabric-skimping, miserly, military, masculine, so-called styles which had defeminised so many fashion-conscious women were finally to be consigned to history?

The New Look, which filtered gradually across to these shores in 1947, was the vision of fashion designer Christian Dior – a man whose astute commercial instincts were equalled only by his roman-ticism and intuitive understanding of the 1940s *Zeitgeist*. On 12 February 1947, in the midst of the bleakest winter in living memory, Dior's new couture house released a collection featuring sumptu-ously billowing skirts swirling below waspy waists, with curved shoulders, fluttering bows and generous bosoms, requiring up to 40 metres of material to create. Dior, a keen gardener all his life, named his new collection '*Corolle*', a botanical term which means the crown of petals encircling a flower's centre. His dream was nothing less than the reinvention of womankind as flowers in bloom: Eden regained.

After six years of khaki battledress, masculine overalls, hair above the collar, queue misery and utility furniture, nothing could have tapped more successfully into women's deepest longings for a return to femininity.

But over the summer and autumn of 1947, as skirts crept inexorably longer, alarm mounted. Should we refuse to manufacture the New Look on the grounds that it was a shameful waste of fabric and against the national interest, as President of the Board of Trade Sir Stafford Cripps advocated, or would that – as Anne Scott-James, editor of *Harper's Bazaar* insisted – be export suicide? That October, clothing coupons were cut to four a month. 'Much as the average woman in this country may want to follow present-day fashions, it is quite impossible for her to do so,' wrote one lady to *The Times*.

Feeling like top dog in Dior's New Look. Punch, *1948.*

Whether or not women *could* adopt the look, the question remained as to whether they *should*. For feminists, the New Look seemed to be a visible intent to turn the clock back on emancipation. The war had offered women so many freedoms; wearing uniform had given them pride and independence. So what did Monsieur Dior think he was doing by padding out their bosoms, strangling their waists and send-

ing them tottering out into the streets hampered by such oceans of
surging fabric that they could barely walk, let alone run for a bus or
climb aboard a train? He was out of touch with the modern world,
claimed MP Mabel Ridealgh: 'Women today are taking a larger part
in the happenings of the world and the New Look is too reminiscent
of a caged bird's attitude.'

Mrs Ridealgh had a point. Dior was in love with *La Belle Epoque*,
and there is an argument that the 'New' Look was, in reality, una-
shamedly nostalgic and backward-looking; of a piece, in fact, with
the submissive, *Brief Encounter* mentality which so gripped British
womanhood at that time.★ For thousands of harassed, dowdy
women who had spent blacked-out evenings reading the popular
romances of Georgette Heyer, the New Look spoke of a more gracious time: a bygone age when waists were tiny and frocks were
floaty, when men helped tender damsels in and out of carriages. 'Oh
yes, I'd have liked to have been born in the age when they wore
crinolines . . . so lovely,' sighs Thelma Rendle (née Ryder). The
1940s were discovering a 'New', 'Old' Look: one which had nothing
to do with square-bashing or esprit de corps, and everything to do
with romanticism and femininity. It was unequivocally gorgeous –
and Britain's women loved it.

Shirley Goodhart was one. Jack had found work in Leeds; to her
joy she had become pregnant in the spring of 1947 and gave birth to
a baby girl in January 1948. As soon as she was up and about, and
relieved to be finally out of smocks, she wheeled the pram down into
Leeds city centre to look for 'new-style clothes'. She was disappointed to find the fuller-skirted models weren't yet available – 'most
shops still selling off old styles'. But, undaunted, she bought fabric
and a cheap paper pattern inspired by Dior and got out her scissors.

★ In *Austerity Britain* (2007), David Kynaston airs the opposing argument, put forward by cultural historian Angela Partington, that the New Look made a defiant
statement, that it was 'stroppy', feisty and mould-breaking. Partington compares
its 'strong colours [and] severe shapes' with the 'twee . . . sensible' utility styles of
the earlier 1940s and points out that many working-class women subverted the
'designer' New Look to match their own requirements. But to describe the curva-
ceous silhouettes of 1947-8 as 'severe' is surely stretching a point, while 'twee'
doesn't exactly sum up – to me anyway - the skimpiness and rigidity of wartime
styles.

February 2nd 1948

Helen is 4 weeks old today. Found time to continue making my new dress, and put it all together ready for trying on. I thought that it was supposed to be 'new length' but I find that I shall have to put a false hem in order to make it long enough.

With her figure back in trim, Shirley was in the forefront when the New Look hit the Leeds shops in April:

April 23rd

I've bought a new suit; the third 'new style' item in my wardrobe. There is an increasing minority of 'new style' among the women in Leeds.

The controversy surrounding the New Look was a miniature version of the greater debate, which would not die down, around the place of women in post-war Britain. Fashion, or freedom? Wives, or career women? Flowers, or feminists? But the New Look's brief sway was, for those who wore it and loved it, an uplifting interlude. It was a love affair with hope, and a covenant from the Great God Fashion that, though food and fuel were short, and though ice and floods might engulf the nation, a full feminine skirt promised that all might still be well with the world.

A Love Match

The hot summer of 1947, followed by an equally glorious (for some) royal wedding, made the belt-tightening and gloom of that year a little more bearable. Attlee's government needed all the help it could get that August, when – owing to an export–import gap now estimated at £600 million – it was forced to announce that the country was back to a wartime economy, that tea and meat rations were to be cut, pleasure motoring would be abolished, and foreign travel suspended. The Empire, too, was falling victim to financial retrenchments. On 15 August 1947 the independence of India – the 'jewel in the crown' – was made effective. International anxieties resurfaced as the sinister terminology of the Cold War gained currency. Britain was weak and poor, its ancient might overshadowed by new powers.

Anything that helped boost morale was welcome: a wonderful

exhibition of French tapestries at the Victoria and Albert Museum was a highlight of the year for art-lovers. Ealing Studios started production of a run of heart-warming comedies, beginning with *Hue and Cry*, filmed on location in bomb-scarred London. Cambridge won the Boat Race and finally admitted women to full membership of the University. The shops were starting to stock expensive luxury goods again: artificial flowers, handbags and cosmetics.

But sometimes it was hard to endure the de-energising diet. Shirley Goodhart found herself seized by longings for 'large helpings of meat', while poor Maggie Joy Blunt wrote a frenzied, mouth-watering paean to her favourite dishes of hallowed memory:

Oh, those pre-war days! . . . Foie gras with whipped cream & hard-boiled egg set in aspic with green peas – Pineapple cream made with real fruit – strawberry meringue pudding . . . Veal cutlets rolled in beaten egg & grated cheese & grilled . . . Asparagus . . . I'm dribbling now.

In September you could still bathe in the sea, and October saw a beautiful Indian summer – which perhaps compensated for the burdensome cut in the bacon ration, the railway ticket price rise, the selling of Government gold reserves to ease the debt and the worrying news that India and Pakistan were now at war.

20 November 1947 was overcast and damp. The romantic novelist Miss Florence Speed was glad, however, that it didn't rain. She and her sister Mabel listened on the wireless to the wedding ceremony of Princess Elizabeth and Lieutenant Philip Mountbatten and, along with millions of listeners worldwide, heard the pair make their vows before the altar of Westminster Abbey.

The whole thing was very moving. Mabel said 'Why do these things always bring tears to our eyes?'
Why? But it did . . .
At dinner we had a little sherry to drink the health of bride & groom.

On that grey day, Britain's royal nuptials were a pageant of colour and hope, and a reminder that wars might come and go, but the magnificent traditions that made Britain great hadn't changed. Dabbing their eyes, the two spinsters Florence and Mabel Speed felt uplifted and moved beyond expression. Princess Elizabeth's big day locked down a prototype of aspirational post-war womanhood: follow my example, the occasion seemed to say, and catch your Prince.

But average, imperfect young women like Doffy Brewer were simply outclassed. For five years Doffy had done her bit training gunners in the ATS, playing her part in the important defences against the V1 and V2 rockets. After demob in 1945 it was back to the family home at Romford, and teaching. She was twenty-seven.

I was very ordinary, not particularly pretty, terribly shy – particularly with boys – and not grown-up enough. I remember reading a letter in a magazine – this girl was upset because she couldn't get a boyfriend, and the agony aunt's reply was: 'Girls are like cherries: some ripen in June, some in July, some don't ripen till October. Be patient with yourself.' And I thought, 'That's me.'

But Doffy's philosophy had to compete with her mother's tireless attempts to get her hitched.

My mother had three men that she'd lined up for me. Oh yes, she was no slouch, my mother!

The first was Ken. Poor old Ken. He took me out to dinner in the West End, and I ordered a salad, thinking I would appear dainty. But he was famished, so he ordered a meat pudding. And this marvellous vast salad arrived, alongside this minuscule meat pudding. Well, I wanted to laugh, but Ken was very solemn. He didn't laugh about it at all. So I never went out with him again.

That was one off my mother's list.

And then there was a chap who was on our staff at school. He was a bit creepy and pompous. He always seemed to have 'wise' words. I went into his classroom one day and found his ten-year-olds doing an old-fashioned writing lesson. He had them all copying these lines from the blackboard: 'Something Attempted – Something Done – Has Earned A Night's Repose.' Oh dear! Well, I couldn't marry a man like that, could I?

And unfortunately the other one was married already, and I would never have married a divorced man, I just couldn't do it. I really couldn't.

Doffy's scruples, patience, and sense of the ridiculous were to keep her single for another twelve years. John Kerr – 'the nicest man I've ever met' – did not come into her life until 1959.

*

After losing two fiancés in the war, Helen Forrester had also resigned herself to a single future. Soon after the war ended, she got a job with the Metal Box Company. The packaging industry gave her career prospects, reasonable pay and a responsible, confidence-boosting position: it was 'a fascinating world for a woman to be in'. But with no expectation of marriage she felt an underlying hopelessness.

However, in 1948 Helen met the man who would become her husband: an Indian theoretical physicist named Avadh Bhatia. She did not write a memoir about this life-changing event. But in 1959 she published a novel entitled *Thursday's Child*, which opens with the heroine, Peggie, breaking down in tears on hearing that her fiancé, Barney, has been killed:

I was stupefied . . . It was said that lightning did not strike twice in the same place, and it seemed impossible to me that in one war a woman could really lose two fiancés . . .

'Kill me, Lord, kill me too,' I shouted in my agony.

Helen's son, Robert Bhatia, offers a caution about his mother's first novel. 'She always swore that it was not autobiographical.' Nevertheless, he notes that she clearly drew on her relationship with Avadh Bhatia and his home country in writing *Thursday's Child*.

'Peggie' meets 'Ajit Singh' at a Liverpool club set up to help the city's numerous immigrants integrate with the locals. They drink tea together:

I took a good look at him. He was dressed in an old tweed jacket and baggy, grey trousers; his white shirt made his skin look very dark but his features were clear cut and delicate; both in expression and outline his face reminded me of a Saint in an old Italian painting.

Ajit (like Avadh) is in Liverpool to study. Avadh, who came from a high-caste, privileged, traditional Indian background, had already received an advanced degree from the University of Allahabad and was now in England writing a thesis for his doctorate. In the novel their relationship develops slowly. Ajit invites Peggie to meet other members of the Indian community; in return he is asked back to the family home, though her broken heart is not yet mended. But the more time they spend together, the more Peggie grows to like and respect him. As a Hindu, he teaches her about Shiva, the destroyer, and Brahma, who creates. 'So life is born anew and nothing is wasted.' One winter's day they walk out of the city by the sea wall, and eat sandwiches together in a sheltered hollow of the dunes. Gradually she confides in him and tells him of her past griefs. Ajit listens, then takes her hand:

'Let me marry you. Let me show you what life and love can really be.'

I started up as if to run away, but he would not let go of my hand.

'Don't go away. Hear me to the end.'

I looked down at him and was astonished at the beauty which flooded his face; it was transfigured . . . I knew I was seeing something rare . . .

'I have loved you from the first day I saw you . . .'

Helen Forrester's marriage to Avadh Bhatia was a deliverance. After the war the savour had gone out of Liverpool and all it stood for. As a choice of mate Avadh couldn't have been more unconventional, nor represented more of an escape from the sorrowful stranglehold of her past.

Soon after their marriage in Britain, the couple started a new life in Ahmadabad, the largest city in Gujarat, on the edge of the desert. In *Thursday's Child* Helen Forrester evokes the shock of arrival amid the deafening bustle of streets, thronged with children and beggars, tongas, bicycles, camels and cars. Temple bells clanged and radios blared. In India she learned to bargain for everything, she learned to distinguish the rank smell of a jackal, to wear a sari and to give orders to the servants. She tells of the culture shock entailed in adapting to her new in-laws, and how she felt 'pummelled by new experiences'. There was the vice-like heat to acclimatise to, and a landscape of cactus and sand. Monkeys lived in the mango trees, and an incessant creak came from the tethered ox whose exertions drew water from the well. She became accustomed to the sight of snakes, scorpions and locusts, and she caught dysentery. 'Although I hardly realised it at the time, I was slowly becoming part of India. Each friend I made, each custom I learned to understand and tolerate, was a thread which bound me closer to her and made me part of her multicoloured pattern.' Helen's lifelong marriage to Avadh remained loving and supportive, based on profound communication. 'How much I owe him for making my life anew,' she wrote. 'My cup runneth over.' But, humbled after so many years of unhappiness, she never questioned Avadh's precedence. 'They always lived where his work took him,' says their son. Eventually they moved to Canada; at the high point of his career Dr Bhatia was director of the Theoretical Physics Institute at the University of Alberta. 'My mother was a devoted faculty wife. And when she began to write, she did so in the last half-hour of the day, when other duties were done.'

Today, Robert Bhatia remains proud of Helen's capacity to transcend the misery and hardships of her early life:

She got away from her terrible previous environment completely. But emotionally she never completely left it. She never truly got over losing two fiancés. Was she happy? How can I answer that? There was always a twinge of sadness and bitterness for much of her life. I think she was angry at the cards life had dealt her, and after all that she had experienced she sometimes had trouble relating to people who had not been through the war.

Life had beaten her down, but she turned herself around. Her secret was her courage, and her maturity. She was talented, and yes, truly, she was a competent, strong, and successful person.*

★

The idea of marriage, whether within or outside her social tribe, was still problematical for Phyllis Noble. Again and again she had been caught up by her passions, but her greatest fear was that passion was a trap. She would end up like her mother, whose life – cumbered with shopping, washing and meals – had hit a cul-de-sac. But could she envisage a future without motherhood? In the autumn of 1947, when she embarked on her course of study to become an almoner – or hospital social worker – she was twenty-five years old. Her father had begun to mutter that she would soon be on the shelf. But Phyllis knew that there was time enough.

Hospital social work was a small profession, but Phyllis had found herself on the end of a government-backed recruitment drive. Dwindling numbers of almoners needed to be made good, and many patients wounded in the war were in dire need of social rehabilitation. Once the new National Health Service came into being – scheduled

---

* Helen Forrester's books have sold 4 million copies, and in 1988 she was granted an Honorary Degree by the University of Liverpool. She is still alive and living in Canada, but her powers are fading, and her memory is inconsistent. Dr Avadh Bhatia died in 1984.

for summer 1948 – the need would be all the greater. Phyllis was in at the beginning of a Labour-initiated sea-change in social services. The post-war world would see the obsolescence of the WVS-style Lady Bountiful, with her easy authority and 'duchess touch', to be replaced by full-scale professionalisation of the sector. Phyllis would be attending an 'emergency' course lasting just one year.

For Phyllis 1947–8 was a year of profound intellectual release; of reading, self-examination and mental discovery:

Sleep considerably delayed last night [she wrote in October 1947] by mental excitement consequent on Prof. Marshall's lecture on 'Social Structure'.

Psychology lectures awoke unprecedented questions in her brain. She explored the agnostic writings of Winwood Reade* and read *My Apprenticeship* by Beatrice Webb. The Webbs' extraordinary partnership – intellectual, ascetic, though childless – inspired her. Marriage could surely be something higher and better than slavery dressed up as sexual attraction. Sidney Webb was unprepossessing, but he was brilliant. 'It is only the head that I am marrying,' Beatrice had written. Together, they were guided by their socialist mission and their avowed aim to reduce the sum of human suffering; there was no hint of servitude or dependency in the Webbs' relationship, which proved that there could be such a thing as a marriage of minds:

[They] made me realise that there could be perhaps a form of marriage which was a beginning and not, as I had always feared, the end of life.

Sometimes, Phyllis's head was so busy she needed time to process her thoughts and find a perspective. She walked one November evening across London Bridge and crossed the churchyard of Southwark Cathedral. Six years earlier the same cityscape would have resounded to the detonations of high explosive and the ear-splitting rattle of anti-aircraft fire. The sky would have been alight with apocalyptic flames and criss-crossed with searchlights, with the Thames warehouses a blinding furnace, presenting a scene of terror as people scurried for shelter. Now the serene vision of a lofty plane tree silhouetted against

* Winwood Reade (1838–75), romantic Victorian traveller, doctor and controversialist, author of *The Martyrdom of Man* (1872).

the evening sky caused Phyllis to catch her breath – '[making] me gasp for the dear dead spirit'. Inside the cathedral an organist practised, the echoing chords enhancing the tranquillity:

I could be calmed by the reflection of man's transiency as an individual; yet power as a stream – represented, perhaps, by this imposing, strong, building. The sound of trains rumbled outside & pressed in. It was inevitably to minimise one's own petty affairs, by reflecting how the scenery around those walls must have changed, & changed again, before reaching the present confused, noisy & dirty pass.

Life, it still seemed to Phyllis, was a mess.

As far as her own petty affairs were concerned, confusion prevailed; her new-found philosophy had not yet taken root. At a New Year's gathering at the Strand Palace Hotel she was partnered with a charming married man who – it was explained – was on his own because his wife was expecting a child. In the early hours he burst into Phyllis's bedroom, where, after some kerfuffle, she gave in to his energetic persuasion. Escaping from the hotel the next morning was potentially deeply shaming – 'in the late 1940s adultery (or, in my case, fornication) in a hotel room was not taken lightly' – but her seducer managed things with the utmost aplomb. It was clear he was a practised cheat.

Dirt and poverty were also now part of Phyllis's everyday experience. In January 1948 she was despatched to Deptford to do field-work with the Family Welfare Association. On the 13th she recorded her first home visit to an Irish slum family in her journal. 'To think,' she wrote, '[that] such squalor can still exist!'

Surely I can never forget that smoke-filled room: the mouldy cabbage in the corner, the bowl with its dirty water, the toddler with transparent shirt and no shoes on the bare boards. And it will be some while, certainly, before I forget the shock of horror on hearing – 'There's another behind you' – turning to see on the springs of the bed amongst the rags, that tiny 1 month old mite . . .

We are still suffering from the effects of the Industrial Revolution. Equally true that two major wars have aggravated a vast problem . . .

At present, I feel only the scratching against a stone!

The next two months were to bring her up against a Dickensian London she had barely imagined, of hunger and ignorance, hostels and down-and-outs. The experience would shape her political convictions and her life's work. In March, she made an investigative visit to a homeless men's hostel in Kennington. One of the supervisors, a good-humoured, enthusiastic and studious young man, showed her around, and they got into conversation about society and its problems. He was impressively eloquent, well read and well informed. That evening she wrote in her diary:

Peter Willmott was extremely interesting. A person I should very much like to know!

Peter, it turned out, was as attracted to Phyllis as she was to him.

That spring of 1948, things moved very fast. Phyllis agrees now that it was unlike any of her previous relationships. From their first meeting she felt instinctively that this was someone she could be happy with. 'It was a *coup de foudre*.' That same day Peter Willmott had confided to a friend, 'I have met the girl I want to marry.' Their relationship progressed at breakneck tempo, and inevitably there were stumbles. Peter talked Phyllis into attending Mass at Brompton Oratory, though they were both staunch agnostics; it would be a cultural experience, he explained. But when she turned up in green slacks he expressed disapproval. Another time he objected because she licked her knife. Just how progressive was he, she wondered furiously. Was this middle-class young man, despite his professed impartiality and freedom from prejudice, just as class-bound and sexist as the rest of them? 'But the magnetic spell between us quickly drew us together again. Being apart was too painful.'

Phyllis's family were soon pestering to see 'the latest', but for as long as possible she delayed taking Peter back to Lee for a Sunday roast dinner to meet them. What would her lover make of their unintellectual conversation, their ramshackle working-class home, the steamy little kitchen festooned with drying underwear? Her mum would be sweating over the range, piling everyone's plates high with mashed potatoes and greens (inevitably followed by a boiled suet pudding). Her dad would be a bit too blustery after a few pints in the local. For despite Phyllis's declared lack of class bias, there was still shame attached to her proletarian origins. Her worries were soon allayed by Peter's affectionate reaction. 'I really like the way you are with your family. And they are obviously so fond of you.'

Every spare hour outside work Phyllis now spent with Peter Willmott. His shabby flat over the hostel in Kennington was a romantic
refuge from petit-bourgeois domesticity. They would eat bread and
cheese sitting on the worn rug in front of the spluttering gas fire,
then make love in Peter's institutional metal bed. He rarely changed
the sheets, but to her eyes it was all 'admirably carefree and Bohemian'. But Phyllis was still in a minority in feeling entitled to a sex
life before marriage; the prevalent British view, as revealed in a survey made by Mass Observation in 1949, was still small-c conservative;
few people thought moral standards were improving at this time,
extra-marital relationships were frowned upon, and a majority were
against pre-marital sex.

In May Phyllis went to St Thomas's Hospital to finish her training
as a student almoner in Casualty. Here her job was to discuss her
patients' worries. Did they need referrals? Did they have domestic,
financial, nutritional or mental problems? She was also expected to
explain to each patient that the hospital depended on voluntary contributions, reinforcing the point by rattling the little tin box on her
desk and asking for a donation to hospital funds. 'I seldom managed
this part of the interview without embarrassment on my side, and
too often on that of the patients, whose worn clothes and worried
faces showed clearly enough how little they could afford.'

On 5 July 1948 all that ended. As the date approached for the
birth of the National Health Service, there was great joy and
excitement in Casualty. Shortly before the appointed day, Phyllis
and her colleagues threw out the little tin boxes. 'It was the symbolic new beginning of a health service that was intended to be
free for all.'

Modern Times

For many who had worked and campaigned for a better post-war
Britain, the National Health Service represented the fulfilment of all
that they had dreamed of, the dawning of 'a new world, a new day.'

On Day One a Leeds woman went straight out to the pub to celebrate with her friends. Her mother, as she recollected, was at the dentist's surgery on that momentous morning, waiting to have her teeth pulled and replaced with dentures; one of her sisters was first in line at the optician's for new NHS spectacles, while the other, who had been made to pay a midwife 12s 6d to have her first baby – ('it was rather bad . . . no gas and air') – rejoiced to have her second, easy delivery for nothing: 'She thought it was absolutely wonderful, because besides having a free midwife, she had a nurse came in every day . . . bathed the baby, showed her how to look after it . . . '. In Manchester another woman shopped her way round the services, starting out with a doctor's prescription, then on for an eye test, followed by a visit to the chiropodist and back to the doctor's again for a hearing test, before suggesting that she might as well call in on the undertaker's on her way home . . .

Women had always been on the sharp end when it came to dealing with everything from coughs and sneezes, to births, deaths, toothache and chickenpox, and the National Health Service had an immediate impact on them. For years their own ailments had been neglected as too expensive to treat. A female doctor working in general practice in a poor district was overwhelmed by the difference she was able to make in the first six months of the new service, as women flooded in with chronic conditions like hyperthyroidism or varicose ulcers. They had lived all their lives stoically accepting that 'you never go to a doctor because it's always far too expensive'. Now they could, and did. 'Suddenly they could be treated.' Other health professionals, like nurses, were uplifted beyond measure by the overnight availability of elementary supplies: 'Suddenly you'd got it all, this gorgeous soft cotton wool, beautiful clean bandages . . . we talked about it for weeks afterwards.' Patients were delighted by the contrast. Domestic servant Margaret Powell had first been hospitalised in 1944 and then again in 1948; her first experience, with a gastric ulcer, had been nasty, scary and humiliating. The food and amenities were 'deplorable', the lack of privacy – with public bedpan sessions, and one toilet roll between four – was distressing. When she returned after July 1948 with breast cancer, 'what a change I found':

You were treated as though you mattered. Even the waiting room was different. No dark green paint, whitewash and wooden benches. There were separate chairs with modern magazines.

For a week she was on the ward:

And again what a difference I saw . . . The bed that I'd had before was like lying on the pebbles on Brighton beach . . . But now I had a rubber mattress. I felt as though I could have lain there forever.

And the food was beautiful.

Margaret felt she was in a luxury hotel. Each bed had its own curtains, the meals were many and various, served on brightly coloured trays. There were even fish knives.

★

Welfare for women was, at last, becoming a reality. Family Allowances took effect from 1946. By 1948 the Family Planning Association had sixty-five clinics, and by the following year new ones were opening at a rate of five weekly. National Maternity Services accompanied the inauguration of the NHS. Recommendations for day nurseries, baby-sitting facilities and home helps were in the pipeline. There would be community centres, communal laundries and restaurants. The Labour government took every opportunity to congratulate itself on the rosy cheeks and improved height and weight of thousands of post-war boom babies; in these respects the good intentions of ministers and social reformers to improve the lot of women seemed to be bearing fruit: the harvest of peace was delivering undreamed-of progress and benefits, especially to poor working-class women.

The later 1940s also offered glimpses into an even more rewarding future: one in which the housewife might cease to be a beast of burden, lay down her load and – with time on her hands – turn, like men, to careers and causes. Social involvement for women meant reading intelligently, attending meetings and lectures, playing as full a part as they could. For women to remain at home was insufficient today. In his essay 'Woman's Place' William Emrys Williams,★ director of the Bureau of Current Affairs, wrote:

★ A brilliant journalist and passionate educationist, for thirty years W. E. Williams was editor-in-chief of Penguin Books. He also helped set up the Council for the Encouragement of Music and the Arts (CEMA), which developed into the Arts Council. His wife, Gertrude Rosenblum, became Professor of Social Economics at the University of London.

Woman's place is Everywhere.

She has the same responsibilities as men.

The war has precipitated the answer.

The new buzz-phrase was 'post-war participation', and it was actually beginning to look achievable.

Was it possible that the long hours spent queuing outside individual shops were numbered? In January 1947 the *Daily Express* ran an enticing piece entitled 'QUEUES: This may be the answer'. The illustration showed a stylish young woman pushing a wheeled double-decker trolley; the article explained how she would do her shopping in a new form of 'help-yourself market', proceeding through a one-way turnstile into aisles full of shelves, from which she would fill her trolley with tins and packages, before submitting the contents to a cashier who would ring them up on a register and pass them for packing to an attendant. The supermarket – American-style – was born. 'The women there like it – and I think shoppers here would too.' By the end of that year ten such stores had opened in Britain.

What could be done about the queues? 'We may have to adopt the American help-yourself idea,' suggested the Daily Express.

And was it possible that the time spent on housework might finally be reduced? Most housewives at this time still spent up to eleven hours a day on their tasks. But labour-saving gadgetry was starting to appear on the market: the twin-tub, the Frigidaire and the electric toaster. Since the 1946 'Britain Can Make It' exhibition Mrs Post-war had had her heart set on such futuristic delights. Shirley Goodhart was one young wife who purchased a Hoover vacuum cleaner in 1949: 'Such a joy to get our bedroom carpet clean without the effort of lying under the bed with a handbrush.' And, judging by the deluge of requests for post-war career advice to women's magazines, women did indeed have ambitions that extended beyond keeping their homes immaculate:

I shall soon be leaving school and I would like to work in a film studio.

I am terribly anxious to get a job abroad as my divorce has just come through and I want to get right away from all the unhappiness connected with my past life.

But, despite the recommendations of a Royal Commission report, equal pay was still being sidelined. Noisy equal-pay activists were regarded as a sectional minority, and the Labour Party felt able to risk losing their vote. In 1948 the patriarchy still found it too hard to accept that women might have the same skills, intellect and competence as men; nor could they contemplate any erosion of their power base.

The Pram in the Hall

Since the age of sixteen Phyllis Noble had dreamed of a life different to that of her mother. Education had shown her the way. Books and ideas seemed to promise an abundant harvest, a life of the mind, and, after the war, she had entered a profession where her skills were needed and appreciated. The road lay open. But the claims of love were immediate and pressing.

On 31 July 1948 Phyllis Noble's hopes of a modern marriage were, to the limits that she could have hoped for, fulfilled. Peter Willmott had been offered a place to study Economics and Politics at Ruskin College, Oxford, and, faced with enforced separation, they decided to get married straight away. Having agreed, Phyllis was jittery. 'I suppose if it doesn't work out we can always get a divorce,' she said, but Peter soberly discouraged any flippancy on the matter. Her mother panicked at the spectacle of Phyllis throwing herself away on a penniless student. 'He's got nothing,' she wailed. Mrs Noble was made so distraught by her daughter's plans for a no-frills wedding with no guests and no reception that Phyllis eventually caved in and invited her family to see them being married by Donald Soper, the famous Methodist minister, at Kingsway Hall. To her relief, Peter's family were dissuaded from making the journey. On the day, she put on her best interview suit – green gaberdine – teamed with a pink felt hat and dainty veil and caught the bus to Holborn. The Nobles were there in force; but Peter, exhausted from doing night duty at the hostel, was late. Their two witnesses arrived shortly afterwards, and without further ado the ceremony was under way. When it was all over the company repaired to the pub for a cursory drink to toast the newly wed pair before they fled for Charing Cross. As they reached the honeymoon pub in a Kentish village their nervous excitement slowly ebbed. Peter could barely speak from tiredness, and on reaching their bedroom dropped instantly into a deep and childlike slumber. 'This, I thought, is surely an odd and lonely start to a marriage.' They had known each other barely four months.

Some excerpts from Phyllis's diary for 1948:

20th August 1948

A new page for Mrs Willmott!

7th September 1948

Such continuous happiness is almost unbearable – certainly contains an element of anguish. After 5 weeks life still really consists only of Peter.

3rd November 1948

Impossible to express the deep excitement which tingles and sings inside on looking around at 'our home' . . . To me it is already all I want a home to be – not too large, not too small, mainly furnished with books, made alive by our love.

Phyllis had found her life's partner.

But by the end of 1948, when she discovered she was pregnant, their life together took a new turn. Peter was working for the Labour

Party, and having a baby would mean no room in the Canonbury flat. So when Peter's father offered them accommodation under his roof in Essex the Willmotts, like many other homeless young couples, had no option but to accept. In August 1949 Lewis was born. For Phyllis, freedom, ambition and choice were all deferred, as motherhood brought with it a rush of conflicting emotions. There was intense joy but also, with Peter's commute and demanding job taking up most of the long day, debilitating loneliness. And, as any new mother knows, intellectual activity went on hold. Books, ideas and 'post-war participation' were suspended. After broken nights and mornings spent boiling nappies, Phyllis's face would be streaming with tears as she pushed her pram between the endless hedgerows of that featureless countryside. Her picture of a marriage that would exclude her from 'real life' was materialising in just the way she had always dreaded. What had become of her 'marriage of minds'? Was she becoming her mother? It was indeed a punishment, a sentence to servitude and hard labour. 'I'm so tired of my life here in such a weary, weary way,' she wrote early in 1950:

This year, I shall not find spring singing through me with upsurging hopes. Although each day I am expectant for I know not what, each day I am worn out by waiting – for Peter, for the future, for life to begin again.

But Phyllis had married a man who accepted her for who she was. Outfacing her mother's disapproval – 'as a daughter she thought I was odd . . . abnormal' – she struggled on and resumed her career at the earliest opportunity.

That was over sixty years ago. Phyllis was widowed in 2000. 'We were married for forty-two years. I'm a relic. I'm just amazed I could have survived him. Peter was so much more sensible than I was – the guy rope tying me to the ground; he was a wonderful man.'

★

For Joan Wyndham, being lonely and hard-up had never cramped the bohemian in her; and anyway, what bona fide bohemian had ever had any money?

Joan was the kind of optimistic young woman for whom hope would always triumph over experience. In 1946 she was jobless, and her boyfriend, Kit Latimer, had broken her heart by announcing his intention of marrying a rival ex-WAAF. Back in Fitzrovia, she took to drinking with the Ceylonese poet Meary Tambimuttu, who had been a wartime sex symbol and was as indigent, romantic and generous as she was. His bed was full of bugs, so she never slept with him, but in a profligate moment at the Hog in the Pound Tambi produced an engagement ring set with three opals. Joan went to wash her hands, and the gems – all imitation – immediately dropped out and disappeared down the waste. Mortified at the thought of hurting Tambi's feelings, she ran for the back door and never returned.

As the cold winter of 1947 set in, Joan kept warm in bed with the painter Lucian Freud. But Freud quickly replaced her with a new muse, Kitty Garman. Once the weather improved Joan and a girlfriend hitch-hiked to Cornwall and made for the Scilly Isles, where they camped out in a sea-cave with a group of young French proto-hippies who lived on boiled limpets and roasted seagulls. It was a happy time, which lasted until the local police evicted them. Joan then decided to track down her smart but reprobate father, the spendthrift journalist Dick Wyndham, at his mill house in Sussex. The autumn saw Joan in Oxford. At a party she met a tall, blond, clever philosophy undergraduate named Maurice (Mo) Rowdon: 'We took one look at each other and spent the rest of the night talking and dancing. A few days later I moved in with him.'

In March 1948 Joan too became pregnant. She and Mo Rowdon decided to get married, though their infant daughter was already three weeks old by the time Joan finally got to the altar. In the halcyon early days of her marriage Joan suddenly got the news that Dick Wyndham – who had been reporting the first salvos between the newly formed state of Israel and its Arab neighbours for the *Sunday Times* – had been shot dead by a sniper. There were terrible pangs for a father whom she had barely known – mingled with the overt hope that she and Mo would surely, now, come into a fortune. But by the time the lawyers had paid off Dick's debts and calculated death duties, there was only enough to buy a small cottage near Sevenoaks, to which they decamped that summer:

Domesticity – how I hated it! Much as I loved my daughter, I wasn't too keen on the rest of the stuff that goes with motherhood. Those were the days when nappies were soaked in pails, boiled up on top of the stove and hung out to dry in the garden. In spite of rationing I cooked a huge fantastic meal twice a day, and grew fat and ugly.

I had a pleasant house in one of the prettiest villages in Kent, an adoring husband and a lovely daughter – so why was I so bloody miserable?

Rural heaven, the timeless peace of an English valley, couldn't compete with her formative years spent in the Chelsea Blitz. For Joan, post-war participation meant parties, and not the political kind. At the age of twenty-seven, how could being a housewife measure up to the sheer adrenalin rush of making love as the bombs rained down, dropping amphetamines in an air-raid shelter or dancing, drunk on crème de menthe, to a soundtrack of sirens? Joan tried growing vegetables, acquired a cat and a rabbit and made friends with the only Communists in the village. But it was no good. 'All the time I was dreaming of Negro nightclubs, young bearded boys in tight black trousers, and smart literary parties full of my father's old friends.' The city in wartime had marked her. Nothing would ever quite live up to it again.

'There is no more sombre enemy of good art than the pram in the hall,' wrote Cyril Connolly in *Enemies of Promise* (1938). Exiled to Kent, Joan Wyndham would probably have recalled this famous dictum from her father's literary drinking companion. Joan had met Connolly in 1945, describing him as 'fat and piggy with one of those clever-ugly faces like Dylan Thomas had'. Certainly, Connolly saw his notional pram (he had no children at the time) and the responsibilities it represented as more of a threat to male creativity than female. His assumptions, and those of his sex, were that the pram's occupant would be taken care of by the female parent, whose 'good art' was presumably of lesser importance.

Nina Bawden's creative talents were shelved when she turned down a £900-a-year job in journalism because of her pregnancy. The newlywed acquired instead a substantial Rolls Royce of a perambulator, immensely heavy and cumbersome. Getting this monster up the steps to the front door left Nina exhausted, but it was 'light and springy on the flat'. Nicholas, born in summer 1947, lay in it, and was now the focus of her existence:

I would have given my life for him had the need arisen. But I was alone with him all day and longed for someone to talk to who could talk back to me. Eventually, I met another girl in a similar plight. We pushed our prams to the park together on fine afternoons and, when it rained, sat in each other's houses smoking and drinking gin or whisky while our babies played behind the sofa and pulled each other's hair. Babies and boredom, boredom and babies – when the whisky ran out, we made up our faces, exchanged clothes, did our hair, and the afternoon still yawned ahead.

★

For too many women joining the ranks of wives and mothers in the second half of the 1940s, it felt as though the war had offered them a glimpse of how life could be – a tantalising taste of liberty – only for it to be snatched away again. 'Grossly unfair' was how ATS volunteer Hilda Marter described her own situation in 1945. Hilda, who had married shortly before the outbreak of war, joined the ATS after her husband was posted abroad and spent four years seeing action on the command post of an anti-aircraft battery. It was 'an important job . . . that I enjoyed and . . . being my own person – instead of a housewife pandering to my husband's every need . . . gave me a confidence I had never had before.' At last her husband got leave – just as she was expecting to be sent out to Belgium. At such a time it was out of the question to ask him to use a condom – 'tantamount to asking for a divorce' – and to her utter dismay, Hilda became pregnant. All hopes of promotion, travel and status were suspended. Her husband departed again, and she was left alone with a new baby in an insanitary, run-down cottage. 'I often wonder what sort of career I might have been able to follow had I been able to choose my own destiny.' Despite her unchallengeable competence and professionalism, women like Hilda still felt incapable of challenging their husbands.

The sexual stereotypes were as axiomatic for many women as they were for men. Ursula Bloom, who came from a slightly older generation, struggled to express the misgivings she felt at modern men helping in the home:

Men and women have drawn level in the race for life, but the condition is such a new one that any woman worth her salt still cannot bear to see a man doing the jobs that should be entirely hers, without a sense of embarrassment.

It is a difficult matter trying to re-educate oneself to the new system.

In the same vein, Barbara Cartland was unable to countenance outside careers for married women. She herself had declined an invitation to stand for parliament because the hours conflicted with the children's bedtime and the peaceful after-dinner interlude 'when a man likes to sit beside the fire and talk over what has happened during the day.' She was lucky, as a novelist, in being able to drop everything when her husband returned from his office. And if confident, privileged women like her felt unable to make claims, how much more so did the working-class factory women interviewed by the social researcher Ferdinand Zweig? 'The one thing which struck me in my inquiry was the sense of inferiority which many, if not most, women have. They accept man's superiority as a matter of fact.'

In the later 1940s, despite all that they had proved both to themselves and to men, most women still lacked any sense that they were entitled to stand equally beside their 'lords and masters'.

*

In 1947 a galaxy of distinguished women came together who, over the course of the next four years, would meet to discuss where their sex stood in the mid-twentieth century. Eminent representatives of the business, charitable, employment and educational fields, scientists, journalists, feminists and trade unionists attended.* This rolling conference, entitled 'The Feminine Point of View', set out to explore how far emancipation had really come, why its impact had been restricted, and what could be done to enable women to achieve their potential.

In 1951 Olwen Campbell, one of the sponsors of the conference, wrote a report of its deliberations and conclusions. The great and good who had gathered over that four-year period had concluded that a feminine influence would unquestionably have a benign impact on our world. Women's contribution was, they now urged, of the utmost value – 'We believe that the world desperately needs her point of view':

---

* They included Eva Hubback, Principal of Morley College, Ann Temple of the *Daily Mail*, the scientist and pacifist Professor Kathleen Lonsdale, the birth control pioneer Dr Helena Wright, Juanita Frances, activist and editor of the feminist forum *Wife and Citizen*, Mary Field, film producer and president of the British Federation of Business and Professional Women, and the trade union leader Dame Florence Hancock.

The ultimate aim, which we should never lose sight of, is nothing less than a society shaped and run equally by men and women and pursuing the best ideals and hopes of both.

Polite and moderately worded as it was, the professed aspiration of these thoughtful and educated ladies was not so much to engage in a battle with men, but to redeem humanity itself. Like Vera Brittain five years later (in *Lady into Woman*) they were pursuing not so much equality for themselves, but a 'woman's service for peace', a future for the human race. A lofty aim indeed, which might have carried more weight had their rhetoric not been so polite, so conciliatory. They had perhaps heeded the fate of those activists whose campaign for equal pay had been sidelined.

These women were as sick of bombs and battles as everybody else, and even in dissent the participants saw themselves as more 'feminine' than feminist. They came from a world, and spoke to a public, in which 'all girls want to marry and nearly all will marry'. They held firmly to their interpretation of the female character, with its traditional qualities of compassion, intuitive sympathy, aversion to violence, selflessness and reverence for individual life. They accepted that the ministrations of home and family fell primarily on the female. Olwen Campbell and her company were not about to jettison their foundation garments, march as sisters or chain themselves to railings. That was still a long way off.

And perhaps that was why – despite their excellent analysis, compelling arguments and the conclusive need for a new approach that would break the cycle of aggressive wars – the 1950s would see the institution of marriage enjoying unprecedented stability, with little change either in women's status or women's self-estimation. Perhaps, too, it was why change, when it did come in the 1970s, had to be played out according to men's rules: those of noisy protest, angry demonstration and belligerent force.

Millions Like Them

The children of the Armistice had travelled a long road since 1939. We have a tendency to romanticise the Second World War, to build up comforting pictures of heroism featuring armadas of small ships, defiance of danger on the high seas, the gallantry of Spitfire crews, the fearless comradeship of the Blitz and feats of bravery on the Normandy beaches, all to the accompaniment of wailing sirens and the ringing rhetoric of Winston Churchill. We tend to see it as a man's war.

The woman's war had its moments of glory too. But they were often simpler: celebrating a sinking with a bottle of cheap wine labelled 'Matapan'; the joy of a double-yolked egg; beautiful shiny lace-up shoes; a mattress remodelled from sugar sacks; cream cakes on the Cobb; jitterbugging; floating on Martini . . . And the tough times were correspondingly banal: days on the factory floor, followed by 'straight to bed, buggered'; rising at 4 a.m. for a working day on the Sheffield trams; frozen early mornings in the conifer plantations of northern Scotland; grief and ennui; 'Missing, presumed killed'; pouring rain, and counting the bricks in the wall; rubble; destruction; death on the ward; the swabbing of shit from traumatised soldiers after D-day; lisle stockings and snapped knicker elastic; waiting, hoping and despairing. And this time the accompaniment is Vera Lynn's crystalline voice singing:

> There'll be bluebirds over
> The white cliffs of Dover,
> Tomorrow, just you wait and see.
> There'll be love and laughter,
> And peace ever after,
> Tomorrow – when the world is free.

Though the perfect peace was as empty a promise as the bluebirds, not everything had been lost. In jungles and deserts, the ideal of home had kept many millions of soldiers going through the weary years of war. Treasured in each wallet or kitbag, the creased and dogeared black-and-white photograph of a smiling girlfriend or wife would sustain its memory. From all the struggle and heartache of the war Home and Hearth had emerged as the repository of all things good, all things worth fighting for, with Woman at its heart. Electricity and technology were transforming it from a prison to a power base. For the next decade and onwards, Home would be woman's empire.

'*With these modern inventions housework's a pleasure.*'
In 1946, a Hoover seemed to promise true joy.

War had brought her pride, and a sense of value. Friendships forged out of common experiences endured. Voluntarism thrived. A generation emerged from ten years of rationing unable to contemplate waste or debt, incapable of using more than a quarter of an inch of toothpaste, resistant to the modern culture of excess. Many who lived through the war continue to share a powerful patriotism and sense of national unity. And ten years of suffering and boredom bred millions of stoical survivors. If the women who came of age in the 1940s have just one thing in common, it is their characteristic quality of patience. Their mantra: 'We didn't analyse. We just got on with it. We lived from day to day.'

And as the war receded into history, most of them were quietly relieved to have come through, grateful for what remained of life's blessings.

This story began with snapshots from the lives of some of the participants in 1939. It draws to a close a decade later with some pages from the post-war album. Here they are, a bit older, some with small children and husbands, in sepia and black-and-white, smiling bravely for the camera. Most of them by now will be familiar.

First, a wedding photograph; taken at St Mark's Church, North Audley Street, Mayfair. Blooming and smiling, with a long veil, ruffled full-length lace wedding dress and carnation bouquet, Helen Vlasto has married her long-term sweetheart Dr Aidan Long. Her private means, and his post in a London hospital, enable her to return to the life for which she was born, that of a lady of leisure. The Longs are rich, and outnumbered – even in these austerity days – by their staff: maids, a chauffeur and cooks. But grief is lying in wait for Helen when her baby daughter, born in 1947, dies after just a few days. Helen, who has relied all her life on her looks and good fortune, becomes ever more unwilling to engage with matters of substance. The days fill with aimless activity: letters to write, hairdressing appointments, cocktails at six. It is as if the war had never happened; Helen's life has gone on hold. '[She] was an extraordinarily late-developer,' says Helen's son. 'But [writing her memoirs] was a turning point. She was able to reinvent herself and in her late 50s and 60s acquired a rapidly forming "gravitas".'

Ilkley Road, Barrow-in-Furness: a December night in 1948, with the rain lashing outside, and a fire crackling. Diarist Nella Last is recording a tetchy row between herself and her husband, Will. Tea – a generous spread of hard-boiled egg with grated cheese, wholemeal bread, butter and jam and toasted fruit bread – has been cleared away, when Will (who continues to run his joinery business) starts to drone with misery about the threatened departure of one of his apprentices. Driven away by Mr Last's grumbles and fault-finding, the boy is off to join the navy. But Nella has no sympathy with her husband. She lashes out and tells him plainly that the only thing that keeps her chained to the stove and sink is her own self-respect as a housewife. It's not surprising you lose everyone who ever works for you, she tells him. 'You never say a thing is nice or give a word of thanks for any effort, and you pounce on any little error or fault.' And if he didn't start trying soon, she'd be the next one packing her bags.

A cottage in Slough, a few weeks later. Maggie Joy Blunt's guests have left and, thankful to be on her own again with her beloved cats, she reflects on the isolation of her post-war existence: 'I am at heart a solitary, selfish creature and am sure I should find marriage irksome eventually.' Life holds challenges enough for Maggie; she has decided to put effort into changing the world through politics and will campaign in the next election for the Liberal Party. There is charitable work to do, friends, the theatre, a writing project that will occupy much of her time, and plans to open a bookshop. 'My philosophy for years now has been to take things as they come, to live the life you have in hand as fully as you can, & let the future take care of itself.'

A summer day in Piccadilly: Madeleine Henrey and her husband have returned to their Shepherd Market flat. Bobby is at school now, and Madeleine is writing the story of her Normandy farm. But Madeleine finds she can't concentrate, and the Bond Street shops beckon. A sunny London morning and the thought of new hats still have the power to tempt a woman like Madeleine and, basket in hand, she heads out. Here in the West End many of the buildings have been cleaned up – at least on the outside – but the little shops with their heraldic crests which once sold kid evening gloves that buttoned up above the elbow all seem to have closed. Still, rumour has it that the price of knitting wool has come down and, even better, that nylon stockings are in. It is a matter of time before the big stores will yet again be full of lovely, shimmering fabrics. No man can experience the joy Madeleine feels at stroking the tempting softness of a bolt of *crêpe de chine*. 'I am thankful to be a woman.'

Ham Spray House: at the foot of the Wiltshire downs, Frances and Ralph Partridge continue to lead quietly civilised lives, in which books and the company of friends predominate. Their son, Burgo, now fourteen, is entering a difficult adolescence. The summer of 1949 is sultry; the only cool time is the early morning, and Frances walks barefoot on her dew-laden lawn before breakfast. Later in the day, a circle of deckchairs under the beech tree is a shady refuge for drinks and conversation. On 6 August Frances rereads her wartime diaries and reflects on how life has changed since the days when her interest was exclusively, hectically engaged by public horrors:

Now we have lived through three years of total peace; we still have rationing but don't fear it getting worse (as we did then); there have been political crises and alarms for us to read and talk about ad lib. The chief change is that today our minds are much more often full of the books we are reading, the work we are doing, and above all the vicissitudes in the lives of Burgo and many friends whose troubles are very much our concern.

Her pacifist convictions remain unaltered.

Oundle, Northamptonshire: another wedding picture. Lorna is smiling for the camera, after trading her maiden name, Bradey, for Kite. Ralph, her husband, is a career soldier with the British Army of Occupation in Germany, a onetime patient of hers. In Hanover in 1948 they renewed their romance, and he proposed after a night at the opera. Lorna's marriage to Ralph Kite means automatic resignation from Queen Alexandra's Imperial Military Nursing Service. She has a child now, she works in the army thrift shop, dutifully attends coffee mornings, hosts curry lunches and tries to avoid becoming too like the other 'kitten' wives on the base at Sölingen near Düsseldorf. But there is nothing to do, and it is, in many ways, a mind-numbing existence. Lorna, high-spirited, sociable and sexy, is too uncompromising to fit neatly into the 'devoted military wife' slot. She has always lived life to the full, always loved to party, and the role of flirt comes more naturally to her than that of docile housewife. And, though their marriage is strong and loving, any spare energy is expended on stormy rows with her husband.

A railway station in Sussex: Anne Popham, back from Germany since 1947, has found a job as an exhibitions organiser for the newly formed Arts Council of Great Britain, work which has brought her back into contact with the world of contemporary artists. One of these, a tall, talented man with red hair, asks her out. He seems kind, clever and impressively well informed about politics and current affairs and yet he also seems deeply unsure of himself. An invitation follows to his parents' Sussex home, where Anne sits to him for her portrait. The family welcomes her; she feels admired, appreciated. He sculpts a head of clay, caressing the terracotta cheekbones, moulding her lips with sensitive, spatula-like fingers. She feels beautiful. When he takes her to catch her train she reaches up and briefly kisses him. They look at each other with new eyes.

Ontario, Canada: Mavis Lever, married name Mavis Batey, has travelled to Ottawa, where her husband Keith has accepted a position on the staff of the High Commission. After five years of fever-pitch work at Bletchley, Mavis is relieved not to have to keep up the pace. 'We could never have slogged the way we did without the excitement of the war. Mercifully, I decided to have a baby.' So she has packed her Harris tweed suit and boarded a liner for the other side of the world. She also takes with her her secret life of codes and intercepts, but for another twenty-five years she will not reveal a word about her wartime occupation. In Canada a second baby is born. Far from home in a land of plenty, Mavis enjoys the heaven of disposable nappies; also chocolate, and steak. Inexperienced as a cook, one of our foremost code-breakers is almost floored by the expectation that she will whip up a three-course diplomatic dinner for her husband's colleagues – 'How do you feed an Ambassador when your repertoire doesn't extend beyond corned beef and bread-and-butter pudding?' The Bateys return to England in 1950: with her family growing up, Mavis discovers a surprising new outlet for her forensic talents and love of literature, becoming the secretary and later president of the Garden History Society.

Edinburgh: Jean Park (née McFadyen), has 'landed on her feet'. After months of frustration living with the in-laws in Edinburgh, she has the luck to find a flat in the church manse. Brenda, the minister's wife, is pregnant and has advertised the accommodation in return for help in the house. A happy time follows: 'We got on great. I only worked for her up until lunchtime, and my time was my own after that.' Brenda and she share out the washing, the baking, and – when the time comes – baby tips. Jean's own daughter is born in 1948. How far has she come from her lonely teenage days, skivvying in the great landowner's remote castle in the glens? In her view, cleaning for Brenda at the manse was a world away. 'My life had changed completely. It definitely gave me confidence. I would never have done all these things if it hadn't been for the war.' Her relationship with her employer and landlady is one of mutual respect and firm friendship.

Blackheath, London: an envelope drops through Miss Mary Cornish's letterbox, from nineteen-year-old Fred Steels. It contains greetings, and reminiscences about the days they spent together after Lifeboat Number 12 was cast adrift on the Atlantic ocean. 'It is just over 4 years since we wrote to each other,' he tells her,

but I do know that it is just over 8 years since we shared our nightmare experience, and I want you to know that I for one will never forget what you did for us during that experience.

Miss Cornish reads it and adds it to a growing bundle of correspondence from the boys – Paul Shearing, Ken Sparks and Billy Short

– who still write to her, addressing her as 'Auntie Mary'. She is fifty now and has returned to her life as a music teacher. If anything, her ordeal has sharpened her appetite for life: for music, gardens, books, travel and friendships. The fortitude and mental grip that helped Mary Cornish survive shipwreck and despair now propel her forward; she possesses, as her niece says, 'a fiery spirit'.

Leamington Spa, Warwickshire: the wedding of Alan Milburn to Judy Pickard is taking place, just over a year after his return from Oflag VIIB. To his mother's relief, Alan spends the six months following his release on light duties in a mixed battalion only 10 miles from Burleigh, the home in Balsall Common where she has spent so many anxious hours awaiting news of his safety. During this time he is billeted at a hotel named The Oaks, and it is here that he meets Judy, whose mother is the proprietor. Judy finds her new mother-in-law, Clara Milburn, to be a firm and friendly woman – 'unique in many ways'. In her sixties, she continues practical and as busy as ever, gardening, reading, writing, painting and tending to her husband Jack's needs. With Alan settled, she eagerly awaits the arrival of a Milburn grandson (and it *must* be a boy), for in Clara's world view Milburn men still lead the human procession, while Milburn women are there to applaud, to wait and to sew on their buttons.

South Kensington: Frances Parker (née Faviell) is remaking her life in London after the extremities of the Blitz, the anguish of post-war Berlin. The bombs had razed 33 Cheyne Place to the ground; she and Richard have moved to an airy and comfortable modern house with a large studio in a quiet street behind Fulham Road. John is at school. Back in her old haunts, Frances picks up the artistic social life that she left behind in 1939. She has time and peace of mind, too, to give to painting, and canvases accumulate. The studio is stacked high with portraits of her many friends, lovingly executed miniatures, the occasional exuberant flower piece: a rhododendron, joyfully magenta in its blue vase. But the war memories persist. Painful and difficult though she finds it, Frances embarks on a book about her time in Berlin, followed by a book about the Chelsea Blitz. Writing them is both liberating and cathartic, and the books are well received. But *A Chelsea Concerto* will be her last. Frances Faviell now confronts a war that is unwinnable, for at fifty-seven she is dying of an untreatable cancer.

North Berwick, the Firth of Forth: it's the Sunday before Kay Mellis's wedding to Alastair Wight. In Scotland in 1950, working-class tradition still requires the engaged couple to hold open house for well-wishers, who are expected to call by bearing gifts: useful household items like wringers, sewing-machines and carpet sweepers. Kay's mum has made it clear that she and Alastair ought to stay in to greet the many guests from their close-knit Edinburgh neighbourhood. But Kay and Alastair, who have known each other since childhood, have other ideas:

That weekend we decided that we weren't going to be staying in on a Sunday, we were going to North Berwick on the bus. My mother wasn't best pleased because she thought people would come and we wouldn't be there. But still, away we went.

The couple walk along the bay arm in arm, past the outdoor salt-water swimming pool and round the picturesque harbour. Perhaps they reminisce about Kay's Land Army days: the back-breaking years when girls like her 'weren't allowed to be miserable' despite her sore hands, raw from hoeing, and the rats that plagued her nights. Or maybe she remembers John, the kindly farmer who employed her – 'I was his chick' – or the reels in the village hall after the day's work was done.

But most likely she and Alastair talk about how life will be when they are married. Dress-making is her love; she won't have to give that up. His steady job with a printing machinery firm will ensure them an adequate income.

The war ending was going to be the start of something wonderful. We'd rent a house, it wouldn't be bought, you know what I mean? – and we'd get some furniture. A Chesterfield suite, a dining room suite and a bedroom suite.

On that sunny afternoon, with the sea sparkling and the gannets calling from the Bass Rock, Vera Lynn's promise of peace is being fulfilled for Kay and Alastair:

We had a lovely time in North Berwick. We had a bag of chips out of the chip shop. And I felt we had done what we wanted to do that day. Maybe we didn't do the right thing. But we did it because it was what *we* wanted to do.

They feel lucky to be alive and in love. In a week they will be man and wife. They dream of a peaceful future. They will have a family and, in time, grandchildren. Kay's sewing-machine will whirr all day, and there will be all the fabric she ever wanted.

Kay Wight is in her late eighties now. She and Alastair still live quietly in their modest home in an Edinburgh suburb. She tut-tuts a little about modernity – 'Kids now grow up before their time. Och, it's a disaster!' – about the way her granddaughters don't learn to cook – 'What's better than a plate of mince and tatties? Don't get me started!' – and about the way women wear trousers to dances – 'There's nothing worse.' She laments the loss of community: 'Life was so different then – your aunties and uncles and everybody lived nearby. Your whole life was different, you know what I mean? If you were bombed out it was a case of "Come in, come in." There was always a door open.' And teenagers get away with disrespect to the old in a way that to her is incomprehensible:

So I say, all right, I'll go back to my wee old chair.

It is the fate of every generation, as it grows old, to be pushed to one side by the young. The achievements and sacrifices of the 1940s women have bought us peace, but we take them for granted. Their values are rejected as old-fashioned and irrelevant. We patronise them a little and, ultimately, forget them. The process is necessary, but we also lose by it. For if we are ever to learn from history, we must get under the skins of the people who made it: our mothers, our aunts, our grandmothers, Kay Wight, and millions like her. They are us, and we will, in our turn, be like them.

Appendix: Military and Civilian Casualties among Women 1939–1945

Women's Auxiliary Services

	Killed	Wounded	Missing	POW
Wrens	102	22		
ATS (including Army Nursing Services)	335	302	94	20
WAAFs	187	420	4	
Total	624	744	98	20

Civilians*

Killed or missing, believed killed	Injured / detained in hospital
25,399	37,822

* figures include female Civil Defence workers.

Figures from: 'Command Paper 6832 – Strength and Casualties of the Armed Forces and Auxiliary Services of the United Kingdom 1939 to 1945', in W. Franklin Mellor, ed., *History of the Second World War, United Kingdom Medical Series: Casualties and Medical Statistics* (Her Majesty's Stationery Office, London, 1972), pp. 834–9.

Notes on Sources

The following notes give only principal sources consulted and are firmly aimed at the general reader rather than the academic. For all publication details please refer to the Select Bibliography on page 480.

At the risk of disappointing lovers of statistics, I have not credited the use of every figure throughout the book; statistical research on the Second World War is readily available. My principal statistical references derive from the following books:

Calder, Angus, *The People's War: Britain 1939–1945*.

Halsey, A. H., *Trends in British Society since 1900: A Guide to the Changing Social Structure of Britain*.

Howlett, Peter, *Fighting with Figures: A Statistical Digest of the Second World War*.

Kynaston, David, *Austerity Britain 1945–51*.

Longmate, Norman, *How We Lived Then: A History of Everyday Life during the Second World War*.

Noakes, Lucy, *Women in the British Army: War and the Gentle Sex 1907–1948*.

Summerfield, Penny, *Women Workers in the Second World War: Production and Patriarchy in Conflict*.

Winter, J. M., 'The Demographic Consequences of the War', in H. L. Smith, ed., *War and Social Change: British Society in the Second World War*.

Zweiniger-Bargielowska, Ina, *Austerity in Britain: Rationing, Controls and Consumption, 1939–1955*.

Certain sources recur throughout the book; in such cases I have annotated them, for the sake of brevity, with abbreviations as follows:

AC/ENEMY	Aileen Clayton, *The Enemy is Listening*
AC/PP	Aileen Clayton, private papers
AP/A	Anne Popham, author interview
AP/PP	Anne Popham, private papers

BBC/PW	BBC People's War Website
BC/YO	Barbara Cartland, *The Years of Opportunity*
CL/A	Christian Lamb, author interview
CL/HAT	Christian Lamb, *I Only Joined for the Hat*
CM/MM	Clara Milburn, *Mrs Milburn's Diaries*
CW/A	Cora Williams, author interview
DB/A	Dorothy Brewer-Kerr, author interview
DB/GIRLS	Dorothy Brewer-Kerr, *The Girls Behind the Guns*
DW/DV	Doris White, *D for Doris, V for Victory*
EJH/A	Elizabeth Jane Howard, author interview
EJH/S	Elizabeth Jane Howard, *Slipstream*
FF/BEAR	Frances Faviell, *The Dancing Bear*
FF/CHELSEA	Frances Faviell, *A Chelsea Concerto*
FM/A	Flo Mahony, author interview
FP/EL	Frances Partridge, *Everything to Lose*
FP/PW	Frances Partridge, *A Pacifist's War*
HF/LIME	Helen Forrester, *Lime Street at Two*
HF/L'POOL	Helen Forrester, *By the Waters of Liverpool*
HF/THURS	Helen Forrester, *Thursday's Child*
HL/CI	Helen Long, *Change into Uniform*
JK/A	Joan Kelsall, author interview
JoyT/A	Joy Trindles, author interview with her children
JoyT/PP	Joy Trindles, private papers
JoyT/PW	Joy Trindles, article, BBC People's War
JP/A	Jean Park, author interview
JT/A	Joan Tagg, author interview
JW/AO	Joan Wyndham, *Anything Once*
JW/LB	Joan Wyndham, *Love is Blue*
JW/LL	Joan Wyndham, *Love Lessons*
KW/A	Kay Wight, author interview
LK/MD	Lorna Kite, *Mentioned in Despatches*
Mar.P/A	Margaret Pawley, author interview
Mar.P/OI	Margaret Pawley, *In Obedience to Instructions*
MB/A	Mavis Batey, author interview
MB/NGS	Margery Berney, *No Glass Slipper*

MD/A	Mary Angove, author interview
MH/FARM	Madeleine Henrey, *A Farm in Normandy and The Return to the Farm*
MH/JOURNAL	Madeleine Henrey, *Madeleine's Journal*
MH/LONDON	Madeleine Henrey, *London Under Fire*
MO	Mass Observation Archive
MP/A	Marguerite Patten, author interview
MP-D/NY	Mollie Panter-Downes, *The New Yorker*
MS/MEM	Monica Symington, *A Memoire: The War and Its Aftermath*
NB/TIME	Nina Bawden, *In My Own Time*
NL/NLP	Nella Last, *Nella Last's Peace*
NL/NLW	Nella Last, *Nella Last's War*
NM/NOTES	Naomi Mitchison, *Among You Taking Notes*
PB/A	Pip Brimson, author interview
PB/PP	Pip Brimson, private papers
PB/WAAF	Pip Brimson, *A WAAF in Bomber Command*
PC-H/A	Patience Chadwyck-Healey, author interview
PW/A	Phyllis Willmott, author interview
PW/CAW	Phyllis Willmott, *Coming of Age in Wartime*
PW/CCA	Phyllis Willmott, Diary, Churchill College Archive
PW/GG	Phyllis Willmott, *A Green Girl*
PW/JS	Phyllis Willmott, *Joys and Sorrows*
SH-J/A	Sheila Hails, author interview
TR/A	Thelma Rendle, author interview
VA/A	Verily Anderson, author interview
VA/SPAM	Verily Anderson, *Spam Tomorrow*
VA/SQUARE	Verily Anderson, *Our Square*

Notes

Prelude

pages 1–2. 'a very ordinary girl . . .': PW/GG; PW/CAW; PW/CCA.
pages 2–3. 'For skinny Jean McFadyen . . .': JP/A.
page 3. 'Patience Chadwyck-Healey . . .': PC-H/A.

pages 4–5. 'Kay Mellis, now in her late eighties . . .': KW/A.

page 5. 'Margaret Herbertson, a diplomat's daughter . . .': Mar.P/A.

pages 5–6. 'Phyllis ('Pip') Beck . . .': PB/PP; PB/WAAF.

page 6. 'Twenty-five year-old Margery Berney . . .': MB/NGS.

page 6. 'Mary Cornish shares a flat . . .': author interviews with Elizabeth Paterson (Mary Cornish's niece), 2009, and Maggie Paterson (niece-in-law), 2009.

pages 6–7. 'Thelma Ryder, at seventeen . . .': TR/A.

page 7. 'Clara Milburn is fifty-five . . .': CM/MM.

page 7. 'Helen Vlasto is spending . . .': HL/CI; author correspondence with Christopher Long (son of Helen Long née Vlasto).

pages 7–8. 'Monica Littleboy, daughter of a manager . . .': MS/MEM.

page 8. 'Anne Popham, aged twenty-two . . .': AP/A.

page 8. 'Nella Last has lived . . .': NL/NLW

page 8. 'Mavis Lever, a well-read sixth-former . . .': MB/A.

pages 8–9. 'Helen Forrester's family . . .': HF/L'POOL.

page 9. 'Madeleine Henrey, the chic French wife . . .': MH/LONDON.

Chapter 1: We're at War

page 10. 'Joan Wyndham started to keep a diary . . .': JW/LL.

page 10. 'Margaret Perry from Nottingham . . .': Margaret Perry's untitled memoir is held in the collection of working-class autobiographies at Brunel University.

page 11. 'Mary Hewins from Stratford-upon-Avon . . .': Angela Hewins, *Mary, after the Queen*.

page 11. 'Debutante Susan Meyrick . . .: cited in Anne de Courcy, *Debs at War: 1939-1945 – How Wartime Changed Their Lives*.

page 11. 'Mary Angove down in the West Country . . .': MD/A.

page 11. 'Flo Mahony, now in her late eighties . . .': FM/A.

page 11. 'get a little extra soap darling . . .': MP/A.

page 11. 'buy up hairpins, Kirby grips . . .': cited in Norman Longmate, *How We Lived Then: A History of Everyday Life during the Second World War*.

page 11. 'Dolly Scannell's baby . . .': Dorothy Scannell, *Dolly's War*.

page 11. 'Kathleen Hale's husband . . .': Kathleen Hale, *A Slender Reputation*.

page 11. 'Virginia Graham ordered . . .': Janie Hampton, ed., *Joyce and Ginnie: The Letters of Joyce Grenfell and Virginia Graham*.

pages 11–12. 'Edna Hughes from Liverpool . . .': cited in Colin and Eileen Townsend, *War Wives: A Second World War Anthology*.

page 12. 'Some are learning to be cooks . . .': *Woman's Own*, 9 September 1939.

page 12. 'a popular perception of the ATS . . .': see Lucy Noakes, *Women in the British Army: War and the Gentle Sex 1907–1948*.

page 13. 'Patience admits . . .': PC-H/A.

page 13. 'Twenty-four-year-old Verily Bruce . . .': VA/A; VA/SPAM.

pages 13–15. 'Frances Faviell, thirty-seven . . .': FF/CHELSEA.

page 15. 'Helen Forrester was also aware . . .': HF/L'POOL.

page 16. 'Joan Wyndham was busy . . .': JW/LL.

page 16. 'Another woman recollected . . .': cited in Norman Longmate, ed., *The Home Front: An Anthology of Personal Experience 1938–1945*.

pages 17–18. 'Helen Vlasto, on holiday with her family . . .': HL/CI.

page 17. 'Nature is providing . . .': cited in Longmate, ed., *The Home Front*.

page 18. 'Sixteen-year-old Pip Beck . . .': PB/PP.

page 18. 'Phyllis Noble was "very scared" . . .': PW/CCA.

page 18. 'I get emotional remembering it . . .': MD/A.

page 18. 'one sixteen-year-old . . .': cited in Longmate, ed., *The Home Front*.

page 18. 'Another – in the middle . . .': LK/MD.

pages 18–19. 'Marguerite Eave had just moved . . .': MP/A.

page 19. 'Frances Faviell, who . . .': FF/CHELSEA.

pages 19–20. 'In Streatham, Pat Bawland . . .': author interview with Pat Evans, née Bawland, 2008.

pages 20–21. 'forty-nine-year-old housewife Nella Last . . .': NL/NLW.

page 21. 'Patience Chadwyck-Healey . . .': PC-H/A.

pages 21–2. 'Frances Faviell watched carloads . . .': FF/CHELSEA.

page 22. 'fourteen-year-old Nina Mabey . . .': NB/TIME.

pages 22–3. 'the Forrester family were visited . . .': HF/L'POOL.

page 23. 'Mrs Lilian Roberts . . .': see www.wartimememories.co.uk.

pages 23–4. 'The diarist Frances Partridge . . .': FP/PW.

pages 24–5. 'The Women's Voluntary Service . . .': see Charles Graves, *Women in Green: The Story of the W.V.S.*; see also James Hinton, *Women, Social Leadership and the Second World War: Continuities of Class*.

page 25. 'Rene Smith, a respectable newlywed . . .': cited in Townsend and Townsend, *War Wives*.

page 25. 'The Tyson family . . .': see Ben Wicks, *No Time to Wave Goodbye*.

page 26. 'Nina Mabey was primarily dismayed . . .': NB/TIME.

page 26. 'Despite much kindness . . .': HF/L'POOL.

page 26. 'Our familiar world . . .': PW/CAW.

pages 26–8. 'Nella Last recorded . . .': NL/NLW.

page 28. 'A woman spotted . . .': MP-D/NY.

page 28. 'One young woman literally bumped . . .': cited in Townsend and Townsend, *War Wives*.

page 28. 'the housewife Clara Milburn . . .': CM/MM.

pages 28–9. 'the writer and journalist Mollie Panter-Downes . . .': MP-D/NY.

page 29. 'This war really isn't at all bad . . .': JW/LL.

page 29. 'Clara Milburn noted . . .': CM/MM.

page 30. 'a speech broadcast on the wireless . . .': cited in introduction to *Joyce Grenfell: The Time of My Life, Entertaining the Troops – Her Wartime Journals*, ed. James Roose-Evans.

pages 30–31. 'In a St Albans store . . .': MO.

page 31. 'there were still croissants . . .': JW/LL.

page 31. 'music teacher Mary Cornish . . .': author interviews with Elizabeth Paterson (Mary Cornish's niece), 2009, and Maggie Paterson (niece-in-law), 2009.

pages 31–2. 'Vera Welch's career . . .': author interview with Dame Vera Lynn, 2009.

page 32. 'Marguerite Eave found herself . . .': MP/A.

pages 32–6. 'Helen Forrester was one . . .': HF/L'POOL.

page 35. 'For Frances Faviell in Chelsea . . .': FF/CHELSEA.

page 36. 'trainee beautician Monica Littleboy . . .': MS/MEM.

pages 36–7. 'the story of Anne Popham . . .': AP/A.

page 37. 'Young Pip Beck . . .': PB/PP.

page 37. 'Frances Campbell-Preston . . .': Frances Campbell-Preston, *The Rich Spoils of Time*.

page 38. 'For fifteen year-old Pat Bawland . . .': author interview with Pat Evans, née Bawland, 2008.

page 38. 'Kay Mellis in Edinburgh . . .': KW/A.

pages 38–9. 'the King spoke to the nation . . .': cited in FF/CHELSEA.

Chapter 2: All Our Prayers

page 40. 'Madeleine Henrey felt . . .': MH/FARM.

pages 40–42 'Lorna Bradey, aged twenty-four . . .': LK/MD.

pages 43–5. 'Clara Milburn was exasperated . . .': CM/MM.

pages 44–5. 'the novelist Barbara Pym . . .': Barbara Pym, *A Very Private Eye: An Autobiography in Letters and Diaries.*

pages 45–6. 'Frances Faviell went . . .': FF/CHELSEA.

pages 46–7. 'Joan Wyndham, aged seventeen . . .': JW/LL.

page 48. 'Everyone is getting married . . .': cited in Sandra Koa Wing, ed., *Our Longest Days: A People's History of the Second World War.*

page 48. 'Randolph Churchill . . .': in Eric Taylor, *Forces Sweethearts: Service Romances in World War II.*

page 48. 'Margery Berney was another . . .': MB/NGS

page 49. 'Eileen Hunt made her way . . .': BBC/PW, article ID: A4056914.

page 49. 'Women want to be partners . . .': cited in Jane Waller and Michael Vaughan-Rees, *Women in Wartime: The Role of Women's Magazines 1939–45.*

page 49. 'Miss E. de Langlois . . . Mrs Gilroy . . . Mrs Hope . . .': all in *Daily Sketch*, May 1940.

page 50. 'WAR WORKERS' SUNDAY DASH . . .': *Daily Sketch*, 27 May 1940.

page 50. 'Mass Observation took . . .': in Dorothy Sheridan, ed., *Wartime Women: An Anthology of Women's Wartime Writing for Mass Observation 1937–45.*

page 50. 'A BLACK DAY . . .': in ibid.

pages 50–51. 'So cruel . . .': in ibid.

pages 51–3. 'The writer Naomi Mitchison . . .': NM/NOTES.

pages 52–3. 'Frances Partridge, also . . .': FP/PW.

pages 53–5. 'On 20 May QA Lorna Bradey . . .': LK/MD.

page 55. 'Mrs Milburn heard . . .': CM/MM.

page 55. 'For the 224,585 British troops . . .': figure from Robert Goralski, *World War II Almanac 1931–1945: A Political and Military Record.*

page 56. 'Peggy Priestman . . .': BBC/PW, article ID: A4051018.

page 56. 'VAD Lucilla Andrews . . .': Lucilla Andrews, *No Time for Romance.*

page 56. 'Kathy Kay's platoon . . .': BBC/PW, article ID: A2278389.

pages 56–7. 'Mary Angove was another . . .': MD/A.

page 57. 'WAAF Joan Davis . . .': BBC/PW, article, ID: A4052413.

pages 57–9. 'In Villers-sur-Mer . . .': MH/FARM.

pages 59–60. 'But the ordeal . . .': LK/MD.

pages 60–61: 'Clara Milburn heard . . .': CM/MM.

page 61. 'Frances Campbell-Preston . . .': Campbell-Preston, *The Rich Spoils of Time.*

page 61. 'News was even slower . . .': BC/YO.

page 61. 'Today I have just heard . . .': CM/MM.

page 62. 'Is it any good fighting . . .': Mass Observation diarist Muriel Green, in Sheridan, ed., *Wartime Women*.

page 62. 'an office worker . . .': cited in Longmate, *How We Lived Then*.

page 62. 'Nella Last was listening . . .': NL/NLW.

page 62. 'In Essex . . .': cited in Joshua Levine, ed., *Forgotten Voices of the Blitz and the Battle for Britain*.

page 62. 'Naomi Mitchison had given . . .': NM/NOTES.

page 63. 'Do not believe rumours . . .': cited in FF/CHELSEA.

page 63. 'the publicity picture . . .': *Daily Sketch*, 19 June 1940.

pages 63–4. 'What General Weygand . . .': see F. W. Heath, ed., *A Churchill Anthology – Selections from the Writings and Speeches of Sir Winston Churchill*.

page 64. 'When people have decried [him] . . .': Joan Seaman, cited in Levine, *Forgotten Voices*.

page 64. 'We would really . . .': Joan Varley, cited in ibid.

page 64. 'Every man and woman . . .': *The Times*, 19 June 1940.

pages 64–8. 'WAAF Aileen Morris . . .': AC/ENEMY.

Chapter 3: Wreckage

pages 69–70. 'Helen Forrester was . . .': HF/L'POOL.

pages 70–72. 'Sonia Wilcox . . .': information supplied by Jonathan Keates.

page 72. 'Shirley Hook's wedding plans . . .': MO.

pages 72–5. 'Verily Bruce's otherwise . . .': VA/A; VA/SPAM.

pages 75–7. 'Helen Forrester and Harry O'Dwyer . . .': HF/L'POOL.

pages 77–81. 'The story of Mary Cornish . . .': Elspeth Huxley, *Atlantic Ordeal*; Tom Nagorski, *Miracles on the Water: The Heroic Survivors of the U-boat attack on the SS* City of Benares *– One of the Great Lost Stories of WWII*; Janet Menzies, *Children of the Doomed Voyage*; Mary Cornish's private papers in the possession of Maggie Paterson; author interviews with Maggie Paterson and Elizabeth Paterson.

pages 81–2. 'Hermann Göring, Commander-in-Chief . . .': cited in John Keegan, *The Second World War*.

page 82. 'Joan Tagg, aged fifteen . . .': JT/A.

page 82. 'In London, Sheila Hails . . .': SH-J/A.

page 82. 'Virginia Woolf described . . .': *The Diaries of Virginia Woolf*, vol. 5, ed. Anne Olivier Bell, entry dated Friday 16 August 1940.

pages 82–3. 'Frances Faviell and her fiancé . . .': FF/CHELSEA.

pages 83–4. 'Virginia Woolf had written an essay . . .': Virginia Woolf, 'Thoughts on Peace in an Air Raid', from *The Death of the Moth and Other Essays*.

page 85. 'Charles Graves, the historian . . .': Graves, *Women in Green*.

page 85. 'Tea became the common healer . . .': Hilde Marchant, *Women and Children Last – A Woman Reporter's Account of the Battle of Britain*.

page 85. 'Yorkshire farmer's wife . . .': see Eric Taylor, *Heroines of World War II*.

page 86. 'Albert Powell from Lewisham . . .': Margaret Powell, *Climbing the Stairs*.

pages 86–7. 'Phyllis Noble decided . . .': PW/CAW, PW/CCA.

page 87. 'Magnificently terrifying . . .': MH/LONDON.

page 87. 'A lethal fairyland . . .': Agnes Fish, *Recollections of Farnsworth and Kearsley 1900–1945*.

page 87. 'the female shelterers went prepared . . .': see Doris Barry in Mavis Nicholson, *What Did You Do in the War, Mummy? Women in World War II*.

page 87. '*Woman's Own* readers . . .': cited in Waller and Vaughan-Rees, *Women in Wartime*.

pages 87–8. 'Two young Bermondsey women . . .': Ruth Durrant, contributor to *The Wartime Memories Project* website www.wartimememories. co.uk/women.html.

page 88. 'The indefatigable Mass Observers . . .': cited in Tom Harrisson, *Living through the Blitz*.

page 88. 'Air-raid warden Barbara Nixon . . .': Barbara Nixon, *Raiders Overhead: A Diary of the London Blitz*.

page 88. 'One woman nightly drank . . .': cited FF/CHELSEA.

page 88. 'Flo Mahony's brand . . .': FM/A.

page 88. 'I'm ill . . .' [and other quotations]: cited by Harrisson, *Living through the Blitz*.

page 88. '63,000 of them . . .': statistics cited in Harold L. Smith, 'The Effects of War on the Status of Women', in H. L. Smith, ed., *War and Social Change – British Society in the Second World War*.

pages 88–9. 'One woman had to be taken . . .': Marchant, *Women and Children Last*.

page 89. 'The writer Fiona MacCarthy . . .': Fiona MacCarthy, *Last Curtsey – The End of the Debutantes.*

pages 89–90. 'One of those who moved in . . .': Diana Cooper, *Trumpets from the Steep.*

page 90. 'Restaurants and dancing . . .': VA/SPAM.

page 90. 'The best swing band . . .': JW/LL.

pages 90–91. 'While London blazed, Mary Cornish . . .': Mary Cornish's private papers in the possession of Maggie Paterson; author interviews with Maggie Paterson and Elizabeth Paterson.

pages 91–3. 'In 1939 Frances Faviell . . .': FF/CHELSEA.

pages 93–4. 'Barbara Nixon encountered . . . ': Barbara Nixon, *Raiders Overhead.*

page 94. 'For Edith . . .': BBC/PW, article ID: A2499519.

page 94. 'Dianna Dobinson's flat . . .': BBC/PW, article ID: A1127549.

page 94. 'Seventeen-year-old Londoner . . .': author interview with Cora Williams, née Styles, 2008.

page 94. 'Elizabeth Bowen emerged . . .': from Elizabeth Bowen, 'London, 1940', in *Collected Impressions.*

pages 95–6. 'Hilde Marchant, a journalist . . .': Marchant, *Women and Children Last.*

page 96. 'A woman working as a driver . . .': cited in Sheridan, ed., *Wartime Women.*

page 96: 'Sheila Hails was coming home . . .': SH-J/A.

pages 96–7. 'A nurse who survived . . .': cited by Taylor, *Heroines of World War II.*

page 97. 'Mass Observation interviewed . . .': cited in Harrisson, *Living though the Blitz.*

page 97. 'As Barbara Cartland said . . .': BC/YO.

pages 98–9. 'twenty-four-year-old Anne Popham . . .': AP/PP.

page 99. 'We all had miserable days . . .': KW/A.

page 99. 'We were much more accepting . . .': JT/A.

page 99. 'You just go on with your life . . .': TR/A.

page 99. 'You just grin and bear it . . .': author interview with Vera Roberts, 2008.

page 100. 'In Coventry and Warwickshire . . .': Taylor, *Heroines of World War II.*

pages 100–101. 'Joan Kelsall still lives . . .': JK/A.

page 101. 'Alma Merritt and her family . . .': letter from Mrs Merritt to the author.

page 101. 'Joyce Hoffman's family . . .': letter from Mrs Hoffman to the author.

pages 101–2. 'The Wall family . . .': letter from Phillip Wall to the author.

page 102. 'Clara Milburn arose . . .': CM/MM.

page 102. 'like old sheets . . .': in Angela Hewins, *Mary, after the Queen*.

page 102. 'I coped by getting angry . . .': JK/A.

page 102. 'Cora Styles was sixteen . . .': CW/A.

page 102. 'Marguerite Patten reserves . . .': MP/A.

pages 102–3. 'Mrs Milburn went out . . .': CM/MM.

pages 103–4. 'Joan Wyndham had fallen . . .': JW/LB.

page 104. 'Mary Wesley's wartime . . .': see Patrick Marnham, *Wild Mary: The Life of Mary Wesley*.

page 104. 'Phyllis Noble noticed . . .': PW/CAW.

pages 104–5. 'In the London underground . . .': Harrisson, *Living through the Blitz*.

page 105. 'I had seen a couple . . .': FF/CHELSEA.

Chapter 4: 'Ready to Win the War'

pages 106–7. 'In the summer of 1941 . . .': author interview with Kaye Bastin, née Emery, 2008.

page 108. 'Pip Beck joined the ARP . . .': PB/PP.

page 109. 'Mass Observation offered the case-history . . .': Harrisson, *Living through the Blitz*.

page 109. 'Sometimes it is the small . . .': HF/L'POOL.

page 109. 'Barbara Cartland put in a plea . . . ': BC/YO.

pages 109–10. 'Nella Last reached . . .': NL/NLW.

pages 110–11. 'Frances Faviell . . .': FF/CHELSEA; interview with Mrs Pamela Hanbury.

page 111. 'Nella Last's reflections . . .': NL/NLW.

page 113. 'We all feel very strongly . . .': *Daily Sketch*, 21 March 1941.

page 113. 'The Labour Party conference . . .': *The Times*, 15 April 1941.

page 113. 'The army had a sleazy reputation . . .': see Noakes, *Women in the British Army*.

page 114. 'In the end . . .': Mary Grieve, *Millions Made My Story*.

page 115. 'Edith Summerskill . . .': from 'Conscription and Women', in *The Fortnightly*, March 1942.

page 115. 'Most of us felt . . .': FF/CHELSEA.

page 115. 'For a housewife . . .': cited in Penny Summerfield, *Women Workers in the Second World War: Production and Patriarchy in Conflict*.

page 115. 'Monica Littleboy's experience . . .': MS/MEM.

pages 115–16. 'Mrs M. in the Midlands . . .': cited in Townsend and Townsend, *War Wives*.

page 116. 'Young women like Phyllis Noble . . .': PW/CAW; PW/CAA.

pages 117–20. 'One of these young women . . .': DB/GIRLS.

pages 120–23. 'Doris, a sunny-tempered . . .': DW/DV.

pages 123–7. 'Twenty-one-year-old Mavis Lever . . .': MB/A; *The Bletchley Park War Diaries July 1939–August 1945*. See also www.royalnavy.mod.uk/history/battles/.

pages 127–9. 'After her narrow escape . . .': LK/MD.

pages 130–33. 'For her part . . .': DW/DV.

page 131: 'A frequent wartime catastrophe . . .'; Tottenham Court Road: BBC/PW, article ID: A2429561; Sheffield: see Edie Rutherford in Koa Wing, ed., *Our Longest Days*; Truro: Charmian Martin's war memories at www.thisiscornwall.co.uk; Cairo: see Grenfell, *The Time of My Life*.

page 131: 'No man wants to come home . . .': see Waller and Vaughan-Rees, *Women in Wartime*.

page 132. 'When Doffy Brewer left home . . .': DB/GIRLS.

pages 132–3. 'Barbara Cartland . . .': BC/YO.

page 133. 'One ATS officer . . .': cited in de Courcy, *Debs at War*.

page 133. 'Jenny Nicholson, the author . . .': Jenny Nicholson, *Kiss the Girls Goodbye*.

page 134. 'every troop locker . . .': see John Costello, *Love, Sex and War 1939–1945*.

page 134. 'thereby ruining . . .': MP-D/NY.

page 135. 'clothes-conscious Madeleine Henrey . . .': MH/LONDON.

page 135. 'It's getting easy . . .': NL/NLW.

pages 135–6. 'Phyllis Noble's job . . .': PW/CAW.

pages 136–8. 'For Helen Forrester . . .': HF/LIME.

page 138. 'As one woman said . . .': cited in Longmate, *How We Lived Then*.

pages 138–9. 'Newlywed Kaye Bastin . . .': author interview with Kaye Bastin, née Emery, 2008.

page 139. 'There was Mrs Louis . . .': cited in May Rainer, *Emma's Daughter*; this unpublished memoir is held in the collection of working-class autobiographies at Brunel University.

pages 139–40. 'There was Elizabeth Jane Howard . . .': EJH/A; EJH/S.

page 140. 'Margaret Perry . . .': Margaret Perry's untitled memoir is held in the collection of working-class autobiographies at Brunel University.

pages 140–41. 'Barbara Cartland worked . . .': BC/YO.

Chapter 5: 'Your Country Welcomes Your Services'

pages 142–3. 'At Ham Spray House . . .': FP/PW.

page 144. 'Christian Oldham, the convent-educated . . .': CL/A; CL/HAT.

page 145. 'An ATS recruit recalled . . .': Sylvia Mundahl Harris, *The View from the Cookhouse Floor*.

page 145. 'The knickers were long-legged . . .': FM/A; JT/A.

page 145. 'Just imagine . . .': cited in Vera Lynn with Robin Cross and Jenny de Gex, *Unsung Heroines: The Women Who Won the War*.

page 146. 'A dazzling Wren . . .': see *The Wartime Scrapbook: On the Home Front 1939 to 1945*, compiled by Robert Opie.

page 146. 'Clara Milburn and her husband . . .': CM/MM.

page 146. '*The Daily Mail* invited readers . . .': cited in Cooper, *Trumpets from the Steep*.

page 146. 'Vera Roberts trained . . .': author interview with Vera Roberts, 2008.

pages 146–7. 'she would immediately stride . . .': cited in Nicholson, *Kiss the Girls Goodbye*.

page 147. 'It still wasn't . . .': see M-O Bulletin on *Women in Public Houses*, in Sheridan, ed., *Wartime Women*.

page 147. 'Those ATS girls . . .': cited in Hylton, *Their Darkest Hour*.

page 147. 'nothing but a league . . .': see Noakes, *Women in the British Army*.

page 147. 'officers' groundsheets . . .': examples given in Hylton, *Their Darkest Hour*.

page 148. 'In her account . . .': Hilary Wayne, *Two Odd Soldiers*.

page 148. 'I never had any trouble . . .': cited in de Courcy, *Debs at War*.

page 148. 'Eileen Rouse came back . . .': author interview with Eileen Morgan, née Rouse, 2008.

page 148. 'For Pat Bawland . . .': author interview with Pat Evans, née Bawland, 2008.

page 149. 'Flo Mahony's feelings . . .': FM/A.

pages 149–52. 'Twenty-year-old Jean McFadyen . . .': JP/A.

pages 152–3 'Kay Mellis was another . . .': KW/A.

page 153. 'Another propagandising . . .': Vita Sackville-West, *The Women's Land Army*.

pages 153–4. 'Shirley Joseph described . . .': Shirley Joseph, *If Their Mothers Only Knew: An Unofficial Account of Life in the Women's Land Army*.

page 154. 'Monica Littleboy held out . . .': MS/MEM.

page 154. 'Mary Fedden chose . . .': from Nicholson, ed., *What Did You Do in the War, Mummy?*

page 155. 'Patience Chadwyck-Healey would . . .': PC-H/A.

pages 155–6. 'Christian Oldham in the Wrens . . .': CL/HAT.

page 156. 'For Audrey Johnson . . .': cited in CL/HAT.

page 157. 'evacuated from Ilford . . .': NB/TIME.

page 157. 'WAAF Flo Mahony . . .': FM/A.

page 158. 'Mavis Lever was well aware . . .': MB/A.

page 158. 'Patience Chadwyck-Healey couldn't bear . . .': PC-H/A.

page 158. 'And according to Joan Wyndham . . .': JW/LB.

page 158. 'Ex-debutante Wren . . .': de Courcy, *Debs at War*.

page 158. 'When Barbara Pym . . .': Pym, *A Very Private Eye*.

page 158. 'I was used to dear . . .': de Courcy, *Debs at War*.

page 158. 'One well-educated Wren . . .': private information.

pages 159–63. 'The story of Christian Oldham's life . . .': CL/A; CL/HAT.

pages 163–9. 'Eighteen-year-old Pip Beck . . .': PB/PP; PB/WAAF.

page 167 'Not a Cloud in the Sky . . .': lyrics taken from version written and composed by Tommie Connor and Eddie Lisbona.

page 170. 'Frances Partridge's small corner . . .': FP/PW.

pages 170–71. 'Sheila Hails was born . . .': SH-J/A.

pages 171–2. 'Not all female conscientious objectors . . .': see Denis Hayes, *Challenge of Conscience*.

page 172. 'the artist Mary Fedden . . .': Nicholson, ed., *What Did You Do in the War, Mummy?*

page 173. 'Cliff seems . . .': NL/NLW.

page 173. 'Three years today . . .': CM/MM.

pages 173–5. 'Anne Popham's lover . . .': AP/A; AP/PP.

Chapter 6: The Girl That Makes the Thing-ummy Bob

page 176. '250,000 20–21-year-olds . . .': taken from *The Daily Sketch*, 1942.

page 176. 'A convocation of . . .': cited in Grieve, *Millions Made My Story*.

page 177. 'Rage stirred . . .': see Edith Olivier, *Night Thoughts of a Country Landlady*.

pages 177–8. 'But in Barrow-in-Furness . . .': NL/NLW.

page 178. 'Vere Hodgson . . .': Vere Hodgson, *Few Eggs and No Oranges: The Diaries of Vere Hodgson 1940–45*.

page 178. 'one WAAF to put on two stone . . .': JT/A.

page 178. 'a nutritious picnic treat . . .': *The Good Housekeeping Book of Thrifty War-Time Recipes* (approved by the Ministry of Food).

page 178. '*Woman's Own* gave recipes . . .': *Woman's Own*, 1943.

page 178. '*The Daily Express* . . .': see *The Wartime Scrapbook*.

pages 178–9. 'Nella Last was proud . . .': NL/NLW.

page 179. 'the Advice Division . . .': newspaper cutting cited in Bette Anderson, *We Just Got on with It – British Women in World War II*.

page 179. 'Try cooking cabbage . . .': *The Wartime Scrapbook*.

pages 179–80. 'In 1942 the home economist . . .': MP/A.

pages 180–81. 'We never went without . . .': FM/A.

page 181. 'Eileen Rouse says . . .': author interview with Eileen Morgan, née Rouse, 2008.

pages 181–4. 'One of these was Zelma Katin . . .': Zelma Katin, *Clippie: The Autobiography of a War Time Conductress*.

page 184. 'Mrs Milburn marvelled . . .': CM/MM.

pages 184–5. 'the writer Amabel Williams-Ellis . . .': Amabel Williams-Ellis, *Women in War Factories*.

pages 186–7. 'Until 1942 Thelma Ryder lived . . .': TR/A.

page 187. 'Emily Jones's face . . .': Margaretta Jolly, ed., *Dear Laughing Motorbyke: Letters from Women Welders of the Second World War*.

pages 188–9. 'Elsie Whiteman and . . .': Sue Bruley, ed., *Working for Victory: A Diary of Life in a Second World War Factory*.

page 190. 'Among the Yorkshire welders . . .': Jolly, ed., *Dear Laughing Motorbyke*.

pages 190–91. 'My initiation . . .': cited in Longmate, ed., *The Home Front*.

page 191. 'Margaret Perry was another . . .': Margaret Perry's untitled memoir is held in the collection of working-class autobiographies at Brunel University.

page 191. 'The welders seem not . . .': Jolly, ed., *Dear Laughing Motorbyke*.

page 191. 'One investigation . . .': see Pearl Jephcott, *Rising Twenty: Notes on Some Ordinary Girls*.

page 192. 'Making a thing . . .': see 'The Thing-Ummy-Bob', written by Gordon Thompson and David Heneker.

pages 192–3. 'In their off-duty . . .': Jolly, ed., *Dear Laughing Motorbyke*.

page 193. 'Amabel Williams-Ellis's book . . .': Amabel Williams-Ellis, *Women in War Factories*.

page 194. 'One day . . . a gang of us . . .': cited in Townsend and Townsend, *War Wives*.

page 194. 'a joke started . . .': see Costello, *Love, Sex and War*.

pages 194–5. 'When the GIs from Steeple Morden . . .': see Elfrieda Berthiaume Shukert and Barbara Smith Scibetta, *War Brides of World War II*.

page 195. 'As Madeleine Henrey wrote . . .': MH/LONDON.

pages 196–7. 'When African American . . .': see Shukert and Scibetta, *War Brides*.

page 197. 'Frances Partridge wrote . . .': FP/PW.

pages 197–9. 'Dolly Scannell, a married . . .': Scannell, *Dolly's War*.

page 199. 'Margaret Tapster used to dance . . .': BBC/PW, article ID: A5827665.

page 199. 'While American women . . .': see Shukert and Scibetta, *War Brides*.

pages 199–200. '[Eddie] told me . . .' [also Ruth Patchen story]: see http://uswarbrides.com/bride_stories/index.html.

page 200. 'Nineteen-year-old Mary Angove . . .': MD/A.

pages 200–201. 'Barbara Cartland would be . . .': BC/YO.

pages 201–4. 'Corporal 'Mike' Morris's . . .': AC/ENEMY.

pages 204–8. 'A startlingly pretty debutante . . .': HL/CI.

page 208. 'Clara Milburn listened . . .': CM/MM.

page 208. 'the London diarist . . .': Hodgson, *Few Eggs and No Oranges*.

pages 208–9. 'Kathleen Church-Bliss . . .': Bruley, ed., *Working for Victory*.

page 209. Frances Partridge hardly . . .': FP/PW.

page 209. 'Two Sundays ago . . .': see *A Churchill Anthology*.

page 209. 'Nella Last listened . . .': NL/NLW.

Chapter 7: Sunny Intervals

page 210. 'WAAFs like R/T operator . . .': PB/WAAF.

page 210. 'Wren Pat Bawland . . .': author interview with Pat Evans, née Bawland, 2008.

page 210. 'Hearts do break . . .': cited in Townsend and Townsend, *War Wives*.

pages 211–13. 'Today, Cora Williams . . .': CW/A.

page 214. 'a Blitz survey . . .': cited in Harrisson, *Living through the Blitz*.

pages 214–15. 'Nella Last and her husband . . .': NL/NLW.

page 214. 'Doffy Brewer still remembers . . .': DB/A.

page 214. 'Doris Scorer's days off . . .': DW/DV.

page 215. 'Mary Fedden went . . .': from Nicholson, ed., *What Did You Do in the War, Mummy?*

page 215. 'Barbara Pym was . . .': Pym, *A Very Private Eye*.

page 215. 'Clara Milburn found . . .': CM/MM.

pages 215–16. 'Susan Woolfit's war work . . .': in Jenny Hartley, ed., *Hearts Undefeated – Women's Writing of the Second World War*.

page 216. 'You lived at that period . . .': CW/A.

pages 216–20. 'Phyllis Noble longed . . .': PW/CAW; PW/CCA.

pages 220–23. 'Joan Wyndham's war . . .': JW/LB.

pages 223–4. 'Elizabeth Jane Howard . . .': EJH/A; EJH/S.

pages 224–5. 'Meanwhile, Phyllis Noble . . .': PW/CAW; PW/CCA.

page 226. 'Meanwhile, male attitudes . . .': : see Costello, *Love, Sex and War*.

page 226. 'Ex-WAAF Joan Tagg . . .': JT/A.

page 227. 'one US staff sergeant . . .': Costello, *Love, Sex and War*.

page 227. 'they often issued a supercharge . . .': see MH/LONDON.

page 227. 'Flo Mahony was a WAAF . . .': FM/A.

pages 227–8. 'I've been working in London . . .': cited in Nicholson, *What Did You Do in the War, Mummy?*

page 228. 'A slice off a cut loaf . . .': cited in Townsend and Townsend, *War Wives*.

page 228. 'Disturbing clashes . . .': examples cited in Waller and Vaughan-Rees, *Women in Wartime*.

page 229. 'Jane Howard's baby . . .': EJH/S.

page 229. 'the correspondence columns . . .': in *The Times*, 1942.

page 229. 'Mass Observation interviewed . . .': cited in Sheridan, ed., *Wartime Women*.

page 230. 'It's one in the eye . . .': NM/NOTES.

page 230. 'On 23 March 1943 . . .': NL/NLW.

page 230. 'it was a fate . . .': JT/A.

pages 230–31. 'One ATS Officer . . .': cited in de Courcy, *Debs at War*.

page 230. 'Far worse was . . .': LK/MD.

page 231. 'Barbara Cartland stressed . . .': BC/YO.

pages 231–2. 'Seventeen-year-old Vivian Fisher's . . .': cited in Ben Wicks, *Welcome Home: True Stories of Soldiers Returning from World War II*.

page 232. 'Another woman whose husband . . .': cited in Townsend and Townsend, *War Wives*.

page 232. 'A soldier based . . .': cited in Grenfell, *The Time of My Life*.

page 232. 'The agony aunts . . .': see Waller and Vaughan-Rees, *Women in Wartime*.

page 232. 'Pregnant mums . . .': see Longmate, *How We Lived Then*.

pages 232–3. 'Madeleine Henrey . . .': MH/LONDON.

pages 233–4. 'Verily Bruce was another . . .': VA/A; VA/SPAM.

pages 235–9. 'In 1942–3 QA Lorna Bradey's . . .': LK/MD.

pages 240–41. 'In the summer of 1943 . . .': NB/TIME.

page 241. 'Shirley Goodhart . . .': MO.

pages 241–2. 'Margery Baines (née Berney) . . .': MB/NGS.

page 242. 'People talk . . .': MP-D/NY.

page 242. 'Naomi Mitchison took . . .': NM/NOTES.

pages 242–3. 'Land girl Kay Mellis's . . .': KW/A.

page 243. 'Lovely breakfasts . . .': CM/MM.

page 243. 'I just wanted . . .': PC-H/A.

page 243. 'In 1944 the author . . .': Margaret Goldsmith, *Women and the Future*.

pages 243–5. 'Nella Last listened . . .': NL/NLW.

Chapter 8: Over There

page 246. 'No chance of chicken . . .': Hodgson, *Few Eggs and No Oranges*.

page 246. 'Naomi Mitchison hung . . .': NM/NOTES.

page 246. 'Wren Maureen Bolster . . .': Maureen Wells, *Entertaining Eric: A Wartime Love Story*.

page 246. 'In Inverness, Joan Wyndham . . .': JW/LB.

page 246. 'Nella Last wished . . .': NL/NLW.

pages 246–7. 'In Croydon, Elsie Whiteman . . .': Bruley, ed., *Working for Victory*.

page 247. 'Clara Milburn went . . .': CM/MM.

page 247. 'Some of you may . . .': reported in *The Times*, 28 December 1943.

page 247. 'Mike Morris of the "Y" . . .': AC/ENEMY.

page 248. 'Some people think . . .': cited in Koa Wing, ed., *Our Longest Days*.

page 248. 'I'm just living for the day . . .': cited in Tamasin Day-Lewis, ed., *Last Letters Home*.

pages 249–51. 'Joyce Grenfell had packed . . .': see Grenfell, *The Time of My Life*; Hampton, ed., *Joyce and Ginnie*.

pages 251–4. 'Vera Lynn's travel experiences . . .': author interview with Dame Vera Lynn, 2009; interview with Nigel Farndale, *Daily Telegraph*, 17 August 2009.

pages 254–5. 'At the famous Windmill Theatre . . .': see Doris Barry in Nicholson, *What Did You Do in the War, Mummy?*

page 255. 'Theatre director Nancy Hewins . . .': see entry in *Oxford Dictionary of National Biography*.

pages 255–6. 'twenty-two-year-old Isa Barker . . .': author interview with Isa Rankin, née Barker, 2008.

page 256. 'ATS recruit Vera Roberts . . .': author interview with Vera Roberts, 2009.

pages 256–9. 'For Helen Forrester . . .': HF/LIME.

pages 259–60. 'Monica Littleboy . . .': MS/MEM.

page 260. 'On 2 April a friend . . .': FP/PW.

page 260. 'Up in Scotland . . .': NM/NOTES.

page 260. 'Verily Anderson . . .': VA/SPAM.

pages 260–61. 'When Vera Brittain . . .': Vera Brittain, *Testament of Experience: An Autobiographical Story of the Years 1925–1950*.

page 261. 'a nuisance to anyone . . .': MO.

page 261. 'The routine . . .': DW/DV.

page 261. 'Mavis Lever was able . . .': MB/A.

page 261. 'SOE agents . . .': see Mar.P/OI.

pages 262–3. 'Senior Wren Christian Lamb . . .': CL/HAT.

page 263. 'WAAF Edna Hodgson . . .': BBC/PW, article ID: A2300400.

page 263. 'like Maureen Bolster . . .': Wells, *Entertaining Eric*.

pages 263–4. 'On his last leave . . .': HF/LIME.

page 264. 'Sylvia Kay . . .': BBC/PW, article ID: A3094238.

page 264. 'ATS volunteer Mary Macleod . . .': BBC/PW, article ID: A4910528.

page 264. 'A young Irish nurse . . .': BBC/PW, article ID: A8999004.

page 264. 'QA Maureen Gara . . .': Obituary of Lieutenant-Colonel Maureen Gara, *Daily Telegraph*, 27 December 2009.

page 264. 'Meanwhile, Monica . . .': MS/MEM.

page 264. 'On 24 May Elsie Whiteman . . .': Bruley, ed., *Working for Victory*.

pages 264–5. 'Twenty-eight-year-old Aileen Hawkins . . .': see Obituary of Aileen Hawkins in *The Thomas Hardy Fellowship Newsletter* 13 (Winter 2006), ed. John Pentney; poem in Anne Powell, ed., *Shadows of War: British Women's Poetry of the Second World War*.

pages 265–6. 'We are gated . . .': Wells, *Entertaining Eric*.

page 266. 'D-day had been scheduled . . .': see Antony Beevor, *D-Day: The Battle for Normandy*.

page 266. 'On the Isle of Wight . . .': MS/MEM.

page 266. 'The typists working . . .': BBC/PW, article ID: A4910528.

page 266. 'Clara Milburn hung . . .': CM/MM.

pages 266–7. 'Verily Anderson and Julie . . .': VA/SPAM.

page 267. 'Sheets hung out . . .': cited in Longmate, ed., *The Home Front*.

page 267. 'Sheila Hails, marooned . . .': SH-J/A.

pages 267–8. 'Mollie Panter-Downes . . .': MP-D/NY.

page 268. 'For London-based Frenchwoman . . .': MH/LONDON; MH/FARM.

pages 268–9. 'All around us . . .': Rozelle Raynes, *Maid Matelot*.

pages 269–70. 'From the Isle of Wight . . .': MS/MEM.

page 270. 'in Nancy O'Sullivan's . . .': BBC/PW, article ID: A8999004.

page 270. 'In Portsmouth . . .': The D-day and Normandy Fellowship website, http://ddnf.org.uk/, D-Day Memories of Naina Cox.

pages 270–71. 'Monica Littleboy accompanied . . .': MS/MEM.

page 271. 'Maureen Bolster was . . .': Wells, *Entertaining Eric*.

pages 271–3. 'That June, Helen Forrester . . .': HF/LIME.

page 273. 'Wrens like Ena Howes . . .': BBC/PW, article ID: A4162187.

pages 273–4. 'Iris Ogilvie . . .': see Cross and de Gex, *Unsung Heroines*; also obituary of Iris Ogilvie, *Daily Telegraph*, 10 January 2006.

pages 274–8. 'QA Joy Taverner . . .': JoyT/A; see also BBC/PW, article
   ID: A1096580 (reprinted with permission); excerpt from 'Until Belsen'
   in Powell, ed., *Shadows of War*.

Chapter 9: No Real Victory

pages 279–80. 'Miss Florence Speed . . .': Florence Speed, Diary of Miss F.
   M. Speed, Imperial War Museum, Department of Documents, IWM
   86/45/2.

page 280. 'London is in a chastened . . .': Hodgson, *Few Eggs and No
   Oranges*.

page 280. 'the "up-for-the-day . . ."':MP-D/NY.

pages 280–81. 'I don't like these Bombs . . .': in Campbell-Preston, *The
   Rich Spoils of Time*.

page 281. 'As code-breaker . . .': MB/A.

pages 282–3. 'In 1943 ATS . . .': DB/GIRLS.

page 283. 'Horrible creatures . . .': CM/MM.

page 283. 'We all thought . . .': cited in Koa Wing, ed., *Our Longest Days*.

pages 283–4. 'Swamped as she was . . .': MB/NGS.

page 284. 'Maggie Joy Blunt . . .': MO; and see Simon Garfield, *Our Hidden
   Lives – The Remarkable Diaries of Post-war Britain*.

page 284. 'Barbara Cartland questioned . . .': BC/YO.

page 284. 'In summer 1944 . . .': cited in David Kynaston, *Austerity Britain
   1945–1951*.

page 285. 'Writing in 1953 . . .': Vera Brittain, *Lady into Woman: A History
   of Women from Victoria to Elizabeth II*.

page 286. 'What would you be doing . . .': DB/GIRLS.

page 286. 'I long for an excuse . . .': MO.

page 288. 'one smart lady . . .': BBC/PW, article ID: A2915705.

page 288. 'We were a lot fitter . . .': BBC/PW, article ID: A4050749.

page 288. 'Frances Faviell bicycled . . .': FF/CHELSEA.

page 288. 'Don't forget . . .': JT/A.

page 289. 'The public has been asked . . .': MP-D/NY.

page 289. 'Lady Clementine Beit . . .': see Peggy Scott, *British Women at
   War*.

page 290. 'When you feel tired . . .': cited in Longmate, *How We Lived Then*.

page 291. 'Constance Galilee . . .': BBC/PW, article ID: A2915705.

page 291. 'I've hardly anything . . .': MO.

page 291. 'The thoughtful Barbara Cartland . . .': BC/YO.

page 291. 'One diarist described . . .': MO.

page 292. 'Phyllis Noble's mum . . .': PW/CAW.

page 292. 'Frances Partridge was one . . .': FP/PW.

page 292. 'In September 1943 . . .': Speed, Diary.

page 292. 'For Sheila Hails . . .': SH-J/A.

pages 292–3. 'It took the war . . .': NL/NLW.

page 293. 'Our mums could cook . . .': JT/A.

pages 293–7. 'One of them was Margaret Herbertson . . .': Mar.P/OI; Mar.P/A.

pages 297–301. 'QA Joy Taverner . . .': JoyT/A; JoyT/PP; JoyT/PW; excerpt from 'Until Belsen' in Powell, ed., *Shadows of War*.

page 298. 'A British reporter . . .': transcript of Richard Dimbleby's report given on www.spartacus.schoolnet.co.uk/2WW.

page 301. 'Maggie Joy Blunt could . . .': MO.

page 301. 'Anne Popham's job . . .': AP/A.

pages 301–2. 'Maggie Joy Blunt was equally . . .': MO.

page 302. 'Joan Wyndham's party spirits . . .': JW/LB.

page 302. 'Clara Milburn listened . . .': CM/MM.

page 302. 'Vere Hodgson shared . . .': Hodgson, *Few Eggs and No Oranges*.

page 302. 'Naomi Mitchison had witnessed . . .': NM/NOTES.

page 302. 'Sheila Hails, a pacifist . . .': SH-J/A.

pages 302–3. 'Frances Partridge, as usual . . .': FP/PW.

page 303. 'Thelma Ryder's concerns . . .': TR/A.

page 303. 'There is no such thing . . .': 'September 1, 1939', first published in book form in W. H. Auden, *Another Time*.

page 304. 'In 2003 Joy Taverner's . . .': JoyT/PW.

pages 304–7. 'Maggie Joy Blunt was appalled . . .': MO.

Chapter 10: A Brave New World

page 308. 'Mary Angove let rip . . .': MD/A.

pages 308–9. 'Verily Anderson and . . .': VA/SPAM.

pages 308–9. 'The German war . . .': see *A Churchill Anthology*.

page 309. 'Looking on, Mollie Panter-Downes . . .': MP-D/NY.

pages 309–10. 'Marguerite Patten's mother . . .': MP/A.

page 310. '"A magic night" . . .': BBC/PW, article ID: A2756351.

page 310. 'Vere Hodgson recorded . . .': Hodgson, *Few Eggs and No Oranges*.

page 310. 'Like thousands . . .': BBC/PW, article ID: A1951355.

page 310. 'Teenager Anne Thompson . . .': BBC/PW, article ID: A40575117.

page 310. 'In Oxford . . .': NB/TIME.

page 311. 'Like many others . . .': cited in Koa Wing, ed., *Our Longest Days*.

page 311. 'Muriel Green got drunk . . .': cited in ibid.

page 311. 'Joan Wyndham headed . . .': JW/LB.

page 311. 'One young woman . . .': cited in Wicks, *Welcome Home*

page 311. 'Another woman . . .': cited in Longmate, ed., *The Home Front*.

pages 311–12. 'Soldiers like Jack Clark . . .': cited in Day-Lewis, ed., *Last Letters Home*.

page 312. 'By 1945 QA Lorna Bradey . . .': LK/MD.

pages 312–13. 'Margaret Herbertson remained . . .': Mar.P/OI.

page 313. 'Widowed at the age . . .': CW/A.

page 313. 'Monica Littleboy . . .': MS/MEM.

pages 313–14. 'Thelma Ryder didn't . . .': TR/A.

page 314. 'The diarist Shirley Goodhart . . .': MO.

pages 314–16. 'On VE-day Jack Milburn . . .': CM/MM.

pages 316–17. 'Patrick Campbell-Preston . . .': Campbell-Preston, *The Rich Spoils of Time*.

page 317. 'Jean McFadyen was still working . . .': JP/A.

pages 317–19. 'Doris Scorer's boyfriend . . .': DW/DV.

page 319. 'Frank was to prove . . .': information from Roger Kitchen, Wolverton, and recorded interview with Doris White, Living Archive Online, Milton Keynes.

page 319. 'Helen Forrester couldn't help . . .': HF/LIME.

pages 319–20. 'WAAF driver Flo Mahony . . .': FM/A.

page 320. 'Flo Mahony's friend . . .': JT/A.

pages 320–22. 'Still in Italy . . .': Mar.P/OI.

page 322. 'QA Lorna Bradey . . .': LK/MD.

page 323. 'Zelma Katin had become . . .': Katin, *Clippie* .

page 323. 'Naomi Mitchison's socialism . . .': Naomi Mitchison to Tom Harrisson, 9 October 1944, cited in Jenni Calder, *The Nine Lives of Naomi Mitchison*.

page 323. 'Vera Brittain had spent . . .': see entry in *Oxford Dictionary of National Biography*.

page 324. 'On VE-day Nella . . .': NL/NLW.

pages 324–6. 'The wife of a Surrey vicar . . .': see entry in *Oxford Dictionary of National Biography*; also Paul Addison, *Now the War Is Over: A Social History of Britain 1945–51*; and *The Times*, 9 July 1946, 12 September 1947.

page 327. 'Shirley Goodhart's Mass Observation . . .': MO.

pages 327–8. 'The Oxford student . . .': NB/TIME.

page 328. 'The Labour manifesto . . .': see Kynaston, *Austerity Britain*.

pages 328–9 'Naomi Mitchison had mixed . . .': NM/NOTES, and Calder, *The Nine Lives*.

page 329. 'Britain was still living . . .': see Kynaston, *Austerity Britain*.

page 329. 'Nella Last couldn't get . . .': NL/NLW.

page 329. 'In Slough, Maggie Joy Blunt . . .': MO.

page 329. 'Barbara Pym often felt . . .': Pym, *A Very Private Eye*.

page 329. 'Mary Wesley remarked . . .': see Marnham, *Wild Mary*.

pages 329–30. 'In Paris . . .': Cooper, *Trumpets from the Steep*.

page 330. 'People laughed when . . .': cited in Longmate, *How We Lived Then*.

pages 330–31. 'The middle-aged novelist . . .': Ursula Bloom, *Trilogy*.

pages 331–2. 'But Nina Mabey couldn't be there . . .': NB/TIME.

page 332. 'Naomi Mitchison had come down . . .': Calder, *The Nine Lives*.

pages 332–3. 'Some Tories, like Virginia Graham . . .': see Anne Harvey's preface to Virginia Graham, *Consider the Years*.

page 333. 'Nella Last called in . . .': NL/NLW.

page 333. 'Ursula Bloom felt . . .': Ursula Bloom, *Trilogy*.

page 334. 'Thelma Ryder felt . . .': TR/A.

pages 334–5. 'At last, at long last! . . .': cited in Koa Wing, *Our Longest Days*.

page 335. 'Eileen Jones . . .': BBC/PW, article ID: A4506851.

page 335. 'One despairing woman . . .': Mass Observation, *Peace and the Public*.

page 335. 'Ursula Bloom spent . . .': Bloom, *Trilogy*.

page 335. 'Nella Last felt . . .': NL/NLW.

page 335. 'Frances Partridge . . .': FP/PW.

page 336. 'The *Daily Mail* columnist . . .': *Daily Mail*, 9 August 1945.

pages 336–7. 'On VJ-day Lorna Bradey . . .': LK/MD.

pages 337–8. 'For Phyllis Noble . . .': PW/CAW.

page 338. 'Helen Forrester too . . .': HF/LIME.

pages 338–9. 'Monica Littleboy's memories . . .': MS/MEM.

pages 339–40. 'Thelma Ryder was luckier . . .': TR/A.

Chapter 11: Picking Up the Threads

pages 341–2. 'When the war ended . . .': MO.

page 343. 'Ex-FANY Margaret Herbertson . . .': Mar.P/A.

page 343. 'Mike Morris . . .' etc: for all sources see under individual names in abbreviations list.

page 344. 'The rejoicing had gone sour . . .': Bloom, *Trilogy*.

page 344. '*Woman's Own* columnist . . .': *Woman's Own*, March 1946.

page 345. 'One uniformed bride-to-be . . .': cited in Sheridan, ed., *Wartime-Women*.

pages 345–6. 'Nurse Helen Vlasto . . .': HL/CI.

page 346. 'the white flame . . .': NL/NLW.

pages 346–7. 'Ex-Flight Officer Wyndham . . .': JW/AO.

pages 347–8. 'Wren telegraphist . . .': letter to author from Anne Glynn-Jones.

page 348. 'Flo Mahony thrived . . .': FM/A.

page 348. 'An edifice seemed . . .': PB/WAAF.

page 348. 'Stoker Wren Rozelle Raynes . . .': Raynes, *Maid Matelot*.

page 349. 'But Jean McFadyen . . .': JP/A.

pages 350–51. 'When Joan and Les Kelsall . . .': JK/A.

page 351. 'Four walls and a roof . . .': cited in Kynaston, *Austerity Britain*.

pages 351–2. 'the squatting bandwagon . . .': see Addison, *Now the War Is Over*.

page 352. 'The journalist Mollie Panter-Downes . . .': MP-D/NY.

pages 352–3. 'Nella Last was open-eyed . . .': NL/NLP.

page 353. 'The new world was hard . . .': Bloom, *Trilogy*.

page 353. 'All too often . . .': MP-D/NY.

pages 353–4. 'The writer Angela du Maurier . . .': Angela du Maurier, *It's Only the Sister: An Autobiography*.

page 354. 'The diarist Maggie Joy Blunt . . .': MO.

page 354. 'Nevertheless, Mary Manton . . .': *Daily Sketch*, November 1945.

pages 354–5. 'Sylvia Duncan was another . . .': *Daily Sketch*, February 1946.

page 355. '"E", writing to the *Daily Mail* . . .': *Daily Mail*, 16 October 1945.

page 355. 'Nella Last tried to identify . . .': NL/NLP.

page 355. 'There is not room . . .': *Daily Mail*, 16 August 1945.

pages 355–6. 'Helen Forrester put her devastated . . .': HF/LIME.

page 356. Flo Mahony was demobilised . . .': FM/A.

pages 356–8. 'VAD Helen Vlasto . . .': HL/CI.

pages 358–9. 'Joan Wyndham put £5 . . .': JW/AO.

pages 359–61. 'Verily Anderson was almost never . . .': VA/SPAM.

page 361. 'Good morning, my sweet . . .': cited in Susan Briggs, *Keep Smiling Through: The Home Front 1939–45*.

page 362. 'the historian Harold L. Smith . . .': Smith, 'The Effect of War on the Status of Women'.

pages 362–4. 'One of these was Dolly Scannell . . .': Scannell, *Dolly's War*.

page 363. 'Don't expect to pick up . . .': cited in Summers, *Stranger in the House*.

page 365. 'Probably, "When I was in Peshawar in '43" . . .': These examples cited by ibid., Alan Allport, *Demobbed: Coming Home After the Second World War*, and various contemporary newspaper articles and correspondence.

page 365. 'Desert rat Charles Hopkinson . . .': cited in Wicks, *Welcome Home*.

pages 365–7. 'Once demobbed, Chas Scannell . . .': Scannell, *Dolly's War*.

page 366. 'Cookery expert Marguerite Patten's . . .': MP/A.

page 367. 'Ann Temple's finger . . .': article and correspondence in *Daily Mail*, 16 October 1945.

page 369. 'the big-hearted tolerance of Greg James . . .': cited in Summers, *Stranger in the House*.

page 369. 'the murderous rage of Private Reginald Keymer . . . Sergeant Albert Nettleton . . . Private Cyril Patmore . . . ex-serviceman Leonard Holmes . . .': see Allport, *Demobbed*.

pages 369–70. 'One of the few things . . .': MB/NGS.

page 370. 'I am going to have . . .': *Woman*, 23 February 1946.

page 370. 'I am ashamed to say . . .': *Woman*, 16 February 1946.

page 370. 'I am engaged . . .': *Woman's Own*, March 1946.

pages 371–3. 'Shortly after the liberation . . .': MH/FARM.

Chapter 12: A Bitter Time

page 374. 'the romantic fiction author Miss Florence Speed . . .': Speed, Diary.

pages 374–5. 'Three months earlier . . .': from reports in *The Times*, the *Daily Sketch*.

pages 375–81. 'More than 100,000 of these had married . . .': see Shukert and Scibetta, *War Brides*; and http://uswarbrides.com.

pages 376–8. 'Victoria Stevenson . . .': *Woman's Own*, March 1946.

page 377. 'But Elizabeth Jane Howard . . .': EJH/A.

pages 378–9. 'When she first met Kenneth Davis . . .': MD/A.

pages 379–80. 'Peggy came from a . . .': Margaret H. Wharton, *Recollections of a GI War Bride: A Wiltshire Childhood*.

pages 380–81. 'Elizabeth Jane Howard's account . . .': EJH/A.

page 380. 'As one ex-Wren bride recalled . . .': http://uswarbrides.com.

page 381. 'Fred – Fred – dear Fred . . .': from *Brief Encounter*, script by Noël Coward, directed by David Lean.

pages 382–3. 'One 8th Army driver . . .': cited in Allport, *Demobbed*.

page 383. 'One psychologist . . .': Reg Ellery, *Psychiatric Aspects of Modern Warfare*, cited in ibid.

pages 383–4. 'In the spring of 1946 . . .': NB/TIME.

pages 384–5. 'Or take the case of . . .': CL/A, CL/HAT.

pages 385–6. 'Patience Chadwyck-Healey was another . . .': PC-H/A.

page 386. 'Frances Campbell-Preston was another . . .': Campbell-Preston, *The Rich Spoils of Time*.

page 386. 'Pip Beck – ex-WAAF . . .': PB/A.

page 386. 'Cora Johnston, née Styles . . .': CW/A.

page 386. 'Flo Mahony, ex-WAAF . . .': FM/A.

page 387. 'Eileen Morgan, née Rouse . . .': author interview with Eileen Morgan, née Rouse, 2008.

pages 387–9. 'Like so many, Margery Baines . . .': MB/NGS.

pages 389–90. 'WAAF Pip Beck . . .': PB/A; and author interview with Peter Brimson, 2010.

pages 390–91. 'After Cora Johnston's husband . . .': CW/A.

page 391. 'Joy Taverner married . . .': author interview with Michael Trindles and Sue Green (son and daughter of Joy Trindles, née Taverner); JoyT/PP.

pages 391–3. 'In the autumn of 1945 . . .': MS/MEM.

pages 393–5. 'Phyllis Noble was blessed . . .': PW/CAW, PW/JS.

page 395. 'My generation was . . .': SH-J/A.

pages 395–6. 'Frances Partridge was another . . .': FP/EL.

page 396. 'Vera Lynn also . . .': author interview with Dame Vera Lynn, 2009.

pages 396–8. 'WAAF Mike Morris . . .': AC/PP.

pages 398–401. 'In November 1945 . . .': AP/A, AP/PP.

page 401. 'When QA Lorna Bradey . . .': LK/MD.

pages 401–3. 'But the artist Frances Faviell . . .': FF/BEAR.

pages 403–4. '*A Woman in Berlin* . . .': Anonymous, *A Woman in Berlin*, translated by Philip Boehm.

page 403. 'As Virginia Woolf had written . . .': from Woolf, 'Thoughts on Peace in an Air Raid'.

page 404. 'By the time Phyllis Noble . . .': PW/JS.

page 404. 'blizzards were making headlines . . .': *The Times*, the *Daily Sketch*.

pages 404–5. 'Maggie Joy Blunt went shopping . . .': MO.

pages 405–6. 'The nation shivered . . .': for an account of the cold winter of 1947 see Kynaston, *Austerity Britain*.

page 406. 'Bakers were prohibited . . .': *Daily Express*, 12 February 1947.

page 406. 'The *Daily Mirror* offered suggestions . . .': *Daily Mirror*, 14 February 1947.

page 406. 'Margaret Herbertson, who . . .': Mar.P/A.

page 406. 'Thrifty Nella Last . . .': NL/NLP.

page 406. 'Maggie Joy Blunt struggled . . .': MO.

pages 407–10. 'Frances Faviell's account . . .': FF/BEAR.

Chapter 13: There'll Be Bluebirds

page 411. 'I'm not clever . . .': NL/NLP.

page 412. 'Mary Grieve, the editor . . .': Grieve, *Millions Made My Story*.

page 412. 'The rich could not pay more . . .': Bloom, *Trilogy*.

page 412. 'Frances Campbell-Preston's family . . .': Campbell-Preston, *The Rich Spoils of Time*.

page 413. 'The war certainly taught . . .': BC/YO; and Henry Cloud, *Barbara Cartland: Crusader in Pink*.

page 413. 'Allowing for the general impoverishment . . .': George Orwell, *The Collected Essays, Journalism and Letters of George Orwell*, vol. 4.

pages 413–14. 'In 1948 the sociologist . . .': Jephcott, *Rising Twenty*.

page 414. 'Nella Last began to assess . . .': NL/NLP.

page 415. 'I'm having a deliberately . . .': MO.

page 415. 'The holiday-camp phenomenon . . .': Valerie A. Tedder, *Post-war Blues*.

pages 415–16. At the other end of the social scale . . .': MP-D/NY.

pages 416–19. 'The New Look . . .': see Pearson Phillips, 'The New Look', in Michael Sissons and Philip French, eds., *Age of Austerity*; and Harry Hopkins, *The New Look: A Social History of the Forties and Fifties in Britain*.

page 417. 'as Anne Scott-James . . . insisted . . .': letter to *The Times*, 29 September 1947.

page 417. 'Much as the average woman . . .': letter to *The Times*, 1 October 1947.

page 418. 'Women today are taking . . .': Mabel Ridealgh, MP, cited in Sissons and French, eds., *Age of Austerity*.

page 418. 'Oh yes, I'd have liked . . .': TR/A.

pages 418–19, 420. 'Shirley Goodhart was one . . .': MO.

page 420. 'Maggie Joy Blunt wrote . . .': MO.

page 420. 'The romantic novelist . . .': Speed, Diary.

page 421. 'young women like Doffy Brewer . . .': DB/A.

pages 421–4. 'After losing two fiancés . . .': HF/LIME; HF/THURS; and author interview with Robert Bhatia.

pages 424–8. 'The idea of marriage . . .': PW/JS; PW/CCA; PW/A.

pages 428–9. 'On Day One a Leeds woman . . .': examples cited in Addison, *Now the War Is Over*.

pages 429–30. 'Domestic servant Margaret Powell . . .': Powell, *Climbing the Stairs*.

pages 430–31. 'In his essay, "Woman's Place" . . .': William Emrys Williams, 'Women's Role', in *Current Affairs Magazine*, 11 January 1947.

page 432. 'Shirley Goodhart was one young wife . . .': MO.

page 432. 'post-war career advice . . .': examples from *Everywoman*, 1948.

pages 432–4. 'Since the age of sixteen . . .': PW/JS; PW/CCA; PW/A.

pages 434–6. 'For Joan Wyndham . . .': JW/AO.

pages 436–7. 'Nina Bawden's creative talents . . .': NB/TIME.

page 437. 'Grossly unfair . . .': cited in Wicks, *Welcome Home*.

page 437. 'Ursula Bloom, who . . .': Bloom, *Trilogy*.

page 438. 'In the same vein, Barbara Cartland . . .': BC/YO.

page 438. 'the social researcher Ferdinand Zweig . . .': Ferdinand Zweig, *Women's Life and Labour*.

pages 438–9. 'In 1947 a galaxy . . .': Olwen W. Campbell, *The Report of a Conference on The Feminine Point of View*.

page 442. 'First, a wedding photograph . . .': HL/CI; author correspondence with Christopher Long.

page 442. 'Ilkley Road, Barrow-in-Furness . . .': NL/NLP.

pages 442–3. 'A cottage in Slough . . .': see Garfield, *Our Hidden Lives*.

page 444. 'A summer day in Piccadilly . . .': MH/JOURNAL.

pages 444–5. 'Ham Spray House . . .': FP/EL.

page 444. 'Oundle, Northamptonshire . . .': LK/MD; author interview with Ralph Kite (son of Ralph and Lorna Kite, née Bradey).

page 444. A railway station in Sussex . . .': AP/A.

pages 444–5. 'Ontario, Canada . . .': MB/A.

page 445. 'Edinburgh: Jean Park . . .': JP/A.

pages 445–6. 'Blackheath, London . . .': author interviews with Elizabeth Paterson (Mary Cornish's niece), 2009, and Maggie Paterson (niece-in-law), 2009; and private papers of Mary Cornish, courtesy of Maggie Paterson.

page 446. 'Leamington Spa, Warwickshire . . .': CM/MM.

page 447. 'South Kensington . . .': FF/CHELSEA; author interview with Mrs Pamela Hanbury.

pages 447–8. North Berwick, the Firth of Forth . . .': KW/A.

Select Bibliography

Biography, Memoirs, Diaries, Autobiography

The impossibility of doing full justice to the vast abundance of war memoirs that exists will be apparent to anybody researching the period, and this selection represents the tip of a sizeable iceberg.

Anderson, Verily, *Spam Tomorrow*, Rupert Hart-Davis, London, 1956.

Andrews, Lucilla, *No Time for Romance*, Harrap and Co., London, 1977.

Anonymous, *A Woman in Berlin*, trans. Philip Boehm, Virago, London, 2005.

Barraud, E. M., *Set My Hand upon the Plough*, Littlebury and Co., Worcester, 1946.

Bawden, Nina, *In My Own Time: Almost an Autobiography*, Virago, London, 1995.

Beck, Pip, *A WAAF in Bomber Command*, Goodall Publications, London and St Albans, 1989.

Bloom, Ursula, *Trilogy*, Hutchinson, London, 1954.

Bowen, Elizabeth, 'London, 1940', in *Collected Impressions*, Longmans, Green and Co., London, 1950.

Brewer Kerr, Dorothy, *The Girls Behind the Guns*, Robert Hale, London, 1990.

Brittain, Vera, *Testament of Experience: An Autobiographical Story of the Years 1925–1950*, Victor Gollancz, London, 1957.

Broad, Richard and Suzie Fleming, eds., *Nella Last's War: A Mother's Diary 1939–45*, Falling Wall Press, Bristol, 1981.

Bruley, Sue, ed., *Working for Victory: A Diary of Life in a Second World War Factory*, Sutton Publishing, Stroud, 2001.

Calder, Jenni, *The Nine Lives of Naomi Mitchison*, Virago, London, 1997.

Campbell-Preston, Frances, *The Rich Spoils of Time*, The Dovecote Press, Wimborne Minster, 2006.

Cartland, Barbara, *The Years of Opportunity 1939–1945*, Hutchinson and Co., London, 1948.

Clayton, Aileen, *The Enemy Is Listening: The Story of the Y Service*, Hutchinson and Co., London, 1980.

Cloud, Henry, *Barbara Cartland: Crusader in Pink*, Weidenfeld and Nicolson, London, 1979.

Cooper, Diana, *Trumpets from the Steep*, Rupert Hart-Davis, London, 1960.

Day-Lewis, Tamasin, ed., *Last Letters Home*, Macmillan, London, 1995.

Donnelly, Peter, ed., *Mrs Milburn's Diaries: An Englishwoman's Day-to-Day Reflections 1939–45*, Harrap, London, 1979.

Du Maurier, Angela, *It's Only the Sister: An Autobiography*, Peter Davis, London, 1951.

Faviell, Frances, *A Chelsea Concerto*, Cassell and Co., London, 1959.

Faviell, Frances, *The Dancing Bear: Berlin de Profundis*, Rupert Hart-Davis, London, 1954.

Forrester, Helen, *By the Waters of Liverpool*, The Bodley Head, 1981.

Forrester, Helen, *Lime Street at Two*, The Bodley Head, 1985.

Forrester, Helen, *Thursday's Child*, Hodder and Stoughton, 1959.

Garfield, Simon, ed., *We Are at War: The Remarkable Diaries of Five Ordinary People in Extraordinary Times*, Ebury Press, London, 2005.

Grenfell, Joyce, *Joyce Grenfell: The Time of My Life, Entertaining the Troops: Her Wartime Journals*, ed. James Roose-Evans, Hodder and Stoughton, London, 1989.

Grieve, Mary, *Millions Made My Story*, Victor Gollancz, London, 1964.

Hampton, Janie, ed., *Joyce and Ginnie – the Letters of Joyce Grenfell and Virginia Graham*, Hodder and Stoughton, London, 1997.

Henrey, Mrs Robert, *The Farm in Normandy and The Return to the Farm*, J. M. Dent and Sons, London, 1952.

Henrey, Mrs Robert, *London Under Fire*, J. M. Dent and Sons, London, 1982.

Henrey, Mrs Robert, *Madeleine's Journal*, J. M. Dent and Sons, London, 1953.

Hewins, Mary, *Mary, after the Queen*, Oxford University Press, 1986.

Hodgson, Vere, *Few Eggs and No Oranges: The Diaries of Vere Hodgson 1940–45*, Persephone Books, London, 1999.

Howard, Elizabeth Jane, *Slipstream: A Memoir*, Macmillan, 2002.

Hurst, Margery, *No Glass Slipper*, Sphere Books, London, 1968.

Huxley, Elspeth, *Atlantic Ordeal*, Chatto and Windus, London, 1941.

Jolly, Margaretta, ed., *Dear Laughing Motorbyke: Letters from Women Welders of the Second World War*, Scarlet Press, London, 1977.

Joseph, Shirley, *If Their Mothers Only Knew: An Unofficial Account of Life in the Women's Land Army*, Faber and Faber, London, 1946.

Katin, Zelma, *Clippie: The Autobiography of a War Time Conductress*, John Gifford, London, 1944.

Kite, Lorna, *Mentioned in Despatches: World War II as Seen through the Eyes of a Nurse*, unpublished, Archive of Working-class Autobiographies, Brunel University.

Koa Wing, Sandra, ed., *Our Longest Days: A People's History of the Second World War*, Profile Books, London, 2008.

Lamb, Christian, *I Only Joined for the Hat: Redoubtable Wrens at War: Their Trials Tribulations and Triumphs*, Bene Factum Publishing, London, 2007.

Leslie, Anita, *A Story Half-told: A Wartime Autobiography*, Hutchinson, London, 1983.

Levine, Joshua, *Forgotten Voices of the Blitz and the Battle for Britain*, Ebury Press, London, 2007.

Long, Helen, *Change into Uniform: An Autobiography 1939–1946*, Terence Dalton, Lavenham, 1978.

MacCarthy, Fiona, *Last Curtsey: The End of the Debutantes*, Faber and Faber, London, 2006.

Malcolmson, Patricia and Robert, eds., *Nella Last's Peace: The Post-war Diaries of Housewife, 49*, Profile Books, London, 2008.

Marnham, Patrick, *Wild Mary: The Life of Mary Wesley*, Chatto and Windus, London, 2006.

Mitchison, Naomi, *Among You Taking Notes: The Wartime Diary of Naomi Mitchison*, ed. Dorothy Sheridan, Victor Gollancz, London, 1985.

Mundahl-Harris, Sylvia, *The View from the Cookhouse Floor*, Caedmon of Whitby, 1995.

Nicholson, Mavis, *What Did You Do in the War, Mummy? Women in World War II*, Chatto and Windus, London, 1995.

Nixon, Barbara, *Raiders Overhead: A Diary of the London Blitz*, Scolar Press, London, in association with Gulliver Publishing Co., Banbury, 1980.

Partridge, Frances, *A Pacifist's War*, The Hogarth Press, London, 1978.

Partridge, Frances, *Everything to Lose: Diaries 1945–1960*, Victor Gollancz, London, 1985.

Pawley, Margaret, *In Obedience to Instructions: FANY with the SOE in the Mediterranean*, Leo Cooper, Barnsley, 1999.

Perry, Margaret, untitled memoir, unpublished, Archive of Working-class Autobiographies, Brunel University.

Powell, Margaret, *Climbing the Stairs*, Peter Davies, London, 1969.

Pym, Barbara, *A Very Private Eye: An Autobiography in Letters and Diaries*, Macmillan, London, 1984.

Raynes, Rozelle, *Maid Matelot*, Nautical Publishing Company, Lymington, Hampshire, 1971.

Scannell, Dorothy, *Dolly's War*, Macmillan, London, 1975.

Smith, Lyn, *Young Voices: British Children Remember the Second World War*, Viking, London, 2007.

Speed, Florence, Diary of Miss F. M. Speed, Imperial War Museum, London, Department of Documents, IWM 86/45/2.

Symington, Monica, *A Memoire: The War and Its Aftermath*, Imperial War Museum, London, Department of Documents, IWM 01/19/1.

Taylor, Eric, *Heroines of World War II*, Robert Hale, London, 1991.

Tedder, Valerie A., *Post-war Blues*, Leicester City Council, 1999.

Townsend, Colin and Eileen, *War Wives: A Second World War Anthology*, Grafton Books, London and Glasgow, 1989.

Wayne, Hilary, *Two Odd Soldiers*, George Allen and Unwin, London, 1946.

Wells, Maureen, *Entertaining Eric: A Wartime Love Story*, Ebury Press, London, 2007.

Wharton, Margaret H., *Recollections of a G.I. War Bride: A Wiltshire Childhood*, Alan Sutton Publishing, Gloucester, 1984.

White, Doris, *D for Doris, V for Victory*, Oakleaf Books in association with Peoples Press, Milton Keynes, 1981.

Willmott, Phyllis, *A Green Girl*, Peter Owen, London, 1983.

Willmott, Phyllis, *Coming of Age in Wartime*, Peter Owen, London, 1995.

Willmott, Phyllis, *Joys and Sorrows: Fragments from the Post-war Years*, Peter Owen, London, 1995.

Woolf, Virginia, *The Diaries of Virginia Woolf*, vol. 5, ed. Anne Olivier Bell, The Hogarth Press, London, 1984.

Wyndham, Joan, *Love Lessons: A Wartime Diary*, Heinemann, London, 1985.

Wyndham, Joan, *Love Is Blue: A Wartime Diary*, Heinemann, London, 1986.

Wyndham, Joan, *Anything Once*, Sinclair-Stevenson, London, 1992.

History, Sociology, Documentation, Advice

Books about the Second World War proliferate at an alarming rate; few researchers can hope to do more than skim the surface, and the following list is highly selective. Material on the post-war world is thinner on the ground. I have accordingly given my choice of books on the later 1940s a section to itself.

Pre-war and Second World War

Adam, Ruth, *A Woman's Place 1910–1975*, Chatto and Windus, London, 1975.

Adie, Kate, *Corsets to Camouflage: Women and War*, Hodder and Stoughton, London, 2003.

Anderson, Bette, *We Just Got on with It: British Women in World War II*, Picton Publishing, Chippenham, 1994.

Beevor, Antony, *D-Day: The Battle for Normandy*, Viking, London, 2009.

Bletchley Park, *The Bletchley Park War Diaries July 1939–August 1945*, printed in aid of the Bletchley Park Trust.

Boston, Anne and Jenny Hartley, eds., *Wave Me Goodbye and Hearts Undefeated*, Virago, London, 2003.

Bowley, Ruth, *Women – in a Man's World?* Bureau of Current Affairs, London, 1949.

Braybon, Gail and Penny Summerfield, *Out of the Cage: Women's Experiences in Two World Wars*, Pandora, London, 1987.

Briggs, Asa, *Go to It! Working for Victory on the Home Front 1939–1945*, Mitchell Beazley, London, 2000.

Briggs, Susan, *Keep Smiling Through: The Home Front 1939–45*, Weidenfeld and Nicolson, London, 1975.

Brittain, Vera, *Lady into Woman: A History of Women from Victoria to Elizabeth II*, Andrew Dakers, London, 1953.

Calder, Angus, *The Myth of the Blitz*, Jonathan Cape, London, 1991.

Calder, Angus, *The People's War: Britain 1939–1945*, Jonathan Cape, London, 1969.

Costello, John, *Love, Sex and War: Changing Values 1939–1945*, William Collins Sons and Co., London, 1985.

De Courcy, Anne, *Debs at War: 1939–1945: How Wartime Changed Their Lives*, Weidenfeld and Nicolson, London, 2005.

Donnelly, Mark, *Britain in the Second World War*, Routledge, London and New York, 1999.

Gardiner, Juliet, *The Thirties: An Intimate History*, HarperPress, London, 2010.

Gardiner, Juliet, *Wartime Britain 1939–1945*, Headline, London, 2004.

Goldsmith, Margaret, *Women and the Future*, Lindsay Drummond, London, 1946.

Goralski, Robert, *World War II Almanac 1931–1945: A Political and Military Record*, Hamish Hamilton, London, 1981.

Graves, Charles, *Women in Green: The Story of the W.V.S.*, Heinemann, London, 1948.

Gubar, Susan, '"This is My Rifle, This is My Gun": World War II and the Blitz on Women', in Margaret Randolph Higonnet et al., eds., *Behind the Lines: Gender and the Two World Wars*, Yale University Press, New Haven and London, 1987.

Halsey, A. H., ed., *Trends in British Society since 1900: A Guide to the Changing Social Structure of Britain*, The Macmillan Press, London and Basingstoke, 1972.

Harrisson, Tom, *Living through the Blitz*, Collins, London, 1976.

Hayes, Denis, *Challenge of Conscience: The Story of the Conscientious Objectors of 1939–1949*, Allen and Unwin, London, 1949.

Heath, F. F., ed., *A Churchill Anthology: Selections from the Writings and Speeches of Sir Winston Churchill*, Odhams Books, London, 1965.

Hinton, James, *Women, Social Leadership, and the Second World War: Continuities of Class*, Oxford University Press, 2002.

Holdsworth, Angela, *Out of the Doll's House: The Story of Women in the Twentieth Century*, BBC Books, London, 1988.

Howlett, Peter, *Fighting with Figures: A Statistical Digest of the Second World War*, HMSO (Central Statistical Office), 1995.

Hylton, Stuart, *Their Darkest Hour: The Hidden History of the Home Front 1939–1945*, Sutton Publishing, Stroud, Gloucestershire, 2001.

Keegan, John, *The Second World War*, Hutchinson, London, 1989.

Kramer, Ann, *Land Girls and Their Impact*, Remember When, an imprint of Pen and Sword Books, Barnsley, 2008.

Lewis, Roy and Angus Maude, *The English Middle Classes*, Phoenix House, London, 1949.

Longmate, Norman, *How We Lived Then: A History of Everyday Life during the Second World War*, Hutchinson, London, 1971.

Longmate, Norman, ed., *The Home Front: An Anthology of Personal Experience 1938–1945*, Chatto and Windus, London, 1981.

Lynn, Vera, with Robin Cross and Jenny de Gex, *Unsung Heroines: The Women Who Won the War*, Sidgwick and Jackson, London, 1990.

Marchant, Hilde, *Women and Children Last: A Woman Reporter's Account of the Battle of Britain*, Victor Gollancz, London, 1941.

McBryde, Brenda, *Quiet Heroines: Nurses of the Second World War*, Chatto and Windus, London, 1985.

Menzies, Janet, *Children of the Doomed Voyage*, John Wiley, Chichester, 2005.

Minns, Raynes, *Bombers and Mash: The Domestic Front 1939–1945*, Virago, 1980.

Nagorski, Tom, *Miracles on the Water: The Heroic Survivors of the U-boat Attack on the SS* City of Benares – *One of the Great Lost Stories of WWII*, Constable and Robinson, London, 2007.

Nicholson, Jenny, *Kiss the Girls Goodbye*, Hutchinson and Co., London, 1944.

Noakes, Lucy, *Women in the British Army: War and the Gentle Sex 1907–1948*, Routledge, London, 2006.

Orwell, George, *The Collected Essays, Journalism and Letters of George Orwell*, vol. 4, eds. Sonia Orwell and Ian Angus, Penguin Books in association with Secker and Warburg, Harmondsworth, 1970.

Panter-Downes, Mollie, *London War Notes 1939–45*, ed. William Shawn, Longman, London, 1972.

Powell, Anne, ed., *Shadows of War: British Women's Poetry of the Second World War*, Sutton Publishing, Stroud, 1999.

Sackville-West, Vita, *The Women's Land Army*, Imperial War Museum, London, 1944.

Scott, Peggy, *British Women at War*, Hutchinson and Co., London, 1940.

Sheridan, Dorothy, ed., *Wartime Women: An Anthology of Women's Wartime Writing for Mass Observation 1937–45*, Heinemann, London, 1990.

Shukert, Elfrieda Berthiaume and Barbara Smith Scibetta, *War Brides of World War II*, Presidio Press, Novato, CA, 1988.

Smith, Harold L., 'The Effect of the War on the Status of Women', in H. L. Smith, ed., *War and Social Change: British Society in the Second World War*, Manchester University Press, 1986.

Summerfield, Penny, *Reconstructing Women's Wartime Lives: Discourse and Subjectivity in Oral Histories of the Second World War*, Manchester University Press, 1998.

Summerfield, Penny, *Women Workers in the Second World War: Production and Patriarchy in Conflict*, Croom Helm, London, 1984.

Taylor, Eric, *Forces Sweethearts: Service Romances in World War II*, Robert Hale, London, 1990.

Tyrer, Nicola, *Sisters in Arms: British Army Nurses Tell Their Story*, Weidenfeld and Nicolson, London, 2008.

Tyrer, Nicola, *They Fought in the Fields: The Women's Land Army: The Story of a Forgotten Victory*, Sinclair-Stevenson, London, 1996.

Waller, Jane, and Michael Vaughan-Rees, *Women in Wartime: The Role of Women's Magazines 1939–1945*, Macdonald and Co., London, 1987.

Watkins, Gwen, *Cracking the Luftwaffe Codes: The Secrets of Bletchley Park*, Greenhill Books, London, 2006.

Wicks, Ben, *No Time to Wave Goodbye*, Bloomsbury, London, 1988.

Williams-Ellis, Amabel, *Women in War Factories*, Gollancz, London, 1943.

Woolf, Virginia, 'Thoughts on Peace in an Air Raid', in *The Death of the Moth and Other Essays*, The Hogarth Press, London, 1942.

Zweig, Ferdinand, *Women's Life and Labour*, Gollancz, London, 1952.

Post-war

Addison, Paul, *Now the War Is Over: A Social History of Britain 1945–51*, BBC and Jonathan Cape, London, 1985.

Allport, Alan, *Demobbed: Coming Home after the Second World War*, Yale University Press, New Haven and London, 2009.

Campbell, Olwen W., *The Report of a Conference on The Feminine Point of View*, Williams and Norgate, London, 1952.

Garfield, Simon, ed., *Our Hidden Lives: The Remarkable Diaries of Post-war Britain*, Ebury Press, London, 2004.

Hennessy, Peter, *Never Again: Britain 1945–51*, Jonathan Cape, London, 1992.

Hodson, J. L., *The Way Things Are: Being Some Accounts of Journeyings, Meetings, and What Was Said to me in Britain between May, 1945 and Jan., 1947*, Victor Gollancz, London, 1947.

Hopkins, Harry, *The New Look: A Social History of the Forties and Fifties in Britain*, Secker and Warburg, London, 1963.

Howard, Kenneth, *Sex Problems of the Returning Soldier*, Sydney Pemberton, Lever Street, Manchester, 1945.

Jephcott, Pearl, *Rising Twenty: Notes on Some Ordinary Girls*, Faber and Faber, London, 1948.

Kynaston, David, *Austerity Britain 1945–1951*, Bloomsbury Publishing, London, 2007.

Lewis, Jane, *Women in Britain since 1945: Women, Family, Work and the State in the Post-war Years*, Blackwell, Oxford, 1992.

Mass Observation, *Peace and the Public*, Longmans, Green and Co., London, 1947.

Newsom, John, *The Education of Girls*, Faber and Faber, London, 1948.

Sissons, Michael, and Philip French, eds., *Age of Austerity*, Hodder and Stoughton, London, 1963.

Slater, Eliot and Moya Woodside, *Patterns of Marriage: A Study of Marriage Relationships in the Urban Working Classes*, Cassell and Co., London, 1951.

Summers, Julie, *Stranger in the House: Women's Stories of Men Returning from the Second World War*, Simon and Schuster, London, New York etc., 2008.

Wicks, Ben, *Welcome Home: True Stories of Soldiers Returning from World War II*, Bloomsbury, London, 1991.

Wilson, Elizabeth, *Only Halfway to Paradise: Women in Postwar Britain 1945–1968*, Tavistock Publications, London, New York, 1980.

Winter, Jay, 'The Demographic Consequences of the War', in H. L. Smith, ed., *War and Social Change: British Society in the Second World War*, Manchester University Press, 1986.

Zweiniger-Bargielowska, Ina, *Austerity in Britain: Rationing, Controls and Consumption 1939–1955*, Oxford University Press, 2000.

Archives and Websites

The American War Bride Experience: http://uswarbrides.com.

BBC People's War: www.bbc.co.uk/ww2peopleswar.

Collection of Working-class Autobiographies, Brunel University.

The D-Day and Normandy Fellowship website: http://ddnf.org.uk/.

The Imperial War Museum.

Mass Observation Archive, Sussex University Library.

Newspaper Collection, British Library at Colindale.

The Oxford Dictionary of National Biography online: www.oxforddnb.com.

The Royal Navy website: www.royalnavy.mod.uk.

The Wartime Memories Project: www.wartimememories.co.uk.

World War-2.net: www.worldwar-2.net.

Acknowledgements

This book would not have been possible without the help of a large number of people; I am grateful to all of them. With such a range of contributions, it seems invidious to prioritise my thanks, nevertheless I owe a special debt of gratitude to Eleo Gordon, my tireless and magnificent editor at Viking, whose idea the book was, and another one to my husband William Nicholson, who has never failed to encourage, advise, read and reread. Affectionate thanks also to my agent, Caroline Dawnay, and to Venetia Butterfield at Viking for her confidence in me.

I am particularly grateful to a number of people who have given me special help; thank you to the late Russell Ash, Lord Briggs, Janie Hampton, Nicola Tyrer and Sarah Waters. I would also like to acknowledge specific research assistance from Paul Beecham, Henrietta Bredin, Anna Fewster, Sabine Goodwin, Miles Mantle, Julia Nicholson and Teddy Nicholson.

The book would not exist in its present form without the inclusion of interviews with the elderly ladies who contributed their memories, their time and their hospitality: the late Verily Anderson, Kaye Bastin, Mavis Batey, the late Pip Beck, Anne Olivier Bell, Dorothy Brewer-Kerr, Mary Davis, Pat Evans, Dame Mary Glen-Haig, Elizabeth Jane Howard, Sheila Hugh-Jones, Joan Kelsall, Christian Lamb, Dame Vera Lynn, Flo Mahony, Patience Maxwell, Eileen Morgan, Jean Park, Marguerite Patten, Margaret Pawley, Isa Rankin, Thelma Rendle, Vera Roberts, Betty Smith, Marjorie Smith, Joan Tagg, Kay Wight, Cora Williams and Phyllis Willmott.

In some cases I have spoken to or corresponded with the friends or relatives of women who wanted a helping hand or could no longer speak for themselves: thank you to Judith Bastin, Robert Bhatia, Peter Brimson, Mary Clayton, Bess Cummings, Charlotte Deane, Catherine Green, Sue Green, Jonathan Keates, Ralph Kite, Christopher Long, Maggie Paterson, Elizabeth Paterson, Alexandra and Gordon Tregear and Michael Trindles.

Thanks, too, to the people who were so helpful in bringing me together with my interviewees: Ruth Boreham, Richard Cable, Martyn Cox, Sue Gibbs, Janet Hodgson, Jonathan Hugh-Jones, Ruth Jennings, Virginia Lewis-Jones, Anne Morrison, Deborah Mulhearn, Jane Myles, Tom Nagorski, Alastair Upton, and Tessa Volders. A number of kind people replied to my requests for memories or information: my thanks to Mary-Rose Benton, Mrs T. Dufort, Mrs V. Falck, Jean Faulks, Averil Kear, Anne Lewis-Smith, Anne McGravie, Joyce Openshaw, Patricia Potton, Beryl Staley and Philip Wall.

Librarians and archivists are my heroes (and heroines, of course). Particular thanks to Fiona Courage, Karen Watson and their colleagues at the Mass Observation archive at Sussex University; also to the staff of the London Library; and to Sophie Bridges, Paula Gerrard, Emma Goodrum, Dr Lesley Hall, Isabel Hernandez, David Jamieson, Matthew McMurray, Dr Juliette Pattinson, Katrina Presedo, Andrew Riley, Andy Smith and Julie-Ann Vickers.

Research for a book of this kind can lead an author on some fascinating diversions through academic institutions, local history societies, oral history societies, military associations, niche magazines and the like; en route, I've had help from a number of people involved with such organisations, notably Ruth Brown, Squadron Leader Beryl E. Escott, Pat Farrington, Juliette Gammon, Frank Haslam, Steve Humphries, Dr Irene Maver, Naomi McMahon, Mrs Julie Somay, Lis Tighe, Eve Watson, Dave Welsh, Andrew Westwood-Bate, Jo White, John Wilson, and Angela Wintle. I've also been given useful leads by Andrew Bibby, Daniel Hahn, Sam Humphrey and Janet Menzies.

My year-long quest to unearth the post-war career of the mysterious author Frances Faviell deserves a paragraph of acknowledgements to itself. I was spurred on by James Beechey, Frances Christie, Chris Faviell, Sabina ffrench Blake, Mrs Peggy Guggenheim, Duff Hart-Davis, Bea Hemmings, Wendy Hitchmough, Max Hodgkin, Colin McKenzie, Richard Morphet, John Moynihan, Jonathan Prichard, Richard Shone, Father Jonathan Swindells and Henry Wyndham. Our joint efforts were finally crowned when I managed to trace, firstly, Mrs Pamela Hanbury, whose mother, it turned out, had been Faviell's closest friend, and finally (through the help of Stephen Woolley) John Parker, Faviell's son.

A number of friends and strangers have offered kind and unprompted assistance on different occasions. For this, grateful thanks to Alex Dufort, Dr Margaretta Jolly, David Kynaston, Dr James Le Fanu, Dr David Mellor, Di Speirs and Julie Summers. Answers to specific queries were ably supplied by Liz Bassett and Felicity Thompson.

The challenge of indexing a book studded with namechecks has been splendidly met by Douglas Matthews; my thanks, too, to Katherine Stroud and to the team at Viking: Ben Brusey, Lesley Hodgson, Keith Taylor and David Watson who have been diligent and enthusiastic throughout.

★

In addition, the author gratefully acknowledges the kind permission of copyright holders to quote from a number of authors and sources, as follows: lines from 'September 1, 1939': Copyright © 1940, The Estate of W. H. Auden; excerpts from *In My Own Time* by Nina Bawden reproduced with permission of Curtis Brown Ltd, London on behalf of Nina Bawden, copyright © Nina Bawden; 'The White Cliffs of Dover', written by Nat Burton and Walter Kent, used by Permission of Shapiro Bernstein & Co. Limited, all rights reserved, International Copyright secured; 'There'll Always be an England', words and music by Ross Parker and Hugh Charles © Copyright 1939 Dash Music Company Limited, all rights reserved, International Copyright Secured, reprinted by permission; *Brief Encounter* © NC Aventales AG 1945, www.noelcoward.com, use of quote by permission of Alan Brodie Representation Ltd, www.alanbrodie.com; excerpts from *London Under Fire* © Mrs Robert Henrey, and *A Farm in Normandy* and *The Return to the Farm* by Madeleine Henrey both published by J. M. Dent & Sons, an imprint of The Orion Publishing Group, London; material from the Mass Observation archive reproduced with permission of Curtis Brown Ltd, London, on behalf of the Trustees of the Mass Observation Archive, copyright © The Trustees of the Mass Observation Archive; extracts from *A Pacifist's War* and *Everything to Lose*, copyright © Frances Partridge, reproduced by permission of the author c/o Rogers, Coleridge & White Ltd., 20 Powis Mews, London W11 1JN; excerpts from *Change into Uniform* reprinted with thanks to the late author and journalist Helen Long, née Vlasto. Extracts from *Love Lessons* by Joan Wyndham (Heinemann, 1985), *Love is Blue* by Joan Wyndham (Heinemann, 1986) and *Anything Once* by Joan Wyndham (Sinclair-Stevenson, 1992) are printed by permission of United Agents Ltd on behalf of The Estate of Joan Wyndham. Acknowledgements are due to the Trustees of the Imperial War Museum, with particular thanks to Gordon and Alexandra Tregear, for the use of unpublished excerpts from the writings of Monica Symington née Littleboy, and to Mrs Ouida V. Ascroft for the use of unpublished excerpts from the writings of Miss F. M. Speed, both now held in the Department of Documents at the Imperial War Museum.

Permission to quote from *A WAAF in Bomber Command* is given by Peter Brimson, Pip Beck's son; quotations from *The Years of Opportunity* by Barbara Cartland reprinted by kind permission of Cartland Promotions; permission to use quotations from her own work, without payment, is granted by Margaret G. Pawley; and quotation from the lyric 'Not a Cloud in the Sky' by kind permission of Peermusic (UK) Ltd, London. Particular thanks to John Parker for his (retrospective) permission for the use of material from two of his mother's books: *The Dancing Bear – Berlin de Profundis*, published by Rupert Hart-Davis, and *A Chelsea Concerto*, published by Cassell plc, a division of the Orion Publishing Group, both by Frances Faviell.

Grateful thanks too, to Rachel Anderson for permission to quote from *Spam Tomorrow* by Verily Anderson, 'Payment for use of the quotations selected, waived as agreed by Verily before her death on 16 July 2010'; to Mrs Dorothy Brewer-Kerr for permission to quote excerpts from *Girls Behind the Guns*; to Christopher Clayton, for permission to quote from *The Enemy is Listening: The Story of the Y Service* by Aileen Clayton; to Robert Bhatia on behalf of his mother, Helen Forrester, for the use of quotations from *By the Waters of Liverpool*, *Lime Street at Two* and *Thursday's Child*; to Ralph Kite, the son of Lorna Kite, for the use of quotations from the unpublished writings of his mother; to Susan S. Green for the use of quotations from the published and unpublished writings of her mother, Joy Trindles; and to Mrs Phyllis Willmott for permitting quotations from *Coming of Age in Wartime*, *Joys and Sorrows* and from her unpublished diary held in Churchill College Archive.

*

Acknowledgements are also due to the following whose works have been quoted from: Lucilla Andrews, *No Time for Romance*; *A Woman in Berlin*; Ursula Bloom, *Trilogy*; Vera Brittain, *Lady into Woman*; Sue Bruley, ed., *Working for Victory*; Frances Campbell-Preston, *The Rich Spoils of Time*; Joyce Grenfell, *The Time of My Life*; Eric Hobsbawm, *Age of Extremes: The Short Twentieth Century*; Elizabeth Jane Howard, *Slipstream*; Kenneth Howard, *Sex Problems of the Returning Soldier*; Margery Hurst, *No Glass Slipper*; Shirley Joseph, *If Their Mothers Only Knew: An Unofficial Account of Life in the Women's Land Army*; Zelma Katin, *Clippie;* Christian Lamb, *I Only Joined for the Hat*; Hilde Marchant, *Women and Children Last: A Woman Reporter's Account of the Battle of Britain*; Judy Milburn and Peter Donnelly on behalf of the estate of Clara Milburn for permission to quote from *Mrs Milburn's Diaries: An Englishwoman's Day-to-Day Reflections 1939–1945*; Naomi Mitchison, *Among You Taking Notes*; Jenny Nicholson, *Kiss the Girls Goodbye*; quotations from Iris Ogilvie from Vera Lynn, with Robin Cross and Jenny de Gex, *Unsung Heroines: The Women Who Won the War*; Margaret Powell, *Climbing the Stairs*; Barbara Pym, *A Very Private Eye*; Rozelle Raynes, *Maid Matelot*; Dorothy Scannell, *Dolly's War*; Maureen Wells, *Entertaining Eric*; Margaret Wharton, *Recollections of a GI War Bride: A Wiltshire Childhood*; Virginia Woolf, *The Diaries of Virginia Woolf* and 'Thoughts on Peace in an Air Raid', from *The Death of the Moth and Other Essays*.

While every effort has been made to trace the copyright holders of a number of other works quoted in this book, it has proved impossible in certain cases to obtain formal permission for their use. The publishers would be glad to hear from any copyright holders they have not been able to contact and to print due acknowledgements in future editions. Works whose copyright holders have so far proved untraceable are as follows: the lyric beginning 'Good morning my sweet . . . ' reprinted in *Keep Smiling Through – The Home Front 1939–45* by Susan Briggs; *London War Notes* by Mollie Panter-Downes; *D for Doris, V for Victory* by Doris White, published by Oakleaf Books; and the poem 'End of D-Day Leave' by Aileen Hawkins, reprinted in *Shadows of War: British Women's Poetry of the Second World War*, edited and introduced by Anne Powell.

Index

He just wanted a decent book to read ...

Not too much to ask, is it? It was in 1935 when Allen Lane, Managing Director of Bodley Head Publishers, stood on a platform at Exeter railway station looking for something good to read on his journey back to London. His choice was limited to popular magazines and poor-quality paperbacks – the same choice faced every day by the vast majority of readers, few of whom could afford hardbacks. Lane's disappointment and subsequent anger at the range of books generally available led him to found a company – and change the world.

'We believed in the existence in this country of a vast reading public for intelligent books at a low price, and staked everything on it'
Sir Allen Lane, 1902–1970, founder of Penguin Books

The quality paperback had arrived – and not just in bookshops. Lane was adamant that his Penguins should appear in chain stores and tobacconists, and should cost no more than a packet of cigarettes.

Reading habits (and cigarette prices) have changed since 1935, but Penguin still believes in publishing the best books for everybody to enjoy. We still believe that good design costs no more than bad design, and we still believe that quality books published passionately and responsibly make the world a better place.

So wherever you see the little bird – whether it's on a piece of prize-winning literary fiction or a celebrity autobiography, political tour de force or historical masterpiece, a serial-killer thriller, reference book, world classic or a piece of pure escapism – you can bet that it represents the very best that the genre has to offer.

Whatever you like to read – trust Penguin.